CU00751812

Robert John (Bob) Hunter was born in rural Meath in 1938 and was educated at Wesley College and Trinity College, Dublin. After graduation in 1960, he began research on the Ulster Plantation in the counties of Armagh and Cavan, 1608–41. This interest in the Plantation, and early modern Irish history generally, was to dominate his life.

In 1963 he was appointed Assistant Lecturer in History at Magee College, thus beginning an association with the city of Derry/Londonderry that was to continue for the rest of his life. The creation of what was to become the University of Ulster also saw him teaching regularly in Coleraine.

Through his meticulous research, he developed an encyclopaedic knowledge of his subject, traversing such themes as the development of towns, the role of the English planters, the history of trade and migration and the intellectual and cultural life of Ulster more generally.

Though his untimely death in 2007 was to cut short his ambitions for further writing, he was nevertheless to leave behind more than thirty articles, essays, reviews, etc., which were the result of painstaking study conducted with a careful eye for detail and relevance.

John Johnston is a native of Belfast and a graduate of Queen's University and holds postgraduate degrees from the University of London and the Open University. He has been a secondary school teacher and a further education lecturer and now works as a civil servant. He lives in Germany.

'Men and arms'
The Ulster settlers, *c.* 1630

Edited by

R.J. Hunter

Prepared for publication
by John Johnston

Published in association with the R.J. Hunter Committee.
The Committee works to acknowledge the contribution R.J. Hunter made to
the study of our past by making more widely known the results of his research,
as well as giving limited support to others engaged in associated endeavours.

The Committee is grateful for the assistance of John Johnston
in producing this volume.

Published 2012, reprinted 2015
by Ulster Historical Foundation
49 Malone Road, Belfast, BT9 6RY
www.ancestryireland.com
www.booksireland.org.uk

Except as otherwise permitted under the Copyright, Designs
and Patents Act 1988, this publication may only be
reproduced, stored or transmitted in any form or by any
means with the prior permission in writing of the publisher
or, in the case of reprographic reproduction, in accordance
with the terms of a licence issued by The Copyright
Licensing Agency. Enquiries concerning reproduction outside
those terms should be sent to the publisher.

© R.J. Hunter
978-1-908448-94-1

Cover design:
John Speed's map of Ireland published in *The Theatre of the Empire of Great Britaine*, 1612,
courtesy of the Cardinal Tomás Ó Fiaich Memorial Library and Archive.
Halberd, early modern weapon, possibly late sixteenth or early seventeenth century,
courtesy of Hermann Danzmayr | Dreamstime.com

Printed by SPRINT-print Ltd.
Design by Cheah Design

CONTENTS

Ioan. Strad. Academie. Floreten. figuravit.   Raphael. Sadeler. scalp. et excud.

At Rex, ne iuuenum incipiant frigescere uires,   Venatu inuigilet, pubemq exerce

Pax olea incedit dum redimita comas,   Per iuga sit ludus cursu ag

Ille autem ante alios pernix uolet aequore, nec sit
Tranare insolitus flumina magna labor.

Venatio, the allegory of the hunt:
The Ulster settlers produced
hunting versions of pikes and
firearms for the muster. The print
shows Diana, the goddess of the
hunt, holding a hunting pike
(about two-thirds the length of a
military pike), with a hunting gun
and powder flask to the right of
her feet. With weapons like these,
the lord deputy, Sir Thomas
Wentworth, declared, the settlers
were 'a company of naked men'
armed only with 'birding pieces'.

Johannes Sadeler I (sculp. et
excud.): Johannes Stradanus (fig),
A page from a series of allegorical
portrayals of trades (1597),
engraving Venatio (the Hunt),
Inventory Number: Gr 2023 f.
Städtisches Museum Schloss
Rheydt, Mönchengladbach.

PREFACE

The Muster Roll of the Province of Ulster is a large, leather-bound volume in the British Library, where it is shelved as Additional Manuscript 4770. The volume consists of 283 folio sheets, each slightly larger than a page of A4, on which are recorded the names of 13,147 adult males from the nine counties of Ulster. Each county forms a separate section of the volume and the men who mustered are listed under the names of their landlords; beside each man's name there is a description of the weapons he was carrying or a note that he was unarmed. The lists cover the first 276 folios and the remaining seven folios are a 'breviate' or summary of the whole book. Most of the men who mustered were English and Scottish settlers and, in the absence of comprehensive parish and estate records, the muster roll is the nearest one has to a census of the British population of early seventeenth-century Ulster.

In the late 1960s or early 1970s Robert Hunter began a project to publish each section of the muster. William Copeland Trimble had published the muster roll for county Fermanagh in the *History of Enniskillen* in 1919,[1] and T.G.F. Paterson had published that for county Armagh in 1970.[2] Robert therefore began with the muster roll for county Donegal, which he published in 1972,[3] and in 1978 he and Michael Perceval-Maxwell collaborated on an edition of the muster roll for county Cavan.[4] The muster roll for county Fermanagh seems to have been the next section which Robert intended to publish, but for whatever reason he put the project into abeyance and did not resume working on it until 1998. Over the following years he collated material for counties Antrim, Down, and Londonderry and had begun working on the muster rolls for counties Monaghan and Tyrone shortly before his death in 2007.[5]

Robert had also changed his intention of publishing the muster roll for each of the counties separately and had decided to publish the muster roll as a single volume. His working papers for the project consist of manila folders, one for each county and one for the introduction to the book. The county folders contain copies of published transcripts of the muster roll, offprints from a microfilm copy of the original manuscript, Robert's holograph transcripts of the offprint, copies of earlier transcripts from the Public Record Office of Northern Ireland (PRONI), and loose notes on individuals mentioned in the muster roll or points for explanation or follow-up.[6] This book is essentially a compilation of those notes, the transcripts of the muster roll, and the annotations on individual settlers.[7] The title of the book – *Men and arms: the Ulster settlers, c. 1630* – is the one Robert had chosen.

Robert had noted in 1972 that a 'more detailed criticism' of the muster roll would 'have to be based on an examination of other primary sources, for example inquisitions printed and manuscript and any estate papers that may be located.'[8] The annotations he subsequently produced were a step towards that 'detailed criticism' and 'examination of other primary sources', in particular material in the National Archives of Ireland (NAI). I have added to his notes through reference to material from sources he did not use and through cross-referencing family names with the online transcripts of the 1641 depositions.[9] The result, I hope, meets Robert's exacting standards of meticulousness and precision.

Personal names are shown in the transcript of the muster roll as they appear in the original manuscript, but otherwise I have silently expanded contractions and used modern spellings and punctuation: modern versions of names are used for the most part in the footnotes. For ease of reference, I have enumerated all of the names in the muster roll: in the original manuscript, the names in counties Armagh, Cavan, Fermanagh, Londonderry, and Tyrone are enumerated but not those in counties Antrim, Donegal, Down, and Monaghan. Secondly, I have adapted Robert's methodology and put details of the weapons being carried at the start of a column rather than trying to bracket names together as is done in the original manuscript. Finally, I have followed long-standing conventions of beginning years on 1 January rather than 25 March, of referring to Laois and Offaly as Queen's County and King's County, and of using Derry for the city and Londonderry for the county.

In producing this edition of the muster roll, I am grateful to the British Library Board, the Public Record Office of Northern Ireland, the National Archives of Ireland, the National Library of Ireland, the Board of Trinity College Dublin, Sheffield City Council: Libraries, Archives, and Information,[10] and The Bodleian Library, University of Oxford for permission to publish and cite documents in their collections, to the committees of the Cumann Seanchais Ard Mhacha, Cumann Seanchais Bhreifne, the Clogher Historical Society, and the Donegal Historical Society and to the Irish Manuscripts Commission for permission to use copyrighted material, to Laura Houghton Hunter for agreeing to give access to her father's papers, and to the Hunter Committee for financial support with the project. I am especially indebted to William Roulston and the Ulster Historical Foundation for their support and encouragement, to Ian Montgomery of PRONI for arranging access to the Hunter Papers before they had been fully catalogued and for providing scanned copies of Robert's transcripts, and to Carole Yates and the team at the Rheindahlen Library for arranging inter-library loans. Lastly, I must thank my wife, Monika, for her patience and support with this project and my sister and brother-in-law, Fiona and Sam Mulholland, for their hospitality during visits to Ireland.

John Johnston
Mönchengladbach, 2012

---

1   William Copeland Trimble, *The history of Enniskillen, with references to some manors in county Fermanagh and other local subjects*, 1 (Enniskillen, 1919) [hereafter, Trimble, *History of Enniskillen*], pp 197–221; Trimble used a transcript of the original manuscript provided by Rev. W.H. Dundas (ibid. p. 200): there is no transcript of the muster roll in the Dundas papers (Public Record Office of Northern Ireland [PRONI], D1588).

2   T.G.F. Paterson, 'An unpublished early seventeenth-century census of the men and arms on the estates of English and Scotch settlers in county Armagh', in *Seanchas Ardmhacha*, 5 (1970) [hereafter, Paterson, 'Armagh'], pp 401–17; Paterson used the transcript of the manuscript in the Armagh Public Library, a copy of which is in the National Library of Ireland [hereafter NLI].

3   R.J. Hunter, 'The settler population of an Ulster plantation county', in *Donegal Annual*, 10 (1972) [hereafter, Hunter, 'Donegal'], pp 124–54.

4   R.J. Hunter and Michael Perceval-Maxwell, 'The muster roll of *c.* 1630: county Cavan', in *Breifne*, 5 (1978) [hereafter, Hunter and Perceval-Maxwell, 'Cavan'], pp 206–12.

5   This paragraph is based on notes and correspondence in Robert's working papers on the muster roll (PRONI, D4446/A/8).

6   The offprint appears to be from the NLI microfilm copy of the original manuscript and the transcripts are from PRONI, D1759/3C/3 and T934/1.

7   Robert's annotations are shown as [RJH] and mine as [JJ].

8   Hunter, 'Donegal', p. 127.

9   www.1641.tcd.ie.

10 Hereafter, Sheffield Archives.

Ioan. Stradanus invent.   Ioan. Collaert sculp.   Phls Galle excud.

Horrida Barbariæ regio nutrire Camelos
28.   Dicitur eximios, miles quos nauticus atram

em patiens venatur : dura palato
grauem ventris placat fistitq̃ latratum .

The Camel Hunt
The men in the print are dressed as the Ulster settlers who mustered around 1630 would have been. The swords the men are wearing are typical of those of that period: they are symbols of social status as much as weapons for personal protection. The man in the foreground is firing a caliver: he is holding the butt against his upper right arm and using his right hand to operate the long sear lever that releases the match which ignites the powder in the firing pan.

Giovanni Stradanus (Jan van der Straat) 1523 Brügge – 1605 Florence otherwise known as Joan Stradanus invent. Joan Collaert sculp. Phl's Galle excud. The Camel Hunt, engraving, Inventory Number: Gr 700. Städtisches Museum Schloss Rheydt, Mönchengladbach.

Pikeman and Musketeer (photograph courtesy of the Honourable Artillery Company, London)
The London Companies equipped the trained bands in Derry and Coleraine with pikes and muskets. When deployed, the musketeers would step forward and discharge their weapons. They would then retire behind the pikemen to reload. The pikemen would step forward and plant their pikes into the earth to create a barrier to an attacking enemy. Coordinating these actions required constant practice and regular drilling, whilst the cost of maintaining the equipment limited membership of the trained bands to the wealthier townsmen.

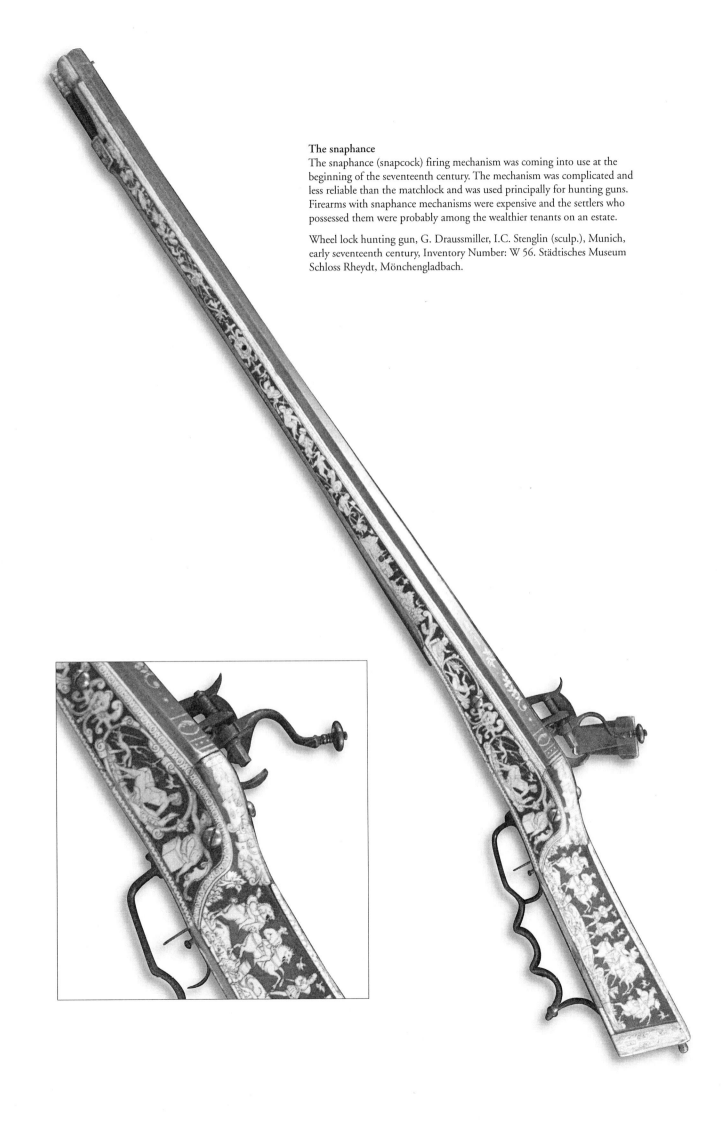

The snaphance

The snaphance (snapcock) firing mechanism was coming into use at the beginning of the seventeenth century. The mechanism was complicated and less reliable than the matchlock and was used principally for hunting guns. Firearms with snaphance mechanisms were expensive and the settlers who possessed them were probably among the wealthier tenants on an estate.

Wheel lock hunting gun, G. Draussmiller, I.C. Stenglin (sculp.), Munich, early seventeenth century, Inventory Number: W 56. Städtisches Museum Schloss Rheydt, Mönchengladbach.

INTRODUCTION

1. Background[1]

The conditions of the plantation in Ulster required English and Scottish undertakers to 'have ready in their houses at all times a convenient store of arms, wherewith they may furnish a competent number of men for their defence, which may be viewed and mustered every half year, according to the manner of England.'[2] The servitor grantees, who were not obliged to introduce colonists, were also to 'have a convenient store of arms in their houses.' Not surprisingly, no such requirement was imposed on the native Irish grantees in the plantation.[3]

It would not be appropriate to attempt to generalise here about the extent to which the undertakers fulfilled their obligation to maintain arms. The muster book of *c.* 1630 is an important source in this respect. As in so many aspects of the plantation, there was considerable variation in performance amongst the grantees. The requirement that the undertakers should have arms 'in their houses' presupposed that their tenantry should live, in accordance with another condition, in villages close to the settlers' strongholds. However, in practice, the settlement pattern that emerged was one which involved both small village nuclei and dispersed settlement. Some grantees, like Sir Stephen Butler in county Cavan who, on Pynnar's evidence, had 'very good' arms for 200 men in his castle 'besides which are dispersed to his tenants for their safeguard',[4] recognised that the logic of such settlement was a measure of dispersal of arms as well. Other undertakers merely passed on the responsibility to their tenantry. Thus John Dillon in county Armagh stated in 1622 that his tenants were 'enjoined by lease to find a musket, a pike, a sword, and dagger.'[5]

However, although the government surveys of the plantation taken periodically from 1611 onwards enquired into the amounts of arms, mustering, or the regular training of the tenantry in their use, which was a government responsibility, was for long neglected. It was not until 1618 that this was put in hand for the country at large. The reason was not primarily due to the situation in Ireland, or Ulster which had in the previous years been disturbed. The outbreak of war on the continent had caused alarm in England and a mustering of the English forces was ordered in the February of that year.[6] It seems reasonable to suggest that the decision for Ireland had the same background. On 8 May the king, on the advice of the Irish deputy, Oliver St John, decided to appoint two muster-masters, Nicholas Pynnar, and Captain George Alleyne who became responsible for Ulster and Leinster.[7]

Alleyne's inspection was the first to be carried out in plantation Ulster.[8] He provided figures – not names – of those who attended for the nine counties of Ulster with a report on the difficulties he encountered. Calculating on the basis that the six escheated counties contained 197,000 acres and that twenty-four men were to be mustered on every thousand acres, he computed that 4,728 men should appear; that is he took the numbers of tenants required by the articles of plantation as being the norm also for muster purposes. In all he recorded that 1,966 men appeared or only some forty per cent of his required total.[9]

It emerges in 1624 at a time of crises in Anglo-Spanish relations which was having reverberations in Ulster that mustering there had not been continued. In that year, when it was decided to expand the regular army in Ireland, a recommendation was also made for the revival of the muster in Ulster.[10] With the outbreak of war between England and Spain following on the accession of Charles I and lasting until 1630, the fear of insurrection or internal disturbance in Ulster, where the plantation was taking effect, received an added dimension with the possibility of invasion. By late in 1625 a substantial proportion of the standing army had been transferred to Ulster.[11] The appointment of provost marshals, an already well-tried expedient for dealing with unrest, was also resorted to. However, the troops were ill disciplined, the provost marshals were ineffectual, and complaints from the northern counties flowed into Dublin Castle over the winter.[12]

A renewed concern with mustering and training the 'risings out' – the feudal equivalent of a militia – was therefore manifest during these emergency years. Risings out were held in county Antrim and county Down in 1626.[13] The calling of half-yearly musters in Ulster was authorised in August 1627, with the undertakers' commitment reduced to having 'in every thousand acres ... five pikemen ready, beside arms and fine shot', although this was later amplified to having five pikes and five calivers or muskets per thousand acres.[14] The death of George Alleyne delayed starting the musters, but in September 1628, following on royal instructions of the previous July to the lord deputy,[15] Lieutenant William Graham was appointed, for life, muster-master for Ulster and Leinster with the power to demand the same fees as his predecessor, Captain Alleyne, had received previously.[16] The muster roll, commonly dated as *c.* 1630, may then be ascribed to Graham.

The return – a somewhat slipshod undated transcript in a difficult hand apparently transcribed from field papers[17] – was compiled from musters carried out between the spring of 1629 and the spring of 1633.[18] It was not the first muster to be carried out: the return for county Cavan notes the appearance of defaulters from the previous muster and errors 'in the other book'.[19] While it does not represent a census, the muster roll is the most exhaustive listing of the settler population that is available. Not only is it a means of assessing the planting achievement of the individual grantees, but it is also a firm reference against which other sources providing names may be compared to assess, for example, settler mobility.[20] The number of men who mustered was 13,147.[21] The quantity of weapons produced – 3,154 pikes and halberds and 1,920 firearms[22] – appeared to satisfy the criterion of five pikes and five firearms per thousand acres and the distribution of weapons broadly reflected the distribution of manpower. The figures, however, were less reassuring when examined more closely. Most of the pikes and firearms were to be found on a few estates in each county and only eight of the estates and corporate towns had colours and drummers, the instruments for command and control. Hence, whilst they might be able to defend themselves as individuals, the settlers could not form coherent bodies of armed men that would be capable of defending their communities.

The accuracy or reliability of the muster book is probably variable. An analysis of its contents for Londonderry shows that its return for that county approximates very closely to the total of British males present.[23] This is also the case with county Cavan, while the coverage for county Armagh must be regarded as conservative. Recalcitrance in mustering was characteristic of England at this time[24] – and this could well have been reflected amongst the colonists in Ireland – but Graham's return in comparison with Alleyne's is itself evidence of his greater thoroughness and may indicate greater concern in this matter by the government in this period in comparison with 1618.[25]

It appears too that Graham continued to execute his functions for a long time. Wentworth who examined Graham's statistics early in 1634 was concerned by what they revealed, observing that the Ulster colony was but 'a company of naked men', underarmed or in many cases provided with arms of 'altogether unserviceable' types such as 'birding pieces'.[26] His policy would be, he stated, to encourage Graham in every way. Graham still held the position in 1640, though then his function would appear to have been complicated by divergence of attitude amongst the colonists themselves.[27]

2. Additional Notes

These notes, collated from R.J. Hunter's working papers, are issues that he had identified for inclusion in the introduction to *Men and arms*.

2.1. The Career of William Graham

William Graham was the second son of Sir Richard Graham, who had come to Ireland with his younger brother, Sir George Graham, during the Nine Years' War (1594–1603). At the end of the war the brothers were granted lands in Kildare, Queen's County, and Wicklow,[28] on which they settled other members of the clan after the abortive plantation of Roscommon,[29] and in 1615 they were granted 2,000 acres of servitor lands in the barony of Tullyhaw, county Cavan.[30] As servitors, the brothers were not obliged to settle British tenants on their property but they built a 'bawn of stone and lime, sixty feet square and ten feet high, with a little house in it.'[31]

William Graham himself first comes to notice in 1624, when he received 'payment for apprehending two notorious malefactors' in county Monaghan. Later, as provost marshal of county Wicklow between 1626 and 1627, he was associated with the schemes of the lord deputy, Lord Falkland, and Sir William Parsons to expropriate the Byrnes of Ranelagh.[32] His rise was therefore probably a result of his connection with Falkland and Parsons and – through his cousin, Sir John Graham – with their patron, the duke of Buckingham.[33] About the time he was appointed muster master, Graham had moved with his family to Lisnamallard, one of the churchlands he had leased in Clankelly barony, county Fermanagh.[34] The manner in which he carried out his duties as muster-master fostered resentments and in 1640 there were complaints about him in the Irish parliament.[35] Perhaps fearful of where his unpopularity might lead, Graham joined the Irish uprising, and he and his family, along with other Scots, took part in the plundering and killing of the English settlers at Newtownbutler on 25 October 1641 and later at Clones in county Monaghan.[36]

William Graham's fate is unknown but some of his relations remained in Fermanagh: in 1688 Marie Graham, the widow of his brother, Arthur, held 'the four tates of Ballycollagh' that her husband had rented from the bishop of Clogher for £10 0s 0d.[37] Others returned to the family properties in Leinster: one of William Graham's sons, Richard, became a prominent Jacobite in Queen's County. Another son, John, was resident at Glaslough, county Monaghan in the 1660s and eventually inherited the family's properties. He kept the estate at Bawnboy but sold the rest 'for fear of a further confiscation.'[38]

2.2. The Dating of the Muster Roll

The muster roll, although conventionally described as 'c. 1630', was produced by William Graham between 1628, when he was appointed muster-master, and 1634, when he presented his findings to Sir Thomas Wentworth, the lord deputy.[39] The order in which the counties appear in the muster roll – Cavan, Armagh, Fermanagh, Tyrone, Londonderry, Antrim, Donegal, Down, and Monaghan – is probably the sequence in which the musters were conducted. It would have taken about five minutes to parade each man, to inspect his weapon, and to record his name. Graham would therefore have needed three weeks for each muster in counties Cavan, Armagh, and Fermanagh, four weeks for the musters in counties Tyrone, Londonderry, Antrim, and Donegal, six or eight weeks for the muster in county Down, and less than a week for the muster in county Monaghan.

After his appointment as muster-master in September 1628, Graham wrote to landlords, warning them of the forthcoming muster and telling them where to assemble their tenants.[40] Given the farming calendar, the best time for holding the musters would have been in the spring, after the fields had been ploughed and seeds had been sown. The sequence in which estates mustered suggests that Graham worked to a programme he had agreed with each landlord, and the musters seem to have been held at market towns or in estate villages. The time Graham would have spent travelling around the province would have extended the time needed to muster each county by up to a fortnight. The whole process, including the time needed to compile the summary for presentation to the lord deputy, would therefore have taken up to twelve months to complete and appears to have been done in four stages. The Cavan, Armagh, and Fermanagh musters were carried out in the spring of 1629. The Fermanagh muster roll shows 'Mrs Hamilton, widow to the lord archbishop of Cashel' as the 'undertaker of 1,500 acres' in the barony of Magheraboy and John Sedborough as the 'undertaker of 1,000 acres' in the barony of Clankelly. Malcolm Hamilton, archbishop of Cashel, died on 29 April 1629 and Sedborough, whose demesne was the neighbouring townland to Graham's property, died before July 1629.[41] The Cavan and Armagh muster rolls precede that for Fermanagh and so, assuming that six weeks were needed for mustering each county, the county Cavan musters were probably carried out before Easter (5 April),[42] those in county Armagh between Easter and Whitsun (23 May), and those in county Fermanagh by the end of June 1629.

The dating of the other musters is less straightforward. The mustering of county Tyrone was probably carried out in the spring of 1630 and a tenancy agreement shows that the muster of Londonderry was completed before July 1631.[43] The appearance of Peter Hill and Sir John Clotworthy as landlords in county Antrim shows that the muster there was carried out after the deaths of their fathers, Moses Hill and Sir Hugh Clotworthy, in February 1631.[44] The county Donegal muster does not include James May, who was made a freeholder on the Wilson estate at Convoy on 25 April 1631 and who was attainted for high treason on 5 May 1632: the muster for this county must therefore 'have taken place [either] before he arrived ... [or] after his execution.'[45]

Graham could not have conducted the Antrim and Donegal musters between 1 March and 24 April 1631, and the appearance of Christopher Freeman as lessor of the Fishmongers' Company means that the muster of that estate took place after January 1631.[46] The musters of the city and liberties and of the McClelland and Harrington estates were therefore possibly conducted immediately after the muster of county Tyrone in the spring of 1630, and the musters for the remainder of Londonderry and of county Antrim were held in the spring of 1631. The Donegal muster would then have been carried out after Easter (1 April) 1632, the musters of county Down and county Monaghan would have been held in the spring of 1633, and Graham would have spent the autumn of that year compiling the summary for presentation to the lord deputy.

2.3. Families and Kinship

As 'the first comprehensive list we possess of the English and Scotch emigrants who became domiciled' in the province, the muster roll 'is a document of equal interest to the genealogist and the historian.'[47] The information it contains supplements that in the reports of the 1622 commission,[48] whilst analyses of surnames reveal the areas in England, Scotland, and Wales from which the settlers originated.[49] Such analysis can be taken further: 'a small minority of the Scottish settlers have epithets and Gaelic forms of first names, whilst the majority of the Scots have English forms [of] Christian names. It is probably a reasonable assumption that the former group were Irish-speaking and the latter English-speaking.'[50] However, a more complete picture of the British community in early seventeenth-century Ulster can be constructed if the muster roll is examined in conjunction with other sources, such as estate papers and probate records.

The requirement for undertakers to settle twenty-four men from ten families per thousand acres meant that each family consisted of a father and one or more grown-up sons. When the family arrived in Ulster around 1615, the father would have been aged at least forty and the younger of the sons would have been at least eighteen years of age. By 1630, the father would have been in his late fifties or early sixties, the sons would have been in their thirties or forties, and some of the grandsons might have been old enough to muster. Although much would depend on the men's ages and on whether they could have had adult sons when the musters took place, a family connection is likely if a surname recurs two or three times in the muster list for an estate, and so the size of the settler population can be extrapolated through the frequency with which surnames appear in the muster roll.[51]

There are, for instance, twenty-eight surnames among the forty-four men who mustered on Edward Hatton's estate at Magheraveely in county Fermanagh. Eighteen of the surnames appear once in the muster list, eight of them twice, and two of them (Beatty and Little) five times each. With two families called Beatty and two families called Little, there were in all thirty British families on the estate.[52] 'If, to take account of some few absentees or because some families ... might have been represented by only one member, some increase should be made, then fifty to sixty might be the truer figure' for the number of adult males on the estate.[53] There would have been a similar number of females and so, assuming that the numbers of children and adults were the same, there would have been more than two hundred British people living around Magheraveely in 1630.

Family connections can also be established where members of a family were living on different estates. Thomas Carrington and his brother, Richard, for instance, mustered with their sons –

Christopher, Thomas, and Walter – on Sir Edward Bagshaw's estate in county Cavan but 'Richard Carington younger' mustered on Francis Sacherevell's estate at Legacorry, county Armagh: since these are the only men in the muster roll to be named Richard Carrington, it is reasonable to identify them as father and son. Likewise, Edward and Giles Whitehead are the only men with that surname in the muster roll: the former mustered on Sir Stephen Butler's estate at Belturbet in county Cavan and the latter on Sir William Brownlow's estate at Lurgan in county Armagh. There is no apparent connection between the men, but the will of Henry Smith of Lurgan reveals that Giles Whitehead was his grandson and that Giles's uncles were John Smith, who mustered at Lurgan, and William Smith, who mustered on Henry Stanhow's estate at Clontylaw.[54]

Connections like these reveal the movement of younger sons within the province. Humphrey Darbyshire, a leaseholder on the Sacherevell estate in 1622,[55] does not appear in the muster roll but the three men in it who are called Darbyshire are likely to have been his sons. Thomas Darbyshire mustered on the Sacherevell estate, and Lawrence and John Darbyshire mustered on Anthony Cope's estate at Loughgall: the eldest son, Thomas, had therefore taken over the family farm and his younger brothers had moved onto a neighbouring estate. Movement like this would have been common during the 1620s and 1630s and was a factor in the expansion of British landholding as men like the Darbyshire brothers took leases on townlands that had previously been let to native Irish tenants.[56]

Finally, the weapons that were produced for the muster are indications of their owners' wealth and social status. Firearms – in particular, 'the most advanced weapon, the snaphance' – were expensive, and so those who held them were probably wealthier than those who had 'simple weapons such as a sword, pike, [or] halberd.'[57] Using possession of firearms as a test, one can distinguish leaseholders from copyholders on the Archdale estate in county Fermanagh and assess Robert Adair's success in 'creating quite a sizeable upper stratum of tenants with a much broader base of sub-tenants' on the estate he had inherited in county Antrim.[58] One cannot, however, generalise about social structures and relationships from the weapons that men were carrying or were not carrying: in Londonderry, two of the Companies' chief tenants – George Canning of the Ironmongers and Peter Barker of the Drapers – mustered without arms and one of the wealthiest men in county Cavan, Richard Castledine, only carried a sword.

3.   Editorial Note [JJ]

Robert was editing the muster roll from published material for counties Armagh, Cavan, and Donegal and from transcripts for the other counties. He had produced full transcripts for counties Antrim, Down, and Monaghan and partial transcripts for counties Fermanagh, Londonderry, and Tyrone. I have used published material to supplement the transcripts for Fermanagh and Londonderry and my own transcript to supplement that for Tyrone.

Family relationships have only been noted in the muster roll where these can be positively identified, as when two men share the same forename and surname and one is suffixed 'elder' and the other 'younger', or where a relationship is explicitly stated in another source, such as the 1622 undertakers' certificates. Caution is especially needed with the 1641 depositions because the deponents usually only gave information about themselves. In her deposition of January 1642 Anne Cooke, for instance, describes herself as 'of Belturbet in the county of Cavan, widow'. She relates how 'Phillip O'Reilly and his soldiers' robbed her of 'cattle, household goods, debts, and her interest in a lease and a freehold to the value of sevenscore pounds.' She tells us that 'one of her children is since starved by the means of the rebels.'[59]

What she does not tell us is the name of her husband. Eight men named Cooke were living in Belturbet in 1630: we can discount one of them – William – because he was still alive in May 1642, but we are still left with seven – four of whom are called Anthony – from which to choose.[60]

1   Taken from Hunter, 'Donegal', pp 124-7 and supplemented with material from Robert Hunter's working papers: I am grateful to the Donegal Historical Society for permission to reproduce and adapt the original text.

2   T.W. Moody (ed.), 'The revised articles of the Ulster plantation, 1610' in *Bulletin of the Institute for Historical Research*, 12 (1935), pp 178–83; for a study of the English system, see Lindsay Boynton, *The Elizabethan militia, 1558–1633* (London, 1967). 'A convenient store of arms' for an undertaker of a 'great proportion' of 2,000 acres was 'twelve muskets and calivers, [and] twelve hand weapons for the arming of twenty-four men' (*Calendar of Carew MSS, 1603–24*, p. 269), or enough weapons to arm half of the adult males on the estate [JJ].

3   T.W. Moody (ed.), 'Ulster plantation papers, 1608–13', number 18, in *Analecta Hibernica*, 8 (1938).

4   George Hill, *An historical account of the plantation in Ulster at the commencement of the seventeenth century, 1608–20* [hereafter, Hill, *Plantation*], p. 465.

5   NLI, MS 8014/8; Victor Treadwell (ed.), *The Irish commission of 1622: an investigation of the Irish administration, 1615–22 and its consequences, 1623–4* (Irish Manuscripts Commission: Dublin, 2006) [hereafter, Treadwell (ed.), *Irish commission*], p. 547: the London Companies and some of the leading undertakers imported weapons from England and the Low Countries (see, for example, James Morrin (ed.), *A calendar of the patent and close rolls of chancery in Ireland for the reign of Charles I, years 1 to 8 inclusive* (Dublin, 1863) [hereafter, Morrin (ed.), *Patent rolls, Charles I*], pp 200–1). Dillon's approach, however, was the more typical one. Sir Thomas Ridgeway, for instance, 'enjoined' prospective tenants on his estate at Augher in county Tyrone in 1613 'to furnish themselves with sufficient arms' (Historical Manuscripts Commission, *Report on the Hastings manuscripts*, 4 (London, 1947), pp 179–80) and two fee-farm grants of land on the Taylor estate in county Cavan in 1613 and 1615 were made in consideration of the 'bodily service' of the tenants and their successors 'to be at all time for ever done at the time of muster being thereunto called' (NAI, M6956/4, 5) [RJH]. Requiring tenants to provide their own weapons created a problem, as the settlers took their arms with them when they moved to other estates and incoming tenants did not have weapons. Consequently, as happened with Sir Stephen Butler's property in county Cavan, an estate that had been well armed in 1619 or 1622 became effectively disarmed by 1630 [JJ].

6   Boynton, *Elizabethan militia*, p. 237.

7   Bodleian Library, Oxford, Carte MS 62, f. 481; the patent renewed Pynnar's appointment as muster-master of Connacht and Munster, a post he had held since 1615 (*Calendar of patent rolls, Ireland, James I*, p. 338), and replaced Richard Bingley with Alleyne; Bingley had been muster-master of Leinster since 1609 (*Calendar of state papers, Ireland, 1608–10*, p. 197) and muster-master of Ulster since 1610 (ibid. pp 496–7) [JJ].

8   His report, with transcripts of related documents, is in BL, Add. MS 18,735 (*Calendar of state papers, Ireland, 1615–25*, pp 226–30).

9   Some detected faults of arithmetic in the original manuscript and slight inaccuracies in the calendared version have been corrected [RJH].

10   Ibid. pp 510–11; Aidan Clarke, 'The army and politics in Ireland, 1625–30', in *Studia Hibernica*, 4 (1964), pp 28–53; see also David W. Miller, 'Non-professional soldiery, c. 1600–1800', in Thomas Bartlett and Keith Jeffery (eds.), *A military history of Ireland* (Cambridge, 1996), pp 316–17.

11   *Calendar of state papers, Ireland, 1625–32*, pp 50–1.

12   Ibid. pp 173, 207; for an example of a provost marshal being ineffectual, see Hunter, 'Donegal', pp 150–3.

13   *Calendar of state papers, Ireland, 1625–32*, p. 441.

14   Instructions to the lord deputy, 16 August 1627 (ibid. pp 263–4); further instructions to the lord deputy, 5 June 1628 (ibid. p. 350).

15   Ibid. 367; Morrin (ed.), *Patent rolls, Charles I*, pp 380–1.

16   Ibid. p. 385; NAI, Lodge MSS, misc. enrolments, p. 41.

17   BL, Add. MS 4770 (hereafter, Muster Roll): an example of the difficulty of reading the manuscript is Graham's 'V and Ws [which] sometimes leave the possibility for ambiguity open: the reader should consider the possibility of substituting one for the other, e.g. Vyne may be Wyne' (note by RJH, spring 1999 [PRONI, D4446/A/6]).

18   See Additional Notes 2.2.

19   Muster Roll, fols 9v, 18, and 19; George Alleyne probably compiled 'the other book' [JJ].

20   British settlers in early seventeenth-century Ulster were very mobile: only a third of the men who mustered on Sir Anthony Cope's estate at Loughgall in county Armagh were from families that had been present in 1622, and barely a quarter of those who mustered on the Balfour estate at Lisnaskea in county Fermanagh appear in the rent roll that was compiled in May 1636 [JJ].

21   This is a corrected figure taking into account inaccuracies of arithmetic for counties Armagh, Cavan, and Donegal [RJH]: the totals for county Down are also inaccurate [JJ].

22   The firearms were calivers, muskets, and snaphances; the caliver and musket were developments of the arquebus and had matchlock actions: the snaphance was an early form of the flintlock action (V.B. Norman and Don Pottinger, *English weapons and warfare, 449–1660* (London, 1979), p. 190).

23   Moody, *Londonderry*, pp 278–9, 319–22.

24   Boynton, *Elizabethan militia*, pp 269–87; recalcitrance is a reflection of the demilitarisation of early seventeenth-century British society (John Kenyon and Jane Ohlmeyer, 'The background to the civil wars in the Stuart kingdoms', in John Kenyon and Jane Ohlmeyer (eds.), *The civil wars: a military history of England, Scotland, and Ireland, 1638–60* (Oxford, 1998), pp 4–6).

25   There is no evidence, for example, that Graham accepted Alleyne's convention that only twenty-four males were musterable per thousand acres. Leases of this period contained relevant stipulations. Thus a fee-farm grant of land in Cavan in November 1636 required the tenants to be 'always furnished to their power and ability with good sufficient arms and weapons both for the defence of themselves and the country of the said plantation against the rebels and other [of] his majesty's enemies' (NAI, M6956/8). Another Cavan lease of *c.* 1635 required the tenant to appear at all musters and outrisings and contribute with the rest of the tenants to a group of 'ten able men, well armed with pike and musket for the king's service' and the defence of the landlord when required (NAI, Deeds, wills, and instruments ... post mortem, 25, pp 254–65).

26   Sheffield Archives, WWM/StrP/5/37–48.

27   E. Berwick (ed.), *The Rawdon papers* (London, 1819), p. 63.

28   RJH, Notes on William Graham (PRONI, D4446/A/7/2); Bernard Burke, *Vicissitudes of families*, third series (London, 1863), pp 143–7; Hill, *Plantation*, p. 337; the description of William Graham in 1624 as being 'of The Mote in county Cumberland'

(*Calendar of patent rolls, Ireland, James I*, p. 582), the clan's principal seat near Longtown on the Anglo-Scottish border, suggests that Sir Richard and Sir George Graham were members of the leading family within the clan.

29 As part of the pacification programme that followed the union of the crowns, fifty families were deported from Eskdale to Roscommon in 1606. Sir Richard and Sir George Graham are the 'two gentlemen of their own name' who met the families at Dublin. Most of the families moved onto Sir Richard and Sir George's estates when the Roscommon plantation collapsed (George Macdonald Fraser, *The steel bonnets: the story of the Anglo-Scottish border reivers* (London, 1971), pp 323–4). Graham is still a common surname in Kildare, Laois, and Wicklow [JJ].

30 Hill, *Plantation*, pp 337–8.

31 Ibid. p. 474; this was the origin of Bawnboy. In 1622 the bawn, house, and '200 acres of land' were let 'for twenty-one years' to 'Lieutenant William Rutledge [who] dwelleth' in the house: the remainder of the land was 'set to the Irish from year to year' (Treadwell (ed.), *Irish commission*, p. 523).

32 *Calendar of patent rolls, Ireland, James I*, p. 582; Burke, *Vicissitudes of families*, p. 152; Nicholas Canny, *Making Ireland British, 1580–1650* (Oxford, 2001), pp 264–5; for William Graham's lands in Queen's County and county Wicklow, see NAI, Lodge MS, 5, 90 and 357.

33 Burke, *Vicissitudes of families*, p. 151; Sir John Graham was Buckingham's master of horse.

34 Graham was probably a tenant of 'Mr William Stammers [who] holdeth these two tates [Lisnamallard and Lurganboy] of freehold land, 1 May 1637' (NAI, RC5/28).

35 Grievances against Lieutenant William Graham, in *Journal of the house of commons, Ireland* (1641), p. 334 [RJH].

36 Depositions mentioning Graham's participation in the uprising: TCD, MS 831, fols 023r–024v; MS 833, fols 260r–260v; MS 835, fols 073r–073v, 091r–092v, 115r–115v, 135r–135v, 147r–147v, 155r–155v, and 182r–182v; MS 838, fols 62–67v.

37 Inquisition on the death of Roger Boyle, bishop of Clogher, 19 April, 4 James II (NAI, RC 9/1, p. 294).

38 Burke, *Vicissitudes of families*, pp 159–60.

39 Parts of this and the following paragraphs have appeared in John Johnston, 'An Irish county in 1630: the muster roll of county Monaghan', in *Clogher Record*, 20 (2010), pp 233–42. I am grateful to the Clogher Historical Society for permission to reproduce extracts from that article. Data from Robert Hunter's working papers have led me to revise the dating that was suggested in the article [JJ].

40 The assumption that Graham wrote to the undertakers before holding the muster is based on his statement that 'the servitors in the county of Donegal who inhabit the barony of Kilmacrenan and the barony of Tyrhugh caused not their British to appear at the general muster at the time and places appointed according to the warning given them' (Muster Roll, f. 280) [JJ].

41 Henry Cotton, *Fasti ecclesiae Hiberniae*, 1 (2nd edition, Dublin, 1851), p. 13; Inquisitions of Ulster, Fermanagh, (33) and (55) Charles I.

42 www.staff.science.uu.nl/~gentleman0113/easter/easter_text2b.htm, accessed 17 February 2012.

43 T.W. Moody, *The Londonderry plantation: the City of London and the plantation in Ulster, 1607–41* (Belfast, 1939), p. 278, footnote 3.

44 Sir Moses Hill died on 10 February and Sir Hugh Clotworthy on 28 February 1631 (NAI, BET1/9, p. 58) [RJH].

45 RJH, Note on NAI, Ferguson MSS, 12, 183, 207–8 (PRONI, D4446/A/7/4).

46 R.J. Hunter, 'The Fishmongers' Company of London and the Londonderry plantation, 1609–41', in Gerard O'Brien (ed.), *Derry and Londonderry: history and society* (Dublin, 1999) [hereafter, Hunter, 'Fishmongers' Company'], p. 240.

47 Paterson, 'Armagh', p. 402.

48 Canny, *Making Ireland British*, pp 208–11.

49 Michael Perceval-Maxwell, *The Scottish migration to Ulster in the reign of James I* (London, 1973), chapters 8 and 9; Philip Robinson, *The plantation of Ulster: British settlement in an Irish landscape, 1600–70* (Dublin, 1984) [hereafter, Robinson, *Plantation of Ulster*], chapters 4 and 5; settlers in county Fermanagh who originated in Norfolk, for example, can be identified through their surnames [RJH]. Graham's spellings of Welsh names (Evance for Evans and Joanes for Jones, for example) suggest that these settlers may still have been Welsh-speaking [JJ].

50 Note by RJH (PRONI, D4446/A/8).

51 Extrapolation from the muster roll data for the province as a whole gives a total population of at least 30,000, but 'it is fairly clear that under-recording [in this and other musters] is a serious problem' and so 'an estimate nearer to 40,000 might be more appropriate [for the total British population of the province]' (W.A. Macafee, 'The movement of British settlers into Ulster during the seventeenth century', in *Familia: Ulster Genealogical Review*, 2 (1992), pp 94–5).

52 Note in PRONI, D4446/A/8.

53 R.J. Hunter, 'The Bible and the bawn: an Ulster planter inventorised', in Ciaran Brady and Jane Ohlmeyer (eds.), *British interventions in early modern Ireland* (Cambridge, 2005), p. 125.

54 RJH, Note based on NAI, BET 1/58 (PRONI, D4446/A/8); Inquisitions of Ulster, Armagh, (3) Charles I: Edward Whitehead was probably Giles's father and the husband of Henry Smith's second daughter, Dorothy; the elder daughter is probably the Mary Smith who was killed at Shewis, 1641 (Deposition of Ann Smith and Margret Clark, 16 March 1643 [TCD MS 836, fols 073r–074v]) and the youngest daughter, Elizabeth, may have been married to Robert Whitehead of Iniskeen, county Monaghan (Deposition of Elizabeth Whitehead, 18 June 1642 [ibid. fols 178r–178v]) [JJ].

55 Treadwell (ed.), *Irish commission*, p. 545.

56 Raymond Gillespie, 'The origins and development of an Ulster urban network, 1600–41', in *Irish Historical Studies*, 24 (1984), pp 18–19; John Johnston, 'Settlement on an Ulster estate: the Balfour rentals of 1632 and 1636', in *Clogher Record*, 12 (1985), pp 92–102.

57 Raymond Gillespie, *Colonial Ulster: the settlement of east Ulster, 1600–41* (Cork, 1986) [hereafter, Gillespie, *Colonial Ulster*], p. 117.

58 John Johnston, 'The plantation of county Fermanagh, 1610–41: an archaeological and historical survey' (unpublished M.A. thesis, Queen's University Belfast, 1976), pp 193–6; Gillespie, *Colonial Ulster*, p. 118.

59 Deposition of Anne Cooke, 19 January 1642 (TCD, MS 832, fols 211r–211v).

60 Muster Roll, fols 3–6; Deposition of William Cooke, 19 May 1642 (TCD, MS 833, fols 120r–120v).

County Cavan

[f. 3][1]

The Muster Roll of the County of Cavan[2]

Barony of Loughty

Sir Steaphen Butler, knight, undertaker of 2000 acres: his men and arms

Swords only
1. Sammuell Fullwood
2. Edward Sherynd
3. Anthony Aphy[3]
4. William Baker[4]
5. William Searle
6. Thomas Walker
7. John Carr[5]
8. William Smyth[6]
9. John Hames
10. William Venables
11. John Hickman[7]
12. Thomas Pyman
13. James Graham
14. James Greere
15. Nicholas Sympson younger[8]
16. Richard Cooling

[f. 3v]
17. William Cooke[9]
18. Michall Cooke
19. Peter Cooke
20. Zachary Warrell
21. James Woods[10]
22. Edward Davis
23. Anthony Cooke

Swords and Pikes
24. John Heron[11]
25. William Pennington
26. Christopher Anson[12]
27. Thomas Hunter
28. John Greere
29. Christopher Maynes
30. William Maynes

No Arms
31. Alexander Copeland
32. Symond Braydin
33. George Brookes
34. Mathew Enerrington[13]
35. John Ogill[14]

36. James Woods
37. Thomas Rayman
38. Gawyn Ellot
39. William Manson
40. Henry Warran
41. William Astwood[15]

[f. 4]
42. Nicholas Brooker
43. William Woods
44. Nathaniell Sharp
45. Christopher Goodwin
46. Anthony Cooke
47. Thomas Vynables
48. Robert Chapman
49. Edward Davis
50. William Reynold[16]
51. Richard Pyman
52. William Gather[17]
53. George Sharp
54. William Cante[18]
55. Thomas Borkeberry
56. Nicholas Sharp
57. Henry Lawader

---

1. Graham's numbering of the pages starts here with folio 1: the folios were later renumbered to include the two blank pages at the start of the volume. This numbering is conventionally used for references to pages of the muster roll.

2. Hunter and Perceval-Maxwell, 'Cavan', pp 208–21: I am grateful to the committee of Cumann Seanchais Bhreifne for permission to reproduce this text.

3. Numbers 3 and 163 are likely to be father and son: the spelling of the surname suggests that the family was still Welsh speaking (the modern spelling is Pugh); Hunter and Perceval-Maxwell, 'Cavan', p. 208 gives the name as Aply.

4. Robbed, 1641 (Examination of William Baker, 25 July 1642 [TCD MS 817, fols 065r–067v]); possibly the son of John Baker (Sir Edward Fish, number 3).

5. Hanged Belturbet, January 1642 (Deposition of William Bloxam, 28 November 1642 [TCD MS 833, fols 109r–109v] and Examination of Peter Rickebee, 1 April 1654 [ibid. fols 295r–296v]).

6. Merchant; resident Belturbet; losses £857 0s 0d (Deposition of William Smith, 7 July 1642 [ibid. fols 189r–190v]).

7. Yeoman; resident 'Tunckeerveta'; losses £145 12s 0d; brother-in-law, Donnell O'Leary, looked after family (Deposition of John Hickman, 6 February 1643 [ibid. fols 156r–156v]).

8. Nicholas Simpson senior did not muster.

9. Yeoman; resident Belturbet; losses £116 10s 0d (Deposition of William Cooke, 19 May 1642 [ibid. fol. 120r]).

10. Joanne Woods 'the younger … widow aged forty-seven years' reported losses of £100 0s 0d. One of the three men named Woods (numbers 21, 36, and 43) is her husband and another one in her father-in-law: he and her mother-in-law were alive in October 1641 (Depositions of Joane Woods, elder and younger, undated [TCD MS 832, fols 166v–167r]).

11. Innkeeper; resident Belturbet; losses £414 0s 0d; his son was called Brian (Deposition of John Heron, 11 January 1642 [TCD MS 833, fols 006r–007v]). Two other men (numbers 161 and 164) are listed as John Heiron: I have identified number 24 as John Heron, the innkeeper, because his name is spelled the same way in the muster roll and in the deposition [JJ].

12. Hunter and Perceval-Maxwell, 'Cavan', p. 208 gives this name as Awson.

13. Possibly Musgrave Arrington 'of the Ibries in the parish of Dromlane'; losses £18 0s 0d (Deposition of Musgrave Arrington, 7 January 1642 [TCD MS 832, fols 180r–180v]).

14. Tanner; resident Belturbet; estimated losses £385 0s 0d (Deposition of William Ellicott, John Heron, and George Ellwood, 24 March 1642 [TCD MS 833, fols 103r–103v]); described as 'gentleman' (Deposition of Thomas Wenslowe, 16 January 1644 [TCD MS 835, fols 249r–249v]); hanged in Fermanagh (Deposition of William Gibbs, 31 January 1644 [TCD MS 833, fols 249r–250v]).

15. Shoemaker; resident Belturbet; losses £375 0s 0d (Deposition of William Astwood, 12 May 1642 [TCD MS 832, fols 181r–182v]).

16. One William Reynolds described himself as 'of Lisanaore in the parish of Templeport …, gentleman' and reported losses of £364 8s 0d (Deposition of William Reinoldes, 6 April 1643 [TCD MS 832, fols 059r–059v and MS 833, fols 260r–260v]): another William Reynolds described himself as a 'yeoman' of Currgarrah and reported losses of £102 0s 0d (Deposition of William Reinolds, 12 July 1643 [ibid. MS 832, fols 128r–129r and MS 833, fols 258r–259v].

17. This may be 'old William Carter', who was killed with his wife at Belturbet, 30 January 1642 (Deposition of William Gibbs, 31 January 1644 [ibid. fols 249r–250v]).

18. Yeoman; resident at Edenterriffe; losses £820 0s 0d; wife died at Ardbrackan during the flight to Dublin (Deposition of Richard Lewys, 30 December 1641 [TCD MS 832, fols 198r–198v; ibid. fols 034r–035v]).

58. William Hanck
59. Thomas Clarke
60. Thomas Woodward
61. Peter Hilton
62. William Taylor
63. Jaly Forborne[19]
64. Thomas Forborne
65. Anthony Forborne[20]

[f. 4v]

66. Thomas Dawson
67. Richard Narath
68. Oliver Smyth[21]
69. John Smyth[22]
70. Nicholas Smyth[23]
71. John Watson[24]
72. John Bradshaw
73. Ralph Campion
74. Cuthbert Greire
75. William Heckreck
76. John Crawdock
77. George Chardreck
78. George Butler
79. John Hutchison
80. Thomas Goathead
81. Richard Typar

82. William Parr[25]
83. William Graves
84. Daniell Ebbots
85. William Bradshaw
86. Robert Underwood
87. John Marham
88. Richard Cahowne
89. George Elwood[26]

[f. 5]

90. Edward Browne[27]
91. Richard Gamble
92. William Coop
93. John Morton
94. Ralph Coowling
95. Thomas Price
96. John Wood
97. Richard Thurbane[28]
98. John Newman
99. John Vaus
100. Anthony Cooke
101. William Gibbs[29]
102. Ralph Browne
103. Thomas Reynolds
104. Thomas Cloff

105. John Wilkinson[30]
106. Sampson Smyth
107. Benjamin Taylor[31]
108. Charles Best[32]
109. John Warran[33]
110. Thomas Fenshaw
111. Edward Whitehead
112. Michaell Cranfeild
113. Richard Rowles
114. Edward Marston[34]
115. Walter Moore[35]

[f. 5v]

116. Peter Scot
117. Henry Reynold[36]
118. John Sawson
119. Edward Davis
120. William Reynolds[37]
121. Robert Chapman
122. Richard Pyman
123. John Bell
124. William Anston[38]
125. William Reyner
126. Edmond Sherin[39]
127. Seth Field

19 The Fairburns were brothers and 'men of considerable estate and quality in both counties of Cavan and Fermanagh.' They 'were possessed of an estate of inheritance worth £100 0s 0d per annum, so that the same being rightly valued together with their personal estate, it doth amount to £1.500 0s 0d or thereabouts' (Deposition of Oliver Smith, 22 June 1647 [TCD MS 833, fols 285r–286v]).

20 Anthony Fairburn was a tanner; he was resident at Derrycarry (Butlersbridge) when he, his wife, his father, and his brother – both of whom were called John – were murdered, 1642 (Deposition of Symon Wesnam, 23 July 1642 [ibid. fol. 188v]); his losses were estimated at £1500 0s 0d (Deposition of Richard North, 22 June 1647 [ibid. fol. 285r]).

21 Gentleman; aged forty-six; resident 'Crahard'; losses £1.071 0s 0d; Smith had built up an estate consisting of six townlands in Cavan and Fermanagh (Deposition of Oliver Smith, 31 January 1642 [ibid. fols 287r–288r]). He lent £150 0s 0d to Anthony Fairburn, repayable over twenty years at £15 0s 0d a year on surety of a mortgage on Derrycarry (Deposition of Symon Wesnam, 23 July 1642 [ibid. fol. 188v]), and certified that Eleanor and Abraham James had lost £2.417 0s 0d (Deposition of Oliver Smith et al., 14 February 1642 [TCD MS 835, fols 172r–172v]).

22 Younger brother of Oliver Smith (Deposition of Oliver Smith, 31 January 1642 [TCD MS 833, fols 287r–288r]); identified as one of 'such protestants as … went to mass' (Deposition of Arthur Culme, 9 May 1642 [ibid. fols 127r–132v]); killed 1642; losses £32 0s 0d (Deposition of widow, Elizabeth Smith, 1 June 1642 [ibid. fols 192r–192v]).

23 Resident Ryneary; losses £275 0s 0d (Deposition of his brother-in-law, Martine Killhare, 13 January 1642 [ibid., fols 031r–032v]); identified as one of 'such protestants as … went to mass' (Deposition of Arthur Culme, 9 May 1642 [ibid. fols 127r–132v]).

24 Resident 'Polebrallogh'; held three townlands from 'Lieutenant John Campbell'; losses £72 5s 0d (Deposition of John Watsone, 11 November 1642 [ibid. fols 202r–203v]).

25 Farmed Aghriplowes; losses £30 0s 0d (Deposition of his widow, Elizabeth Parr, 22 March 1642 [ibid. fols 044r–044v]).

26 Felt maker; resident Belturbet; losses £142 0s 0d (Deposition of George Elwood, 26 March 1642 [ibid. fols 148r–149v].

27 Baker; resident Belturbet; losses £585 13s 4d (Deposition of Edward Browne, 5 April 1647 [ibid. fols 283r–283v]).

28 'Gentleman'; resident 'Kilconny'; losses £659 19s 8d (Deposition of Richard Thurbane, 4 August 1643 [ibid. fols 271r–271v]).

29 Butcher; resident Belturbet (Deposition of William Gibbs, 31 January 1644 [ibid. 249r–250v]); losses £178 16s 8d (Deposition of wife, Jane Taylor, 8 January 1642 [ibid. fols 067r–067v]).

30 Cooper; resident Belturbet; losses £161 0s 0d (Deposition of John Wilkinson, 8 January 1642 [ibid. fols 087r–087v]).

31 Tanner; farmed 'Comleine', near Belturbet; losses £178 16s 8d (Deposition of Jane Taylor, 8 January 1642 [ibid. fols 067r–067v]).

32 Chapman; resident Belturbet; losses £60 (Deposition of Charles Best, 8 January 1642 [TCD MS 832, fols 187r–187v]).

33 Brother-in-law of Rev. Martin Baxter of Carndallan (Deposition of William Baxter, 22 September 1642 [TCD MS 835, fols 192r–193v]); resident Belturbet and landlord to John West (number 154); owed Philip Ward £2 8s 0d (Deposition of Phillip Ward, 7 January 1642 [TCD MS 833, fols 085r–085v]).

34 Wife and children drowned Belturbet, 30 January 1642 (Examination of Peter Rickebee, 1 April 1654 [ibid. fols 295r–296v]).

35 Killed, 1642 (Depositions of Robert Bairde, 9 November 1642 [ibid. fols 102r–103v] and Patrick Bell, 9 November 1642 [ibid. fols 107r–108v]).

36 Yeoman; 'of Cornemuckley … aged forty-three years or thereabouts'; losses £598 10s 0d (Deposition of Henry Reynolds, 4 January 1642 [ibid. fols 057r–057v]); held Drumalee from Frances Perkins for £20 0s 0d (Deposition of Frances Perkins, 24 March 1642 [ibid. fols 045r–046v]).

37 See number 50.

38 Hunter and Perceval-Maxwell, 'Cavan', p. 209 gives this name as Austin.

39 Sherwin took out a lease on Creeny for eighty-seven years in May 1640 (Inquisitions of Ulster, Cavan (67), Charles I) but said he had been resident on the townland since 1619. He described himself as a 'gentleman' and held land in counties Cavan, Fermanagh, and Monaghan. His assailants in October 1641 included his landlord, Philip Hugh Mac Shane O'Reilly, and his losses totalled £2.238 10s 0d (Deposition of Edmund Sherwyn, 10 January 1642 [TCD MS 833, fols 064r–065v]).

128. Izack Ralph[40]
129. Ephraim Ralph
130. John Ralph
131. Andrew Peter
132. William Bloxholme[41]
133. Henry Lawander
134. George Netter[42]
135. John Coxes
136. John Walker[43]
137. William Butler
138. Izack Butler
139. George Maynes

[f. 6]

140. John Johnes[44]
141. John Ebbots
142. Daniell Ebbots
143. Beniamin Henington
144. Robert Crane
145. Thomas Carter
146. Theogennes Fynnaby
147. Olyver Bryan
148. Anthony Cooke
149. Robert Chapman
150. Thomas Taylor[45]
151. John Fourber
152. Anthony Fourber
153. Richard North[46]

[f. 6v]

154. John West[47]
155. Robert Chapman

156. John Smyth[48]
157. Peter Hilton
158. Thomas Sharp
159. Nicholas Clark
160. Thomas Goathead
161. John Heiron
162. Richard Wetten
163. Anthony Aphy[49]
164. John Heiron

[164 men;] 31 [30] Swords; 7 Pikes[50]

[f. 7]

Barony de Tulknock [Tullyhunco], Cavan

Sir Francis Hammelton, knight and baronet, undertaker of 3000 acres in the barony above said, the names of his men and arms as followeth

No Arms
1. Thomas Murrow
2. John Michell

Sword Only
3. George Nixon

No Arms
4. Thomas Maywitie[51]

Sword and Pike
5. William Bell[52]
6. John Ediby
7. William Sharp[53]
8. Mathew Gray

Pike only
9. John Gillispick

Sword and Pike
10. Archball Johnston[54]
11. John Bell
12. Robert Delap
13. Thomas Joanes[55]

Sword only
14. Richard Joanes
15. William Joanes[56]

Sword and Musket
16. Robert Hunt[57]

No Arms
17. Gilbert Murrowes
18. Patrick Murrowes

Sword and Snaphance
19. William Hunt

Sword and Pike
20. Robert Berry

---

[40] Numbers 128 to 130 are probably related: the use of Old Testament forenames is to be noted [RJH].

[41] 'Of Polenemadre near Belturbet … gentleman'; farmed three townlands, with a house on each; losses £1.630 0s 0d (Deposition of William Bloxam, 28 November 1642 [TCD MS 833, fols 109r–109v]).

[42] Yeoman; losses of £201 0s 0d (Deposition of George Netter, 24 January 1643 [ibid. fols 255r–255v]).

[43] Killed Lare, February 1642 (Depositions of William Jamesone, 8 July 1642 [ibid. fols 160r–160v] and of Jenett Kearnes, Brian Sherin and William Beatagh, 13 February 1644 [ibid. fols 254r–254v]).

[44] Resident Belturbet; killed, January 1642 (Deposition of William Gibbs, 31 January 1644 [ibid. fols 249r–250v]).

[45] 'Of Belturbet … gentleman … aged three score years or thereabouts'; held nine townlands in counties Cavan and Fermanagh and five houses in Belturbet; losses £703 0s 0d (Deposition of Thomas Taylor, 3 January 1642 [ibid. fols 070r–070v]).

[46] 'Of Drumcarplin … farmer aged fifty-five years or thereabouts'; losses £400 0s 0d (Deposition of Richard North, undated [TCD MS 832, fol. 169r]) or £410 0s 0d (Deposition of Richard North, 12 January 1642 [TCD MS 833, fols 041r–041v]).

[47] Gentleman; farmed three townlands near Belturbet; losses £411 10s 0d; purchased Cahard from Richard Smith and built his house, valued at £60 0s 0d, there (Deposition of John West, 10 February 1642 [ibid. fols 083r–083v]).

[48] Possibly 'John Smith late of Lismore near Kilmore … carpenter aged forty-five years' (Deposition of John Smith, 26 July 1642 [TCD MS 832, fols 169v–171v]).

[49] See number 2.

[50] Errors in the totals are shown in square brackets.

[51] Son of number 83.

[52] William and John Bell are probably the sons of John Bell (numbers 5, 11, and 31): another son, Patrick, was too young to muster; he was farming Aghknock, 1641 (Deposition of Patrick Bell, 9 November 1642 [TCD MS 833, fols 107r–108v]).

[53] Held Shantomyne and Corrikirie from Roger Moynes (Deposition of William Sharpe, 9 November 1642 [ibid. fols 184r–184v]); possibly father of John Sharpe (Deposition of Patrick Atkinson, 21 July 1642 [ibid. fols 183r–183v]); escaped to Dublin, October 1641 (Deposition of Faithfull Teate, Elizabeth Day and William Thorp, 20 April 1642 [ibid. fols 061r–062v]).

[54] The nine men named Johnston (numbers 10, 38, 54, 64, 67, 68, 72, 87, and 97) are drawn from at least three separate families.

[55] Gentleman; resident 'Drominan'; 'aged three score and odd' years (Deposition of Thomas Jones, 26 July 1642 [TCD MS 833, fols 164r–164v]; father of William Joanes (number 15) [and possibly of Richard Jones (number 14)]; losses £229 0s 0d (Deposition of William Jones and Thomas Jones, 26 July 1642 [ibid. fols 163r–163v]).

[56] 'Of Cornedrom … gentleman'; son of Thomas Jones (number 13) (ibid.).

[57] 'Late of Curre …, gentleman …, aged … fifty years or thereabouts'; losses £180 0s 0d (Examination of Robert Hunt, undated [TCD, MS 832, fols 164r–164v]); could also be 'Robert Hunte of Cor …, gentleman aged thirty-seven years'; losses £302 4s 0d (Deposition of Robert Hunte, 15 May 1643 [TCD MS 833, fols 252r–252v]); Robert (number 16) and William (number 19) Hunt may have been sons of Stephen Hunt, one of the freeholders (Hill, *Plantation*, pp 469–70).

Sword and Caliver

21. John Graham[58]

[f. 7v]

Snaphance only

22. Henry Ban

Pike only

23. James Ban

Sword and Pike

24. Frauncis Kee
25. Adam Anderson
26. John Lassy

No Arms

27. Thomas Mumberson[59]

Sword and Pike

28. John Cowen
29. Andrew Wood

Sword and Snaphance

30. George Frissell

Sword and Pike

31. John Bell

Sword and Musket

32. Alexander Hume

Sword and Pike

33. John Killpatrick

No Arms

34. James Moffet
35. James Kilcrag[60]

Sword and Pike

36. Jeremy Boston
37. Thomas Finlaw

No Arms

38. Martin Johnston

Sword only

39. Bryan Shedy
40. John Sympson[61]

Sword and Snaphance

41. Andrew Gilespy

Sword and Pike

42. Thomas Twigg

Sword and Musket

43. Gilbert Wance

Pike only

44. James Bernes

[f. 8]

Sword and Pike

45. Thomas McCor
46. William Richardson

No Arms

47. Oliver Owdny[62]
48. Nicholas Owdny

Sword and Snaphance

49. Thomas Twedy
50. George Hammelton

Sword and Musket

51. John Dixon
52. James Morison

No Arms

53. Alexander Kincraig

Sword and Pike

54. John Johnston
55. James Anderson
56. George Anderson

Snaphance only

57. Archball Renny

Sword only

58. Thomas Renny

Sword and Snaphance

59. Hugh Renny

Sword and Pike

60. John Mory

Sword and Snaphance

61. Thomas Coop

Sword and Musket

62. John Cooper[63]

Sword and Pike

63. James Hammelton

These appeared without arms

64. Thomas Johnston
65. David Wawigh
66. Thomas Roger
67. Patrick Johnston

[f. 8v]

68. Walter Johnston[64]
69. Thomas Mitchell
70. Patrick Mewres
71. John Little
72. Andrew Johnston
73. Thomas Morman
74. Robert Shawe
75. Thomas Trotter
76. James Ewrat
77. Andrew Herriott
78. Adam Elliott
79. John Remy
80. Thomas Remy
81. Seymour Styell
82. Robert Nixon
83. Thomas Mawitie elder[65]
84. John Mawitie[66]
85. James Mawitie
86. Nathaniell Mawitie
87. William Johnston
88. Alexander Frissell
89. John Rankyne
90. John Delap

[f. 9]

91. Edward Cary
92. John Forker
93. William Shelson
94. Robert Anderson
95. Thomas Leassy
96. John Leassy

---

58   Killed, 1641 (Deposition of John Simpson, 2 March 1644 [TCD MS 833, fols 264r–264v]).

59   Possibly son of Adam Maunderson, leaseholder, 1629 (Hill, *Plantation*, p. 470).

60   Owed £1 5s 0d to Robert Symons (Craig, number 16) (Deposition of Robert Symons, 12 October 1642 [TCD MS 833, fols 185r–185v]).

61   John Simpson described himself as 'late of Killashandra …, gentleman, lieutenant to Sir Francis Hamilton …, [and] aged about thirty-nine years'; he reported 'the loss of his goods, chattels, and means [to] the sum of £100 at least' (Deposition of John Simpson, 2 March 1644 [ibid. fols 264r–264v]).

62   Nicholas Udney leased Cran on John Hamilton's estate for five years from 1 April 1621 (Inquisitions of Ulster, Cavan (18) Charles I).

63   'Gentleman'; losses £484 0s 0d (Deposition of Edward Cooper, 24 May 1642 [TCD MS 833, fols 122r–122v]).

64   Owed 9s 0d to Robert Symons (Deposition of Robert Symons, 12 October 1642 [ibid. fols 185r–185v]).

65   Father of number 4 and probably related to numbers 84 to 86.

66   Leaseholder for twenty-one years, 1629 (Hill, *Plantation*, pp 469–70); owed 14s 0d to Robert Symons (Deposition of Robert Symons, 12 October 1642 [TCD MS 833, fols 185r–185v]).

97.   Symon Johnston
98.   Robert Hammelton
99.   John Thomson
100.   Robert Chrighton
101.   Christopher Sympson
102.   Edward Knight
103.   George Story
104.   William Roger
105.   William Coussings[67]
106.   Robert Really[68]
107.   James Really
108.   Moyses Really
109.   Richard Lighterfoote[69]
110.   John Gellaspy
111.   Henry Fetterson
112.   Bartholemew Bockham
113.   William Hammelton
114.   Francis Coussings

[f. 9v]

115.   John Garyner[70]
116.   Edward Cooper[71]
117.   John Sallowes
118.   George Lawder[72]
119.   William Cadell
120.   James Lawder
121.   Francis Mophet
122.   Thomas Graham[73]
123.   James Hammelton
124.   William Gillespy
125.   John Mophet
126.   William Young
127.   Patrick Graham
128.   Edward Coop
129.   Andrew Glaspeck
130.   William Glaspeck
131.   Henry Pench
132.   Thomas Coop
133.   John Coop
134.   Thomas Remick
135.   John Murry
136.   Thomas Muffes

Those men who made default at the general muster appeared at the last muster without arms.
113 [136] Men; 24 [46] Swords; 25 [29] Pikes; 6 Muskets; 1 Caliver; 9 Snaphances

[f. 10]

Barony of Tullyknock [Tullyhunco], Cavan

Sir James Crag knight and undertaker of 2000 acres in the barony above said, the names of his men and arms as followeth

Sword and Pike
1.   Alexander Watson

Pike Only
2.   John Bull

Halberd Only
3.   William Johnston

No Arms
4.   Hugh Bull

Sword and Musket
5.   Henry Garvye

No Arms
6.   Andrew Cowell

Sword and Pike
7.   Archball Gourdner

Musket only
8.   Alexander Johnston

Sword and Pike
9.   Gawin Fitzpatrick

Pike only
10.   William Ruddell

Sword and Pike
11.   George Taylor
12.   Edward Leake

Sword and Musket
13.   Henry Baxter[74]
14.   Christopher Hunt

Sword and Pike
15.   James Fyndloe
16.   Robert Symons[75]
17.   Andrew Frizell

Sword and Musket
18.   William Leake
19.   William Symons[76]

No Arms
20.   Richard Baker

Pike only
21.   Ralph Tomlison[77]

No Arms
22.   James Galespeck

[f. 10v]

Sword and Musket
23.   Thomas Fayne

Pike only
24.   William Galespeck

Sword and Pike
25.   David Galespeck

---

67   Killed, May 1642 (Deposition of John Simpson, 2 March 1644 [ibid. fols 264r–264v]).
68   Robert, James, and Moses Really (numbers 106 to 108) are either the sons of John Reley, to whom Sir George Mainwaring let Corlysally for forty-one years, 20 August 1616 (Inquisitions of Ulster, Cavan (23) Charles I), or related to the servitor, 'Captain Reley [who] hath 1.000 acres, called Lisconnor' in Tullaghgarvey (Nicholas Pynnar, Survey of the plantation (1619), in Hill, *Plantation*, p. 459).
69   Freeholder, 1629 (ibid. pp 469–70).
70   Killed, 1641 (Examination of Robert Hunt, undated [TCD MS 832, fols 164r–164v]).
71   Gentleman; brother of John Cooper (number 62); losses £382 0s 0d (Deposition of Edward Cooper, 24 May 1642 [TCD MS 833, fols 123r–123v]).
72   Freeholder, 1629 (Hill, *Plantation*, pp 469–70).
73   Killed, 1641 (Deposition of John Simpson, 2 March 1644 [TCD, MS 833 fols 264r–264v]).
74   Gentleman; immediate losses £760 0s 3d, future losses £20 a year from his freehold (Deposition of Henry Baxter, 21 June 1643 [TCD MS 833 fols 217r–218v]).
75   'Yeoman'; losses £617 7s 0d, including debts totalling £27 8s 0d owing from other British tenants (Deposition of Robert Symons, 12 October 1642 [ibid. fols 185r–185v]); father-in-law of Martin Baxter who owed £53 5s 0d to Philip Ward (Deposition of Phillip Ward, 7 January 1642 [ibid. fols 085r–085v]).
76   Owed £4 0s 0d to Edward Howey, 1641 (Deposition of Alice Hovay, 7 January 1642 [ibid. fols 012r–013v]); his 'cowman and servant', Patrick Magowan, was one of the rebels, 1641 (Deposition of Elizabeth Ward, 13 September 1642 [ibid. fols 198r–198v]).
77   'Yeoman'; killed, December 1641; resident Crena; losses £422 0s 0d (Deposition of widow, Jane Tomlinson, 9 August 1642 [ibid. fols 197r–197v]).

No Arms
26. James Anderson

Pike only
27. William Symonton

No Arms
28. John Fyndloe[78]

Pike and Sword
29. David Phillips[79]

No Arms
30. Lawrence Plant
31. George Sterling
32. Henry Litster
33. Richard Hoopes
34. Henry Hoopes[80]
35. John Gardner
36. John Pattent
37. William Goslop
38. Robert Johnston[81]
39. Richard Lowharret
40. George Best
41. John Baker
42. Henry Chambers
43. William Thomson
44. Mychall Miller
45. Robert Had
46. John Dixon
47. Roger Clayton[82]

[f. 11]

48. William Morris
49. Hugh Remick
50. Symond Anderson
51. William Johnston
52. John Lawson
53. John Dickeson
54. Henry Hoopes younger[83]

54 Men; 16 Swords; 15 Pikes; 6 [7] Muskets; 1 Halberd

[f. 11v]

Cavan
Barony of Tulliknock [Tullyhunco]

Sir Archball Atchison knight, undertaker of 1000 acres in the barony above said, the names of his men and arms as followeth

Sword only
1. William Wood

Sword and Snaphance
2. Alexander Wood

Sword only
3. John Atcheson
4. William Wilson

Sword and Pike
5. Thomas Todrick

Sword and Snaphance
6. James Mill

Sword and Pike
7. John Gilpatrick
8. Jeremy Synier

Sword and Snaphance
9. William Ranny

Sword and Pike
10. George Lairmounth
11. Richard Sexes

Halberd only
12. Edmond Diss

Sword and Pike
13. Patrick Brewshanks
14. Georg Shewernam
15. William Gibson

Snaphance only
16. John Glen

Sword and Snaphance
17. Ralph Wilson

No Arms
18. Ralph Lotchwarret
19. George Best
20. George Tully

20 Men; 14 Swords; 8 [9] Pikes; 5 Snaphances

[f. 12]

Cavan
Barony of Loughty

Sir Edward Bagshaw knight, undertaker of 1500 acres: the names of his men and arms

No Arms
1. Edward Copeland
2. Benedict Catnam[84]
3. Sammuell Catnam[85]
4. Sammuell Sharp
5. Henry Allen
6. Richard Dawson
7. John Goodbody
8. Thomas Carington[86]
9. John Ward
10. Edward Butler
11. Richard Couch
12. Robert Plootes
13. Thomas Styles

Snaphance only
14. Francis Lug

Pike only
15. Griffin Evance

---

78 John Finlay and Patrick Finlay leased Tullylurkan on John Hamilton's estate for seven years from 12 May 1620 (Inquisitions of Ulster, Cavan (18) Charles I).

79 His widow was killed at Belturbet in January 1642 (Deposition of William Gibbs, 31 January 1644 [TCD MS 833, fols 249r–250v]).

80 Father of number 54 and probably of number 33.

81 'Of Oghall in the county of Cavan, yeoman' (Deposition of Robert Johnson, 21 January 1642 [TCD MS 833, fols 019r–019v]).

82 'Of Sallaghwee … yeoman aged fifty years'; losses £865 0s 0d (Deposition of Roger Cleayton, 23 November 1642 [ibid. fols 117r–117v]).

83 Son of number 34.

84 Killed, October 1641 (Depositions of John Baker, 17 September 1642 [TCD MS 833, fols 100r–101v] and Arthur Culme, 9 May 1642 [ibid. fols 127r–132v]; possibly father of Samuel Cotnam (number 3) (Deposition of Samuell Cotnam, 28 February 1642, [ibid. fols 126r–126v]) and of Benedict Cotnam on the Moynes estate; possibly related to 'Thomas Cottenham of the Quivy …, yeoman' (Deposition of Oliver Smith et al., 14 February 1642 [ibid. MS 835, fols 172r–172v]).

85 'Gentleman'; farmed Derryvony and Coragh townlands; losses £794 0s 0d; reported death of father and probable death of his son (Deposition of Samuell Cotnam, 28 February 1642 [TCD MS 833, fols 126r–126v]).

86 Numbers 8 and 23 are probably father and son; one of them was a weaver, who lived at Ballenesse and suffered losses of £150 0s 0d (Deposition of widow, Audrey Carington, 27 October 1645 [ibid. fols 282r–282v]). Richard Carrington (number 22) is Thomas Carrington senior's brother and the father of Richard Carrington junior, who appears as number 13 on Francis Sacherevall's estate, county Armagh. Christopher and Walter Carrington (numbers 24 and 25) are probably the younger sons.

Sword only
16.   Robert Norrice

No Arms
17.   Oliver Brian

Sword and Snaphance
18.   Mathew Rolph
19.   Thomas Wentworth

Snaphance only
20.   Francis Robison

Sword only
21.   Richard Bennet[87]

Pike only
22.   Richard Carington elder

[f. 12v]

No Arms
23.   Thomas Carington
24.   Christopher Carington

Musket only
25.   Walter Carington

Pike only
26.   John Ward

Sword only
27.   Roger Killhare[88]

No Arms
28.   Thomas Robison
29.   Phillip Ward
30.   Frauncis Long

31.   Richard Cox
32.   Robert Plots

32 Men; 5 Swords; 3 Pikes; 1 Musket;
4 Snaphances

[f. 13]

Cavan

Barony de Loughty

The Lady Waldrune, undertaker
of 2000 Acres: the names of her
men and arms as followeth[89]

Sword and Pike
1.   Thomas Led

Sword only
2.   Richard Hamberby

No Arms
3.   John Wisson

Sword and Pike
4.   George Chapman

Sword only
5.   Richard Casselden[90]

Pike only
6.   John Twig

Sword and Pike
7.   Steaphen Sligh

Sword and Snaphance
8.   William Casselden[91]

Pike only
9.   Anthony Birsid

No Arms
10.   William Rattall
11.   David Callet
12.   George Stosbany
13.   William Robinson
14.   Peter Cross[92]
15.   John Cross
16.   Thomas Woodyeare
17.   William Stortwant
18.   Anthony Stortvant[93]
19.   Thomas Lynol
20.   John Parker
21.   Arthur Clark
22.   Dominick Parker[94]
23.   John Towend
24.   Christopher Bowser
25.   Thomas Crowne
26.   Henry Throne
27.   William Goodman
28.   Edward Newman

[f. 13v]

29.   Jeremy Twig
30.   John Brodhorse[95]
31.   John Gamble[96]
32.   John Cuoston
33.   John Greene the elder[97]
34.   John Greene the younger
35.   Thomas Greene
36.   William Knowels
37.   Gawyn Ellot
38.   Nynyan Ellot[98]
39.   Peter Clarke[99]
40.   William Wadare

---

[87]   Carpenter; resident Kilcorbie; losses £170 0s 0d (Deposition of Richard Bennett, 4 August 1644 [TCD MS 833, fols 220r–220v]).

[88]   Roger Killhare died before 1641. His widow, Elizabeth, and Martin, one of his sons, held three townlands, one of them Drumlane, and suffered losses totalling £331 0s 0d. The other son, Godfrey, occupied the townland of Munlogh and suffered losses of £104 0s 0d. Nicholas Smyth (Sir Stephen Butler, number 70) was Roger Killhare's son-in-law (Depositions of Martine Killhare, 13 January 1642 [ibid. fols 029r–033v]).

[89]   The Waldron, later the Farnham, estate included parts of what had been Lisreagh, which had been the property of Sir George Mainwaring. The bulk of the Lisreagh estate passed to Roger Moynes, January 1628 and became Moynehall (Hill, *Plantation*, pp 461–6).

[90]   Richard Castledine was one of the original settlers in county Cavan: Sir George Mainwaring let him 'one water-mill and mill house, with parcel of the two poles of Drynan, for thirty-one years', 1 August 1618 (Inquisitions of Ulster, Cavan (23) Charles I). Castledine's estate at Farnham was worth £2.228 0s 0d, 1641 (Deposition of his son-in-law, John Waldron, undated [TCD MS 832, fols 144r–144v]): Castledine described himself as a gentleman and estimated his losses at £2.085 0s 0d (Deposition of Richard Castledine, 19 July 1642 [TCD MS 833, fols 113r–116v]).

[91]   Resident Inishmore; losses £102 0s 0d (Deposition of William Castledine, 5 January 1642 [TCD MS 832, fols 202r–202v]).

[92]   Killed, 1641 (Deposition of William Reinolds, 12 July 1643 [TCD MS 833, fols 258r–259v]).

[93]   Robbed and stripped at Butlersbridge, 1641 (Deposition of William Ragg, 8 January 1642 [ibid. fols 058r–058v]).

[94]   Yeoman; resident Dromonam; losses £1.266 9s 9d (Deposition of Joane Parker, 2 June 1647 [TCD MS 833, fols 286r–286v]); killed, 1642 (Depositions of Robert Bairde, 9 November 1642 [ibid. fols 102r–103v] and Patrick Bell, 9 November 1642 [ibid. fols 107r–108v] and Information of Manus McCowen, 11 May 1653 [TCD MS 838, fols 140r–140v]).

[95]   One of the original settlers; leased Aghnaghlogh from Sir George Mainwaring for forty-one years, 25 July 1617 (Inquisitions of Ulster, Cavan (23) Charles I).

[96]   Probably the son of Robert Gamble, to whom Sir George Mainwaring let two townlands for forty-one years, 2 October 1617 (Inquisitions of Ulster, Cavan (23) Car. I); resident Butlersbridge; aged fifty in 1641; losses £87 0s 0d (Deposition of John Gamble, 10 January 1642 [TCD MS 832, fols 229r–229v]).

[97]   Father of number 34 and probably of number 35.

[98]   Reportedly apostate (Deposition of Arthur Culme, 9 May 1642 [TCD MS 833, fols 127r–132v]).

[99]   Resident 'Derregide'; losses £290 0s 0d (Deposition of Peter Clarke, 22 January 1642 [TCD MS 832, fols 203r–203v]).

41. Gabriell Kirby
42. William Swanson[100]
43. Thomas Carter[101]
44. Walter Humes
45. Nicholas Parker
46. Robert Twig
47. Jefferey Twig[102]
48. Thomas Round
49. Edward Throne[103]
50. Walter Holmes[104]
51. Henry Roe
52. Edward Throne
53. William Rastoll[105]
54. Thomas Rastoll

54 Men; 5 [6] Swords; 4 [5] Pikes;
1 Snaphance

[f. 14]

Cavan
Barony de Loughty

Brockell Taylor esquire,
undertaker of 1500 acres:
the names of his men and
arms as followeth

Halberd only
1. Austen Page

No Arms
2. Richard Webster[106]

Musket only
3. Thomas Stamone[107]

Sword and Pike
4. Thomas Barthow
5. Nathaniell Teat
Drum
6. Adam Dewsberry

Snaphance only
7. William Palmer

Sword only
8. George More

No Arms
9. John Lokington[108]

Sword and Snaphance
10. Phebe Bignall[109]

Sword and Pike
11. John Ayer

Sword and Snaphance
12. Thomas Hill

Musket only
13. John Parnell

Snaphance only
14. Thomas Perkinson
15. Henry Brookes

Sword and Snaphance
16. Moyses Hibbots[110]

Sword and Pike
17. Daniell Hibbots

Sword and Snaphance
18. John Hibbots[111]

Pike only
19. John Humphreyes

Sword and Pike
20. Thomas Oxorth

Snaphance only
21. Vincent Oxorth

[f. 14v]
22. Thomas Porter[112]

Sword and Pike
23. William Quisy[113]
24. John Robinson

Pike only
25. John Reader

Snaphance only
26. James Stanyon[114]

Sword and Pike
27. John Stoniford
28. Richard Dixon[115]

Pike only
29. Robert Taylor

---

100 Possibly the son of Nicholas Swanson, who was 'aged seventy-two years or thereabouts' when he and his family were driven from their farm, losing £331 6s 8d (Deposition of Nicholas Swanson, 31 January 1642 [TCD MS 833, fols 066r–066v]).

101 Killed with Gamaliell, his son, Belturbet, January 1642 (Deposition of Richard Bennett, 4 August 1644 [ibid. fols 220r–220v]); Gamaliell Carter was known as Chem (Deposition of William Gibbs, 31 January 1644 [ibid. fols 249r–250v]).

102 Owed £4 0s 0d to Robert Symons (Deposition of Robert Symons, 12 October 1642 [ibid., fols 185r–185v]); killed, 1641 (Deposition of William Reinolds, 12 July 1643 [ibid. fols 258r–259v]).

103 'Edward Throne an English protestant [was] living lately [1641] in a lonely house near Farnham': his losses amounted to £9 10s 0d (Deposition of his widow, Anne Throne, 5 January 1642 [ibid. fols 074r–074v]).

104 Yeoman; 'late of Dredagh'; losses £343 10s 0d; named those killed at Ballyhaise (Deposition of Walter Holmes, 2 June 1647 [ibid. fols 284r–284v]).

105 Resident 'Tullylough', 1641; losses £65 0s 0d (Deposition of William Rasdall, 15 May 1643 [ibid. fols 261r–261v]).

106 Killed at Ballyhaise (ibid.).

107 Thomas Stamone or Stamore may be a relative of William Stammers who held Williams Graham's 'two tates [Lisnamallard and Lurganboy in Fermanagh] of freehold land' in 1637 (NAI, RC5/28) [RJH].

108 Numbers 9 and 83 are father and son; 'John Lockington the elder of Swethland' and his brother Edward (Bishop of Kilmore, number 5) were among the original settlers in the county. John Lockington senior described himself as a tanner and claimed losses amounting to £167 0s 0d (Deposition of John Lockinton, 28 February 1643 [TCD MS 833, fols 171r–171v]). He was named as one of the 'English that go to mass' (Deposition of Symon Wesnam, 22 July 1642 [ibid. fols 204r–206v]). John Lockington junior was murdered at Ballyhaise (Deposition of William Rasdall, 15 May 1643 [ibid. fols 261r–261v]).

109 Tanner and one of the 'English that go to mass' (Deposition of Symon Wesnam, 22 July 1642 [ibid. fols 204r–206v]).

110 'Gentleman'; resident Inishlegg; losses £576 0s 0d (Deposition of Moses Ibott, 6 July 1643 [ibid. fols 253r–253v]); gunsmith; wife, Meriall, daughter of Anthony Fairburn (Sir Stephen Butler, number 65) (Deposition of Richard North, 22 June 1647 [ibid. fol. 285r]).

111 'Of Enysbegge … yeoman'; losses £248 5s 0d (Deposition of John Hibbetts, 19 July 1643 [ibid. fols 008r–008v]).

112 Lost £182 0s 0d (Deposition of Thomas Porter, 26 May 1642 [ibid. fols 180r–180v]).

113 William Quincy's father, Henry, was a carpenter who became a freeholder, 1615 (Hill, *Plantation*, p. 461); William Quincy's losses, 1641 totalled £450 0s 0d (Deposition of William Quency, 26 January 1642 [TCD MS 833, fols 056r–056v]).

114 Possibly father of Richard Stannyan, resident at Ballyhaise and lost £38 0s 0d, 1641 (Deposition of Richard Stannyan, 23 November 1642 [ibid. fols 193r–193v]).

115 Assaulted and robbed in October 1641 (Deposition of William Thorpe, 10 January 1642 [ibid. fols 072r–072v]).

Sword and Pike

30. William Perkins[116]

No Arms

31. John Thorp[117]
32. William Thorp[118]
33. John Dewsberry[119]
34. James Graham
35. John Greeare
36. Cuthbert Greeare
37. Thomas Little
38. James Greeare
39. John Wilson
40. Robert Allen
41. John Russell
42. Thomas Brag
43. Thomas Newman[120]

[f. 15]

44. William Henderson
45. Jessie Wiggins
46. John Wilson
47. Symond Wisname[121]
48. William Hill
49. William Grove
50. William Par
51. Beniamin Kinnington
52. Brian Barnes[122]
53. Myles Par[123]

54. Myles Par younger
55. William North[124]
56. Thomas North
57. George Butler
58. George Chadick
59. Jeffery Wilcox
60. William Heckeriff
61. Christopher Maynes[125]
62. John Brookes[126]
63. John Crawdock
64. Robert Crosse
65. Richard Witton
66. William Maynes
67. William Kellum
68. Richard Peale
69. Thomas Gouthwet

[f. 15v]

70. Richard Cheston
71. Richard Pepper
72. John Gardner
73. Robert Reader[127]
74. James Reader
75. Phillip Pepper
76. William Gardner[128]
77. George Hecklefeild
78. Henry Hecklefeild[129]
79. George Naylor[130]
80. John Rowkins[131]

81. John Dewsberry
82. Thomas Greeare
83. John Lockington[132]
84. William Falk
85. William Millington

85 Men; 15 Swords; 11 Pikes; 10 Snaphances; 1 Halberd; 1 Musket; [1 Drum]

[f. 16]

Cavan
Barony de Loughty

Mr Moynes[133] esquire, undertaker of 2000 acres: the names of his men and arms

No Arms

1. John Douglas

Caliver only

2. Allen Dowe

Sword only

3. John Butler

---

[116] Resident Ballyhaise; losses £100 0s 0d (Deposition of William Perkins, 4 January 1642 [ibid. fols 049r–049v]); held Enshanah for £6 2s 0d from Francis Perkins (Deposition of Frances Perkins, 24 March 1642 [ibid. fols 045r–045v]).

[117] Assaulted and robbed, October 1641(Deposition of William Thorpe, 10 January 1642 [ibid. fols 072r–072v]); losses £136 0s 0d (Deposition of Margery Thorp, 7 March 1642 [ibid. fols 073r–073v]).

[118] Resident Ouley, near Ballyhaise, 1641; losses £155 10s 0d (Deposition of William Thorp, 10 January 1642 [ibid. fols 072r–072v]).

[119] Held Atteduffe from Francis Perkins for £6 0s 0d (Deposition of Frances Perkins, 24 March 1642[ibid. fols 045r–045v]); carrier; resident Castleterra; losses £107 10s 0d (Deposition of John Dewsbury, 2 April 1642 [ibid. fols 144r–144v]).

[120] Sixty year lease on 300 acres, 1615 for £61 10s 0d a year (Hill, *Plantation*, p. 461); losses £229 0s 0d; (Deposition of Thomas Newman, 12 January 1642[TCD MS 833, fols 038r–038v]).

[121] 'Gentleman'; resident Carrickmore; losses £167 0s 0d (Deposition of Symon Wesnam, 22 July 1642 [ibid. fols 204r–206v]); son, Thomas, killed Ballyhaise (Depositions of Elizabeth Day, 21 August 1643 [ibid. fol. 245r–245v] and William Rasdall, 15 May 1643 [ibid. fols 261r–261v]).

[122] Possibly also known as Henry Barnes and, if so, the father of Henry Barnes junior; the Barnes farmed Derrihow and lost £360 0s 0d (Deposition of Henry Barnes, 17 January 1642 [TCD MS 832, fols 185r–185v]).

[123] Father of number 54 and probably 50.

[124] 'Of Corincooney … weaver'; losses £184 0s 0d (Deposition of William North, 30 June 1642 [TCD MS 833 fols 179r–179v]).

[125] Tailor; resident Butlersbridge; losses £27 0s 0d (Deposition of Christopher Meanes, 29 March 1642 [ibid. fols 176r–176v]).

[126] 'Yeoman aged forty years or thereabouts'; losses £20 0s 0d (Deposition of John Brooks, 5 January 1642 [TCD MS 832, fols 193r–193v]).

[127] Robert Reader died before 29 November 1630 (NAI, M6956/8): his widow and son, Thomas 'concluded a deal with the landlord concerning their freehold property' [RJH]. The 'naked and mad Englishman called Robert Reader' who was killed by Farrell McBrian Oge O'Reilly in 1641(Deposition of Symon Wesnam, 22 July 1642 [TCD MS 833 fols 204r–206v]) may have therefore been another of his sons or a son of either John Reader (number 25) or James Reader (number 74) [JJ]. Thomas Reader farmed Kilvanny and reported losses of £990 0s 0d (Examination of Thomas Reader, 23 January 1642 [ibid. fols 094r–095v]).

[128] 'Of Knockfadda in the parish of Ballyhaise … [and a] farmer, aged sixty-three years or thereabouts' (deposition, undated [TCD MS 832, fol. 165r]); later described himself as 'yeoman' and reported losses of £316 0s 0d (Deposition of William Garton, 10 January 1642 [ibid. fols 228r–228v]); owed £2 0s 0d to Philip Ward (Deposition of Phillip Ward, 7 January 1642 [TCD MS 833, fols 085r–085v]).

[129] Described himself as 'of Lisneshanny … gentleman, aged thirty-two years or thereabouts'; held eight townlands in Castlerahan and four burgage plots in Belturbet; losses £890 0s 0d (Deposition of Henry Hocklefield, 5 January 1642 [ibid. fols 009r–010v]).

[130] His widow, Isabel, was aged thirty-two, 1641; their lease on Keadew had fourteen years to run and their losses amounted to £150 0s 0d (Deposition of Issabell Nayler, 5 January 1642 [ibid. fols 037r–037v]).

[131] Son-in-law of William Cooke (Sir Stephen Butler, number 17); losses £160 10s 0d (Deposition of William Cooke, 24 May 1642 [ibid. fols 121r–122v]).

[132] See number 9.

[133] Roger Moynes had acquired the estate of Sir George Mainwaring, January 1629 but died before July of that year, and the estate was granted to his widow, Abigail, and John Greenham (Hill, *Plantation*, pp 466–7). The estate later passed to Moynes's son, Roger, who was killed during the attempted relief of Drogheda in 1642. Roger Moynes junior's widow, Dorothy, reported losses of £1.613 0s 0d in goods, chattels, livestock, fodder, and rents (Deposition of Dorothy Moigne, 5 March 1642 [TCD MS 833, fols 036r–036v]).

Sword and Caliver
4. John Guy[134]

Caliver only
5. George Gray[135]

No Arms
6. Robert Newton[136]

Musket only
7. Thomas Darlin[137]

Pike only
8. William Newton

Sword and Pike
9. Thomas Oliver[138]

Sword and Snaphance
10. Hamlet Steele[139]

Pike only
11. William Ownes

Caliver only
12. Ralph Asbrooke

No Arms
13. Nicholas Heath
14. Mathew Hitchcock
15. John Wheler
16. Gregory Flecker
17. Rynyon Ellot
18. John Taylor[140]
19. Benedict Cotnam[141]
20. Mathew Ross

21. Richard Corrington
22. William Bristow[142]
23. John Goodbody
24. Richard Benidict
25. Roger Killer
26. John Ward[143]
27. Georg Bullock[144]
28. Griffin Evance

28 Men; 4 Swords; 1 [3] Pike;
1 Musket; 3 Calivers; 1 Snaphance

[f. 16v]

Cavan
Barony de Loughty

Mr Amis and Mr Greeneham,[145]
undertakers of 1500 acres: the
names of their men and arms

Sword and Pike
1. William Dowkes[146]
2. Henry Callendyn

Sword and Musket
3. John Sympson[147]

Sword and Pike
4. George Evance[148]

Sword and Snaphance
5. George Whittakers

No Arms
6. Edward Havy[149]

Pike only
7. Edward Samcock

No Arms
8. James Williamson
9. William Johnston

9 Men; 5 Swords; 4 Pikes; 1 Musket;
[1 Snaphance]

[f. 17]

Cavan
Barony de Clankey

Sir Henry Pearce baronet,
undertaker of 3000 acres: the
names of his men and arms

Sword and Target
1. Ralph Robinson

Sword and Pike
2. George Steill[150]
3. John Lighterfoote

Pike only
4. John Oswell

Sword and Pike
5. Thomas Ragdall

Sword and Caliver
6. William Price[151]

---

[134] Possibly the son of Thomas Guy, to whom Sir George Mainwaring let two townlands for 25 years, 25 March 1628 (Inquisitions of Ulster, Cavan (23), Charles I; Hill, *Plantation*, p. 466).

[135] 'Husbandman'; resident at Oghall; losses £60 0s 0d (Deposition of George Graye, 14 June 1643 [TCD MS 833, fols 251r–251v]).

[136] Robert Newton, one of the original settlers, granted Aghnagloch on a 41 year lease from Sir George Mainwaring, 20 August 1616. William Newton (number 8) is one of Robert Newton's sons; another son, John, reported losses of £195 0s 0d (Deposition of John Newton, 21 May 1642 [ibid. fols 177r–177v]).

[137] Resident, 1641 (Deposition of Thomas Dawline, 14 February 1642 [TCD MS 832, fols 220r–220v]).

[138] Yeoman; aged 25; resident Corlislee; losses £77 10s 0d (Deposition of Thomas Olipher, 9 February 1642 [TCD MS 833, fols 042r–043v]).

[139] Innkeeper Cavan town, 1641; losses £180 0s 0d; killed Virginia, 13 October 1643 (Deposition of his widow, Alice Steele, 8 January 1642 [ibid. fols 268r–268v]).

[140] One of the original settlers; freeholder, 26 July 1613 (Inquisitions of Ulster, Cavan (23) Charles I).

[141] See Sir Edward Bagshaw, number 2.

[142] Killed 1641; held two townlands; losses £300 0s 0d (Deposition of his cousin, Daniell Morriss, 6 June 1642 [TCD MS 835, fols 212r–212v]).

[143] Resident Portmoylin; losses £122 0s 0d ([Deposition of his wife, Ellin Ward [ibid. fols 079r–079v]).

[144] Silvanus Bullock, possibly the son of George Bullock, described himself as 'of Belturbet … gentleman' and reported losses £23 0s 0d (Deposition of Silvanus Bullock, 29 January 1642 [TCD MS 832, fols 194r–194v]).

[145] John Greenham, 'a Dublin purchaser', was granted sole possession of the manor of Tonnagh on 14 July 1629 (Morrin (ed.), *Patent rolls, Charles I, 1–8*, p. 476; Hill, *Plantation*, p. 467).

[146] Yeoman; resident Kilnacorra; losses £441 0s 0d (Deposition of William Douckes, 8 January 1642 [MS 832, fols 224r–225v]); father of Thomas and John Douks 'of Clancurran' on the Bishop of Kilmore's estate (Deposition of Jane Douks, 8 January 1642 [ibid. fols 226r–226v]).

[147] 'Of Killenanam …, yeoman'; losses £418 (Deposition of John Symson, 23 March 1642 [TCD MS 833, fols 186r–186v]).

[148] 'Late of the black bull …, yeoman'; losses £686 0s 0d (Deposition of widow, Ursula Evans, 27 July 1643 [ibid. fols 246r–247v]).

[149] Resident Crumlin; losses £229 0s 0d (Deposition of Alice Hovay, 7 January 1642 [ibid. fols 012r–013v]); other members of the family who made depositions were John and Robert Hovey (13 January 1642 [ibid. fols 014r–015v]; the losses of the former were £43 11s 0d and those of the latter £96 10s 0d, making the family's total losses £379 1s 0d.

[150] Leased Cornelyon, 10 April 1627; wife Eliza and daughter Mary (Inquisitions of Ulster, Cavan, (19) Charles I).

[151] Leased Corvilliemahie, 10 April 1627; wife, Ellen and son, Anthony (ibid.).

11

Pike only

7.   John Loch[152]

Sword and Pike

8.   Robert Hammelton[153]
9.   Thomas Leakin elder[154]

Pike only

10.   Thomas Leakin younger

Caliver only

11.   John Robinson

No Arms

12.   Ralph Brian
13.   James Steward[155]
14.   Thomas Belshes
15.   David Wallet
16.   Robert Welsh

16 Men; 7 Swords; 6 [8] Pikes;
2 Calivers; [1 Target]

[f. 17v]

Cavan
Barony de Clanky

John Hammelton Esquire, undertaker of 1000 acres: the names of his men and arms as followeth

Sword and Snaphance

1.   Alexander Anderson[156]
2.   Alexander Davidson[157]

Sword and Caliver

3.   John Hammelton

No Arms

4.   George Carrudhouse

Sword and Snaphance

5.   James Glen

Pike only

6.   William Mirdoch[158]

Sword and Pike

7.   John Johnston[159]
8.   William Johnston

No Arms

9.   John Gibson

Pike only

10.   Patrick Gourdon

Sword and Snaphance

11.   John Steyne
12.   Hugh McConnochy

Sword and Musket

13.   John Hammelton

Pike only

14.   John Lowson

Sword and Snaphance

15.   John Mitchell[160]

No Arms

16.   George Caratheres
17.   John Gourden
18.   James Johnston
19.   John McGir
20.   Mathew Gemmell
21.   James Gemmell

[f. 18]

22.   William Murdo
23.   Thomas Belstes
24.   John Johnston
25.   Alexander Anderson
26.   John McGir
27.   John Gourden
28.   David Galbreath
29.   Frauncis Graham[161]
30.   Mathew Genvill
31.   John Lawson
32.   John Hammelton
33.   Thomas Hammelton
34.   George Irwin
35.   John Gillespi
36.   John Willy[162]
37.   Thomas Fraser
38.   John Hope
39.   William Hope
40.   Robert Rea
41.   John Carrudhouse
42.   John Hammelton younger[163]
43.   James Gleene
44.   John Bell
45.   John Wright
46.   James Johnston
47.   William Johnston
48.   John Johnston
49.   James Genniwill
50.   John Gennivill
51.   William Gennivill
52.   John Young
53.   William Wallas
54.   Allen Armestrong

A mistake in the other book: 44 for 54
44 [54] Men; 10 Swords; 3 [5] Pikes;
1 Musket; 1 Caliver; 6 Snaphances

---

[152] Leased Lisneclea, 1 April 1627; wife, Jennett and son, James (ibid.).

[153] Probably related to John Hamilton who leased Dromhillagh, 19 April 1627; John Hamilton's son was called Nicholas (ibid.).

[154] Numbers 9 and 10 are father and son.

[155] Held Corbeagh for his life and those of his wife, Ann, and daughter, Mary (ibid.); 'of Killalisse …, gentleman'; losses £152 0s 0d (Deposition of James Stewart, 12 November 1642 [TCD MS 833, fols 196r–196v]).

[156] Anderson, one of the original settlers, received a twenty-one year lease for three-fourths of Knocknalosset, 21 April 1619 (Inquisitions of Ulster, Cavan (18), Charles I). He described himself as 'of Coronary in the county of Cavan, gentleman' and reported losses of £339 0s 0d (Deposition of Alexander Anderson, 26 June 1642 [TCD MS 832, fols 179r–179v]. He let Drumgoon to Francis Graham (number 29) (Deposition of Francis Graham, 2 November 1643 [TCD MS 833, fols 153r–154v]).

[157] Davidson, one of the original settlers, received a lease of Glasdrumman for his own life and that of his wife, Jennett, on 2 December 1618 (Inquisitions of Ulster, Cavan (18), Charles I).

[158] Numbers 6 and 22 are probably father and son; James and Robert Murdoch may also be sons; William Murdoch was resident at Correnerier and reported losses of £67 0s 0d (Depositions of James, Robert, and William Murdoghe, 12 November 1642 [TCD MS 833, 172r–175v]).

[159] Seven men (numbers 7, 8, 18, 24, 46, 47, and 48) are named Johnston. The distribution of names within the list suggests that there are at least two families, numbers 7 and 8 and numbers 46 to 48. Numbers 18 and 24 may be members of either family or of other families.

[160] John Mitchell was resident at Corwhowrin and aged over eighty when he was killed at Bailieborough, 1641 (Depositions of Alexander Anderson, 26 July 1642 [TCD MS 833, fols 96r–97v], William Sharpe, 9 November 1642 [ibid. fols 184r–184v], and James Stewart, 12 November 1642 [ibid. fols 196r–196v].

[161] Yeoman; resident Drumgown (Deposition of Francis Greham, 2 November 1642 [ibid. fols 153r–154v]).

[162] Twenty-one year lease of Kilnacrew, 15 April 1627 (Inquisitions of Ulster, Cavan (18), Charles I).

[163] John Hamilton senior could be numbers 3, 13, or 32.

[f. 18v]

Cavan

Barony de Clankey

William Balye[164] esquire,
undertaker of 1000 acres:
the names of his men and
arms as followeth

Sword and Pike
1. James Bayly[165]

No Arms
2. Thomas Baly

Sword and Pike
3. Edward Bayly[166]

Sword only
4. Alexander Bayly
5. Robert Rosse

Musket only
6. John Eccles

Sword only
7. Andrew Black[167]

Sword and Pike
8. Walter Miller[168]

Sword and Pike
9. John Moscommon younger[169]

Sword and Musket
10. John Herron

Sword and Pike
11. William Little
12. James Tindall[170]

No Arms
13. Alexander Paterson

Sword and Musket
14. John Crookes

Sword and Pike
15. Robert Cutberson[171]
16. James Cutberson[172]
17. John Cutberson

Sword and Caliver
18. John Steaphenson[173]

[f. 19]

Sword and Pike
19. David Barbor[174]
20. Alexander Tyndall[175]
21. Adam Bayly[176]

Sword and Musket
22. John Hammelton[177]
23. John Balie

No Arms
24. George Cambell

Sword only
25. Alexander McIllhench

Sword and Snaphance
26. John Willy

Sword and Pike
27. Robert Wood

No Arms
28. John Owin
29. William Ray
30. John Steward
31. John Johnston
32. James Tate
33. George McChench
34. John Maxwell
35. John Bayly

The sum mistaken in the other book
34 [35] Men; 5 [23] Swords; 3 [14]
Pikes; 2 [1] Snaphances; [4 Muskets;
1 Caliver]

---

164 Bailey was resident at Bailieborough Castle when the rising broke out, October 1641. He fled after surrendering livestock worth £700 0s 0d (Deposition of Andrew Black 3 February 1644 [TCD MS 833, fols 221r–221v]), but his wife, who was living in the castle, was taken hostage until she could purchase her freedom (Deposition of John Stevinson, 29 October 1642 [ibid. fols 194r–195v]).

165 Fee farmer of Moltelagh and Lisnalsk,1619 (Hill, *Plantation*, p. 456); resident Bailieborough when killed, 1641 (Depositions of Alexander Anderson, 26 July 1642 [TCD MS 833, fols 96r–97v], Symon Ghrame, 12 November 1642 [ibid. fols 151r–151v], James Stewart, 12 November 1642 [ibid. fols 196r–196v], and Jenett Kearnes, Brian Sherin and William Beatagh, 13 February 1644 [ibid. fols 254r–254v]).

166 Fee farmer, 1619 (Hill, *Plantation*, p. 456) and tenant of Sir Henry Pearce (Inquisitions of Ulster, Cavan (19), Charles I); let Annaghlive to John Ireweene and to Marteine Little (Deposition of Marteine Little, 9 November 1642 [TCD MS 833, fols 150r–150v and 167r–167v]); owed 'twenty shillings sterling' to John Miskimmin (number 9), 1641 (Deposition of John McSkimmeine, 12 November 1642 [ibid. fols 187r–187v]) and £168 0s 0d to Alexander Cummings, vicar of Kilkan and Knockbryde; killed at Julianstown, 1641 (Deposition of Alexander Comine, 2 March 1642 [TCD MS 832, fols 205r–205v]); losses £861 6s 8d (Deposition of widow, Jane Baylie, 7 September 1642 [TCD MS 833, fols 104r–104v]).

167 Yeoman, resident at Caldwally (Deposition of Andrew Black, 3 February 1642 [ibid. fols 221r–221v]).

168 Leaseholder, 1629 (Hill, *Plantation*, p. 456).

169 Resident Errigal; losses £35 0s 0d (Deposition of John mcSkimmeine, 12 November 1642 [TCD MS 833, fols 187r–187v]).

170 James Tindall or Alexander Tyndall (number 20) was the husband of Grisell Tindale and died before 1641 (Deposition of Jane Cuthbertson, 3 February 1644 [ibid. fols 243r–244v]).

171 Numbers 15 to 17 may be sons of Gilbert Cuthbertson, leaseholder in 1629 (Hill, *Plantation*, p. 456); Robert Cuthbertson was resident at Lisanalsky when he was killed, 1641 (Depositions of Alexander Anderson, 26 July 1642 [TCD MS 833, fols 96r–97v], Symon Ghrame, 12 November 1642 [ibid. fols 151r–151v], James Stewart, 12 November 1642 [ibid. fols 196r–196v], and Jenett Kearnes, Brian Sherin and William Beatagh, 13 February 1644 [ibid. fols 254r–254v]).

172 Resident Lare; lost £40 0s 0d (Deposition of wife, Jane Cuthbertson, née Barlie, 3 February 1644 [ibid. fols 243r–244v]).

173 Leaseholder, 1629 (Hill, *Plantation*, p. 456); resident Killashandra; clerk of Killan and Knockbride; 'of Correnerie in the county of Cavan, gentleman'; losses £133 10s 0d (Deposition of John Stevinson, 29 October 1642 [TCD MS 833, fols 194r–195v]).

174 Fee-farmer on John Hamilton's estate and leaseholder on William Bailey's estate, 1629 (Hill, *Plantation*, p. 456; Inquisitions of Ulster, Cavan (18) Charles I); 'a pillaged man'; owed £8 0s 0d to Symon Ghrame (Drumgown churchlands, number 2) (Deposition of Symon Ghrame, 12 November 1642 [TCD MS 833, fols 151r–152v].

175 See number 12.

176 Adam and John Bailey (numbers 21 and 23) were brothers (Deposition of Jenett Kearnes, Brian Sherin and William Beatagh, 13 February 1644 [ibid. fols 254r–254v]). John Bailey was a leaseholder in 1629 (Hill, *Plantation*, p. 456). They were resident at Lare when they were killed, 1641 (Depositions of Alexander Anderson, 26 July 1642 [ibid. fols 96r–97v], Symon Ghrame, 12 November 1642 [ibid. fols 151r–151v], James Stewart, 12 November 1642 [ibid. fols 196r–196v] and John Sharpe, 9 November 1642 [ibid. fols 183r–183v]).

177 John Hamilton (number 22), William Ray (number 29), James Tate (number 32), and John Bailey (number35) were leaseholders, 1629 (ibid.).

[f. 19v]

Cavan
Barony de Clankey

Mrs Hammelton, widow of William Hammelton esquire, undertaker of 1000 acres in the barony above said, the names of her men and arms as followeth[178]

Sword and Pike
1. John Mitchell
2. John Gibson
3. William Ree

Sword and Snaphance
4. James Hammelton
5. John Steaphen

5 Men; 5 Swords; 3 Pikes; 2 Snaphances

[f. 20]

Cavan
Barony de Loughty

Sir Edward Fish baronet, undertaker of 2000 acres: the names of his men and arms

No Arms
1. John Sowgdan[179]
2. Thomas Sowgdan[180]
3. John Baker[181]
4. John Powell[182]
5. Edward Johnston[183]
6. Sammuell Howdsworth
7. Thomas Glasier
8. John Taylor[184]
9. Henry Fetherstone
10. John Ward
11. Alexander Walles
12. John Chapman
13. Andrew Prawdlaw
14. James Creighton
15. Rynyon Creighton
16. Richard Powell
17. Thomas Staton
18. Robert Girlie
19. Richard Smith[185]
20. Edward Bishop
21. George Brocker[186]
22. William Talbot
23. John Taylor
24. Thomas Goodwin
25. Thomas Sudgeston
26. John Baker[187]
27. John Powell

[f. 20v]

28. Edward Johnston
29. Samuell Houldsworth
30. Thomas Smith[188]
31. George Smith
32. Tymothy Glaser
33. Henry Fetherstone
34. Alexander Walsh
35. Robert Crosby
36. John Chapman
37. Andrew Prowdlow
38. James Creighton

Sword and Snaphance
39. Thomas Jenise

Sword only
40. Peter Jenise

Snaphance only
41. John Allen

Sword and Snaphance
42. George Brooker younger[189]

Sword only
43. William How

Sword and Snaphance
44. Philip Whitman[190]
45. Oliver Pinder[191]

Pike only
46. Thomas Greves

Snaphance only
47. Richard Deere

---

[178] William Hamilton, the younger brother of Sir James Hamilton, Viscount Clandeboy, lived at Ballymachan, near Belfast and died, late 1628; his widow, Jane, was the executrix of his will (Morrin (ed.), *Patent rolls, Charles I, 1–8*, p. 517; Hill, *Plantation*, p. 455).

[179] John Sugden had received a fee-farm of two townlands from Fishe, 1628 (Inquisitions of Ulster, Cavan (26), Charles I) and had leased another five before 1641. He resided at Lisnamaine, near Belturbet. His servant, George Smyth (number 31), described his master as a gentleman and reported that his master's losses including 'leather and hides out of his tan yard', amounted to £1.440 0s 0d (Deposition of George Smyth, 24 April 1642 [TCD MS 833, fols 269r–269v]). Sugden's elder son, Edward, reported that his father had died at Croghan Castle (Deposition of Edward Sugden, 13 September 1643 [ibid. fols 269v–270v]).

[180] Younger son of John Sugden (number 1).

[181] Baker, one of the original settlers, received a lease of one townland for his life and those of his wife, Maria, and son, William (see Sir Stephen Butler, number 4), 1616 (Inquisitions of Ulster, Cavan (26), Charles I). John Baker (number 26) is also a son. In his deposition (17 September 1642 [TCD MS 833, fols 100r–101v]), John Baker senior describes himself as 'of Derricrinnill … gentleman' and reported losses of £475 0s 0d. He remained on his farm until August 1642.

[182] One of the Powells (numbers 4, 16, or 27) was the husband of Millicent Powell: he died before 1641. She reported losses amounting to £40 0s 0d through the rising (Deposition of Milisent Powell, 5 January 1642 [ibid. fols 054r–054v]).

[183] Numbers 5 and 28 are father and son; one of them joined the rebels, 1641 (Deposition of John Wheelewright, 18 August 1643 [ibid. fols 272r–272v]).

[184] John Taylor was one of the original settlers and took out leases for twenty-one years on three townlands, 1616; the lease for two townlands was with Daniel O'Leary and the second lease was with his wife, Anne (Inquisitions of Ulster, Cavan (26), Charles I).

[185] Richard Smith, a neighbour of John Sugden (Deposition of George Smyth, 26 April 1642 [TCD MS 833, fols 269r–269v]), held Crahard by the year, 1628 (Inquisitions of Ulster, Cavan (26), Charles I) but sold the townland to John West when he moved onto Sir Stephen Butler's estate (Deposition of John West, 10 February 1642 [TCD MS 833, fols 083r–083v]). This exchange of holdings shows how settlers moved from one estate to another [JJ].

[186] George Brooker leased a townland for twenty-one years from John Fishe, 1616 (Inquisitions of Ulster, Cavan (26), Charles I); father of number 42.

[187] See number 3.

[188] Thomas Smith may be the gunsmith, who gave a lengthy account of the murders at Belturbet, 1642 (Deposition of Thomas Smith and Joane Killin, 8 February 1644 [TCD MS 833, fols 265r–266v]).

[189] Son of number 21.

[190] Yeoman; aged forty-five; losses £360 0s 0d (Deposition of Phillip Whitman, 4 January 1642 [ibid. fols 086r–086v]).

[191] Leased a townland in partnership with John Taylor (number 8), 1615 (Inquisitions of Ulster, Cavan, (26) Charles I); tanner; resident Knogham; losses £902 2s 0d (Deposition of Oliver Pynder, 7 January 1642 [TCD MS 833, fols 050r–051v]).

Sword and Pike

   48.   Robert Burrus[192]

48 Men; 7 Swords; 2 Pikes;
5 [6] Snaphances

[f. 21]

Cavan
Barony de [Castlerahan]

The names of the British tenants and their arms residing on the servitors land of the earl of Fyngall in the barony above said

Sword only

   1.   John Nix[193]

Halberd only

   2.   Henry Nix the younger

Sword only

   3.   Thomas Locke
   4.   Thomas Spreckly
   5.   Joseph Earth

No Arms

   6.   James Gray
   7.   William Robison
   8.   Henry Nix
   9.   Lawrence Nix
   10.   Edward Richard
   11.   Leonard Beckwith
   12.   Richard Cade[194]
   13.   William Belfeild
   14.   William Grimshaw

   15.   Thomas Bignall[195]
   16.   Richard Loc
   17.   James Gray
   18.   William Robison
   19.   Henry Nix
   20.   John Nix
   21.   Joseph Nix
   22.   William Grimshaw
   23.   Thomas Lock
   24.   Edward Richardson
   25.   Lawrence Beckworth
   26.   Richard Cade
   27.   Thomas Bignall
   28.   Thomas Sprockes

28 Men; 4 Swords; 1 Halberd

[f. 21v]

Cavan
Barony de Castleraine

The names of the tenants of the bishop of Kilmore and their arms in his churchlands being 2000 acres

Sword only

   1.   Thomas Dowxkes[196]

Sword and Caliver

   2.   John Dowxkes

No Arms

   3.   Christopher Ellot

Sword and Pike

   4.   Richard Dichare

Halberd only

   5.   Edward Lockington[197]

Pike only

   6.   John Sutton

Snaphance only

   7.   John Henids[198]

Sword and Snaphance

   8.   Edward Crosse

No Arms

   9.   William Taylor
   10.   George Tuchberry
   11.   Edward Clarke
   12.   Anthony Culum[199]
   13.   William Fry
   14.   John Sympson[200]
   15.   Alexander Sympson
   16.   Dominck Parker[201]
   17.   Anthony Slortenant
   18.   Thomas Taylor[202]
   19.   William Slortenant
   20.   Thomas Lynald
   21.   John Parker[203]
   22.   Edward Singcock

[f. 22]

   23.   Thomas Wooyeare
   24.   David Killet
   25.   John Dicher
   26.   Thomas Gamble
   27.   Thomas Hexter
   28.   John Hexter
   29.   Peter Cross
   30.   John Crosse
   31.   Thomas House

---

[192] Leased one townland for sixty years, 1628 (Inquisitions of Ulster, Cavan (26), Charles I); 'of Farnham'; losses £41 6s 0d (Deposition of Robert Barowe, 29 January 1642 [TCD MS 832, fols 186r–186v]).

[193] There were two families called Nixon in Virginia (Nix is a short-form of the name). One family consists of Henry Nixon senior (number 8), Henry Nixon junior (number 2) and probably of John and Lawrence Nixon (numbers 1 and 9). The second family is Henry, John, and Joseph Nixon (numbers 19 to 21). John Nixon was a tanner and reported losses of £57 10s 0d, 1641 (Deposition of John Nix, 21 May 1642 [TCD MS 833, fols 178r–178v]).

[194] Numbers 12 and 26 are father and son; Richard Cade is Richard Gates, whose losses, 1641 amounted to £75 12s 0d (Deposition of his wife, Jan Gates, 29 January 1642 [TCD MS 832, fols 231r–231v]).

[195] Thomas Bignall is the father of Phebe (Brockwell Taylor, number 10) and Thomas Bignall (number 27) and the brother of William Bignall, who mustered on Sir Stephen Butler's Fermanagh estate; Thomas Bignall was resident at Virginia, 1641 and lost £250 0s 0d (Deposition of his widow, Mary Bignell, 21 April 1643 [TCD MS 833, fols 222r–222v]).

[196] Thomas and John Dowkes (numbers 1 and 2) are the sons of William Dowkes (Amis and Greenham, number 1).

[197] One of the original settlers in the county, Lockington had a thirty-nine year lease on Corlorgragh and Dreenan from Sir George Mainwaring, 1 August 1618 (Inquisitions of Ulster, Cavan (23) Charles I).

[198] Resident Drumhill; losses £304 13s 0d (Deposition of John Hines, 12 January 1642 [TCD MS 833, fols 016r–017v]).

[199] Custodian of Cloughoughter Castle (Deposition of his 'kinsman', Arthur Culme, 9 May 1642 [ibid. fols 127r–132v]).

[200] Tanner; killed, 1641 (Examination of Robert Hunt, undated [TCD MS 832, fols 164r–164v] and Deposition of John Simpson, 2 March 1644 [ibid. fols 264r–264v]).

[201] Yeoman; resident Dromonam; losses £1.266 9s 9d (Deposition of his widow, Joane Parker, 2 June 1647 [TCD MS 833, fols 286r–286v]).

[202] Mason, resident Kilmore; losses £280 0s 0d (Deposition of Thomas Taylor, 12 January 1642 [ibid. fols 068r–068v]).

[203] John or William Parker was 'formerly … [the] schoolmaster' and was 'hanged upon a sallow tree' near Keelagh Castle (Deposition of John Simpson, 2 March 1644 [ibid. fols 264r–264v]).

32. Thomas Sympson
33. John Grozer
34. William Johnes
35. Steaphen Symson
36. William Parker[204]

36 Men; 4 Swords; 2 Pikes; 1 Caliver; 1 Halbert; [2 Snaphances]

[f. 22v]

Cavan

The names of the townsmen of Cavan and their arms as followeth

Sword and Musket
1. Eluathain Brooke

Sword and Snaphance
2. Lawrance Dards[205]

Sword and Pike
3. William Anes[206]

No Arms
4. John Ouldsbroone
5. John Whitman[207]
6. James Atkins
7. Lucke Whirwoods
8. Thomas Awnes
9. Richard Shepy
10. Robert Hunt
11. Robert Dawlin
12. Thomas Dawlin[208]
13. William Woorthington
14. John Browne
15. Lawrence Moore
16. John More
17. William Clifford
18. Allen Cooke
19. Robert Woorth
20. Robert Dannet
21. Henry Hunt
22. Peter Usher
23. Robert Awnes
24. John Dowdall[209]
25. Nathaniell Dardes
26. John Hill
27. Robert Wright

These two last reside in the parish of Killeserdinyue
A mistake in the sum: 18 [27] Men; 3 swords; 1 Musket; 1 Pike; [1 Snaphance]

[f. 23]

Cavan

The names of the British and their arms inhabiting on the churchlands of Drowmgowne

Sword and Pike
1. Frauncis Graham[210]
2. Symond Graham[211]

Swords Only
3. Frauncis Graham younger
4. John Willie
5. John Young
6. Robert Ray
7. John Hope

7 Men; 2 Swords; 2 Pikes

---

[204] See number 21.
[205] Losses £59 5s 0d, 1641 (Deposition of Lawrance Dawds, 24 February 1642 [TCD MS 833, fols 141r–141v]).
[206] The modern spelling of the surnames for numbers 3, 8, and 23 is Owens.
[207] Merchant; losses £800 0s 0d (Certificate of John Whitman, 10 June 1643 [TCD MS 836, fols 113r–113v]); sovereign of the town; amended losses £1.000 0s 0d (Deposition of John Whitman, 14 July 1643 [TCD MS 833, fols 273r–274v]).
[208] Resident, 1641 (Deposition of Thomas Dawline, 14 February 1642 [TCD MS 832, fols 220r–220v]).
[209] Named as one 'of such landed men as before are in rebellion of the county of Cavan' (Deposition of Thomas Crant, 13 February 1642 [ibid. fols 212r–219v] and Deposition of George Creighton, 15 April 1643 [TCD MS 833, fols 227r–242v]).
[210] Simon and Francis Graham are the sons of Francis Graham; losses £127 10s 0d (Deposition of Francis Greham, 2 November 1642 [TCD MS 833, fols 153r–154v]).
[211] Lent £8 0s 0d to David Barbor, who mustered on William Bailey's estate (Deposition of Symon Ghrame, 12 November 1642 [ibid. fols 151r–152v]).

County Armagh

[f. 24]

The Muster Roll of the County of Armagh[1]

Barony de Oneallane

Anthony Cope esquire, undertaker of 3000 acres: the names of his men and arms as followeth

Sword only
1. William Pearson[2]

Sword and Musket
2. Henry Pilkinton[3]
3. Nicholas Gregg[4]
4. Nicholas Cooke[5]

Sword and Pike
5. William Richardson[6]

Sword only
6. Edward Gregg[7]
7. Philip Box
8. Edward Box
9. John Manton
10. Edward Eaton[8]

Pike only
11. Symond Gower[9]

No Arms
12. William Jennings younger[10]

Sword and Pike
13. Edward Adams[11]

Pike only
14. Christopher Spencer[12]

Caliver only
15. William Spencer[13]

Sword only
16. Anthony Tinkeler[14]

Musket only
17. Richard Roberts[15]

Pike only
18. William Beare[16]

Sword only
19. Joseph Hanley[17]

[f. 22v]

Snaphance only
20. John Richardson[18]
21. Trypinion Stockwood

Sword only
22. John Reedburne

Musket only
23. Henry Sheath[19]

Pike only
24. Robert Shearly[20]

Sword and Musket
25. Symond Clarke

Caliver only
26. Henry Hunt[21]

---

[1] Robert Hunter was working from a copy of Paterson, 'Armagh'; I am grateful to the committee of the Cumann Seanchais Ard Mhacha for permission to reproduce that article.

[2] Cope had appointed Pearson as overseer of the estate in 1611 (*Calendar of Carew MSS, 1603–24*, p. 225); he held a three-life freehold of sixty acres and a leasehold of 'one and three-quarters [of a] townland and a windmill', 1622 (Treadwell (ed.), *Irish commission*, pp 542, 555–6).

[3] Pilkington held 'three-quarters of a townland for three lives', 1622 (ibid. p. 555). He was killed, 1641 and was described as 'gentleman … of Loughgall'; (Depositions of Edward Saltenstall and George Littlefeild, 1 June 1642 [TCD MS 836, fols 069r–079v] and of Christian Stanhawe and Owen Frankland, 23 July 1642 [ibid. fols 075r–076v]). He was possibly the husband of Elizabeth Pilkington and hence the father-in-law of Richard Newberry (number 106); losses reportedly £615 0s 0d (Deposition of Richard Newberrie, 27 June 1642 [ibid. fols 060r–061v]).

[4] Gregg held 'forty acres and a water mill' from Cope, 1622 (Treadwell (ed.), *Irish commission*, p. 556). He was the father of John Gregg (number 96) and the brother of Edward Gregg (number 6). He was aged sixty-six, 1641 and suffered losses amounting to £200 0s 0d (Depositions of John Greg, 7 January 1642 [ibid. fols 004r–005v] and of Alice Gregg, 21 July 1643 [ibid. fols 095r–096r]).

[5] Cooke held twenty acres, 1622 by lease from Cope (Treadwell (ed.), *Irish commission*, p. 555).

[6] William Richardson was a sub-tenant of John Alcock (number 125) and held 'twenty acres and more' directly from Cope, 1622 (ibid. pp 542, 556). Richardson was possibly the first husband of Eleanor Fullerton and hence the father of John Richardson (number 153). Her second husband, William, was the rector of Loughgall (Deposition of Ellenor Fullerton, 16 September 1642 [TCD MS 836, fols 050r–051v]).

[7] Brother of Nicholas Gregg (number 3) (Deposition of Alice Gregg, 21 July 1643 [ibid. fols 095r–096r]).

[8] Held a 'quarter townland and better', 1622 (Treadwell (ed.), *Irish commission*, p. 556).

[9] Gower or Govers held a townland, 1622 (ibid. p. 555) and was one of the three tenants whose names are recorded in the inquisitions (Inquisitions of Ulster, Armagh (11) and (30), Charles I).

[10] Jennings's father, William Gemmings, held 'about twenty acres' from Cope, 1622 (Treadwell (ed.), *Irish commission*, p. 542).

[11] Sub-tenant of John Alcock, 1622 (ibid.); possibly the son of John Adams, one of Cope's principal tenants (Inquisitions of Ulster, Armagh (11) and (30), Charles I).

[12] Sub-tenant of Nicholas Alcock, 1622 (Treadwell (ed.), *Irish commission*, p. 542).

[13] 1622: resident at Loughgall (ibid. p. 543).

[14] 1622: sub-tenant of John Boylton, leaseholder of John Dillon (ibid. p. 547).

[15] 1622: resident at Loughgall (ibid. p. 543).

[16] Possibly father of Erasmus Beere, gentleman of Ballygassoon (Examination of his widow, Jane Beere, 4 June 1653 [TCD MS 838, fols 098r–099v]).

[17] Possibly the son of Richard Hanley, who held a fifteen acre freehold, 1622 (Treadwell (ed.), *Irish commission*, p. 542); killed, 1641 (Examination of Thomas Taylor, 24 February 1653 [TCD MS 836, fols 179r–180v]).

[18] Gentleman; killed, 1641 (Depositions of Christian Stanhawe and Owen Frankland, 23 July 1642 [ibid. fols 075r–076v] and of Edward Saltenstall and George Littlefeild, 1 June 1642 [ibid. fols 069r–079v]).

[19] Possibly son of George Sheath, who held 'about sixty acres for three lives' on Cope's estate and was a freeholder of 100 acres on Sir John Dillon's estate (Treadwell (ed.), *Irish commission*, pp 555, 558).

[20] Chandler; resident at Loughgall, 1622 (ibid. p. 543).

[21] Relative of Christopher Hunt, who had a leasehold of sixty acres, 1622 (ibid.).

Pike only
27. Frauncis Redbourne
28. George Norris

Caliver only
29. John Stones[22]

Sword and Caliver
30. John Taylor[23]

Pike only
31. Henry Humphreys[24]

Sword only
32. Robert Hall
33. Nathaniell Stones

Snaphance only
34. Thomas Chamberlaine[25]

Sword and Snaphance
35. Robert Parker

Sword and Caliver
36. Richard Peacok

Sword only
37. James Brambey

No Arms
38. Ralph Buckle
39. Hercules Adams[26]
40. Symond Mortimer[27]
41. Marke Skarlet[28]
42. William Clarke[29]
43. William Watnall
44. Richard Buggie[30]

[f. 25]

45. Gyles Adams[31]
46. John Adams younger[32]
47. Thomas Manton[33]
48. William Davis[34]

49. George Bridges[35]
50. Thomas Twilly
51. Robert Williams
52. Edward Stanhow[36]
53. Jacob Dobson
54. Martin Twilly
55. John Adams the older[37]
56. James Simmes[38]
57. Edward Cooper
58. Thomas Robins
59. John Ellcock younger[39]
60. John Wright[40]
61. John Hall[41]
62. Henry Bibyes
63. Richard Warran[42]
64. Thomas Spencer[43]
65. William Clarke younger[44]
66. Timothy Bennet
67. Richard Jeffes[45]
68. Thomas Jeffs

---

[22] John Stones was one of the three lives named in Robert Stone's lease of 'a house and six acres of land in Annareagh for three lives' from John Heron, 1616 (Inquisitions of Ulster, Armagh, (5) Charles I). The others were Nathaniell Stones (number 33) and Richard Burkett (Waldrum, number 37).

[23] Taylor was a cottager, 1622 (Treadwell (ed.), *Irish commission*, p. 543). He is possibly the father of Thomas Taylor, tanner of Clanbrassil, who buried Henry Pilkington [number 2 above], 'a neighbour of his that was hanged near his own dwelling towards Loughgall' (Examination of Thomas Taylor, 24 February 1653 [TCD MS 836, fols 179r–180v]).

[24] Leased a townland from Cope, 1622 (Treadwell (ed.), *Irish commission*, p. 556).

[25] Leaseholder on Sir John Dillon's estate, 1622 (ibid. p. 557).

[26] Sub-tenant of John Alcock, 1622 (ibid. p. 542).

[27] Sub-tenant of John Alcock and leased 'about 25 acres' from Cope, 1622 (ibid. pp 542, 556).

[28] Sub-tenant of John Alcock, 1622 (ibid. p. 542).

[29] Father of William Clarke, younger (number 65): his wife, Margery, was aged sixty-nine in 1641: his son estimated his mother's losses at £35 0s 0d (Deposition of William Clarke, 7 January 1642 [TCD MS 836, fols 002r–003v]). William Clarke senior was a sub-tenant of John Alcock, 1622 (Treadwell (ed.), *Irish commission*, p. 542).

[30] Buggie was a sub-tenant of Gregory Wright, one of the freeholders, 1622. He had 'lately … left the land and gone out of the country.' 'Widow Buggie' was presumably Richard Buggie's mother (ibid. pp 542–3). Richard Buggie had therefore gone to England to arrange his father's affairs and later returned to Ireland.

[31] Killed, 1641 (Examination of James Jackson, 5 March 1654 [TCD MS 836, fols 232r–233v]).

[32] Son of number 55.

[33] Manton, who leased a townland and a 'quarter townland and better' from Cope, was reported 'lately to have left the land and gone out of the country', 1622 (Treadwell (ed.), *Irish commission*, pp 543, 556).

[34] Resident at Loughgall, 1622 (ibid. p. 542).

[35] Bridges, number 49 or 126, (ibid. p. 555) was one of Cope's principal tenants (Inquisitions of Ulster, Armagh, (11) and (30), Charles I).

[36] Purchased Derrycorry and Clanvickish from William Stanhow, his brother, in 1626 (Inquisitions of Ulster, Armagh, (3) Charles I); Examination of Bryan McCarbary og McCana, 12 May 1653 [TCD MS 836, fols 216r–217v]).

[37] Adams held a townland, 1622 (Treadwell (ed.), *Irish commission*, p. 555) and was one of the tenants whose names are recorded in the inquisitions (Inquisitions of Ulster, Armagh, (11) and (30), Charles I); he was the father of number 46.

[38] Simms leased 'about forty acres' from Cope, 1622 (Treadwell (ed.), *Irish commission*, p. 556). He was the father-in-law of John Gregg (number 96) and was aged fifty when he was killed in 1641. His losses amounted to £150 0s 0d (Deposition of John Greg, 7 January 1642 [TCD MS 836, fols 004r–005v]).

[39] Son of number 125.

[40] Either John Wright senior, father-in-law of William Clarke the younger (number 65), or John Wright junior, his brother-in-law; John Wright senior's losses £326 0s 0d and those of John Wright junior £60 0s 0d (Deposition of William Clarke, 7 January 1642 [ibid. fols 002r–003v]); John Wright senior, a smith, was a sub-tenant of John Alcock, 1622 (Treadwell (ed.), *Irish commission*, pp 542–3).

[41] Killed, 1641 (Information of Margaret Clarke, 16 March 1643 [TCD MS 836, fols 035r–036v]).

[42] 'Of Anexsory in the parish of Levalleglish in the barony of Oneilland and county of Armagh, yeoman, a British protestant of the age of forty-six years'; losses £921 10s 0d; tenant of John Alcock; son-in-law of Thomas Cattle (number 69), and the brother of William Warren (John Dillon, number 13) (Deposition of Richard Warrin, 7 January 1642 [ibid. fols 009r 010v]).

[43] Leaseholder on Sir John Dillon's estate, 1622 (Treadwell (ed.), *Irish commission*, p. 558).

[44] Tanner; 'of Agralohoe'; losses £436 0s 0d (Deposition of William Clarke, 7 January 1642 [TCD MS 836, fols 002r–003v]); son of number 42; Clarke was aged forty-five and resident at Killultagh, county Antrim when he made his deposition (Examination of William Clark, 28 February 1654 [TCD MS 838, fols 177r–178v]).

[45] Resident Loughgall, 1622 (Treadwell (ed.), *Irish commission*, p. 543); the family was still present as Timothy Jeffes was killed at Portadown, 1641 (Deposition of Robert Maxwell [TCD MS 809, fols 005r–012v]).

69. Thomas Cotle[46]
70. Thomas Bradley[47]
71. Thomas Roberts
72. William Parker
73. Anthony Kitte[48]
74. Thomas Butler[49]
75. Richard Taylor[50]

[f. 25v]

76. Henry Robins
77. William Pert
78. Thomas Py
79. John Adams[51]
80. John Meallaway
81. Richard Robinson
82. Richard Roberts[52]
83. William Hopkins[53]
84. John Wright[54]
85. Thomas Leech
86. Thomas Martin[55]
87. Humphrey Brouchas
88. Christopher Black[56]
89. John Swerwood
90. Thomas Nicholson[57]
91. Robert Atkins[58]
92. Lawrance Darbishere[59]

93. John Darbishere[60]
94. Anthony Knight
95. Henry Hallaway
96. John Gregg[61]
97. George Browne[62]
98. George Brown younger
99. John Massy
100. George Seggs
101. Richard Butter
102. William Turner
103. Griffin Powell
104. Richard Farnell
105. James Steward
106. Richard Newberry[63]
107. Arthur Hunt[64]
108. John Raeffearne

[f. 26]

109. John Barbie
110. Edward Jerwis
111. William Davis[65]
112. Richard Elcock[66]
113. Ezekiell Palmer[67]
114. Thomas Wright
115. Robert Stones
116. Richard Humphreys[68]

117. John Spencer
118. John Roberts
119. Humphrey Woods
120. John Johnston
121. John Powell
122. Thomas Stoodman
123. Marke Reedborne[69]
124. Thomas Tornetton
125. John Elcock[70]
126. George Bridges[71]
127. Sampson Flowery
128. Christopher Adams
129. Thomas Jeffs
130. William Parker
131. John Candras
132. Richard Roberts
133. Edward Taylor[72]
134. William Marriot[73]
135. Francis Sherly
136. James Crossen

[f. 26v]

137. James Whitman
138. George Sheat
139. John Massy

---

46   Sub-tenant of Nicholas Alcock, freeholder, 1622 (Treadwell (ed.), *Irish commission*, p. 541); father-in-law of Richard Warren (number 63); aged sixty when killed, 1641; his losses were reportedly £375 0s 0d and those of his son, Thomas, £80 0s 0d (Deposition of Richard Warrin, 7 January 1642 [TCD MS 836, fols 009r–010v]).

47   Possibly father of James Bradley of Narrow Water, county Down; James Bradley, who was aged thirty-two when he made his deposition, took refuge in Sir William Brownlow's castle at Lurgan, 1641 (Examination of James Bradley, 21 May 1653 [ibid. fols 261r–261v]).

48   Present, 1622 (Treadwell (ed.), *Irish commission*, p. 562).

49   Held forty acres by lease from Cope, 1622 (ibid. p. 543).

50   Held three townlands by lease from Anthony Cope, 1622 (ibid. pp 555–6).

51   Adams held 'forty acres' from Cope, 1622 (ibid. p. 556). The commissioners annotated repetitions in Cope's certificate: there is no annotation against John Adams's name so he and number 55 are different John Adamses.

52   Present, 1622 (ibid. p. 563).

53   Possibly son of John Hopkins who held sixty acres of Mullanasilla on a three-life lease from John Dillon, 1622 (ibid. p. 547).

54   See number 60.

55   Killed at Lurgan, 1641 (Deposition of Katherin Cooke, 24 February 1644 [TCD MS 836, fols 092r–093v]).

56   Possibly son of William Black, resident 1622 (Treadwell (ed.), *Irish commission*, p. 563).

57   Brother or son of William Nicholson, clerk who was a sub-tenant of William Pearson, 1622 (ibid. p. 543).

58   Possibly son of John Atkins, who held a third share of a three-life lease on Killemany from John Dillon, 1622 (ibid. p. 546).

59   Lawrence, John, and Thomas Derbyshire (numbers 92 and 93 and Francis Sacherevell, number 80) are probably the sons of Humphrey Derbyshire, who held a three-life lease on the Sacherevell estate, 1622 (ibid. p. 545).

60   Resident at Loughgall (Deposition of Katherin O'Kerrie, 19 July 1643 [TCD MS 836, fols 097r–097v]).

61   'Of Cloveneden … yeoman of the age of thirty-five years'; losses £755 0s 0d; father Nicholas Gregg (number 3), father-in-law James Simms (number 56) (Deposition of John Greg, 7 January 1642 [ibid. fols 004r–005v]).

62   Numbers 97 and 98 are father and son.

63   'Of Creenaghe near Loughgall in the County of Armagh gentleman'; possibly son-in-law of Elizabeth Pilkington and hence of Henry Pilkington (number 2); losses £870 0s 0d (Deposition of Richard Newberrie, 27 June 1642 [TCD MS 833, fols 060r–061v]).

64   Possibly son of Christopher Hunt, who had a leasehold of sixty acres, 1622 (Treadwell (ed.), *Irish commission*, p. 543).

65   Present, 1622 (ibid. p. 563).

66   Held a townland from Cope, 1622 (ibid. p. 556).

67   Resident Loughgall, 1622 (ibid. p. 543).

68   Killed, 1641 (Deposition of Edward Saltenstall and George Littlefeild, 1 June 1642 [TCD MS 836, fols 069r–079v]).

69   Resident at Loughgall, 1622 (Treadwell (ed.), *Irish commission*, p. 543).

70   Freeholder of 100 acres, 1622 (ibid. p. 542); let two water mills for grinding corn to John Gregg (number 96) for 21 years; valued at £150 0s 0d (Deposition of John Greg, 7 January 1642 [TCD MS 836, fols 004r–005v]); father of number 59 [and possibly 112].

71   See number 49.

72   Cottager, sub-tenant of Francis Sacherevell, 1622 (Treadwell (ed.), *Irish commission*, p. 545); resident at Loughgall, 1641 (Deposition of Katherin O'Kerrie, 19 July 1643 [TCD MS 836, fols 097r–097v]).

73   Gentleman of Loughgall; murdered with his son, 1641 (Deposition of Edward Saltenstall and George Littlefeild, 1 June 1642 [ibid. fols 069r–079v]).

140. William Black[74]
141. John Harris
142. John Wilson[75]
143. Thomas Wynter
144. John Hill
145. John Beke
146. John Steward
147. Edward Shadwell[76]
148. Robert Parker
149. Richard Peacock[77]
150. Robert Hall
151. John Taylor
152. Henry Hunt[78]
153. John Richardson[79]
154. George Morris[80]
155. Symond Clarke

155 Men; 18 swords; 7 Pikes;
5 Muskets; 2 Calivers;
4 Snaphances

[f. 27]

Armagh
Barony de Oneallan

John Dillon, esquire, undertaker of 1500 acres: the names of his men and arms as followeth

Sword and Pike
1. Andrew Hutchison[81]
2. Richard Chandler[82]

Sword only
3. Robert Geratt

Caliver only
4. Thomas Lealand[83]

Sword and Caliver
5. Robert Roe[84]

Sword and Musket
6. Sammuell Betts
7. John Salterston[85]

No Arms
8. John Newman[86]
9. George Brookes
10. William Matlo[87]
11. Robert Millington[88]
12. Walter Scull
13. William Warren[89]
14. Thomas Masson
15. Thomas Woodward[90]
16. Edward Trundall
17. Henry Newberry[91]
18. Richard Wrench[92]
19. William Throne[93]
20. Psevall Newberry
21. Francis Lealand[94]
22. John Burdet
23. John Russell
24. Nathaniell Dillon[95]
25. Abraham Starr

---

[74] 1622: resident at Loughgall (Treadwell (ed.), *Irish commission*, p. 543).

[75] Held sixty acres of Mullanasilla on a three-life lease from John Dillon, 1622 (ibid. p. 547).

[76] 'Mr Edward Chadwell' of Loughgall was killed with 'his wife', December 1641 (Examination of Michaell Harrison, 11 February 1653 [TCD MS 836, fols 127r–138v]).

[77] Numbers 149 and 151 were resident at Loughgall 1622: (Treadwell (ed.), *Irish commission*, p. 543).

[78] Possibly related to Christopher Hunt, who had a leasehold of 60 acres, 1622 (ibid.).

[79] Possibly the son of William Richardson (number 5); killed, 1641 (Deposition of Ellenor Fullerton, 16 September 1642 [TCD MS 836, fols 050r–051v]).

[80] Survived drowning at Portadown, 1641 (Examination of William Clarke, 7 January 1642 [ibid. fols 177r–178v]).

[81] Possibly son of John Hutchison who held Cloghan with Thomas Newberry, 1622 (Treadwell (ed.), *Irish commission*, p. 546); Hutchison was resident at Hockley before 1641 but was living at Knockcarne, near Lisburn in the 1650s; he was aged forty-two when he made his deposition (Examination of Andrew Hutchinson, 19 April 1653 [TCD MS 836, fols 248r–249v]).

[82] Held sixty acres of Mullanasilla on a three-life lease, 1622 (Treadwell (ed.), *Irish commission*, p. 547).

[83] Brother of Francis Lealand (number 21); 'workman to Sir Phelim O'Neill' (Deposition of Francis Leiland, 19 July 1643 [TCD MS 836, fols 098r–099v]).

[84] 'Gentleman'; held Ballybrannan and sixty acres in Dromadd on a three-life lease, 1622 (Treadwell (ed.), *Irish commission*, p. 546).

[85] Salterston had a quarter share of a three-life lease on Grange, 1622 (ibid.). The 'junior two of John Salterston's sons' were among those who 'being English turned unto them [the Irish] and went with them to Lisnagarvey and fought there against the English' (Deposition of John Wisdome, 8 February 1642 [TCD MS 836, fols 014r–015v]). Edward Salterston, one of John Salterston's sons, described himself as 'of the Grange … gentleman' and reported his father's losses as amounting to £1,700 0s 0d (Deposition of Edward Saltenstall and George Littlefeild, 1 June 1642 [ibid. fols 069r–079v]).

[86] Leaseholder, 1622 (Treadwell (ed.), *Irish commission*, p. 557).

[87] Held sixty acres of Mullanasilla on a three-life lease, 1622 (ibid. p. 547).

[88] Robert Millington held Drumnasoo with Michael Obbyns and Henry Newberry (number 17), 1622. Robert and Ellen Millington were killed, 1641 (Deposition of Joane Constable, 6 June 1643 [TCD MS 836, fols 087r–090v] and Examination of Andrew Hutchinson, 19 April 1653 [ibid. fols 248r–249v]).

[89] Brother of Richard Warren (Anthony Cope, number 63); losses £80 0s 0d; killed, 1641 (Deposition of Richard Warrin, 7 January 1642 [ibid. fols 009r–010v]).

[90] Resident Hockley; killed, 1641 (Deposition of Edward Saltenstall and George Littlefeild, 1 June 1642 [ibid. fols 069r–079v]).

[91] Held Drumnasoo with Michael Obbyns and Robert Millington, 1622 (Treadwell (ed.), *Irish commission*, p. 546); another member of the family, Thomas Newberry, held Cloghan jointly with John Hutchison, father of Andrew Hutchison (number 1); Thomas Newberry was killed, 1641 (Deposition of Elizabeth Price, 26 June 1643 [TCD MS 836, fols 101r–105v]).

[92] Richard Wrench is probably the son of John Wrench, to whom William Stanhow let six townlands for twenty-one years in 1613 (Inquisitions of Ulster, Armagh, (3) Charles I). Wrench senior lived at Benburb (Treadwell (ed.), *Irish commission*, p. 544).

[93] Throne and his wife, Alice, were among those burned to death at Shewis, 1641 (Deposition of Joane Constable, 6 June 1643 [TCD MS 836, fols 087r–090v]).

[94] Lealand, 'of Drumadmore in the parish and county of Armagh, yeoman', was one of the original settlers and had 'lived within the parish and county of Armagh for the space of thirty years together last past and above'; he reported losses of £180 0s 0d (Deposition of Francis Leiland, 19 July 1643 [ibid. fols 098r–099v]).

[95] Held Altaturke as freehold, 1622 (Treadwell (ed.), *Irish commission*, p. 546).

26. John Leurock
27. James Chappell[96]
28. William Brookes
29. Mathew Martin
30. Thomas Small
31. William Harrison
32. Erasmus Dillon[97]
33. Bernard Roberts
34. Richard Stubs[98]

34 Men; 6 Swords; 2 Pikes; 2 Muskets;
2 Caliver

[f. 27v]

Armagh
Barony de Onealland

Mr Waldrum,[99]

undertaker of 2000 acres:

the names of his men and
arms as followeth

Sword and Snaphance
1. Robert Nicholson
2. Edward Black

Snaphance only
3. William Taylor[100]

Sword only
4. Anthony Part

Musket only
5. William Copeland[101]

Sword and Snaphance
6. Nathaniell Browne

Sword and Musket
7. William Shelton

Sword only
8. John Dawkins[102]

Sword and Musket
9. John Russell

Sword only
10. Edward Russell
11. Charles Stakes

Snaphance only
12. Robert Foster

No Arms
13. Randall Lilly
14. Edward Helfoord
15. Sammuell Sherlocke
16. William Berry[103]
17. Edward Tacy

18. John Pattisn[104]
19. Robert Gibbon[105]
20. Robert Bonner[106]
21. Robert Caulfield
22. William Stocker
23. Abell Barnett
24. Thomas Foster[107]
25. William Herbert
26. Richard Maure
27. John Maure
28. Richard Sommerscall[108]
29. George Stanion
30. John Shaw
31. Robert Haywood[109]
32. Nicholas Winson
33. Richard Clarke
34. John Cole
35. Gyles Blacklock[110]
36. Thomas Greene[111]
37. Richard Burcot
38. John Newman
39. George Brunt
40. Thomas Anderson
41. Thomas Markham
42. John Florry[112]
43. Hugh Sutton
44. Michaell Greene
45. Gyles Blakelock[113]

45 Men; 9 Swords; 5 Snaphances;
2 Muskets

---

[96] Chappell was resident in Armagh when he was killed, 1641 (Deposition of Edward Saltenstall and George Littlefeild, 1 June 1642 [TCD MS 836, fols 069r–079v]).

[97] Freeholder; one of those who 'being English turned unto them [the Irish] and went with them to Lisnagarvey and fought there against the English' (Deposition of John Wisdome, 8 February 1642 [ibid. fols 014r–015v]).

[98] Resident at Annaghclare, which he held with sixty acres of Mullanasilla on a three-life lease, 1622, when he was killed, 1641 (Treadwell (ed.), *Irish commission*, pp 546–7; Depositions of Francis Leiland, 19 July 1643 [TCD MS 836, fols 098r–099v] and of Elizabeth Price, 26 June 1643 [ibid. fols 101r–105v]).

[99] 'Mr Waldrum' is probably the father of Eliza Waldron, the wife of John Obbyns, whose father, Michael, was undertaker of Ballywarren, the modern Portadown. Michael Obbyns had been outlawed because of debts in 1626 and died on 26 September 1629 (Inquisitions of Ulster, Armagh, (22) Charles I; Hill, *Plantation*, p. 558). Eliza Waldron had a jointure on the estate and Graham's description of her father as the proprietor of the estate suggests he was acting as trustee for his daughter and son-in-law.

[100] Freeholder on Sir John Dillon's estate, 1622 (Treadwell (ed.), *Irish commission*, p. 557); tanner; survived drowning at Portadown, 1641 (Examination of William Clarke, 28 February 1653 [TCD MS 836, fols 177r–178v] and of Thomas Taylor, 24 February 1653 [ibid. fols 179r–180v]).

[101] Leaseholder on Sir John Dillon's estate, 1622 (Treadwell (ed.), *Irish commission*, p. 558); killed at Kinard, 1641 (Examination of William Skelton, 20 February 1653 [TCD MS 836, fols 171r–174v]).

[102] Cottager and sub-tenant of Henry Sacherevell, 1622 (Treadwell (ed.), *Irish commission*, p. 545).

[103] Relation of either Moses Berye or John Berrye, the former a freeholder and the latter a leaseholder, on Sir John Dillon's estate, 1622 (ibid. p. 557).

[104] Resident Lurgan; yeoman; house and one acre on a twenty-one year lease, 1622 (ibid. p. 553).

[105] Leaseholder on Sir John Dillon's estate, 1622 (ibid. p. 557).

[106] Leaseholder on Sir John Dillon's estate, 1622 (ibid.); he may be the same Robert Bonner who assigned a freehold on the Fishmongers' estate in Londonderry to Francis Hayward (Hunter, 'Fishmongers' Company', p. 254).

[107] Resident Armagh; killed, 1641 (Deposition of Edward Saltenstall and George Littlefeild, 1 June 1642 [TCD MS 836, fols 069r–079v]).

[108] Leaseholder on Sir John Dillon's estate, 1622 (Treadwell (ed.), *Irish commission*, p. 557).

[109] His wife was killed, January 1642 (Examination of Frances St John, 21 April 1653 [TCD MS 837, fols 038r–039v]).

[110] Numbers 35 and 45 are the son and grandson of Egidius Blacklock, to whom John Heron let 'the lands of Cannaneale … for twenty-one years', 1614 (Inquisitions of Ulster, Armagh, (5) Charles I).

[111] Yeoman; resident Drumcree; losses over £100 0s 0d (Deposition of Thomas Greene and Elizabeth Greene, 10 November 1643 [TCD MS 836, fols 094r–094v]).

[112] Tenant of Sir John Dillon, 1622 (Treadwell (ed.), *Irish commission*, p. 557).

[113] See number 35.

[f. 28v]

Armagh
Barony de Oneallan

Mr Stanhow, undertaker of 1500 acres: the names of his men and arms as followeth

Sword only
1. Henry Read[114]

Snaphance only
2. John Gray[115]

No Arms
3. Henry Kerfoote

Snaphance only
4. Thomas Kerfoote
5. Richard Mantle[116]

No Arms
6. Ralph Pollock

Snaphance only
7. George Clerke[117]

No Arms
8. Zacary Foster
9. William Smith[118]

Snaphance only
10. Thomas Butler
11. George Branston
12. Robert Branston
13. James How[119]

Pike only
14. Robert Jackson[120]

No Arms
15. Henry Tyllyfley

Sword and Snaphance
16. Nicholas Goddar[121]

16 Men; 2 swords; 1 Pike; 9 snaphances

[f. 29]

Armagh
Barony de ONeallan

Francis Satcheuerall esquire, undertaker of 2000 acres: the names of his men and arms

Snaphance only
1. John Edmond[122]

Sword and Pike
2. William Hebone

Sword only
3. James Smith[123]

Snaphance only
4. John Richardson

Sword only
5. John Nixon
6. John Boy
7. Gregory Jackson[124]

Sword and Pike
8. John Towell[125]

Sword only
9. John Garrat
10. Sammuell Potter[126]

Snaphance only
11. Robert Wilkinson[127]

Sword and Snaphance
12. Richard Smith

Sword only
13. Richard Carington[128]
14. Nicholas Woods[129]
15. David Williams[130]
16. George Woodier

---

[114] Held 'one balliboe [and] has a house and lives in it', 1622 (Treadwell (ed.), *Irish commission*, p. 544).

[115] Possibly son of either Oliver or Richard Gray, leaseholders on Sir John Dillon's estate, 1622 (ibid. pp 547, 558).

[116] Possibly son of William Mantell, a yeoman, who had leased a house and ten acres for thirty-one years from Sir William Brownlow, 1622 (ibid. p. 554).

[117] Held 'a parcel of a third part of a townland, about twenty acres', 1622 (ibid.); leased two townlands for twenty-one years, 1626 (Inquisitions of Ulster, Armagh, (3) Charles I); leaseholder on Sir John Dillon's estate, 1622 (Treadwell (ed.), *Irish commission*, pp 557–8).

[118] Leased one townland, 1622 (ibid. p. 544) and three townlands on one-year lease, 1627 (Inquisitions of Ulster, Armagh, (3) Charles I); elder son of Henry Smyth and brother of John Smyth (Brownlow, number 34) of Lurgan [RJH].

[119] Killed, 1641 (Deposition of Christian Stanhawe and Owen Frankland, 23 July 1642 [TCD MS 836, fols 075r–076v]).

[120] Possibly constable at Holywood, 1642 (Examinations of Katherine McGarry, 10 May 1653 [TCD MS 838, fols 247r–248v] and Daniel MacThomas O Gilmore, 28 April 1653 [ibid. fols 249r–250v]).

[121] Possibly son of John Goddard, who held sixty acres in fee simple on Michael Obbyns's estate, 1622 (Treadwell (ed.), *Irish commission*, p. 563); killed, 1641 (Deposition of Christian Stanhawe and Owen Frankland, 23 July 1642 [TCD MS 836, fols 075r–076v]).

[122] Possibly son of Thomas Edmundes, who had a three-life lease on twenty acres, 1622 (Treadwell (ed.), *Irish commission*, p. 545); killed, 1641 (Deposition of Margaret Phillis, 15 March 1643 [TCD MS 836, fols 066r–066v]).

[123] Three-life lease on 20 acres, 1622 (Treadwell (ed.), *Irish commission*, p. 545).

[124] Killed, 1641 (Deposition of Margaret Phillis, 15 March 1643 [TCD MS 836, fols 066r–066v]), as were his wife and his sister, Ann (Deposition of Katherin Cooke, 24 February 1644 [ibid. fols 092r–093v]).

[125] Possibly John Teale, sub-tenant on Sir Archibald Acheson's estate, 1622 (Treadwell (ed.), *Irish commission*, p. 545).

[126] Possibly son of Henry Potter, sub-tenant of Henry Sacherevell, 1622 (ibid.); another member of the family, Humphrey, was killed at Kinard, November 1641 (Examination of Michaell Harrison, 11 February 1653 [TCD MS 836, fols 127r–138v]).

[127] Three-life lease on twenty acres, 1622 (Treadwell (ed.), *Irish commission*, p. 545); father of number 21; he and his wife, aged sixty, killed, 1641; a younger son, Hugh, resident Kilmore (Deposition of Katherin Cooke, 24 February 1644 [TCD MS 836, fols 092r–093v]).

[128] Son of Richard Carrington (Cavan, Sir Edward Bagshaw, number 22); Richard Carrington junior later returned to the family farm at Drumcole in county Cavan; he was aged forty when killed, 1641; his widow reported losses of £500 0s 0d, later amended to £610 0s 0d (Depositions of Grace Carinton, 21 and 28 April 1642 [TCD MS 833, fols 110r–111v and 199r–199v]).

[129] Three-life lease on fifteen acres, 1622 (Treadwell (ed.), *Irish commission*, p. 545); wife, Frances, and a child killed, 1641 (Information of Margaret Clarke, 16 March 1643 [TCD MS 836, fols 035r–036v] and Deposition of Ann Smith and Margret Clark, 16 March 1643 [ibid. fols 073r–074v]).

[130] Three-life lease on fifteen acres, 1622 (Treadwell (ed.), *Irish commission*, p. 545); described himself as 'of Sucstowne', 1641; losses £98 6s 4d (Deposition of Davie Williams, 12 January 1642 [TCD MS 836, fols 013r–013v]).

17. Henry Hampton[131]
18. John Williams
19. John Gryndall
20. Francis Grindall
21. Robert Wilkinson younger[132]

[f. 29v]

Pike only

22. Arthur Miller[133]

Sword only

23. John Jackson[134]
24. William Bonner[135]
25. James Powell[136]

Sword and Snaphance

26. James Hobs[137]

Caliver only

27. George Williams[138]

Sword and Snaphance

28. Nicholas Williams

Sword only

29. Edward Meres[139]
30. Luke Johnston

Pike only

31. John Phillis[140]

32. Michaell King[141]
33. Thomas Phillis[142]

Snaphance only

34. Edward Fenton
35. Robert Morris
36. Thomas Harris[143]

Sword only

37. Richard Dutton
38. Mungo Dawe

Sword and Snaphance

39. Henry Dowe

Sword and Pike

40. Edward Sharp
41. Robert Smith[144]

Sword only

42. Edward Symons[145]

Pike only

43. Francis Sams

Sword only

44. Henry Satcheverall[146]
45. Wm Satcheverall

Sword and Snaphance

46. Thomas Kirke

[f. 30]

No Arms

47. William Spery
48. James Norton
49. Lawrence Barnell
50. Richard Messenger
51. George Symson[147]
52. Sammuell Garrat
53. Thomas Parker
54. Thomas Moore
55. Nicholas Wilkinson
56. John Wilkinson
57. Robert Kirke
58. William Williams
59. John Higs[148]
60. Thomas Williams[149]
61. William Clarke
62. George Herrod
63. Nathaniell Williams
64. John Clarke[150]
65. James Boy
66. William Ware[151]
67. John Carruddas[152]
68. Trynion Hodgenson
69. William Donne
70. William Troult

[131] His wife, Jane, was 'the most forward and cruellest rebel', 1641 (Information of Margaret Clarke, 16 March 1643 [ibid. fols 035r–036v]).

[132] Son of number 11.

[133] Resident Loughgall, 1622 (Treadwell (ed.), *Irish commission*, p. 541).

[134] Leaseholder on Sir John Dillon's estate, 1622 (ibid. p. 558).

[135] Three-life lease on sixty acres, 1622 (ibid. p. 545).

[136] Powell and his wife were killed, 1641 (Depositions of Margaret Phillis, 15 March 1643 [TCD MS 836, fols 066r–066v] and of Joane Constable, 6 June 1643 [ibid. fols 087r–090v]).

[137] Possibly James Hobson, a yeoman, with twenty-one year lease on a house and twenty acres at Lurgan, 1622 (Treadwell (ed.), *Irish commission*, p. 553).

[138] 'Of Drumcor … yeoman'; losses £110 0s 0d, 1641 (Deposition of William Duffeild ex parte George Williams, 11 August 1642 [TCD MS 836, fols 047r–047v]).

[139] Held a small parcel of land, 1622 (Treadwell (ed.), *Irish commission*, p. 545); killed, 1641 (Deposition of Margaret Phillis, 15 March 1643 [TCD MS 836, fols 066r–066v]).

[140] Cottager or sub-tenant on the estate of Sir Archibald Acheson, 1622 (Treadwell (ed.), *Irish commission*, p. 546); father of Thomas Phillis (number 33); killed 1641 (Deposition of Margaret Phillis, 15 March 1643 [TCD MS 836, fols 066r–066v]).

[141] Possibly the son of Roger or Edward King, the former a freeholder and the latter a leaseholder, on Sir John Dillon's estate, 1622 (Treadwell (ed.), *Irish commission*, p. 557).

[142] Linen weaver; son of number 31; killed, 1641; losses £151 0s 0d (Deposition of his wife, Margaret Phillis, 15 March 1643 [TCD MS 836, fols 066r–066v]).

[143] Cottager and sub-tenant of Francis Sacherevell, junior, 1622 (Treadwell (ed.), *Irish commission*, p. 545).

[144] Tailor; resident at Shewis when killed, 1641 (Information of Margaret Clarke, 16 March 1643 [TCD MS 836, fols 035r–036v] and Deposition of Ann Smith and Margret Clark, 16 March 1643 [ibid. fols 073r–074v]).

[145] Possibly son of Richard Symons, who had a twenty-one year lease on Drumnahunchin, 1622 (Treadwell (ed.), *Irish commission*, p. 545).

[146] Henry Sacheverell described himself as 'of Ballybreagh in the county of Armagh, gentleman' and reported losses amounting to £2,015 0s 0d from his properties in Armagh, Dublin, King's County, Louth, and Monaghan (Deposition of Henry Sacheverell, 27 September 1643 [TCD MS 836, fols 106r–106v]). Henry, William, and Francis Sacherevell (numbers 44, 45, and 88) are the sons of Francis Sacherevell, the undertaker (see Hill, *Plantation*, p. 562).

[147] Sub-tenant on Sir Archibald Acheson's estate; appeared with sword and pike, 1622 (Treadwell (ed.), *Irish commission*, p. 561).

[148] Three-life lease on twenty acres, 1622 (ibid. p. 545); 'one Higgs' killed near Benburb, December 1641 (Examination of Michaell Harrison, 11 February 1653 [TCD MS 836, fols 127r–138v]).

[149] Numbers 60 and 61 each had a three-life lease for twenty acres, 1622 (Treadwell (ed.), *Irish commission*, p. 545).

[150] 'Of Annaclea in the parish and County of Armagh'; losses £103 16s 8d; his house was the scene for one of the massacres in the county, 1641 (Information of his wife, Margaret Clarke, 16 March 1643 [TCD MS 836, fols 035r–036v]).

[151] Possibly son of Matthew Ware, sub-tenant on Sir Archibald Acheson's estate, 1622 (Treadwell (ed.), *Irish commission*, p. 548).

[152] Killed, 1641 (Deposition of Edward Saltenstall and George Littlefeild, 1 June 1642 [TCD MS 836, fols 069r–079v]).

71. Morrise Pritchard
72. Donnell Matchet[153]
73. Ralph Hill[154]
74. Thomas Black
75. Gilbert Harrison
76. Roger Carr
77. Robert Dawson

[f. 30v]

78. Edward Dawson
79. Thomas Weasworth
80. Thomas Darbishere[155]
81. James Mcbeake
82. John Johnston
83. Michaell Mastoune[156]
84. George Pressike
85. Robert Neale[157]
86. John Hobkins
87. George Hunkinson
88. Francis Satcheverall[158]
89. Roger Medcalf[159]
90. Thomas Enman[160]
91. Thomas Gates[161]
92. Nathaniell Leach[162]
93. Hugh Moore[163]
94. James Boy
95. Robert Carruddas
96. Henry Dickinson
97. Thomas Odomes

98. William Wat
99. John Haughton[164]
100. William Dower
101. James Pringle[165]
102. Thomas Harris[166]
103. Charles Maccum
104. Robert Morris

[f. 31]

Armagh
Barony ONealland

Richard Cope esquire, and Mr Obbins, undertakers of 2000 acres: the names of their men and arms

Sword only
1. John Symonds[167]

Caliver only
2. Arnold Franklin[168]

Snaphance only
3. Robert Woorkman

Pike only
4. Thomas Jefferey

Sword and Caliver
5. Henry Hollinwort

Caliver only
6. Thomas Coe[169]

Sword and Caliver
7. George Win

Sword only
8. John Carter[170]

Snaphance only
9. Richard Robinson[171]
10. Robert Huckerby

Sword only
11. Thomas Burrowes
12. Nicholas Porter[172]
13. Thomas Ally[173]

Snaphance only
14. John Johnston

Caliver and Bandelier
15. Thomas Lougby

Sword and Pike
16. Ganther Hide[174]

---

[153] Matchett's father, James, was granted 'the small proportion of Kerhanan' [Tanderagee], 1610. He sold the estate to Sir Oliver St John, viscount Grandison and became rector of Kilmore, taking a three-life lease on the townlands of Drumard and Anaboe. Daniel Matchett was aged twenty-four in 1611, when he was acting as agent for his father (Hill, *Plantation*, p. 261; Treadwell (ed.), *Irish commission*, p. 545); he died after escaping with his family, 1641. His widow described him as 'of Kilmore in the County of Armagh, gentleman' and stated that their losses amounted to £1,323 0s 0d (Deposition of Ellen Matchett, 3 September 1642 [TCD MS 836, fols 058r–059v]).

[154] Killed, with his wife, 1641 (Information of Margaret Clarke, 16 March 1643 [ibid. fols 035r–036v] and Deposition of Ann Smith and Margret Clark, 16 March 1643 [ibid. fols 073r–074v]).

[155] Son of Humphrey Darbyshire, who had a three-life lease on sixty acres, 1622 (Treadwell (ed.), *Irish commission*, p. 545); his younger brothers, Lawrence and John, are numbers 92 and 93 on Anthony Cope's estate.

[156] Possibly son of William Mastone, a cooper, who had a house and fifty acres near Lurgan on a thirty–one year lease, 1622 (ibid. p. 554).

[157] Three-life lease on Raughmulcrany, 1622 (Ibid. p. 545).

[158] Francis Sacherevell, the eldest of the undertaker's sons, was aged twenty-two and held the townlands of Mulladry and Drumnahunshin, 1622 (ibid.). He was resident at Legacorry, 1641 and reported losses amounting to £3,674 0s 0d (Deposition of Frauncis Sacheverell, 21 July 1643 [TCD MS 836, fols 107r–111v]).

[159] Possibly father of James and Mary Metcalfe, who were burned to death at Shewis, 1641 (Deposition of Joane Constable, 6 June 1643 [ibid. fols 087r–090v]).

[160] Lease for twenty-one years on a parcel of land near Legacorry, 1622 (Treadwell (ed.), *Irish commission*, p. 545).

[161] Possibly son of John Gates who held a townland in fee simple on Michael Obbyns's estate, 1622 (ibid. p. 563).

[162] Third share of a three-life lease on Killemany, John Dillon's estate, 1622 (ibid. p. 546).

[163] Cottager or sub-tenant on Sir Archibald Acheson's estate, 1622 (ibid.); killed, 1641 (Deposition of Margaret Phillis, 15 March 1643 [TCD MS 836, fols 066r–066v]).

[164] Cottager or sub-tenant of James Matchett, 1622 (Treadwell (ed.), *Irish commission*, p. 545); killed, 1641 (Deposition of Elizabeth Rolleston, 21 August 1642 [TCD MS 836, fols 068r–068v]).

[165] Possibly son of William Pringle, cottager or sub-tenant on Sir Archibald Acheson's estate, 1622 (Treadwell (ed.), *Irish commission*, p. 546).

[166] Possibly related to number 36.

[167] Eventual purchaser of Francis Sacherevell's estate (Hill, *Plantation*, p. 562).

[168] Wife killed, January 1642 (Examination of Frances St John, 21 April 1653 [TCD MS 837, fols 038r–039v]).

[169] Possibly son of Roger Coe, a cottager or sub-tenant of Henry Sacherevell, 1622 (Treadwell (ed.), *Irish commission*, p. 545).

[170] Possibly son of Thomas Carter, a yeoman, who held a house and twenty-five acres on Sir William Brownlow's estate for 21 years (ibid. p. 554).

[171] Possibly son of William Robinson, who held 'part of a townland [with] three or four cottagers' on a twenty-one year lease, 1622 (ibid. p. 563).

[172] Lease of twenty acres on the Grandison estate at Tanderagee; mustered there with a caliver, 1622 (ibid. p. 514).

[173] Held 'a ploughland' in fee simple and leased another townland with John Partridge, 1622 (ibid. p. 563).

[174] Goulther Hide was a cottager or sub-tenant of Henry Sacherevell, 1622 (ibid. p. 545).

No Arms
17.   Richards Boyes
18.   William Coop younger[175]
19.   Anthony Dillon[176]
20.   Edward Gill[177]
21.   Thomas Workeman[178]
22.   John Robinson[179]
23.   Nathaniell Robinson
24.   William Coop[180]

24 Men; 8 Swords; 2 Pikes;
3 Calivers; 4 snaphances

[f. 31v]

Armagh
Barony de Oneallan

Sir William Brownlow knight, undertaker of 2500 acres: the names of his men and arms as followeth

Sword and Snaphance
1.   Thomas Spence

Pike only
2.   Peter Harland[181]

Sword and Pike
3.   John Hobson[182]

Sword and Caliver
4.   Christopher Relise

Sword and musket
5.   William Ward[183]

Sword and Pike
6.   James Thompson

Sword and Caliver
7.   William Horner[184]

Sword and Pike
8.   William Heathwood
9.   John Winter

Sword and Caliver
10.   James Atkinson[185]
11.   William Nicholson[186]

Sword and Snaphance
12.   Arthur Burt

No Arms
13.   Francis Robson[187]

Sword and Pike
14.   Richard Yates

Pike only
15.   William White[188]

Sword and Pike
16.   Thomas Yates[189]

Sword and Caliver
17.   Lancelot Pearson[190]

Pike only
18.   John Camsy

Sword and Pike
19.   John Ridgedale[191]

Sword and Snaphance
20.   Thomas Cowert

Sword and Caliver
21.   Robert Preciss

Sword and Pike
22.   James Allen

Sword and Caliver
23.   Thomas Hoocker[192]

[f. 32]

Pike only
24.   Walter Scot
25.   Robert Gibbs[193]
26.   Roger Gibbs

No Arms
27.   John Scot

Caliver only
28.   Leonard Pearson

Snaphance only
29.   William Trewman[194]

No Arms
30.   Richard Walker[195]

---

[175] Son of number 24.

[176] Freeholder on John Dillon's estate, 1622 (ibid. p. 546).

[177] Possibly the father of 'Alexander Gill of Lurgan in the county of Armagh [who was] aged forty-six years [when his deposition was] taken … the 20th day of May 1653' (Examination of Alexander Gill [TCD MS 836, fols 254r–255v]); Alexander Gill did not muster.

[178] Possibly the son of Simon Workman or of William Workman, each of whom held sixty acres in fee simple, 1622 (Treadwell (ed.), *Irish commission*, p. 563).

[179] John Robinson, a weaver, had a twenty-one year lease on a house and ten acres on Sir William Brownlow's estate, 1622 (ibid. p. 554).

[180] Father of number 18 above; leaseholder on Sir John Dillon's estate, 1622 (ibid. p. 557).

[181] Turner; house and fifty acres on a twenty-one year lease, 1622 (ibid. p. 552).

[182] Yeoman; house and two acres on a twenty-one year lease, 1622 (ibid. p. 553).

[183] Smith; house and one acre on a twenty-one year lease, 1622 (ibid. p. 552); his son, Thomas, killed, November 1641 (Examination of William Codd, 3 June 1653 [TCD MS 836, fols 268r–269v]).

[184] Husbandman; house and one acre on a twenty-one year lease, 1622 (Treadwell (ed.), *Irish commission*, p. 553).

[185] Tailor; house and two acres on a twenty-one year lease, 1622 (ibid.); 1634: Thomas Atkinson – possibly one of his sons – was named as an overseer of Henry Smythe's will (see number 34) (NAI, BET1/58 [RJH]).

[186] Weaver; house and eight acres on a twenty-one year lease (Treadwell (ed.), *Irish commission*, p. 554).

[187] Possibly son of John Robson, husbandman, who had a twenty-one year lease on a house and twenty acres, 1622 (ibid.): John Robson is number 7 on John Hamilton's estate.

[188] Mason; house and twenty-two acres on a twenty-one year lease (ibid. p. 552).

[189] Labourer; house and eleven acres on a twenty-one year lease (ibid. p. 554).

[190] He or Leonard Pearson (number 28) is the father of 'Robert Person of Clanbrasill in the County of Armagh, weaver, aged thirty-eight years or thereabouts [whose deposition was] taken at Carrickfergus upon oath the 18th of May 1653' (Examination of Robert Person [TCD MS 836, fols 262r–263v]).

[191] Husbandman; house and twenty-two acres on a twenty-one year lease (Treadwell (ed.), *Irish commission*, p. 552).

[192] Son of William Hooker, husbandman, who had a house and 100 acres on a twenty-one year lease, 1622 (ibid.).

[193] Yeoman; house and twenty acres on a twenty-one year lease, 1622 (ibid. p. 554).

[194] Truman is probably the son of Wilfred Trueman, who had a house and a sixty acre freehold outside Lurgan and was described as 'gentleman', 1622 (ibid.). William Truman was resident in Armagh when he was killed, 1641: his widow reported losses amounting to £208 18s 0d (Deposition of Elizabeth Trewman, 14 May 1643 [MS 836, fols 117r–117v]).

[195] Shoemaker; house and ten acres for thirty-one years (Treadwell (ed.), *Irish commission*, p. 555).

Sword and Pike

31. Stephen Jackson[196]
32. William Farris

Sword and Caliver

33. Edward Boone

Sword only

34. John Smythe[197]

Pike only

35. James Minard

Sword only

36. Gyles Whithead[198]
37. William Hunter[199]
38. Henry Hunter[200]

Pike only

39. Robert Harrison

Sword only

40. Robert Covert

No Arms

41. John Cooper[201]

Sword and Pike

42. Thomas Thompson[202]

42 Men; 27 Swords; 16 Pikes;
1 Musket; 8 Calivers;
4 Snaphances

[f. 32v]

Barony of Fewes

The Lord Mountnorrice; undertaker of 1000 acres: the names of his men and arms as followeth[203]

Sword and Pike

1. William Dowglas

Snaphance only

2. James Impson

Sword only

3. Peter McCulaph[204]
4. John Grimton[205]
5. Thomas Trumble

Caliver only

6. William Ellot[206]

Pike only

7. George Crafford
8. Thomas More

Caliver only

9. William Irwin

Snaphance only

10. Henry Moore

Sword only

11. Thomas Tattyne[207]

12. William Clay[208]
13. John Hollinwood[209]
14. Nathaniell Abeston
15. John Reedford

Caliver only

16. Richard Moore[210]

Sword only

17. Oliver Kennitee[211]

Snaphance only

18. William Shawe

Caliver only

19. Andrew Williams

Snaphance only

20. Thomas Hallwood

Sword and Caliver

21. William More

[f. 33]

No Arms

22. John Boware[212]
23. Ingram Curtis
24. Richard Fallerton
25. Peter Trumble[213]
26. John Trumble[214]
27. William Nixon
28. William Moore
29. John Thompson[215]

---

196 Possibly son of James Jackson, joiner, who had a house and two acres at Lurgan on a twenty-one year lease (ibid. p. 553).

197 John Smythe is the younger son of Henry Smythe, a yeoman, who had a house and eighty acres in freehold for three lives at Lurgan, 1622 (ibid.) and who died in the autumn of 1634 (NAI, BET1/58). Giles Whitehead (number 36) is Henry Smyth's grandson [RJH]. William Smythe, the elder son, mustered at Clontylaw (Stanhow, number 9 is the only William Smythe or Smith in the county) [JJ].

198 Nephew of John Smythe (number 34); killed, November 1641 (Examination of William Codd, 3 June 1653 [TCD MS 836, fols 268r–269v]).

199 Husbandman; house and ten acres for twenty-one years, 1622 (Treadwell (ed.), *Irish commission*, p. 554); killed, 1642 (Information of Manus McCowen, 11 May 1653 [TCD MS 838, fols 140r–140v]).

200 Husbandman; house and forty acres for twenty-one years, 1622 (Treadwell (ed.), *Irish commission*, p. 552); killed, 1642 (Information of Manus McCowen, 11 May 1653 [TCD MS 838, fols 140r–140v]).

201 Turner; house and forty acres for twenty-one years, 1622 (Treadwell (ed.), *Irish commission*, p. 552); named as an overseer of Henry Smythe's will, 1634 (see number 34).

202 Shoemaker; house and twelve acres for twenty-one years (Treadwell (ed.), *Irish commission*, p. 552).

203 Richard Rolleston, the original undertaker, mortgaged the manor of Teemore to Sir Francis Annesley, Lord Mountnorris between 1619 and 1622 (Hill, *Plantation*, p. 561). The Rollestons were still resident on the property, 1641 (Deposition of Elizabeth Rolleston, 21 August 1642 [TCD MS 836, fols 068r–068v]).

204 Leaseholder on John Hamilton's estate, 1622 (Treadwell (ed.), *Irish commission*, p. 548).

205 Killed, 1641 (Deposition of Elizabeth Rolleston, 21 August 1642 [TCD MS 836, fols 068r–068v]).

206 Possibly son of Robert Elliott, who held sixty acres on a three-year lease, 1622 (Treadwell (ed.), *Irish commission*, p. 544).

207 Rolleston had made Tatton a freeholder, 1611 (Hill, *Plantation*, p. 560): described as a soldier; held half a townland, 1622 (Treadwell (ed.), *Irish commission*, p. 543); killed, 1641 (Deposition of Elizabeth Rolleston, 21 August 1642 [TCD MS 836, fols 068r–068v]).

208 Possibly son of Peter Clay who held fifteen acres on a three-year lease, 1622 (Treadwell (ed.), *Irish commission*, p. 544); killed, 1641 (Deposition of Elizabeth Rolleston, 21 August 1642 [TCD MS 836, fols 068r–068v]).

209 Sub-tenant of Sir Henry Bourchier, who held 120 acres on a lease, 1622 (Treadwell (ed.), *Irish commission*, p. 543).

210 One of Rolleston's freeholders, 1611 (Hill, *Plantation*, p. 560); present, 1622 (Treadwell (ed.), *Irish commission*, p. 565).

211 Held 100 acres for four years, 1622 (ibid. p. 544).

212 Described as a soldier and as holding half a townland for life, 1622 (ibid. p. 543); resident Marlacoo when killed, 1641 (Deposition of Elizabeth Rolleston, 21 August 1642 [TCD MS 836, fols 068r–068v] and Examination of Christian Hunter, 6 May 1653 [ibid. fols 212r–213v]).

213 Weaver; sub-tenant of Robert Montgomery of Edenykennedy on Sir Archibald Acheson's estate, 1622 (Treadwell (ed.), *Irish commission*, p. 560).

214 One of John Hamilton's tenants, 1618 (Inquisitions of Ulster, Armagh, (4) Charles I).

215 Killed, 1641 (Deposition of Elizabeth Rolleston, 21 August 1642 [TCD MS 836, fols 068r–068v]).

30. William Thompson[216]
31. David Roe
32. Alexander Thompson
33. John Dow
34. Robert Arnold[217]
35. Ralph Jackson[218]

34 Men; 11 Swords; 3 Pikes;
3 Calivers; 4 Snaphances

[f. 33v]

Barony of Fewes

Sir Archball Atchison knight,
undertaker of 3000 acres: his
men and arms as followeth

Sword only
1. Robert Wood[219]
2. Edward Johnston[220]

No Arms
3. Alexander Ross[221]

Pike only
4. Andrew Pitt

No Arms
5. John Betty
6. Robert Ekey

Sword only
7. George Gourdon[222]
8. William Maxwell[223]

Sword and Snaphance
9. Robert McCarton

Pike only
10. Alexander Dunken

Caliver only
11. Thomas Black[224]

Sword and Pike
12. Adam Bayteye[225]

Sword only
13. Thomas Bayly

Pike only
14. Alexander Scot[226]

Sword and Caliver
15. John Scot

Sword only
16. Archball Young

Snaphance only
17. Robert Gercen[227]

Sword only
18. John Johnston

Sword and Pike
19. Robert Turner
20. John Mcquhan[228]
21. Edward McKetney[229]

[f. 34]

22. William Irwin
23. John Payne
24. William Montgomery[230]
25. William Leadley[231]
26. Gawen Glendony
27. William Armstrong
28. John Cerruddas[232]
29. John Lough[233]

Sword only
30. William Hynde
31. Thomas McGahan[234]
32. William McKetteny[235]
33. Andrew Sprot[236]
34. James Scot
35. Robert Thompson
36. Robert Johnston

Sword and Pike
37. Adam Turner[237]

Pike only
38. Ralph Scot

Sword and Caliver
39. Robert Foster

Sword and Pike
40. John Gibson[238]
41. Donnell McCartney
42. John Sprot

Sword only
43. Thomas Blackwood

---

[216] Sub-tenant on Sir Archibald Acheson's estate, 1622 (Treadwell (ed.), *Irish commission*, p. 561).

[217] Possibly father of Richard Arnold, killed, 1641 (Deposition of Elizabeth Rolleston, 21 August 1642 [TCD MS 836, fols 068r–068v]).

[218] Shown as number 34.

[219] Held 120 acres of Coolmillish, allegedly in freehold, 1622 (Treadwell (ed.), *Irish commission*, p. 547).

[220] Held 120 acres of Coolmillish, allegedly in freehold; sub-tenant of John McQuhan (number 20) at Creggan; constable of Clancarny and appeared with a sword, a pike, and a horseman's staff, 1622 (ibid. pp 547, 561–2).

[221] Weaver; resident in Clancarny; appeared with a sword and a 'banded staff', 1622 (ibid. p. 562).

[222] Possibly son of John Gourdon, resident of Clancarny, who appeared with a sword and horseman's staff, 1622 (ibid.).

[223] Lease on 100 acres of Drumlack, 1622 (ibid. p. 547).

[224] Resident in Clancarny; appeared with a sword, 1622 (ibid. p. 562).

[225] Lease on 100 acres of Bryandrum, 1622 (ibid. p. 547).

[226] Lease on 100 acres of Bryandrum, 1622 (ibid.).

[227] Sub-tenant on Drumlack, 1622 (ibid. p. 548).

[228] Held Lurgyross on a twenty-one year lease, 1622 (ibid. p. 549).

[229] Edward and William McKetney (numbers 21 and 32) may be the sons of Robert Caitney, who had a lease on 100 acres of Drumlack, 1622 (ibid. p. 547).

[230] Possibly son of Robert Montgomery, who held Edenykennedy in freehold, 1622 (ibid. p. 560).

[231] Sub-tenant of Patrick Acheson on Derlett, 1622 (ibid.).

[232] Possibly son of George Cardhouse, who held sixty acres on a seven-year lease, 1622 (ibid. p. 549).

[233] Sub-tenant of Andrew Sturgeon at Cloghoge, 1622 (ibid. pp 561).

[234] Son or brother of number 20: John Mawhan the younger, a sub-tenant of Patrick Acheson's at Drumgane, appeared with a sword and pike, and John Mawhan the elder had two swords and a pike, 1622 (ibid. pp 560–1).

[235] Brother of Edward McKetney (number 21 above).

[236] Sub-tenant of Andrew Sturgeon at Cloghoge; appeared with sword, 1622 (ibid. p. 561).

[237] Sub-tenant of John Mcquhan (number 20) at Creggan; appeared with 'a banded staff only', 1622 (ibid.).

[238] Sub-tenant of Andrew Sturgeon at Drumnahunshin and of John Mcquhan (number 20) at Lurgyross (ibid.); possibly son of Jacob Gibson who had held part of Carricklane, 1622 (ibid. p. 548).

Sword and Caliver
44. James White[239]
45. Quinton Nixon[240]
46. Archball Cothers

[f. 34v]

Sword and Pike
47. Edward Gibson[241]

Sword and Caliver
48. John Irwin[242]

Caliver only
49. Patrick Creery[243]

Sword, caliver, and bandoliers
50. Adam Young

Pike only
51. David Ould

No Arms
52. James Gyld[244]
53. James Wilson[245]
54. John Mackney[246]
55. William Johnston

[f. 35]

Armagh
Barony de fewes

John Hammelton esquire, undertaker of 2500 acres: the names of his men and arms

Sword only
1. James Harrison[247]
2. John Flewry

Pike only
3. David Thomson

Sword only
4. John Greere[248]
5. Gilbert Greere
6. James Greere
7. John Robson[249]
8. Thomas Grindell[250]

Snaphance only
9. John Harknes

Sword only
10. Thomas Custis[251]

Sword and Snaphance
11. David Murrey

Pike only
12. Martin Browne

Sword only
13. Anthony Grindall[252]
14. Thomas Norwich

Sword and Pike
15. William Bell[253]
16. William Murrey

Caliver only
17. Robert Jordainie

Pike only
18. Andrew Jordainie

Sword and Snaphance
19. John Carlell

Sword only
20. James Roe[254]

Pike only
21. James Fryer
22. David Leach[255]
23. William Leach

[f. 35v]

Musket only
24. Robert Sturgion[256]

Sword and Pike
25. John Hodg
26. James Hodg

Sword only
27. Francis Carrudas[257]

No Arms
28. William Carrudas

Pike only
29. John Moffat[258]
30. Thomas Clarke

Sword and Pike
31. Mungo Birres

---

239 Leaseholder on John Hamilton's estate, 1622 (ibid.).
240 Possibly son of Robert Nixon, who had a lease on 100 acres of Bryandrum, 1622 (ibid. p. 547).
241 Possibly son of William Gibson, sub-tenant on Drumgane, 1622 (ibid. p. 559).
242 Lease on 100 acres of Carricklane; sub-tenant of Andrew Sturgeon on Drumnahunshin; appeared with a sword and a horseman's staff, 1622 (ibid. pp 547, 561).
243 Sub-tenant of John Mcquhan (number 20) at Creggan; appeared then with pike, 1622 (ibid. p. 561).
244 Resident Clancarny; appeared with a sword and piece, 1622 (ibid. p. 562).
245 Resident Clancarny; sub-tenant of John Sturgeon at Creggan; appeared with sword and pike, 1622 (ibid.).
246 Lease on 100 acres of Bryandrum, 1622 (ibid. p. 547).
247 Brother of John Harrison, younger (Armagh town, number 107).
248 Possibly John Grane, one of John Hamilton's tenants, 1617 (Inquisitions of Ulster, Armagh, (4) Charles I).
249 Husbandman; twenty-one year lease on a house and twenty acres on Sir William Brownlow's estate, 1622 (Treadwell (ed.), *Irish commission*, p. 554); possibly rented part of Cloghoge on Sir Archibald Acheson's estate from Andrew Sturgeon and appeared with a sword, 1622 (ibid. p. 561).
250 'Of Curragh in the County of Armagh, gentleman'; losses £554 10s 0d (Deposition of Thomas Grundell [TCD MS 836, fols 053r–054v]); his father, Ralph, had received Ballinecorra as a freehold from Sir James Craig in 1614 (Inquisitions of Ulster, Armagh, (4) Charles I) and held 120 acres, 1622 (Treadwell (ed.), *Irish commission*, p. 548).
251 Curtis's father, John, was one of the original settlers; he had received Ballygroobany as a freehold from Sir James Craig in 1614 (Inquisitions of Ulster, Armagh, (4) Charles I) and held sixty acres, 1622 (Treadwell (ed.), *Irish commission*, p. 548).
252 Held twenty acres of Ballynahinch on a three-life lease from Francis Sacherevell and thirty acres on John Hamilton's estate, 1622 (ibid. pp 545, 548).
253 Killed near Armagh, 1641 (Deposition of John Wisdome, 8 February 1642 [TCD MS 836, fols 014r–015v]).
254 Son of either Thomas or Robert Roe, cottagers, 1622 (Treadwell (ed.), *Irish commission*, p. 549).
255 One of John Hamilton's tenants, 1617 (Inquisitions of Ulster, Armagh, (4) Charles I).
256 Seven members of the Sturgeon family – Andrew, Andrew junior, Herbert, John, John 'of the Kill', Robert, and William – were leaseholders or sub-tenants on Sir Archibald Acheson's estate, 1622 (Treadwell (ed.), *Irish commission*, pp 549, 561).
257 One of John Hamilton's tenants, 1617 (Inquisitions of Ulster, Armagh, (4) Charles I).
258 Possibly son of James Moffatt, one of John Hamilton's tenants, 1617 (ibid.), cottager, with 'six acres and four cows' grazing', 1622 (Treadwell (ed.), *Irish commission*, p. 549).

Sword only
32.   Fergus Flack[259]

Pike only
33.   John Henderson[260]

Sword and Pike
34.   John Sherley[261]

Pike only
35.   Robert Christall
36.   George Bell[262]
37.   John Carlell
38.   David Gass
39.   Philip Morton

Sword and Pike
40.   George Bell

Pike only
41.   John Lockmer

Sword and Pike
42.   Alexander Hamelton
43.   Alexander Browne

Pike only
44.   Gilbert McMurrey

Sword and Caliver
45.   John Allen[263]

Caliver only
46.   David Houston

Sword only
47.   John Browne[264]

Sword and Pike
48.   John Fleck

[f. 36]
49.   Patrick Granton[265]

Sword and Caliver
50.   Thomas Parker[266]

Sword only
51.   Robert Ellot[267]

Sword and Snaphance
52.   John Ellot[268]

Sword and Caliver
53.   Alexander Calagh

Sword and Musket
54.   John Park

Sword and Pike
55.   Mathew German[269]
56.   Thomas Florry
57.   John McCall

Sword and Snaphance
58.   Robert Thomson

Caliver only
59.   John Trumble[270]

Sword and Pike
60.   John Deanes[271]

Pike only
61.   James Key

Caliver only
62.   John Wilkin[272]

Pike only
63.   Francis Wilson

Sword only
64.   John Krick[273]
65.   Patrick Richy[274]

Sword and Snaphance
66.   James Richy

Sword and Pike
67.   Thomas Hodg

Pike only
68.   Richard Forbee

Sword and Pike
69.   George Hay[275]

Pike only
70.   Patrick Gorden

Sword and Pike
71.   John Johnston[276]

Sword only
72.   John Cass

[f. 36v]

Pike only
73.   James Fryer

Sword only
74.   John Graham

Pike only
75.   Thomas McKnight[277]

Sword only
76.   John Murmon

Sword and Pike
77.   Alexander McCloose

---

[259] One of John Hamilton's tenants, 1617 (Inquisitions of Ulster, Armagh, (4) Charles I) and a sub-tenant on Sir Archibald Acheson's estate, 1622 (Treadwell (ed.), *Irish commission*, p. 561).

[260] Butcher; sub-tenant on Sir Archibald Acheson's estate, 1622 (ibid. p. 560).

[261] Possibly son of Laurence Shirloe, one of John Hamilton's tenants, 1617 (Inquisitions of Ulster, Armagh, (4) Charles I).

[262] Sub-tenant of Robert Maxwell, 1622 (Treadwell (ed.), *Irish commission*, p. 549).

[263] One of John Hamilton's tenants, 1617 (Inquisitions of Ulster, Armagh, (4) Charles I).

[264] One of John Hamilton's tenants, 1617 (ibid.); 'cottager', 1622 (Treadwell (ed.), *Irish commission*, p. 549).

[265] One of John Hamilton's tenants, 1617 (Inquisitions of Ulster, Armagh, (4) Charles I); held twenty-four acres with George Parker (see number 50), 1622 (Treadwell (ed.), *Irish commission*, p. 549).

[266] Possibly son of George Parker, one of John Hamilton's tenants, 1617 (Inquisitions of Ulster, Armagh, (4) Charles I), who held twenty-four acres with Patrick Granton (number 49), 1622 (Treadwell (ed.), *Irish commission*, p. 549).

[267] Elliott was one of the original settlers; received a twenty-one year lease of Balliletrie from Sir James Craig, 9 September 1614; lease renewed after Hamilton took possession of Craig's estate, 1617 (Inquisitions of Ulster, Armagh, (4) Charles I); resident, 1622 (Treadwell (ed.), *Irish commission*, p. 548).

[268] Sub-tenant on Sir Archibald Acheson's estate, 1622 (ibid. pp 560–1).

[269] Killed, 1641 (Deposition of Elizabeth Rolleston, 21 August 1642 [TCD MS 836, fols 068r–068v]).

[270] One of John Hamilton's tenants, 1617 (Inquisitions of Ulster, Armagh, (4) Charles I).

[271] Tenant, 1617 (ibid.); cottager, 'with four acres and four cow's grazing', 1622 (Treadwell (ed.), *Irish commission*, p. 549).

[272] Possibly John Welky, cottager, 'with four acres and four cow's grazing', 1622 (ibid.).

[273] Possibly John Kirk, one of John Hamilton's tenants, 1617 (Inquisitions of Ulster, Armagh, (4) Charles I).

[274] One of John Hamilton's tenants, 1617 (ibid.).

[275] Killed, 1641 (Examination of John Bratten, 28 February 1653 [TCD MS 836, fols 181r–181v]).

[276] One of John Hamilton's tenants, 1617 (Inquisitions of Ulster, Armagh, (4) Charles I).

[277] Sub-tenant of Robert Montgomery on Edenykennedy on Sir Archibald Acheson's estate, 1622 (Treadwell (ed.), *Irish commission*, p. 560).

78. Andrew Nixon[278]
79. Christopher Irwin[279]
80. Symond Carthers

Sword only
81. Andrew Bell[280]

Sword and Caliver
82. George Bell

Sword and Pike

83. David Moffet

No Arms
84. Robert Grindall[281]
85. William Palmer[282]
86. Thomas Bridome
87. John Grundall[283]
88. John Armstrong
89. Robert Hammelton[284]
90. Michell Rae[285]
91. John Fargisonne[286]
92. William Atcheson
93. Gilbert McCanny
94. John Greere[287]
95. John Hall[288]

[f. 37]

96. John Raborne[289]
97. Robert Johnston[290]

98. George Gasse
99. David Cowtard
100. Walter Scot
101. Humphrey Lee
102. David Kirkwood
103. John Armstrong
104. William McClubby
105. William Howy
106. Robert Howy
107. John McDowell
108. John Hammelton[291]
109. Robert Fargissone[292]
110. Robert Thomson
111. Robert Grindall
112. John Cowterd
113. William Steele

[f. 37v]

Armagh
Barony de Onealland

The Lord Grandison, undertaker of 1000 acres: the names of his men and arms as followeth

Pike only
1. Robert Balmer

Sword only
2. Thomas Hall

Sword and Caliver
3. George Rogers[293]

Sword only
4. Roger Birchall[294]

Sword and Caliver
5. Mathew Duke[295]
6. John Williams[296]

Snaphance only
7. Robert Ingledene[297]

Sword and Snaphance
8. Thomas Wilson[298]

Sword only
9. Thomas Barrowes
10. Ralph Jackson
11. Melchesedeck Murteant[299]

No Arms
12. Thomas Warriner
13. Robert Tynsley
14. Humphrey Wisdome
15. William Lambert
16. Edward Calvert[300]
17. James Chambers[301]

---

[278] Possibly son of Clement Nickson, cottager, 1622 (ibid. p. 549).

[279] Possibly son of Edward Irwinge, one of John Hamilton's tenants, 1617 (Inquisitions of Ulster, Armagh, (4) Charles I).

[280] One of John Hamilton's tenants, 1617 (ibid.); sub-tenant of Robert Maxwell, 1622 (Treadwell (ed.), *Irish commission*, p. 549).

[281] Son of Ralph Grindell, principal freeholder; sub-tenant of his father, 1622 (ibid.).

[282] Palmer held a townland from Anthony Cope, 1622 (ibid. p. 556) and was a sub-tenant on the estates of Sir Archibald Acheson and Francis Sacherevell (ibid. pp 561, 563).

[283] Son of Ralph Grundell; sub-tenant of his father, 1622 (ibid. p. 549); wife drowned, 1641 (Deposition of Elizabeth Trewman, 14 May 1643 [TCD MS 836, fols 117r–117v]).

[284] One of John Hamilton's tenants, 1617 (Inquisitions of Ulster, Armagh, (4) Charles I); held 30 acres, 1622 (Treadwell (ed.), *Irish commission*, p. 548).

[285] Son of Adam Rae, one of John Hamilton's tenants, 1617 (Inquisitions of Ulster, Armagh, (4) Charles I).

[286] One of John Hamilton's tenants, 1617 (ibid.).

[287] Cottager, 'with four acres and four cow's grazing', 1622 (Treadwell (ed.), *Irish commission*, p. 549).

[288] One of the original settlers; received three-life lease of Killycapple and Latmacollum from Claud Hamilton, 1614 (Inquisitions of Ulster, Armagh, (4) Charles I); held twenty-four acres with Archibald Greer, 1622 (Treadwell (ed.), *Irish commission*, p. 549).

[289] Possibly son of Thomas Reburne who held fifteen acres, 1622 (ibid.).

[290] Sub-tenant of John Davison (number 30 on the Archbishop of Armagh's lands, 'More in the Barony of Armagh') and John Welch, 1622; probably held 20 acres (ibid.).

[291] Tenant, 1617 (Inquisitions of Ulster, Armagh, (4) Charles I); cottager, 'with four acres and four cow's grazing', 1622 (Treadwell (ed.), *Irish commission*, p. 549).

[292] Tenant in 1617 (Inquisitions of Ulster, Armagh, (4) Charles I); cottager, 'with four acres and four cow's grazing', 1622 (Treadwell (ed.), *Irish commission*, p. 549).

[293] George and John Rogers (number 20) were probably the sons of Francis Rogers, who held twenty-seven acres on a lease and who mustered with a pike, 1622 (ibid. p. 542).

[294] Killed at Lurgan, 1641 (Deposition of Katherin Cooke, 24 February 1644 [TCD MS 836, fols 092r–093v]).

[295] Leaseholder of 26 acres; mustered with a pike, 1622 (Treadwell (ed.), *Irish commission*, p. 514).

[296] Mustered with a musket and caliver, 1622 (ibid. p 541).

[297] Possibly Robert Ingledewe, glover, who had a freehold of a house and thirty acres on Sir William Brownlow's estate, 1622 (ibid. p. 554).

[298] Held fifteen acres on a lease; mustered with a caliver, 1622 (ibid. p. 541).

[299] An Old Testament forename [RJH].

[300] Possibly son of John Calvert, leaseholder of 15 acres, who mustered with a caliver, 1622 (ibid. p. 541) and brother of Robert Calvert (number 22).

[301] Possibly father of Thomas Chambers, who was resident in Armagh and who lost £1,270 10s 0d, 1641 (Deposition of Thomas Chambers, 2 June 1642 [TCD MS 836, fols 042r–043v]).

[f. 38]

18. John Dale[302]
19. Robert Atkinson[303]
20. John Rogers[304]
21. John Gobbet
22. Robert Calvert
23. Lancelot Hodgson
24. Alexander Browne
25. William Atkinson
26. Christopher Seggs
27. John Ward[305]
28. Morrice Williams
29. John Robinson
30. George Stockdal
31. John Meredeth

[f. 38v]

Armagh
Barony de Orier

The Lord Viscount Grandison his British tenants dwelling on his servitors land being 1000 Acres their names and Arms

Sword and Snaphance
1. James Pringle

Sword and Musket
2. John Layfield

Sword only
3. Peter Welsh

Sword and Snaphance
4. Richard Pearson[306]

Sword only
5. Henry Duffield[307]

No Arms
6. Charles Watkins[308]
7. George Copelane[309]
8. Nicholas Wray
9. Phillip Cassment
10. John Ralf
11. Ralph Steward
12. Richard Able[310]
13. Richard Barnet
14. Robert Pringle[311]
15. Francis Watkin
16. Godfrey Watkin
17. Steaphen Booth[312]
18. James Pringle
19. Nicholas Wray
20. Vincen Leigh
21. Charles Watkin

[f. 39]

Armagh
Barony de Orier

Sir Henry Boocer his servitors land being 2000 acres: the names of his men and arms

Sword only
1. Ensign Richard Ball
2. William Greere
3. William Carlel
4. Henry Hunter[313]
5. John Glendony
6. Henry Hunter younger[314]
7. Oliver Kennitee
8. John Hollinwood
9. Thomas Ball
10. Robert Hunter younger[315]

[f. 39v]

Armagh
Barony de Orier

Sir Charles Poyntes knight, his British tenants residing on his natives lands being 500 acres: the names of his men and arms as followeth

Sword only
1. John Browne[316]
2. Walter Scot
3. Thomas Wilson
4. William Wilson[317]

Pike only
5. John Steward
6. James Steward

Caliver only
7. William Irwin

Sword only
8. Christopher Irwin
9. Archball Ellot
10. Richard Browne
11. Owen Powell
12. John Smyth

No Arms
13. John Irwin
14. John Thompson
15. William Dod
16. John Irwin younger

---

302 Held sixty-five acres in freehold and leasehold and mustered with a caliver, 1622 (Treadwell (ed.), *Irish commission*, p. 514).

303 Robert and William Atkinson (number 25) were probably the sons of Richard Atkenson, who had a twenty-acre leasehold and who mustered with a caliver, 1622 (ibid.), but they may also have been the Robert and William Atkinson who were yeomen and who each had a house and thirty acres on twenty-one year leases on Sir William Brownlow's estate, 1622 (ibid. p. 555).

304 Killed at Lurgan, 1641 (Deposition of Katherin Cooke, 24 February 1644 [TCD MS 836, fols 092r–093v]).

305 Mustered with a caliver, 1622 (Treadwell (ed.), *Irish commission*, p. 541); killed, 1641 (Deposition of William Duffeild, 9 August 1642 [TCD MS 836, fols 048r–049v]).

306 Appeared with caliver, 1622 (Treadwell (ed.), *Irish commission*, p. 551).

307 Possibly father of William Duffield of Lissenesky (Deposition of William Duffeild ex parte George Williams, 11 August 1642 [TCD MS 836, fols 047r–047v]).

308 Possibly husband of Ann Watkins; drowned, 1641 (Deposition of Margret Bromley, 22 August 1642 [ibid. fols 040r–041v]).

309 Killed, 1641 (ibid.)

310 Smith; resident Tanderagee before 1641; died near Belfast, 1652 (Examination of his widow, Anne Ebell, 3 June 1653 [TCD MS 838, fols 304r–305v]).

311 Held sixty acres of Mullanasilla on a three-life lease from John Dillon, 1622 (Treadwell (ed.), *Irish commission*, p. 547).

312 Possibly son of James Booth, resident on the Grandison estate, 1622 (ibid. p. 564).

313 Father of number 6; one of John Hamilton's tenants, 1617 (Inquisitions of Ulster, Armagh, (4) Charles I).

314 Son of number 4.

315 Robert Hunter senior did not muster.

316 Possibly one of John Hamilton's tenants, 1617 (Inquisitions of Ulster, Armagh, (4) Charles I).

317 Smith; killed near Armagh, 1641 (Deposition of John Wisdome, 8 February 1642 [TCD MS 836, fols 014r–015v] and Examination of James Sym, 19 May 1653 [ibid. fols 227r–227v]).

[f. 40]

17. Robert Steavensonne[318]
18. James Anderson
19. Roger Wilkinsonne
20. Robert Fryer
21. John Richardson
22. Archbald Richardson
23. Christopher Wilson
24. John Taylor
25. Richard Cooke[319]
26. George Vincent
27. William Ellot
28. Roger Williamson

[f. 40v]

Armagh
barony de Oneallan

The British Dwelling on the land of the Right Reverend Father in god the Lord Primate of Armagh

Snaphance only
1. John Woodward[320]

Sword and Pike
2. John Deane

Snaphance only
3. Ralph Clayton[321]

Sword only
4. Frauncis Hobson

Snaphance only
5. Sammuell Newberry

Pike only
6. Ralph Newberry

No Arms
7. William Anson
8. William Barnes[322]

More in the barony de Fewes

No Arms
9. John Montgomery
10. John Greere[323]
11. John Conningham
12. Robert Jordaine
13. Alexander Mungomery
14. Mathew Mophet

More in the Barony of Armagh

Sword only
15. Edward Brookes
16. William Brookes
17. Edmond Brookes[324]
18. Mathew Broadhead
19. Nicholas Clarke

[f. 41]

20. Symond German
21. Thomas Richardson
22. Peter Ridly
23. Henry Wilkinson
24. John Porter

Sword and Snaphance
25. Francis Allen[325]

Sword only
26. John Allen younger
27. Edward Allen
28. John Palmer

Sword and Musket
29. Richard Wallem

Sword and Snaphance
30. Richard Hall

Snaphance only
31. John Barnes

Sword only
32. Gilbert Gawhones
33. Godfrey Greeire
34. Richard Tuby
35. Archball Ellot
36. Sammuell Herbert
37. George Littlefield[326]
38. George Tate[327]
39. William Story
40. Robert White[328]
41. Silvester Amis

Snaphance only
42. John Mortrom[329]
43. William Fargheher

Sword and Caliver
44. John Davison[330]

[f. 41v]

No Arms
45. John Keaser[331]
46. Thomas Rixon
47. Thomas Arpe
48. Andrew Clarke
49. John Allen[332]
50. Michaell Smyth elder[333]
51. Thomas Connerly
52. John Richardson
53. William Slater
54. George Daskins

---

[318] Killed Marlacoo, 1641 (Examination of Christian Hunter, 6 May 1653 [ibid. fols 212r–213v]).

[319] Killed, 1641 (Deposition of Elizabeth Rolleston, 21 August 1642 [ibid. fols 068r–068v]).

[320] 'Yeoman'; resident at Kilmore; owed money to Thomas Chambers; reportedly joined the Irish, 1641 (Deposition of Thomas Chambers, 2 June 1642 [ibid. fols 042r–043v]).

[321] Killed, 1641 (Deposition of Margaret Phillis, 15 March 1643 [ibid. fols 066r–066v]).

[322] Sub-tenant of John Boylton, one of John Dillon's leaseholders, 1622 (Treadwell (ed.), *Irish commission*, p. 547).

[323] 'Young John' Greer held Ballylane on Sir Archibald Acheson's estate, 1622 (ibid. pp 548, 560) and was killed, 1641 (Deposition of Elizabeth Rolleston, 21 August 1642 [TCD MS 836, fols 068r–068v]).

[324] Edmund Brookes held a quarter share of a three-life lease on Grange on John Dillon's estate, 1622 (Treadwell (ed.), *Irish commission*, p. 546).

[325] Numbers 25, 26, and 27 are the sons of number 49.

[326] Littlefield described himself as a yeoman; he was resident in Loughgall in 1641 and reported losses amounting to £57 0s 0d (Deposition of Geoge Littlefeild, 1 June 1642 [TCD MS 836, fols 055r–056v]). John Wisdom claimed Littlefield was one of those who 'being English turned unto them [the Irish] and went with them to Lisnagarvey and fought there against the English' (Deposition of John Wisdome, 8 February 1642 [ibid. fols 014r–015v]). Wisdom's statement is, however, scored out, which would suggest that the commissioners taking the depositions accepted Littlefield's claim that he had escaped from captivity.

[327] Possibly son of Arthur Tate, leaseholder of ninety acres on Anthony Cope's estate, 1622 (Treadwell (ed.,), *Irish commission*, p. 543).

[328] Leaseholder on John Hamilton's estate, 1622 (ibid. p. 548).

[329] Resident Armagh when killed, 1641 (Examination of John Henderson, 2 May 1653 [TCD MS 836, fols 250r–251v]).

[330] One of John Hamilton's tenants, 1617 (Inquisitions of Ulster, Armagh, (4) Charles I) and resident, 1622 (Treadwell (ed.), *Irish commission*, p. 548).

[331] 'Clerk of the church of Clonfeacle', 1641 (Deposition of John Parrie, 31 May 1642 [TCD MS 836, fols 062r–065v]).

[332] One of Anthony Cope's tenants, 1622 (Treadwell, *Irish commission*, p. 541); father of number 26 and probably of numbers 25 and 27.

[333] Michael Smyth junior appears not to have mustered.

55. Alexander Mosser
56. Walter Herbert
57. William Ranolds
58. Arthur Gisley

More out of the town and liberties of Armagh

Sword only
59. James Greere
60. Leonard Willan
61. Mathew Usher
62. George Singleton
63. John Cox

Sword and Pike
64. Richard Esson

Sword only
65. Francis Graham

Snaphance only
66. John Woulds

Sword and Pike
67. William Graves younger[334]

Sword and Snaphance
68. Edward Walker

Sword only
69. George Teddy

[f. 42]

Sword and Snaphance
70. Robert Payne

Sword and Musket
71. Patrick Moody

Drummer
72. James Moody

Sword only
73. John Payne
74. Thomas Steavenson

Sword and Caliver
75. John Low

Sword only
76. John Graunt

Sword and Pike
77. Christopher Symons[335]
78. Bryan Oathes

Pike only
79. George Loe[336]

Sword only
80. David Ethington

Sword and Snaphance
81. John Smith

Sword only
82. John Whittington
83. John Whittington
84. John Dawson[337]
85. William Lawrance
86. James Gore[338]

Pike only
87. Thomas Alman

Sword only
88. Peter White

Sword and Snaphance
89. John How

Sword only
90. John Henderson[339]
91. Richard Francis
92. William Carlell[340]

Sword and Snaphance
93. James Sheall

Caliver only
94. Robert Massy

[f. 42v]

Sword and Snaphance
95. Nicholas Cox
96. Henry Walterton

Sword and Caliver
97. Thomas Barly[341]

Sword only
98. Gilbert Allert

Sword and Snaphance
99. Arthur Graham

Sword and Musket
100. Henry Corvinn

Sword and Pike
101. Thomas Jack

Caliver
102. Thomas Phillips

Sword only
103. William Burnham

Sword and Pike
104. Symond Michelson[342]

Sword only
105. William Tomlinson
106. Robert Steavenson[343]
107. John Steavenson
108. John Harrison younger[344]

No Arms
109. Thomas Smith
110. Alexander Pagget

---

334 William Graves senior may be number 83 on Sir Stephen Butler's estate in county Cavan [JJ].

335 Possibly the father of Crispian Symonds, shoemaker, killed, 1641 (Deposition of Edward Saltenstall and George Littlefeild, 1 June 1642 [TCD MS 836, fols 069r–079v]).

336 Held sixty acres of Drumadd on a three-life lease from John Dillon, 1622 (Treadwell (ed.), *Irish commission*, p. 546).

337 Resident in Armagh, 1641 (Examination of Magdalen Duckworth, 10 February 1653 [TCD MS 836, fols 121r–122v]).

338 Possibly son of William Gore, 'gardener' who held 'a third [of a townland]' in fee simple on Michael Obbyns's estate, 1622 (Treadwell (ed.), *Irish commission*, p. 563).

339 Resident Armagh, 1641 (Examination of John Handerson, 8 April 1653 [TCD MS 836, fols 208r–209v]); described himself as 'of Lurgan ... aged sixty-eight years or thereabouts [when his deposition was] taken at Lisnagarvey 2 May 1653' (Examination of John Henderson, 2 May 1653 [ibid. fols 250r–251v]).

340 Leaseholder on John Hamilton's estate, 1622 (Treadwell (ed.), *Irish commission*, p. 548); died before 1641; his widow was still living in the town when the rising started; John Dawson (number 25) was her landlord (Examination of Magdalen Duckworth, 10 February 1653 [TCD MS 836, fols 121r–122v]).

341 Killed, 1641 (Examination of John Handerson, 8 April 1653 [ibid. fols 208r]).

342 Resident Armagh when killed, 1641 (Examination of John Henderson, 2 May 1653 [ibid. fols 250r–251v]).

343 Killed, 1641 (Deposition of Elizabeth Rolleston, 21 August 1642 [ibid. fols 068r–068v]).

344 Brother of James Harrison (John Hamilton, number 1): John Harrison senior did not muster in County Armagh.

111. Peter Seckly
112. Richard Sudwick[345]
113. Richard Chappell[346]
114. Thomas Tedder
115. Thomas Corbit
116. John Moody
117. William Taft[347]
118. Thomas Burden

[f. 48]

119. Edward Messy
120. William Skandall
121. George Taylor[348]
122. Joseph Baylif[349]
123. Thomas Whitakers[350]
124. William Blakeborone
125. John Martin[351]
126. William Rigs
127. Walter Stafford
128. Silvester Ramsy[352]
129. Nathaniell Lord[353]
130. Richard Baddaly[354]
131. Andrew Wylly[355]
132. William Irwin
133. Godfrey Greeire
134. Randal Hencher
135. William Curtis
136. Robert Browne
137. Robert Griffin[356]
138. Robert Patterson
139. Richard Partage
140. Thomas Hall
141. Symond Ellet[357]
142. Henry Markham[358]
143. Godfrey Grere

144. Ralph Tyrell
145. Roger Key
146. Henry Grace
147. Jeffery Rutledg
148. Leonard Swift
149. Mathew Black

[f. 43v]

Armagh

The Lord Calfield, his abbey lands being 3000 Acres: his men and arms

Sword and Musket
1. Edward May
2. Henry Davis
3. Henry Draper

Sword and Caliver
4. Thomas Vannanker
5. James Badlock[359]
6. James Bedlock younger

Sword and Pike
7. Edward Whittingham[360]

Sword and Musket
8. William Dunbebin[361]

Sword and Pike
9. John Morgan[362]
10. John Dunkin
11. Lawrance Smith
12. Thomas Wray

Sword only
13. Hugh Vananker
14. Robert Smith

Sword and Pike
15. Robert Graves

Sword and Snaphance
16. Thomas Barber

Sword and Musket
17. Richard Lock

Sword and Caliver
18. John Ager[363]

Sword and Snaphance
19. Edward Prison[364]

Sword and Pike
20. Thomas Hall
21. Evance Meredeth

Sword and Musket
22. James Sommerell

[f. 44]

23. Francis Weldon

Sword and Caliver
24. Frauncis Feeble
25. Richard Collins

Sword and Halberd
26. Richard Parr

---

[345] Sovereign of Armagh, 1641 (Deposition of John Parrie, 31 May 1642 [ibid. fols 062r–065v]).

[346] Killed, 1641; losses £3,243 2s 0d (Deposition of his widow, Charity Chappell, 2 July 1642 [ibid. fols 044r–045v]).

[347] William Taft may have been the son of Hugh Taft, whose widow and family were living at Tanderagee, 1622 (Treadwell (ed.), *Irish commission*, p. 564). John Taft, brother-in-law of Richard Able (Grandison, servitor's lands, number 12) may have been another of Hugh Taft's sons: John Taft and his family were killed at Tanderagee in 1643 (Examination of Anne Ebell, 3 Jun 1653 [TCD MS 838, fols 304r–305v]).

[348] George Pipes, the 'inn holder', found shelter in the house of 'one Mr Taylor', 1641 (Deposition of George Pipes, 24 July 1643 [TCD MS 836, fols 100r–100v]).

[349] Possibly son of Henry Bayliffe, sub-tenant of John Alcock, freeholder on Sir Anthony Cope's estate, 1622 (Treadwell (ed.), *Irish commission*, p. 542).

[350] 'Gentleman'; killed, 1641 (Deposition of Edward Saltenstall and George Littlefield, 1 June 1642 [TCD MS 836, fols 069r–079v]).

[351] Held twenty acres on the Mountnorris estate and a sub-tenant on Sir Archibald Acheson's estate, 1622 (Treadwell (ed.), *Irish commission*, pp 544, 560); killed, 1641 (Deposition of Joane Constable, 6 June 1643 [TCD MS 836, fols 087r–090v]).

[352] Killed, 1641 (Examination of John Henderson, 2 May 1653 [ibid. fols 250r–251v]).

[353] Sub-tenant of John Davison and John Welsh on John Hamilton's estate, 1622 (Treadwell (ed.), *Irish commission*, p. 549).

[354] Possibly son of John Baddeley, resident on Anthony Cope's estate, 1622 (ibid. p. 562).

[355] Sub-tenant of John Davison and John Welsh on John Hamilton's estate, 1622 (ibid. p. 549); possibly father of John Wyly, who was killed with his wife, 1641 (Deposition of Joane Constable, 6 June 1643 [TCD MS 836, fols 087r–090v]).

[356] Possibly the father of John Griffin, clerk who was killed, 1641 (Depositions of Christian Stanhawe and Owen Frankland, 23 July 1642 [ibid., fols 075r–076v] and of Edward Saltenstall and George Littlefeild, 1 June 1642 [ibid. fols 069r–079v]).

[357] Sub-tenant of Mark Acheson on Glasdrummond on Sir Archibald Acheson's estate, 1622 (Treadwell (ed.), *Irish commission*, p. 560).

[358] Leaseholder on Sir John Dillon's estate, 1622 (ibid. p. 557).

[359] Numbers 5 and 6 are father and son.

[360] Sub-tenant of Nicholas Alcock, freeholder on the Cope estate at Loughgall, 1622 and leased a townland on the Stanhow estate (Treadwell (ed.), *Irish commission*, p. 542, 544).

[361] Sub-tenant of Nicholas Alcock, freeholder on the Cope estate at Loughgall, 1622 (ibid. p. 542).

[362] John Morgan was the son of David Morgan, to whom John Heron let 'the lands called Capponey, for three lives', 1616 (Inquisitions of Ulster, Armagh, (5) Charles I).

[363] Leaseholder on Sir John Dillon's estate, 1622 (Treadwell (ed.), *Irish commission*, p. 558).

[364] Possibly son of George Paison, leaseholder on Sir John Dillon's estate, 1622 (ibid.).

Sword and Pike
27. Richard Pare

Sword and Musket
28. Robert Atcheson

Sword only
29. William Bride

Sword and Pike
30. William Copeland[365]
31. John McEwan[366]
32. James Roane[367]

Sword and Snaphance
33. Frauncis Graham

Sword and Musket
34. Richard Walker
35. Roger James

Sword and Halberd
36. Henry Dalton[368]

Sword and Snaphance
37. Richard Blundell[369]

Sword and Pike
38. John Halnes

Sword and Snaphance
39. Ralph How[370]

Sword and Caliver
40. Richard Warran[371]

Sword and Musket
41. John Heyden

Sword and Pike
42. Dennis Ding

Sword and Halberd
43. Hugh Fews

Sword and Pike
44. Richard Lock
45. Thomas Denis

[f. 44v]

46. Richard Bridges

Sword and Musket
47. Edward Godfrey
48. John Cutris
49. John Perkin

Sword and Pike
50. William Perkin

Sword and Caliver
51. Alexander Gorden

Sword and Pike
52. Robert Bridges
53. William Graham[372]
54. John Crosby
55. John Agger[373]

Sword and Caliver
56. Alexander Trotter

[f. 45]

Armagh
Barony de Fewes

Mr Richardson[374]
his tenants on his churchlands,
the names of his men

No Arms
1. Norman Youghell
2. John Youghell
3. Robert Ellot
4. Robert Hall
5. Francis Johnston[375]
6. John Readfoord
7. Richard Moore
8. John Pike

---

[365] Leaseholder on Sir John Dillon's estate, 1622 (ibid.).

[366] Sub-tenant of Robert Montgomery on Edenykennedy on Sir Archibald Acheson's estate, 1622 (ibid. p. 560).

[367] Killed, 1641 (Deposition of Edward Saltenstall and George Littlefeild, 1 June 1642 [TCD MS 836, fols 069r–079v]); resident 'Magharnahaly'; losses more than £2,000 0s 0d; Rowan's family, apart from Robert, the youngest child, was wiped out when fleeing to Clandeboy (Deposition of Edward Wilson ex parte Robert Rowan, 12 October 1642 [TCD MS 839, fols 028r–028v]).

[368] Held fourteen acres on the Grandison estate and mustered with a caliver, 1622 (Treadwell (ed.), *Irish commission*, p. 541).

[369] Father of William Blundell of Grange, killed, 1641 (Information of Margaret Clarke, 16 March 1643 [TCD MS 836, fols 035r–036v], Deposition of Ann Smith and Margret Clark, 16 March 1643 [ibid. fols 073r–074v], and Deposition of Edward Saltenstall and George Littlefeild, 1 June 1642 [ibid. fols 069r–079v]).

[370] Sub-tenant of Nicholas Alcock, freeholder on the Cope estate at Loughgall (Treadwell (ed.), *Irish commission*, p. 542).

[371] Killed, 1641 (Deposition of Elizabeth Price, 26 June 1643 [TCD MS 836, fols 101r–105v]).

[372] Sub-tenant on Sir Archibald Acheson's estate and appeared with a sword, 1622 (Treadwell (ed.), *Irish commission*, p. 561).

[373] Sub-tenant of Robert Maxwell on John Hamilton's estate, 1622 (ibid. p. 549).

[374] John Richardson, a 'preacher of God's word', as he described himself in his will, was the minister of Levalleglish parish, county Armagh. He was the second son of John Richardson, gentleman, of Warmington in Warwickshire and married Eleanor, the eldest daughter of William Barnet of Harwich. John Richardson died, 25 September 1634 (Note by RJH based on NAI, BET1/58, pp 57–8 and BL Add MS 4820, f. 170 [PRONI, D4446/A/8]).

[375] Weaver; resident in Clancarny, 1622; appeared with a sword (Treadwell (ed.), *Irish commission*, p. 562).

County Fermanagh

[f. 46]

The Muster Roll of the County of Fermanagh

Barony de Magherstafeny and Clankelly

James, Lord BALLFOWRE, Baron of Claunally, undertaker of 5000 acres; the names of his men, and arms, as followeth[1]

Sword and Pike
1. Donnell Lenox[2]

Sword only
2. Robert Calwell[3]
3. James Rosse
4. James Hendry
5. Walter Murray
6. Richard Murray
7. John Michell[4]

Sword and Pike
8. William Greg[5]
9. Robert Graham[6]

Sword only
10. Robert Michell

Sword and Pike
11. Robert Scot
12. John Gregg[7]

Sword only
13. William Little

Sword and Pike
14. Robert Scot
15. Robert Gregg[8]

[f. 46v]

Sword only
16. John Little[9]

Sword and Snaphance
17. Archbell Johnston[10]

Snaphance only
18. Robert Tellyfeare[11]

Pike only
19. George Frihall[12]

Sword and Pike
20. William Murray[13]

Sword only
21. William Porter[14]

Snaphance
22. John Mundall

Sword only
23. Symon Henderson[15]
24. Adam Armstrong

Pike only
25. Alexander Grindeston[16]

Sword only
26. John Beaty

Pike only
27. John Beaty

Sword only
28. Andrew Irwin[17]
29. John Goodman
30. Francis Johnston[18]
31. Frauncis Johnston
32. John Beaty
33. James Johnston[19]
34. Quintan Noble
35. James Graham

Pike only
36. Robert Graham
37. Adam Beaty younger

Sword only
38. Christopher Carruddas[20]
39. Archball Scot

[f. 47]

40. Lodwick Steward
41. James Clarke[21]
42. James Armstrong[22]
43. William Dunweedy
44. Malcolm M'Farlan

No Arms
45. John Sympson

---

1 The muster roll for the Balfour estate was analysed in Johnston, 'Settlement on an Ulster estate'.
2 Leased two townlands and had two properties in the town of Ballybalfour (Balfour Rental, 1632 and 1636).
3 Robert Caldwell and Walter and Richard Murray were resident in Ballybalfour; Caldwell may have been one of the original settlers (ibid. 1636).
4 Held Killicadine and Killmccrannell for £7 0s 0d, 1632 and Garticarne for £7 0s 0d, 1636 (ibid. 1632 and 1636).
5 Held Lisnaskea with number 12 for £16 0s 0d, 1632 and for £15 0s 0d, 1636 (ibid.).
6 Held Aghamore and Durosse with number 15 for £7 0s 0d (ibid. 1632).
7 See number 8: also held Drombaddabegg on a three-year lease from All Saints 1635 for £7 0s 0d (ibid. 1636).
8 See number 9.
9 Held Croaghan and part of Carrowmccosker for £13 10s 0d (ibid. 1632).
10 Archibald and George Johnston held Coolaran for £5 10s 0d; 'Archie Johnston' also held a third of Carrowmccosker for £7 10s 0d (ibid.).
11 Held Fawny and Dresternan for £7 0s 0d, 1632 and for £11 0s 0d, 1636 (ibid. 1632 and 1636).
12 Held Cosswash and the mill for £17 0s 0d (ibid. 1632).
13 Held Ferwash for £3 10s 0d (ibid. 1632); resident Ballybalfour (ibid. 1636).
14 Held Coolcaran at will for £7 0s 0d (ibid.).
15 Henderson and Adam Armstrong (number 24) held Foyermore and Foyergrewine for £17 0s 0d a year (ibid. 1632); Henderson was the sole tenant, 1636 and the rent had been reduced to £16 0s 0d (ibid. 1636).
16 Held Terrefreshin with his fellow mason, John Churnside (number 51) at will for £7 0s 0d a year (ibid.).
17 Held Lislostie for £24 0s 0d a year, 1632 and for £30 0s 0d a year, 1636 (ibid.); participant in assault on Newtownbutler, 25 October 1641 (Deposition of Elizabeth Coats, 4 January 1642 [TCD MS 835, fols 091r–092v]).
18 Numbers 30 and 31 may be father and son: they held Drombaddamore for £5 0s 0d (Balfour Rental, 1632).
19 Held Dromconn and Drombaddabegg for £10 0s 0d (ibid.); held Drumbaddamore for £6 0s 0d, 'but a little before May Day he ran away in the night … and lives with Archibald Hamilton' (ibid. 1636).
20 Held Derryree for £7 0s 0d, 1632 and for £9 0s 0d, 1636 (ibid.).
21 Resident Ballybalfour; held Lisneile at will for £7 0s 0d a year until All Saints 1635 (ibid.).
22 Held Legogharkan, Kewmoghan, Aghnacloye, and Tonagh for £21 0s 0d (ibid. 1632).

46. William Ricarby[23]
47. John Rathborne[24]
48. William Glene
49. John Grahame[25]
50. John Little
51. John Chyrnesyde[26]
52. Arthur Beaty[27]
53. James Balfoore[28]
54. John Johnston[29]
55. Symond Little
56. William Ellot[30]
57. James Rea[31]
58. William Beaty
59. David Beaty[32]
60. Adam Beaty
61. William Dunbar
62. Robert Armstrong
63. George Read[33]
64. Daniell Lenox
65. Alexander Balfoure[34]
66. David Story[35]
67. Alexander Shere
68. John Browne

[f. 47v]

69. John Farwhere[36]
70. Gilbert Adamson
71. Thomas Cragg
72. Thomas Farbouse[37]
73. George M'Kenrick
74. William Little
75. Richard Henderson
76. William Mophet
77. Symon Mophet
78. Robert Gradin
79. John Irwin
80. David Irwin
81. Matthew Beaty[38]
82. William Fargisonne
83. William Little
84. Walter Little

85. James Little
86. John Beaty
87. Andrew Little
88. Robert Christoll
89. Walter Ranick
90. Gabrarll Gibson[39]
91. Robert Somerwell
92. James Byny
93. Thomas Smyth
94. Alexander Moorhead
95. Robert Smith
96. Michael Wilson
97. Thomas Little
98. David Scot
99. James Mountgomery

[f. 48]

Barony de Magherbuy

Sir William Cole, knight, undertaker of 1000 acres: the names of his men and arms as followeth

Sword only
1. John Pagget

Sword, Pike, Cuirass, and Headpiece
2. John Gibbs

Caliver and Sword
3. Roger Skales

Sword and Pike
4. Adam Johnston

Sword only
5. James Johnston
6. Adam Browne
7. Arthur Johnston

Sword and Pike
8. Adam Nixon
9. Thomas Beaty

Sword only
10. Richard Johnston

Sword and Pike
11. William Nordus

Sword only
12. Francis Johnston

Sword and Musket
13. Thomas Johnston

Sword and Pike
14. William Johnston
15. Robert Johnston

Sword and Musket
16. John Armestrong

Sword and Pike
17. William Johnston

Sword only
18. Lancelot Armestrong
19. John Gillpatrick

Sword and Caliver
20. John Hadson

Sword and Pike
21. Thomas Upperry[40]

Sword and Caliver
22. Charles Forrest

Sword only
23. William Grocer
24. John Oglee

---

23 House in Ballybalfour; possibly original settler (ibid. 1636).
24 Resident Ballybalfour; 'the lame fellow that writ for my Lord' (ibid.).
25 Held Dromcroo for £5 0s 0d (ibid. 1632).
26 See number 25; held Tulleene for three years from All Saints 1635 at £7 0s 0d (ibid. 1636).
27 Held Cullein for £6 0s 0d (ibid. 1632).
28 Resident at Ballybalfour; held Enigriffen for £3 0s 0d, Enisluth for £2 10s 0d, Enislin [for £2 10s 0d, and Aghakilmaid for £12 0s 0d (ibid. 1636).
29 Held Croghan 'from year to year' at £9 0s 0d (ibid.).
30 Yeoman; resident Gortgorgan; losses £527 0s 0d, 1641 (Deposition of William Ellicott, 8 January 1642 [TCD MS 835, fols 102r–102v]).
31 James Reagh, Edward Beatty, and David Beatty (number 59) held Leragh and Gontecharne for £6 0s 0d a year (Balfour Rental, 1632).
32 See number 57.
33 Resident Ballybalfour (ibid. 1636).
34 Resident Naan Island; arranged for Phillip O'Cleryan to hold Rosinakoole for £5 0s 0d and Rose Island for £16 0s 0d (ibid.).
35 Resident Ballybalfour (ibid.).
36 Held Sheebegg for £6 0s 0d, 1632; died before 1636; widow resident Ballybalfour (ibid. 1632 and 1636).
37 'Of Maguiresbridge', 1638 (Inquisitions of Ulster, Fermanagh, (39), Charles I).
38 Held Tulleinn for £5 0s 0d (Balfour Rental, 1632).
39 Killed, 1641 (Deposition of Margery Barlow, 27 February 1643 [TCD MS 835, fols 191r–191v]).
40 This name is Welsh and is now spelled Perry [RJH].

Sword and Caliver
25. Alexander Ogle

[f. 48v]

Sword only
26. William Scot

Sword and Halberd
27. Nicholas Ossenbrooke[41]

Sword and Pike
28. William Ossenbrooke[42]

Sword and Caliver
29. John Taylor
30. John Johnston

Sword and Pike
31. Roger Pearse

Sword and Caliver
32. Randall Pearse

Sword and Pike
33. Henry Bradley
34. Christopher Harlore

Sword and Musket
35. Symond Charlesworth

Sword only
36. George Courser
37. John Ellot

Sword and Caliver
38. Abraham Wadsworth

Sword and Pike
39. Thomas Abbot

Sword and Caliver
40. Richard Beaty

Sword only
41. James Brinan

Sword and Pike
42. Fargus Graham

Sword only
43. Henry Johnston
44. George Smala

Sword and Pike
45. William Wiggin

Sword only
46. Thomas Pockridg[43]

Pike and Sword
47. Thomas Little

Swords only
48. John Johnston
49. Richard Whitings

No Arms
50. Frauncis Charlesworth
51. Phillip Ossenbrooke
52. Thomas Harlore
53. Thomas Perry
54. Thomas Forrest
55. James Raikie
56. James Dundoes
57. William Sovage younger[44]
58. George Graham
59. John Fare
60. John Portis
61. John Thomson
62. James Armestrong
63. Alexander Skeares
64. John Car
65. Robert Portis
66. Patrick Ewart
67. Thomas Sanderson
68. James Ewart

[f. 50]

Barony de Lourgg

Mr Archdall, undertaker of 2000 acres his men and Arms as followeth

Sword and Caliver
1. James Johnston
2. Robert Johnston

Sword only
3. David Johnston[45]
4. Henry Jarvis

Sword and Snaphance
5. Archball Armstrong

Sword only
6. William Marshall[46]
7. Andrew Johnston

Sword and Caliver
8. John Jackson
9. Thomas Robert
10. William Ellot

Sword only
11. Symond Hudson

Sword and Caliver
12. James Coulter

Sword only
13. William Browne[47]
14. Thomas Little

Sword and Caliver
15. William Ellot
16. Alexander Armestrong

Sword and Musket
17. Robert Willson

Sword only
18. John Irwin

No Arms
19. William Ellot
20. George Irwin

Sword and Musket
21. Robert Willson

Sword only
22. John Irwin

---

41 One of the original burgesses of Enniskillen (Trimble, *History of Enniskillen*, p. 188).

42 William Ossenbrooke, who may have been Nicholas Ossenbrooke's son, survived capture by the rebels, 1641 and was living in Tirhugh barony, county Donegal in 1654 (Examination of Richard Fawsett, 30 and 31 March 1654 [TCD MS 835, fols 262r–264v]).

43 William Pockridge, his father, was buried in the churchyard in 1628; Thomas Pockridge's memorial is in St Macartin's cathedral, Enniskillen [RJH].

44 William Savage senior is either number 14 on Sir John Hume's estate or number 10 on Leonard Blennerhasset's.

45 Robert Hunter's transcript for Fermanagh breaks here and resumes with the Heygate estate (f. 58v): the transcript for the intervening estates is based on the Tenison Groves transcript (PRONI, T808/15164) and on Trimble, *History of Enniskillen*, pp 197–221.

46 Resident Castle Waterhouse; killed Newtown, 1641 (Depositions of Elizabeth Adwick, 4 January 1642 [TCD MS 835, fols 071r–071v] and Richard Knowles, 10 January 1642 [ibid. fols 129r–130v]); losses £60 0s 0d (Deposition of Anne Marshall, 3 January 1642 [ibid. fols 136r–136v]).

47 Wounded and killed at Newtown, 1641 (Depositions of Anne Booth, 8 January 1642 [ibid. fols 078r–079v] and Richard Knowles, 10 January 1642 [ibid. fols 129r–130v]).

Musket only

23.   John Houlden

Halberd only

24.   Peter Lourdg

Pike only

25.   Charles Cute

Sword and Snaphance

26.   John Armestrong

Sword only

27.   David Byers[48]

No Arms

28.   George Irwin
29.   Thomas Lewes
30.   Edward Brama
31.   Nicholas Richmond
32.   Thomas Whitby
33.   Richard Foster
34.   Thomas Anderson
35.   Henry Robinson
36.   John Robinson[49]
37.   Richard Wilson
38.   Izack Trott
39.   Thomas Moore[50]
40.   John Wilson
41.   John Birs

[f. 51]

Barony of Magheraboy

Mrs Hammelton, widow to the lord archbishop of Cashel deceased,[51] undertaker of 1500 acres: the names of her men and arms as followeth

Sword only

1.   William Crawford[52]

Sword and Pike

2.   William Beaty
3.   John Wilson
4.   David Johnston

Sword and Caliver

5.   John M'Creeke

Sword and Pike

6.   Gawen Ellot

Sword only

7.   James Sommerwell[53]
8.   William Ellott

Sword and Pike

9.   Robert Foster

Sword only

10.   William Rennick

Sword and Pike

11.   John Graham
12.   James Nicall
13.   William Waterson
14.   Mungo Ellot
15.   William Sympson

Sword only

16.   Thomas Sympson

Sword and Pike

17.   Robert Ellot
18.   George Armstrong
19.   William Ellot
20.   John Young[54]

Sword only

21.   Alexander Young
22.   Thomas Steele

No Arms

23.   Marke Ellot
24.   James M'Calstander

[f. 51]

Barony de Magherboy

Sir John Hume knight, undertaker of [3500] acres: the names of his men and arms, as followeth

Sword and Pike

1.   Thomas Cranston[55]

Sword and Snaphance

2.   John Hemingston

Pike only

3.   George Calder

Sword and Snaphance

4.   Thomas Pott

Sword and Pike

5.   William Cranston

Pike only

6.   Thomas Smith, elder[56]

Sword only

7.   John Thompson

Sword and Snaphance

8.   Alexander Carr

Sword and Pike

9.   James Skrest

Sword only

10.   John Miller
11.   William Chrisies
12.   James Dundas[57]

---

48   Freeholder (Hill, *Plantation*, p. 487).

49   Robinson and his family later moved to Newtown, from where they fled to Dublin in 1641. Their losses amounted to £123 0s 0d, of which 'three score pounds' were 'wines [such] as sack, white wine, claret wine, and aquavit'. Robinson mustered as a soldier in Dublin but was killed when another soldier had a negligent discharge (Deposition of his widow, Ursula Robinson, 23 June 1642 [TCD MS 835, fols 213r–213v]).

50   Freeholder (Hill, *Plantation*, p. 487).

51   Malcolm Hamilton was nominated to become archbishop of Cashel, 8 March 1623 and was consecrated, 29 June 1623; he died, 25 April 1629 (Cotton, *Fasti ecclesiae Hiberniae*, 1, p. 13). His will was made, 27 August 1627 and was proved, 7 May 1629. The sons from his first marriage were Archibald, Hugh, and John and the sons from his second marriage were Thomas and Malcolm. His daughters were Marion and Agnes (NAI, BET1/9, p. 55). John Hamilton matriculated at the University of Glasgow, 1628 and Malcolm Hamilton junior matriculated, 1633 [RJH].

52   Jean Hamilton's maiden name was Jean Crawford; William Crawford is probably one of her relatives and was the agent or seneschal [RJH]; he held a townland on a twenty-one year lease (Inquisitions of Ulster, Fermanagh, (24) Charles I).

53   Freeholder; one of Archbishop Hamilton's executors (ibid.); Somerville's daughter, Jane, married John Hamilton, third son of Archbishop Hamilton (J.B. Leslie, *Clogher clergy and parishes* (Enniskillen, 1929), p. 90).

54   Held two townlands on a lease from the archbishop's executors (Inquisitions of Ulster, Fermanagh, (24) Charles I).

55   Leaseholder on Mrs Hamilton's estate (Inquisitions of Ulster, Fermanagh, (24) Charles I).

56   Thomas Smith junior may be number 5 in the list of Enniskillen townsmen.

57   Described as 'yeoman' when juror Enniskillen, 1622 (Inquisitions of Ulster, Fermanagh, (3) James I).

Sword and Pike

13. John Allen[58]
14. William Savage
15. George Graham
16. George Atkinson
17. George Rankin
18. George Fayre
19. John Partish
20. John Neal
21. James Graham
22. William Wilkin
23. Thomas Spence

Sword only

24. Alexander Atkinson
25. Martin Ellot

Sword and Pike

26. Alexander Morison

Sword and Snaphance

27. William Roberts

Sword and Pike

28. James Hermiston

Sword only

29. John Greere, younger[59]
30. George M'Millane

Sword and Pike

31. William Fayre
32. William Ayre[60]
33. John Spence

Sword and Snaphance

34. John Watterson

Sword and Pike

35. David Browne
36. James Browne
37. Thomas Goodfellow

Pike only

38. James Wood
39. James Anderson

Sword only

40. Thomas Trotter

Pike only

41. George Gibson

Sword and Pike

42. Frauncis Trotter

Sword only

43. John Goodfellow[61]

Sword and Caliver

44. John Hall[62]

Sword and Pike

45. Thomas Lawhart

Pike only

46. Alexander Anderson[63]

Sword and Pike

47. William Brock
48. John Brock
49. John Black
50. William Kinge
51. Robert Black

Sword only

52. John Clarke

Sword and Pike

53. Henry Black

Sword and Halberd

54. Alexander Hume[64]
55. Patrick Hume[65]

Sword and Pike

56. John Thompson
57. Michael Dixon

Sword only

58. George Robinson

No Arms

59. Alexander Spence
60. Alexander Patterson

61. George Armstrong
62. George Chirsyde
63. John Goodfellow, younger[66]
64. James Brock
65. John Rannick
66. Rynyon Bell
67. John Thomson
68. John Trumble
69. Thomas Atkinson
70. Vincent Cocking
71. Nicholas Roger
72. Adam Williamson
73. John Huggins
74. George Car
75. William Ross
76. Thomas Coningham
77. Gabrahell Coningham
78. Alexander Chirsyde
79. George Dick[67]
80. David Anderson
81. Christopher Anderson
82. Robert Younger
83. William Henderson
84. Thomas Younger
85. Patrick Smelly
86. John Clarke
87. Alexander Anderson, elder[68]
88. John Greere[69]
89. John Renton
90. Alexander Bell

[f. 53]

Barony de Magherboy

George Hume esquire, undertaker of 1000 acres: the names of his men and arms as followeth

1. Alexander Hogg
2. John Richardson
3. James Hermidston

Sword only

4. John Hemidston

---

58 James Dundas is mentioned in an inventory at Enniskillen, 1622 (Trimble, *History of Enniskillen*, p. 126); his son, Thomas, was captured by the rebels, 1641, but survived and was living at Hare Island, 1654 (Examination of Richard Fawsett, 30 and 31 March 1654 [TCD MS 835, fols 262r–264v]).

59 Also known as Langford Greer; killed at Tully Castle, 1641 (ibid.); son of number 89.

60 'Of Carrickreagh, gentleman', 1639 (Inquisitions of Ulster, Fermanagh, (40) Charles I).

61 Father of number 37 and number 63.

62 Originally leaseholder of Malcolm Hamilton; moved onto Hume estate around 1620 (Inquisitions of Ulster, Fermanagh, (24) Charles I).

63 Son of number 87.

64 'Gentleman', juror, Enniskillen, 1622 (Inquisitions of Ulster, Fermanagh, (3) James I).

65 Subject of a £50 0s 0d bond to give deposition (Deposition of Patrick Hume, 1 April 1654 [TCD MS 835, fols 260r–260v]).

66 Son of number 43 and brother of number 37.

67 Possibly George Dixon; killed, Newtown, 1641 (Deposition of Robert French, 12 March 1643 [TCD MS 835, fols 109r–110v]).

68 Father of number 46.

69 Father of number 29; leaseholder on archbishop of Cashel's estate, Castletown [Monea] (Inquisitions of Ulster, Fermanagh, (24) Charles I).

Pike only

5. Andrew Hume

Sword only

6. Robert Henderson

Pike only

7. John Ripeth

Sword and Snaphance

8. George Craford

Sword and Pike

9. Robert Bowmaker

Snaphance only

10. John Gibson

Sword only

11. John Fayre[70]

Sword and musket

12. John Fayre, younger

Sword and Pike

13. Clement Nixon
14. Robert Portas

Snaphance only

15. Patrick Ewart

Sword only

16. William Michell

Sword and Pike

17. William Liddall

Sword and Snaphance

18. Andrew Herit

Sword only

19. John Croser

Sword and Pike

20. Thomas Sanderson
21. William Dunsy
22. Alexander Johnston

Sword and Snaphance

23. James Waugh
24. James Armestrong

Sword and Pike

25. William Armestrong

No Arms

26. Alexander Trotter
27. James Trotter
28. John Bowmaker
29. James Ellot

[f. 54]

Barony de Lourgg

Sir Gerrard Lowther, kt. Undertaker of 2000 acres: the names of his men and arms, as followeth

Sword and musket

1. Walter Ares

Musket only

2. Richard Good[71]

Sword and Musket

3. John Simble

Sword and Pike

4. John Maxwell

Sword and Caliver

5. Andrew Bayty

Sword and Pike

6. George Bayty

Sword only

7. John Johnston

Sword and Pike

8. William Bayty, younger[72]

Sword and Caliver

9. Richard Baity

Sword and Musket

10. Leonard Slater
11. Christopher Cawarty

Sword and Pike

12. Francis Johnston
13. Peter Blare
14. Lancelot Carleton[73]
15. Ambrose Carleton
16. Francis Carleton

Sword and Musket

17. William Moffet

Sword and Pike

18. William Irwin

Sword and Caliver

19. James Irwin

Sword and Pike

20. Andrew Johnston

Sword and Caliver

21. James Johnston
22. Hugh Baety
23. David Baety
24. William Thompson
25. John Thomson

Sword and Musket

26. John Reedman[74]
27. James Davison

Sword and Pike

28. Christopher Calvert[75]

Sword and Musket

29. Robert Maxwell

Sword and Caliver

30. Robert Johnston
31. David Watson
32. John Little
33. John Finding
34. John Graham

Sword only

35. Walter Baety

Sword and Pike

36. Robert Good[76]
37. John Peacock

---

[70] Numbers 11 and 12 are father and son.

[71] Richard (number 2), Robert (number 36), and John (number 42) Good are brothers: their father, John Good senior, did not muster.

[72] Son of number 45 below.

[73] Numbers 14 to 16 are 'most likely from the Carletons of Penrith, Cumberland and neighbouring places in Westmorland, near Lowther: Carleton of Brampton Foot, county Cumberland (Burke, *Landed Gentry*)' but 'Ambrose and Francis Carleton are "possible Norfolk names"' [RJH].

[74] Possibly father of Thomas Redman, son-in-law of Francis Blennerhasset, and 'most barbarously and cruelly hanged up to death on Tenterhooks' at Lowtherstown, 1641 (Deposition of Ann Blenerhasset, 31 March 1643 [TCD MS 835, fols 236r–236v]).

[75] Related to Christopher Calvert, number 2 on Thomas Flowerdew's estate [RJH].

[76] Brother of numbers 2 and 42.

38. Thomas Noble
39. John Nixon
40. James Maxwell
41. Francis Irwin
42. John Good, younger[77]
43. Ralph Wyndstones
44. John Baety

No Arms
45. William Beaty[78]
46. John Smythe
47. Robert Johnston

[f. 55]

Mr Hannings, undertaker of 1000 acres: the names of his men and arms as followeth

Musket only
1. William Amcres

Sword and Snaphance
2. Edward Scammell, younger[79]

Snaphance only
3. Edward Bampton

Sword only
4. Thomas Widson

Sword and Pike
5. Samuel Brumer

Sword and Snaphance
6. Thomas Richardson

Sword only
7. John Woke

Pike only
8. John Smith

Caliver only
9. John Ellis

Pike only
10. Haman Father

Halberd only
11. Richard Orme[80]

Pike only
12. Ralph Whittaker

Sword and Pike
13. Edward Browne
14. William Ogle

Sword and Caliver
15. Evance Westhead

Sword and Pike
16. Allen Gibb
17. Christopher Johnston[81]

Sword only
18. William Bell[82]

Sword and Caliver
19. Richard Raynick
20. Robert Hantsworth
21. John Roggers

No Arms
22. Mathew Helswords[83]
23. John Hyde
24. Joseph Wats

[f. 56]

Barony de Lourgg

Mr Flowerdew, undertaker of 2000 acres: the names of his men and arms as followeth

Sword and Pike
1. Christopher Irwin

Sword and Caliver
2. Christopher Calvert[84]
3. John Tymeyng

Sword and Pike
4. Gerrard Reedman

Musket only
5. William Barefoote

Sword and Pike
6. John Yedding
7. Rowland Glover[85]
8. Vincent Reede

Sword and Caliver
9. John Irwin

Sword and Pike
10. Thomas Browne[86]

Sword and Snaphance
11. Steaphen Smith

Pike only
12. Thomas Lifer

Snaphance only
13. Richard Coult

No Arms
14. Ambross Carleton[87]
15. Francis Carleton
16. Andrew Johnston
17. John Readman
18. Francis Irwin
19. Thomas Johnston
20. George Yeddin
21. Thomas Barefoote
22. Thomas Hogg
23. Thomas Harrison
24. Thomas Laughlane
25. William Widson
26. Edward Thomson
27. Patrick Wallas
28. Humphrey Carfil
29. William Mason
30. John Little

---

77 Brother of numbers 2 and 36.
78 Father of number 8 above.
79 He or his father was 'of Drummal', 1628 (Inquisitions of Ulster, Fermanagh, (1) Charles I).
80 Leased Drumee for sixty-one years from Sir William Cole in 1613 (ibid. (4) Charles I).
81 Son of William Johnson of Hunningston, county Fermanagh, who died December 1627: Christopher Johnson's brother, Thomas, resident Warwickshire (NAI, BET1/31, p. 133).
82 Killed with his son, 1641 (Depositions of Robert Flacke, 12 August 1642 [TCD MS 835, fols 201r–202v] and Elizabeth Fletcher, 16 August 1643 [ibid. fols 242r–242v]).
83 Resident Newtown; killed, 1641 (Deposition of Margery Barlow, 27 February 1643 [ibid. fols 191r–191v]).
84 Related to Christopher Calvert, number 28 on Sir Gerald Lowther's estate [RJH].
85 Rowland Glover can be linked to Richard Glover of Norwich (RJH: Information from P. Rutledge, Norfolk Record Office, 11 July 1978, referring to Norwich MS 12368 [PRONI, D4446/A/8]).
86 Leased 'Corneloct' from William Bickerdick; losses £28 0s 0d (Deposition of Thomas Browne, 11 January 1642 [TCD MS 835, fols 086r–086v]).
87 Ambrose Carleton was a 'kinsman to' Lieutenant William Graham and joined him in rebellion, 1641 (Depositions of Robert Barton, 5 January 1642 [ibid. fols 073r–073v] and Elizabeth Coats, 4 January 1642 [ibid. fols 091r–092v]).

[f. 57]

Barony de Lourgg

Francis Blennerhasset esquire, undertaker of 1500 acres: the names of his men and arms as followeth[88]

Sword only
1. Robert Askin

Sword only
2. William Helliard

Snaphance only
3. *William Crome[89]

Pike only
4. Bryan Kellane

Sword only
5. Richard Hesket
6. Richard Beard[90]
7. Thomas Johnston
8. William Mawe[91]
9. Richard Lilly
10. William Cox
11. *Richard Natley
12. *William Notley
13. Richard Hall
14. Tiege Bire
15. George Harrison
16. Richard Hill
17. Walter Natley
18. Christopher Thurston
19. John Bird
20. Mathew Erskin
21. William Armstrong
22. William Slater
23. Thomas Barton
24. Richard Bucket

[f. 57]

Barony de Lurgg

Mr Leonard Blennerhasset, undertaker of 2000 acres: the names of his men and arms as followeth

Sword and Snaphance
1. Thomas Pock[92]

Sword and Pike
2. William Powell
3. Edward Martin

Sword only
4. Robert Westby

Pike only
5. John Kirke
6. Thomas Satcheverell

Sword and Snaphance
7. Robert Rycroft[93]

Snaphance only
8. Christopher Thoxter

Pike only
9. Robert Barton

Snaphance only
10. William Savage[94]
11. Jeremy Emery[95]

Sword only
12. Leonard Toby
13. *William Halland

Sword and Pike
14. [Robert] Rackins[96]
15. William Grace[97]
16. *Richard Notley
17. George Barton
18. Thomas Palmer
19. Thomas Westby, elder[98]
20. Thomas Westby, younger
21. John Vernam[99]
22. William Hamilton

[f. 5]

Barony de Clankelly

Sir Hugh Woorell knight, undertaker of 1000 acres:[100] the names of his men and arms, as followeth

Sword only
1. Hugh Worell
2. George Worrell[101]
3. Charles Worrell

Pike only
4. Thomas Dewsbery[102]

Sword and Snaphance
5. Robert Moore
6. William Armstrong[103]

Sword only
7. Thomas Armstrong

No Arms
8. Thomas Bent
9. Michaell Amerson

---

88 Killed Ballyshannon, 1641; losses in counties Cavan, Fermanagh, and Monaghan £1.860 0s 0d (Deposition of his widow, Ann Blennerhasset, 31 July 1643 [ibid. fols 236r–236v]).

89 Names preceded with an asterisk are identifiably from Norfolk [RJH].

90 Captured by the rebels, 1641; still alive, 1654 (Examination of Richard Fawsett, 30 and 31 March 1654 [ibid. fols 262r–264v]).

91 Possibly father of Jathnell Mawe, who held Fargrim near Magheraveely, 1641 (Deposition of Jathnell Mawe, 3 January 1642 [ibid. fols 138r–138v]).

92 Tenant of Leonard Blennerhasset's father, Thomas (Inquisitions of Ulster, Fermanagh, (2) Charles I).

93 Killed, 1641 (Deposition of Robert Flacke, 12 August 1642 [TCD MS 835, fols 201r–202v]).

94 Freeholder, 1634 (Inquisitions of Ulster, Fermanagh, (48) Charles I).

95 Held Drumnarullagh for £1 0s 4d, 1632 (ibid.); described as 'of Kesh, yeoman', 1639 (ibid. (40) Charles I).

96 The manuscript at this point is illegible; Robert Rackins became a tenant on the estate between 1614 and 1619 (ibid. (2) Charles I) and I have presumed that he is the man named here [JJ].

97 Possibly father of Edward Grace, who was captured by the rebels, 1641 and who was living at Boa Island, 1654 (Examination of Richard Fawsett, 30 and 31 March 1654 [TCD MS 835, fols 262r–264v]).

98 Numbers 19 and 20 are father and son.

99 Freeholder, 1634 (Inquisitions of Ulster, Fermanagh, (48) Charles I).

100 Sir Hugh Wyrrell died later in 1629 and the estate was granted to his executors, Sir Thomas Rotherham, Stephen Allen, and Rev. Martin Baxter, 6 March 1630 (Morrin (ed.), *Patent rolls, Charles I*, pp 530–1; Inquisitions of Ulster, Fermanagh, (32), Charles I; Hill, *Plantation*, p. 484).

101 'Of Ballagh … gentleman'; losses £440 16s 6d, 1641 (Deposition of George Wirrall, 18 July 1642 [TCD MS 835, fols 231r–232v]).

102 'Of Drumralla … webster'; losses £112 10s 0d (Deposition of Elizabeth Dewsberry, 7 January 1642 [ibid. fols 100r–100v]).

103 Resident Magheraveely; killed, 1641 (Deposition of Cormack McDonell, 30 June 1654 [ibid. fols 265r–266v]).

10. Arthur Graham[104]
11. William Graham
12. George Graham
13. Edward Graham
14. Thomas Graham
15. John Bell
16. John Wesson
17. William Amerson
18. Rist Moore
19. Walter Graham

[f. 58v]

Barony de Clankelly[105]

James Higget, Lord Bishop of Kilfenora,[106] undertaker of 1000 acres: the names of his men and arms, as followeth

Sword only
1. Thomas Lane[107]

Sword and Pike
2. John Presly[108]

Sword only
3. Thomas Dillon

Sword and Pike
4. William Little

Pike only
5. Richard Hayle[109]

Sword and Pike
6. Arthur Foster
7. Thomas Little

Pike only
8. Symond Presly[110]

Sword only
9. Morrish Middlebrooke[111]

Snaphance only
10. Thomas Knowells[112]

Sword and Snaphance
11. Thomas Presly[113]

Sword and Pike
12. Lewis Ridg
13. William Wallis

Snaphance only
14. Anthony Barlow[114]

Pike only
15. Francis Tod

Sword only
16. Andrew Little

Sword and Pike
17. David Lenton
18. William Graham

No Arms
19. Symond Burny[115]
20. Edward Clarke[116]
21. William Tomson
22. James Burny

[f. 59]

Barony de Clankelly

Charles Waterhouse esquire, undertaker of 1000 acres: the names of his men and arms as followeth[117]

Sword and Snaphance
1. John Wright[118]

Sword and Pike
2. William Bishop

Pike only
3. Richard Nevill

Sword only
4. Nicholas Wally

Pike only
5. Christopher Bowser[119]

---

104 Brother of William Graham the muster-master (Deposition of Elizabeth Coats, 4 January 1642 [ibid. fols 091r–092v]); resident Ballybalfour, 1641 (Deposition of Lawrence Knowles [ibid. MS 834, fols 124r–124v]).

105 Robert Hunter's transcript resumes at this point.

106 Nominated bishop of Kilfenora, 28 February; consecrated, 9 May 1630; died, 30 April 1638 (Leslie, *Clogher clergy and parishes*, p. 42) [RJH].

107 Killed Newtown, 1641; described as 'a very ancient man' (Deposition of Lawrence Knowles, 7 January 1642 [TCD MS 835, fols 011r–011v]) and as a 'gentleman aged fourscore years or thereabouts' (Deposition of Richard Knowles, 10 January 1642 [ibid. fols 129r–130v]).

108 'Gentleman'; juror Magheraveely, 1621 (Inquisitions of Ulster, Fermanagh, (2) James I); resident Ballywillin; died before 1641; property left to his children: Grace, Susan, Anne, James, and Simon; widow married Francis Lovett (Deposition of Grace Lovett, 5 January 1642 [TCD MS 835, fols 133r–134v]).

109 Killed, 1641 (Deposition of William Baker, 8 January 1644 [ibid. fols 234r–234v]).

110 Son of number 2 (Deposition of Grace Lovett, 5 January 1642 [ibid. fols 133r–134v]).

111 Aged 44, 1642; 'of Knockmakegan … yeoman'; losses £420 0s 0d (Deposition of Morris Midlebrooke, 7 January 1642 [ibid. fols 141r–141v]).

112 'Gentleman', resident Castlecoole [Newtown], juror Enniskillen, 1638 (Inquisitions of Ulster, Fermanagh, (39) Charles I); 'yeoman', age 41, losses £873 0s 0d (Deposition of Thomas Knowles, 3 January 1642 [TCD MS 835, fols 131r–132v]); brother of Cavan, Sir Stephen Butler, number 20 (Deposition of Lawrence Knowles, 7 January 1642 [ibid. fols 011r–011v]).

113 'Gentleman', juror Enniskillen, 1622 (Inquisitions of Ulster, Fermanagh, (3) James I); renewed tenancy with Simon Presly (number 8), 1 May 1637 (ibid. (25), Charles I); resident Lisnehelly, 1639 (ibid. (40) Charles I); killed Newtown, 1641 (Depositions of Elizabeth Dewsberry, 7 January 1642 [TCD MS 835, fols 100r–100v] and Richard Knowles, 10 January 1642 [ibid. fols 129r–130v]).

114 Farmer; hanged, 1641; losses £300 0s 0d (Deposition of his widow, Margery Barlow, 27 February 1643 [ibid. fols 191r–191v]).

115 Burny (numbers 19 and 22) is a Norfolk name [RJH].

116 Possibly son of John Clarke, juror Magheraveely, 1621 (Inquisitions of Ulster, Fermanagh, (2) James I); resident Tantybulk in 1641, 'gentleman'; losses in Fermanagh and Cavan £129 12s 0d (Deposition of Edward Clarke, 12 August 1642 [TCD MS 835, fols 195r–195v]).

117 Waterhouse was one of the three leaseholders to whom Sir Stephen Butler let the manor of Derryany, which he had purchased from George Smelhome in 1618. Each leaseholder was still apparently in possession of his lands in 1629 (Inquisitions of Ulster, Fermanagh (11) Charles I), so the other leaseholders – Richard Buckland and Robert Montgomery – may have been Waterhouse's partners.

118 A 'butcher and innkeeper', he reported losses of £74 0s 0d 'in money …, thirty stone or thereabouts of tallow …, [and] the benefit of one lease of an house lately built by himself with an homestead thereto belonging' as well as 'household goods, wearing clothes, four beeves ready killed, beer for his inn keeping and other household provision' for which he did not give a value (Deposition of John Right, 5 January 1642 [TCD MS 835, fols 158r–158v]).

119 See Cavan, Waldron, number 24: Christopher Bowser the elder was killed with his son, Christopher the younger, and daughter at Newtown, 1641 [Depositions of Elizabeth Adwick, 4 January 1642 [ibid. fols 071r–071v] and Robert French, 12 March 1642 [ibid. fols 109r–110v]); Joan Bowser, widow of Christopher Bowser, described her husband as 'a man of good fashion' and reported losses amounting to £235 0s 0d; she

No Arms

6. William Kettle
7. Thomas Bulman[120]
8. Christopher Wilkinson[121]
9. Humphrey Halland
10. John Pageat
11. Henry Clarke
12. Nicholas Pageat

[f. 59v]

Barony de Clankelly

Edward Hatton, Archdeacon of Ardagh, undertaker of 1000 acres: the names of his men and arms, as followeth[122]

Sword and Pike

1. John Baety[123]

Pike only

2. George Beaty
3. William Beaty[124]

Sword and Pike

4. James Steward
5. John Little[125]

Sword only

6. Thomas Little

Sword and Caliver

7. John Tibs[126]
8. Maximillion Tibs[127]

Sword and Pike

9. John Breaton[128]

Pike only

10. Bastyn Cottingham[129]

Sword and Pike

11. Myles Acree[130]

Pike only

12. John Burse[131]
13. Richard Aston[132]
14. Thomas Aston[133]

Snaphance only

15. William Fulke

Sword only

16. Roger Maddeson[134]

Sword and Pike

17. John Beaty, younger[135]

18. Colinton Maird[136]
19. Peter Maddyson[137]

Snaphance only

20. John Irwin

Sword and Pike

21. Robert Graham
22. John Wayst

Pike only

23. James Birney[138]

Sword and Snaphance

24. Richard Bradarne

Pike only

25. John Vich
26. Archball Armestrong[139]

No Arms

27. William Wilson[140]
28. Martin Little
29. Thomas Seaton[141]
30. John Felix
31. John Hall
32. James Little
33. John Carver

---

identified William Graham, 'the muster master of the north', as her husband's killer (Deposition of Joan Bouser, 11 January 1642 [ibid. fols 080r–080v]).

[120] Killed Newtown, 1641; described as 'worth many thousands and a great freeholder' (Depositions of Joan Bouser, 11 January 1642 [ibid.] and Robert French, 12 March 1642 [ibid. fols 109r–110v]).

[121] Father of Henry and Francis Wilkinson, who were killed at Newtown, 1641 and whom Joan Bowser described as 'good rich men' (Depositions of Elizabeth Adwick, 4 January 1642 [ibid. fols 071r–071v]) and of Joan Bouser, 11 January 1642 [ibid. fols 080r–080v]).

[122] For a detailed analysis of this estate, see Hunter, 'The Bible and the bawn', pp 116–34.

[123] There are two families named Beatty on the estate: one family consists of numbers 1 to 3 and the other numbers 17 and 43 [RJH].

[124] Killed, 1641 (Deposition of Katherin Maddison, 17 November 1642 [TCD MS 835, fols 210r–210v]).

[125] Numbers 5, 6, 28, 32, and 44 are probably members of the same family [RJH].

[126] Numbers 7 and 8 are related; the family is from Blisworth Hundred, Wimersley, Northamptonshire [RJH].

[127] Resident Ringvilla; killed near Shannock, October 1641; losses £469 0s 0d (Deposition of Alice Tibbs, 4 January 1642 [TCD MS 835, fols 179r–180v]); brother-in-law of Thomas Middlebrooke, number 2 on Sir Stephen Butler's estate (Deposition of Thomas Midlebrooke, 4 January 1642 [ibid. fols 142r–142v]).

[128] Numbers 9 and 24 are related; 'Breaton and Bradane are versions of Bretton or Braydin (cf. Symon Braydin on [the] Butler estate, Loughtee, in muster roll' [RJH].

[129] Killed, October 1641 (Depositions of Patrick O'Brian, 29 January 1642 [TCD MS 835, fols 082r–083v] and Hugh Stoaks, 7 January 1642 [ibid. fols 174r–174v]); member of a clerical family [RJH].

[130] Killed in October 1641 (Depositions of Patrick O'Brian, 29 January 1642 [ibid. fols 082r–083v], Hugh Stoaks, 7 January 1642 [ibid. fols 174r–174v]), and Simon Crane, 9 August 1642 [ibid. fols 198r–199v]); brother-in-law of Mary and Francis Sillyard (Deposition of Mary Sillyard, 17 April 1643 [ibid. fols 248r–248v]); owned a sword, 1641 (Deposition of Cormack McDonell, 30 June 1654 [ibid. fols 265r–266v]).

[131] Burse and his wife were resident in Newtown when he was killed, October 1641; his widow reported losses 'of thirty and five shillings in ready money, besides the lease of her house and garden and some goods to the value of three pounds sterling' (Deposition of Elizabeth Boursee, 19 January 1642 [ibid. fols 087r–087v]).

[132] Numbers 13 and 14 are related [RJH].

[133] Killed, 1641 (Depositions of Patrick O'Brian, 29 January 1642 [ibid. fols 082r–083v] and Hugh Stoaks, 7 January 1642 [ibid. fols 174r–174v]).

[134] Numbers 16 and 19 are related [RJH].

[135] See number 1.

[136] Juror Maghraveely (Inquisitions of Ulster, Fermanagh, (2) James I) and Enniskillen, 1622 (ibid. (3) James I); tenant of John Sedborough (ibid. (40) and (55) Charles I).

[137] Witness, by mark, to James Hatton's will [RJH]; killed in 1641; losses £452 0s 0d (Deposition of his widow, Katherin Maddison, 17 November 1642 [TCD MS 835, fols 210r–210v]).

[138] Related to number 37 [RJH]; killed, 1641 (Deposition of Robert Aldrich, 10 February 1644 [TCD MS 834, fols 168r–169v]).

[139] Numbers 26 and 41 are possibly father and son [RJH].

[140] Numbers 27 and 42 are related [RJH]; resident Clabby, 1639 (Inquisitions of Ulster, Fermanagh, (40) Charles I).

[141] Born about 1598, Winton, East Lothian; Christopher Seaton born there, 20 February 1617; member of a clerical family [RJH].

34. John Each
35. Gawin Johnston[142]
36. Thomas Michell[143]
37. James Burny
38. Archball Johnston[144]
39. John Slack[145]
40. John Burse
41. Arch: Armstrong
42. Archball Wilson
43. John Beaty
44. John Little

[f. 60]

Mr Sedburrogh, undertaker of 1000 acres: the names of his men and arms, as followeth

Pike only
1. Thomas Tybbeall[146]

Caliver only
2. Joseph Dixon

Pike only
3. William Baxter[147]
4. Richard Crosse[148]

No Arms
5. Thomas Childermes

Snaphance only
6. William Holliwood
7. Edward Halliwood[149]

Pike and Sword
8. Robert Hudson
9. Thomas Pearson
10. Robert Clearetowne

Pike only
11. Richard Roland

Sword and Pike
12. Hugh Stokes[150]
13. John Padge

Pike only
14. William Lackbone
15. Thomas Day[151]

Sword and Snaphance
16. William Dye

[f. 61]

Barony de Magherboy

Sir John Dunbar knight, undertaker of 1000 acres: the names of his men and arms as followeth[152]

Sword and Pike
1. William Johnston
2. John Mophet

Snaphance only
3. John Gilmore

Sword and Pike
4. George Sheano

Sword and Musket
5. Thomas Trotter[153]

Sword and Pike
6. William Graham
7. Thomas Graham

Sword and Musket
8. George Torkinton
9. Randall Bowen
10. Walter Johnston

The half barony of Knockneeny

Mr Adwick, undertaker of 1000 acres: the names of his men and arms[154]

Sword and Pike
1. Otywll Bridghowse

Snaphance only
2. Christopher Dallson
3. John Bryare

Pike only
4. Hugh Sherwood[155]

Snaphance only
5. Steaphen Cooke[156]

---

[142] Numbers 35 and 38 are related [RJH].

[143] Killed, 1641 (Deposition of Katherin Maddison, 17 November 1642 [TCD MS 835, fols 210r–210v]).

[144] 'Son in law to' Lieutenant William Graham; joined rebellion, 1641 (Depositions of Robert Barton, 5 January 1642 [ibid. fols 073r–073v] and Elizabeth Coats, 4 January 1642 [ibid. fols 091r–092v]).

[145] Son of James Slack, rector of Enniskillen and husband of Martha, Edward Hatton's daughter; witness to will of James Hatton, the undertaker's son (NAI, RC/28p) [RJH].

[146] 'Gentleman'; juror Enniskillen, 1622 (Inquisitions of Ulster, Fermanagh, (3) James I); tenant, 1629 (ibid. (40) and (55) Charles I).

[147] 'Gentleman'; resident Rathmoran; losses in Cavan and Fermanagh £1.048 0s 0d; son of Rev. Martin Baxter of Carndallan, county Cavan, losses £2,000 0s 0d; nephew of John Warren of Belturbet (Deposition of William Baxter, 22 September 1642 [TCD MS 835, fols 192r–193v]).

[148] Possibly father of Henry and Joseph Crosse, who were killed, 1641 (Depositions of Patrick O'Brian, 29 January 1642 [ibid. fols 082r–083v] and of Alice Champyn, 14 April 1642 [ibid. fols 196r–197v]) and of John Cross 'of Lissanabrocke', losses £165 0s 0d (Deposition of Margaret Crosse, 25 February 1642 [ibid. fols 098r–098v]) and related to Thomas Crosse 'of Lissanaknocke in the parish of Drummully … an English protestant aged threescore years or thereabouts', losses £180 0s 0d (Deposition of Thomas Crosse, 25 February 1642 [ibid, fols 099r–099v]).

[149] Killed near Clones, 1641 (Deposition of John Marten, 14 January 1642 [TCD MS 834, fols 127r].

[150] 'Gentleman'; juror Enniskillen, 1622 (Inquisitions of Ulster, Fermanagh, (3) James I); tenant, 1629 (ibid. (40) and (55) Charles I); 'of Tawnate … gentleman'; losses £220 0s 0d (Deposition of Hugh Stoaks, 7 January 1642 [TCD MS 835, fols 174r–174v]).

[151] Thomas and William Day (numbers 15 and 16) may have been the sons of Randolph Day, who was a tenant, 1629 (Inquisitions of Ulster, Fermanagh (40) and (55) Charles I).

[152] Seventeen families were resident on Dunbar's estate, 1622 (Treadwell (ed.), *Irish commission*, p. 536). The number of men mustered and the weapons carried are exactly what Dunbar was required to produce for inspection, and so there were probably more settlers on the estate than the muster roll would suggest [JJ].

[153] Killed at Tully Castle, 1641 (Deposition of Patrick Hume, 1 April 1654 [TCD MS 835, fols 260r–260v]).

[154] George Adwick had married the widow of Thomas Creighton, who had purchased the manor of Aghalane from Thomas Monypenny, Lord Kinkell. In 1619, Adwick was also in possession of Sir Hugh Wirral's estate in county Cavan and of James Traile's estate in Fermanagh (Hill, *Plantation*, pp 464–5, 477–8). Adwick said that his losses, 1641 amounted to £317 0s 0d and that the rebels had 'spared his life because as they said, he was so very old' (Deposition of George Adwick, 4 August 1643 [TCD MS 835, fols 230r–230v]).

[155] Numbers 4 and 6 are probably related.

[156] 'Of Mullynacoagh in the parish of Kinawley, half barony of Knockinny and county of Fermanagh, yeoman, aged forty-one years'; losses £65 0s 0d (Deposition of Stephen Cooke, 7 July 1642 [TCD MS 835, fols 094r–094v]).

No Arms

  6.   Thomas Sherwood

[f. 62]

Barony de Knocknyny and Coole

Sir Stephen Butler knight, undertaker of 3000 acres: the names of his men and arms[157]

Sword and Snaphance

  1.   Edward Rogers[158]

Sword only

  2.   Thomas Midlebrooke[159]

Sword only

  3.   Bartholomew Caps

  4.   Thomas Meanese[160]

Sword and Snaphance

  5.   John Meanse[161]

  6.   John More[162]

  7.   Oliver Wyndser, younger[163]

  8.   John Kettle[164]

Halberd only

  9.   Thomas Coop

Sword and Pike

  10.   Thomas Walker[165]

Sword and Snaphance

  11.   William Morton[166]

  12.   Richard Morton[167]

Snaphance only

  13.   Robert Allen[168]

  14.   William Berry[169]

Sword only

  15.   William Rogers

Sword and Pike

  16.   William Flent

Pike only

  17.   Henry Dalmore

Sword and Pike

  18.   Robert Heaklefeild[170]

Snaphance only

  19.   Edward Knowels

  20.   Laurence Knowels[171]

Pike only

  21.   Robert Barton[172]

Sword only

  22.   Thomas Pearce

Pike only

  23.   John Penne

Sword and Pike

  24.   Martin Evance

Sword only

  25.   Thomas Turnor

Sword and Snaphance

  26.   John Mayres[173]

  27.   Edward Mayres[174]

---

[157] For an analysis of the social structure of this community, see Canny, *Making Ireland British*, pp 349–53.

[158] 'Gentleman', 1622 (Inquisitions of Ulster, Fermanagh, (3) James I) and 'of Leitrim, gentleman', 1639 (ibid. (1) Charles I); losses £302 0s 0d (Deposition of his wife, Ellen Rogers, 5 January 1642 [TCD MS 835, fols 159r–159v]).

[159] Aged thirty-one; 'of Legmacaffry … yeoman'; losses £164 14s 0d; brother-in-law of Maximilian Tibbs (Hatton, number 8) (Deposition of Thomas Midlebrooke, 4 January 1642 [ibid. fols 142r–142v]).

[160] 'Of Castlecoole' [Newtownbutler], 1628 (Inquisitions of Ulster, Fermanagh, (1) Charles I); let property in leasehold to other settlers (see Deposition of Elizabeth Moore, 10 January 1642 [TCD MS 835, fols 089r–089v]).

[161] 'Of Mullaghsillagh, yeoman', 1639 (Inquisitions of Ulster, Fermanagh, (40) Charles I); killed, 1641 (Depositions of Elizabeth Dewsberry, 7 January 1642 [TCD MS 835, fols 100r–100v] and Robert Aldrich, 10 February 1644 [TCD MS 834, f. 168r]).

[162] Killed, 1641 (Deposition of Margery Barlow, 27 February 1643 [TCD MS 835, fols 191r–191v]).

[163] Brother of William Windsor (number 42 below).

[164] 'Farmer, an English Protestant, late of Newtown'; losses £80 0s 0d (Deposition of John Kettle, 5 January 1642 [TCD MS 835, fols 128r–128v]).

[165] Yeoman; 'aged forty-six years or thereabouts'; had taken 'one lease of half the tate of land [ ] of Bunn … for twenty-eight years from the first day of May last [1641] at and under the annual or yearly rent of fifty-seven shillings [£2 17s 0d]'; losses £64 0s 0d (Deposition of his brother Thomas Walker (number 43), 2 June 1642 [ibid. fols 228r–228v]).

[166] 'Of Kinneneber of the parish of Drummully, half barony of Coole and county of Fermanagh, yeoman, aged thirty-nine years or thereabouts'; losses £600 0s 0d; held land on Aghalane and Castle Brindsley estates (Deposition of William Morton, 5 January 1642 [ibid. fols 147r–148v]); Rice and John Morton possibly younger brothers and resident in Coole and Knockninny baronies (Depositions of Johan Morton, 3 January 1642 [ibid. fols 146r–146v] and John Morton, 3 January 1642 [ibid. fols 149r–149v]).

[167] Morton described himself as a 'gentleman'. His wife described him as a yeoman and said that he had taken a ninety-one year lease on Gubb for £1 4s 0d a year, May 1640. They suffered losses amounting to £400 0s 0d, 1641. They escaped with their four children to Dublin (Depositions of Barbary Morton, 3 January 1642 [ibid. fols 145r–145v] and Richard Morton, 15 May 1643 [ibid. fols 246r–246v]).

[168] Held land on a seventy-one year lease from Edward Sibthorpe, a freeholder of John Sedborough (Inquisitions of Ulster, Fermanagh, (55) Charles I).

[169] William Berry was the son of Joseph Berry, 'an ancient aged man, past four score years of age': William and Joseph Berry were killed, 1641 (Deposition of Ellen Adams, 23 August 1647 [TCD MS 835, fols 257r–258v]). William may have been the brother of John Perry, who described himself as 'of Newtown alias Castlecoole … yeoman, aged fifty-eight years or thereabouts' and reported losses of £177 0s 0d; John Perry's other children were John and Sara (Deposition of John Perry, 10 January 1642 [ibid. fols 155r–155v]).

[170] Tanner; resident Newtown, 1641; losses £500 0s 0d; much of the family died after fleeing to Dublin (Deposition of Mary Hocklefeild, 30 May 1653 [ibid. fols 244r–244v]).

[171] 'Of the parish of Newtown'; losses £506 0s 0d; brother of Thomas Knowels (Deposition of Lawrence Knowles, 7 January 1642 [ibid. fols 011r–011v]).

[172] 'Of Newtown alias Castlecoole … blacksmith, aged threescore and five years or thereabouts'; losses £66 0s 0d (Deposition of Robert Barton, 5 January 1642 [ibid. fols 073r–073v]).

[173] John and Edward Mayres (numbers 26 and 27) were brothers of Dorothy Rampayne; killed, 1641 (Deposition of Dorothy Rampaine, 4 September 1643 [ibid. fols 247r–247v]).

[174] 'Lived within two miles of Newtown' (ibid.).

Pike only

28. George Broadshaw[175]

Snaphance only

29. Symond More[176]

Sword and Pike

30. Robert Willson
31. Philip Skelton

Sword only

32. Humphrey Wheeler[177]
33. Edward Kent
34. Robert Williamson

No Arms

35. Thomas Greene
36. John Rogers
37. William Troleman
38. Thomas Sympson [178]
39. William Seatwo[179]
40. Roger Markhand
41. Robert Lunne[180]

42. William Windsore[181]
43. Robert Walker[182]
44. Thomas Allen[183]
45. William West
46. John West
47. William Bootes
48. Mathew Freman
49. James Booth, younger[184]
50. John Booth
51. Robert Temple[185]
52. Christopher Cotes[186]
53. Thomas Lawrence
54. Valentine Cranly
55. Walter Newbone[187]
56. Bennet Taylor
57. Robert Walker
58. Richard Walker[188]
59. Thomas Pip
60. Thomas Bell
61. George Ward[189]
62. William Fenton[190]
63. Jonathan Allen
64. Walter Free

65. John Tuttle[191]
66. Thomas Middlebroke[192]
67. Thomas Tutle
68. Thomas Freman
69. Thomas Handbridg
70. Thomas Adwick[193]
71. Thomas Sprag[194]
72. Roger Machan[195]
73. Francis Sympson[196]
74. Henry Woods
75. Christopher Bridon
76. John West

[f. 63v]

77. John Chadwick[197]
78. William Machan[198]
79. John Browne
80. Henry Berry
81. Henry Rogers
82. John Barton[199]
83. William Antryn
84. Thomas Hancock[200]

---

175 'Of Castleroe', 1639 (Inquisitions of Ulster, Fermanagh, (40) Charles I); possibly the father of John Braishawe of Agharoossky, losses £243 0s 0d (Deposition of Avis Braishawe, 4 April 1642 [TCD MS 835, fols 081r–081v]).

176 Possibly husband of Elizabeth Moore; tenant of Thomas Meanese (number 4); losses £149 5s 0d; held prisoner by the Irish, 1641 (Deposition of Elizabeth Moore, 10 January 1642 [ibid. fols 089r–089v]).

177 Possibly father of Robert Wheeler, who was killed, 1641 (Deposition of Dorothy Rampaine, 4 September 1643 [ibid. fols 247r–247v]).

178 'Gentleman', 1622 (Inquisitions of Ulster, Fermanagh, (3) James I); resident Clonelty; he and his wife were 'very old' when they escaped to England, 1641 (Deposition of his son, John Simpson, 16 May 1642 [ibid. fols 226r–227v]); losses £210 0s 0d (Deposition of Thomas Simpson, 31 July 1643 [ibid. fols 250r–250v]).

179 Probably Seaton: clerical family [RJH]; killed, 1641 (Depositions of Margery Barlow, 27 February 1643 [TCD MS 835, fols 191r–191v] and Katherin Maddison, 17 November 1642 [ibid. fols 210r–210v]).

180 Killed at Newtown, 1641 (Deposition of Richard Knowles, 10 January 1642 [ibid. fols 129r–130v]).

181 'Of Aghanahinch … tanner'; losses £1,032 0s 0d; died after flight to Dublin in 1642 (Depositions of Agnes Winsor, 5 January 1653 [ibid. fols 061r–061v] and 4 January 1642 [ibid. fols 188r–188v]).

182 'Yeoman aged thirty-two years or thereabouts'; farmed Bunn with his brother (number 10); losses £53 0s 0d (Depositions of Thomas Walker, 2 June 1642 [TCD MS 835, fols 228r–228v] and Robert Walker [ibid. fols 229r–229v]).

183 Killed, 1641 (Deposition of William Baker, 8 January 1644 [TCD MS 835, fols 234r–234v]).

184 Tailor; farmed Lettergreen; losses £205 0s 0d; joined Edward Aldrich's company at the siege of Drogheda (Deposition of Anne Booth, his wife, 8 January 1642 [TCD MS 835, fols 078r–079v]); James Booth senior did not muster.

185 Held Trasna island for £4 10s 0d, 1631 (A true particular of the proportion … of Dresternan, 8 June 1631 [PRONI, D1939/21/3]).

186 Resident Donagh; killed with son, also Christopher, 1641; losses £377 0s 0d (Deposition of his widow, Elizabeth Coats, 4 January 1642 [TCD MS 835, fols 091r–092v]); 'gentleman' (Deposition of Elizabeth Dewsberry, 7 January 1642 [ibid. fols 100r–100v]); daughter married Andrew Mainwaring, 'gentleman'; dowry £100 0s 0d (Deposition of Andrew Mainwaring, 15 February 1642 [TCD MS 809, fols 297r–297v]).

187 Witnessed killing of Thomas Hancock (number 84), 1641 (Deposition of Robert Hancock, 8 January 1642 [TCD MS 835, fols 115r–115v]).

188 'Of Newtown … grocer … aged forty-one years or thereabouts'; losses £792 0s 0d (Deposition of Richard Walker, 3 January 1642 [ibid. fols 182r–182v]).

189 'Of Castlenew', 1639 (Inquisitions of Ulster, Fermanagh, (40) Charles I); killed near Newtown, 1641 (Deposition of Barbary Morton, 3 January 1642 [TCD MS 835, fols 145r–145v]).

190 Possibly 'William Benington, gentleman' of Killyclowny; losses £56 4s 0d (Deposition of Mary Bennington, 7 January 1642 [ibid. fols 074r–075v]).

191 John Tythill held Kinnicane on the manor of Legan [Callowhill] for three years at £9 0s 0d a year (Balfour Rental, 1636).

192 Present, 1641 (Deposition of Avis Braishawe, 4 April 1642 [TCD MS 835, fols 081r–081v]).

193 'Gentleman'; went to West Indies, 1639; losses £138 10s 0d (Deposition of his wife, Elizabeth Adwick, 4 January 1642 [ibid. fols 071r–071v]).

194 'Of Brenish … skinner and parchment maker … Aged forty four years or thereabouts'; losses £36 0s 0d (Deposition of Thomas Spraige, 3 January 1642 [ibid. fols 173r–173v]).

195 Numbers 72 and 78 are probably the father and brother of 'Thomas Machem of Newtown … cordwainer'; losses £65 0s 0d (Deposition of Agnes Machem, 4 January 1642 [ibid. fols 135r–135v]).

196 Son of number 38; resident Clonelty with father and brother, John; losses £100 0s 0d; escaped to Dublin but killed whilst soldier at Drogheda (Deposition of John Simpson, 16 May 1642 [ibid. fols 226r–227v]).

197 Killed Newtown, 1641 (Deposition of Richard Knowles, 10 January 1642 [ibid. fols 129r–130v]).

198 See number 72.

199 'Of Mullaned'; losses £263 10s 0d (Deposition of Ellinor Barton, 5 January 1642 [ibid. fols 072r–072v]).

200 Resident Lurganboy; killed, 1641 (Deposition of son, Robert Hancock, 8 January 1642 [ibid. fols 115r–115v]).

85. William Parsons
86. Symond Wentford
87. William Perkins[201]
88. William Bignall[202]
89. Thomas Sanderson[203]
90. Francis Chonell[204]
91. William Morris
92. Thomas Whittaker

[f. 64]

Barony de Magherbuy

The names of the townsmen of Enniskillin and their arms

Sword only
1. Frauncis Bird   Provost
2. Gerrard Wiggan[205]
3. David Williams
4. Thomas Browning

Sword and Pike
5. Thomas Smith[206]

Sword only
6. Andrew Lewis
7. Ralph Pickering

Sword and Pike
8. Andrew Ward

Sword only
9. William Johnston
10. John Harrison

Sword and Pike
11. Thomas Little

Sword only
12. Gilbert Johnston

Sword and Pike
13. William Wheatlow

Sword only
14. Thomas Hogg
15. James Johnston

Sword and Pike
16. Mungo Rotherfield[207]

Sword and Caliver
17. Thomas Hill

Sword only
18. William Orum

Sword and Caliver
19. James McKilmay

Sword only
20. George Bochonan

Sword and Pike
21. John Davis

Sword only
22. Robert King[208]

Sword and Caliver
23. John Amerson[209]

Sword and Pike
24. John Ford

Sword only
25. John Hays

Sword and Pike
26. Richard Nyst
27. John Padge
28. William Hogg

Sword only
29. Richard Smyth

Sword and Caliver
30. John Davison
31. William Boochannan
32. John Blany

Pike only
33. John Radcliff

Sword and Halberd
34. John Carroll
35. John Mouse

Sword only
36. David Logan

No Arms
37. Richard Maior
38. William Grible
39. John Frith
40. Jeremy Gleene
41. John Maxwell
42. George Gylesby
43. Robert Ree
44. Rynyon Watson
45. George Nichols
46. John Caldwell[210]
47. Christopher Charleton
48. Rynyon Armstrong
49. Thomas McCartan younger[211]
50. David Minshaw
51. Brian Johnston
52. Thomas Yates

[f. 65]

Barony de Tyrkenedy

The Lord Dillon's servitors land, being 1500 acres: the names of his men and arms as followeth

Sword only
1. Randall Ellot

---

[201] Resident Trory, near Enniskillen, 1628 (Inquisitions of Ulster, Fermanagh, (1) Charles I); killed near Newtown, 1641(Deposition of Barbary Morton, 3 January 1642 [ibid. fols 145r–145v]).

[202] See Cavan, earl of Fingal, number 15. Bignall and Francis Channell (number 89) leased Corclare, Termacarsie, Drumanybegg, and Drumanycappell for 60 years at £6 10s 0d a year, 1629 (PRONI, D/1939/21/3]). They divided the holding: Bignall taking Drumanybegg and Drumanymore and Channell Corclare, Termacarsie, and Drumanycappell (Balfour Rental, 1636). In his deposition, Bignall said he was a millwright, aged sixty, that he held three farms worth £26 0s 0d at Derrycree, and that his wife and child had died during the flight to Dublin (16 January 1644 [TCD MS 835, fols 235r–235v]).

[203] Possibly Thomas Sanders 'of Drumbrughas in the parish of Kinawley'; losses £90 0s 0d (Deposition of Thomas Sanders, 7 January 1642 [ibid. fols 160r–160v]).

[204] See number 88.

[205] Son of Alexander Wigham, one of the town's original burgesses (Trimble, *History of Enniskillen*, p. 174); resident Enniskillen, 1628 (Inquisitions of Ulster, Fermanagh, (1) Charles I).

[206] Possibly the son of number 5 on Sir John Hume's estate.

[207] The Christian name suggests his origins were in the Glasgow region [RJH].

[208] King was a merchant: he supplied Sir William Cole's regiment with clothing and equipment after 1643 (Trimble, *History of Enniskillen*, p. 234).

[209] 'Gentleman'; juror Enniskillen, 1638 (Inquisitions of Ulster, Fermanagh, (39) Charles I); possible relationship to William Ameres [Emerson] (Hunnings) [RJH].

[210] Died after 1634 (funeral certificate in BL, Add MS 4820, f. 16) [RJH].

[211] 'Late of Lurgandarragh in the county of Fermanagh, a British protestant'; losses £308 0s 0d (Deposition of Thomas mcCartny, 4 April 1642 [TCD MS 835, fols 194r–194v]); Thomas McCartney senior did not muster.

2. Hugh Nixon[212]
3. Christopher Nixon[213]
4. Robert Ellot[214]
5. Martin Ellot[215]
6. John Armestrong
7. John Nixon

Sword and Pike

8. Martin Ellot, elder[216]

Sword only

9. John Nixon
10. Gawin Baiteye
11. Richard Graham

Sword and Pike

12. John Armestrong
13. William Armestrong
14. Rynnyon Armestrong

Sword only

15. Quinton Nixon
16. Gawin Nixon
17. William Armstrong
18. John Ellot
19. Thomas Armstrong
20. Robert Ellot, younger[217]
21. William Armstrong

Sword and Pike

22. Andrew Armestrong

Sword only

23. Walter Frizell
24. Robert Crosby
25. Symond Armstrong
26. Thomas Noble[218]

No Arms

27. Thomas Noble, elder

[f. 66]

Barony de Tyrkenedy

Sir William Cole, for his Servitors lands, being 1000 acres: his men and arms

Sword and Pike

1. Edward Carnaby

Sword only

2. William Skayles
3. Alexander Wiggon[219]

Sword and Pike

4. Symond Rutleidg
5. William Armestrang

Sword only

6. Symon Armstrang
7. John Armstrange
8. John Steeles

Pike and sword

9. John Hayes[220]

Sword only

10. Andrew Wiggan
11. John Steele

Sword and Pike

12. David Ellot
13. Andrew Armstrang

[f. 67]

Barony de Tyrkenedy

Captain Roger Atkinson,[221] his servitors lands 1000 acres: the names of his men and arms

Sword only

1. George Wilson
2. William Moore
3. Peter Duffin
4. John Skarlet, younger[222]
5. John Skarlet, elder
6. Thomas Zack
7. John Hunter
8. John Brewer

No Arms

9. Zachary Rampayne[223]
10. William Barret
11. Robert Prowing
12. John Duffyn[224]
13. John Duffin, younger
14. Thomas Calbreath
15. Francis Brangan
16. John Shearerton
17. William Johnston
18. Robert Story
19. John Ellot
20. Thomas West
21. Toby Brewer
22. Thomas Atkinson
23. Andrew Williamson
24. Thomas Calbreath
25. William Zack

Sir Ralph Gower knight, his servitors lands being 1000 acres: the names of his men and arms

No Arms

1. Charles Brookes[225]
2. Edward Maxwell
3. David Johnston
4. John Micheall
5. John Ellot[226]

---

[212] Killed Lowtherstown with wife, 1641 (Deposition of Riccard Bourke, 12 July 1643 [TCD MS 835, fols 238r–239v]).

[213] Nixon rented Tymery for one year at £5 0s 0d, 1636 (Balfour Rental, 1636).

[214] Father of number 20.

[215] Son of number 8.

[216] Father of number 5.

[217] Son of number 4.

[218] Numbers 26 and 27 are father and son.

[219] One of first burgesses of Enniskillen, 1613 (Trimble, *History of Enniskillen*, p. 174); resident Larvey, 1639 (Inquisitions of Ulster, Fermanagh, (40) Charles I); family connections with Lincolnshire (will of Thomas Mountford [NAI, PROB 11/137, fols 438v–40]) [RJH].

[220] Resident Newtown; tanner; aged fifty; wife Susan; losses £132 0s 0d (Deposition of John Hayes, 5 January 1642 [TCD MS 835, fols 116r–116v]).

[221] Atkinson sold his estate to Arthur Champion of Shannock; losses £3,168 11s 6d (Deposition of Roger Atkinson, 26 June 1643 [TCD MS 835, fols 233r–233v]).

[222] Numbers 4 and 5 are father and son; one of them was resident 'Killhola', 1628 (Inquisitions of Ulster, Fermanagh, (1) Charles I).

[223] 'Of Aghrinaghe … gentleman'; killed, 1641; losses £1,730 0s 0d (Deposition of his widow, Dorothy Rampaine, 4 September 1643 [TCD MS 835, fols 247r–247v]).

[224] Numbers 12 and 13 are father and son.

[225] 'Gentleman'; juror Enniskillen, 1622 (Inquisitions of Ulster, Fermanagh, (3) James I); stood surety for Sir John Dunbar as High Sheriff of Fermanagh, 1619 (Treadwell (ed.), *Irish commission*, p. 410).

[226] Father of numbers 8 and 9.

6. Symond Creighton
7. Christopher Sympson
8. John Ellot, younger
9. William Ellot
10. Thomas Beaty
11. John Beaty
12. Thomas Atwill
13. Philip Hall
14. Steaphen Hall
15. James Gray
16. John Kidly
17. William Hall[227]
18. Nicholas Ossenbrooke[228]
19. Philip Ossenbrooke
20. Richard Johnston
21. John Johnston
22. John Armestrang
23. Lancelot Armestrang
24. William Johnston
25. David Johnston
26. Symond Armestrang
27. Thomas Ellot
28. Archbell Ellot[229]
29. Thomas Armestrang
30. Archbell Ellot, younger
31. William Ossenbrooke

Barony de Tyrkenedy

The Lord Hasting's churchlands, being 1500 acres: the names of his men and arms as followeth

Sword and Pike
1. Thomas Slack

Sword only
2. Richard Gutridg[230]

Sword and Caliver
3. Thomas Fawscet[231]

Sword only
4. John Beaty
5. John Ellot

Sword and Caliver
6. William Ellot

Sword only
7. Thomas Ellot

Sword and Pike
8. Archball Ellot
9. Thomas Armstrong[232]

Sword only
10. Gawin Cooke
11. John Murdo
12. John Craford
13. Thomas Humfrey

Sword and Snaphance
14. Thomas Armstrang, younger[233]
15. John Bews

Pike only
16. Richard Cooke

No Arms
17. Archball Armstrong
18. Thomas Bews
19. Robert Teckison
20. Thomas Blayney
21. Anthony Prior
22. Robert Nixon
23. John Jackson
24. Thomas Beaty
25. John Pog
26. Steaphen Hall
27. John Reilly
28. James Gray
29. Gilbert Johnston
30. Symond Armstrong
31. John Humfrey
32. Richard Crowken, younger[234]
33. William Graham
34. Patrick Frizell
35. Andrew Sympson
36. William Jengs
37. James Irwin
38. George Crawford
39. William Mophet
40. Thomas Ellot

[f. 68]

Barony de Magherboy

Mr Archdal's tenants on his churchlands, being 1000 acres: the names of his men and arms as followeth

Sword only
1. William Johnston[235]

Sword and Pike
2. William Johnston, younger
3. Richard Packrag
4. George Waret
5. William Balls

Calivers only
6. Symond Johnston
7. John Little

No Arms
8. Arch: Little
9. Ralph Wyndstandby
10. George Chittock
11. Andrew Cockraine
12. Alexander Wiggin
13. Thomas Wiggin
14. Robert Armstrang

[f. 69]

Barony de Lurgg

Leonard Blennerhasset his churchlands, being 500 acres: his men and arms as followeth

No Arms
1. Richard Cardy
2. George Irwin
3. Richard Irwin
4. Edward Cutler
5. Robert Ellot
6. John Crozer
7. Henry Greene

---

[227] Rented twenty acres from Malcolm Hamilton (Inquisitions of Ulster, Fermanagh, (24) Charles I); one of the first burgesses of Enniskillen (Trimble, *History of Enniskillen*, p. 174).

[228] Numbers 18, 19, and 31 are probably relatives of Nicholas Ossenbrooke, one of the original burgesses of Enniskillen. The Nicholas Ossenbrooke listed here was farming Mullaghree, 1628 (Inquisitions of Ulster, Fermanagh, (1) Charles I).

[229] Father of number 30.

[230] Resident Lisgoole, 1628 (Inquisitions of Ulster, Fermanagh, (1) Charles I); provost of Enniskillen, 1638 (ibid. (38) Charles I).

[231] Possibly the father of Richard Fawsett, prisoner of the rebels and witness to killings at Tully Castle, 1641 (Examination of Richard Fawsett, 30 and 31 March 1654, 1654 [TCD MS 835, fols 262r–264v]).

[232] Father of number 14.

[233] Son of number 9.

[234] Richard Crowken senior did not muster.

[235] Freeholder on Castle Archdale (Hill, *Plantation*, p. 487); father of number 2.

Barony de Lurgg

The Lady Brewerton's churchlands,[236] being 2000 acres: the names of her men and arms

Sword only
1. John Wallas
2. William Morris

Sword and Pike
3. John Moore
4. Thomas Abrow
5. Thomas Beaty
6. John Ore
7. George Beaty

Sword only
8. William M'Culin

Sword and Pike
9. John M'Culm

Sword only
10. Walter Beaty
11. John Beaty

No Arms
12. James Henderson
13. Robert Gower
14. William Moore
15. James Beary

[f. 71]

Half Barony de Clankelly

Lieutenant William Graham,[237] his churchlands, being 500 acres: the names of his men and arms

Sword and Pike
1. Edward Graham[238]
2. Hugh Graham
3. William Graham

Sword and Musket
4. John Graham[239]
5. William Graham

Sword and Snaphance
6. Francis Graham[240]

Sword and Caliver
7. Herbert Graham
8. John Bell

The Barony de [Magheraboy]

Mr Fullerton's glebelands, being 120 acres: his men and arms, as appeared

Sword and Snaphance
1. James Enerat
2. Thomas Tuttorr

[f. 71v]

Barony de Clankelly

Mr Willoby, his Churchlands being 500 acres his men and arms as followeth

Sword only
1. John Johnston

Sword and Pike
2. Robert Johnston
3. Edward Johnston[241]

Pike only
4. Edward Johnston, younger[242]

No arms
5. John Mihell

Sword only
6. George Lawesdall

Mr Hugh Montgomery his Churchlands,[243] being 1000 acres: his men and arms

Sword only
1. Edward Wear
2. John M'Gregor
3. Thomas Greg
4. Sammuel Hetton
5. Neal Montgomery[244]
6. William Clarke
7. Charles Murray

Pike only
8. Abraham Wilkinson

Sword and Pike
9. William Montgomery
10. John Mungomery

No Arms
11. James Hay

---

236 Susan Brereton was the daughter of Lord Brabazon, earl of Meath. Her first husband was George Montgomery, bishop of Clogher (NAI, BET1/41, p. 135) and Sir John Brereton, King's Serjeant at Law was her second husband; his will was proved, 30 October 1629 (NAI, BET1/10, p. 118): 'another judge getting land in Ulster, this time as a tenant' [RJH].

237 This is the compiler of the muster roll. The churchlands in question are near Roslea.

238 Son of William Graham (Deposition of Elizabeth Coats, 4 January 1642 [TCD MS 835, fols 091r–092v]).

239 Son of William Graham (Burke, *Vicissitudes of families*, pp 160–1).

240 Son of William Graham (Deposition of Elizabeth Coats, 4 January 1642 [TCD MS 835, fols 091r–092v]).

241 Numbers 3 and 4 are father and son.

242 Leased Aghadizart for three years from All Saints 1635 at £16 0s 0d (Balfour Rental, 1636).

243 George Montgomery, bishop of Clogher settled Hugh Montgomery, his kinsman on the churchlands of Derrybrusk and appointed him receiver of rents for the diocese. Hugh Montgomery died before 1641. His son, Nicholas married Sir John Dunbar of Derrygonnelly's granddaughter (*Montgomery MSS*, pp 99–100, 388–389).

244 This name is printed as Neal Montgomery (Trimble, *History of Enniskillen*, p. 219) but it should probably read Nich[olas] Montgomery [JJ].

County Tyrone

[f. 72]

The Muster Roll of the County of Tyrone[1]

[Tyrone Barony de Clougher][2]

Sir James Erskin knight, undertaker of 3000 acres: the names of his men and arms

Sword and Musket
1. John Johnston

Sword and Caliver
2. Robert Haliburton

Sword only
3. Andrew McCrery[3]

Sword and Pike
4. William Sterling[4]

Sword only
5. John Morgan
6. Patrick Bell[5]

Sword and Halberd
7. Robert Pearce[6]

Sword and Caliver
8. John Headen younger[7]

Sword only
9. John Clarke
10. William McKeone

Sword and Pike
11. William Lecock[8]

Sword only
12. William Barnet
13. Thomas Leadstone[9]

Sword and Musket
14. John Really[10]

Sword and Pike
15. Peter Realye
16. Andrew Donnell

Sword only
17. Alexander Wright

Sword and Caliver
18. Richard Fixter[11]

[f. 72v]

19. William Bell[12]

Sword and Pike
20. Thomas Gillespy

Sword and Musket
21. William Erskin

Sword and Pike
22. James Waddell

Sword and Caliver
23. Andrew McCormack

Sword only
24. John Hanna
25. John Carrudhowse

Sword and Pike
26. William More younger[13]
27. George Armstrong
28. William Klingane
29. William Bell

Sword and Snaphance
30. John Phare

Snaphance only
31. William Holyday[14]

Sword and Pike
32. Allen More[15]
33. James More

Sword and Snaphance
34. William Moore[16]

Sword only
35. Thomas Browne
36. David Bell

Sword and Pike[17]
37. Nynnyon McLoane[18]

---

1 Robert Hunter began transcribing the Tyrone section of the muster roll shortly before his death. His transcript ends with Richard Fixter (number 18) and I have produced the remainder of the transcript [JJ].

2 There is no heading on the first folio: the heading above appears from folio 73v onwards.

3 Originally tenant of Sir William Stewart (Inquisitions of Ulster, Tyrone, (49) Charles I).

4 William Sterling resident near Ballymoney, county Antrim; worked as surgeon Coleraine, 1641 (Examination of William Sterling, 2 March 1653 [TCD MS 838, fols 060v–061r]).

5 One of the 'inferior burgesses' of Augher, 1622 (Treadwell (ed.), *Irish commission*, p. 575); the nine men called Bell (numbers 6, 19, 29, 36, 99, 121, 128, 132, and 135) are drawn from three, possibly four, families.

6 One of the 'superior burgesses' of Augher, 1622 (ibid.).

7 See number 64.

8 The modern spelling of the surname would be Alcock.

9 Leaseholder Augher, 1622 (Treadwell (ed.), *Irish commission*, p. 576).

10 One of the 'superior burgesses' of Augher, 1622 (ibid. p. 575).

11 One of the 'superior burgesses' of Augher, 1622 (ibid.).

12 'William Bell of Roughan the elder … gentleman' reported losses amounting to £698 0s 0d (Deposition of William Bell, 28 April 1642 [TCD MS 839, fols 027r–027v]), while 'William Bell of Ballylagan gentleman' said his losses were £331 0s 0d (Deposition of William Bell, 30 April 1642 [ibid. fols 029r–029v]). The deponents may be father and son and are probably two of the three men named William Bell who are listed here (numbers 19, 29, and 132).

13 The six men called Moore are drawn from at least two families. Numbers 26 and 34 are father and son, and numbers 32 and 33 may be from the same family; numbers 101 and 138 are probably from other families.

14 Cottager, 1622 (Treadwell (ed.), *Irish commission*, p. 575).

15 'Gentleman'; held 100 acres on two three-life leases, 1622 (ibid. pp 575–6).

16 'Gentleman'; held 180 acres on two three-life leases and sixty acres on a twenty-one year lease, 1622 (ibid.).

17 The deletion of caliver in the original manuscript and its replacement with pike is evidence of Graham's efforts to parade the men according to the weapons they held and to produce an accurate return [RJH].

18 Tenant of number 32, 1622 (Treadwell (ed.), *Irish commission*, p. 575).

Sword and Caliver
38. John McLoane

Sword and Pike
39. Edward Lockerby

Sword only
40. John Meliken[19]

[f. 73]

Sword and Pike
41. Martin Thompson
42. John Graham

Sword only
43. John Martin[20]

Musket only
44. Thomas Scot[21]

Sword and Pike
45. Murtogh Nisbet[22]
46. Thomas Read

Sword only
47. Francis Gilpatricke

Sword and Caliver
48. David Meliken

Sword only
49. James Gordon

Sword and Caliver
50. John Bennet elder[23]

Pike only
51. John Dixon[24]

Sword and Pike
52. Fargus Graham

Sword only
53. Michaell Elton

Sword and Musket
54. John McJury

Sword only
55. Andrew Ellot

Sword and Pike
56. James Welch[25]
57. William Noble
58. Robert Nisbet
59. Robert Symmington younger[26]

[f. 73v]

Sword and Snaphance
60. James Meliken

Sword and Pike
61. James Henderson

Pike only
62. Symond Armstrong

Sword and Pike
63. John Lenton

No Arms
64. John Headen elder[27]
65. Adam Chearall
66. John Gambell
67. James Anderson[28]
68. Morgan Parkes[29]
69. John Graham

70. Thomas McCarmack
71. Robert Watt[30]
72. John Caughton
73. Edwin Irwin
74. Daniell Gilpatrick
75. John McNaught[31]
76. John Henderson[32]
77. John Scot[33]
78. William Lurk
79. Patrick Small
80. Adam Johnston
81. William Smyth
82. William Clarke[34]

[f. 74]

83. Robert Ellot
84. William Ellot
85. John Douglas
86. Cyprian Baker[35]
87. William Murrow[36]
88. Patrick Read
89. Charles Halkeny[37]
90. Zachary Barnet
91. John Alexander[38]
92. James Clarke[39]
93. William Grainger
94. Paul Sympson
95. Thomas McCarmack
96. George Dixon
97. Thomas McGeoch
98. Robert Rooke
99. Thomas Bell
100. George Turner
101. Thomas Moore[40]
102. James Moorehead
103. Christopher Little
104. William Kirkpatrick
105. Adam Johnston

[19] Cottager on Lord Ridgeway's estate and held sixty acres on George Ridgeway's estate for twenty-one years, 1622 (ibid.).

[20] Tenant of Alexander Dunbar, who held 120 acres on a twenty-one year lease from George Ridgeway, 1622 (ibid.).

[21] Held sixty acres of a three-life lease, 1622 (ibid.).

[22] Murdoch Nesbit senior and junior each held 120 acres on a four-life lease, 1622 (ibid. p. 576); this is probably Murdoch Nesbit junior.

[23] John Bennett senior, father of number 109, held 120 acres on a twenty-one year lease and may have been one of the 'superior burgesses' of Augher, 1622 (ibid. p. 575).

[24] Cottager, 1622 (ibid.).

[25] James Welch, a 'tailor at Dungannon', was the gaoler of the British in the town, 1641 (Examination of John Morris, 27 May 1653 [TCD MS 838, fols 296r–296v]).

[26] Robert Symmington senior is not recorded in the muster roll: possibly he was too old to muster. Robert Symmington senior or junior was a tenant of Murdoch Nesbit junior, 1622 (Treadwell (ed.), Irish commission, p. 576).

[27] Numbers 8 and 64 are father and son; John Headen senior was one of the 'inferior burgesses' of Augher, 1622 (ibid. p. 575).

[28] Son of Richard Anderson, a leaseholder at Augher, 1622 (ibid. p. 576).

[29] One of the 'inferior burgesses' of Augher, 1622 (ibid.).

[30] Sub-tenant on Ballyloughmagniffe (Hugh Mitchell's, later Sir Henry Titchbourne's, estate), 1622 (ibid. p. 577).

[31] Tenant of Alexander Dunbar, who held 120 acres on a twenty-one year lease, 1622 (ibid. p. 576).

[32] Cottager, 1622 (ibid. p. 575).

[33] Cottager at Augher, 1622 (ibid. p. 576).

[34] Forty-acre leasehold on Sir Henry Mervin's estate, 1622 (ibid. p. 573).

[35] Possibly son of Simon Baker, an 'inferior burgess' of Augher, 1622 (ibid. p. 575).

[36] Previously a tenant of Sir William Stewart (Inquisitions of Ulster, Tyrone, (49) Charles I).

[37] Possibly Charles Hawkins, an 'inferior burgess' of Augher, 1622 (Treadwell (ed.), Irish commission, p. 575).

[38] Leaseholder, Augher, 1622 (ibid. p. 576).

[39] Leaseholder, Augher, 1622 (ibid.).

[40] Cottager, 1622 (ibid. p. 575).

106. William Pasely
107. Richard Waltham[41]

[f. 74v]

108. Edward Conningham
109. John Bennet younger[42]
110. Thomas Penney elder[43]
111. Thomas Penney younger
112. Symond Snowball
113. Robert Griffin
114. Walter Scot[44]
115. David Scot
116. John Scot
117. Walter Noble[45]
118. Thomas Crag
119. John Ramsey
120. James Patton
121. Francis Bell
122. John Dick
123. John Fenwick
124. Alexander Scot
125. John Crag[46]
126. Alexander Scot
127. Richard Armstrong
128. John Bell[47]
129. John Henderson
130. John McLoane[48]
131. John Sharp
132. William Bell
133. John Hanna
134. James Waddell
135. David Bell
136. William Erskin
137. James Waddell
138. Allen Moore

[f. 75]

Tyrone
Barony de Clougher

Sir William Steward knight,[49]
undertaker of 4000 acres:
his men and arms as followeth

Sword and Pike
1. Thomas McCallen
2. John Scot
3. William Myn[50]

Sword only
4. George Dymster

Sword and Pike
5. William Derkoe
6. John McCrery[51]
7. William Moore[52]

Sword only
8. Roger Mynne

Pike only
9. William Mynne

Sword and Pike
10. John Mynne
11. William Wilson[53]
12. Gawen Beaty[54]

Sword only
13. John Sincleare[55]

Sword and Pike
14. Oghthrip McDowgall[56]

Sword only
15. John Carson

Sword and Pike
16. David mcLearne[57]

Sword only
17. Archball Hammilton[58]

Pike only
18. John Maccrery elder[59]

Sword and Caliver
19. John Davison
20. John Gibson

Pike only
21. Thomas Crag

Sword only
22. Robert Scot

Sword and Musket
23. John Graham

Sword and Pike
24. John Bell
25. George Willson
26. John Thomson[60]
27. John Thomson younger
28. John Pocock

---

41 One of the 'superior burgesses' of Augher and freeholder of 120 acres, 1622 (ibid. pp 575–6).

42 Son of number 50; cottager, 1622 (ibid.).

43 Numbers 110 and 111 are father and son; Thomas Penney senior was a 'superior burgess' of Augher and held 120 acres on a three-life lease, 1622 (ibid.) and to whom Sir William Cope let 200 acres for twenty-one years (ibid. p. 593).

44 Sub-tenant on Sir William Parsons's estate, 1622 (ibid. p. 580).

45 Sub-tenant on Sir William Parsons's estate, 1622 (ibid.).

46 Tenant of Murdoch Nesbit junior, 1622 (ibid. p. 576).

47 Cottager, 1622 (ibid. p. 575).

48 Names from serial 130 onwards are squeezed into the bottom right-hand corner of the folio, appearing almost as an addendum to the main list.

49 Stewart estimated his losses, 1641 at more than £4,000 (Deposition of Sir William Stewart, 12 October 1643[TCD MS 839, fols 045r–046v]).

50 William Meene (number 3), Roger Meene (number 8), and John Meene number 10) were leaseholders (Inquisitions of Ulster, Tyrone, (49) Charles I).

51 Numbers 6 and 18 are father and son.

52 William Moore had a 21-year lease on sixty acres, 1622 (Treadwell (ed.), *Irish commission*, p. 578; Inquisitions of Ulster, Tyrone, (49) Charles I).

53 Five men are named Wilson. John Wilson (number 34) is the son of John Wilson (probably number 33) who had a third share of a 21-year lease on 60 acres, 1622. His partners were Michael McCullough (see number 95) and John McIlmurry (Inquisitions of Ulster, Tyrone, (49) Charles I; Treadwell (ed.), *Irish commission*, p. 578). William and George Wilson (numbers 11 and 25) may be related to number 33, but John Wilson (number 38) is probably a member of a different family.

54 Four men are named Beatty. Adam and John Beatty are probably the sons of John Beatty (numbers 58, 61, and 71); Gavin (number 12) does not fit into that pattern of forenames and so he is probably from a different family.

55 John and James Sinclair (number 59) may be the sons of David 'Sinclair, gentleman', who had a sixty acre freehold, 1622 (Treadwell (ed.), *Irish commission*, p. 578).

56 'Wehtrie McDowgall' was a tenant of George Sanderson, a freeholder on Alexander Sanderson's estate, 1622 (ibid. p. 581).

57 'Gentleman'; sixty acre freehold, 1622 (ibid. p. 578; Inquisitions of Ulster, Tyrone, (49) Charles I).

58 Seventeen-year lease on sixty acres, 1622 (Treadwell (ed.), *Irish commission*, p. 578).

59 Father of number 6.

60 Numbers 26 and 27 are father and son.

[f. 75v]

29. John Jordaine[61]
30. John Jordaine younger
31. John Paye
32. Thomas Payne[62]

Sword only
33. John Wilson[63]

Sword and Pike
34. John Wilson younger

No Arms
35. Alexander Curly
36. John Fargison[64]
37. George Michell
38. John Wilson
39. William Nelson
40. Andrew Nelson[65]
41. John Keg
42. James Graham
43. Herbert Ellot
44. David Little[66]
45. Robert Edger
46. John Edger
47. John Myn
48. William Graham
49. George Curly
50. William Leallon
51. James McKean
52. Thomas Mason
53. James Myn
54. John Myn
55. William Forrest

[f. 76]

Danyell Lasy [Deletion in original MS]
56. Francis Carruddas
57. Adam Beaty

58. James Sincleare[67]
59. John McLeallon
60. John Beaty
61. George Huchison
62. Arch Fullerton
63. John Delap[68]
64. William Graham
65. George Corbit
66. Patrick Huchison
67. Patrick Monngomery
68. John Scersby[69]
69. John Armstrong[70]
70. John Beaty
71. Nicholas Foster
72. Jo Armstrong
73. Richard Armstrong
74. John Payne
75. William Dunbar
76. William Craford

[f. 76v]

Sword and Musket
77. Duncan McFarlan

Sword, Musket, and Bandoliers
78. William Young

Sword and Musket
79. Nicholas Conningham[71]

Sword and Pike
80. James Cacone

Sword and Snaphance
81. John McFarlan

Sword only
82. Patrick McFarlan

Sword and Snaphance
83. Andrew Leene

Sword and Pike
84. Charles Pock

Sword and Musket
85. Thomas Calwell

Sword and Snaphance
86. William Largg[72]

Sword and Musket
87. Alexander Crawfoord

Sword and Pike
88. Robert Middleton

Sword and Caliver
89. John Read
90. Alexander Bonnty
91. Andrew Hay

Sword and Pike
92. William Russell

Sword and Musket
93. George Gordon

Sword and Pike
94. James Myning
95. Nicholas McColagh[73]

Sword and Musket
96. John Rea[74]

Sword and Caliver
97. Walter Robinson

Musket only
98. Andrew Clarke
99. Edward Forbus

---

[61] Numbers 29 and 30 are father and son and may be the son and grandson of Saunders Jordan, who leased sixty acres from Sir Robert Newcomen, 1622 (Treadwell (ed.), *Irish commission*, p. 569).

[62] Cottager, 1622 (ibid. p. 575).

[63] Numbers 33 and 34 are father and son; there are several families named Wilson on the estate (see number 11).

[64] Tenant of Alan Moore, 1622 (ibid. p. 576).

[65] Cottager on Sir Andrew Stewart's estate, 1622 (ibid. p. 584).

[66] David Little is probably the son of Andrew Little, who shared a fifteen-year lease on sixty acres with his brothers, Christopher and 'Clancy' (ibid. p. 578): the brothers had moved to Richard Cope's estate before 1630 and appear there as numbers 4 and 23.

[67] See number 13 above.

[68] Killed, 1641 (Deposition of George Burne, 12 January 1644 [TCD MS 839, fols 038r–039v]).

[69] John Sowersby; killed, 1641 (Deposition of Gartrude Carlile, 13 Mar 1643 [ibid. fols 031r–032v]).

[70] John Armstrong, a cottager on William Turvin's (later Archibald Hamilton's) estate, mustered with a pike, 1622 (Treadwell (ed.), *Irish commission*, p. 577); he may be the father of Joseph and Richard Armstrong.

[71] Possibly the son of John Cunningham, who had a 100 acre freehold, 1622 (ibid. p. 570).

[72] Large took over William Carmichael's 100 acre freehold, 1622 (ibid. p. 571): Carmichael either moved to a 120-acre freehold on Sir George Hamilton's estate at Derrywoon (ibid. p. 570) or became a cottager on Sir Andrew Stewart's estate (ibid. p. 583).

[73] Son of 'Michael McCullogh, gentleman', who had a third share of a 21-year lease on sixty acres on Sir William Stewart's estate, 1622 with John McIlmurry and John Wilson (number 33 above) (ibid. p. 578).

[74] Sub-tenant on Alexander Sanderson's estate, 1622 (ibid. p. 581).

Sword and Caliver
100. William Barkley[75]
101. William Barkley younger
102. John Smith

Sword and Pike
103. James Lawrences

[f. 77]

Sword and Caliver
104. Duncan Bacehanon

Sword and Musket
105. Daniell Kettagh

Sword only
106. John Calweill

Sword and Caliver
107. Arthur Peate

Pike only
108. William Neterage

Sword and Snaphance
109. James McCrabb
110. William Reynalagh
111. Alexander McCaslane

No Arms
112. Danwill Hendrick
113. Duncan mcFarlan

Sword and Snaphance
114. John Fynlay

No Arms
115. Andrew Robertson
116. Robert Peate
117. James Dromeed
118. Danyell Robertson
119. John Bruse
120. Patrick Bruse
121. John Calwel   merchant

122. John Cordiner
123. David Lowry
124. Donwell Henrick
125. Duncan Derry
126. Robert Steward[76]
127. Mathew Heckcles
128. John Okelly
129. James Watson
130. Henry Mackey

[f. 77v]

Tyrone Barony de Clougher

Sir Henry Tychborne knight, undertaker of 2200 acres

Sword and Snaphance
1.   James Willson

Pike only
2.   William Pakeston

Sword and Pike
3.   Andrew Hartland

Sword and Snaphance
4.   William Roberts

Sword and Pike
5.   James McKeone

Sword only
6.   John Pake[77]

Sword and Caliver
7.   Gawin Hall[78]
8.   John Hall[79]

Sword and Pike
9.   William Young

Sword and Halberd
10.   Thomas Read

Sword only
11.   David Hall[80]

Sword and Pike
12.   James Ballfoure[81]

Sword and Caliver
13.   Robert Graham[82]

Pike only
14.   Adam Bracklocklock[83]

Sword and Pike
15.   Edward Pocoke

Pike only
16.   John Beaty[84]

Sword and Pike
17.   George McCartan

Sword only
18.   John Graham[85]
19.   James Jammison

Pike only
20.   John Little[86]

Sword and Pike
21.   George Wacker

Sword and Caliver
22.   Thomas Wacker

Sword and Pike
23.   Adam Beaty[87]

[f. 78]

24.   John Frezell
25.   Adam Willson

Sword only
26.   Symond Hall

---

75   Numbers 101 and 102 are father and son; William Barclay senior may be the son of 'David Barkley, laird of Ladyland', who had a 140-acre freehold, 1622 (ibid. p. 578); David Barclay was afterwards knighted, and obtained extensive lands from Sir William Stewart (Inquisitions of Ulster, Tyrone, (49) Charles I).

76   Hundred-acre leasehold from Sir Robert Newcomen, 1622 (Treadwell (ed.), *Irish commission*, p. 570).

77   Possibly the son of Thomas Pook, sub-tenant of Thomas Wilson (number 1) and Robert Hall (number 33 or number 45), 1622 (ibid. p. 577).

78   Six men are named Hall. Robert Hall (number 33 or number 45) held sixty acres in freehold, 1622 (ibid.); Simon (number 26) and Robert may be his sons, while Gavin and John Hall (numbers 7 and 8) and possibly David Hall (number 11) may be members of a different family.

79   See number 7.

80   See number 7.

81   James and Alexander Balfour had a twenty-one year lease on 120 acres, 1622 (Treadwell (ed.), *Irish commission*, p. 577).

82   Robert Graham held thirty acres on a ten-year lease on the estate of William Turvin, later that of Archibald Hamilton, 1622, when he mustered with a pike (ibid.).

83   Sub-tenant of Robert Hall (number 33 or number 45), 1622 (ibid.).

84   Resident Ballynelurgan [Fivemiletown], 1622 (ibid.).

85   Three of the four men named Graham were called John and so there were at least two families named Graham on the estate (numbers 18 and 31 and numbers 40 and 41).

86   Sub-tenant on Sir William Parsons's estate, 1622 (ibid. p. 580).

87   'Gentleman'; thirty acre freehold with Adam Scot, 1622 (ibid. p. 577).

Sword and Pike

27. Andrew Greere
28. William Scot

No Arms

29. Thomas Demster
30. James Baxter
31. John Graham
32. Adam Beaty
33. Robert Hall
34. David Poke[88]
35. Robert Blacklock
36. George Singcleare[89]
37. William Crery
38. John Walker[90]
39. Edward Wilson[91]
40. James Graham
41. John Graham
42. James Mickle[92]
43. Arthur Grame[93]
44. John Wessy
45. Robert Hall
46. John Quhally
47. Thomas Derryman

Barony Straban

Sword and Snaphance

48. Roger Clencross

Sword only

49. John McCordy

Sword and Pike

50. Thomas McCordy

Sword and Snaphance

51. Dunkin Loughlyne

No Arms

52. Gilbert McCordy
53. Thomas Holland[94]
54. Andrew Holyday[95]

[f. 78v]

Tyrone
Barony de Clougher

Sir William Parsons knight and baronet, undertaker of 1500 acres: the names of his men and arms

Sword and Caliver

1. John Carness[96]

Sword only

2. John Scot
3. William McIlltough

Sword and Caliver

4. Adam Armstrong[97]

Sword and Pike

5. John Hammilton[98]
6. James Hammilton
7. Martin Cody[99]
8. John Moore[100]
9. Francis Beaty
10. Alexander Hathorne

Sword only

11. William Hyndze

Halberd only

12. John Jewyn[101]

Sword and Pike

13. Thomas Gillaspy

Sword and Caliver

14. John Gillaspy

Sword and Pike

15. John Moore[102]

Sword only

16. William Anderson

Sword only

17. John Brackton[103]
18. Thomas Brackton

Sword and Snaphance

19. James Bracton
20. John Brackton younger

---

88 Possibly brother of number 6.

89 'William Sinclair, laird of Rosteen', probably the father of George Sinclair, had a sixty-acre freehold, 1622 (Treadwell (ed.), *Irish commission*, p. 577).

90 Walker shared a sixty acre freehold with William Craig, 1622 (ibid.).

91 'Of Latmackmurphy in the parish of Aghalow in the Barony of Dungannon and County of Tyrone gentleman' (Deposition of Edward Wilson ex parte Robert Rowan, 12 October 1642 [TCD MS 839, fols 028r–028v]).

92 Held a tenement in Ballynelurgan for twenty-one years, 1622 (Treadwell (ed.), *Irish commission*, p. 577).

93 Arthur Graham had leased 100 acres for thirty-one years on the estate of William Turvin (later that of Archibald Hamilton), 1622 (ibid. p. 576).

94 Possibly son of Henry Holland, one of the workmen Sir Thomas Ridgeway promised would become freeholders (Carew, Survey of the Plantation (1611), in Hill, *Plantation*, p. 538).

95 Leaseholder of sixty acres for twenty-one years on Sir Robert Newcomen's [later Sir William Stewart's] estate, 1622 (Treadwell (ed.), *Irish commission*, p. 570).

96 'John Karnes, gentleman' had a sixty acre freehold on Sir William Stewart's estate and a twenty-one year lease for two townlands on Sir William Cope's estate, 1622 (ibid. pp 578, 594). By 1641, he had moved to 'Personstoun' [Beragh], where he had 'a fair stone house well [built] new over with shingles, and about three other stone houses of nine couples and other fair English houses of timber' and let six townlands for £30 0s 0d a year. As well as raising cattle and sheep, he established a tannery and had business interests in counties Antrim and Donegal (he was clerk of the peace for county Donegal and feodary (an official of the Court of Wards) for counties Antrim and Donegal: these posts were worth £30 0s 0d a year). 'About a short time before the … Irish rebellion, he bought 1,500 acres of land [in county Tyrone] from Richard Coop of Blittoch, esquire and from his son Nicholas Alcock', paying 'in ready gold and money £1,230 0s 0d.' – in other words, he bought out his landlord. Cairns reckoned that he could have let the property for £160 0s 0d a year and that his losses excluding the Cope property, totalled £1,430 10s 0d (Deposition of John Kairnes, 14 April 1642 [TCD MS 839, fols 033r–034v]).

97 The six men named Armstrong are drawn from three families (number 4, numbers 36, 38, and 39, and numbers 50 and 52).

98 John Hamilton, 'gentleman' and Adam Glendinning [Lindsay, number 15] held 'sixty acres jointly' for twenty-one years, 1622 (Treadwell (ed.), *Irish commission*, p. 579).

99 Martin Cody senior and Martin Cody junior were cottagers on David Kennedy's (later John Symington's) estate, 1622 (ibid. p. 584).

100 Son of William Moore, who had a three-life lease on 180 acres, 1622 (ibid. p. 579).

101 John Owen shared a twenty-one year lease for sixty acres 'in Esker More' near Beragh with John Nelson, John senior, John Nelson junior, and Thomas Bratton (numbers 17 to 20), 1622 (ibid. p. 579). William Nelson (number 23 or number 41) is probably a son of John Nelson.

102 See number 8.

103 Father of numbers 18 to 20; John Brackton senior, John Brackton junior, and Thomas Britton shared a twenty-one year lease for sixty acres 'in Esker More' [near Beragh] with John Irwin and John Nelson, 1622 (Treadwell (ed.), *Irish commission*, p. 579).

Sword and Pike

21. Robert Crookeshankes[104]
22. Henry Crookeshanckes

Sword only

23. William Nelson

[f. 79]

24. Gilbert Kirke

Sword and Pike

25. Gilbert Middiken
26. James Beaty
27. John Beaty elder[105]

Sword and Musket

28. John Beaty younger

Sword and Pike

29. James Gillaspy
30. William Anderson
31. Richard Irwin

Sword and Halberd

32. Andrew Ellot

Sword and Pike

33. William Gildony

No Arms

34. James Hall
35. Andrew Dixon
36. Symond Armstrang[106]
37. George Irwin
38. Symon Armstrang younger[107]
39. Rynnon Armstrang[108]
40. John Graham[109]
41. William Nelson

42. Jenkin Todd
43. Robert Gillinows
44. David Johnston
45. Michaell Davidson
46. William Davis
47. Walter Bell
48. Edward Little
49. William Willson
50. William Armstrang
51. William Noble[110]
52. Ebby Armstrang
53. Thomas Cady
54. John Roper
55. Robert Irwin
56. John McKerrall
57. James Hyndze
58. James Graham
59. William Cory

[f. 79v]

Tyrone
Barony de Clougher

Richard Coape esquire, undertaker of 1500 acres: his men and arms as followeth[111]

Sword and Pike

1. George Steward[112]

Pike only

2. George Carson

Sword and Pike

3. William Bell
4. Christopher Little[113]

5. Robert Wilson
6. John Wilson

Sword only

7. John Mungomery[114]

Sword and Pike

8. Thomas Steward
9. Robert Graham
10. Robert Scot

Sword and Caliver

11. Edward Little

Sword and Pike

12. Archball Glendonagh[115]

Sword and Pike

13. John Glendonagh
14. William Glendonagh
15. Andrew Glendonagh
16. George Thomson[116]

Sword and Snaphance

17. Nicholas Lyttle

Pike only

18. Andrew Armstrang[117]

No Arms

19. Adam Johnston
20. John Thompson
21. George Beaty[118]
22. Nicholas Thomson[119]
23. Clement Lyttle[120]
24. Archbald Wilson
25. Archbald Graham
26. Nynyan Gledony[121]

---

[104] Leaseholder on Sir George Hamilton's estate, 1622 (ibid. p. 569).

[105] Tenant of number 8, 1622 (ibid.); father of number 28 and possibly of number 26.

[106] Numbers 36 and 38 are father and son.

[107] See number 36.

[108] Ninian Armstrong, a cottager on William Turvin's (later Archibald Hamilton's) estate, 1622, mustered with a 'Scots lance' (Treadwell (ed.), *Irish commission*, p. 577).

[109] Numbers 40 and 58 are probably related.

[110] Tenant of William Moore (see number 8), 1622 (Treadwell (ed.), *Irish commission*, p. 580).

[111] Richard Cope was the grandson of Sir Anthony Cope, the original grantee. He sold the property in the spring or summer of 1641 to John Cairns (f. 78v), one of the principal leaseholders for £1,230 0s 0d 'in ready gold and money' (Deposition of John Kairnes, 14 April 1642 [TCD MS 839, fols 033r–034v]).

[112] Sub-tenant of 'William Stewart, gentleman', who had a twenty-one year lease on two townlands, 1622 (Treadwell (ed.), *Irish commission*, p. 594).

[113] Christopher Little shared a fifteen year lease on sixty acres on Sir William Stewart's estate with his brothers, Andrew (Sir William Stewart, number 44) and 'Clancy' [Clement (number 23)] Little, 1622 (ibid. p. 578). Edward and Nicholas Little (numbers 11 and 17) are probably the sons of Christopher and Clement Little.

[114] Sub-tenant of 'William Stewart, gentleman', 1622 (ibid. p. 594).

[115] There are two possibly related families called Glendonagh on the estate; numbers 12 to 15 are probably from the same family; numbers 26 and 28 may be from another family. Archibald Glendonagh was a sub-tenant of Thomas Penney of Augher, who had a 21-year lease on 200 acres, 1622 (ibid. p. 593).

[116] Sub-tenant of Thomas Penney of Augher, 1622 (ibid.).

[117] Cottager on Sir Andrew Stewart's estate, 1622 (ibid. p. 584).

[118] Son of Edward Beatty, sub-tenant of 'William Stewart, gentleman', 1622 (ibid. p. 594).

[119] Cottager on William Turvin's (later Archibald Hamilton's) estate and mustered with a 'Scots lance', 1622 (ibid. p. 577).

[120] Possibly 'Clancy' Little, brother of Andrew and Christopher Little; see number 4.

[121] See number 12.

27. George Russell[122]
28. Adam Glendoney[123]

[f. 80]

Tyrone
Barony de Clougher

John Leigh esquire, undertaker of 2000 acres: the names of his men and arms

Sword and Pike
1. Robert Bennet

Sword and Musket
2. Edward Cooke[124]

Sword and Pike
3. John Beaty[125]
4. Alexandre Perry[126]

Sword and Musket
5. Henry Cooke

Sword and Pike
6. John Cassydon

Sword and Musket
7. William Typpyne

Sword only
8. Francis Carlill

Snaphance only
9. Richard Hall

Sword and Pike
10. William Newmand

No Arms
11. Edward Baly
12. Richard Typpyr[127]
13. Owen Carran
14. Thomas Bell

15. Edward Hatches
16. Anthony Bayly
17. William Hyng

[f. 80v]

Tyrone
Barony de Clougher

Archball Hammelton esquire, undertaker of 1000 acres: the names of his men and arms

Sword and Pike
1. John McClenan
2. John Coulden

Sword and Snaphance
3. John Crosby[128]

Sword only
4. Archball Ellot[129]

Sword and Caliver
5. John Ellot

Sword and Pike
6. William Ellot

Sword and Musket
7. George Symson

Sword only
8. William Morton
9. John Bell[130]

Sword and Pike
10. Robert Cory[131]

Sword only
11. Sammuell Cory

Sword and Pike
12. John Symington

Sword and Caliver
13. William Symington

Sword and Snaphance
14. Robert Wiggin

Sword and Musket
15. John Weere

Sword and Snaphance
16. Alexander Graham
17. Thomas Graham[132]

Sword only
18. John O Mory
19. Andrew Hammilton
20. Robert Cory younger
21. James Laker

No Arms
22. Alexander Bradfoord
23. Guy Walker
24. Symond Berne[133]
25. Steaphen Greg

[f. 81]

Tyrone
Barony de Dungannon

Sir Andrew Steward knight and baronet, undertaker of 4500 his [acres]: men and arms

Sword only
1. James Steward[134]

Sword and Snaphance
2. John Steward[135]

Sword and Pike
3. John Dyall[136]

---

[122] Had a sixth share in a sixty-one year lease for 120 acres on David Kennedy's (later John Symington's) estate, 1622 (Treadwell (ed.), *Irish commission*, p. 584).

[123] See number 12.

[124] Held sixty acres in freehold and another sixty in leasehold, 1622 (Treadwell (ed.), *Irish commission*, p. 578).

[125] Sixty-acre leasehold, 1622 (ibid.).

[126] Leased twenty acres, 1622 (Ibid.).

[127] Cottager, 1622 (ibid. p. 575).

[128] Cottager, mustered with a pike, 1622 (ibid. p. 577).

[129] Numbers 4 to 6 are probably related.

[130] Two men called John Bell mustered with lances, 1622. They were probably father and son; one held ten acres on a nine year lease and the other was a cottager (ibid.). John Bell here is probably the son.

[131] Samuell and Robert Corry (numbers 11 and 20) are the sons of Robert Corry (number 10).

[132] Cottager and mustered with two pikes and a musket, 1622 (ibid.).

[133] Cottager on Sir Andrew Stewart's estate, 1622 (ibid. p. 583).

[134] 'Gentleman'; held sixty acres for twenty-one years, 1622 (ibid. p. 581).

[135] This may be Sir Andrew's brother (PRONI, *Introduction [to the] Castle Stewart Papers*, 2007).

[136] John Dalzell may be the son of 'William Dalzell, gentleman' who held sixty acres for life, 1622 (Treadwell (ed.), *Irish commission*, p. 581).

Sword and Snaphance

4.   Andrew Steward[137]

Sword only

5.   Alexander Cunny
6.   Patrick Jackson[138]
7.   Robert Arbuthnot[139]
8.   David Steward[140]
9.   Robert Perdy[141]
10. John Miller[142]

Sword and Pike

11. John Humphrey
12. Robert Read

Sword and Snaphance

13. Roger Andrewes

Sword and Pike

14. Andrew Landles[143]
15. Andrew McCaine[144]
16. Robert Michaell[145]
17. James McCroych
18. James Steward
19. James Thomson[146]

Sword only

20. William Thomson

Sword and Pike

21. John McBeid

Sword only

22. Thomas Hume

Sword and Pike

23. John Gorden
24. Thomas Ellot

[f. 81v]

Snaphance only

25. Thomas Gillis[147]

Sword only

26. John Clafford

Sword and Snaphance

27. George Catcherd

Sword and Pike

28. Lancelot Ellot
29. John Girwan
30. Walter Graham[148]

Sword only

31. George Johnston

Sword and Halberd

32. Thomas McNeesh

Sword and Pike

33. John McChapy

Sword and Snaphance

34. Neekeed McCroch

Sword only

35. Robert Coleston[149]
36. William Coleston
37. Thomas Carlill[150]
38. Christopher Harris
39. Richard Coleston
40. John Johnston

Sword and Pike

41. Thomas Rogers
42. George Armestong

No Arms

43. Robert Hall[151]
44. Neenoad McEvale
45. William Thompson
46. Robert Ghasright
47. James Carlill[152]
48. James McCroch

[f. 82]

Sword only

49. Alexander McNaught[153]

Sword and Pike

50. John English[154]
51. John Robinson
52. James Sanderson

Sword and Snaphance

53. Richard Wilson

Sword only

54. John White[155]
55. Archball Johnston

Sword and Snaphance

56. Thomas Dobson

Sword only

57. John Weere

Sword and Pike

58. John Dale
59. Duncan Cory
60. Andrew Landels
61. George Alexander
62. William Steward[156]
63. George Johnston
64. Patrick Wallas[157]

---

[137] This may be Sir Andrew's son (PRONI, *Introduction [to the] Castle Stewart Papers*).

[138] Possibly the son of 'Robert Jackson, gentleman', resident at Stewartstown, 1622 (Treadwell (ed.), *Irish commission*, p. 596).

[139] 'Gentleman', resident at Stewartstown, 1622 (ibid.).

[140] Sub-tenant on Sir William Cope's (later Richard Cope's) estate, 1622 (ibid. p. 594).

[141] Butcher, resident at Stewartstown, 1622 (ibid.).

[142] Carpenter, resident at Stewartstown, 1622 (ibid.).

[143] Possibly son of Hew Landels, malt maker and resident of Stewartstown, 1622 (ibid.).

[144] Cottager, 1622 (ibid. p. 584).

[145] Held 120 acres in freehold, 1622 (ibid. p. 583).

[146] Four men are named Thompson or Thomson; two (numbers 19 and 65) are called James and two (numbers 20 and 45) William; the families are possibly related. William Thompson, a tradesman was resident at Stewartstown, 1622 (ibid.).

[147] Cottager on Lord Ridgeway's (later Sir James Erskine's) estate, 1622 (ibid. p. 575).

[148] Cottager on Lord Ridgeway's (later Sir James Erskine's) estate, 1622 (ibid.).

[149] Thirty acre leasehold on Sir Henry Mervin's estate, 1622 (ibid. p. 573).

[150] Killed, 1641; 'late of Creena … husbandman'; losses £266 0s 0d (Deposition of his widow, Gartrude Carlile, 13 March 1643 [TCD MS 839, fols 031r–032v]).

[151] Possibly related to 'Simon Hall, gentleman' who had a sixty acre freehold, 1622 (Treadwell (ed.), *Irish commission*, p. 580).

[152] Sub-tenant on Sir George Hamilton's estate, 1622 (ibid. p. 570); 'gentleman'; losses £290 0s 0d; he and his wife killed, 1641 (Deposition of Gartrude Carlile, 13 March 1643 [TCD MS 839, fols 031r–032v]).

[153] Cottager, 1622 (Treadwell (ed.), *Irish commission*, p. 583).

[154] Quarter-share of a sixty-one year lease on 120 acres, 1622 (ibid.).

[155] Cottager, 1622 (ibid.).

[156] 'William Steward, son to the [earl of Castlestewart's] uncle', had a 120-acre freehold, 1622 and 'William Stewart, gentleman' held sixty acres for twenty-one years (ibid. p. 581).

[157] Son of 'Gilbert Wallace', a cottager, 1622 (ibid. p. 584).

65. James Thomson
66. John Hercus[158]
67. Robert Ellot
68. Robert Hall[159]
69. John Steward
70. John Gibb[160]
71. Adam Miller
72. Adam Bell
73. William Dale

[f. 82v]

74. James Greir
75. John Pott[161]
76. George Beaty
77. George Rea

[f. 79v]

78. Walter Tower
79. Robert Gillmore
80. Richard Willson
81. John English
82. Edward Sweire

Sword and Snaphance
83. Archball Bellison
84. Thomas Sincleare[162]
85. John Harderson
86. John Mccaddon
87. John Robson
88. Robert Michaell
89. Henry Jammison
90. James Sommerville
91. John Gerin
92. Andrew Steward
93. John Steward
94. Richard Cowelson

[f. 83]

Tyrone
Barony de Dungannon

Henry Steward esquire, undertaker of 1500 acres: the names of his men and arms

Sword and Musket
1. James Sommervill

Sword only
2. Robert Gablead[163]

Sword and Pike
3. David Goodlad

Sword and Snaphance
4. William Goodlad

Sword and Caliver
5. William Thomson

Sword only
6. Robert Mase[164]
7. Robert Mase younger
8. Thomas Robinson

Snaphance only
9. Thomas Avery[165]
10. John Pigget[166]

Sword and Musket
11. William Cannings

Caliver only
12. Henry Avery

Snaphance only
13. James Readfearne

Sword only
14. Henry Piggot

Sword and Pike
15. John Learman[167]

Sword only
16. David Neesmith
17. William Sanderson

Sword and Snaphance
18. Thomas Coleston[168]
19. Robert Barkedyes

Pike only
20. Robert Sothersan

Sword only
21. John Smith[169]

Snaphance only
22. James Williams[170]

[f. 83v]

Sword only
23. Henry Daragh[171]

Sword and Pike
24. George Byrnye[172]

Sword and Musket
25. John Bayly[173]

Sword and Caliver
26. Thomas Steaphenson[174]

[158] Possibly 'John Hervey, gentleman' who had a 300-acre freehold with 'his two sons', 1622 (ibid. p. 580).
[159] See number 43.
[160] Son of David Gibb, tradesman, resident at Stewartstown, 1622 (ibid. p. 594).
[161] Son of Robert Pott, a cottager on Sir Robert Newcomen's (later Sir William Stewart's) estate, 1622 (ibid. p. 569).
[162] Cottager, 1622 (ibid. p. 583).
[163] Robert, David, and William Goodlad (numbers 2 to 4) are probably the sons of Thomas Goodlad, Sir Robert Heyburn's agent, 1622 and freeholder of 180 acres (ibid. p. 580).
[164] Numbers 6 and 7 are father and son; Robert Mayse senior was one of the 'inferior burgesses' of Augher, 1622 (ibid. p. 575); Robert Mayse senior or junior was killed, 1641 (Deposition of Gartrude Carlile, 13 March 1643 [TCD MS 839, fols 031r–032v]).
[165] One of seven tenants who leased 240 acres from Sir Robert Heyburn, 10 May 1620 (Hill, *Plantation*, p. 547; Treadwell (ed.), *Irish commission*, p. 580).
[166] Killed with 'two or three of his sons', 1641 (Deposition of Gartrude Carlile, 13 March 1643 [TCD MS 839, fols 031r–032v]); the sons are probably Henry and John Piggot (numbers 14 and 46).
[167] Possibly the son of Patrick Learman who leased 180 acres, 1622 (Treadwell (ed.), *Irish commission*, p. 580).
[168] Possibly the son and sub-tenant of John Coulson, who leased 240 acres, 1622 (ibid.).
[169] 'John Smythe of Turlawghan' was a tenant of 'Davy Bailey', who leased sixty acres with John Bailey (number 25), 1622 (ibid.).
[170] Possibly a son of Robert Williams, one the workmen Sir Thomas Ridgeway promised would become freeholders (Carew, Survey of the Plantation (1611), in Hill, *Plantation*, p. 538).
[171] Leased sixty acres with 'William Hepborne' (possibly son of Sir Robert Heyburn, the original undertaker), 1622 (Treadwell (ed.), *Irish commission*, p. 580).
[172] Cottager on Sir Andrew Stewart's estate, 1622 (ibid. p. 583).
[173] Leased 60 acres with 'Davy Bailey', 1622 (ibid., p. 580).
[174] Tenant at will on the earl of Abercorn's estate at Strabane, 1622 (ibid. p. 569).

Sword and Pike

27. William Bayly

Sword and Musket

28. James Mackrone

Sword and Caliver

29. Duncan Meny

Musket only

30. John Foster

Sword only

31. Walter Hog[175]

Sword and Pike

32. James Hog
33. Robert McNar
34. William Scot

No Arms

35. William Plowman[176]
36. Thomas Eaton
37. Edward Garlick[177]
38. James Wood[178]
39. John Smyth younger[179]
40. Edward Garlick
41. James Learman
42. Robert Mase
43. John Learman
44. John Smyth[180]
45. Henry Avery
46. John Piggot

[f. 84]

Tyrone
Barony de Dungannon

Captain Alexander Sanderson, undertaker of 1000 acres: his men and arms as followeth

Sword and Snaphance

1. George Brecking

Sword and Pike

2. Thomas Creighton

Sword and Snaphance

3. Hector Ellot[181]

Sword and Caliver

4. Gilbert Hardy

Sword and Pike

5. George Gath[182]

Sword and Snaphance

6. John Rosse

Sword only

7. James Shaw[183]

Sword and Snaphance

8. George Douglas

Sword and Pike

9. Mathew Peteroul
10. William Gillaspy
11. Robert Baird
12. James Beaty

Sword only

13. William Myllikin
14. Hugh Craford
15. John Armstrang
16. Archbald Armstrang

Sword and Pike

17. James Fostall
18. William Bretting

[f. 84v]
No Arms

19. John Bably

20. James Shaw
21. Robert Parson
22. John Parson
23. Archbald Sanderson
24. John Creighton
25. John Gath younger[184]
26. John Cowayne
27. John Douglas
28. John Dunbar[185]
29. William Grocer
30. Humphry Boward
31. John Graham
32. Robert Armstrang
33. John Shaw
34. Richard Gillaspy
35. Adam White
36. Robert Gray

[f. 85]

Tyrone
Barony de Dungannon

Mr Symonton, undertaker of 1000 acres: his men and arms

Sword and Pike

1. George Eccles

Sword only

2. John Jackson

Sword and Snaphance

3. John Greire
4. Henry Jammison
5. James Cranston

Sword and Pike

6. James Gath

Sword and Snaphance

7. George Burned[186]
8. Hugh Reed

---

[175] 'Walter Hog of the Cavan' was a tenant of 'Davy Bailey' who leased 60 acres with John Bailey (number 25), 1622 (ibid. p. 580).

[176] One of seven tenants who leased 240 acres from Sir Robert Heyburn, 10 May 1620 (ibid. p. 580; Hill, *Plantation*, p. 547); killed, 1641 (Deposition of Gartrude Carlile, 13 March 1643 [TCD MS 839, fols 031r–032v]).

[177] 'Edward Garlique of Bovane' was a tenant of 'Davy Bailey' who leased sixty acres with John Bailey (number 25), 1622 (Treadwell (ed.), *Irish commission*, p. 580).

[178] Killed, 1641 (Deposition of Gartrude Carlile, 13 March 1643 [TCD MS 839, fols 031r–032v]).

[179] Son of number 44.

[180] Father of number 39.

[181] Possibly the son of Archibald Elliott, a copyholder in the town of Tullylagan [modern Sandholes], 1622 (Treadwell (ed.), *Irish commission*, p. 582).

[182] George and John Gath (numbers 5 and 25) are probably brothers; their father, John Gath senior, did not muster. He was a tenant of John Treythane, who held 100 acres for twenty-one years, 1622 (ibid. pp 581–2).

[183] Copyholder in Tullelagen, 1622 (ibid.).

[184] See number 5.

[185] Cottager, 1622 (ibid. p. 583).

[186] George Burnet was probably a relation of William Burnet, who was 'dwelt before and at the beginning of the Irish Rebellion [in October 1641] at Cookstown' and who was living in 'the Parish of Dunneen in the County of Antrim' [Toomebridge] in 1653 (Examination of William Burnett, 14 March 1653 [TCD MS 838, fol. 077v]).

Pike only
9. David Henderson

No Arms
10. James Young[187]
11. Archbald Sparckle
12. James Grere
13. Robert Grere[188]
14. —[189]
15. David Jammison
16. John Steward
17. George Beaty
18. Robert Daragh
19. John Watterson
20. Symond Armstrang[190]
21. John Jobe
22. Robert Bennet
23. Rowland McMullan
24. John Young[191]
25. Thomas Young[192]
26. John Bell
27. Robert Fenton
28. George Gath

[f.85v]

Tyrone
Barony de Dungannon

Alexander Richardson esquire, undertaker of 1000 acres: his men and arms as followeth

Sword and Pike
1. Thomas Carr[193]

Pike only
2. Adam Sommervill[194]
3. Andrew Ellot[195]
4. William Russell
5. William Cadarisse

Sword and Snaphance
6. Ralph Haborne

Pike only
7. John Mynnis
8. John McKey
9. Robert Ellot
10. William Scot[196]
11. Walter Sommerville

Sword and Snaphance
12. John Browne[197]
13. James Ellot
14. Patrick Herron

Sword and Pike
15. George Sybyny

Sword only
16. Francis Ellot
17. Marke Ellot

Sword and Pike
18. Andrew Ellot
19. William Russell[198]

No Arms
20. Archbald Kill
21. Francis Russell
22. Francis Ellot
23. Symond Henderson
24. Marke Ellot
25. Archbald Ellot
26. George McEnall

[f. 86]

Tyrone
Barony de Dungannon

Robert Lyndsay esquire, undertaker of 1000 [acres:] his men and arms

Sword and Caliver
1. Roger McMurlan

Sword and Snaphance
2. Robert Nixon[199]
3. John Style[200]
4. David English[201]

Sword only
5. David Thomson[202]

Sword and Snaphance
6. John Walse
7. William Sammuell

Sword and Pike
8. Jenkin Bell[203]

Sword and Snaphance
9. George Hetherrington
10. Rynyon McCaffie

Sword and Pike
11. William Ellot
12. John Ellot

Sword only
13. Robert Baxty
14. Archbald Ellot

Sword and Pike
15. Adam Glendunning

Sword only
16. James Sommervile

Sword and Pike
17. George Carr

Sword only
18. James Harper

---

187 James Young was killed 'by some of the Irish going from Lissan towards Moneymore' at Christmas 1641 (Examination of Neile oge ó Quin [ibid. fols 038r–039v]).

188 Sub-tenant on Alexander Sanderson's estate, 1622 (Treadwell (ed.), *Irish commission*, p. 580).

189 Number 14 is missing in the original manuscript: the numbering goes from 13 to 15.

190 Son of Lorne Armstrong, a cottager, 1622 (ibid. p. 584).

191 Killed at Lissan around Christmas 1641 (Examinations of James Steile, 14 March 1654 [TCD MS 838, fols 076v–077r] and Margaret Armstrong, 18 March 1653 [ibid. fol. 080v]).

192 Sub-tenant on Andrew Sanderson's estate, 1622 (Treadwell (ed.), *Irish commission*, p. 581).

193 Held a seven-year lease of 'Tatte Kyell and Tyrvone', 1622 (Treadwell (ed.), *Irish commission*, p. 583).

194 Somerville shared a 21-year lease of 'Bromlistagh and Lathnacrosse' with James Scott, 1622 (ibid. p. 583).

195 The nine men called Elliott (numbers 3, 9, 13, 16, 17, 18, 22, 24, and 25) are probably drawn from at least three families.

196 Possibly son of Adam Somerville's partner, James Scott.

197 Son of 'William Brunne', a sub-tenant 'dwelling upon the Drome', 1622 (Treadwell (ed.), *Irish commission*, p. 583).

198 Brother of Francis Russell (number 21); the brothers had a twenty-one year lease of sixty acres on David Kennedy's (later John Symington's) estate, 1622 (ibid. p. 584).

199 Possibly son of Henry Nixon, a tenant of William Rowle, 1622 (ibid. p. 582).

200 Son of 'James Steill', one of the 'tenants of Marasudan', 1622 (ibid.).

201 Tenant of John Hayly, who held sixty acres on a nineteen year lease, 1622; he held the lease 'by right of the late William Bonner' (ibid.).

202 Tenant of Helena Forester, who had a sixty acre freehold, 1622; she was the widow of Alexander Forester (ibid.).

203 Bell was a tenant of Henry Acheson in Fews Barony, county Armagh and mustered with a sword, 1622 (ibid. p. 548).

Sword and Pike
19. John Sommervile
20. Adam Bell

Drummer
21. John Creighton

Sword only
22. Barnard Lyndsay
23. William Rowle[204]
24. James Hasty

No Arms
25. William Scot
26. William Bruce[205]
27. Francis Carr[206]
28. James Sincleare
29. Robert Crawford[207]
30. John Irwin
31. James Glenduning
32. Patrick Cadash

[f. 86v]

33. Andrew Fargison
34. Rynyon Pearson
35. William Maxon
36. Andrew Berry
37. Andrew McKedyon
38. George Seebit
39. Robert Steele[208]
40. William Steele
41. John Rud
42. Robert Ellot
43. John McConnell
44. Robert McGriffin
45. George Glynon
46. James Walker
47. Luke Acheson
48. John Cass
49. James Foster
50. John Gourdon
51. James Sanderson
52. Robert Ellot
53. Andrew McDilshonder
54. William Sanderson

55. William Ellot
56. James Hasty
57. John Creighton
58. James Lurg
59. Archbald Ellot
60. Jenkin Bell
61. John Walsh
62. Robert Nixon[209]
63. David Thomson
64. William Rowl
65. George Carr

[f. 87]

Tyrone Barony de Omy

The Lord Hastings, undertaker of 2000 acres: his men and arms as followeth

Sword only
1. Lawrence Nerthenwil[210]

Sword only
2. Conn Roberts[211]
3. Rise Roberts

Sword and Pike
4. Richard Scot
5. Richard Jones

Sword only
6. Thomas Landy
7. Francis Bird

Snaphance only
8. Edward Moore

Sword only
9. William Edwards

Sword and Snaphance
10. Charles Bastards[212]

Sword only
11. Joseph Bastards

Sword and Snaphance
12. John Steward

Snaphance only
13. Edward Moore

Sword only
14. Lewis Jones

Sword and Snaphance
15. Charles Grome
16. John Bisse
17. Thomas Clarke

Sword and Musket
18. John Taylor[213]

Sword and Caliver
19. Francis Haward

Musket only
20. Robert Gardner

Sword and Caliver
21. Robert Borrell[214]

Sword only
22. Griffin Uprichard

Snaphance only
23. Richard Waterhouse[215]

No Arms
24. Thomas Hog
25. John Bastards

[f. 87v]

Barony de Omy

Sir Pearce Crosby knight, undertaker of 3000 acres: his men and arms as followeth

Sword only
1. John Miller

---

[204] Held 120 acres on a seven-year lease, 1622 (ibid. p. 582).

[205] William Bruce the younger was a cottager on Sir Robert Newcomen's (later Sir William Stewart's) estate, 1622 (ibid. p. 570).

[206] Tenant of John Richardson, freeholder of 120 acres, 1622 (ibid. p. 582).

[207] Tenant of William Rowle (number 64), 1622 (ibid.).

[208] 'Robert Steill Arlatt' was a tenant of William Rowle, 1622 (ibid.).

[209] See number 2.

[210] Netherville held the townland of Cookeragh, which he let to Irish tenants (Inquisitions of Ulster, Tyrone, (35) Charles I).

[211] Conn (number 2) and Reece (number 3) Roberts may be the sons of John Roberts, who had a sixty acre leasehold, 1622 (Treadwell (ed.), *Irish commission*, p. 574).

[212] Bustard (the modern spelling of the family's name) was also a tenant on James Mervin's estate (Inquisitions of Ulster, Tyrone, (35) Charles I); other members of the family are Joseph (number 11) and John Bustard (number 25). Another member of the family is William Bustard, who held 240 acres in freehold and leasehold on the Hastings estate, 1622 (Treadwell (ed.), *Irish commission*, p. 574), and whose widow reported losses amounting to £340 0s 0d, 1641 (Deposition of Ann Bastard, 3 June 1643 [TCD MS 839, fols 106r–106v]).

[213] John Taylor held 120 acres in freehold and leasehold on the earl of Castlehaven's estate, 1622 (Treadwell (ed.), *Irish commission*, p. 572).

[214] Thirty acre leasehold, 1622 (ibid. p. 574).

[215] 'Widow Waterhouse', his mother, had thirty acres in leasehold, 1622 (ibid.).

Sword and Snaphance
2.   John Anderson
3.   James Maughan

Sword only
4.   Alexander Gilpatricke
5.   John Steward
6.   John Maxwell
7.   David Sheapheard
8.   Robert Scot
9.   James Kirke
10.   Thomas Maughan
11.   William Neylly
12.   John McCala
13.   John Greire
14.   John Burnet

Snaphance only
15.   Daniell Lastly

Sword only
16.   Francis Parry

Sword and Pike
17.   Alexander Coloston
18.   Patrick McNicol

Sword only
19.   William Breaty

Sword and Snaphance
20.   Archbald Robinson

Sword only
21.   Robert Hammilton

Sword and Pike
22.   William Robertson

[f. 88]

Sword and Pike
23.   John McCrue[216]

Sword and Snaphance
24.   Daniell McNeekell

Sword only
25.   Richard Byers
26.   Robert Turner[217]

Sword and Pike
27.   James Maston

Sword only
28.   John Maston

Sword and Pike
29.   Gilbert O Crag

No Arms
30.   Archbald Maughan
31.   Archbald Douglas
32.   John Robertson[218]
33.   David Forley
34.   John McConnell
35.   William Ballyntyn
36.   Arch: Sholes
37.   John Ballyntyn
38.   Robert Hammilton
39.   William Breaty
40.   Francis Perry[219]
41.   John Burnet
42.   John McCala
43.   William Robertson
44.   Robert Scot
45.   John Maxwell
46.   James Kirk
47.   John Anderson

[f. 88v]

Barony de Omy

Captain Mervin, undertaker of 6000 acres: his men and arms

Sword and Pike
1.   Nicholas Bront

Sword only
2.   Richard Hallon
3.   William Shaw[220]

Sword and Snaphance
4.   James Perry

Sword only
5.   John Hammilton

Sword and Snaphance
6.   Edmond Mervin
7.   William Powell

Sword and Pike
8.   William Black

Sword and Pike
9.   William Frezell

Musket and Bandoleirs
10.   Edward Marvin

Sword, Musket, and Bandoleirs
11.   William Moore

Sword and Caliver
12.   John Wood elder[221]

Musket only
13.   John Wood younger

Sword, Musket, and Bandoleirs
14.   William Wood

Sword and Snaphance
15.   John Hogge

Sword only
16.   Richard Conny

Caliver and Bandoleirs
17.   Thomas Hadick

Snaphance only
18.   James Browne

Sword only
19.   David Dony

Sword and Pike
20.   Richard Maxwell
21.   George Stanning

Sword only
22.   James Wylly[222]

Sword and Snaphance
23.   John Gourden

Sword and Pike
24.   John Newtown

[f. 89]

25.   Robert Beaty

Sword and Snaphance
26.   Archbald Scot

---

[216] Father of number 55 on Captain Mervin's estate, below.
[217] Cottager on Lord Ridgeway's (later Sir James Erskine's) estate, 1622 (Treadwell (ed.), *Irish commission*, p. 575).
[218] Cottager, 1622 (ibid. p. 572).
[219] Son of Thomas, James, or Orlando Perry, tenants on the earl of Castlehaven's estate, 1622 (ibid.).
[220] 'Gentleman'; sixty acre freehold and sixty acre leasehold, 1622 (ibid. p. 573).
[221] Numbers 12 and 13 are father and son.
[222] Sixty acre leasehold, 1622 (Treadwell (ed.), *Irish commission*, p. 573).

Sword only
27. Thomas Mervin

Pike only
28. George Browne

Sword and Snaphance
29. Peter Style

Sword only
30. John Rasedeyhe

Sword and Pike
31. John Lewis

Sword, Musket, and Bandoleirs
32. James Person
33. Robert Waterrall

Sword and Pike
34. James Waterall

Musket and Bandoleirs
35. Owen Lewis[223]

Pike only
36. John Clark

Sword and Pike
37. Francis Armstrong

Sword, Musket, and Bandoleirs
38. John Anthony

Sword and Snaphance
39. John Reyney

Sword and Pike
40. Robert Hammilton
41. William Armstrong
42. John Anderson

Sword only
43. Francis Leskeyne
44. Adam Sowerty

Sword and Pike
45. William Duff McDony
46. Richard Steaphenson
47. Edward Poe[224]

[f. 89v]

No Arms
48. Christopher Browne
49. John Michaell[225]
50. Anthony Pot[226]
51. James Reyney
52. Robert Armstrong
53. Gilbert Gray
54. Richard Beyor
55. John McCru younger[227]
56. John Cloughan
57. Robert Crosby

[f. 90]

Barony de Strabane

Malcolm Dromond esquire, undertaker of 1000 acres: his men and arms

Sword and Pike
1. John Large
2. William Sharpe[228]
3. Patrick Bradene
4. Thomas McGowne[229]
5. Richard Turner
6. William Read[230]
7. John Bard
8. Thomas Monzy
9. Donnald McKillip
10. John McGregor
11. John Beier

Sword and Snaphance
12. John Harnor
13. Andrew Coskey

Sword and Caliver
14. Patrick Graham

Sword only
15. William Johnston

[f. 90v]

Barony de Strabane

Sir George Hammilton knight, undertaker of 2500 acres: his men and arms

Sword and Snaphance
1. William Miller

Sword and Pike
2. John Porter[231]

Sword and Caliver
3. James Wilkin

Sword and Snaphance
4. Steaphen Lowry[232]

Sword only
5. John Murrey

Sword and Pike
6. Peter Laughlyne

Sword and Snaphance
7. James Mathew
8. Daniell Wood

Sword and Pike
9. Daniell Browne

Sword and Snaphance
10. John Michaell
11. James Cross
12. John Holmes
13. Claudius Paul

Sword Only
14. Clawdius Willson
15. George Nesbit

Sword and Pike
16. David Murray

Sword and Halberd
17. James Lowry

Sword and Snaphance
18. John Granger

Sword and Pike
19. Robert Brewell

Sword only
20. Robert Wart
21. James Lynne

---

[223] Sixty acre leasehold, 1622 (ibid.).

[224] Hundred and twenty acre freehold and sixty acre leasehold, 1622 (ibid.).

[225] Thirty acre leasehold, 1622 (ibid.).

[226] Possibly the son of Robert Pott, a cottager on Sir Robert Newcomen's (later Sir William Stewart's) estate, 1622 (ibid. p. 569).

[227] Son of number 23 on Sir Pearce Crosby's estate.

[228] Leaseholder; described as 'yeoman', 1622 (Treadwell (ed.), *Irish commission*, p. 571).

[229] Possibly son of John Magowan, leaseholder; described as 'a redshank' and as 'yeoman', 1622 (ibid.).

[230] Leaseholder; described as 'yeoman', 1622 (ibid.).

[231] Possibly son of Patrick Porter, tenant at will on the Donalong estate, 1622 (Treadwell (ed.), *Irish commission*, p. 568).

[232] Possibly son of John Lowry, cottager, 1622 (ibid.).

Sword and Snaphance
22. Danniall McIlwaine

Sword and Pike
23. Danniell Hill

Sword only
24. Robert Granger[233]

[f. 91]

Sword and Snaphance
25. Robert Macklin

Sword only
26. Andrew Clay

Sword and Snaphance
27. John Macklyne

Sword only
28. Alexander Browne

Sword and Pike
29. Robert Wallas

Sword and Snaphance
30. Andrew Browne

Sword and Pike
31. Gillcolim McCollim

Sword and Snaphance
32. Alexander Fenton

Sword and Pike
33. Georg Bron   Recusant[234]

Sword only
34. James Barhill
35. David McDoall
36. John Browne[235]
37. James Hall
38. William Daragh
39. Art McArt

Sword and Snaphance
40. William Greenly

Sword only
41. Robert McAllen

Sword and Pike
42. Adam Wen
43. Archbald Brooke

Sword only
44. James Longtowne

Sword and Snaphance
45. Robert Lowther

Sword only
46. William Nicholl

Sword and Caliver
47. John Ore elder
48. John Ore younger
49. Alexander Clenny
50. James Clenny
51. Gawin Steele[236]

No Arms
52. Patrick Hunter
53. John Wilson
54. Mathew Kayle

[f. 91v]

Barony de Strabane

The Countess of Abbercorne, undertaker of 2000 acres: the names of her men and arms

Sword only
1. Thomas Pardune
2. John Lawson
3. Archbald Barr younger

Sword and Pike
4. John Arbarhale

Sword and Snaphance
5. Arthur Hammilton

Sword and Pike
6. John Coghrayne
7. John Mathewson

Sword and Snaphance
8. William Cayl
9. James Dunkin
10. William McClement

Sword only
11. James Long
12. John Shaw
13. William Gurlay[237]
14. Robert Bigor
15. John Wilson[238]
16. James Edger
17. Alexander Browne
18. Gilbert McCracharan

Sword and Snaphance
19. John Birkmyre

Sword and Pike
20. James Gilmour
21. Gilbert McKee

Sword only
22. James McNeight

[f. 91]

23. Robert Wood

Sword and Snaphance
24. John McNaught

Sword only
25. John mcQurarty
26. William Ferbish

Sword and Snaphance
27. James Staynyhill
28. John Carmighell[239]

Sword only
29. John Staynihill

Sword and Pike
30. James Cary

Sword and Snaphance
31. James Browne

Sword only
32. Donny McGill

Sword and Snaphance
33. David Rowlstone

Sword and Pike
34. David McLeallan
35. William McLeallan

---

[233] Tenant at will on the Donalong estate, 1622 (ibid. p. 567); killed, 1641 (Examination of Elizabeth Jefferdson, 7 March 1653 [TCD MS 839, fols 049r–050v]).

[234] Roman Catholic.

[235] Stone house in Ardstraw and leasehold tenancy, 1622 (Treadwell (ed.), *Irish commission*, p. 569).

[236] Possibly son of Andrew Steele, leaseholder, 1622 (ibid.).

[237] Killed, 1641 (Deposition of George Burne, 12 January 1644 [TCD MS 839, fols 038r–039v]).

[238] Tenant at will on the Donalong estate, 1622 (Treadwell (ed.), *Irish commission*, p. 567).

[239] Leaseholder on Sir George Hamilton's estate, 1622 (ibid. p. 569).

Sword and Snaphance
36. James Balfoare

No Arms
37. James Boyd
38. Thomas Rudderfoord
39. David Wein
40. Thomas Porke

[f. 92v]

Barony de Strabane

The Master of Abbercorne, undertaker of 2500 acres: his men and arms

Sword and Pike
1. Conchor McAleyster
2. John Anderson[240]
3. John Templeton

Sword and Snaphance
4. Homer Maxwell

Sword and Pike
5. John Kynard

Sword and Snaphance
6. George Cass

Sword and Pike
7. Walter Ro

Sword and Snaphance
8. Robert Hammilton[241]
9. William Kunningham[242]
10. Arthur Littlejohn
11. David Templeton

Sword only
12. James Fleming[243]

Sword and Snaphance
13. John Willson

Sword only
14. William Bochanan

Sword and Musket
15. William Dugall

Sword and Pike
16. William Bochanan

Sword and Caliver
17. John Barnes

Sword and Snaphance
18. Hugh McEnor
19. John Greene

Sword only
20. Nole mcIldony

Sword and Snaphance
21. Thomas Conningham

Sword only
22. John Kinkeard
23. Andrew Kinkeard

Sword and Snaphance
24. Thomas Carr

[f. 93]

Sword and Snaphance
25. Daniell Kinkeard

Sword and Pike
26. Patrick Browne
27. Thomas McKillmene

Sword and Snaphance
28. Duniell Galbreath

Sword and Pike
29. Andrew Carr[244]

Sword only
30. Daniell Gambell

Sword and Pike
31. John Steaphenson[245]

Sword only
32. John Ald

Sword and Snaphance
33. George Hammelton

Sword only
34. John Ore

Sword and Snaphance
35. James Hoggshead

Sword only
36. William Fullerton
37. John Scot

Sword and Snaphance
38. Alexander Jonkin

Sword only
39. Daniell McFatter

No Arms
40. James Cutbertson[246]
41. Thomas Browne
42. Robert Calwell
43. George Bruse[247]
44. John Kinkeard
45. Hugh Hunter
46. John Sluane
47. Archbald Maxwell
48. John McKarnes
49. John Ore
50. Daniell McKeir
51. William Willson

[f. 93v]

Barony de Strabane

Sir William Hammilton knight, undertaker of 2750 acres: his men and arms as followeth

Sword and Pike
1. James Conningham
2. James McCarney
3. William Nicholl
4. Mathew Crafoord[248]
5. Charles Pock
6. James Pock
7. John Winter
8. Alexander Quinton
9. John Davison
10. James Quinton
11. Daniell McKey

Sword and Snaphance
12. John Browne
13. Robert Hammilton

---

[240] Tenant at will on the Strabane and Donalong estates, 1622 (ibid. p. 568).
[241] Tenant at will on the Strabane estate, 1622 (ibid. p. 567).
[242] Tenant at will on the Strabane estate, 1622 (ibid.).
[243] Possibly the son of John Fleming, tenant at will on the Strabane estate, 1622 (ibid. p. 569).
[244] Andrew Kerr senior was a tenant at will on the Strabane estate, 1622 (ibid.): this may be his son.
[245] John Stephenson senior and John Stephenson junior were tenants at will on the Strabane estate, 1622: this is probably John Stephenson junior (ibid.).
[246] Probably son of Thomas Cuthbertson, tenant at will on the Strabane estate, 1622 (ibid.).
[247] Sub-tenant on Sir George Hamilton's estate, 1622 (ibid. p. 570).
[248] Tenant at will on the Strabane estate, 1622 (Treadwell (ed.), *Irish commission*, p. 567).

14. Andrew Hay
15. Thomas Pettegson
16. Francis Irwin

Sword only
17. John Mathew

Sword and Snaphance
18. William Laughlin
19. Robert Wood
20. Henry Crookeshank
21. Archbald Glen

Sword and Pike
22. Alexander Glen
23. Gilbert Grooden

[f. 94]

Sword and Caliver
24. Thomas Morhead

Sword and Pike
25. William Nicholl
26. Thomas Parke

Sword and Snaphance
27. Gawin Steele
28. Alexander Steward[249]
29. John Walker

Sword and Pike
30. Malcolme McCabe
31. Walter McPerson

Sword and Snaphance
32. Hugh Hammilton[250]
33. Hugh Hammilton younger[251]
34. Andrew Davison

Sword and Pike
35. Christopher Irwin[252]
36. James Kenny
37. James Hymphil
38. Robert Holan
39. John Scot

Sword and Snaphance
40. John Grange
41. John Queenton

Sword and Pike
42. John Hood

No Arms
43. John Walker

[f. 94v]

Barony de Strabane

The names of the men and arms of the town of Strabane

Sword only
1. James Gib   Provost

Sword and Snaphance
2. Hugh Knyland
3. Robert Comyn
4. Henry Wood

Snaphance only
5. Walter Wright

Sword only
6. James Reynold
7. William Coningham[253]

Snaphance only
8. Georg Paterson

Sword only
9. John Wallis elder[254]

Sword and Snaphance
10. Noel McIlwayne
11. John Home

Sword and Pike
12. John More

Sword and Snaphance
13. Patrick Caweill

Bearer of the Colours
14. Robert Algeir[255]

Sword and Pike
15. Thomas Colinn

Sword and Snaphance
16. Thomas Young[256]
17. John Hector

Sword and Pike
18. William Craghead

Sword and Caliver
19. Andrew Kelly
20. Robert Robertson younger[257]

Sword and Pike
21. Robert Robertson elder

Sword and Snaphance
22. John Robertson

[f. 95]

Sword and Snaphance
23. Robert Wallis
24. Gabriell Homes younger[258]
25. James Wallis

Sword only
26. Adam Kennittee

Sword and Snaphance
27. Thomas Young elder[259]

Sword and Musket
28. George Bruse

Sword only
29. John Wallis younger[260]
30. William Young

Sword and Snaphance
31. James Scot younger[261]
32. Alexander McKenes

---

[249] 'Alexander Stewart, gentleman' leased 180 acres of Robert Lindsay's estate for nineteen years, 1622 (ibid. p. 582).

[250] Father of number 33; Hugh Hamilton of Moyagh, 'gentleman' had a sixty acre freehold and Hugh Hamilton of Lisdovin a sixty acre freehold and a stone house on the Dunalong estate, 1622 (ibid. p. 568).

[251] Son of number 32.

[252] Held 200 acres in freehold and leasehold on the estate of William Turvin (later that of Archibald Hamilton) (ibid. p. 576).

[253] This man or number 162 was a tenant at will on the Strabane estate, 1622 (ibid. p. 567).

[254] Father of number 29.

[255] Robert Algeo had a stone house and a leasehold tenancy on Sir George Hamilton's estate at Ardstraw, 1622 (Treadwell (ed.), *Irish commission*, p. 569).

[256] Son of number 27.

[257] Numbers 20 and 21 are son and father.

[258] Gabriel Holmes senior did not muster.

[259] Father of number 16.

[260] Son of number 9.

[261] Son of number 70.

Sword and Pike
33. James Flamming

Sword only
34. Jobough Canahill

Sword and Snaphance
35. Hugh McKener

Sword and Pike
36. Robert Leidy

Snaphance only
37. Robert Young elder[262]

Sword and Snaphance
38. Gilbert Johnston[263]

Sword only
39. James McCuler

Sword and Snaphance
40. John Bochanan
41. William Hunter

Sword only
42. Duncan McFarlan

Sword and Snaphance
43. John Smyth

Sword only
44. Robert McMurra

Sword and Pike
45. William McKeene
46. William Bisland
47. John McMichell

Sword and Caliver
48. John Bisland

[f. 95v]

49. Bryan Galbreath

Sword and Pike
50. John Roger
51. William Kennittee

Sword and Snaphance
52. Robert Moderwell

Sword and Halberd
53. Andrew Hay

Pike only
54. John Smyth

Sword and Snaphance
55. George Homes

Sword and Pike
56. John Hynes

Sword only
57. Robert Smith

Sword and Pike
58. James Andrew

Sword only
59. Robert Yury

Sword, Snaphance, and Bandoleirs
60. John Learman

Sword and Halberd
61. Robert Latty

Sword and Snaphance
62. William Young

Sword only
63. Hugh Maxwell

Sword, Snaphance, and Bandoleirs
64. Andrew Grannger

Sword and Pike
65. David Barbor

Sword and Snaphance
66. Gawen Hammelton

Sword and Pike
67. John Smyth

Sword and Caliver
68. Allan Cuthbert

Sword and Pike
69. William Paterson

Sword and Snaphance
70. James Scot[264]
71. Duncan Turner
72. James Blayne

Sword and Caliver
73. John Hammilton

[f. 96]

Sword and Pike
74. John King
75. John Curry

Sword and Snaphance
76. Robert Leith

Sword and Pike
77. Patrick Muddy
78. William Browne

Sword and Snaphance
79. Robert Morison

Sword, Caliver, and Bandoleirs
80. Walter Moryson

Sword and Snaphance
81. George Scot
82. Thomas McClintock

Sword and Pike
83. Thomas Wallice

Sword and Snaphance
84. James Cuming

Sword and Pike
85. James Archbold elder[265]

Sword and Snaphance
86. David Miller
87. James Archbold younger[266]

Sword and Pike
88. James Pattowne
89. Edward Richardson[267]
90. John Rakin

Sword and Snaphance
91. John Crag

---

[262] Father of number 173; possibly the same man who, 1622, was a cottager on Sir Andrew Stewart's estate (Treadwell (ed.), *Irish commission*, p. 583).

[263] Possibly cottager of the estate of William Turvin (later that of Archibald Hamilton) and mustered with no arms, 1622 (ibid. p. 577).

[264] Father of number 31.

[265] Father of number 87.

[266] Son of number 85.

[267] Cottager on Sir Andrew Stewart's estate, 1622 (Treadwell (ed.), *Irish commission*, pp 583–4).

Sword and Pike
  92. John Browne

Sword and Musket
  93. John McKarmick

Sword and Snaphance
  94. William Sommervill

Sword, Musket, and Bandoliers
  95. Arthur Luggy

Sword and Snaphance
  96. Patrick Hammilton[268]

Sword only
  97. David Robinson

Sword, Snaphance, and Bandoliers
  98. Robert Lonny

Sword only
  99. William Hammilton[269]

[f. 96v]

Sword and Snaphance
  100. John Kiell

Sword and Pike
  101. William Bicbon

Sword and Caliver
  102. James Cocheran

Sword and Snaphance
  103. William Knox

Sword only
  104. Robert Wilson

Sword and Snaphance
  105. John Wilson

Sword and Pike
  106. George McLong
  107. James Conningham
  108. Hugh Calder

Sword only
  109. George Buntyne

Sword and Caliver
  110. John Smyth

Sword and Pike
  111. Robert McRyre
  112. James Roger

Sword and Snaphance
  113. James Mathew
  114. Gabraell Mathew

Snaphance only
  115. David McKenny

Sword and Musket
  116. John Burnes

Sword and Pike
  117. William Crag

Sword and Snaphance
  118. John Thompson

Sword and Snaphance
  119. William Wilson

Sword only
  120. William Wright

Sword and Pike
  121. James Hanna
  122. John Kinningham

Sword only
  123. Donnell McCleane

Sword and Snaphance
  124. Robert Conningham

Sword and Pike
  125. Andrew Ore
  126. Arthur Maxwell

[f. 97]

  127. William Goody
  128. James Parsons
  129. Daniell Gambell

Sword and Caliver
  130. James Browne

Sword and Pike
  131. Archbald McNeal[270]

Sword only
  132. James Haterick

Sword and Pike
  133. Robert Russell

Sword only
  134. Daniell Purdon

Sword and Pike
  135. David Coningham

Sword only
  136. William Ewart
  137. John Paterson younger[271]

Sword and Snaphance
  138. John Hames younger[272]

Sword only
  139. Andrew Cassen
  140. Hugh Sommervil

Sword and Pike
  141. Adam Knox

Sword only
  142. John Humes[273]
  143. Robert Lyndsey
  144. David White
  145. John Ore

No Arms
  146. John Delap
  147. William Cuthbert
  148. John Jackson
  149. James Bishond
  150. James Coming
  151. Archbald Robinson
  152. William Henderson

[f. 97v]

  153. Andrew Hammilton
  154. John Luggy
  155. David Morrison
  156. Andrew Moderwell
  157. William Catherson
  158. John McMichaell

---

[268] Son of 'Patrick Hamilton, clerk' who held 420 acres in freehold, 1622 (ibid. p. 568).

[269] This man may be 'William Hamilton, merchant', who was the provost of Strabane, 1622 and who had a 120 acre freehold 'with a house' on the earl of Abercorn's Strabane estate and a sixty acre leasehold on the earl of Castlehaven's estate (ibid. pp 567, 572).

[270] Possibly the son of Gilchrist McNeile, tenant at will on the Strabane estate, 1622 (Treadwell (ed.), *Irish commission*, p. 567).

[271] Son of number 174.

[272] Son of number 142.

[273] Father of number 138.

159. Alexander Conningham
160. James McKasby
161. John Younger
162. William Conningham[274]
163. David Montcrieff
164. James Crome
165. Hugh Sommervil
166. William Cader
167. Thomas Alexander
168. Robert Bennet
169. Walter Long
170. James Nesmith
171. John Douglas
172. John Crome
173. Robert Young younger[275]
174. John Patterson elder[276]
175. John Smallet
176. David Montcrieff
177. Robert Patterson
178. John Gouchom

[f. 98]

179. William How
180. John Miller
181. John Hutton
182. David Long
183. Robert Long
184. John Homes
185. John Yates
186. Daniell Fargison
187. Archball Kaill
188. John Ellot
189. John Johnston
190. Gilchrist McMoale
191. Dowgall gray McMeiny
192. Adam McLang
193. Robert Bilfkeir
194. James Conningham
195. Robert McTyre
196. Hugh Maxwell
197. John Cunningham[277]
198. Claudius Alegoo
199. Andrew Ore
200. Donnell McClone
201. James Hanna
202. John Thompson
203. John Burnes
204. James Mathew
205. John Smyth
206. Hugh Calder

207. Robert Wilson
208. William Knox

[f. 98v]

Tyrone
Barony de Dungannon

The Right Reverend Father in God Lord Primate of Armagh, his churchlands in the barony above said being 4000 acres: his men and arms

Sword only
1. Richard Jonncy[278]

Sword and Pike
2. John Armstrong[279]

Sword and Snaphance
3. James Standish

Sword and Pike
4. James Button
5. Thomas Wooker
6. William Walker

Sword only
7. Robert Randall[280]

Pike only
8. Robert Craisbrooke

Sword and Snaphance
9. Edward Lyncicam

Sword and Pike
10. John Gurney

Sword and Snaphance
11. David Young
12. Henry Wright
13. John Wright[281]

Sword only
14. Gebey Smyth

Pike only
15. John Davye[282]
16. John Southerne

Sword and Pike
17. John Cluny

Sword only
18. James Steed

Pike only
19. James Arbuch
20. John Wilson

Sword and Snaphance
21. John McKnocker

[f. 99]

Sword and Pike
22. John Bond

Sword only
23. John Ellot
24. Robert Allasiny
25. James Steward
26. Thomas Condall
27. William Knigsonne
28. John Patersonne

Sword and Snaphance
29. William Malanes

Sword and Pike
30. George Miller
31. Andrew Cayle

Sword and Snaphance
32. David Kayle

Sword only
33. John Baly

Sword and Snaphance
34. James Coopson

Sword only
35. David Nixon
36. William Armstrong

Sword and Pike
37. Symond Armstrong

Sword only
38. David Purris
39. Water Rayny

---

[274] See number 7.

[275] Son of number 37.

[276] Father of number 137.

[277] Tenant at will on the Strabane estate, 1622 (Treadwell (ed.), *Irish commission*, p. 567).

[278] Possibly father of Anthony Johnsey, who was killed, 1641(Examination of Edmond Knowles, 25 March 1653 [TCD MS 839, fol. 066r]).

[279] Killed with his wife, 1641 (ibid.).

[280] Father of John Randall, who was living at Carrickfergus in 1653 (ibid.) or the Robert Randall to whom Robert Dale referred his questioners (Examination of Robert Dale, 21 May 1653 [TCD MS 839, fols 082r–083v]).

[281] Possibly a tenant of Sir William Stewart (Inquisitions of Ulster, Tyrone, (49) Charles I).

[282] Possibly son of 'Watkin Davy', leaseholder on Alexander Richardson's estate, 1622 (Treadwell (ed.), *Irish commission*, p. 583).

Pike only

40. William Breslane

Sword only

41. Thomas Trumble

Sword and Pike

42. Robert Ellot

Snaphance only

43. Gawen Douglas

Sword and Pike

44. Thomas Jones

[f. 99v]

Pike only

45. Michaell McByrd

Sword only

46. Archbald Armstrong
47. Christopher Scot

No Arms

48. Thomas Irwin[283]
49. Morgan Edwards
50. John Scot
51. George Pollard
52. Patrick Robinson
53. Richard Douglas
54. John Gibson
55. Andrew Johnston
56. William Read
57. Robert Loweth
58. John Scot

[f. 100]

Tyrone
Barony de Clougher

James Lord Bishop of Clougher, his Tenants on his Churchlands being 3000 acres: his men and arms

Sword, Pike, and Gorget

1. Thomas Bull

Sword only

2. Ambrosse Smith

Pike with Complete Arms

3. Norris Morgan
4. John Hill

Sword and Musket

5. Edmond Palmer

Sword only

6. James Mungomery[284]

Sword and Pike

7. John Kenedy[285]

Sword only

8. Gilbert McKitterick

No Arms

9. William Dunwoody

Halberd only

10. Robert Richy[286]
11. David Thompson

Drummer

12. William Baly

Pike only

13. Richard Smythson

Halberd only

14. Ralph Carrington

Sword and Musket

15. John Mungomery[287]

Sword only

16. Robert Mungomery[288]
17. John Ritchy

Halberd only

18. Andrew Breaton

Sword only

19. James Sanderson
20. Richard Graham
21. Thomas Wright

Sword and Snaphance

22. John Duncan

Sword and Pike

23. John Nesbit

Sword and Snaphance

24. James Lockhart

[f. 100v]

Sword and Pike

25. John Gledston

Halberd only

26. Thomas Wilson[289]

Sword only

27. Patrick Holiday

Pike only

28. Cutbert Martin

Sword only

29. Thomas Martin

Sword and Musket

30. Gilbert McChower
31. William Hanna

Sword only

32. John McGilpyne

Sword and Snaphance

33. William Kee

Sword only

34. James Mountgomery
35. Steaphen Hunter

Sword and Musket

36. James MacKeane

Sword only

37. Adam Cakrell

Pike only

38. Robert Leaw

Sword and Pike

39. John Wright[290]

Snaphance only

40. John Wilson

---

283 Possibly a sub-tenant on Robert Lindsay's estate, 1622 (ibid. p. 582).
284 Sub-tenant on Sir William Cope's (later Richard Cope's) estate, 1622 (Treadwell (ed.), *Irish commission*, p. 594).
285 Stood surety for Fenton Parsons as High Sheriff of Tyrone, 1622 (ibid. p. 412).
286 Leasehold tenant on Sir George Hamilton's estate, 1622 (ibid. p. 569).
287 'Gentleman'; twenty-one year lease on 120 acres on Sir William Stewart's estate, 1622 (ibid. p. 578).
288 Twenty-one year lease on 180 acres on Sir William Stewart's estate, 1622 (ibid.); possibly stood surety for Sir John Dunbar as High Sheriff of Fermanagh, 1618 (ibid. p. 410).
289 Possibly Hugh Mitchell's agent at Ballyloughmagniffe [Fivemiletown], 1622 (ibid. p. 577); Sir Henry Titchbourne acquired the estate in 1628 (Inquisitions of Ulster, Tyrone, (6) Charles I).
290 Possibly a tenant of Sir William Stewart (Inquisitions of Ulster, Tyrone, (49) Charles I).

Sword only

41. Adam Browne

Sword and Pike

42. Alexander mcKetterick[291]

Sword only

43. Gilbert Ramsay
44. William Draydon[292]
45. William Draydon younger[293]
46. Thomas Beaty[294]

[f. 101]

No Arms

47. Christopher Saintson
48. Thomas Moore
49. Gilbert Mungomery elder[295]
50. Gilbert Mungomery younger
51. Adam Blacklock
52. John Smyth
53. David Hathorne
54. Mathew Duncan
55. Thomas Duncan
56. Alexander Barnes
57. John Mordogh
58. William Wright[296]
59. William Homes
60. John Burny
61. John Adamson
62. David Millikin
63. John McGilroy[297]
64. John Madrestonne

[f. 101v]

Barony de Omy

William Hammilton esquire, his churchlands being 1000 acres: his men and arms

No Arms

1. Robert Steele
2. John Steele
3. John Steward
4. Nenyon Steele
5. Archbell Cawtart
6. John Cawtart
7. Symond McBleere
8. Andrew Cawtart
9. Robert Armstrong
10. Hugh Irwin
11. Edward Mophet
12. Thomas Mophet
13. Mathew Mophet
14. Patrick Steward

[f. 102]

Tyrone
Barony de Dungannon

The Lord Viscount Chichester out of his town of Dungannon and the rest of his servitors lands being 2000 acres: his men and arms

Sword and Snaphance

1. Francis Jackson[298]

Sword only

2. James Ellot
3. Alexander Beard
4. Robert Horson[299]
5. John Ellot[300]

Sword and Musket

6. James Scot

Sword only

7. Thomas Fisher[301]
8. Anthony Howler
9. Christopher Wasson[302]
10. Robert Toby

No Arms

11. Jefferey Joanes
12. George Pikes[303]
13. John Godfrey
14. Morris Coop
15. William Broad
16. Gyles Smyth

[f. 102v]

17. Christopher Wilson
18. Thomas Gray
19. Danniell Barres[304]
20. John McVaugh
21. John Sepobaton[305]
22. John Short
23. Robert Sorlow
24. John Walton
25. George Smith[306]
26. Richard Smith
27. Humphrey Godfrey
28. John Beard
29. Art Ally
30. Hector Dromfeild
31. George Caxanell

[f. 103]

Tyrone
Barony de Dungannon

The Lord Viscount Powerscourt, his servitors lands 2120 acres: his men and arms as followeth

---

[291] McKetterick was originally a tenant of Sir William Stewart, from whom he had a nineteen year lease on sixty acres, 1622 (Treadwell (ed.), *Irish commission*, p. 578). McKetterick had only recently moved to the bishop's lands because the 1628 inquisition records him as still present on Stewart's estate (Inquisitions of Ulster, Tyrone, (49) Charles I).

[292] Father of number 45; cottager on Lord Ridgeway's (later Sir James Erskine's) estate, 1622 (Treadwell (ed.), Irish commission, p. 575).

[293] Son of number 44.

[294] Sub-tenant on Ballyloughmagniffe, 1622 (ibid. p. 577).

[295] Numbers 49 and 50 are father and son.

[296] Sub-tenant on Sir William Parsons's estate, 1622 (ibid. p. 580).

[297] Cottager on Lord Ridgeway's (later Sir James Erskine's) estate, 1622 (ibid. p. 575).

[298] Burgess, 1622 (ibid. p. 598).

[299] Possibly the father-in-law of Ann Orson [TCD MS 838, fols 124r–124v]; she escaped with her father to Glenavy, county Antrim in 1641; she and her husband, Richard, were living in Drogheda in 1653 (Examination of Thomas Dixon, 15 March 1653 [TCD MS 836, fols 120r–120v]).

[300] Freeman and resident, 1622 (Treadwell (ed.), *Irish commission*, p. 598), he may have been the father of John Elliott, who was aged 30 and living at Killultagh, county Antrim in 1653 (Examination of John Ellott, 3 May 1653 [TCD MS 838, fols 177r–178v]).

[301] Possibly son of Robert Fisher (?), freeman and resident, 1622 (Treadwell (ed.), *Irish commission*, p. 598).

[302] Possibly son of 'Walter Brussan', freeman and resident, 1622 (ibid.).

[303] Possibly 'George Pipps', freeman and resident, 1622 (ibid.).

[304] Freeman and resident, 1622 (ibid.).

[305] This is probably Semple; James Sompile was a freeman and resident, 1622 (ibid.).

[306] Burgess, 1622 (ibid.).

Sword only
1. Hamlet Moore Esquire[307]

Sword only
2. Edmond Blomer Esquire[308]
3. Thomas Smyth

Sword and Snaphance
4. John Olly
5. William Wilkes

Sword and Caliver
6. William Wilkinson[309]

Sword only
7. Thomas Barnes

Sword and Snaphance
8. Thomas Curtis[310]

Sword only
9. Richard Curtis[311]
10. William Baly

Sword and Snaphance
11. John Brome
12. George Smith

Sword only
13. Edmond Blomer[312]
14. Nicholas Blomer
15. Andrew Blomer

Sword and Snaphance
16. Edward Yarrow

Sword and Musket
17. Robert Alcock

Sword and Pike
18. Edward Avary

Snaphance only
19. William Bouth

Sword and Caliver
20. Woolfryd Trewman

Sword and Snaphance
21. John Trewman

[f. 103v]

22. Robert Trewman
23. Francis Trewman

Sword only
24. William Harris
25. Robert Ward
26. John Gore elder[313]
27. William Myles[314]

Sword and Snaphance
28. Thomas Stanby

Sword only
29. Thomas Harris
30. Francis Gore

Sword and Snaphance
31. Thomas Freeman

Sword only
32. John Bradley
33. George Reynolds

Sword and Caliver
34. Robert Lockwood

No Arms
35. Andrew Clarke
36. Thomas Curtis[315]
37. John Boulton[316]
38. John Gore[317]

39. Christopher Fausset[318]
40. John Gibbs[319]
41. William Husselton
42. Robert Walton
43. Thomas ap Thomas
44. Robert Gore
45. Nicholas Reynolds
46. Zachary Humfreyes

[f. 104]

Tyrone
Barony de Dungannon

The Lord Calfeild his servitors lands 1240 Acres: his men and arms as followeth

Sword only
1. Francis Caxorne
2. Edward Haward

Sword and Caliver
3. Abraham Knowles
4. Robert Owen

Sword only
5. Robert David
6. Robert Eales

Sword and Snaphance
7. John Howard
8. John Dory

Sword and Pike
9. Edward Pepper

Sword and Snaphance
10. William Steward
11. Robert Steward

Sword only
12. Robert Hamwell

---

307 Resident 1622 (Treadwell (ed.), *Irish commission*, p. 587).

308 Resident 1622 (ibid.).

309 Wilkinson, who appears to have been reputedly a healer, was resident in Benburb when he was killed, 1641 or 1642 (Examination of Thomas Dixon, 15 March 1653 [TCD MS 836, fols 120r–120v]).

310 This man and number 36 are father and son. Both were resident, 1622, the father being described as a husbandman and the son as one of the 'men unmarried' (Treadwell (ed.), *Irish commission*, p. 587).

311 One of the 'men unmarried', 1622 (ibid.); possibly a son of Thomas Curtis.

312 Numbers 13 to 15 were 'men unmarried' and resident, 1622 (ibid.).

313 Father of number 44.

314 Shoemaker; resident, 1622 (Treadwell (ed.), *Irish commission*, p. 587).

315 See number 8.

316 Husbandman; resident, 1622 (Treadwell (ed.), *Irish commission*, p. 587).

317 Son of number 26.

318 'Christopher Fossett, a glover, [was killed] in Benburb town at the house of one William O'Daylings', 1641 (Examination of Magdalen Guilly, 8 May 1653 [TCD MS 838, fols 141r–142v]).

319 John Gibbs was a tailor when he living in Benburb, 1622 (Treadwell (ed.), *Irish commission*, p. 587). He was still resident there, 1641 but he had moved to Glenavy, county Antrim, 1653. He was then aged 58 and described himself as a yeoman (Deposition of John Gibbs [TCD MS 839, fols 058r–059v]).

[f. 104v]

Tyrone
Barony de Dunganon

Sir Bawersley Newton knight, his servitors lands 2000 acres: his men and arms as followeth

Sword and Pike
1. Robert Homell
2. Robert Haborne[320]
3. John Symonton
4. John Moffet
5. Arthur Ellet

Pike only
6. Arch Ellot

Sword and Pike
7. Richard Johnston
8. James Graham
9. James Lawson
10. Andrew Welles[321]

Sword and Musket
11. John Sympson

Sword and Caliver
12. William Barber
13. John Wells

Caliver only
14. William Ellot
15. Gawen Ellot

Sword and Snaphance
16. Thomas Armstrong

Snaphance only
17. William Gibbins

Sword and Snaphance
18. John Gibbins

No Arms
19. John Dawson
20. James Kirkpatrick
21. Peter Watson
22. William Baety
23. James Baety
24. John Richy
25. James Richy
26. John Lenton
27. William Anderson
28. James Jackson
29. John Martin
30. James Miller

---

[320] Had a 200 acre leasehold on Sir Robert Newcomen's (later Sir William Stewart's) estate, 1622 (Treadwell (ed.), *Irish commission*, p. 570).
[321] Cottager on Sir Andrew Stewart's estate, 1622 (ibid. p. 584).

County Londonderry

[f. 105]

The Muster Roll of the County of Londonderry

The names of the men and arms of the City and Liberties of London Derry[1]

Sword only
1. Steaphen Akenhead

Sword and Musket
2. John Hodgkins

Sword only
3. Hugh Beylands
4. Thomas Drury

Sword and Pike
5. William Glass

Sword only
6. George Lyon
7. Thomas Plunket[2]
8. William Gardner[3]

Musket
9. William Gardner younger[4]

Sword and Pike
10. James Campion
11. James Hay
12. Robert Russell
13. John Evance

Sword and Musket
14. John Smyth[5]

Sword and Pike
15. Neal McKee

Sword only
16. William Sampson

Sword and Musket
17. John Sampson
18. Gilbert McLealand

[f. 105v]
19. William Davy

Halberd only
20. Thomas Skynner

Sword and Pike
21. John Bores

Sword and Musket
22. William Cooke

Sword only
23. Joseph Gray

Sword and Pike
24. Robert Blackwood
25. John Crookeshanks

Sword and Musket
26. Nynnyon Boyd[6]
27. John Gibson

Sword and Snaphance
28. John Rowe[7]

Sword and Pike
29. Gawin Henry

Sword and Musket
30. James Boyd

Sword only
31. John Gamble

Sword and Pike
32. John Rankin

Sword and Musket
33. John Smyth
34. Thomas Boyd
35. William Wylde
36. John McKey

Sword and Pike
37. John Cass
38. William Dunbar

Sword only
39. Alexander Alexanders

Sword and Pike
40. John Steward[8]
41. William Lucas

Sword and Snaphance
42. Robert Rutter

[f. 106]

Sword only
43. Robert Thomson[9]
44. Anthony Knowles[10]

Halberd only
45. John Chiles

Sword only
46. Thomas Nealson
47. Edward Goodyeer

Sword and Halberd
48. John Yorke

Sword only
49. Henry Keene

Sword and Pike
50. Alexander Kyng

---

[1] Robert Hunter had not transcribed the muster roll for the city and liberties: I have cross-checked my transcript against that of Billy McAfee (http://www.billmacafee.com/1630musterrolls/1630musterrollsderry.pdf, accessed 21 February 2011).

[2] Householder, 1609 (Hill, *Plantation*, p. 402).

[3] Numbers 8 and 9 are father and son.

[4] William Gardner accompanied Rev. Charles Anthony, vicar of Ballaghy 'to raise forces to beat back the enemy' and remained with Archibald Stewart in county Antrim, 1641 (Deposition of Charles Anthony, 12 June 1642 [TCD MS 839, fols 096r–097v]).

[5] Nine men are called Smyth: recurrences of forenames – James (numbers 309 and 474) and John (numbers 14, 33, 79, 139, and 474) – suggest that the men were drawn from at least three families.

[6] Eleven men are called Boyd: recurrences of forenames – John (numbers 152, 491, 553, and 583) and Thomas (numbers 34, 347, and 330) – suggest the men were drawn from at least three families.

[7] Mustered as a 'pikeman armed' Coleraine, 1622 (PRONI D2096/1/1B).

[8] The distribution of the five men named Stewart (numbers 40, 97, 110, 197, and 198) suggests they are drawn from at least two families.

[9] Seven men are named Thomson (numbers 43, 218, 493, 528, 531, 544, and 568): recurrences of forenames – Alexander (numbers 544 and 568) and Robert (numbers 43 and 528) – suggest that the men are drawn from at least two families.

[10] Mustered as a halberdier Coleraine, 1622 (PRONI D2096/1/1B).

Sword only
51. Francis Barnsly[11]

Sword and Pike
52. Robert Parkes
53. William Anderson
54. Thomas Kelly

Sword only
55. Abraham Hall

Sword and Pike
56. Thomas Cravan[12]

Sword only
57. Archbald Dunkan

Sword and Musket
58. Owen Hewes

Sword only
59. John Cooke
60. John Anderson
61. John Ledlat

Sword and Musket
62. Peter Sherly
63. John Bell
64. William Mommell
65. Robert Browne

Sword only
66. John Sturgon

Sword and Musket
67. David Young

Sword and Pike
68. John Baker[13]

Sword only
69. James Griffin

Sword and Musket
70. John Calwell

Sword only
71. Alexander Landsey

Sword and Pike
72. Gawin Cragg[14]

Sword only
73. James Moore
74. Gawen Crag younger
75. William Allan[15]
76. James Flemming
77. Alexander How
78. Gawen Robinson
79. John Smyth
80. Thomas Semple

Musket only
81. John Calveill
82. William Calveill

Sword only
83. George Barker
84. James Atkin[16]

Musket only
85. John Miller[17]

Sword only
86. Roger Hancock
87. John Cleid
88. Robert Young
89. William Allen
90. Hugh Allan
91. Patrick Allen
92. George Poke

[f. 107]

93. Henry Davison
94. George Long
95. John Bar
96. Arthur Rise
97. William Steward
98. William Gamble
99. Archbald McCracken
100. Patrick Sidbert
101. Archbell Readall
102. Patrick Hall
103. James Stynson
104. Peter Hayton
105. Robert Miller
106. Robert Graidy

107. Robert Watson
108. Walter Galbreath
109. William Heath

110. John Steward
111. John Casson
112. John Wilson
113. Gabraell Wilson
114. Thomas Browne
115. John Allen
116. Robert Makeir
117. William Hund

[f. 107v]

Sword and Pike
118. Robert Hunter

Sword only
119. Edward Bland
120. William Young
121. James Densye
122. John Donaldson

Sword and Pike
123. William Mathew

Sword only
124. John Newen

Sword and Pike
125. Gawen Smelly

Sword only
126. Alexander McGee
127. Andrew McKee
128. Peter Knox
129. William Greg
130. Andrew Greg

Pike only
131. Robert Fulton
132. William Forbes

Sword and Musket
133. John Price[18]

Sword only
134. Peter Halton
135. Symond Hare

136. Mungo Parden

Sword and Musket
137. John McKenny

---

[11] Mustered as a 'musket and caliver man' Coleraine, 1622 (ibid.).

[12] Thomas and Ralph Cravan (numbers 56 and 383) are brothers: their father, Ralph Cravan senior, did not muster.

[13] Alderman, 1613 (Hill, *Plantation*, p. 427); possibly stood surety for Robert Cartwright as High Sheriff of Donegal, 1617 (Treadwell (ed.), *Irish commission*, p. 409).

[14] Numbers 72 and 74 are father and son. Three other men (numbers 149, 392, and 514) are named Craig. One of them (number 514) is called Gavin and so these five men are drawn from at least two families.

[15] Eight men are named Allan or Allen: recurrences of forenames – John (numbers 115, 399, and 547) and William (numbers 75, 89, and 375) – suggest that the men were drawn from two or three families.

[16] Possibly the son of William Atkins, burgess, 1613 (Hill, *Plantation*, p. 427).

[17] Six men are named Miller: they are drawn from at least two families because three of them (numbers 105, 142, and 566) are called Robert.

[18] Possibly son of Robert Price, burgess, 1613 (Hill, *Plantation*, p. 427).

Sword and Snaphance
138. John Hare

Sword and Pike
139. John Smyth

Sword only
140. Richard Passy
141. Christopher Coutch

Musket and Bandoliers
142. Robert Miller

[f.108]

143. Alexander Pitts
144. John Sadler[19]
145. John Watson
146. John Jammison
147. Mathew Carbut[20]

Sword and Snaphance
148. John Harrison[21]

Sword only
149. John Crag

Sword and Snaphance
150. Richard Stockes

Sword and Musket
151. Andrew Boyd

Sword and Pike
152. John Boyd

Sword and Musket
153. William Flemming

Sword only
154. Edward Nichols

Sword and Musket
155. Jud Kendrick
156. Edward Black
157. John Bulles elder[22]
158. John Ballas younger

Sword only
159. Steaphen Godfrey

Sword and Pike
160. William Smyth

Sword only
161. John Snoeland
162. George Hunter

Sword and Musket
163. William Briers

Sword and Pike
164. Olfeard Olfeard[23]

Sword only
165. James McCaw

Sword and Musket
166. Thomas Passy

[f. 108v]

Sword and Musket
167. John Smith Taylor
168. Leonard Davis
169. Thomas Woldridg

Sword only
170. Andrew Crookeshanks

Sword and Musket
171. John Sterling

Sword only
172. John Hinkeson

Sword and Pike
173. Charles Burton
174. William Gibson
175. James Dunkin
176. Francis Dallaway

Sword and Musket
177. Thomas Dawson

Sword and Pike
178. Robert Coop
179. Robert Cammell[24]
180. Anthony Farmer
181. Anthony Mercer

Sword and Musket
182. John Hankes
183. John Fowell
184. Jesse Smith[25]
185. Sammuell Doway

Sword, Musket, and Bandoliers
186. Richard Bennet

Sword and Halberd
187. John Really

Sword and Pike
188. Captain Whittakers

Musket and Bandoliers
189. Steaphen Grane
190. Thomas Gamble

[f.109]

Sword and Halberd
191. Robert Barnes

Sword and Pike
192. Neest Johnston

Sword and Musket
193. David Rannick

Sword only
194. William Clements

Sword and Pike
195. Jeremiah Deacon[26]
196. John Lewis

Sword and Musket
197. James Steward

Sword, Snaphance, and Bandoliers
198. Thomas Steward

Musket only
199. Mathew Browne

Caliver only
200. James Morrison

Sword, Musket, and Bandoliers
201. Walter Hammilton

Musket and Bandoliers
202. Roger Lee

Sword and Halberd
203. Thomas Harcough
204. Gabraell Large

---

[19] Possibly son of Henry Sadler, alderman, 1613 (ibid.).

[20] Possibly son of 'Mrs Corbett', householder, 1609 (ibid. p. 402).

[21] Possibly son of Hannibal Harrison, householder, 1609 (ibid.).

[22] Numbers 157 and 158 are father and son.

[23] Olphert, Thomas, and Patrick Olphert (numbers 164, 384, and 439) are the sons of Wybrants Olphert.

[24] Cammell is a phonetic rendering of Campbell; given the use of Gaelic forenames, the family may have originated in the Western Isles [RJH].

[25] Alderman, 1613 (Hill, *Plantation*, p. 427).

[26] Jeremiah Deacon may be related to Edward Deacon, who mustered as a 'pikeman unarmed' at Coleraine, 1622 (PRONI D2096/1/1B).

Sword only
205. Thomas Poulteney

Sword, Musket, and Bandoliers
206. Richard Berry

Sword only
207. John Sadock

Sword, Musket, and Bandoliers
208. John Cambell

Sword and Halberd
209. John Mason

Sword and Pike
210. William Turnstall

Sword and Musket
211. Edward Blunket[27]

Sword only
212. Humfrey Baliff

Sword and Halberd
213. William Fixter

[f. 109v]

214. Thomas Brookes

Sword and Musket
215. George Cambell

Sword only
216. Walter Jacket

Sword and Musket
217. William Semple

Sword, Musket, and Bandoliers
218. John Thomson
219. John Welsh

Sword only
220. Straford Watts

Sword and Pike
221. Toby Smith[28]

Sword only
222. William Appleton

Sword and Pike
223. John Rogers

Sword and Musket
224. Hugh Carbut

Sword only
225. Nathaniell Huscock
226. William Burnes

Sword and Musket
227. David Hammelton

Sword only
228. John Gylles
229. John Prigeon
230. John Cawlian

Sword and Musket
231. Robert Shaw

Sword and Pike
232. James Hunter
233. Christopher Gifford

Sword and Musket
234. William Longe

Sword, Musket, and Bandoliers
235. Patrick Riche

Sword and Musket
236. Eskill Clegg[29]

[f. 110]

Sword and Halberd
237. Robert Goodwin elder[30]

Sword and Pike
238. Robert Goodwin younger[31]

Sword and Musket
239. John Sollers

Sword and Pike
240. Henry Wray[32]

Sword only
241. John McMath

Sword and Pike
242. Henry Osborne

Sword only
243. George Sear

Sword and Musket
244. Robert Lasson

Sword and Pike
245. Gabraell Sprouse
246. Robert Kill

Sword and Musket
247. Richard Cooke

Sword only
248. William Michell
249. John Broster

Sword and Pike
250. Thomas Craford

Sword only
251. Thomas Wright

Sword and Musket
252. Zachary Peares

Sword only
253. John Eling[33]
254. Edward Broster
255. James Perpoynt
256. Walter Petfeild
257. John Reede

Snaphance only
258. Nicholas Propter

Sword only
259. Peter Monserance

Sword, Musket, and Bandoliers
260. Alexander Lee

[f. 110v]

Sword only
261. John Petfeild
262. Richard Petfeild

Sword, Musket, and Bandoliers
263. Roger Waltham

Sword and Musket
264. John Hay

---

[27] Possibly Plunkett (http://www.billmacafee.com/1630musterrolls/1630musterrollsderry.pdf, accessed 21 February 2011).
[28] Merchant (Hunter, 'Fishmongers' Company', p. 242).
[29] Possibly a Cheshire name [RJH].
[30] Father of number 238; clerk and chamberlain of the city, 1613 (Hill, *Plantation*, p. 427).
[31] Son of number 237.
[32] Possibly son of John Wray, householder, 1609 and alderman in 1613 (Hill, *Plantation*, p. 427).
[33] This man may 'Captain Eeling' (or his son), householder, 1609 (ibid. p. 402).

Sword only

265. Robert Douglas
266. George Rosse[34]
267. David Bougham

Snaphance only

268. Muns Moote

Sword only

269. William Ross
270. George Cogheran
271. John Cogheran
272. John White
273. Georg Begg
274. David Fullerton
275. John Yate

Sword and Pike

276. John Jammison

Sword only

277. John Ross[35]
278. Thomas Moore
279. John Clark
280. Laughlyne Rosse

Sword and Pike

281. Ralph Williamson
282. Henry Freeman
283. Edward Freeman
284. James Hammilton
285. William House elder[36]

[f. 111]

Sword only

286. William House younger
287. Alexander Douglas
288. John Douglas
289. Allen Arbuck

Sword and Musket

290. John Mackee

Sword only

291. Alexander McKee
292. William Henry
293. John Cutbertson

Musket only

294. David Adam

Sword only

295. George Douglas

Sword and Musket

296. Symond Hare

Sword only

297. James Ramfrey
298. Robert Mont

Sword and Musket

299. William How

Sword only

300. John Lyne[37]
301. John Blackborne
302. William Wetherowe
303. John Hay
304. Lawrence Workman
305. John Ormoyle
306. William Doake
307. David Hendman
308. John Brampton
309. James Smyth
310. Archbald re
311. John Dickes
312. William Hammell

Sword and Snaphance

313. John Sleman

[f. 111v]

Sword only

314. Alexander Robertson[38]

Sword and Musket

315. John Robertson

Sword only

316. David Pock
317. John McMaister
318. Robert Irwin
319. Robert Irwin
320. Mathew Black
321. Thomas Haw

322. Robert Cogheran
323. William Sympson
324. William Leap
325. John Packer

Sword and Musket

326. Thomas Toller

Sword only

327. William Murray
328. John Harper
329. Alexander Farmer
330. Thomas Boyd
331. Alexander Robertson
332. Adam Smyth
333. John Wallas
334. John Wood[39]
335. James Mathewes
336. John Arthur[40]
337. John Speare
338. Patrick Ore
339. Thomas Carnell
340. Thomas Peoples

[f. 112]

341. John Wassen
342. Robert Blackwood
343. John Cowan
344. John Arthur
345. James Swoorley
346. William Karsson
347. Thomas Boyd
348. John McKenly
349. John Keemyn[41]
350. Robert Worke
351. James Keymyn
352. William Poke
353. Richard Home
354. John Langmoor
355. John Smely
356. Hugh Gait

No Arms

357. John Donnelson
358. David Hoggard
359. James Bogg
360. Phillip Lawsonn
361. Anthony Lawsonn

---

[34] Five men are named Ross; the different spellings suggest that George and Laughlin Ross (numbers 266 and 280) may be members of one family, and William and John Ross (numbers 269 and 277) members of another family; Robert Ross (number 555) is so distant from the others that he would appear to have been from a separate family.

[35] Ross paid a fine of 20s to Sir Henry Docwra before 1609 for a house and inherited 'a house in the High Street, [for which he paid] a hogshead of beans, and in money, 20s' (Hill, *Plantation*, p. 402).

[36] Numbers 285 and 286 are father and son.

[37] Possibly the son of William Lyne, sheriff, 1613 (Hill, *Plantation*, p. 427).

[38] Two of the four men named Robertson are called Alexander (numbers 314 and 331) and two are called John (numbers 315 and 513). Numbers 314 and 315 are probably related and numbers 331 and 513 are members of a different family or of two separate families.

[39] Held 'one quarter of land called Mullenan' in 1609 (Hill, *Plantation*, p. 401).

[40] The three men called John Arthur (numbers 336, 344, and 579) are from at least two separate families.

[41] Now spelled Cummings (http://www.billmacafee.com/1630musterrolls/1630musterrollsderry.pdf, accessed 21 February 2011).

362. David Young
363. Lewis Davis
364. William Well
365. John Moorehead
366. Hugh Wilde[42]
367. John Well
368. Griffin Hues

[f. 112v]

369. Robert Carlill
370. James Cowey
371. Randall Dowdall
372. John Parke
373. Edward Qualane
374. Robert Tash
375. William Allen
376. Thomas Peareman
377. John Peareman
378. Gilbert mcKenny
379. Alexander Glass
380. James Jennings[43]
381. Patrick Patterson
382. Gillmore McCorbe
383. Raph Cravan younger
384. Thomas Alpher
385. William Michell
386. Alexander Atkinson
387. John Guy
388. James Ascorne
389. Latham Skynner
390. Hugh Sempell
391. Arthur Robinson
392. James Crag
393. John McCowan
394. William McLentog
395. James Huston
396. James Allyson

[f. 113]

397. John Adam
398. Robert Cleid
399. John Allen
400. James Poke
401. William McCarroll
402. Mungo Syd
403. William McCordall
404. Henry Wood
405. William Wally
406. John Allyson
407. Alexander Hutchon
408. John Allison
409. George Warden
410. Thomas Leacklen
411. John Robert

412. Henry Johnyson
413. William Kelly
414. Thomas Mill
415. Michaell Scot
416. William Morison
417. William Neesbit
418. Andrew Haman
419. Alexander Neesbit
420. Mathew Laman
421. John Stabridg
422. Steaphen Rayman

[f. 113v]

423. William Carter
424. James Long
425. William Hogg
426. Alexander Richee
427. Thomas Rust
428. Sammuell Dawson
429. William Barr
430. Thomas Burgess
431. Edward Sherington
432. John Woldreadg
433. Richard Wastle
434. Tymothy Ruddock
435. William Whittackers
436. Archbald Smyth
437. Gilbert Parsy
438. John Harrington
439. Patrick Olfords
440. Peter Morgan
441. Richard Joanes
442. Christopher Sandyes
443. Robert Cole
444. Edward Baber
445. Andrew Hammilton
446. Henry Pridion
447. John Stratfield
448. John Wesscoat

[f. 114]

449. John Cole
450. Edward Russell
451. George Messongor
452. John Goldsmith
453. John Conningham
454. William Rogers
455. Thomas Booth
456. Richard Symonds
457. Andrew Neesbit
458. Hugh Michell
459. William Plunket
460. Hugh Coop
461. John Waden

462. John Pit
463. Henry Hatton
464. Zachary Halton
465. William Hatton
466. John Pinnock
467. Thomas Bramson
468. Thomas Knoles
469. Richard Hatton
470. Thomas Stayne
471. William Wallice
472. Mathew Williams
473. Gilbert McRatter
474. James Smyth
475. William Huston

[f. 114v]

476. Alexander Mill
477. John Watson
478. John Lowry[44]
479. William Logg
480. William Cutbertson
481. Robert Cutbertson
482. John Loughead
483. William Thompson
484. John Picke
485. Hugh Cummell
486. Alexander Cooke
487. James Adam
488. Luke Roger
489. John McNicholl
490. John Lyon
491. John Boyd
492. John Maxwell
493. Arch. Thomson
494. John Deal
495. Abraham Carnes
496. James Maxwell
497. David Hunter
498. Mathew Warren
499. William Culiland
500. Donnel McMurrin

[f. 115]

501. Shane Begard
502. John Fynly
503. Hugh Bylands
504. Walter McEldow
505. Steaphen Miller
506. Patrick Bog
507. Neese Cammell
508. John Norris
509. Gillaspy Cammell
510. James McGill
511. Griffin Knight

---

[42] Hugh Wild, a tailor, was killed at Ballinderry, county Antrim, 1641 or 1642 (Examinations of John Porter, 12 May 1653 and Anne Moore, 13 May 1653 [TCD MS 837, fols 161r–163v]).

[43] Possibly son of Richard Jenny, burgess, 1613 (Hill, *Plantation*, p. 427).

[44] This man (or number 586) may have been the son of Sandy Lowry, householder, 1609 (Hill, *Plantation*, p. 402).

512. Archbell Hurd
513. John Robertson
514. Gawen Crage
515. Andrew Hamman
516. William Stabridg
517. George Nesbit
518. Richard Griffin
519. Jefferey Ley
520. John Griffin
521. Patrick Griffin
522. James Browne
523. David Poke
524. Alford Hancely

[f. 115v]

525. Allen Craford
526. John Palmer
527. William Cross
528. Robert Thomson
529. John Hanford
530. John Cooke
531. Edward Thomson
532. Edward Walker[45]
533. Edward Chambers
534. John Jack
535. Isack Smith
536. Richard Burgess
537. Thomas Baker
538. Thomas Skerlet
539. John Woodrose
540. Francis Smith
541. Phillip Rankine
542. John Conningham
543. John Ben
544. Alexander Thomson
545. Henry Finsh[46]
546. William Conningham
547. John Allen
548. Thomas Freman

[f. 116]

549. John Cassrone
550. Alexander Thorton[47]
551. Hugh Fushy
552. John Archy
553. John Boyd
554. Thomas Lee

555. Robert Ross
556. Richard Bassy[48]
557. Robert Cogheran
558. James Cogheran
559. John Gay
560. Peter Crafoord
561. William Anderson
562. John Filsell
563. James Hayre
564. Robert Robinson
565. George Fynley
566. Robert Miller
567. Mungo Kill
568. Alexander Thomson
569. David Miller
570. Thomas Hill

[f. 116v]

571. Richard Scot
572. Adam McKanly
573. George Willson
574. James Osborne
575. Alexander mcCole
576. Robert Boyd
577. Donnell McCarkan
578. William Morison
579. John Arthur
580. Donnell Shane
581. David Hunter
582. John Deale
583. John Boyd
584. Luke Roger
585. William Logg
586. John Lowry
587. James Smith
588. Thomas Knobbs
589. John Pit
590. Hugh Coop
591. Thomas Booth
592. John Cole
593. Edward Baker
594. Peter Morgin
595. William Bar
596. Thomas Rust
597. Thomas Mill
598. John Robert
599. John Alson

[f. 117]

Londonderry

Sir Robert Macclelan knight, chief tenant to the company of [Haberdashers], being 3000 acres: the names of his men and arms as followeth

Sword and Pike
1. Gawen Kelsa

Sword and Snaphance
2. William Glendidge

Sword and Caliver
3. John Patterson

Sword and Snaphance
4. George Glendidge

Sword and Caliver
5. William mcCleland
6. John George
7. John Douglas
8. John Martin
9. John Marson

Sword and Snaphance
10. Thomas Moore [49]
11. William Moore
12. John McCronill

Sword and Pike
13. William Glenn
14. Thomas Patten[50]
15. Patrick McQuhitaugh[51]
16. John Boyd
17. William Boyd younger[52]
18. John Gleene

Sword and Snaphance
19. Thomas Lenton

Sword, Caliver, and Bandoliers
20. Robert Lenton

---

[45] Son of Robert Walker, householder, 1609 (Hill, *Plantation*, p. 402).

[46] Henry Finch – a merchant and a freeholder on the Fishmongers' estate – organised one of the companies to defend Derry in 1642 (Hunter, 'Fishmongers' Company', pp 243, 252).

[47] Possibly the son of Thomas Thornton, householder, 1609 (Hill, *Plantation*, p. 402).

[48] The surname is also spelled Passy.

[49] Five men are called Moore: numbers 10 and 11 are possibly father and son, whilst numbers 33, 102, and 127 may be related or from separate families.

[50] Thomas Patten junior is number 84 on Sir Thomas Phillips's estate.

[51] The Scots form of McQuitty is to be noted [RJH].

[52] William Boyd (number 17) and, possibly, John Boyd (number 16) are sons of William Boyd of Coleraine, where he is number 303. John Boyd (number 86 below) may also be a member of the family.

Sword and Pike
21. William Frasser
22. Adam McCleland

Sword and Musket
23. James Adamson

[f.117v]

Sword and Snaphance
24. John Black

Sword and Pike
25. Andrew Hany
26. Symond Barnes

Sword and Caliver
27. Thomas McCracane

Sword and Pike
28. John Hany
29. James Kersone
30. James Scot
31. Andrew mcMichane

Sword and Snaphance
32. William Montieth

Sword and Pike
33. John Moore

Sword and Caliver
34. Roger McCleland
35. Dono McLeland

Sword and Pike
36. Dono Teich

Sword and Caliver
37. John Panie

Sword and Pike
38. Thomas mcMyne

Sword and Caliver
39. Roger McNaght

Sword and Pike
40. Patrick Foster

Sword and Caliver
41. John Michaell

Sword and Pike
42. John Huston
43. John Irwin

Sword and Caliver
44. James Kirkpatrick

Sword and Snaphance
45. William Bell
46. George Murray

Sword and Pike
47. Andrew Logan

Sword and Caliver
48. Thomas Steavenson

Sword and Pike
49. John Corsby
50. John Lawson[53]

[f. 118]

Sword and Snaphance
51. Thomas Lawson

Sword and Caliver
52. John Gleen
53. Robert Anderson

Sword and Pike
54. John Barde

Sword and Caliver
55. John Anderson
56. James Pyper

Sword and Pike
57. Thomas Mungomery
58. Patrick Bradfoote
59. Roger Scahane
60. John Guy

Sword and Caliver
61. Thomas McCleland

Sword and Pike
62. Robert Hunter

Sword and Caliver
63. John McClarty

Sword and Pike
64. James McKinshry

Sword and Snaphance
65. John McKinshry

Sword and Halberd
66. Gilbert McGarny

Sword and Pike
67. Alexander McKeene
68. John Hare
69. William Danes

Sword and Caliver
70. Edward Payne
71. Hugh Biggard

Sword and Musket
72. Patrick Smith

Sword and Pike
73. John Payne

Sword and Snaphance
74. Robert Maxwell

Sword and Caliver
75. Robert Pepper

Sword and Pike
76. Alexander Pepper

[f. 118v]

Pike only
77. William Muriall

Sword and Pike
78. Thomas Nicholson

Sword and Snaphance
79. William Thomson

Sword and Pike
80. James McWilliam
81. Barnard Deanes

Sword and Snaphance
82. Alexander Patton

Sword and Pike
83. John McCleland

Sword and Snaphance
84. James Hendry

Sword and Pike
85. Thomas Mason

Sword and Snaphance
86. John Boyd

Sword and Pike
87. Robert Baird

---

[53] John and Thomas Lawson (numbers 50 and 51) are probably father and son, while John Lawson (number 118) and Thomas Lawson (number 126) are from another family or are members of separate families.

Sword and Snaphance

88. John Cocherone[54]

Sword and Pike

89. Harbert Killpatrick

Sword and Snaphance

90. Robert Adamson

Sword and Pike

91. William Bayrd

Sword and Snaphance

92. Alexander White

Sword and Caliver

93. Hugh Tany[55]

Sword and Musket

94. John Watt

Sword and Caliver

95. James March

Sword and Pike

96. Henry Kelso[56]
97. Mathew Small

No Arms

98. John Dinsmoore
99. John Liston
100. Symon Frasch
101. John Oliver[57]
102. David Moore

[f. 119]

103. William Ross
104. William Christon
105. Robert Carnes
106. William Sloane
107. John Oswall[58]
108. Andrew Bell
109. William Lastly
110. Gawen Nicholson
111. Robert Cocherah
112. Thomas Calwell
113. John McCleland
114. Robert McCleland
115. John Stones
116. John McQueston
117. Alexander mcQueston

118. John Lawson
119. Andrew Logan
120. Robert Pepper
121. John Payne
122. John Hare
123. John Guy
124. John Bard
125. John Glene
126. Thomas Lawson
127. John Moore

[f. 119v]

Londonderry

Sir Robert McCleland knight, chief tenant of the Clothworkers proportion, being 3000 acres: his men and arms as followeth

Sword only

1. Gawen Car

Pike only

2. John McCleland

Sword only

3. James Michell
4. Robert Robinson

Pike only

5. David Cupar

Sword and Pike

6. James Browne
7. Donnell Marshall

Pike only

8. Alexander Frow

Sword only

9. Arthur Lang
10. Robert Little
11. Thomas Little
12. Hugh Little

Sword and Pike

13. James Piggin

Sword only

14. Robert Garvin
15. William Cracton

16. Thomas Gilmoore
17. Andrew Gilmoore
18. James Gilmoore
19. Andrew Ross
20. John Cabeine

Sword and Pike

21. David Ramsey
22. Alexander Sampson

[f. 120]

Sword only

23. Andrew Thomson
24. John Hunter
25. John Rydley
26. Robert Edward
27. George Lang
28. Robert Delap
29. Adam Fargison

Sword and Pike

30. John Irwin

Sword only

31. William Binning[59]
32. Robert Style
33. Andrew Little
34. John Cleary
35. Thomas Patrick

Sword and Musket

36. John Allen

Sword and Pike

37. John Graham

Sword only

38. William Farker
39. William Gate
40. John Gilliner
41. John Laughry
42. John Lang
43. James Lang
44. David Hunter
45. Robert McKin
46. James Little
47. George Bell
48. Robert Beard

---

54 See Clothworkers, number 50.

55 For Hugh Tany junior, see Antrim, Dunluce, number 397.

56 The earl of Antrim owed Henry Kelso £100 0s 0d, 1638 (Hill, *MacDonnells*, p. 477).

57 Originally from Kirkudbright (John Oliver, *Aspects of Ulster* (Antrim, 1994), pp 42–3).

58 Oswald [RJH].

59 The Northern Ireland telephone directory shows one Binnings in Newtownards; the name Binnie occurs eight times in the province, two of them in Portballintrae [note by RJH].

[f. 120v]

49. William Bog
50. John Knogheran younger[60]
51. William Beaty
52. Robert Hall

Sword and Pike

53. William White
54. Wylliam Wyne[61]

No Arms

55. Alexander Kinnitt
56. James Miller
57. John Cabbin
58. John Johnston
59. Thomas Johnston
60. William Calson
61. Alexander Piggin
62. John McCleland
63. John McMyn
64. Robert Maxwell
65. Peter Gasse

127/192 Men

[f. 121]

Londonderry

Mr Harrington, undertaker of 3000 acres: his men and arms as followeth

Sword and Pike

1. Captain Kilner

Sword and Musket

2. Robert Downes

Sword and Pike

3. Henry Warner

Sword and Caliver

4. Bartholomew Dawson

Sword and Pike

5. Henry Coop elder[62]

Sword and Caliver

6. Henry Coop younger

Sword, Pike, and Corselet

7. Thomas Darling
8. William Holden
9. James Carmichaell

Sword and Halberd

10. Richard Cooke

Sword and Caliver

11. Thomas Raying

Sword, Pike, and Corselet

12. Richard Wakey

Sword and Caliver

13. Edward Swan
14. John Wright[63]

Sword and Snaphance

15. John Wright younger
16. James Payne

Sword and Caliver

17. Robert Payne

Sword, Pike, and Gorget

18. Thomas Reynolds

Sword and Pike

19. John Alcock[64]

Sword and Snaphance

20. Jeremy Ross
21. Anthony Ross

[f. 121v]

22. John McMullan
23. Thomas Kelson

Sword and Caliver

24. John Anderson
25. James Anderson[65]

Sword and Snaphance

26. Michaell Robinson
27. William Clyfton

Sword, Pike, and Corselet

28. Andrew McWilly[66]

Sword, Pike, and Gorget

29. Done McQuilly

Sword and Snaphance

30. John Tarrant

Sword and Caliver

31. Andrew McFarlagh
32. Gawin Ackin[67]
33. James Duning

Sword and Snaphance

34. John Smyth

Sword and Pike

35. Richard Griffin

Sword and Snaphance

36. Thomas Sempell
37. Adam Gate
38. Alexander Huen
39. Gawen Robinson
40. James Browne

Sword and Caliver

41. Thomas Trotter

Sword and Snaphance

42. John Lewis
43. Thomas King[68]
44. John Harper

[f. 122]

No Arms

45. Clemment Munnings
46. Israell Ruddock[69]

---

60 Probably Cochrane (http://www.billmacafee.com/1630musterrolls/1630musterrollsderry.pdf, accessed 21 February 2011); John Cochrane senior may be number 88 on the Haberdashers (Sir Robert McClelland) estate: other possibilities are Derry, number 271 and Fishmongers (Mr Freeman junior), number 33.

61 Wynne is a Welsh name, but Graham writes W as V and so this could be Vyne [RJH].

62 Numbers 5 and 6 are father and son.

63 Numbers 14 and 15 are father and son.

64 Possibly son of Christopher Alcock, householder in Derry, 1609 (Hill, *Plantation*, p. 402) or of Nicholas Alcock, agent for the Clothworkers, 1615 (ibid. p. 441).

65 Resident at Aghadowey, 1641 (Examinations of Martin Taaffe, 30 March 1653 [TCD MS 838, f. 041v] and Nicholas Fulton, 22 March 1653 [ibid. fols 082v–083r])

66 Numbers 28, 29, and 55 are probably related. McWilly and McQuilly may be versions of McQuillan, and the adoption of English forenames suggests that the family had become English-speaking [RJH].

67 'Presumably Gavin nowadays' [RJH].

68 Resident at Vinterstown [Bellaghy], 1641 (Examination of John Turner, 7 March 1653 [TCD MS 838, fols 065v–066r]).

69 The use of Israel and Elias (number 52 below) as Christian names is to be noted [RJH].

47. James Houston[70]
48. James Houston younger
49. William McKillington
50. James Carmighell
51. John Fyndon
52. Elias Smyth
53. Martin Davis
54. William Moore
55. John McQuilly
56. Robert Allyson
57. William Duning

[f. 122v]

Mr Freman the elder [sic], undertaker of 3000 acres: his men appeared with the City and Liberties of London Derry

[f. 123]

London Derry

Mr Freman the younger, chief tenant of the Company of Fishmongers, being 3000 acres[71]

Sword and Snaphance
1. Robert Hughston

Sword, Pike, and Corselet
2. John Davison

Sword and Caliver
3. George Asky[72]
4. John Homes

Sword, Pike, and Headpiece
5. John Moore

Sword, Pike, and Corselet
6. John Thomson
7. Thomas Smyle

Sword and Snaphance
8. David Delap
9. James Clohorone[73]
10. John Griffin
11. Patrick Griffin
12. James Cloheron younger
13. George Beggy

14. David Fullerton
15. John Gate

Sword, Pike, and Corselet
16. David Giffeinge

Sword and Snaphance
17. William Phillicote

Sword, Pike, and Corselet
18. Robert Moore

Sword and Snaphance
19. Robert Clogheron
20. John White

[f. 123v]

No Arms
21. John Hughstone
22. Peter Kishall
23. John Miller
24. George Willson
25. George Bassly
26. John Taylor
27. Ralph Burrowes
28. Thomas Throne
29. Neal McKenly
30. Robert McKenly
31. John McKenly
32. Georg Clogheron
33. John Clogherone
34. James Flemming
35. John McGawen
36. William McKee
37. Archbald Ruddall
38. John Wright
39. Joseph West
40. Richard Bassly
41. Steaphen Heard
42. John Gate

[f. 123]

The Lady Cooke, undertaker of 3000 Acres

[f. 124v]

Mr Wall, chief tenant to the Merchant Taylors, undertakers of 3000 Acres: his men and arms

Sword and Pike
1. John Grenagh

Sword, Caliver, and Bandoliers
2. Francis Gill

Sword and Musket
3. George Bick
4. Robert Dobby

Musket only
5. Robert Hopene

Sword and Musket
6. William mcTeere
7. James Hammelton
8. Robert Hammelton
9. Patrick McTeere

Musket only
10. George Kirkpatrick
11. Hugh Farnald

Pike only
12. William Coop

Sword and Pike
13. William Stanly[74]

Pike only
14. Donnell McClaydd

Sword and Snaphance
15. Francis Bacraby

Musket only
16. John Smith

Sword and Caliver
17. Nicholas Gill

Musket only
18. Rowland Creighton

Sword and Pike
19. Robert Blare
20. James Knocks

Pike only
21. Henry Reny

---

[70] Numbers 47 and 48 are father and son.

[71] This part of the muster roll was compiled after January 1631, when Christopher Freeman became the lessor of the company's estate (Hunter, 'Fishmongers' Company', p. 240).

[72] Askew was associated with the Leathersellers Company, which had been one of the minor companies that were partners of the Fishmongers (ibid. p. 234); resident Ballykelly, 1623 (ibid. p. 224).

[73] Five men are named Cochrane: the distribution and spelling of the surname suggests that 9 and 12 (father and son) were one family and 19, 32 and 33 were another family.

[74] Possibly related to Christopher Stanley, who mustered as a 'pikeman unarmed' at Coleraine, 1622 (PRONI D2096/1/1B).

[f. 125]

Sword and Snaphance
22. James Blare

Sword and Musket
23. Francis Rich

Sword and Caliver
24. John Clemmell

Sword and Snaphance
25. Mathew Hughston

Sword and Musket
26. John Hughston

Sword and Snaphance
27. James Hughston

Sword and Musket
28. Donnagh McRassey

Sword and Pike
29. William Cooke
30. Andrew Read

Sword and Halberd
31. James Speare

Sword and Snaphance
32. Gylaspick Mathey
33. Edward Morton

Musket only
34. William Morton

Sword and Musket
35. George Mynnes
36. Hugh Blare

Sword and Snaphance
37. James Legat

Sword and Musket
38. John Delap

No Arms
39. James Suner[75]
40. Edward Sanderson

41. John Smyth
42. Robert Small
43. Edward Horsfeild
44. Edmund Howard
45. Francis Howard
46. Thomas Howard
47. James Marshall
48. Griffin Howard[76]

[f. 125v]

Londonderry

Mr Canning, chief tenant to the Ironmongers proportion, being 3000 Acres

Sword and Pike
1. Paul Canning[77]
2. Richard Canning
3. William Canning

Sword and Musket
4. Evance Morrisse

Sword only
5. Owen McGilandryes

Sword, Musket, and Bandoliers
6. John McMullan

Sword and Pike
7. John Vincent

Sword and Musket
8. Thomas Moore[78]

Sword and Pike
9. Thomas Stabin
10. Cuthbert Bar
11. Lancelot McKinly
12. Bryan McClenan
13. James Hymphill
14. John McGill

Sword and Musket
15. Elias Church

Sword and Pike
16. Robert Hemphill
17. Thomas Moore younger[79]

Pike only
18. John Henry

Sword and Halberd
19. Thomas Rock

Sword and Pike
20. John Bennet
21. Alexander Gould

Sword and Musket
22. Thomas Neiller

Sword and Pike
23. Allen Smith

[f. 126]

Musket and Bandoliers
24. Andrew Gray

Sword and Musket
25. Owen McGillbredy

Sword only
26. Adam Reed[80]

Sword and Pike
27. William Copeland

Pike only
28. William Chambers

Sword and Pike
29. Thomas Moore elder[81]

Pike only
30. John Ross
31. David Robb

Halberd only
32. Lawrence Wells

Sword, Caliver, and Bandoliers
33. Guy Chamberlyn[82]
34. Alexander Chamberlyn

---

75 Possibly Simer [RJH].
76 Mustered as a 'musket and caliver man' at Coleraine, 1622 (ibid.).
77 Paul, Richard, and William Canning (numbers 1 to 3) are the sons of George Canning (number 113). William, the eldest son, was killed at Garvagh, 1641 (Deposition of Robert Waringe, 12 August 1642 [TCD MS 839, fols 108r–111v]) and Paul Canning became the Company's tenant in 1658 (www.billmacafee.com/estates/landlords/notescompaniesestates.htm, accessed 21 February 2011).
78 Son of Henry Moore (Lady McClelland's churchlands, number 20).
79 Son of number 29.
80 Four men are named Reed (numbers 26, 42, 74, and 75): the distribution of the name in this list suggests that they were drawn from two or three families.
81 Father of number 17.
82 Numbers 33, 34, and 49 are probably related and may be relatives of Abraham Chamberlain of London, who held the fisheries on the Bann [RJH].

Musket only

35. Alexander McAlester[83]

Pike only

36. Cullam McFetriss

Sword only

37. Donnell mcFetriss
    Recusant

Sword only

38. Marto mcMurroghy
    Recusant

Pike only

39. Donnell mcMurroghy
    Recusant

Sword and Musket

40. Moyle Collom

Sword only

41. William Collome

Sword and Pike

42. George Reed
43. John Tome elder[84]

Sword only

44. John Tome younger

Sword and Pike

45. James Gibson

Musket only

46. David Blacker

Pike only

47. John Henderson

Musket only

48. Robert Longmore[85]

Sword, Caliver, and Bandoliers

49. William Chamberlin[86]

[f. 126v]

Sword and Musket

50. Andrew Hunter

Sword only

51. Martin Thomson

Sword and Pike

52. George Asby[87]
53. David Patterson
54. William Spire[88]
55. Adam Spire elder
56. John Keemyng
57. Allen Gout
58. James Spyre elder
59. John Smyth
60. John Spyre
61. Paul Gaut[89]

Sword and Musket

62. Hugh Spyre

Sword and Pike

63. Thomas Gate

Sword and Musket

64. John Thomson
65. Robert Wilson

Sword only

66. Adam Spyre younger[90]

Sword and Pike

67. John Hughston
68. John Smale

Sword and Musket

69. Mungo Smith

Sword and Pike

70. Hugh Willson
71. John McKee

Sword and Musket

72. Lawrence Spire elder[91]

Sword and Pike

73. Thomas Murryne
74. John Reed

[f. 127]

Sword, Caliver, and Bandoliers

75. Robert Reed

Sword and Pike

76. John Anderson
77. Robert Ward
78. William Porter

Sword and Musket

79. William Vincent

Sword and Pike

80. Edward Web

Musket only

81. Robert Epfull[92]

Sword and Musket

82. William Wilk

Sword and Pike

83. Thomas Gibson
84. Robert Smyth

Sword and Musket

85. Nathaniell Carnington
86. Patrick McReady

Sword and Pike

87. Richard Dixon

Musket only

88. Thomas Lull

Sword only

89. James Rod

Sword and Pike

90. Patrick mcGilbredy   Recusant
91. Thomas Hambridg

---

83 One of the perpetrators of the killing of the Irish on Island Magee, 8 January 1642 (Examinations of Bryan McGee, 14 and 27 May 1653 [TCD MS 838, fols 198r–201v] and Margaret Lowreye, 30 April 1653 [ibid. fols 234r–234v]).

84 Numbers 43 and 44 are father and son.

85 William Boyd of Dunluce left Longmore 'one thousand marks Scottish money', 9 December 1624 (Hill, *MacDonnells*, p. 393).

86 See number 33 above.

87 The surname may be Espie [RJH].

88 The nine men named Spyre are drawn from at least three separate families. Numbers 54, 55, and 66 are one family; numbers 58, 117, and possibly 119 are a second family; number 72 is the head of a third family. Numbers 60 and 62 may be members of these families or of a fourth one.

89 Paul Gault was resident at Aghadowey in 1641and fled with the other inhabitants of the village to Coleraine after the British defeat at Garvagh. He was killed in August 1642 when he returned with others to Aghadowey 'to see what was become of their houses and goods' (Examination of Martin Taaffe, 30 March 1653 [TCD MS 838, f. 041v]) and of Nicholas Fulton, 22 March 1653 [ibid. fols 082v–083r].

90 'Adam Speire' was killed at Clogh, county Antrim, January 1642 (Examination of Margarett Dunbar, 8 May 1653 [ibid. fols 237r–237v]).

91 Lawrence Spire junior does not appear in the muster roll.

92 Son of John Epfull, number 121.

Sword and Musket
92. Richard Tyming

Pike only
93. Adam Armestron

Sword only
94. Henry Wings

Pike only
95. Edward Itson

Sword and Musket
96. William Cross elder[93]

Musket only
97. George Cross
98. Thomas Morgan

Halberd only
99. Francis Mason

Sword and Pike
100. Donnell Port

Pike only
101. Robert Eaton

[f. 127v]

Sword and Pike
102. Charles Harrison
103. William Harrison

Pike only
104. Michaell Liggat
105. James Garven

Sword and Pike
106. Sammuell Bramson[94]

Pike only
107. Thomas Hanmor

Sword and Musket
108. William McGill

Pike only
109. Beniamin Tiplady
110. Turlo O Kat

Musket only
111. Turlo Makaspy[95]

Pike only
112. Henry Kinington

No Arms
113. George Canning[96]
114. Robert Mungomery
115. William Wytty
116. Henry Degarnock
117. James Spire younger
118. Barnaby Kerne
119. Robert Spire
120. William Gambell
121. John Epfall[97]
122. John Gyles
123. William Cross[98]

[f. 128]

Londonderry

Mr Church, chief tenant to the proportion of Mercers, being 3000 acres: his men and arms

Sword and Pike
1. Thomas Church[99]
2. Valentyne Hartup
3. Lewis Boyer

Ensign
4. George Church[100]

Sword and Pike
5. Richard Miller

Drum
6. Richard Miller

Sword, Pike, and Corselet
7. Edward Cary

Sword and Pike
8. William Stotesbury[101]

Sword and Caliver
9. Thomas Church younger[102]

Sword and Musket
10. Humfrey Joanes
11. Thomas Hudson

Sword and Caliver
12. Richard Goodwin

Pike complete
13. Thomas Brambe

Sword and Caliver
14. William Gesson

Pike complete
15. John Wilson
16. Richard Michell

Sword and Halberd
17. Richard Drayton

Pikes Complete
18. Gilbert Brop
19. Alexander Wray[103]

Sword and Musket
20. Sammuell Darwin

Sword and Caliver
21. John Stebrank

Sword and Musket
22. John North

---

93 Number 96 is the father of numbers 97 and 123.
94 Mustered at Coleraine as a 'musket and caliver man', 1622 (PRONI D2096/1/1B).
95 The surname could be Espie [RJH].
96 This is the chief tenant: his sons are numbers 1 to 3 [RJH].
97 Father of Robert Apfull (number 81 above); John Apfull was resident at Aghadowey; he died between 25 July, when he wrote his will, and 22 November 1631, when the will was proved (NAI, BET1/1, p. 108) [RJH].
98 Son of number 96 and brother of number 97.
99 Thomas Church is the Mercers' tenant and the father of numbers 4 and 9; the tenants are well-organised, with an ensign and a drummer [RJH]. Church raised two companies of foot to defend Coleraine, December 1641 (Deposition of Charles Anthony, 12 June 1642 [TCD MS 839, fols 096r–097v]).
100 Commanded one of the infantry companies his father (number 1) raised for the defence of Coleraine, December 1641 (ibid.).
101 Stotesbury had moved to Glenavy, county Antrim before 1641: he was reportedly in the company of Michael Dunne, one of the rebel leaders, when the rising began (Examination of Thomas Harpur, 26 May 1653 [TCD MS 838, fols 092r–092v]) and was described as 'a papist' (Examination of Keane Hara, 31 May 1653 [ibid. fols 123r–123v]). Dunne, however, insisted that he and Stotesbury were prisoners (Declaration of Michaell Doyne, undated [ibid. fols 108r–112v]).
102 Son of number 1.
103 Possibly son of John Wray, householder, Derry, 1609 (Hill, *Plantation*, p. 402) and alderman of the city, 1613 (ibid. p. 427).

Sword and Pike
23.   Richard Avery elder[104]

[f. 128v]

Snaphance only
24.   Richard Avery younger

Sword and Caliver
25.   Thomas Corbet   Tucker[105]

Pike complete
26.   William Goodman elder[106]
27.   Valentyne Bradfoord

Sword and Caliver
28.   Thomas Cox

Sword, Musket, and Bandoliers
29.   James Taylor

Pike only
30.   John McGoy

Pike complete
31.   George Camell

Musket only
32.   Thomas Hitchins

Pike complete
33.   Ralph Bartely

Sword and Musket
34.   Thomas Rowly

Pike complete
35.   John Didicot

Sword and Caliver
36.   Denis Weredy

Pike complete
37.   Thomas Short

Sword and Caliver
38.   John Greene
39.   Thomas McFarlin

Caliver only
40.   William Smart
41.   Thomas Gyles elder[107]

Sword and Caliver
42.   John Stanup
43.   William Doggin
44.   Leonard Vincent

Sword and Musket
45.   John Clenton

Sword and Caliver
46.   William Mathers

Sword and Musket
47.   John Michell

[f. 129]

Sword and Caliver
48.   Thomas Barnes

Sword and Snaphance
49.   Thomas Bartrym

Sword and Pike
50.   William Hingson

Sword and Caliver
51.   Robert Ellis
52.   Brian Strabridg
53.   William Goodman younger[108]
54.   Henry Cock

Sword and Snaphance
55.   John Blanchet

Pike complete
56.   Alexander Camell
57.   Robert Camell

Sword and Musket
58.   Henry Birch

Pike complete
59.   John Chambers

Sword and Caliver
60.   Hugh Ocane

Sword and Pike
61.   John Bene

Sword and Caliver
62.   William Buckle
63.   Thomas Smith

Sword and Musket
64.   Arthur Irwin

Sword and Caliver
65.   John Medley
66.   Robert Wilkinson
67.   John Brocter
68.   Thomas Gyles younger[109]

Sword and Musket
69.   James Parson

Sword and Snaphance
70.   Murto Fyn

Sword and Caliver
71.   John Hitchins
72.   Edward Norton

[f. 129v]

73.   Thomas Turner

Sword and Halberd
74.   Thomas Grahams

Sword and Caliver
75.   William Graham
76.   Andrew Gordan
77.   Richard Collins
78.   Edward Ellis
79.   George Moore
80.   Richard Dragford
81.   Francis Clynton[110]
82.   William Hitchins
83.   Thomas Steward
84.   John Clark
85.   Edward Westen
86.   Rowland Allen
87.   John McConnall

---

[104] Numbers 23 and 24 are father and son.
[105] The reference to Corbet's occupation suggests that managing the tuck mill was an important function in the community [RJH].
[106] Father of number 53.
[107] Father of number 68.
[108] Son of number 26.
[109] Son of number 41.
[110] John Vaughan claimed to have recruited 'one Clinton and nine Englishmen more' to settle near Castlefinn, county Donegal, 1613 (Historical Manuscripts Commission, *Report on the Hasting Manuscripts*, 4, pp 171–2; R.J. Hunter, 'Plantation in Donegal', in William Nolan, Liam Ronayne, and Mairead Dunlevy (eds), *Donegal: history and society* (Dublin, 1995), p. 302); Clinton died at Kilrea, 1636 [RJH].

[f. 130]

Londonderry
Barony de Loughinisoline

Henry Conway esquire,[111] chief tenant to the Vintners proportion, being 3000 acres: his men and arms as followeth

Sword only
1. Bernard Laxton

Sword and Pike
2. Richard Glover[112]

Sword only
3. Robert Steavenson[113]
4. Thomas Lewen
5. Ambross Lewen
6. Richard Web
7. Walter Duning

Sword and Pike
8. Richard Walker
9. Nicholas Heath

Sword only
10. Thomas Sparrowes

Pike only
11. Roger Anderson

Sword only
12. Anthony Steaphenson

Drummer
13. John McClene

Sword, Caliver, and Bandoliers
14. John Breir

Sword only
15. Richard Clark

Sword and Caliver
16. Ralph Mathews

Sword and Snaphance
17. Richard Powell

Sword and Pike
18. Thomas Maxwell[114]

Pike and Caliver
19. Alexander Steward[115]

Sword only
20. Gabraell Lynsy

Sword and Pike
21. Cuthbert Nother

Caliver only
22. Robert Steavenson younger

Sword and Snaphance
23. John Egleson

[f. 130v]
24. Thomas Loudy

Sword only
25. Robert Lagan

Sword and Pike
26. John Clay

Sword and Snaphance
27. Thomas Clay

Sword and Pike
28. Walter Spike

Sword only
29. Thomas Holiwell
30. Mortah McHale
31. Robert Frow[116]
32. John Bone
33. John Turner[117]
34. Georg Witty
35. Richard Jennings[118]

Sword and Pike
36. Hugh Vaughan[119]

Sword and Snaphance
37. John Watters[120]

Sword only
38. Edmond Waters
39. James Mouse
40. Evan Price
41. Sammuell Snoden

Sword and Musket
42. John Borrowes

Sword and Snaphance
43. Henry Bretty

Sword only
44. William Dephet

Pike only
45. William Parker

Sword only
46. Robert Joanes[121]

Sword and Caliver
47. John Roberts

[f. 131]
48. Hugh Reede
49. Edward Dabsyre

Sword and Pike
50. Richard Harris

Sword only
51. George Cambell
52. John Gillaspick

Sword and Pike
53. Thomas mcGilduff

Sword only
54. John Watison

Sword and Snaphance
55. Hugh Leagh

---

[111] Conway had married Dame Elizabeth Jones, the widow of Baptist Jones, who had originally leased the Vintners' proportion [RJH].

[112] Tenant on the Fishmongers' estate, 1623 (Hunter, 'Fishmongers' Company', p. 206).

[113] Robert Stevenson (number 3) is the father of Anthony and Robert Stevenson (numbers 12 and 22).

[114] Resident at Vinterstown [Bellaghy], 1641 (Examination of John Turner, 7 March 1653 [TCD MS 838, fols 065v–066r]).

[115] Possibly father of Alistair Stewart, resident Vinterstown, 1641 (ibid.).

[116] Father of numbers 84 and 85.

[117] Resident Vintnerstown, 1641; lost over 140 head of cattle; yeoman, resident Coleraine, 1653; (Examination of John Turner, 7 March 1653 [TCD MS 838, fols 065v–066r]).

[118] Possibly of Richard Jenny, burgess of Derry, 1613 (Hill, *Plantation*, p. 427); killed Magherafelt, 1641 (Deposition of John and James Redferne, 7 November 1642 [TCD MS 839, fols 100r–101v]).

[119] Hugh Vaughan may be the son of John or Henry Vaughan, who were named as aldermen in the 1613 charter of Derry (Hill, *Plantation*, p. 427). John Vaughan was resident and held 'one quarter of land called Lerusk' in 1609 (ibid. p. 401).

[120] John Waters was a burgess of Derry in 1613 (ibid. p. 427); Edmond Waters (number 38) may be his son.

[121] Possibly householder Derry, 1609 (Hill, *Plantation*, p. 402).

Sword only

56. Elias Okes

Sword and Pike

57. John Cambell

No Arms

58. James Fahly
59. William Bell
60. John Huchison
61. Thomas Burnet[122]
62. Morgan Joanes
63. Robert Michell
64. Patrick Shewers
65. Daniell Dephet
66. John Burney
67. William Tutton
68. John Clarke
69. Gyles Pallet
70. John Starky
71. Thomas Smyth
72. Richard Cooke
73. Thomas Trone

[f. 131v]

74. William Rowelly
75. Robert Dillon
76. John Mortimer[123]
77. John Portingall
78. Edward Dixon
79. Robert Wright
80. Griffin Thomas
81. William Naylor
82. Thomas West
83. William Cooke
84. David Frow[124]
85. Robert Frow younger
86. Thomas Turner
87. Robert Women
88. William Michell
89. John Phillips
90. John Craford
91. Robert Safftin

92. Robert Hitchins
93. John Thomson
94. Robert Cumell[125]
95. Arch: Cumell
96. Christopher Gardner
97. John Leadson
98. Thomas Williams
99. Thomas McGilduff
100. John Stenison
101. Nicholas Fray
102. Mathew Key

[f. 132]

London Derry
Barony de Loughynisolyne

Mr Peter Barker, chief tenant of the Drapers proportion, being 3000 acres: his men and arms as followeth

Sword only

1. James Smyth[126]
2. Richard Collins
3. James Young[127]
4. William Widroof
5. John Bigger

Sword and Snaphance

6. James Harshon[128]

Sword only

7. Robert Ownce

Sword and Caliver

8. Francis Irwin
9. Walter Irwin

Sword only

10. Robert Burkhead
11. James Bayty
12. Lancelot Foster

13. Barnaby Standing
14. Patrick Wilson
15. Gabraehell Foster

Sword and Pike

16. Lancelot Prowden

Swords only

17. Robert Henderson
18. John McGee
19. Thomas Foster
20. Mathew Irwin

Sword and Musket

21. Richard Stockkin
22. Richard Russell[129]

[f. 132v]

No Arms

23. Peter Barker[130]
24. Richard Buckhead
25. Daniell Johnston
26. Gerrard Drowry
27. Robert Valintyne
28. Roger Ward
29. George Burkehead[131]
30. Robert Burgess
31. Nicholas Tuff
32. Robert Russell[132]
33. Richard Ogleshew
34. Edward Symerell
35. Nicholas Pearson
36. James Sparke
37. James Grenewood
38. John O Gordon
39. Francis Wright
40. John Braviter
41. Thomas Greenoch
42. Edward Trymble
43. John Tomlyson
44. Isack Joyes
45. John Laughlayne

---

[122] Possibly father of Mary Burnett, wife of, James McColl McDonnell, one of the Irish leaders, 1641 (Examination of John Blaire [TCD MS 838, fols 067v–069v]).

[123] Resident 'on the eastside [of] the Bann', 1641; identified as one of the leading rebels (Examinations of Henry McHenry [TCD MS 838, fols 027r–028v] and John Turner, 7 March 1653 [ibid. fols 065v–066r]).

[124] Numbers 84 and 85 are the sons of number 31.

[125] Now spelled Cornwall (http://www.billmacafee.com/1630musterrolls/1630musterrollsderry.pdf, accessed 21 February 2011).

[126] In Dublin, October 1641 (Depositions of Anne Smyth, Susana Wright, Anne Walton, 15 September 1642 [TCD MS 839, fols 102r–102v]); 'gentleman'; resident Moneymore; his losses £2,771 0s 0d (Deposition of James Smith, 23 February 1642 [ibid. fols 095r–095v]).

[127] 'A Scotchman who dwelt then in Moneymore', Young had a sword and pistol in 1641; he was resident in Antrim in 1652 (Examination of Neile oge ó Quin [TCD MS 838, fols 038r–039v]).

[128] Custodian of Moneymore Castle (Depositions of Anne Smyth, Susana Wright, Anne Walton, 15 September 1642 [TCD MS 839, fols 102r–102v]).

[129] Son of number 32.

[130] This is the chief tenant [RJH].

[131] Bricklayer; resident on estate since 1614; supervised building works; see Rolf Loeber, *A biographical dictionary of architects in Ireland, 1600–1720* (London, 1981), p. 21.

[132] Robert Russell, the father of Richard Russell (number 22), was the Drapers Company's agent [RJH].

[f. 133]

London Derry
Barony of Loughynisolyne

Ralph Whistler esquire, chief tenant to the Salters proportion, being 3000 acres

[f. 133v]

London Derry

The town and liberties of Coleraine, their men and arms

Sword and Pike
1. George Brookes[133]
2. Godfrey Bakane
3. Mathew Poly[134]

Sword and Caliver
4. Allyn Myn
5. John Smyth[135]

Sword and Pike
6. John Caparates
7. Thomas Brotherton[136]

Sword and Halberd
8. Thomas Haylare

Sword and Musket
9. William Betson

Sword and Halberd
10. William Rogers

Swords and Muskets
11. John Reynolds
12. Tymothy Thomas

Sword, Musket, and Bandoliers
13. William Sherewood[137]

Sword and Pike
14. John Gyldson

Sword and Musket
15. John Leigh[138]

Sword and Pike
16. George Costenden

Sword and Musket
17. John Thompson

Sword and Pike
18. Henry Berryford

Sword and Musket
19. Henry Steward

Sword and Pike
20. Nathaniell Davis[139]

Sword and Caliver
21. William Barwick

Sword and Pike
22. Richard Barwick[140]

Sword and Caliver
23. Christopher Haylor

Sword and Musket
24. Isack Barvick

Sword and Pike
25. John Molsworth

Pike only
26. Nicholas mcEnery[141]

Sword and Pike
27. William Welson

[f. 134]

28. George Williamson

Snaphance and Bandoliers
29. Richard Grynn

Sword and Halberd
30. Thomas Creighton

Sword and Caliver
31. Edward Glover[142]

Sword and Pike
32. Mansell Turker

Sword and Halberd
33. Robert Tayre

Sword and Caliver
34. William McInch[143]
35. John mcIntch[144]
36. John Michell

Sword and Snaphance
37. Gawen Parkes

Sword and Musket
38. John Letch

Sword and Pike
39. Mathew mcIntch

Sword and Musket
40. John Farlane younger[145]
41. William Owen
42. Thomas Rawlins

Sword and Caliver
43. John Johnston

Sword and Halberd
44. John Madars[146]

Sword and Pike
45. Humphrey Poddle[147]
46. William Robinson[148]

---

[133] Numbers 1 and 2 mustered as halberdiers, 1622 (PRONI D2096/1/1B).
[134] Mustered as a 'pikeman armed', 1622 (ibid.).
[135] Mustered as a 'musket and caliver man', 1622 (ibid.).
[136] Possibly son of Henry Brotherton, who mustered as a 'pikeman armed', 1622 (ibid.).
[137] Mustered as a 'musket and caliver man', 1622 (ibid.).
[138] Mustered as a 'musket and caliver man', 1622 (ibid.).
[139] Mustered as a 'musket and caliver man', 1622 (ibid.); brother-in-law of George Collymore (number 86) [RJH].
[140] Related by marriage to Simon and Thomas Hillman (numbers 52 and 150) and to John Craig (number 150) (NAI, BET1/31, p. 38 [RJH]).
[141] This surname is 'close to the Gaelic form' [RJH].
[142] Mustered as a 'musket and caliver man', 1622 (PRONI D2096/1/1B).
[143] William McAninch mustered as a 'musket and caliver man', 1622 (ibid.).
[144] Father of number 293.
[145] John Farlane the elder does not appear in the muster roll, but the name John McFarland appears elsewhere in Londonderry and in counties Antrim and Donegal; John McFarland senior may have mustered on one of these estates.
[146] Mustered as a halberdier, 1622 (PRONI D2096/1/1B).
[147] Mustered as a 'musket and caliver man', 1622 (ibid.).
[148] Mustered as a halberdier, 1622 (ibid.).

Sword and Musket
47.   Patrick Deneene

Sword and Pike
48.   Andrew Browne

Sword, Caliver, and Bandoliers
49.   Richard Plack

Sword, Musket, and Bandoliers
50.   John Parker[149]

Sword and Halberd
51.   James Hammilton

Sword and Musket
52.   Symond Hayleman[150]

Sword, Musket, and Bandoliers
53.   Thomas Buckle

Sword and Caliver
54.   John Bratch

Caliver only
55.   Thomas White

[f. 134v]

Sword and Musket
56.   James Wilson

Sword and Pike
57.   Richard Fouchon

Sword and Halberd
58.   Robert Whitechell

Sword and Pike
59.   Edmond Bayly

Sword and Halberd
60.   John Bochonan

Sword and Pike
61.   Ambross Davison[151]
62.   Richard Griffin

Sword and Snaphance
63.   Robert mcGuney

Sword and Musket
64.   John Willson

Sword and Pike
65.   Richard Brookes[152]

Sword and Caliver
66.   William Hyll[153]

Sword and Halberd
67.   William Adams[154]

Sword and Pike
68.   Thomas Adams

Sword and Musket
69.   Robert Scot[155]

Sword and Caliver
70.   Robert Bristo

Sword and Pike
71.   William Hubertson

Sword and Caliver
72.   Sammuell Bridgen

Sword and Snaphance
73.   Joseph Brookes

Sword and Caliver
74.   Robert Gamble

Sword and Musket
75.   John Maydley[156]
76.   John Eaton

Sword and Caliver
77.   Thomas Wooldridg[157]

Sword and Musket
78.   Henry Benner

Sword and Pike
79.   John Conway
80.   George Jackson

Sword and Musket
81.   William Gelderson[158]
82.   William Sharp

[f. 135]

Sword and Pike
83.   Robert Lyn

Sword and Musket
84.   Thomas Drakefoord

Swords and Calivers
85.   Thomas Brownet
86.   George Colemore[159]
87.   John Sampson

Sword and Pike
88.   Thomas Smyth

Swords and Muskets
89.   Francis Cutbert
90.   William Blare

Sword only
91.   Thomas Tayres

Sword and Musket
92.   Richard Tayres
93.   Thomas Willson
94.   Hugh Smyth

Swords and Snaphances
95.   David Grynn
96.   John Foster

Sword and Musket
97.   Richard Prescock[160]

Sword and Pike
98.   William Mitten

---

[149] Mustered as a 'musket and caliver man', 1622 (ibid.).

[150] Simon and Thomas Hillman (numbers 52 and 263) were the sons of Thomas Hillman, a Coleraine alderman who died, 1626. Richard Barwick and John Craig (numbers 22 and 150) were relatives by marriage (NAI, BET1/31, p. 47) [RJH]. Simon Hillman was one of the captains in the defence of Coleraine, 1641 (Deposition of Charles Anthony, 12 June 1642 [TCD MS 839, fols 096r–097v]).

[151] Mustered as a 'pikeman armed', 1622 (ibid.).

[152] Mustered as a 'pikeman unarmed', 1622 (ibid.).

[153] Mustered as a 'pikeman armed', 1622 (ibid.).

[154] Mustered as a 'pikeman unarmed', 1622 (ibid.).

[155] Mustered as a 'musket and caliver man', 1622 (ibid.).

[156] Mustered as a sergeant, 1622 (ibid.).

[157] Possibly son of Walter Woolridge, who mustered as a 'musket and caliver man', 1622 (ibid.).

[158] Possibly son of John Gilderson, who mustered as a halberdier, 1622 (ibid.).

[159] Brother-in-law of Nathaniell Davis (number 20) [RJH].

[160] Possibly son of Roger Prescott, who mustered as a 'pikeman armed', 1622 (PRONI D2096/1/1B).

Sword and Caliver
   99. Bartholemew Robinson
  100. James Thomson

Sword and Pike
  101. Andrew Kirkpatrick

Sword and Snaphance
  102. Steaphen Murtough

Sword and Caliver
  103. William Tylor

Sword and Pike
  104. John Moore

Sword and Snaphance
  105. John Noble

Sword and Pike
  106. Richard Hog

Sword and Snaphance
  107. Paul Gaute

Sword and Pike
  108. Thomas mcEllinure

Sword and Snaphance
  109. Thomas Armestrong

Sword and Musket
  110. Gilbert White

[f. 135v]

Swords and Snaphances
  111. John Reade
  112. James Henderson

Sword, Caliver, and Bandoliers
  113. Richard Clyfton

Sword and Pike
  114. Donnell Roskro

Sword and Snaphance
  115. William Mason[161]

Snaphance only
  116. Andrew Hawthorne

Sword and Musket
  117. Steaphen Rixon
  118. John Cofeild

Sword and Caliver
  119. William Robinson

Sword and Snaphance
  120. John Pitts

Sword and Pike
  121. Alexander Allwell

Sword and Musket
  122. George Allwell
  123. John Gelard

Sword and Pike
  124. Anthony Nuson

Sword and Snaphance
  125. Thomas Raynick
  126. Robert Andrewes

Sword and Musket
  127. Jenken Tewdor

Sword and Pike
  128. Randell Hall
  129. John Spotwood

Sword, Caliver, and Bandoliers
  130. Fargus Fayler

Sword and Musket
  131. Robert Lood

Sword and Pike
  132. Thomas Hargrave

Sword and Caliver
  133. John Coop
  134. Andrew Grynn

Sword and Pike
  135. William Charles
  136. Thomas Gylpatrick

Sword and Snaphance
  137. John Templeton

[f. 136]

Sword, musket, and Bandoliers
  138. Hugh Henderson

Sword and Pike
  139. Michaell Wilkinson
  140. David Wilson
  141. William Wilson
  142. Robert Wakis

Sword and Snaphance
  143. John Wallas[162]

Sword and Pike
  144. John Tomson

Sword and Snaphance
  145. James McElvinne

Sword and Pike
  146. Alexander White

Sword and Halberd
  147. John Barnes

Sword and Snaphance
  148. John Thomson

Sword and Pike
  149. Alexander Willey

Sword and Snaphance
  150. John Crag[163]

Sword and Musket
  151. Robert Faskerley

Sword and Snaphance
  152. Thomas Tirwine

Sword and Pike
  153. John Fargison[164]

Sword and ~~Musket~~ Halberd[165]
  154. John Read elder[166]

Sword and Snaphance
  155. John Read younger
  156. David Logan

---

[161] Possibly son of Robert Mason, who mustered as a halberdier, 1622 (ibid.).

[162] Father of number 222.

[163] Brother-in-law of Richard Barwick (number 22) and cousin of Simon and Thomas Hillman (numbers 52 and 263) (NAI, BET1/31, p. 38 [RJH]).

[164] Fergusson had moved to Bellaghy before 1641; he was aged about 50 and resident at Lackey, near Lisburn when he gave his deposition (Examination of John Fergison, 3 May 1653 [TCD MS 839, fols 115r–115v]).

[165] The alteration from musket to halberd shows that Graham was careful to correct any errors he made in conducting the muster [RJH].

[166] Numbers 153 and 154 are father and son.

Sword and Pike
   157. Thomas Gibson
   158. Dunkan mcFadey

Sword and Musket
   159. Martin mcCranny
   160. John Parsons

Sword, Caliver, and Bandoliers
   161. William Dikres

Sword and Pike
   162. William Naymane

Sword and Caliver
   163. James Steward
   164. Richard Betson[167]

[f. 136v]

Sword only
   165. Thomas Boyd

Sword and Snaphance
   166. Alexander Dicky
   167. Adam Barnet
   168. Andrew Rise
   169. John Steavenson
   170. Hugh Neilson
   171. John Davison
   172. Neyman Garvye
   173. William Tod
   174. James Miller
   175. Thomas Hasselhead[168]
   176. John Anderson
   177. James Crawfoord
   178. John Allson
   179. William Hanny
   180. John Dunlap
   181. John McCourty younger[169]
   182. Thomas Russell
   183. Gilbert Ross
   184. John Hyneman
   185. James Hyneman
   186. George Lange
   187. William Smith
   188. John Galt
   189. John Hunter

[f. 137]

Sword and Caliver
   190. John Hanny

Sword and Pike
   191. John Clarke
   192. John Ben

Sword and Snaphance
   193. William Johnston[170]
   194. John Johnston
   195. John Johnston younger
   196. Thomas Johnston

Sword and Pike
   197. John Come

Sword and Snaphance
   198. John Blany

Sword and Caliver
   199. Adam McClemond

Sword and Snaphance
   200. Archbald Falton
   201. William Ross

Sword and Pike
   202. William Homay

Sword only
   203. Hugh Knox

Sword and Caliver
   204. William Armestrong
   205. William Morton
   206. David Heneman

Sword only
   207. Edward Edge

Caliver only
   208. George Adam
   209. Henry Crayle

Sword and Caliver
   210. James Dunlap

Sword and Pike
   211. Thomas Darlington

Sword and Caliver
   212. Robert Darlington
   213. Thomas Shelly
   214. William Hully
   215. Isack Knox[171]

Sword and Pike
   216. James Houston
   217. William Patchell

[f. 137v]

Sword only
   218. Mathew Hunston
   219. Alexander Inpske[172]

Sword and Pike
   220. John Woodborne

Sword and Halberd
   221. James Browne

Sword and Musket
   222. John Wallice younger[173]

Sword and Halberd
   223. Robert Handley

Sword and Musket
   224. Lawrence Henderson
   225. George Misney

Sword and Pike
   226. John Stockman[174]
   227. William Sempell

Sword only
   228. Thomas Andrew

Pike only
   229. John Cample

Sword and Caliver
   230. Archbald Frizell

Sword and Pikes
   231. John Hollyday

[167] Mustered as a 'musket and caliver man', 1622 (PRONI D2096/1/1B).

[168] Thomas Hasselhead is probably Thomas Haslett, whose 'house in Dunboe parish' was commandeered by the Irish as their headquarters, 1641 (Examination of Donnoghy ó Cahan, 8 March 1653 [TCD MS 838, fols 070v–071r]).

[169] John McGurty senior did not muster: Robert McGurty (number 340) is probably a brother.

[170] William, John senior, John junior, and Thomas Johnston (numbers 193 to 196) are a family group (father and three sons).

[171] 'Biblical Christian name' [RJH].

[172] Ince [RJH].

[173] Son of number 143.

[174] Tanner; resident 'at Desartoghill near Garvagh', 1641 and at Coleraine, 1653 (Examination of Mary Stockman, 8 March 1653 [TCD MS 838, f. 071v]).

232. John Maggwere
233. Archbald Browne
234. John Cuomes
235. Thomas Hugh[175]

Musket only

236. Owen O Gyleire

Pike only

237. William Jarden

Swords and Muskets

238. Hugh McCawe
239. Daniell Ker
240. Patrick Murrey

Musket only

241. Thomas Holmes
242. John Bess
243. Danyell McWhery
244. Richard Pearcy

[f. 138]

Sword and Halberd

245. Patrick Moore

Sword only

246. Donnell McEnery[176]
247. James Blaire
248. John Weire
249. William Oge
250. James Honiman
251. Patrick Gray
252. John Cochras
253. John Holmes
254. John Lamberton
255. William Smyth
256. William McClery
257. James Lyell
258. Thomas Reed
259. James Patterson
260. John Thomson

261. Hugh Blare
262. William Paterson
263. Thomas Hilman
264. Isack Birbeck
265. Godfrey Ball
266. Robert Hughye

Sword and Pike

267. James Gibson
268. Neil mcGillapsey[177]
269. John Niel
270. John Young

[f. 138v]

Musket only

271. John Goody
272. John McCraise[178]
273. Thomas Lines
274. William Patterson
275. James Michell
276. James Mund

No Arms

277. Sampson Brant younger[179]
278. Thomas Taylor
279. Robert Hall elder[180]
280. Ankeen Parnier[181]
281. Phillip Martcall
282. Ralph Brayeer
283. Alexander Bigart
284. William Barrot[182]
285. Robert Mathewes
286. John Willson
287. Edward Roe[183]
288. Thomas Peeke
289. William Hog
290. Thomas Andrews younger[184]
291. Robert Hanly
292. Gilbert Mason
293. John Inch younger[185]
294. James Irwin
295. Hugh Watson[186]

296. Robert Corbet
297. Joseph Watson
298. Robert Carr
299. David Cant
300. Thomas White[187]
301. Thomas White younger

[f. 139]

302. Thomas Delap
303. William Boyd[188]
304. Paul Smart
305. Edward Dawson
306. Thomas Cooke
307. Gabrahell Moore
308. Richard Pearance
309. John Fowler elder[189]
310. Richard Jackson
311. Richard Strayman
312. Robert Patrick
313. Thomas Bowen
314. Robert Morrison
315. John Te Grome[190]
316. Thomas Coch
317. Thomas Allen
318. John Patrick
319. Thomas Rowelly[191]
320. James Smyth
321. Anthony Higgins
322. William Fortick
323. Richard Kent
324. Thomas Peake
325. Robert Major
326. John Bright
327. George Appleby
328. Christopher Stub

[f. 139v]

329. Richard Haynes
330. Thomas Haynes
331. Thomas Gill
332. Richard Rixon

---

[175] He may have moved to Moneymore, where 'Thomas Hughes a glover' had a house 'far from the church', 1641 (Deposition of Robert Waringe, 12 August 1642 [TCD MS 839, fols 108r–111v]).
[176] See number 26.
[177] 'Close to the Gaelic form' [RJH].
[178] Father of number 181.
[179] Son of number 356.
[180] Father of number 352.
[181] Mustered as a 'musket and caliver man', 1622 (PRONI D2096/1/1B).
[182] Numbers 284 and 285 mustered as halberdiers, 1622 (ibid.).
[183] Mustered as a 'pikeman armed', 1622 (ibid.).
[184] Son of number 338.
[185] Son of number 35.
[186] Mustered as a 'musket and caliver man', 1622 (PRONI D2096/1/1B).
[187] Numbers 300 and 301 are father and son.
[188] Possibly father of Haberdashers (Sir Robert McClelland), number 17.
[189] John Fowler junior did not muster.
[190] 'Close to the Gaelic form' [RJH]: now spelled Seagram [JJ].
[191] Mustered as a 'pikeman armed', 1622 (PRONI D2096/1/1B); the will of his widow, Anne, was proved 13 May 1636 (NAI, BET1/58 p. 59) [RJH].

333. John Willson
334. William Chub
335. Richard Bruse
336. John Hilton
337. William Brocker
338. Thomas Andrewes[192]
339. Mathew Tomson
340. Robert McCourty
341. Thomas White
342. John Goody
343. David Cant
344. Thomas Lynes
345. Robert Carr
346. James Michell
347. Robert Corbet
348. James Mund
349. James Irwing
350. Thomas Taylor
351. Gilbert Mason
352. Robert Hall[193]
353. William Hog
354. Ralph Bryer
355. William Patterson
356. Sampson Brant[194]
357. Edward Roe

[f. 140]

Londonderry

Sir Thomas Phillips, his servitors lands, being 3000 acres: his men and arms

Sword and Caliver

1. Christopher Williams
2. Teige Heyland
3. William Heiden
4. John Rosse
5. Francis Coster
6. Robert Martin elder[195]

Sword and Snaphance

7. John Steaphenson
8. Thomas Whitt

Sword and Caliver

9. John Speareman
10. William Fetters
11. Hugh White
12. John Martin elder[196]
13. John Jacks
14. Richard Felton
15. John Waltinstone
16. James Robinson
17. Charles Langdell
18. Alexander Miller
19. Robert More
20. Thomas Conn
21. Robert Martin younger[197]
22. John Wilson
23. Steaphen Robinson
24. David Patten[198]

[f. 140v]

25. Richard Bennet
26. John Sheirley[199]
27. Charles Fisher
28. John Martin younger[200]
29. Herbert Carrudhouse
30. John Wyre
31. William Young
32. John Latham
33. William Wylly
34. John Boyd elder[201]
35. John Gilleland
36. John George
37. Archbell Patten
38. James Fynley
39. Edward Poke
40. James Smyth
41. Archbald Cally
42. William Garthy
43. William Coulton
44. Alexander Roger
45. John White
46. William Smyth
47. John Crawfford younger[202]

Caliver only

48. Donnogh Garrald
49. Francis McMarr
50. Peter Lewis
51. Iver Mullan

Sword and Snaphance

52. Angaies Bourston
53. Robert Patton
54. John Caman
55. John Fetters
56. Christopher Moore[203]
57. Michaell Lamb
58. John Sherley elder[204]
59. David Akin
60. Robert Gillmoore
61. John Boyd[205]
62. John Mountgomery
63. Patrick Fletcher
64. James Robinson
65. Thomas Moore younger[206]
66. Patrick Jackson
67. John Robinson
68. John Houston

Snaphance

69. Robert Lenton

Sword and Snaphance

70. Hugh Jack
71. Thomas Connell
72. Gawin Gilsoe
73. George Robinson
74. James Oliver
75. Robert Shanon
76. Clawdius Sprowell
77. Thomas Moore elder[207]

[192] Father of number 290.
[193] Son of number 279.
[194] Father of number 277.
[195] Father of number 21.
[196] Father of number 28.
[197] Son of number 6.
[198] Thomas Patten (number 84) is the son of number 14 on the Haberdashers (Sir Robert McClelland) estate: the three other men named Patton (numbers 24, 37, and 54) may have been from other families.
[199] Son of number 58.
[200] Son of number 12.
[201] Father of John and Thomas Boyd (numbers 61 and 80).
[202] Son of number 87.
[203] 'Late of Ballinenan in the county of Londonderry, gentleman'; losses £116 0s 0d (Deposition of Christopher More, 7 November 1642 [TCD MS 839, fols 099r–099v]).
[204] Father of number 26.
[205] Son of number 34.
[206] Son of number 77.
[207] Father of number 65.

[f. 141v]

Sword and Musket
78. William Mooregalway

Musket
79. William Michell

Sword and Musket
80. Thomas Boyd[208]
81. James Connell[209]

Sword and Pike
82. Patrick Gibbone
83. Thomas Smith
84. Thomas Patten younger[210]
85. John Martin younger
86. John Yow
87. John Crawford[211]
88. Thomas Sterling
89. Thomas Miller
90. John Kellogh
91. William Dunkin
92. William Gay
93. George Roweth
94. Alexander Steaphenson

Pike only
95. Alexander Browne

No Arms
96. James Parvis
97. Alexander Dunkan
98. John Steward
99. Nynean Watters
100. Anthony Magee
101. John Foord
102. Patrick Laughlyne

[f. 142]

Captain
103. John Cooke

Ensign
104. John Owen

Sergeants
105. Anthony Mathew
106. John Lawson

Drummer
107. George Blare

Pike only
108. Richard Woodfer
109. John Holliday
110. Mathew Robinson
111. George Trotter

No Arms
112. Peter Lewis
113. Richard Bennet
114. William Smith
115. Charles Fisher
116. Alexander Roger
117. John Wyre
118. James Smyth
119. John Latham
120. John George
121. William Young

[f. 142v]

London Derry

Mr Gaidy his churchlands, being 1000 acres: his men and arms as followeth

Sword and Snaphance
1. George Cooke
2. William Ball
3. Robert Hally

No Arms
4. Edward Pitcher
5. Thomas Davis[212]
6. John Davis
7. James Davis
8. Thomas Robinson
9. John Barnefeild
10. John Lenington

[f. 143]

London Derry
Barony de Coolranie

The Lady McCleland her churchlands, 2000 Acres: her men and arms as followeth

Sword and Pike
1. Robert Michell
2. David Fulton

3. Francis Knougheron
4. Thomas Lynye
5. John Parker
6. Nynnyon Black

Pike only
7. John Boyd
8. William Baverlin
9. John Thompson
10. Andrew Thompson
11. Patrick Moorehead
12. John Wallice
13. John Robert
14. David Russell
15. John Luckye

Sword and Musket
16. William Anderson
17. John Fynlay[213]
18. John Fynlay younger

Musket only
19. Robert Murray

No Arms
20. Henry Moore[214]
21. John Mathew
22. Hugh Magoney

[f. 143v]

Sword only
23. John McGilray
24. John Kymin
25. William Armstrong
26. Henry White
27. Hugh Callwell
28. John Crucks
29. William Straythlaine
30. David Crucks
31. John Cragg
32. James Cragg
33. Andrew Richman
34. John Winty
35. George Anderson
36. John Patterson
37. James Smyth
38. John Fulton
39. John Brading
40. John Murray
41. Robert Bipson
42. Andrew Watson
43. John McMullan
44. Thomas Black

---

[208] Son of number 34.
[209] Householder, Derry, 1609 (Hill, *Plantation*, p. 402).
[210] Numbers 84 and 85 are the sons of numbers 14 and 8 respectively on the Haberdashers (Sir Robert McClelland) estate.
[211] Father of number 47.
[212] Thomas, John, and James Davis (numbers 5 to 7) are a family group.
[213] Numbers 17 and 18 are father and son.
[214] Father of Thomas Moore (Canning, number 8); died 1638 (Note by RJH, based on NAI, BET1/41).

45. William Smyth
46. William Style
47. Patrick McIlmartin
48. John Curry

[f. 144]

London Derry

Mr Berresfourd his natives lands, being 1000 acres: his men and arms

Sword and Snaphance
1. George Godfrey[215]

Sword only
2. Barnard Hudman
3. Henry Burdet
4. George Symons
5. James Pearath[216]

Pike only
6. Anthony Wood

Sword and Pike
7. Thomas Johnston

Pike only
8. William Hill
9. Thomas Bountaine[217]

Sword only
10. Thomas Teig

No Arms
11. Peter Symons
12. John Symons
13. Richard Cartwright[218]
14. Gilbert Ellot
15. Robert Greene
16. Nahamen Coop
17. John White
18. John Moore
19. Robert Burden
20. Thomas Phillips
21. John Tatly
22. Alexander Steward
23. James mcCarter

[f. 144v]

24. Leonard Dent
25. Roger Basset
26. George Jordaine
27. John Hamons[219]
28. Alexander Hosty
29. James Mathewes
30. Robert Cole
31. William Parches
32. William Smyth
33. John Byngham
34. Alexander Steward
35. James McCarter
36. George Dickson
37. Andrew Greeble

[f. 145]

London Derry
Barony de Loughinisolyne

The Lord Primate his churchlands, being 1000 acres: his men and arms

Swords only
1. George Trimble
2. William Ellot
3. Thomas Price
4. Robert Smyth

No Arms
5. Nathaniell Hitchins
6. Thomas Hogg
7. Thomas Botkine
8. Hugh Russell[220]
9. John Neytrilton[221]
10. William Thursby
11. Robert Dillon

[f. 145v]

London Derry
Barony de Loughinisolyne

Mr Thomas Dawson his churchlands,[222] being 500 acres: his men and arms

Sword and Snaphance
1. William Wright

Sword and Caliver
2. John Burges

Snaphance only
3. John Connaway

Pike only
4. William Ingle

Sword only
5. Thomas Trewman

No Arms
6. Brian Presson
7. George Read
8. John Dickson
9. Enias Bell
10. Henry Buckham
11. Henry Bringbranke
12. Richard Tyngle
13. Edward Miller

[f. 146]

London Derry
Barony de Loughinisolyne

The Churchlands of Maghera and Desert Martin, being 700 acres: their men and arms

Sword and Pike
1. Richard Leigh

Sword only
2. George Norrice

Sword and Snaphance
3. Nathaniell Harrison

Sword only
4. John Leigh

Sword and Pike
5. John Parker
6. Richard Laden[223]

---

215 Mustered as a 'pikeman armed' at Coleraine, 1622 (PRONI D2096/1/1B).

216 Possibly son of William Parat, who mustered as a 'pikeman armed' at Coleraine, 1622 (ibid.).

217 Killed at Dungiven, 1641 (Deposition of Peter Gates, 6 June 1643 [TCD MS 839, fols 107r–107v]).

218 Possibly 'Cornet Cartwright' (or his son), householder, Derry in 1609 (Hill, *Plantation*, p. 402).

219 One of the organisers of the defence of Magherafelt, 1641 (Deposition of Robert Waringe, 12 August 1642 [TCD MS 839, fols 108r–111v]).

220 'Certain rebels at Magherafelt … sent thither by the wicked traitor Donell O Haggan … stripped Hugh Russell and his wife and children' (ibid.).

221 'Of Moneymore, gentleman' (ibid.).

222 Dawson purchased the lands from Sir Thomas Phillips before 1622 (NAI, CP/N150) [RJH].

223 Ladan may be a misspelling of Lagan (http://www.billmacafee.com/1630musterrolls/1630musterrollsderry.pdf, accessed 21 February 2011).

Sword only

7. Andrew Carter[224]
8. Henry Carter
9. John Oslyn
10. Thomas Berryman
11. Thomas Scot
12. Thomas Leigh
13. Mathew Williamson
14. John Adamson
15. Robert Poke
16. John Cors
17. Robert Oughterson
18. John Adam
19. John Densinyne
20. Cuthbert Donnell
21. William Smyth
22. Robert Eridgson
23. William Harrison

No Arms

26. William Allen
27. Gilbert Bradney
28. Robert Foster
29. Andrew McMullan
30. Walter Glendininne
31. James Cutler
32. George McGill
33. John McHillan
34. Robert Leigh
35. John Glendininne
36. John Robinson
37. John Madoole
38. John Williamson
39. William Oghterson
40. John Oghterson

[f. 146v]

Sword and Snaphance

24. John Delap
25. George McHellan

---

[224] Andrew Carter was killed with his wife and two children at Lissan, near Cookstown, county Tyrone, December 1641 (Examinations of James Steile and Margaret Armstrong, 14 March 1653 [TCD MS 838, fols 076v–077r and 080v]).

County Antrim

[f. 145]

The Muster Roll of the County of Antrym

Barony de Dunluce

The Earl of Antrim his British tenants: their names and arms

Sword only

1. John White[1]
2. John Wilson
3. William Dunlap[2]
4. John Riddell
5. William Gemmill
6. Hugh Galt
7. John Conningham
8. Archbald Hamill
9. Robert Hobkin
10. Andrew Boordlaine
11. Nynyan Hunter
12. George Bard
13. James Gillerson
14. John Adam
15. Robert Adam
16. Daniell Rydings
17. Michaell Mathew
18. John Gilbert
19. James Miller
20. Richard Blankett
21. Thomas Nicoll

[f. 147v]

22. Allen Scot
23. Alexander Grynlay
24. Thomas Hunter
25. Alexander Gemmill
26. John Gillaspy
27. John mcKeene[3]
28. Arch. Thomas
29. Arthur Fulton
30. John Arthur[4]
31. John Longmoore[5]

32. John Rankyn
33. Edward Barr
34. Andrew Steward[6]
35. Robert Smyth
36. John mcGowen
37. John Andrew
38. John Hunter[7]
39. Dunkan McDonnaghy
40. Alexander McCardy
41. Donnell Steward
42. Thomas Chapland
43. Robert Anderson
44. James McQuilly
45. William Harvy
46. David Metland
47. William Gerr

[f. 148]

48. John Dow McGreere
49. Hugh Russell
50. William Thomson
51. Robert Strawbridg
52. Fararther McCloy
53. John Smyth
54. Charles Arthur
55. Andrew Browne
56. William Scot
57. Thomas Smyth
58. John Rasid
59. Edward Lawe
60. John Henderson
61. Hugh Deall
62. Hugh Roger
63. Charles Steavenson
64. John Gillpatrick
65. Nynyan Barkly
66. Hugh Mountgomery
67. Archbald Habkin
68. John Habkin

69. Hugh Thomson
70. Hugh Kidd
71. William Kidd[8]
72. Robert Hall
73. John Thomson

[f. 148v]

74. John McConn
75. Andrew McGlower
76. Robert Henderson
77. Sallomon Habkin
78. Wm. McPettris[9]
79. John Keason
80. Robert Thomson
81. Nynyan Dunlap
82. Alexander Coop
83. Gilbert Kenedy
84. John McCullagh[10]
85. Roger Johnston
86. Thomas Willson
87. Alexander Watson
88. Andrew Dicks
89. Quinton Fulton
90. John Balfoure
91. John Moore
92. John Scot younger[11]
93. John Thomson
94. John Furley
95. William Crag
96. William Kinin
97. Thomas Knock
98. Robert Peoples[12]
99. Andrew Steel

[f. 149]

100. Adam Smyth
101. James Rea
102. Wm. Cleckhorne

---

[1] Father of Glenarm, number 6.

[2] Executor of the will of William Boyd of Dunluce, 9 December 1624 (Hill, *McDonnells*, p. 390).

[3] The McKeenes or MacIains of Ardnamurchan were followers of the MacDonalds in the fifteenth century [RJH].

[4] Resident Dunluce town; killed, 1642 (Examination of David McKenlaies, 2 March 1653 [TCD MS 838, fols 057r–057v]).

[5] John Longmore (number 31 or 255) is probably the son of Robert Longmore, to whom William Boyd of Dunluce left '[one] thousand marks Scottish money', 9 December 1624 (Hill, *McDonnells*, p. 393).

[6] Yeoman; house at Cushendun, 1641 (Examinations of Alexander McKay, 16 March 1653 [ibid. fols 035v–036r] and Andrew Stewart, 4 March 1653 [ibid. f. 063r]).

[7] One of the four men in Dunluce barony named John Hunter (numbers 38, 347, 440, and 469 of the earl's British tenants and number 25 on his servitor lands) was a lawyer (earl of Antrim to William Edmonstone, 5 July 1630, in Hill, *MacDonnells*, p. 199).

[8] Killed, 1641 (Examination of Patrick ó Hara, 16 March 1653 [TCD MS 838, fols 036v–037r]).

[9] William McFetridge's father, Gilbert, leased 200 acres, 6 June 1618. Gilbert McFetridge died, 30 September 1631 and the property passed to his son (Hill, *MacDonnells*, pp 440–1). William McFetridge 'of Loughgeill, gentleman' organised the defence of Dunluce Castle, October 1641 (Examination of William McPheadress, 8 March 1653 [TCD MS 838, fols 072r–072v]).

[10] McCulloch is a Scots name but not from the Isles [RJH].

[11] Son of number 453.

[12] One of the men named Peoples commanded a company of foot at Ballycastle, 1641 (Examinations of Shane O Coll, 28 February 1653 [TCD MS 838, f. 048r] and of Robert Hamill, 4 March 1653 [ibid. fols 064r–064v]).

103. John McClanakan
104. John McMurtry[13]
105. John McMurtry
106. William Hamilton
107. John Mitchell
108. John Mountgomery
109. Thomas mcMourtry
110. Robert Harvye
111. Archbald Tod
112. John Loggan[14]
113. William Loggan[15]
114. David Lyndsay
115. John Lyndsay
116. John Hamill
117. John Getty
118. Adam Galt
119. John Smyrle
120. Thomas Beard
121. John Morish
122. John Morish
123. Robert Steward[16]
124. Adam Neall
125. Robert Moore
126. Thomas Walker
127. Adam Boyd[17]

[f. 149v]

128. Cuthbert Bowell
129. James Orre
130. John Kenedy
131. William Moore[18]
132. Archbald Boyd[19]
133. Rober Carr
134. James Katre
135. Thomas Boyd[20]
136. William Wylly
137. James Smyth
138. William Galt[21]
139. Gillaspy McMyrirty
140. Arch. McNeal
141. Robert Bar younger[22]
142. Donnell Steward
143. John Steward
144. Alexander Steward[23]
145. John Cogheran[24]
146. John Garvan[25]
147. Thomas Boyd
148. Thomas Houston
149. Thomas Lock
150. James Hammelton[26]
151. William Hutchon
152. James Steward[27]

153. Hugh Piples[28]
154. Thomas Boyd
155. David Habkin

[f. 150]

156. Archbald Loggan
157. John Cambell[29]
158. John Dick
159. John Moore
160. David Metland
161. Andrew Logan
162. John Logan younger[30]
163. James Hammelton
164. Patrick Horner
165. John Horner
166. William Johnston
167. Robert Calwell
168. John Carr
169. Thomas Cromy
170. John Bell
171. Robert Boyd
172. William Gemmell
173. Thomas Fulton
174. David Fulton
175. Donnagh McSparran[31]
176. Quinton Steavenson

---

13 McMurty is a common name in the Isles [RJH].

14 Resident Bushmills (Hill, *MacDonnells*, p. 72); brother-in-law of William Boyd of Dunluce (ibid. p. 391); father of number 162.

15 Son of number 112; resident Ballyrashane when killed, February 1642 (Examination of George Tomson, 8 March 1653 [TCD MS 838, fols 069v–070v]).

16 Captain of a company in Archibald Stewart's regiment, 1641 (Examination of Robert Futhy, 2 March 1653 [ibid. fols 059r–060r]).

17 Brother of John Boyd (number 320) and William Boyd (Glenarm, number 140); son of William Boyd of Dunluce (Hill, *MacDonnells*, p. 390).

18 Moore and John Gorm McMartin were in dispute with Robert Peoples (number 98), 1634 (earl of Antrim to William Edmonston, 10 April 1634, in ibid. p. 199).

19 Resident Carncallagh, near Dervock (ibid. p. 72); brother-in-law of Adam, John, and William Boyd (numbers 132 and 320 and Glenarm, number 140) (ibid. pp 390–1); brought news of the rising to Dunluce Castle, October 1641; one of the defenders of Ballintoy church, January 1642 (Examination of Gilduffe O Cahan, 10 March 1654 [TCD MS 838, fols 024r–026v]).

20 Five men on the earl of Antrim's estates are named Thomas Boyd (numbers 135, 147, and 154; servitor lands: number 52; Glenarm: number 87). Thomas Boyd senior, the son of John Boyd, the provost of Irvine, leased Carncoggy, near Dervock in 1614 and was an executor of the will of William Boyd of Dunluce, 1624 and 'curator' [guardian] of Katherine, one of William Boyd's daughters (Hill, *MacDonnells*, p. 72). Thomas Boyd died in 1634 and his son, Hugh, took over the family's property (ibid. p. 440). Thomas Boyd junior was one of those who took refuge in Ballintoy church, January 1642 (Examination of Thomas Boyd, 1 March 1653 [TCD MS 838, fols 052v–053v]) and was one of the witnesses in 1665 in the case against the earl of Antrim's claims to be an 'innocent papist' (Hill, *MacDonnells*, p. 329).

21 Merchant in the town of Dunluce; killed, 1642 (Examination of David McKenlaies, 2 March 1653 [TCD MS 838, fols 057r–057v]).

22 Robert Barr senior did not muster.

23 One of the five men named Alexander Steward (numbers 144, 221, 246, 405, and 478) is 'Alexander Beg Stewart, maltster of her ladyship's own mill' (Examinations of Alice, countess dowager of Antrim, 9 February [ibid. fols 022r–023v] and Edmund ó Haggan, 12 March 1653 [ibid. fols 032r–032v]). Another of the Alexander Stewarts was the son-in-law of Alexander McNaughten, who heads the list of tenants on the earl's servitor lands (Examination of Margarett Dunbar, 8 May 1653 [ibid. fols 237r–237v: the name is spelled Stuart in the original document and Stare in the Internet transcript]). The earl of Antrim owed £200 0s 0d to an Alexander Stewart in 1638 (Hill, *MacDonnells*, p. 477).

24 Killed, 1642 (Examination of John McNeill, 1 March 1653 [TCD MS 838, f. 055r]).

25 Garvin, as lieutenant of Henry Upton's foot company, was responsible for the killing of the Irish at Ballymartin, early 1642 (Examinations of Any ny Cary, 22 April [ibid. fols 160r–161v] and Knogher Agnew, 6 May 1653 [ibid. fols 138r–138v]).

26 James Hamilton got two leases of lands around Ballymoney; each lease was for 301 years, the first being granted, 28 February 1621 and the second, 4 January 1625 (Hill, *MacDonnells*, p. 439). The earl of Antrim owed him £500 0s 0d, 1638 (ibid. p. 477).

27 The Irish leaders met at the house of James Stewart (number 152 or 237 or 321) in Dunluce, morning 24 October 1641 (Examinations of James Widderoe, 2 March 1653 [TCD MS 838, fols 058v–059r] and Gilduffe O Cahan, 10 March 1654 [ibid. fols 024r–026v]).

28 Leased Ballyhibistock, 19 October 1631 (Hill, *MacDonnells*, p. 440).

29 'John Campbell of Ballycastle' married Jeannette Service, the widow of John Hunter (Examination of Jennett Service, 28 February 1653 [TCD MS 838, fols 046r–046v]).

30 Son of number 112.

31 The McSparrans were highland Scots from Bushmills (Examination of Gilduffe O Cahan, 10 March 1654 [TCD MS 838, fols 024r–026v]). The family originated from Argyll [RJH].

177. Gilbert Moore
178. Thomas Orr
179. George Carnes
180. Thomas Watt
181. John Park
182. John Watty
183. John Gibson

[f. 150v]

184. Thomas Old
185. David Powle
186. George Tate
187. John Hamill
188. Alexander Baliff
189. Thomas Fulton
190. Adam Dunlap
191. George Willy
192. William Bowhadan
193. George Douglas
194. Henry Kallender
195. John Blare[32]
196. John Fell
197. Alexander Walker
198. William Adam
199. John Moore
200. John Moore
201. William Renkin
202. David Renkin
203. Wm. McHennet
204. John McChonchoy
205. Archbald Steward[33]
206. Robert Anderson
207. Mungo Eclease
208. William McAlexander[34]
209. George Wasson
210. Hugh Hamill
211. James Smyth
212. James McMurry
213. James Crawffourd

[f. 151]

214. James Dicky
215. Neelly Conchoy
216. John McMurry elder[35]

217. Thomas Hall
218. Andrew Melvill
219. John Foothey
220. Robert Foothey[36]
221. Alexander Steward
222. James Speere
223. Thomas McGragan
224. James Colyer
225. Andrew Doory
226. John Willson
227. John Logan
228. Alexander Hopkin
229. James Templeton
230. John Kenedy
231. John Blythe
232. Alexand. Hume
233. Quinton Kirkwood
234. William Dunbar
235. John McJanet
236. Robert Wodell
237. James Steward
238. Robert Neelson
239. William Elipham
240. Robert Fulton
241. Alexander Henry

[f. 151v]

242. William Dicky
243. George Cup
244. Pallen McFarlin
245. John McFarson
246. Alexander Steward
247. Donnell McNeill[37]
248. Hugh Reed
249. John Bard
250. John Turban
251. Richard Scot
252. James Flesher
253. Thomas Laine
254. John Fargison
255. John Longmore[38]
256. Alexander Smyth
257. Thomas McClewer
258. Robert Mountgomery

Halberd

259. Gilbert Steavenson

Sword and Pike

260. Nicholas Hunter
261. Alexander Spencer

[f. 152]

No Arms

262. Gillorish McGreere
263. John Steward
264. Dunkan McCooke
265. William Steward
266. Archbald Hobkin
267. Hugh Hunter
268. David Paltowne
269. William Cloney
270. Thomas Gawnes
271. James Callwell
272. Robert Browne[39]
273. John McCullane
274. John King
275. Ninian Bard
276. Neal McCleary
277. Dunkan mcCullan[40]
278. Neal mcGrowder
279. John Smyth
280. John Steavenson
281. John Russell
282. Andrew Mingas
283. Hugh Adam
284. Alexander mcConaghay
285. David Wat
286. John mcHilheney
287. John Callam
288. William Gate
289. John mcPhillips

[f. 152v]

290. Alexander mcNeall
291. Alexander mcCurdin
292. Robert mcCardy
293. John Camell
294. Donell mcConnaghay

---

[32] One of the defenders of Oldstone Castle, 1641; held prisoner until May 1642; yeoman; resident Coleraine, 1653 (Examination of John Blaire, 8 March 1653 [TCD MS 838, fols 068v–069v]).

[33] Leased Ballylough, near Bushmills for 101 years at £11 5s 0d a year, May 1621; principal agent for the earl of Antrim on the death of John McNaughton, 1630 and still held appointment, 1655 (Hill, *MacDonnells*, p. 240); resident Ballintoy; commanded British regiment Portnaw, January 1642 (Examination of Robert Futhy, 2 March 1653 [TCD MS 838, fols 059r–060r]).

[34] McAlexander could be a rendering of McAllister [RJH].

[35] John Murray junior is number 6 in the list for Cary barony.

[36] 'Of Ballymoney …, gentleman'; lieutenant of Robert Stewart's company in Archibald Stewart's regiment, 1641–2 (Examination of Robert Futhy, 2 March 1653 [TCD MS 838, fols 059r–060r]).

[37] The name, Donnell or Donald McNeill or MacNeill, appears three times in Dunluce barony (numbers 247, 307, and 329) and originates from the Isles [RJH].

[38] See number 31.

[39] Robert Browne and his son, James (number 404 or 461 below), were among the perpetrators of the killing of the Irish on Island Magee, 8 January 1642 (Examinations of Con O Sheale and Bryan McGee, 21 April 1653 [TCD MS 838, fols 153r–153v and 198r–198v]): Browne denied the charges (Examination of Robert Brown, 27 May 1653 [ibid. fols 310r–311v]).

[40] Possibly McQuillan [RJH].

295. John Parke
296. Donnell mcIllcrylin
297. Daniell Kelly
298. Alexander Gourdon
299. David Steward
300. Symond Lowry[41]
301. Hugh Erd
302. James Thomson
303. Robert McKilmartin
304. Fynlay Spence
305. James Willson
306. John Gemill
307. Donnell McNeal
308. Hugh mcCullam
309. Mathew Steward[42]
310. William Hamill
311. Gilbert Henderson
312. John Willy
313. William Weire
314. Thomas McGrowder
315. Gillcollum McKahan[43]
316. Peter Conningham
317. Edward Mountgomery

[f. 153]

318. James Fleming
319. John Thom
320. John Boyd[44]
321. James Steward
322. Thomas Longmoore
323. John Sterling[45]
324. William Neal
325. John Nicholl
326. John Smyth
327. James Moore
328. Michaell Henderson
329. Donnell McNeal
330. Gilbert Michaell
331. Hugh Maccam
332. John Cannan[46]
333. Robert Smyth
334. Mathew mcilmartin
335. John Logan
336. Alexander Mathew
337. William Logan
338. William Arthur
339. John Randell

340. James Bankehead
341. George Fulton
342. Hugh Thompson
343. John Speere
344. David Watt

[f. 153v]

345. Patrick Hutchon
346. James Gillaspy
347. John Hunter
348. William Neal
349. Robert Culpar
350. Robert Davis
351. Robert Walker
352. John Hall
353. John Hobkin
354. John Gracy
355. John Bunityme
356. John Browster
357. James Dranan
358. James Hogg
359. William Allen
360. John Graham
361. Thomas Stenson
362. John Reed
363. Andrew George
364. Henry Neal
365. John Adam
366. John Wilson
367. John Hall
368. William Newing
369. Donnel mcSpearan
370. Donnell bane Mcallester
371. William Bayding

[f. 154]

372. John Lyon
373. John Logan
374. William Richy
375. David Ligit
376. James Moore
377. Thomas Moore
378. James Hamill
379. John Steaphenson
380. Alexander Browne
381. John Wishen

382. Andrew Wat
383. John Lockhart
384. Robert Porter[47]
385. Francis Porter
386. James Wilson
387. John Moore
388. Robert Porter younger
389. John Patterson
390. Robert Alexander
391. Archbald Akyn[48]
392. John Fynlo
393. Henry Cogherin
394. Thomas Widdriddin
395. Robert Long
396. Robert Wilson
397. Hugh Tany younger[49]

[f. 154v]

398. John mcCabing
399. John Hamill younger
400. Alexander Evorit
401. Thomas Baliff
402. John Scot
403. John McGreere
404. James Browne
405. Alexander Steward
406. Thomas Moorehead
407. Adam Old
408. John Walker
409. John Mathew[50]
410. David Sincleare
411. Alexander McNease
412. Doall McDowallerin
413. John McNicholl
414. Donal Omolldarg
415. Mathew Stanell
416. Alexander mcNeal
417. Gilbert Michell
418. John Tweed
419. Andrew Walker
420. John McClowire
421. James Sperling
422. Hugh Mountgomery
423. William Newing
424. Donnel mcMurchie
425. Robert Spence

---

[41] The Irish who 'beleaguered Coleraine … camped at Peter Lowry's [possibly the son of this man] and the Sterlings' houses about one mile and a half from Coleraine' (Examination of Donnell Gorme McDonnell, 11 March 1653 [TCD MS 838, fols 030r–030v]).

[42] When the rising started, 24 October 1641, the leaders of the Irish in North Antrim had 'been drinking in Mathew Stewart's house some certain time before' (Examination of Hugh Colume, 2 March 1653 [ibid. f. 058r]). Mathew Steward's house was probably an inn.

[43] Gilcollum McKahan is a member of O'Cahan clan [RJH]: the modern version of the name is McCann [JJ].

[44] Brother of Adam (number 127) and William Boyd (Glenarm, number 140); second son of William Boyd of Dunluce (Hill, *MacDonnells*, p. 390).

[45] See number 300.

[46] The earl of Antrim owed 'Mr Kannon' £900 0s 0d, 1638 (Hill, *MacDonnells*, p. 477).

[47] Father of Francis and Robert Porter (numbers 385 and 388).

[48] This version of Aitkin can still be found in Derry [RJH].

[49] For Hugh Tany senior, see Derry, Haberdashers, McClelland, number 93.

[50] Resident of Dunluce town; killed in 1642 (Examination of David McKenlaies, 2 March 1653 [TCD MS 838, fols 057r–057v]).

[f. 155]

426. William Armstrong
427. Donnagh McSparan
428. Donnell McSparan
429. Donnagh bane McAlester[51]
430. Quinton Steavenson
431. William Briding
432. John Lyon
433. John Logan
434. John Wallice[52]
435. Cormick Browne
436. David Hunter
437. Robert Kyd
438. Hugh Fyen
439. Gilcollem McCleary
440. John Hunter
441. Neal McBea
442. John Matty
443. James Mathew
444. Robert McWilliam
445. William Richard
446. John Thomas
447. John Walker
448. John Morton
449. John Parker
450. David Sincleare
451. John Sincleare

[f. 155v]

452. James Sincleare
453. John Scot elder[53]
454. Adam Hall
455. David Bigget
456. John Moore
457. James McNeallan
458. John Ballfoure
459. Mathew Dranan
460. John Kid[54]
461. James Browne
462. George Getty
463. John Getty
464. Gilbert Moore
465. John Hamill

466. Alexander Baliff
467. William Aginloss
468. David Kennety[55]
469. John Hunter
470. Robert Foothey
471. John Logan
472. William Karny
473. James McCord
474. John Maxwell
475. Alexander Spence
476. John Steward
477. John Walker

[f. 156]

478. Alexander Steward
479. William Rinking
480. David Rinking
481. John Peoples[56]
482. John Walkey
483. James Moore
484. Arthur Hammilton
485. Thomas Moore
486. George Carnes
487. James Moore
488. Robert Mason
489. Adam Dunlap
490. Robert Dicks
491. Michaell Tuff
492. Allen mcCallen
493. Farracher McCooke
494. Alexander McCooke
495. James Rinking
496. John Wallice
497. John Boyd
498. Archbald Thomson
499. William McAllester
500. Andrew Gourdon
501. George Cupper
502. John Fell
503. Arch. Steward
504. Andrew Melvin
505. John Fefty
506. James Buchonon

[f. 156v]

507. Alexander Henry
508. Thomas Widdrym
509. John Henry
510. John Kenedy
511. Alexander Chambers
512. James mcMurin
513. John Kackland
514. James Bochanan
515. Anthony Knowells[57]
516. Archbold Maxwell
517. William Crawfourd
518. William Johnston
519. John Hamilton younger[58]
520. John Rodman younger[59]

[f. 157]

The Earl of Antrim's British tenants on his servitors land

Sword

1. Alexander McNaughtan[60]
2. Thomas Nortyn
3. Donnell McNaughtyn[61]
4. Quintan Murer[62]
5. Archbald Murer
6. Robert Young
7. Thomas Armestrong
8. William Louiston
9. Robert Hall
10. John Breiftarth
11. William Moorehead
12. William Dufflemer
13. William Withery
14. Thomas Withery
15. Richard Ramson
16. James Smyth
17. Thomas Thompson
18. Patrick Ladly
19. William Hunter
20. Anthony Connody
21. William Clarke
22. Leonard Seare

---

[51] This is an old Antrim McDonnell name because a branch of the McDonnells had *bane* in it [RJH].

[52] In 1624 William Boyd of Dunluce left 'John Wallace that shooting piece which he hath of mine' (Hill, *MacDonnells*, p. 393).

[53] Father of number 92 above.

[54] Mason, resident at Ballycastle (Examination of Alice, countess dowager of Antrim, 9 February 1653 [TCD MS 838, fols 022r–023v]).

[55] Resident Clough, 1641 (Examination of Margarett Dunbar, 8 May 1653 [TCD MS 838, fols 237r–238v]); possibly son of Walter Kennedy of Armoy, son-in-law of William Boyd of Dunluce and brother-in-law of Adam, John, and William Boyd (numbers 127 and 320 and Glenarm, number 140) (Hill, *MacDonnells*, pp 64, 390–1) and commander of Clough Castle, 1641–42 (ibid. p. 440).

[56] Yeoman; juror, Carrickfergus, 10 April 1630 (Hill, *MacDonnells*, p. 429).

[57] Knowles, an 'English tuck miller', was resident in Ballycastle (Examination of Alice, countess dowager of Antrim, 9 February 1653 [TCD MS 838, fols 022r–023v]).

[58] Son of Cary, number 69.

[59] Son of Glenarm, number 15.

[60] Father in law of Alexander Stuart (British tenants, number 144) (Examination of Margarett Dunbar, 8 May 1653 [TCD MS 838, fols 237r–238v]).

[61] Son of John McNaughton, the earl of Antrim's cousin and agent: John McNaughton established the family at Benvardin, near Dervock; he died in 1630; Donald McNaughton extended the family's properties by leasing four townlands in 1637 (Hill, *MacDonnells*, pp 438–9).

[62] Yeoman; resident Ballycastle (Examination of Quintin Moore, 28 February 1653 [TCD MS 838, f. 048v]).

23. James Garlebang
24. Robert Thomson
25. John Hunter
26. Robert Boyd
27. James Patterson

[f. 157v]

Sword and Pike
28. William Denn
29. John Ratty

Pike only
30. John Gallson
31. John McMaister[63]
32. John Kelson
33. John Murdaugh

Sword, Caliver, and Bandoliers
34. Thomas Casse

Musket and Bandoliers
35. Thomas Kirkwood

No Arms
36. Gilbert mcGillmane
37. John Young
38. John Hogg
39. Thomas Ramson
40. John Johnston
41. John McGee
42. Andrew Gray
43. John Michell
44. Calle Brad
45. Fargus Graham
46. Robert Seir
47. David Browne
48. Robert Jameson
49. Robert Clark[64]
50. John Makee
51. William Smyth

52. Thomas Boyd
53. Andrew Hunter

[f. 158]

54. Adam Mure
55. James Pebult
56. John Browne
57. John Barkly
58. John McWilliam
59. James Thomson
60. Wm. McRory
61. James Ashowre
62. Wm. Moore
63. Toby Armestrong
64. Archbald Armestrong
65. John Henderson
66. John McGill
67. Gilbert Wenge
68. John Gnesse
69. John Nicholl
70. George Cutbert
71. Alexander George
72. John Dobby
73. James Michell[65]
74. William Carmihell
75. Thomas Fargison
76. John Jabe
77. Thomas Garwen
78. Alexander Pathake
79. James mcWilliam

[f. 158v]

Antrim barony de Carry

The Earl of Antrim's British tenants on his natives lands

Sword only
1. Robert Steward[66]
2. John Steward[67]

3. John Steward younger[68]
4. Donnell Roe mcCaw[69]
5. John mcMorerty
6. John McMorry[70]
7. John Tod
8. John Boyd
9. Donnell og McGilcorran
10. John Beabone
11. Patrick Pabels
12. Robert Allen
13. Mungo Gray[71]
14. James Elman
15. John Newin[72]
16. Robert Storourt
17. Hugh Mountgomery
18. Gilbert Gemell[73]
19. William Gemell[74]
20. Fynlay Connaghy
21. David Logan
22. Robert McCarroll
23. Sammuell Smyth
24. Robert Kenedy
25. James Orr

Sword and Targets
26. John Hunter[75]
27. Robert Hunter

Snaphance only
28. Gerrard Joy

[f. 159]

No Arms
29. David Steward
30. John McNell
31. John Fargee
32. Alexander mcCawe
33. John Rannell
34. Thorlagh Firshell
35. Gillcollum McConnaghy
36. Neal McConnaghey

---

[63] 'John McMasters Elder and younger' were among the perpetrators of the killing of the Irish on Island Magee, 8 January 1642 (Examination of Bryan McGee, 21 April 1653 [ibid. fols 198r–198v]).

[64] Later 'Marshall Robert Clearke' (Examination of Owen Magurane, 7 May 1653 [ibid. f. 187r]).

[65] Juror, Carrickfergus, 10 April 1630 (Hill, *MacDonnells*, p. 429); resident Island Magee, 1641 (Examinations of William Graham [TCD MS 838, fols 213r–213v] and James Michell, 1 June 1653 [ibid. fols 223r–224v]).

[66] This is probably 'Robert oge Stewart of the parish of Culfaghtrim, gentleman' (Examination of Robert oge Stewart, 4 March 1653 [ibid. f. 063v]); he is probably the brother of John Stewart (number 2).

[67] Possibly John Oge Stewart, one of the original settlers; leased 200 acres in Grange of Drumtullagh, 1611 (Hill, *MacDonnells*, p. 439).

[68] Son of number 2; held prisoner by the Irish, January 1642 (Examination of Thomas Giffen, 1 March 1653 [TCD MS 838, fols 050v–051r]).

[69] McCaw is 'a frequent McDonnell name' [RJH].

[70] Son of Dunluce: number 126.

[71] Possibly related to David Gray, the 'miller of Mr Stewart's mill near the house of Dunseverick', 1641 (Examination of David Gray, 1 March 1653 [TCD MS 838, f. 052r]).

[72] Killed, 1642 (Examination of Jennett Neaven, his sister, 9 March 1653 [ibid. f. 074v]).

[73] Resident Ballycastle; killed with his son, Robert (Glenarm: 161), 1641 (Examinations of Cormacke ó Dullenan, 16 March 1653 [ibid. f. 037v] and of Geiles Kelsoe, 28 February 1653 [ibid. fols 045v–046r]); the TCD Internet transcript of Dullenan's examination gives Gemmell as Garrell.

[74] Son of Gilbert Gemmell.

[75] Carpenter or joiner; resident Ballycastle (Examinations of Alice Countess Dowager of Antrim, 9 February [TCD MS 838, fols 022r–023v] and of John Hunter's widow, Jennett Service, 28 February 1653 [ibid. fols 046r–046v]).

37. John McHenry[76]
38. John McConceghay
39. Donnell mcGilmartin
40. John mcNeal[77]
41. Aghyn mcCaghyn
42. John mcConnaghey
43. James Gemell
44. Donnell Mor mcCawe[78]
45. Gilnew mcCaw
46. Allen mcMorety
47. Donnell mcCawe
48. Donnell mcAleyster[79]
49. John McCawe
50. David McNeall[80]
51. Michaell Moore
52. John mcGiltorane
53. John Duff Steward
54. Donnell Fryssell
55. John Young[81]
56. Thomas Sterat
57. Thomas Hill

[f. 159v]

58. Hugh Hill[82]
59. Robert Hill
60. Donnell mcGreere
61. John Moore
62. John Arthur[83]
63. Robert Fynlay[84]
64. James Moore
65. John Shpent
66. John Leasson
67. John McConnogh
68. John Neal
69. John Hammilton[85]

70. Neal McCauke
71. John Riogh mcNeal[86]
72. John Duff mcNeal
73. John Streart
74. Robert Ross
75. Robert Fleete
76. Robert Steart
77. Gourdon Ward
78. Thomas Gant
79. John Smyth
80. William Newin
81. Anthony Kenedy
82. Robert Dunlap
83. James Morton
84. John Morton
85. William Fynlay[87]
86. John Fynlay[88]
87. Alexander Roby
88. John Borland
89. Thomas Davison

[f. 160]

Antrym
Barony de Glennarme

The earl of Antrim, his British tenants in the barony above said

Sword only
1. John Ognewe[89]
2. Hugh Crafford
3. James Blare
4. William McKeoghey
5. William Cample

6. John White younger[90]
7. John Whilly
8. Robert Caldwell
9. William Fayrye
10. Bevis Blayre
11. John Kinwood
12. John Conningham
13. Hugh Makye
14. Robert Blaire
15. John Rodman[91]
16. Hugh Delap
17. John Wilson
18. William Alexander
19. Robert Woodsyde[92]
20. Hugh Browne[93]
21. Hugh Millan
22. William Clandnell
23. James Burkhead
24. William Francye
25. James Weare
26. Robert Clandenell
27. Thomas Peoples

[f. 160v]

28. John Boyd
29. Robert Reid
30. George Rid
31. Arch: Miller
32. Alexander McCleare
33. John Roe McMurphey
34. John Smyth
35. Andrew Donnell younger
36. Alexander Russell
37. John Brooke[94]
38. Nicholas Knox

---

[76] The McHenrys of Ballyreagh had been one of the principal Gaelic clans in North Antrim before the arrival of the MacDonnells. Randall MacDonnell granted the family its lands near Ballymoney in a deed dated 5 May 1609 (Hill, *MacDonnells*, p. 439).

[77] Numbers 40 and 50 are probably related [RJH].

[78] See number 4.

[79] The conjunction of Donnell with McAllister is to be noted [RJH].

[80] See number 40.

[81] Resident Ballycastle; died of wounds, June 1642 (Examination of Thomas Giffen [TCD MS 838, fols 050v–051r]).

[82] Resident Ballycastle; killed, 1641 (Examinations of Cormacke ó Dullenan, 16 March 1653 [ibid. f. 037v] and Geiles Kelso, Hugh Hill's widow, 28 February 1653 [ibid. fols 045v–046r]).

[83] Miller at Ballycastle; killed, January 1642 (Examination of Ogan McClery, 28 February 1653 [ibid. f. 049r]).

[84] This may be a brother of William Finlay (number 85): the Finlay brothers were killed at Ramoan church in January 1642 (Examination of Archbald Stewart, 18 May 1653 [ibid. fols 185r–186v]).

[85] Father of Dunluce, number 519.

[86] Numbers 71 and 72 are probably related; their names are from the Isles [RJH].

[87] Possibly a brother of number 63; killed with his son at Ramoan church, 5 January 1642 (Examination of Quintin Moore, 28 February 1653 [TCD MS 838, f. 048v]).

[88] Possibly the son of William Findlay.

[89] John Agnew was the leader of the troopers who carried out the killings of the Irish at Magheramorne, near Larne, February 1642 (Examinations of Owen Magee and Mawd McCawley, 7 May [TCD MS 838, fols 255r–256v]) and of Katherine Magee, 30 April 1653 [ibid. fols 268r–268v]).

[90] Son of Dunluce, number 1.

[91] Father of Dunluce, number 520.

[92] The Woodsides (numbers 19 and 65) are members of the same family. 'Jennett Woodside' was married to Robert Browne (Dunluce: number 272) (Examination of James Collogh, 1 June 1653 [TCD MS 838, fols 208r–209v]) and Agnes Woodside was one of Browne's servants (Examination of Robert Brown, 27 May 1653 [ibid. fols 310r–311v]).

[93] Eldest son of Robert Browne (Dunluce, number 272) (ibid.).

[94] Robert Jameson identified 'John Brookes' as one of those who took him, his sister, Isabel, and his brother, Henry, prisoner, 10 February 1642. Robert Jameson escaped, but Henry was hanged at Glenarm and Isabel was questioned about Ballygally Castle (Examinations of Isabel and Robert Jamieson, 29 January 1653 [TCD MS 838, f. 019r]). This is not the Robert Jameson listed in the muster roll: this one described himself

39. John Donnelson[95]
40. Robert Montsod
41. John Woodside
42. Allan Sempell
43. John Monley
44. William Sandelands
45. James Shaw[96]
46. John Shaw
47. John Boyd
48. John Kinge
49. Adam Boyd
50. John Mory
51. John Young
52. David Storagh
53. Archball Wilson
54. John Clarke

[f. 161]

55. Robert Lost
56. John White
57. Robert Robin
58. Archbald Dinston
59. James Browne
60. Robert Boyd
61. Anthony Steinson
62. John Gibson
63. John Looske
64. John Wilson
65. James Woodsyde
66. William Clarke
67. Brice Dunloth[97]
68. George Logan
69. John Yebells
70. John Browne
71. James Calsy
72. John Scot
73. Robert Boyd
74. Robert Piples
75. John Knox
76. John Ewings
77. Robert Stiught

78. Robert McLoorg
79. David Gregg
80. John Moore
81. Patrick Hughey
82. James Boyd[98]
83. Davyd Steward

[f. 161v]

84. George McConnell
85. William Smyth
86. David Speire[99]
87. Thomas Boyd
88. William Fitcher
89. John Boyd
90. John Fynlay
91. William Smelly

Sword, Caliver, and Bandoliers
92. Gilbert Ognewe
93. Randall Buthell

No Arms
94. John Blaire
95. John Crafford
96. Hugh Crafford
97. Hugh Kirkewood
98. Alexander Shinan
99. Andrew Higard
100. John Smyth[100]
101. John Arnot
102. William Clarke
103. John Loughrig
104. William Speere
105. John Lamond[101]
106. James Allen[102]
107. John Cuthbert
108. Alexander Edmond
109. Patt: Miller
110. Robert Nicold
111. John Miller

[f. 162]

112. John McQuarty[103]
113. John bane McQuarty
114. Gilbert McLeine[104]
115. Donnogh Reigh McLenie
116. Gillcolm McCamer
117. Mourgh McCamer
118. John McMurphy
119. Gillcrist McClarty
120. Thorlogh McPhirchmont
121. John Lym
122. Robert Petterson
123. John Moore
124. Roger Willson
125. William Luggs
126. Mathew Robinson
127. William Huggin
128. Hugh White
129. John Richardson
130. James King
131. Michaell Glencourse
132. Alexander Delap
133. John Moore
134. James Willson
135. John Foud
136. James Muckle
137. Robert Moore
138. Robert Crafford
139. John Camble
140. William Boyd[105]
141. Andrew Artoain

[f. 162v]

142. John Dunbar[106]
143. Gilaspy McMurphy
144. James Morson
145. Donnell McConchey
146. Robert Scot
147. Donnell McKercher
148. William London

as a 'yeoman of the age of 35 years or thereby' (ibid.), so he would have been 12 when the muster roll was compiled. He is probably the son of John Jamieson of Broadisland [Island Magee] and was living in Glenarm in 1653 (Examination of John Brookes, 5 April 1653 [ibid. f. 204r] and deposition of the same, 7 May 1653 [TCD MS 837, f. 125r]).

[95] Held 'three parcels of Ballytubber', 1641 (Down Survey, in Hill, *MacDonnells*, p. 457).

[96] Numbers 45 and 46 are related; James Shaw became a freeholder in 1625 and built Ballygally Castle.

[97] Brice Dunlop's lease of Gortconny, near Ballycastle was renewed, 18 September 1623; Dunlop died 4 April 1674 (Hill, *MacDonnells*, p. 440).

[98] One of the perpetrators of the killing of the Irish on Island Magee, 8 January 1642 (Examination of Bryan McGee, 21 April 1653 [TCD MS 838, fols 198r–198v]).

[99] Brother of Janet Spear, wife of John Smyth (number 100): Janet Spear was killed, 1641 (Examination of Alice countess Dowager of Antrim, 9 February 1653 [ibid. fols 022r–023v]).

[100] Husband of Janet Spear and brother-in-law to David Spear, number 86 (ibid.).

[101] 'Mrs Lawmouth' died after giving birth to a child at Broughshane whilst on the refugee trek from Clogh (Examination of Margarett Dunbar, 8 May 1653 [ibid. fols 237r–238v]).

[102] Yeoman; resident Ballycastle (Examination of James Allen, 1 March 1653 [ibid. f. 050r]).

[103] Numbers 112 and 113 are probably father and son: the use of a Gaelic epithet, *bane*, suggests that the family was Gaelic-speaking [RJH].

[104] The McCleans were 'a big lieutenant family to the Clandonald' at 'Duart on Mull' [RJH].

[105] One of the perpetrators of the killing of the Irish on Island Magee, 8 January 1642 (Examination of Bryan McGee, 21 April 1653 [TCD MS 838, fols 198r–198v]); youngest son of William Boyd of Dunluce (Hill, *MacDonnells*, p. 391); his brothers were Adam and John Boyd (Dunluce, numbers 127 and 320).

[106] 'John Dunbar, his wife, and daughter were in the … castle [at Clogh] at the taking thereof' (Examination of Margarett Dunbar, 8 May 1653 [TCD MS 838, fols 237r–238v]): the text of the deposition shows that Margaret Dunbar is possibly John Dunbar's sister but not his wife.

149. David Roger
150. Andrew Home younger[107]
151. John Walker
152. John Miller
153. William Evein
154. William Greg[108]
155. Robert Andrew
156. Robert Lattar
157. Robert Seyre
158. Lancelot Shaw
159. John Jameson[109]
160. Robert Mure
161. Robert Gemell[110]
162. Robert Luke
163. Hugh Evein
164. James Lattar
165. John Dunlap
166. Ongones McAlexander
167. William Miller
168. Thomas McCalman
169. Thomas Orr[111]
170. James Jameson
171. William Wallace[112]
172. Robert Russell
173. John White

[f. 163]

174. John Horsbruch
175. Nynan Taylor
176. Robert Douglass
177. Thomas Colning
178. John Beatty
179. Thomas Swyman
180. Adam Johnston
181. John Milling
182. Hugh Bit
183. Robert Nicholl
184. Daniell Browne
185. Robert Cahawin
186. Thomas Nicholas
187. Adam Steward
188. Hugh Brickhead

189. John Brickhead
190. George Hare
191. John Peter[113]
192. James Cahowne
193. John Dunlap
194. Alexander Chapatrick
195. James Crafford
196. James Boucher
197. John Miller
198. Robert Luggs
199. John Lipa
200. William Nicholl
201. Andrew Logan
202. Thomas Cahowne
203. David Douglas

[f. 163v]

204. James Miller
205. Patrick Ignawe
206. William McColdan
207. Mungo Young
208. Robert Kirke
209. Patrick Crawfford
210. James Ramsey
211. James Moore
212. Andrew Keere
213. John Drune
214. Robert Boyd
215. Cuthbert Peoples
216. Patt Ognewe
217. Patt Howey
218. Arch. Howye
219. John Caldwell
220. William Smyth
221. Allen Skeogh
222. Alexander Payden
223. Thomas Boyd[114]
224. John Fyndley
225. John Moore
226. William Clarke
227. John Frizell
228. Donnel McKilconney

229. David Steward
230. John Boyd
231. John Mountgomery
232. Adam Steward
233. John Gety

[f. 164]

234. Alexander Clarke
235. Roger Shynean
236. Thomas Millines
237. David Murrey
238. Morymont Collagh
239. William Lewes
240. John Morris
241. John Young
242. David Storagh
243. Alexander Steward
244. Donnell Roe McNeale
245. James Steward
246. Donnell McNeale
247. John Miller
248. James McQuiton
249. Gylernew McCuloe
250. David McCarnid
251. John ballagh McNeil
252. William Cambell
253. John Niell
254. Alexander Hueston
255. Neale McCaine
256. Donnell McAllester[115]
257. James Conningham
258. John Conningham
259. Walter Conningham

[f. 164v]

260. John Dune
261. John Cambell
262. James Baly
263. Robert Peoples
264. Thomas Willy
265. Andrew Rily

[107] Andrew Hume senior did not muster.

[108] Resident Ballygally, 1641; yeoman; aged 60 when he made his deposition (Deposition of William Gregg, 16 May 1653 [TCD MS 837, fols 121r–121v]).

[109] 'John Jamieson [the] elder of Broadisland' was bound by recognisance of £20 0s 0d to give evidence at Carrickfergus against Brian O'Mulligan and others (Recognisance of John Jamieson, Isabel Jamieson and Robert Jamieson, 29 January 1654 [TCD MS 838, fols 019r–019v]).

[110] The son of Gilbert Gemmell and brother of William Gemmell (Cary: 18 and 19): killed with his father near Ballycastle, 1641 (Examination of Geiles Kelso, 28 February 1653 [ibid. fols 045v–046r]).

[111] Possibly father of Robert Orr, a servant of Robert Browne (Dunluce: number 272), 1641 (Examination of Robert Brown, 27 May 1653 [ibid. fols 310r–311v]).

[112] William Wallace was one of the executors of the will of William Boyd of Dunluce, 1624 (Hill, *MacDonnells*, p. 390); he may have been the father of Symon Wallas, who was killed in the winter of 1641–42 (Deposition of William Gregg, 16 May 1653 [TCD MS 837, fols 121r–121v]).

[113] Resident Glenarm, 1641; still resident, 1653 (Recognizance of Andrew Aitton et al., 17 May 1653 [TCD MS 838, fols 205r–205v] and Examination of John Peter, 7 May 1653 [ibid. f. 225r]); John Peter was aged 40 when he made his deposition (Deposition of John Peeter, 7 May 1653 [TCD MS 837, f. 125v]) and, having just turned 18, he would have been one of the youngest settlers to muster in 1631.

[114] Tenant of James Shaw, Ballygally (number 45), 1641 (Examination of Thomas Boyd, 16 April 1653 [TCD MS 838, fols 284r–285v]).

[115] Donald McAllister was either 'Donnell McLester' one of John Edmonstone's troopers and witnessed the killings of the Irish around Larne in January 1642 (Deposition of Donnell McLester of Castlereagh, county Down, 20 May 1653 [TCD MS 837, fols 108r–108v]) or 'Donnell grome McAllester' who was one of the Irish commanders at the assault on Ballintoy church in January 1642 (Examination of Thomas Boyd, 1 March 1653 [TCD MS 838, fols 052v–053v]).

266. William Crafford
267. John Tweed
268. John Dunlap

[f. 165]

Antrym
Barony de Tome

Mr Adares British tenants on his Natives Lands their names and arms

Sword only
1. Patrick McDonnell[116]
2. Thomas Browne
3. Robert Houston[117]
4. William Dunbar
5. George Callwell
6. Thomas Hacket
7. William Kenedy
8. Patrick Cahowne
9. James Smyth
10. Alexander Donnell
11. John Cowen
12. John McAllen
13. Robert Kell
14. Robert Allen
15. John Peoples
16. Dunkan Moore
17. John Swan
18. Gabraell Pollog
19. Andrew McTernaghan
20. John McFadaine
21. Archbald Crockard
22. James Thompson

[f. 165v]

Swords and Pikes
23. James Melikin
24. Neele Kennedy
25. Henry McMullan
26. John Greere
27. William Sharp
28. William Dally

29. John Gowen
30. John Cranny elder[118]
31. Leonard Hurly
32. John Black
33. John Moore
34. William mcKee[119]
35. Andrew Magee
36. James Kilton
37. John McNaught
38. Andrew Wallas
39. Roger Gorden[120]
40. Thomas McKee[121]
41. Thomas McCoskery
42. Thomas Steene
43. Thomas mcCarr
44. James McAllen
45. Andrew Hodleston
46. George McConnell
47. Alexander Williamson
48. A Alexander

[f. 166]

49. Patrick Adare
50. Adam McCarny
51. Thomas McCarny
52. James Clarke
53. John McByrd
54. Alexander McByrd

Pikes only
55. John Taylor
56. James Beaty
57. John Chambers
58. Mathew Chambers
59. Robert Harper
60. John McCarr
61. John Bryan
62. James Cowan
63. John Heddelston

Musket only
64. John Mean

Sword and Target
65. William Moore
66. George Buoy

Sword and Halberd
67. Patrick Adare

Sword and Musket
68. Patrick Young
69. James Browne[122]

Sword and Target
70. Hugh McConnell[123]

Halberd only
71. Quistirne Wilson

Caliver only
72. James Adare

Sword and Caliver
73. Thomas Adare

[f. 166v]

Snaphance only
74. Thomas Alexander

Swords and Snaphances
75. John Beatty
76. Aughey McNeil

Snaphance only
77. Donnell McMullan

Sword and Snaphance
78. Thomas Harbertson

Snaphance only
79. William Adare[124]
80. John Read

Swords and Snaphances
81. John Crany younger[125]
82. James Browne younger[126]
83. George McAlexander
84. Cutbeart Harre
85. James Watt
86. John Fargison
87. John Johnston
88. John Crockard

---

[116] Possibly Isles origin [RJH].

[117] Robert Houston was one of the commanders of the British at Antrim in 1642 (Hill, *MacDonnells*, p. 66).

[118] Father of number 81.

[119] Probably related to number 40 below; possible Isles origin [RJH].

[120] Gordon was identified as one of the troopers responsible for the deaths of William and Mary 'Magocane' [McGeown] at Cloghanduff, near Templepatrick, February 1642 (Examination of Patrick McBegh, 6 May 1653 [TCD MS 838, fols 257r–257v]). In 1653 he was still alive and 'liveth about Maine water' [Ballymena] (Examination of William Macogen [the younger], 19 April 1653 [ibid. fols 265r–265v]).

[121] Probably related to number 34; possible Isles origin [RJH].

[122] Father of number 82.

[123] 'A particular Ulster form of McDonnell, primarily an English usage' [RJH].

[124] Witness to an indenture between Sir Robert Adare and his wife, Jane Edmonstone, on the one part and 'John Edmonstone of Ballibantra, William Houstone, younger, of Culnibackie, Alexander Adare of Ballicheg, all of the county of Antrim, gentlemen, and Thomas Adare, provost of Stranraer' on the other, 8 June 1636, in Hill, *MacDonnells*, p. 200.

[125] Son of number 30.

[126] Son of number 69.

89. Thomas Beatty
90. William Adare
91. Robert Beatty
92. Gilbert McChristian

No Arms
93. John Pelog
94. Hugh Hall
95. John Wallas
96. Randall McGildle
97. Gilbert McBrid
98. Robert Irwin
99. Thomas Adare
100. Robert Kitteredell

[f. 167]

101. Andrew Adare
102. Robert Adare[127]
103. Robert McCullogh
104. John Morrison elder[128]
105. John Morrison younger
106. John McTeraghan
107. William Scot
108. John Maxwell
109. James Browne
110. David Foster
111. John Millikin
112. James Murrey
113. James Adare
114. Gilbert Greere
115. Roger Harrelton
116. John McMullan
117. John Cowen
118. Humphrey Carick
119. John Ballantyne
120. John McFulton
121. Andrew Adare
122. Alexander Adare
123. Andrew Agnece
124. Thomas Callender

[f. 167v]

125. John Hoggin

126. John Steine
127. Hugh Gungione
128. John McConlease
129. John McTernaghan
130. William McBrid
131. Allen Cathcart
132. John Scot
133. John Pollage
134. George Farly
135. Alexander mcSharp
136. John Estone
137. James McConleese

[f. 168]

Antrym
Barony de Belfast

Mr Edmonston, his lands in Broad Iland, the names of his men and arms

Swords only
1. William Wilson[129]
   Recusant
2. Thomas Nelson
3. John Wilson
4. Gilbert McNabine
5. James Buchonan
6. Robert Crafford[130]
7. Alexander Mulnes
8. James Wood
9. John Weare
10. John Donan
11. Walter Marting
12. John Crech
13. John McCarket
14. Edward Logan
15. John Carwer
16. Patrick Buchanon
17. Thomas Robinson
18. John McCord
19. Donald McKinley
20. Thomas Laky

21. Thomas Fryland
22. John McNabin
23. John mcCrere
24. William Home
25. Andrew Dugall
26. William Carr
27. James Herriot[131]

[f. 168v]

28. John McGower
29. John Logy
30. James Edmonston
31. John Righee elder[132]
32. John Bryd
33. John McLucas
34. John Sumer
35. Robert Paul
36. John Craffourd
37. John Crokat
38. James Fewr
39. Robert Tarkart
40. John McDougall[133]
41. Edward Drody
42. Roger McKillowne
43. Patrick McNory
[Two deletions][134]

Swords and Pikes
44. John McNeich
45. Thomas Young
46. Dunkan Wilson
47. James Horslough
48. David Herring
49. James Willey
50. Mathew Young
51. Archbold mcCullogh
52. John Nighlich
53. John Edmonston[135]

[f. 169]

54. James Hadding
55. Dennis Wright

---

[127] Son of William Adare, the proprietor of the estate (Hill, *MacDonnells*, p. 200).

[128] Father of number 105 and, presumably, of James Morrison, who was identified as one of the troopers responsible for the deaths of William and Mary 'Magocane' [McGeown] at Claghanduff, near Templepatrick, February 1642 (Examinations of Patrick McBegh, 6 May 1653 [TCD MS 838, fols 257r–257v] and William Macogen [younger], 19 April 1653 [ibid. fols 265r–265v]); James Morrison was 'aged 22 years [probably should read 32] or thereabouts' and working as a saddler in Carrickfergus in 1653 (Examination of James Morrison, undated [ibid, fols 266r–267v]).

[129] Resident Island Magee, 1641; fled to Scotland when the killings of the Irish started (Examination of William Willson, 1 June 1653 [ibid. fols 218r–219v]); his sister, Mary, remained on Island Magee until his return (Examination of Mary Wilson, 1 June 1653 [ibid. fols 210r–211v]).

[130] Robert Crawford junior was identified as one of the killers of the Irish at Templepatrick, 1642 (Examination of Donell McGillmurtin, 6 May 1653 [ibid. fols 139r–139v]).

[131] The surname originates in Yorkshire but is also found in London and southern Scotland [RJH].

[132] Father of number 69.

[133] 'An Isles name' [RJH].

[134] Graham made the deletions because he had tried to parade the settlers by the arms they were carrying – i.e. those carrying swords were to be followed by those carrying swords and pikes: the two men whose names are deleted appear later in the list: Robert Edmonston, with a snaphance, is number 102 and Thomas Crawford, with a sword and snaphance, is number 103 [RJH].

[135] Commanded a troop of horse, January 1642 (Deposition of Donnell McLester, 20 May 1653 [TCD MS 837, fols 108r–108v]).

56.   Arch. Fyer   Recusant
57.   John Donan
58.   Thomas Neal
59.   Robert Hurslurgh
60.   John Richard
61.   Walter Logan
62.   John McNely[136]
63.   Thomas McCapy[137]
64.   John McCapy
65.   William Johnston
66.   John Stenson
67.   Thomas Cowyn
68.   Nicholl Spence
69.   John Righee[138]
70.   Archbald Herring
71.   John Young
72.   William Wilson
73.   James Sheirtt
74.   William Rydick
75.   Martyn Ghay
76.   James Archenwold
77.   Thomas McCappin younger[139]
78.   John Dunken

[f. 169v]

Pikes only

79.   George Laply
80.   Robert Fyer
81.   John Edmonston
82.   Robert Scot
83.   Robert Knox
84.   John Ramsy
85.   John Keyye[140]
86.   Mathew Hudson
87.   James Bower
88.   Thomas Bard
89.   James McGrame
90.   Andrew Ramsy
91.   David Nygrone
92.   William Carsall
93.   Patrick Fargison
94.   Thomas Gilmore
95.   John Nicholl
96.   George Wasson
97.   John McMaster
98.   John McReath
99.   George Begis
100. John Muthray
101. Hugh Telfer

Snaphance only

102. Robert Edmonston

Sword and Snaphance

103. Thomas Crafford

Target only

104. Thomas Whit

Snaphance only

105. John Donan

[f. 170]

No Arms

106. William Miller
107. John Richard
108. Thomas Browne
109. John McNelly younger[141]
110. Thomas McCrery
111. Robert Williamstone
112. George Herret
113. Alexander Kerr
114. John McCrerye
115. Gilbert Bedgs
116. Gilbert Currne
117. John Fife
118. Patrick McDowgall
119. John Gray
120. John Edmonston
121. David Fife
122. William Cor
123. Thomas Brice
124. Andrew Forsith
125. Robert Cowen
126. Thomas Henderson
127. John McCapein
128. Alexander McCupein
129. David McCullogh
130. Patrick McMein
131. Thomas McBurne
132. William Donnold
133. John Robinson
134. George Douglas
135. William McClentuch
136. John Logy
137. Robert Fyn
138. Robert Scot
139. John Brid
140. John McLucas
141. Robert Knox
142. Hugh Telfer

143. Edward Drody
144. Edward Pall
145. James Willy

[f. 170v]

146. George Johnson
147. John Bell
148. John Koynds
149. John Morish
150. Thomas Damson
151. John McCullagh

Mr Peter Hill[142]
his British Tenants

No Arms

1.   George Hunter
2.   Peter Qwenton
3.   William Willson
4.   Thomas Logan
5.   William Gassron
6.   William Johnston
7.   Adam Fagisson
8.   Archbald Poe
9.   John Home
10.   Robert McGilroy
11.   Robert McGillowse

[f. 171]

Antrym
Barony de Belfast

Mr William Reding his Men

No Arms

1.   James Marag
2.   John McBreding
3.   John McCredy
4.   John Carnaghan
5.   Alexander Ross[143]
6.   John McMagken
7.   John Stoub
8.   John McFadyne
9.   Archbold McCull
10.   John Gibson
11.   Adam Broadfull
12.   John Clemments
13.   Gayne McAdam
14.   John Cassan

---

[136] Father of number 109.

[137] Father of number 77.

[138] Son of number 31.

[139] Son of number 63.

[140] Killed, February 1642 (Examination of Robert Formunt, 1 June 1653 [TCD MS 838, fols 090r–091v] and of John Stewart, 17 March 1653 [ibid. fols 102r–103v]).

[141] Son of number 62.

[142] Son of Moses Hill (died 10 February 1631); Peter Hill died 16 May 1634 [RJH].

[143] Killed in February 1642 (Examinations of James Dermople, 25 March [TCD MS 838, f. 085r] and of John Stewart, 17 March 1653 [ibid. fols 102r–103v]).

15. William Casson
16. William Williams
17. James McBreding

[f. 171v]

Antrym
Barony de Belfast

Mr Dalloway his Men and their Arms

No Arms

1. Dunkan McKinley
2. Thomas Carr
3. Adam Lasson
4. James Guhap
5. John McCullagh
6. Guy Murray
7. John Wilson
8. John Flock
9. Robert Robinson
10. James Dundee
11. John Michell
12. John Maiester
13. John Logan
14. William Bredfoote
15. John Eden
16. Thomas Kerny
17. Alexander Murthee
18. John Crossan
19. Adam McForrin
20. William McForrin
21. William Hogg

[f. 172]

22. John Gibson
23. John Senpy
24. Patrick McFirran
25. John Gibson
26. Robert McCullagh
27. Patrick McCullagh
28. John Rexbrough
29. John McFyrrane

30. Bartholemew McCullogh
31. George Layne
32. John Hamman
33. John Rexburgh
34. Bartholemew McCullagh
35. John Crossan
36. Alexander Adam
37. John Obyne
38. John Mountgomery

[f. 172v]

Antrym
Barony de Masreyne

Sir John Clatwoorthy[144] his Men

No Arms

1. William Lunis
2. James Barber
3. John Barber
4. Robert Barber
5. John Derumple
6. David Raney
7. John Raney
8. John Hurn
9. Michaell Breadfoot
10. George Cogheran
11. Gilbert Grere[145]
12. John Begs
13. George Bronstones
14. John Richee
15. Andrew Bradner
16. Alexander Whit
17. James McBrid
18. Mongo Henderson
19. James McCamond
20. Robert Sybaldes
21. John Sybaldes
22. David Fargison
23. William Leap
24. John Maccord
25. Charles Hornes

[f. 173]

26. Alexander Watson
27. William Horsbrooke
28. Robert Greere
29. John Greere
30. Thomas Black
31. Andrew Wilson
32. Patrick McCoord
33. William Greere
34. David Hud
35. Quintan McAdam[146]
36. Hugh Crafford[147]
37. William Griffin
38. William Steward[148]
39. James Ross[149]
40. Alexander Conningham
41. William Crafford
42. John Davis
43. William Murtagh
44. John Black
45. James Loaden[150]
46. James Tegard
47. John Tegard
48. Hector Kenedy
49. George Cample
50. Alexander Hammilton
51. William McLorgg

[f. 173v]

52. George McAdam younger[151]
53. John Coay
54. William Harper
55. Thomas Greere
56. Robert Forman[152]
57. James Hunter[153]
58. William Garnor[154]
59. David Foreman
60. James Callen
61. Gabby Barber
62. James Herper
63. James Derumple[155]
64. Patrick Black[156]
65. Andrew Derumple
66. Gabby Barbor

---

[144] Sir Hugh Clotworthy died, 28 February 1631 (Note by RJH, based on NAI, BET1/9, p. 58).

[145] Seven men (numbers 11, 28, 29, 33, 55, 135, and 154) are named Greer; the distribution of the surname in the muster list suggests they were drawn from two or three separate families [JJ].

[146] Father of number 52.

[147] One of the killers of the Irish, Templepatrick, 1642 (Examination of Donell McGillmurtin, 6 May 1653 [TCD MS 838, fols 139r–139v]).

[148] William Stewart, a 'boat man at Belfast', was named as one of the assailants of the Irish at Magheramorne, January 1642 (Deposition of Gorre ó Rush, undated (1653?) [TCD MS 837, fols 114r–114v]).

[149] Killed, February 1642 (Examination of John Stewart, 17 March 1653 [TCD MS 838, fols 102r–103v]).

[150] Wounded, February 1642; died later in Scotland (Examination of Patrick Black, 29 March 1653 [ibid. fols. 104r–105v]).

[151] Son of number 35.

[152] Aged 70; resident 'Drumcenevey', 1653 (Examination of Robert Formunt, 1 June 1653 [TCD MS 838, fols 090r–091v]).

[153] Either he or number 130 was killed, February 1642 (Examination of John Stewart, 17 March 1653 [ibid. fols 102r–103v]).

[154] Killed, February 1642 (Examination of Robert Formunt, 1 June [ibid. fols 090r–091v] and of John Stewart, 17 March 1653 [ibid. fols 102r–103v]).

[155] Resident Carnmoney; 'labourer of the Roagh forth', 1653 (Examination of James Dermople, 25 March 1653 [ibid. f. 085r]).

[156] Resident 'in Killelagh at the beginning of the Rebellion' [1641]; aged 50; resident Magheragall, 1653 (Examination of Patrick Black, 29 March 1653 [ibid. fols. 104r–105v]).

67. William Barbor
68. Edward Barbor
69. George McNaught elder[157]
70. John Harper
71. Andrew Slowane[158]
72. William Smyth
73. Andrew McKenny
74. Thomas McCarteney
75. John McCarteney
76. Quintan Crafford
77. James Swan
78. John White[159]

[f. 174]

79. Andrew Michell
80. John McMullan
81. James Reed
82. George Bell
83. Andrew McCraigh
84. Patrick McCraigh
85. James Wilson[160]
86. David Graham
87. John Beatty
88. George Pearson
89. John Kettymoore
90. John Humes
91. John Bell
92. Andrew Walker
93. Gilbert Wallis
94. James Porter
95. Robert Barnet
96. Quinton Pearson
97. Marke Philbye
98. Arthur Jackson[161]
99. Walter Hogg
100. Francis Hutton[162]
101. John Hutton
102. John Alexander
103. Robert Cabbard
104. John Daviss

[f. 174v]

105. Henry Gadash
106. Hugh Conningham[163]

107. Andrew McGilroy
108. John Glover
109. James Johnston
110. William Alexander
111. John Humfrey
112. Thomas Griffin
113. Thomas Hardyn
114. Edward Miller
115. Edward Lattimore
116. Arthur Dename
117. James Ritchmond
118. Robert Hunter
119. David Barbor
120. David Read
121. William Thompson
122. John McAdam
123. John Scot
124. John Browne
125. George Corson
126. George Corson
127. John Molligan
128. Thomas Buchonan
129. John McNallan

[f. 175]

130. James Hunter[164]
131. John McCraigh
132. William Rea
133. John Rea
134. George Kirkwood
135. John Greere
136. George Read
137. David Gibson
138. Hugh Logan
139. Robert Miller
140. William Rany
141. Alexander Prince
142. Thomas Bell
143. John Akye
144. Gilbert Coborn
145. Robert Johnston
146. Alexander Dixon
147. Sammuell Cample
148. Thomas McBlane

149. Patrick McGillure
150. George McMullan
151. John Thomson
152. John McMullan
153. John Bingan
154. John Grere

[f. 175v]

155. Hugh Cample
156. Alexander Catheron
157. John Barbor
158. William Scot
159. George Cample[165]
160. George Cample younger
161. James Moore
162. Alexander Bredfoote
163. Edward Conningham
164. James Armestrong
165. Michaell McCleary
166. Robert Hammilton
167. William Whit
168. James French
169. George Sympson
170. John McMichell[166]
171. George McMichell
172. John McMichell
173. Hugh McMichell
174. George McMichell
175. Patrick Wallice
176. George Dickson
177. James Meyns

[f. 176]

178. James Rassell
179. Andrew McLoorg
180. James Nealson
181. Nicholas McDowell
182. William Read
183. John McAdam
184. William Snort
185. Thomas Waugh[167]
186. John Waugh
187. John Leonox

---

[157] Killed, February 1642 (Examination of Robert Formunt, 1 June 1653 [ibid. fols 090r–091v] and of Patrick Black, 29 March 1652 [ibid. fols 104r–105v]); George McNaught junior did not muster.

[158] Killed, February 1642 (ibid.).

[159] Moved to Templepatrick before 1641; accused by John Stephens of killing his father and brother-in-law, Turlough and James Magee, February 1642 (Examinations of John Stephens, William Magugen, both 19 April, William Jackson, 13 May, and John White, 15 April 1653 [TCD MS 838, fols 243r–246v]).

[160] 'James Wilson of Tunny in county Antrim, aged fifty years' was living at Glenavy in 1641. He had moved to Tunny after the Irish captured Glenavy and was then conscripted into the Irish force that fought at Lisnagarvey (Examination of James Wilson, 9 May 1653 [ibid. fols 294r–294v]).

[161] He may have been a turner by trade: 'one Jackson, a turner's son of Glenavy, living in England, died before the rebellion' (Examination of Ann Orson, undated [ibid. fols 124r–124v]).

[162] Numbers 100 and 101 are related: the earl of Antrim owed one of them £200 0s 0d in 1638 (Hill, *MacDonnells*, p. 477).

[163] 'Late of Downburge in the county of Antrim, gentleman'; losses £977 0s 0d (Deposition of Hugh Cunningham, 21 April 1642 [TCD MS 836, fols 080r–081v]).

[164] See number 57.

[165] Father of number 160 and possibly of 155.

[166] The coincidence of forenames shows that numbers 170 to 174 are members of two closely related families [JJ].

[167] Numbers 185 and 186 are probably related.

188. John Mortagh[168]
189. John Gibson
190. John Hume
191. John Clemments
192. Robert Edington
193. William Jefferey
194. William Samson
195. William Willson
196. Archbald Pay
197. Thomas Forkhead[169]
198. Quintan McCallan
199. David Willson
200. John Carsson
201. William Carsonne

[f. 176v]

202. Francis Halliday
203. James Ramswey
204. William Fayre
205. Robert Gills
206. Thomas Mountgomery
207. Robert Knock
208. Robert Roe
209. Laughlin McLaughlin
210. Donnell McWaugh
     Recusant
211. John Thomas
212. Mark McKeag
213. John McKeag
214. George Hunter
215. Gilbert Griffin
216. John Thurner
217. John Read
218. Andrew Weare
219. George Winchester
220. Thomas Carr
221. Adam Lasson
222. Marke Carr
223. Walter Moure
224. John Moure
225. Owen up Williams
226. Mathew Moure
227. Thomas Loyd
228. William McNeally
229. John Begs

[f. 177]

Antrym
Barony de Masreyne

Mr Henry Uptons
British tenants

Sword and Pike
1. Alexander McCallow
2. Andrew Crawford[170]

Pike only
3. Nicholas Norris
4. John Marke

No Arms
5. Thomas Cuddy
6. James McAleyster
7. John Creighton
8. John Crawford
9. William Egells
10. David Boyd
11. John Cassan
12. John McGay[171]
13. John Greire
14. John Moore
15. Hugh Browne
16. Thomas Macug
17. Thomas Kennedy
18. John Werlyne
19. John Meare
20. John Hunter
21. William Lewis
22. John Browne[172]
23. Andrew Lennock
24. John McConnell

[f. 177v]

25. John Templeton
26. John McCloghan
27. Gilbert McDoell
28. Thomas Bell
29. Fergus McDoell

30. John McCarrdy
31. William Jarden
32. Andrew Charter
33. John Charter
34. Fargus Burden
35. Alexander Burden
36. Alexander McDonnell[173]
37. Alexander McDill
38. James Steinson
39. Robert Magee
40. John Gordan
41. James Dill
42. David Read
43. Robert Parker
44. John McDoell
45. James Read
46. John Miller
47. Archbell Adam
48. Robert Miller[174]
49. John Adam
50. James Blare

[f. 178]

51. Alexander McGlyn
52. John Crafford
53. Rowland Cassan
54. William Moligan
55. John Steward[175]
56. Andrew McCloggig
57. John Nicholl
58. Edward Fargison
59. John Hunter
60. James Miller
61. Mathew Miller[176]
62. Andrew Lyndsay
63. Robert Miller
64. William mcCallow
65. John McBratty
66. Robert Boyd
67. James Quin
68. George McMullan
69. John Lewis
70. John Fulton[177]

---

168 One of assailants of the Irish at Magheramorne, January 1642 (Deposition of Gorre ó Rush, undated [TCD MS 837, fols 114r–114v]); killed near Antrim in February or March 1642 (Deposition of Andrew English, 20 April 1653 [ibid. fols 111r–111v]).

169 The modern spelling is Farquhar [RJH].

170 Andrew and John Crawford (numbers 2 and 8) were named as among the killers of the Irish, Templepatrick, February 1642 (Examination of Donell McGillmurtin, 6 May 1653 [TCD MS 838, fols 139r–139v]).

171 McGay is a phonetic spelling of Magee [JJ].

172 Resident Ballyclare, 1641 (Information of Edward Bell, 5 May 1653 [TCD MS 838, fols 134r–134v]).

173 'Captain Alexander McDonnell' controlled Broughshane after the 1641 uprising (Examination of Margarett Dunbar, 8 May 1653 [ibid. fols 237r–237v]).

174 Participant in the killing of the Irish, Ballymartin, February 1642 (Examination of Any ny Cary, 22 April 1653 [ibid. fols 160r–161v]).

175 Resident Ballymather, 1641; aged 50; resident Templepatrick making deposition (Examination of John Stewart, 17 March 1653 [TCD MS 838, fols 102r–103v]).

176 Smith; born about 1589; resident Calhame, near Ballyclare, 1653 (Examination of Mathew Miller, 15 May 1653 [ibid. fols 314r–315v]).

177 The theft and attempted recovery of John Fulton's cattle sparked the killing of British settlers in Massereene barony in February 1642 (see Examinations of Patrick Black, 29 March [ibid. fols.104r–105v] and of Michaell Doyne, 24 August 1653 [ibid. fols 115r–116v]); Fulton was killed in the fight over his cattle (Examinations of his sons, John, 8 June [ibid. fols 088r–089v] and Thomas, 6 May 1653 [ibid. 100r–101v]).

71. Robert Moore
72. John Baker
73. John Service
74. John Burney
75. Gilbert Pearce[178]
76. James Kirke

[f. 178v]

77. John Henderson
78. John Scot
79. John Tenant
80. James Slonne

81. James Dunkan
82. Edward Barret
83. George Hamilton
84. Francis Hamersly
85. John David
86. John Farnsene
87. John McKee
88. John Thomson
89. John mcIthaney
90. Francis Solspey
91. Robert Warney
92. John Hummersly

[178] Possibly 'a descendant of Captain Piers' (governor of Carrickfergus, 1580s) [RJH].

County Donegal

[f. 179]

The Muster Roll of the County of Donnagall[1]

Barony de Rapho

The Lord Duke of Lynox,
undertaker of 4000 acres:
his men and arms

Swords only

1. Robert Leackye
2. James Wood
3. Andrew Wood
4. Mathew Lyndsey
5. William Douglas
6. Robert Lyndsay
7. Robert Buchanan[2]
8. John Galbreath
9. Alexander Buchanan[3]
10. Alexander Lawder
11. James Denniston elder[4]
12. Andrew Royare[5]
13. William Laughlan
14. John Lowrye
15. John Ralston[6]
16. William Cokeran
17. Hector Hinman
18. Robert Cocheran
19. John Buchanan
20. John McConochy
21. Robert McPeter
22. George Haldin
23. Robert Horner
24. Donell Galey
25. Robert mcKyndely

[f. 179v]

26. Robert Glass
27. Archbell Campbell
28. Fyndley mcKindley
29. Andrew mcTyre

30. Alexander Galbreath
31. John mcKaine
32. John Thromble
33. John Smyth
34. Dunkan mcFarlen[7]
35. Patrick mcNeron
36. Wm. McLentock
37. George Colmories
38. Robert mcFarlan
39. John mcFarlan
40. Patt mcAndrew
41. Patt. McArthur
42. Robert Denyston
43. Donnell mcBaxter[8]
44. John Boyd
45. Humfrey Colquphone
46. William Gulilan
47. John Steward
48. John McIlman
49. John Scot
50. Robert Boyde
51. Thomas Lowrye

[f. 180]

Swords and Snaphances

52. John Wood
53. John Martin[9]
54. John mcLenochan
55. John Cambell elder[10]
56. William Deneston
57. John Buchanan
58. John Cambell
59. John mcFarlan
60. Donnell mcFarlan
61. Robert Michell
62. CostymeRanckeln
63. John Allen
64. Gilbert mcLyntock
65. John Brice[11]

66. James Allan
67. Dunkan Speney
68. Thomas Ramsey
69. John Cock
70. James Cock
71. Andrew Cock
72. William Scot
73. John mcCawly
74. John mcGourden
75. Andrew Lackye
76. James mcKennye
77. James Hustone
78. Robert Lackye

Snaphances only

79. James Dromond
80. Archbald Gambell

[f. 180v]

Swords and Pikes

81. Morrice mcConnell
82. John Cocheran
83. John Snadgarse
84. John Cambell younger[12]
85. Owen mcNair
86. David Lyndsay
87. Alexander mcLentock
88. Robert Aickeene
89. Robert Morison
90. James Kilsoe
91. Donnel mcNichol
92. Dunkan Cambell
93. Donnell mcBaxter elder[13]
94. Robert Barlaine
95. James Richye
96. John Swayne
97. John Valentyne[14]
98. Dunkan Graham

---

[1] Hunter, 'Donegal', pp 130–49: I am grateful to the Donegal Historical Society for permission to use this text. The names are not enumerated in this section of the original document: Graham counted the names after compiling the lists and entered the totals as marginal notes. I have enumerated the names and have not included the marginal notes.

[2] Servant of Marcus Aiken, brother of Rev. Robert Aiken (Examination of John Greenhill, 2 October 1652 [TCD MS 839, fols 139r–140v]); killed, 1641 (Examination of Robert Dall, 30 June 1652 [ibid. fols 141r–142v] and of Alexander Aikins, 18 January 1654 [ibid. 147r–148v]).

[3] Three of the five men named Buchanan (numbers 7, 9, 19, 57, and 163) were called John: the men were drawn from at least two families [JJ].

[4] Father of number 146.

[5] Graham wrote 'g' and 'y' in a very similar fashion: number 12 should read Rogare and number 103 Roger [JJ].

[6] John Ralston was named as a burgess of Bangor in 1613 (*Hamilton MSS*, general appendix, p. lxxix).

[7] The distribution of this surname suggests that at least three families (number 34, 38, and 39; number 59 and 60; and number 111 and 115) were called McFarland. Numbers 102 and 137 may be members of one of these families or of separate families.

[8] Son of number 93.

[9] Martin leased part of Ardrie quarter on the estate of Sir John Cunningham, 1 November 1614 (Inquisitions of Ulster, Donegal, (5) Charles I).

[10] Father of number 84.

[11] Bryce leased part of Dunboy quarter on the estate of Sir John Cunningham, 1 November 1614 (Inquisitions of Ulster, Donegal, (5) Charles I).

[12] Son of number 55.

[13] Father of number 43.

[14] Possibly son of William Valentyne who leased part of Grackhy and Tryan Carrickmore quarters on the estate of Sir James Cunningham, 1 May 1613 (Inquisitions of Ulster, Donegal (5), Charles I).

Pikes only

99. Robert Calmeris
100. Andrew Calmeris

Sword and Halberd

101. Hugh Greire

Sword and Caliver

102. John mcFarlan

No Arms

103. John Royer[15]
104. Morrice Peacock
105. Walter Lowrye
106. William mcNevin
107. Robert Campbell
108. John mcKyndley
109. David mcKan
110. John mcIldonagh
111. Dunkan mcFarlan

[f. 181]

112. John mcAdam
113. Alexander mcBoase
114. Patrick Gwin
115. Dunkan mcFarlan
116. John Crawfford
117. John Sempell
118. James Symison
119. William mcArthur
120. Robert Reroch
121. Thomas Crafford
122. Camack mcCole
123. Henry Cruse
124. John Barlone
125. Thomas Swaine
126. Patrick Porter
127. Randall mcAlexander
128. John Douglas
129. James Logan
130. Alexander Hamond
131. Mathew Gillrew
132. William Hewes
133. Robert Leman

134. Donnell mcCahey
135. Adam Quahone
136. Neece mcGilrouse
137. John mcFarlan
138. Walter Deneston
139. Anthony Steward
140. William Noble
141. John Parmenter[16]

[f. 181v]

142. Andrew Galbreath
143. William Wood
144. John Wood
145. John Steward
146. James Deneston[17]
147. James Muthey
148. Walter Roger
149. John Brittein
150. John Young[18]
151. Gawen McConnell
152. John Watson[19]
153. Walter Henry
154. Robert Cambell
155. Dunkan Crafford
156. George Allyson
157. John Pecock
158. Robert Craufourd
159. Archbald Ballintyne
160. Thomas mcKeeg
161. John Logan
162. Lamock mcColl
163. John Buchanan
164. David Gibb
165. John Pearce
166. John mcGillione

[f. 182]

Barony de Rapho

Sir John Conningham knight,
undertaker of 4.000 acres:
his men and arms

Swords only

1. Robert Boyll[20]
2. Gawen Michell
3. John Malfeild
4. John Wood
5. John Forret
6. James Lennox[21]
7. Patrick Coningham
8. John Longpill
9. William Dunlap[22]
10. Robert Young[23]
11. David Coningham
12. Robert Wallas
13. John Blare
14. Robert Wernogh
15. Patrick Fould
16. Alexander Lawson

Swords and Snaphances

17. Thomas Hislat
18. William mcEask[24]
19. William Saner[25]
20. Patrick mcCleland
21. Andrew Balmanner
22. Alexander Balmanner
23. Robert mcInteer
24. Walter de Jestame
25. Herbert Morison[26]
26. James mcCreay
27. David Ramsay[27]
28. James Young

[f. 182v]

Swords and Pikes

29. James Patterson[28]
30. Art McCary
31. Donnell McKee
32. Killetellon McCury
33. James Robinson[29]
34. John Frizell younger[30]
35. Dunkan mcKinley
36. John Richee
37. John Cambell
38. Adam Fleming

---

15 See number 12.
16 Possibly the son of Christopher Parmenter, agent for William Wilson at Convoy, 1611 (Hill, *Plantation*, p. 514) and brother of Thomas (number 131 on the bishop of Raphoe's lands).
17 Son of number 11.
18 Leased part of Moiagh quarter on the estate of Sir James Cunningham, 1 May 1613 (Inquisitions of Ulster, Donegal (5), Charles I).
19 Leased part of Maghreymore quarter on the estate of Sir James Cunningham, 1 May 1613 (ibid.).
20 Boyle leased part of Dunboy quarter, 1 November 1614 (Inquisitions of Ulster, Donegal, (5) Charles I).
21 James Lennox was a gentleman and esquire mourners at the funeral of Viscount Ards, 1636 (*Montgomery MSS*, p. 136).
22 Numbers 9 and 66 are father and son.
23 The five men named Young (numbers 10, 28, 79, 100, and 117) are drawn from at least two families.
24 William McCassack leased part of Dunboy quarter, 1 November 1614 (Inquisitions of Ulster, Donegal, (5) Charles I).
25 Possibly Sauer [RJH]; William Sare leased part of Dunboy quarter, 1 November 1614 (ibid.).
26 The five men named Morrison (numbers 25, 64, 73, 99, and 108) are drawn from at least two families.
27 Possibly son of John Ramsay, who leased part of Dunboy quarter, 1 November 1614 (Inquisitions of Ulster, Donegal, (5) Charles I).
28 Leased part of Monegragane quarter, 1 November 1614 (ibid.).
29 Leased part of Ardrie quarter, 1 November 1614 (ibid.).
30 Son of number 88.

39. Hugh Thomson
40. William Crafford
41. William Colwell
42. William Steavenson
43. Marcus Odoylson
44. William Marshall
45. Dunkan Lyone
46. Patrick Crafford
47. John Lyone
48. John Mathew
49. John Makee
50. Dunkan McCostune
51. Hugh Barskemny
52. James Hutchison
53. Patrick Delap
54. Hugh Thomson
55. John Gylles
56. James Steill

[f. 183]

57. John Allason
58. William Wilson
59. John Hettels[31]
60. John Hettels younger
61. Steaphen Frag
62. George Scot
63. Henry Gaine
64. James Morrison
65. Killcollume McKeynie
66. Wm Dunlap younger[32]

Swords and Muskets
67. Archbald Fleming
68. Robert Larges
69. James Hate

Sword and Calivers
70. Robert Longpill
71. William Cutberson

No Arms
72. John Fleming[33]
73. James Morrison
74. Gibert Fleming
75. Alexander Thompson
76. John Steavenson

77. James Steward[34]
78. David Tullagh
79. William Young
80. John Watt
81. Patrick Wright
82. John Baytye

[f. 183v]

83. Christopher Walker
84. John Hunter
85. Archbald Hunter
86. Andrew Conningham[35]
87. Donnell McConnell[36]
88. John Frizell[37]
89. William Frizell
90. William Iesack[38]
91. Donnell McIlman[39]
92. John McNevin
93. John Yoole[40]
94. Donnell McKean
95. William Doone
96. Rober Roger
97. Robert Miller
98. Andrew Balmanner
99. James Morison
100. William Young
101. John Bayly
102. John Steaphenson
103. James Cresball
104. John Lyone
105. John Crawfourd
106. Patrick Bright
107. John Wallas
108. John Morrison

[f. 184]

109. James Browne
110. William Snyp
111. Steaphen Cragg
112. James Knox
113. William Crag
114. Mathew Cuningham
115. James Forsyth

116. William McBaine
117. David Young

118. Patt: Fleming
119. Barnard Cuningham[41]
120. James Wilson
121. William Wighton
122. Hugh Sawer
123. Patt Adam
124. John Wallas

[f. 184v]

Barony de Rapho

The Lady Conningham, widow of Sir James Conningham, undertaker of 2000 acres: her man and arms

Swords and Pikes
1. William Conningham[42]
2. James Calquahan
3. Andrew McCorkill
4. John McCorkill
5. Tobias Hood
6. James Davye
7. Peter Starret
8. John Mcquchowne
9. James Knox
10. Adam Garvance

Swords and Snaphances
11. James McAdowe
12. Fyndlay Ewing
13. Dunkan McFarlan
14. Ninian Foulton
15. James Scot
16. William Rankin[43]
17. Daniell Ramsay
18. Martin Galbreath
19. Patrick Porter

Swords and Calivers
20. William McIltherne
21. David Walker
22. John Barbor

Sword and Halberd
23. James Makee

---

[31] Numbers 59 and 60 are father and son.
[32] Son of number 9.
[33] Leased part of Dunboy quarter, 1 November 1614 (Inquisitions of Ulster, Donegal, (5) Charles I).
[34] Robbed, 1641 (Deposition of Christopher Parmenter, 28 July 1650 [TCD MS 839, fols 136r–137v]).
[35] Rented part of Dunboy quarter, 1 November 1614 (Inquisitions of Ulster, Donegal, (5) Charles I).
[36] Rented part of Roughton quarter, 1 November 1614 (ibid.).
[37] Father of number 34.
[38] The modern spelling would be Isaacs [JJ].
[39] Leased part of Playter quarter, 1 November 1614 (Inquisitions of Ulster, Donegal, (5) Charles I).
[40] Possibly Poole [RJH].
[41] Leased part of Moyfadda quarter, 1 November 1614 (Inquisitions of Ulster, Donegal, (5) Charles I).
[42] Lease part of Moyfadda quarter, 1 November 1641 (Inquisitions of Ulster, Donegal, (5) Charles I).
[43] Leased part of Magherymore quarter, 1 May 1613 (ibid.).

[f. 185]

Swords only

24. Andrew George
25. James mcIlman
26. Michaell Rotes[44]
27. Patrick Miller
28. Robert Muntgomery
29. Alexander Conningham
30. Richard Leaky
31. Robert Staret
32. John mcIlhome
33. Sallomon Giffin
34. David Reed
35. Donnell mcDonnell
36. Alexander Carlell
37. William Gafeth

No Arms

38. Gilbert Highgate
39. Patrick Porter
40. Robert Hasta
41. William Gambell
42. John Hunter
43. John Crawfford
44. Robert Johnston
45. Henry Smyth
46. William Boyes
47. David Ramsay
48. William Steward
49. Robert Crafford

[f. 185v]

50. James Conningham
51. Andrew Conningham
52. John Crafford
53. John Hunter
54. John Wilson
55. James Bredyne
56. Mungo Davy
57. William Richey
58. John mcIlhome
59. Henry Hunter
60. John mcHutchon
61. James Rankin
62. William Killy
63. Robert Pots
64. William Gambell
65. John Lyone
66. James Knox

[f. 186]

Barony de Rapho

Sir John Kingsmell knight, undertaker of 2270 acres: his men and arms

Swords only

1. Robert Hammilton
2. Andrew Hammilton
3. Robert Moderwell
4. George Stenson
5. James Symes[45]
6. John Squiverell
7. Robert Warnog
8. John Speare
9. John Wilson
10. James Wilson
11. William Conningham
12. John Bordland
13. Thomas Coopson
14. William Coopson
15. Phillomy Huston
16. Hugh Carnog
17. William Carmighell
18. John Warke
19. William Euch[46]
20. James Crafford
21. James Henderson
22. David Bihit
23. Robert Wilson

[f. 186v]

24. Rise Davis
25. John mcAlpinagh
26. Robert Wallice
27. John Fulton
28. George Young
29. John Patterson
30. John Smyth

Swords and Pikes

31. Gabrahill Morrison
32. Robert Marke
33. John Warnog
34. Walter Lewis
35. Michaell Lewis
36. Allyn mcCall

37. William Davis
38. Thomas Hoggard

Swords and Snaphances

39. Adam Moderwell
40. Alexander Browne
41. James Nealson

No Arms

42. Gilbert Moryson
43. William Fryer
44. Hugh Robinson
45. James Symes younger[47]

[f. 187]

Barony de Rapho

Captain Ralph Mansfield, undertaker of 1000 acres: his men and arms

Swords only

1. Thomas Ellis
2. James Benny
3. William White
4. William Wald
5. John Bell
6. Robert White
7. William Glen

Swords and Pikes

8. James mcTanlease
9. Thomas Dunlelly

Sword and Caliver

10. William Gryffyn

No Arms

11. Robert Adam
12. Ralph Mansfield[48]
13. Thomas Clarke
14. Thomas Gray
15. Thomas Fayrefax[49]
16. Thomas Fayrefax younger

---

44. Possibly Rothes [RJH].
45. Numbers 5 and 44 are father and son.
46. Possibly Ench [RJH].
47. See number 5.
48. This is the undertaker [JJ].
49. Numbers 15 and 16 are father and son.

[f. 187v]

Barony de Rapho

Sir John Willson Baronet,
undertaker of 2550 acres:
his men and arms[50]

Swords only

1. Robert Porter
2. William Makee
3. William Deasly
4. Gabraell Homes
5. John Homes
6. John mcCley
7. David Read
8. Alexander Cambell
9. Wenables Albones
10. Henry Roberts
11. John Frizell
12. John Fulton
13. Robert Ray
14. Donnell Reth[51]
15. Thomas Cranston
16. James Lassles
17. William Lassles
18. William Wilson
19. Richard Browne
20. John Kilpatrick[52]
21. John mcClere
22. Anthony mcClere
23. Michaell mcCleare
24. William Moneyley
25. George Gray younger[53]
26. John Michell
27. John Waynes[54]

[f. 188]

28. John Browne
29. John Hendry
30. David Hunter
31. Robert Read
32. John Weiton
33. James mcGumberry

Swords and Pikes

34. George Irwing
35. John Pitts
36. John Hendry
37. John Davis
38. John mcCowr
39. Thomas Browne
40. Robert Bromside
41. John Kilpatrick[55]

Pike only

42. Alexander McKee

Snaphance only

43. James Fargison
44. John Willson[56]
45. John Halbert
46. John Henderson
47. Thomas Henderson
48. Thomas Lassles

Swords and Snaphances

49. Alexander mcCowr
50. John Rowsell
51. John Fleming

Sword and Musket

52. James Hall

Swords and Calivers

53. Walter Carr
54. William Dixon

[f. 188v]

No Arms

55. Patrick Read
56. Robert Pitts
57. John Edger
58. Patrick mcMullaing
59. James Dunkin
60. Christopher Cale
61. James Nesbit
62. John mcClentock
63. Thomas Davis
64. Robert Robertson
65. Leonard Wisse
66. Robert Ray

[f. 189]

Barony de Rapho

Peter Benson Esquire.,
undertaker of 1.500 acres:
his men and arms

Swords only

1. James O [?] rines[57]
2. John mcCreary
3. James mcCreary
4. Wm. Kirkpatrick
5. Andrew Leapper
6. Jo: Kirkpatrick elder[58]
7. Arch: Mowberry
8. John Kirkpatrick[59]
9. George Harkalls
10. Andrew mcKerry

Swords and Pikes

11. John Bree
12. Thomas Moraphie
13. Thomas Farrell
14. Robert Kirkepatrick[60]

Pike only

15. Gilbert Hesee

Swords and Halberds

16. William Kirkpatrick
17. John Farrell
18. James That[61]

Sword and Musket

19. Thomas Preston[62]

Sword and Caliver

20. Richard Gibson[63]

Swords and Snaphances

21. Richard Roper[64]
22. Patrick Cherry

---

50 Wilson was created baronet, July 1629 [RJH].
51 Possibly Roth [RJH] or Reith [JJ].
52 'Younger' after name erased [RJH]; possibly son of number 41 [JJ].
53 George Gray senior did not muster.
54 Wagires [RJH].
55 Possibly father of number 20.
56 This may be the undertaker or one of his sons.
57 Possibly C [?] rines: this name has been altered [RJH].
58 John Kilpatrick leased part of Knockgarran quarter, 1 May 1616 (Inquisitions of Ulster, Donegal, (10) Charles I); John Kirkpatrick (number 29) is his son.
59 Probably brother of number 14.
60 Robert and James Kilpatrick leased part of Tevickmoy and Dunmoyle quarters, 1 May 1616 (Inquisitions of Ulster, Donegal, (10) Charles I); killed, 1641 (Deposition of Christopher Parmenter, 28 July 1650 [TCD MS 839, fols 136r–137v]).
61 Leased part of Dunmoyle quarter, 1 May 1616 (Inquisitions of Ulster, Donegal, (10) Charles I).
62 Thomas and Henry Preston and Charles Atkinson leased Tedanmore quarter, 1 May 1616 (ibid.).
63 Killed, 1641 (Deposition of James Kenedy [TCD MS 839, fols 131r–131v]).
64 Leased part of Shraghmirler quarter, 1 May 1616 (Inquisitions of Ulster, Donegal, (10) Charles I).

Snaphance only
23. John Davis

[f. 189v]

No Arms
24. Edward Babbington
25. Robert Angleson
26. John Michell
27. Edward Smyth
28. Michaell Blanye
29. Jo: Kirkpatrick younger[65]
30. Alexander Maxwell[66]
31. Richard Babbington
32. Edmond Jesopp
33. William Gibson
34. George Arkales
35. Mathew Browne
36. Andrew mcCheney[67]
37. John mcCheney
38. David Key
39. Alexander Maxfeild

[f. 190]

Barony de Rapho

William Steward Esquire, Lard of Dunduff, undertaker of 1.000 acres: his men and arms

Swords only
1. Archbald Thomson[68]
2. Andrew Thompson
3. Robert Alexander
4. John mcKey[69]
5. David Kenedye[70]
6. Patrick Baruzathyn
7. Anthony Steward[71]
8. John Steward
9. Archbald Steward
10. John Browne
11. Andrew Browne
12. Edward Roger
13. John Moore
14. John mcCullagh
15. John Moire
16. Patrick Conningham
17. John Allyson
18. John Smeally[72]

Swords and Pikes
19. John Davidson
20. Archbald mcEmmory
21. Roary mcCleane
22. Patrick Thomson
23. Donnell Or
24. Mungo David
25. John Cambell[73]
26. John mcLynienie
27. Archbald Hourd[74]
28. William Houston
29. James mcKee
30. Anthony Kenedy
31. George Steward
32. John mcClen
33. John Cambell
34. Hugh Gamill

Swords and Muskets
35. Robert Thomson
36. John Fife[75]

[f. 190v]

Swords and Snaphances
37. James Squire
38. John Conningham[76]
39. Steaphen Marshell
40. John Smyth[77]
41. Michaell Smith
42. Michaell mcCleary
43. Donnell Cambell
44. Archbald Bredene

No Arms
45. John Kelly
46. Humphrey Cooke
47. William Wan
48. Fynley mcKirdly
49. Alexander mcClaney
50. John Conningham
51. John maFay
52. Donnell mcNevin alias mcNit
53. John mcKee younger[78]
54. John mcWalker
55. James mcKergour
56. David Kenedy
57. Alexander mcWilliam
58. Patrick Steward[79]
59. Donnell mcCarslaire
60. James Kenellye
61. John Campbell

[f. 191]

Barony de Rapho

Mr Cahoune Lard of Luce, undertaker of 1,000 acres: his men and arms

Swords and Snaphances
1. John Arrell
2. Patrick Boochanan
3. Humphrey Mountgomery
4. David Hume
5. Walter Barlowe
6. James Leach
7. James Creagh
8. John McGillurne

Swords and Pikes
9. John Blare
10. John Watson
11. John Patterson
12. Thomas Allassonne

---

65 See number 6 above.
66 Son of James Maxwell, who leased part of Dunmoyle quarter, 1 May 1616 (Inquisitions of Ulster, Donegal, (10) Charles I).
67 Numbers 36 and 37 could be McClieney [RJH].
68 Leased part of Drumbarnad quarter, 10 June 1614 (Inquisitions of Ulster, Donegal, (9) Charles I).
69 Leased part of Moneymore quarter, 10 June 1614 (ibid.); father of number 53.
70 David Kennedy may be related to Gilbert Kennedy who leased part of Drumbarnad quarter, 10 June 1614 (ibid.); Anthony and David Kennedy (numbers 30 and 56) may also be relations.
71 The five men named Stewart (numbers 7, 8, 9, 31, and 58) are probably the sons of Walter Stewart, who leased part of Moneymore quarter, and Arthur Stewart, who leased Drumoghill quarter, 10 June 1614 (ibid.).
72 Possibly son of William Smelley who leased part of Moneymore quarter, 10 June 1614 (Inquisitions of Ulster, Donegal, (9) Charles I).
73 Four men (numbers 25, 33, 43, and 61) are named Campbell. As three of them are called John, there were at least two families named Campbell on the estate.
74 Possibly son of John Hood who leased part of Drumbarnad quarter, 10 June 1614 (Inquisitions of Ulster, Donegal, (9) Charles I).
75 John Fyffe leased part of Playter quarter on the estate of Sir John Cunningham, 1 November 1614 (Inquisitions of Ulster, Donegal, (5) Charles I).
76 Leased part of Drumbarnad quarter, 10 June 1614 (Inquisitions of Ulster, Donegal, (9) Charles I).
77 Leased part of Moneymore quarter, 10 June 1614 (ibid.).
78 Son of number 4.
79 See number 7.

Swords only
13. John Foster
14. Arthur mcCurrin
15. Patrick Leach

Sword and Halberd
16. Hugh Mure

No Arms
17. Patrick Morton[80]
18. John Allison
19. John Okenhead

16. George Barret elder[84]
17. George Barret younger
18. Ralph Loyd
19. Richard Lestor
20. John Price
21. Rice Evance[85]
22. Evaine Peirce

Swords only
23. Kinrick Thomas
24. Rice Williams
25. George Newson[86]

22. John Lang
23. Robert Grifeth   cuirasses and gorget
24. John Dealp   cuirasses and gorget
25. John Miller
26. William Miller
27. John mcManus
28. James Martin
29. John mcGilwory
30. William Gambell
31. Arthur mcArthur

[f. 191v]

Barony de Rapho

Captain Robert Davis, undertaker of 2,000 acres: his men and arms

Swords and Pikes
1. David Payne
2. Robert Grame
3. William Johnes
4. James Thompson
5. Richard Davis

Swords and Snaphances
6. John Newton
7. Peter Payne[81]
8. Edward Euance[82]

Snaphance only
9. William Monly

Sword and Halberd
10. William Barr

Sword and Caliver
11. John Parry

No Arms
12. Richard Prick
13. Evane Greefieth
14. David Edmond
15. John Apievin[83]

[f. 192]

Barony de Rapho

Robert Harrington esquire, undertaker of 4000 acres: his men and arms

Swords only
1. Edward Hill
2. Gabraell Griffyeth
3. Patrick Browne
4. William Michell
5. George Michell
6. John Arckly
7. Alexander Twig
8. William Boner
9. Archbald Hunter
10. John Walker
11. William Machan
12. William Sympson
13. James Gurskadyne
14. James Scot
15. Alexander Neesbit

Swords and Pikes
16. Robert Rowchester
17. Robert Wyne
18. Robert Makee
19. James Homes
20. John Nicholas   gorgets[87] complete
21. Walter mcArthur   gorget complete

[f. 192v]
32. Hugh Gwillin
33. John Pepells
34. George Russell
35. Thomas Haward

Pikes only
36. William Ridgate[88]
37. John Gursore

Swords and Muskets
38. James Ranag
39. George Miller
40. Robert Smelly
41. David Gillmore
42. Hugh Gambell
43. James Fleming
44. William Uprichard

Swords and Snaphances
45. Ralph Eorill
46. William Miller
47. Peter Steavenson
48. Gabraell Wilson
49. John Pepells
50. John Fisher
51. Alexander Teus
52. James Darson
53. Patrick mcLintog

Sword and Caliver
54. John Awerd

---

[80] Possibly related to Elizabeth Morton, wife of John Adams (Examination of Alexander Aikins, 8 January 1654 [TCD MS 839, fols 147r–148v]).

[81] Held Cashell and Lure quarters; let parts to Owen Ballagh O'Gallagher and Bryan O'Carrulane (Inquisitions of Ulster, Donegal, (14) and (17) Charles I).

[82] See number 15; killed, 1641 (Deposition of Ann Dutton [TCD MS 839, fols 129r–130v] and Examination of Alexander Aikins, 18 January 1654 [ibid. fols 147r–148v]).

[83] RJH queried this spelling, which is phonetic and would be anglicised as Bevan or Evans [JJ]: numbers 8, 15, and 21 may therefore have been related.

[84] Numbers 16 and 17 are father and son.

[85] See number 15.

[86] Held Altnepestie and Corlackey quarters; let parts to Shane O'Docherty and Tirlough Ballagh McNulty (Inquisitions of Ulster, Donegal, (14) and (17) Charles I).

[87] This and the succeeding objects do not appear in the county abstract [RJH].

[88] One of original settlers; tenant of Sir Maurice Berkeley, the original patentee (Inquisitions of Ulster, Donegal, (12) Charles I).

Swords and Targets
55. Andrew Steavens
56. Patrick mcArrell[89]

[f. 193]

Barony de Rapho

Mr Alexander Steward,
undertaker of 1.000 acres:
his men and arms

Swords and Pikes
1. John mcIlwane
2. Callum mcMuyre
3. James Cambell[90]
4. Robert mcKenily
5. William Toyes[91]
6. William Conningham
7. William Home
8. Neall mcCurid
9. Alexander Cambell

Swords and Snaphances
10. Alexander Cambell
11. John mcKenely
12. Robert Boyd
13. Robert Henedy
14. Storiment Carr

Sword and Musket
15. John Niweme younger[92]

Sword and Target
16. Walter mcFarlen

Swords only
17. John Kennan
18. Ninian Steward

No Arms
19. Andrew Cambell
20. Gilbert mcKenny
21. John Gillaspy
22. Robert Steward
23. John Steward
24. Archbald Steward
25. William Cambell
26. James Fyfe
27. Arch Alexander
28. John Roger
29. John Boyill
30. William Boyill
31. John Cambell
32. Gilbert mcCan

[f. 193v]

Barony de Rapho

James Conningham esquire,
undertaker of 1.000 acres: his
men and arms

Swords only
1. Andrew Crafford
2. John Gills
3. Hugh Lokehart[93]
4. Arch Fynlagh
5. Fynlay mcCredy[94]
6. John Browne[95]

Swords and Pikes
7. John Alexander[96]
8. George White
9. Joseph Browne
10. William Galbreath
11. Hugh Leag
12. Andrew Browne
13. John Harper[97]
14. Thomas Stole
15. Patrick Robison
16. John Enery

Snaphance only
17. Andrew Arnott[98]
18. John Alexander
19. Adnarie Hoomes[99]
20. Robert Graham

Swords and Snaphances
21. John Smyth[100]
22. William Gall[101]
23. Andrew Smyth
24. James Gillmore
25. Robert Roger[102]
26. Thomas Roger
27. Thomas Lars[103]
28. John Adam[104]
29. Robert Davison
30. Michaell Beare

[f. 194]

Swords and Halberds
31. Robert mcKeene
32. Mathew Gieffe[105]

No Arms
33. James Fulloone
34. George Steavenson[106]
35. Andrew Leag
36. John Hururence
37. John Hamilton[107]

---

89 Graham's margin note erroneously shows Patrick Carroll as number 57 [RJH].

90 Six men (numbers 3, 9, 10, 19, 25, and 31) are named Campbell; two of them are called Alexander. They are probably drawn from at least two families.

91 The y has been struck out [RJH]. William Teese leased part of Dryan quarter on the estate of Sir James Cunningham, 1 May 1613 (Inquisitions of Ulster, Donegal (5), Charles I).

92 John Niven senior did not muster.

93 Leased part of Magherybegg quarter, 1 May 1613 (Inquisitions of Ulster, Donegal (5), Charles I).

94 Possibly son of Donnell McCready who leased part of Dryan quarter, 1 May 1613 (ibid.).

95 John and Andrew Browne (numbers 6 and 12) are probably brothers: John Brown leased part of Magherybegg quarter and Andrew Browne part of Magherymore quarter, 1 May 1613 (ibid.); Joseph and James Browne (numbers 9 and 43) may be their sons.

96 Leased part of Eredy quarter, 1 May 1613 (ibid.).

97 Leased part of Magherybegg quarter, 1 May 1613 (ibid.).

98 Leased part of Eredy quarter, 1 May 1613 (ibid.).

99 Possibly Advarie or Advarke [RJH]: Edward Homes leased part of Eredy quarter, 1 May 1613 (ibid.).

100 John and Andrew Smyth (number 21 and 23) are possibly the brothers who leased part of Magherymore quarter, 1 May 1613 (ibid.).

101 Leased part of Magherymore quarter, 1 May 1613 (ibid.).

102 Robert and Thomas Roger may be the sons of John Roger who leased part of Dryan quarter, 1 May 1613 (Inquisitions of Ulster, Donegal (5), Charles I).

103 Possibly Lard [RJH].

104 Killed, 1641 (Deposition of Ann Dutton, 2 November 1642 [TCD MS 839, fols 129r–130v] and examination of Alexander Aikins, 8 January 1654 [ibid. fols 147r–148v]).

105 Possibly Giesse [RJH].

106 Possibly son of Peter Stephenson who leased part of Eredy quarter, 1 May 1613 (Inquisitions of Ulster, Donegal (5), Charles I).

107 Leased part of Eredy quarter, 1 May 1613 (ibid.).

38. James Fulloone
39. Robert Patterson[108]
40. John Cunningham
41. George Naught
42. Hugh Leag
43. James Browne
44. John mcEuan
45. George Speare
46. Mathew mcCadame
47. John Dyne[109]
48. Andrew Dyne
49. Arch Boyle
50. John Calwell
51. Robert mcCamy[110]
52. Robert mcCamy younger
53. Dunkan mcWrick
54. Thomas Richmoule
55. John mcJohn Keine
56. Mungo Willy
57. Andrew Cambell
58. Hugh Mure[111]
59. Andrew Callhown

[f. 194v]

Barony de Rapho

Mr John Steward, undertaker of 1.000 acres: the names of his men and arms

Swords only
1. Arch Steward
2. Andrew Cambell
3. William Cambell
4. Killime mcKaine
5. James Fife
6. John Steward

Pike only
7. John Barkly

Sword and Snaphance
8. William Conningham

Sword and Pike
9. John Bullesine

No Arms[112]
10. Robert Steward
11. John Boyle
12. John Roger
13. Arch Alexander

[f. 195]

Barony de Boylagh and Bannagh

The Earle of Annandall, undertaker of 10.000 acres: the names of his men and arms

Swords only
1. Andrew Nesbit
2. Robert Rinkeny
3. James Read elder[113]

Sword and Snaphance
4. David Greire

No Arms
5. David Fynley
6. Archbald Houet younger[114]
7. George Molligan[115]
8. David Jackson younger[116]
9. John Reynold
10. John Kirkpatrick
11. John Hall
12. John Makye[117]
13. George Miller
14. Andrew mcFarlan

15. Richard Murray
16. Gilbert Shaw[118]
17. Walter Leaky
18. James Read younger[119]
19. John William
20. Edward Griffeth
21. John mcClintog
22. John Menzes
23. Patrick Herron
24. John mcClanes
25. John McCartney
26. John Chancellor

[f. 195v]

27. Robert Walker[120]
28. John Creighton[121]
29. John mcKennet
30. Thomas Blane
31. John Blane
32. Sampson McKee
33. James Blane
34. William Ellot
35. George Ellot
36. John Waus
37. John mcKee
38. Hector Douglas
39. John Gourdon
40. Nichol Walker
41. Alexander Tyndy
42. Martin Shellan
43. Andrew Shella
44. John mcKilvame
45. John Creighton
46. Robert Creighton

47. James Crafford
48. Andrew Dunne
49. David Kernes
50. Robert Kernes
51. David Jackson
52. John Creighton younger[122]

---

[108] Leased part of Magherymore quarter, 1 May 1613 (ibid.); killed, 1641 (Deposition of James Kenedy, 4 March 1643 [TCD MS 839, fols 131r–131v]).

[109] John Dunne, senior and junior leased part of Moiagh quarter, 1 May 1613 (Inquisitions of Ulster, Donegal (5), Charles I).

[110] Numbers 50 and 51 are father and son.

[111] Leased part of Grackhy quarter, 1 May 1613 (Inquisitions of Ulster, Donegal (5), Charles I).

[112] There is no reference to arms here in the manuscript [RJH].

[113] Leased part of Shraghmirler quarter on Peter Benson's estate, 1 May 1616 (Inquisitions of Ulster, Donegal, (10) Charles I); father of number 18.

[114] Brother of number 55; their father, Archibald Howett senior, did not muster.

[115] Brother of number 65: their father, John Mulligan senior, did not muster.

[116] There were two families named Jackson on the estate, as the three men (numbers 8, 51, and 140) are called David Jackson.

[117] Five men are named McKee (numbers 12, 32, 37, 98, and 99); the distribution of the surname within the list and the differences in the spellings suggest that the men are drawn from three families.

[118] Five men in this list are named Shaw (numbers 16, 62, 68, 85, and 142): a sixth did not muster. Two of the men (numbers 62 and 68) are described as 'younger'. The men are therefore drawn from at least two families, but the distribution of names suggests that there might have been up to four families named Shaw on the estate.

[119] Son of number 3.

[120] Numbers 27, 40, 71, and 135 are probably related: if John Waker (number 73) should read John Walker, there would have been two families named Walker on the estate.

[121] Six men are named Creighton (numbers 28, 45, 46, 52, and 59); three of them are called John and so there would seem to have been at least two families named Creighton on the estate.

[122] See number 28.

53. Alexander mcMachan
54. Patrick Dunbar[123]
55. Edward Houet[124]

[f. 196]

56. John Fynlay
57. Thomas Gressy
58. Andrew Keirs
59. Thomas Creighton
60. Robert mcKnaght[125]
61. James mcKnaght younger
62. John Shawe younger[126]
63. John Scot younger[127]
64. Gilbert Shankeland
65. John Milligan younger[128]
66. John Vaux
67. John mcKilmain
68. James Shaw younger[129]
69. John Kirkpatrick
70. Alexander Shilan
71. John Walker
72. Robert Vaux
73. John Waker
74. Michaell mcKilwayne
75. Arch Horner
76. William Cocheran
77. John mcKlaughry[130]
78. John Dunbar
79. Gilbert mcClelan
80. William mcClaughry
81. William mcConnell
82. John mcConnell
83. Dunkan mcKilmore
84. John Camell

[f. 196v]

85. Anthony Shaw
86. Patrick mcHutchin
87. John Bagster
88. Robert mcHutchen
89. John Harvye
90. Steaphen Price
91. James Hugones
92. David Barnes

93. John Smyth
94. James mcKnoe
95. Alexander Murry
96. James Murry
97. John Murry
98. Adam Makee
99. Robert Makee
100. James Frizell
101. John Frizell
102. Thomas Carnes[131]
103. Thomas Carnes younger
104. Fynlay mcCauley
105. Thomas Hutton
106. John Kirk
107. Peter Martin
108. Andrew Robinson
109. Patrick Davison
110. John mcClaughey elder[132]
111. James mcClaughry
112. Alexander Scot
113. William Douglas

[f. 197]

114. Hugh Reed
115. Alexander mcCullog
116. Thomas mcCullogh
117. George mcCullogh
118. Jo: Small younger
119. David Wilson
120. John Karnes
121. Robert Maxwell
122. Thomas Scot[133]
123. George Scot[134]
124. John Johnston
125. William Layser
126. William Kenedy
127. John mcKinley
128. John mcCormick
129. John Leis
130. William Leies
131. John mcKneilly
132. Patrick Dunbar
133. John Camell
134. John Dunbar

135. John Walker
136. Andrew Dunne
137. Andrew Leirs
138. John Fynlay
139. George Ellot
140. David Jackson
141. Robert Kernes
142. James Shaw[135]
143. John Scot[136]

[f. 197v]

Barony de Rapho

Mr Farrell undertaker of 1500 acres which he holdeth by his wife lady to Sir Thomas Couch deceased

[f. 198]

Barony de Rapho

The Lord Bishop of Rapho, his churchlands being 2700 acres: his men and arms

Swords only
1. Archbald Conningham
2. John Smyth
3. John Fulton
4. Mathew Patterson
5. Patrick mcMair
6. John Edward
7. Andrew Steaphenson
8. James Lang
9. William Kingham
10. John Key
11. George Wasson
12. Robert Boochanan
13. William Richie
14. Wm. Nickilvy
15. Thomas Elshintor
16. George Steaphenson

---

[123] The four men named Dunbar were drawn from two families, as two of the men (numbers 54 and 132) are called Patrick and two of them (numbers 78 and 134) are called John.
[124] Brother of number 6.
[125] Numbers 60 and 61 are brothers: James McNaught senior did not muster.
[126] John Shaw senior did not muster.
[127] The five men named Scot (numbers 63, 112, 122, 123, and 143) are drawn from two families; numbers 63 and 143 are father and son, and numbers 112 and 123 are probably the sons of number 122.
[128] Brother of number 7.
[129] Son of number 142.
[130] Son of number 110.
[131] Numbers 102 and 103 are father and son.
[132] Father of number 77.
[133] Leased part of Magherybegg quarter on the estate of Sir James Cunningham, 1 May 1613 (Hill, *Plantation*, p. 507).
[134] See number 63.
[135] Father of number 68.
[136] Father of number 63.

17. John Cocheran
18. Michaell Lyndsay
19. Richard Carson
20. Andrew mcIlvaine[137]
21. William Lyne
22. Claud Donniell
23. John Walker
24. William Henry
25. John Wause
26. Hector Conne
27. Thomas mcArthur
28. Alexander Allen
29. John Harper

[f. 198v]

30. Archbald mcCalla
31. John Allan
32. Robert Wylly
33. William Pock
34. John Walker
35. John Kenedy
36. Robert Fleming
37. James Lard
38. John Morrison
39. Alexander Sterrep
40. Archbald Stenison
41. Robert Bachanan
42. John Graham
43. Thomas Cloughan
44. Dunkan Mountgomery
45. Alexander Gibson
46. Gabraell Maxwell
47. John Laird
48. Archbald Henderson
49. Symond Graham
50. John mcCalla
51. Fyndlay Huston
52. James Makeene
53. William Atkin
54. James Davye
55. Alexander Johnston
56. William Makee
57. John Latay
58. James Hervy
59. John Heslet
60. John Carmouth
61. Thomas Kelson
62. John Calwell
63. Thomas Armor

[f. 199]

Swords and Pikes
64. John Wylly
65. James Dick
66. James Keare
67. John Steaphen
68. George Carmighell
69. John mcPeter
70. James Johnston
71. John Lyndsay
72. Ninian Thompson
73. John mcKinly elder[138]
74. James Spreull
75. James Atterew
76. James Atterew
77. John Willson

Sword and Musket
78. John White

Caliver only
79. Humphrey mcLeny

Swords and Snaphances
80. James Carmighell
81. Richard Horris
82. John Maxwell
83. Archbald Leaviston
84. James Mathey[139]
85. William Lyndsay
86. Robert Barly
87. John Wylly
88. John Dunlap
89. Wm. Carmighell
90. Wm. Carssar'es
91. James Allen younger[140]
92. Robert Lyone
93. John Deneston
94. William Home

[f. 199v]

95. John Stenison
96. John Pirry

Snaphances only
97. John Willy
98. John Wallice

No Arms
99. John Hammilton Esquire
100. George Knox
101. Robert White
102. John Leige
103. Symon Elshinter
104. John Moore
105. Andrew Knox
106. John Leitch
107. Hugh Allan
108. Andrew Steaphen
109. Donnell mcPeter
110. John Snodgrass
111. Christopher Geat
112. Andrew Elshinter
113. Robert Foulton
114. John Allason
115. John Steward
116. Dunkan mcGilmichill
117. Robert Deneston
118. John Roger
119. John mcKee
120. James Mathey
121. John Davy

[f. 200]

122. William Porter
123. Hugh Salsmond
124. John Henderson
125. Thomas Henderson
126. Michaell Henderson
127. Thomas Lassilles
128. Thomas Browne
129. Richard mcCulver
130. Alexander mcCulver
131. Thomas Parmenter[141]
132. John Pitty
133. James Mathey
134. Robert Denton
135. Francis Lacillis
136. Wm. Lasillis
137. John Kirkpatrick
138. Michaell mcCleary
139. William Sterret
140. John Torrenc
141. David Prier
142. John Porter
143. Patrick Knox
144. John Hutchone

[137] Una Stephens named Andrew McIlveen as one of the men who killed her father and brother, Turlough and James Magee, at Templepatrick, county Antrim, February 1642; McIlveen was still living there in 1653, which suggests he may have moved to county Antrim before 1641 (Examination of Woona Stephens, 19 April 1653 [TCD MS 838, fol. 242r]). Another member of the family was called Gilbert (Examination of John White, 15 April 1653 [ibid. fols 245r–246v]).

[138] John McKinley junior did not muster with his father: several men in the county are named John McKinley.

[139] The three men named Mathey (numbers 84, 120, and 133) are called James; this suggests that they are drawn from at least two different families.

[140] James Allen senior did not muster.

[141] Son of Christopher Parmenter, William Wilson's agent at Convoy in 1611 (Hill, *Plantation*, p. 514); probably brother of John Parmenter [Duke of Lennox, number 141]; Christopher Parmenter was resident at Killynure, near Convoy, 1641 and reported losses amounting to £480 0s 0d (Deposition of Christopher Parmenter, 28 July 1650 [TCD MS 839, fols 136r–137v]).

145. James Morison
146. William Boyd
147. Walter Lane
148. Robert Robinson
149. David Crassone
150. Edward Sill
151. William Rankin

[f.200v]

Barony de Rapho

The Deane of Rapho, his churchlands, being 300 acres: his men and arms

Swords only
1. Fynlay mcClentock
2. Thomas mcKeag
3. Dunkan Cambell
4. John Braggat

Sword and Snaphance
5. William Fargison

No Arms
6. John Taylor
7. William Wallace

The Churchlands of Tayboyne: the names of the inhabitants and their arms

Swords and Pikes
1. John Denyn
2. John Strutter

Swords and Snaphances
3. James Hammilton
4. George Morison

No Arms
5. Robert Carsby
6. Robert Callwell

[f. 201]

Barony de Eneshone

The Lo: Chichester, his servitor's lands: his men and arms

Swords only
1. Robert mcKintire
2. James Kintire
3. William Douglas
4. William Maxwell
5. John Hammilton
6. Richard Pyn
7. Richard Benson
8. Andrew Cadwell
9. Nathaniel Couch
10. John Crosse
11. Archbald Conningham
12. Henry Temple
13. Mungo Torents
14. Adam Rosbergh
15. Alexander Lacker
16. John Sampson
17. Paul Faulse
18. James Henderson
19. James Porter[142]
20. William Armone
21. Patrick Wallecs
22. Alexander Adams
23. John Cowbrone
24. John Lyone
25. James Neickill
26. Thomas Glyne
John mcKegge (cancelled)[143]

[f. 201v]

27. Donnell mcManus
28. John Bord
29. John Storret
30. John Nickollon[144]
31. Archbald Barnet
32. Robert Young
33. John Kirkwoode
34. William Kirkwood
35. Abraham Houd
36. Henry Allicock
37. John Chamberlyne
38. Duke Chamberlyne
39. William Chamberlyne
40. Mathew Cadwell
41. John Flyng
42. John Henderson
43. Aghey mcCorkey
44. Andrew Hud
45. Gilbert Woorke
46. Alexander Higat
47. Alexander Worke
48. Thomas Staret
49. Johne Clene
50. John Berry
51. Alexander Cadwell
52. Richard Sampson
53. John Koyne
54. Walter mcCowene
55. Thomas McKeon
56. Robert Coweene

[f. 202]

57. John Staret
58. John Osborne
59. Adam Porter
60. John Ritchie[145]
61. William Porter
62. James Porter
63. William Neely
64. Gabrahell Fayrefax
65. Robert Cary
66. Wm. Cougheron
67. Mathew Alcorne
68. Donnell Denneston
69. Paul Elliot
70. John Knox
71. John Richy
72. Davye Worke
73. John Giffen elder[146]
74. John Mountgomery
75. James mcgee
76. Alexander mcMathew
77. Gilbert mcNeal
78. Alexander Browne
79. Robert Browne
80. Hugh Browne
81. William Wallace
82. John Wallas
83. John Hall
84. Robert mcLenaghan
85. John Elly
86. John Chambers

[f. 202v]

87. Robert Whithill
88. William mcKeone
89. William Nelly
90. Richard Leister
91. Richard Leeth
92. John Bruse
93. John Greig
94. Owen Williams
95. James Leitch

---

[142] Five men are named Porter. Three of them appear close together in the list (numbers 59, 61, and 62) and may be from one family. Numbers 19 and 132 would then be from different families.
[143] This cancelled name is not included in the final count: it could possibly be McClagg [RJH]. John McKeague appears as number 120 below [JJ].
[144] The final 'on' has been corrected from 'yn' [RJH].
[145] The five men named Ritchie are probably drawn from two families, one being numbers 60 and 71 and the other numbers 162, 163, and 165.
[146] John Giffen junior did not muster.

96. John Hilbot
97. William Hibbots
98. James Sorerd
99. Peter Gibson
100. George Redgate
101. George Moorehead
102. James Young
103. Andrew Young
104. Patt Michell
105. George Cary Esquire[147]

Swords and Pikes

106. Thomas Davenport
107. John Browne
108. Andrew Ramson
109. John Hogguyre[148]
110. Nathaniell Willson

Swords and Musket

111. Walter Illiner
112. Thomas Gutery
113. John Scot
114. Edward Parker
115. John Battes
116. Thomas Hodges

Sword and Corselet

117. George Hall

[f. 203]

Sword and Snaphance

118. Robert Hammilton
119. Archbald Collaghan

120. John mcKegg
121. James mcKilveny
122. Mungo Barnet
123. John Fargusonne[149]
124. Humphrey Turay
125. William Hunter

Swords and Halberds

126. Thomas Moore
127. James Michell
128. John Bord
129. Water Salder

Halberds only

130. William Fulton
131. George Burges
132. William Porter

No Arms

133. John Robinson
134. George Butler
135. Bryan Smelly
136. Walter Boy
137. John Lacker
138. Donnagh mcConaghy
139. William Crafford
140. John Glandoney
141. Bartholemew Hog
142. William Newton
143. Edward Rudson
144. Thomas Bruma
145. William Mountgomery
146. Robert Smelly

147. Luke Lassels
148. John Cannall
149. Thomas Orr

[f. 203v][150]

150. Robert Fals
151. Robert Fulton
152. Mungo Warden
153. John Warden
154. John Miller
155. Gilbert mcNeal
156. James Deniston
157. Richard Williams
158. Richard Franncis
159. George Gawen
160. John Price
161. John Michell
162. William Richy
163. Robert Richy
164. Wm. Alcorne
165. David Richey
166. John Guy
167. John mcBy
168. Robert Browne
169. James Conningham
170. Donnell Scot
171. John Hunter
172. James Archbald
173. Henry English
174. John Wray
175. Peter Elder

---

[147] Recorder of Derry (Hunter, 'Fishmongers' Company', p. 239).

[148] This is probably a phonetic rendering of Edger [JJ].

[149] Killed, 1641 (Deposition of James Kenedy, 4 March 1643 [TCD MS 839, fols 131r–131v]).

[150] There is some slight doubt about the arms of those listed on this page of the manuscript: the entry 'no arms' is made against the lower group of names on f. 203 and it has been assumed, although there is no entry about arms on f. 203v, that this applies to these names also [RJH].

County Down

[f. 204]

The Muster Roll of the County of Down

Down

The Earle of Kildare his British tenant their Names and Arms

Swords only

1. Thomas Johnston
2. John McCrary
3. Thomas Newall
4. James Con
5. John Con
6. John McKeaugh
7. James McConn
8. John McRobert
9. John McMurrey
10. Adam McCreary
11. James Kelly
12. John Maxwell
13. David Robinson
14. Richard Turner
15. William Willy
16. Robert Wright
17. John McCreary
18. Alexander Flaintstone
19. Patrick Armestong
20. Thomas Armestrong
21. John Turner
22. Thomas Lyndsey
23. Robert Lyndsey

[f. 204v]

24. Rynyon O Dare
25. Andrew Sybyeth
26. William McClenan
27. Wm. Anderson
28. James Bell
29. John Bell younger
30. Andrew Slone
31. John Denyson
32. John McCourty
33. Andrew Mordagh
34. John Crawfoord
35. Valentine Payne esquire[1]
36. John Taylor
37. William Naught
38. Christopher Duckarne
39. William Conley
40. Richard Mason
41. James Hutchison
42. Robert Hodgson
43. George Frankley
44. John McRobert
45. Henry Carrous
46. John Caughide
47. Phillip Clarke
48. John Curratt
49. James Stonehouse
50. George Hatorne
51. John Michell
52. Henry Haddlestone

[f. 205]

53. James Robinson
54. John Turner
55. John McNaught
56. Patrick McNaught
57. Edward Maxwell
58. Thomas Little
59. John Carsan
60. John Hammilton
61. William Hammilton[2]
62. Robert Crosby
63. Thomas Dixon[3]
64. Francis Keth[4]
65. William Lenton
66. John Comlyne
67. John Wilkin
68. Rynyon Kill
69. John Dixon
70. John Gracye
71. Andrew Lowe
72. David Lowe
73. William Scot
74. John Tate
75. Patrick McKea
76. Alexander McNab
77. Mungo Beaty

Sword and Pike

78. James Melvin Esquire

No Arms

79. Edward Beaty
80. Alexander Hammilton
81. Thomas Miller
82. John Lowe
83. James Hoode
84. James Adamson
85. Guy Gelly
86. John Black
87. John Williamson

[f. 205v]

88. Robert Thompson
89. William McKean
90. William Bell
91. Walter Kelly
92. James Murrey
93. John Bell younger
94. Edward Carlell
95. Hugh Hammilton
96. Robert Leay
97. Ralph Litler
98. Robert Litiwhich
99. John Litiwhich
100. James Davye
101. Thomas Bagan
102. Daniell Calore
103. Henry Calore
104. John Johnston
105. William Steward
106. Robert Camron
107. John Boyd
108. Henry Cutler
109. Thomas Porter
110. Robert Caugh
111. Gilbert Calles
112. John Cooke
113. James Johnston
114. Robert Hurran
115. John Newall
116. John Scot

---

1   Payne was living at Strangford in 1641. He became captain of the settlers and was drilling and training more than 600 men to hold Downpatrick and Lecale against the Irish. According to Payne, Sir James Montgomery deciding to abandon his position led to the fall of Downpatrick and Lecale (Deposition of Valentin Payne, 9 August 1642 [TCD MS 837, fols 019r–020v]).

2   'Will Hamilton' was identified as one of the killers of the Irish in Ardglass, 1643 (Deposition of John MacDonnell, 7 May 1653 [ibid. fols 128r–129v]).

3   Identified as one of the killers of the Irish in 1642 (Deposition of Phellymy Smith, 1 June 1653 [ibid. fols 061r–062v]); 'Dixon came from Bishopscourt to Ardglass of purpose to kill the said [Cormack] Mackgueer because of some difference betwixt the said Mcgueer and a brother of the said Dixon' (Examination of Robert Merriman, 7 May 1653 [ibid. f. 144r]). Dixon is probably the younger son of Robert Dixon (Cromwell, number 60); he was aged 40 when he made his deposition in 1653; he admitted being present at Maguire's death but denied being one of the killers (Examinations of Thomas Dixon, 7 May 1653 [ibid. fols 148r–149v] and 27 May 1653 [ibid. fols 152r–152v]).

4   'Of Ardglass being aged about fifty years' (Deposition of Francis Keith, 7 May 1653 [ibid. f. 132r]).

117. Henry Hudlestone
118. John Cosly
119. Thomas Allan[5]
120. Thomas Allan younger

[f. 206]

121. William Wilson
122. Robert Hostly
123. John Little
124. John Wilson
125. John Watson

[f. 206v]

The Lord Crumwell, his British tenants upon his servitors and churchlands: their names and arms

Sword only

1. Thomas Close
2. Peter Hill[6]
3. James Scot
4. William Turner
5. John Carssan[7]
6. Andrew Spence
7. William Black
8. William Bridges
9. William Turner
10. Robert Breeton
11. John Slark
12. John Ashdon
13. Robert Knock
14. John Rowen
15. Roger Shippheard
16. Thomas Coop
17. John Coop
18. William Athy[8]
19. William Thrift
20. Andrew Young[9]
21. Andrew Young younger

22. John Martin
23. John Bell
24. John McDonnell
25. Henry Smyth[10]
26. Patrick Newhill
27. William Penny
28. John Feathers
29. John Crery

[f. 207]

30. Patrick Kelly
31. William Creary
32. Thomas Bell
33. Thomas Watson
34. William Watson
35. Edward Creighton
36. John Newell
37. William Cormack
38. John Carsan
39. John Cormack
40. John McMakin
41. John McKinshay
42. John Wilson
43. John Lyndsay
44. Robert Frowd
45. Andrew Black
46. John Jening
47. John Steele
48. James Gourdon
49. William Young
50. Gilbert Michell
51. Cuthbert Amon
52. John Browne
53. John Cochan
54. Walter Bell
55. Thomas Spence
56. Claud Hammilton
57. Hugh Griffin
58. William Kining[11]
59. Robert Ranson
60. Robert Dixon[12]

[f. 207v]

61. John Browne
62. Robert Foster younger[13]
63. John Hanna
64. James Hanna
65. Edward Nealson
66. Robert Gibson
67. John Smyth
68. Cuthbert Strong
69. James Scot
70. William Turner
71. John Carsan
72. William Black
73. John Broadfoote
74. Andrew Boyd
75. William Edger
76. Wm. Archbaldson
77. Wm Hammilton
78. John Flack
79. Alexander Fynston
80. John Deniston
81. Patrick Armestrong[14]
82. Thomas Armestrong
83. John Turner
84. Gawen Gelly
85. Alexander Lyndsay
86. Thomas Carruddas
87. Andrew Young younger[15]
88. Herbert Young
89. Thomas Adamson
90. John Smyth
91. John Grat
92. Thomas Kenedy
93. Henry Smyth

[f. 208]

94. Patrick Newell
95. William Penny
96. John Feather
97. William Cormack
98. John Cormack

---

[5] Numbers 119 and 120 may be the grandfather and father of 'Thomas Allen of Ile Lecale [who was] aged twenty-five years' when he made his deposition, describing events at Ballee, January 1642 (Deposition of Thomas Allen, 19 May 1653 [ibid. fols 066r–067v]).

[6] High sheriff and provost marshal for county Down, 1641; organised quarter sessions at Killyleagh to indict more than 100 Irish and Old English men as rebels; losses £3,804 0s 0d (Deposition of Peter Hill, 29 May 1645 [ibid. fols 030r–037v]).

[7] 'John Carshan' (number 5, 38, or 71) was killed at Ballee church, January 1642 (Deposition of John Kimming, 19 May 1653 [ibid. fols 071r–072v]).

[8] Resident Downpatrick; wife, Anne Betts, killed, February 1642 (Examinations of Rowland Browne, 3 June 1653 [ibid. fols 164r–164v], John Smith, 10 June 1653 [ibid. fols 167r–167v], and Henry Smith 3 May 1653 [ibid. fols 181r–181v]).

[9] Numbers 20 and 21 are father and son.

[10] Resident Loughadian, near Poyntz Pass and hence tenant of Marmaduke Whitchurch, 1641; losses £3,762 13s 4d (Deposition of Henry Smith, 11 June 1641 [TCD MS 837, fols 014r–017v]).

[11] After escaping from Ballee church, William Kimming senior found and buried the victims of the massacre at the church in January 1642 (Deposition of William Carshan, 19 May 1653 [TCD MS 837, fols 068r–069v]): the dead included Kimming's sons, Charles and William junior (Deposition of the surviving son, John Kimming of Saul, 19 May 1653 [ibid. fols 071r–072v]).

[12] Father of Robert Dixon younger (number 325), and possibly of Thomas Dixon (Kildare, number 63); resident Bishopscourt (Examination of Thomas Dixon, 7 May 1653 [ibid. fols 148r–149v]).

[13] Robert Foster senior did not muster.

[14] Aged forty; resident Killyleagh, 1653 (Deposition of Patrick Armstrong, 20 May 1653 [TCD MS 837, fols 103r–104v].

[15] Son of number 356.

99. Thomas Standis
100. John McKenester
101. John Willson
102. Patrick Hanan
103. William Black
104. Andrew Black
105. Andrew Spent
106. John McCourty
107. John Irving[16]
108. John Still
109. Edward Bygon
110. James Gourden
111. Andrew Murroch
112. James Rea elder
113. Robert Glentrot
114. John Dixon
115. William Bryeth
116. David Thomas
117. Robert Calwater
118. Owen Johnes
119. Richard Tod
120. Wm Kirkepatrick
121. James Steavenson
122. John McCan
123. John McMathey

[f. 208v]

124. John McMathew
125. Thomas Price
126. John Kawhy
127. John Conningham
128. Thomas Kirkpatrick
129. Robert Burtrick
130. Cloyd Hammilton
131. John Spole
132. John Gillaspeck
133. Frauncis Cunaston
134. Edward Cunaston
135. Edward Hayes
136. Richard Maxwell
137. John Russell
138. John mcMurrin
139. John Loughead
140. Thomas Creary
141. Alexander Carsan
142. John West elder[17]
143. James Cornell
144. Thomas Fad

145. Robert Starling
146. John Robertson
147. Mathew Davis
148. Thomas Weilding
149. John Swell

[f. 209]

150. John McWilliams
151. James Davis
152. William Ard
153. Christopher Nicholson
154. Frauncis Nicholson
155. Edward Syngleton
156. Ralph Smyth
157. Robert Butler
158. Wm. Conningham
159. Richard Huchison
160. Robert Begat
161. William Welshen
162. John Taylor
163. Christopher mcKelson
164. Ralph Angret
165. Robert Begart
166. William Toole
167. Robert Leswith
168. William Steward
169. Robert Cambell
170. John mcRobert
171. John Carrat
172. George Hathorne
173. John Newall
174. William Welshman
175. John Hammilton
176. Richard Maxwell
177. Quinton Agnew
178. James Russell
179. John Russell

[f. 209v]

180. John West elder
181. Mathew Davy
182. John McBrid
183. John McMathew younger[18]
184. William Kirkepatricke
185. John Sproyle
186. Richard Kelsy
187. Richard Coop

188. Robert Cadwalder
189. Owen Johnes
190. Owen Owins

Sword and Pike

191. Thomas Carrudhowse
192. John Carradhouse
193. John Gealton
194. Patrick Hanna
195. John Anderson
196. Robert Coolhart
197. Robert Brittaine
198. James Stanison
199. Richard Gradell

Pike only

200. Robert Knox
201. William Davis
202. William Carlill

Sword and Caliver

203. Robert Harris
204. Andrew English[19]

Sword and Snaphance

205. John Goddy
206. Christopher Saywell

Sword and Musket

207. James Davis
208. Robert Hutchison

[f. 210]

Sword and Halberd

209. James Kelly

Halberd only

210. Thomas Kirkpatrick

No Arms

211. Robert Cole
212. Robert Homes[20]
213. John Smyth
214. Randall Taylor
215. John Hodgson
216. John Streaton
217. John Reader
218. Walter Keil

---

[16] Resident Finnabrogue, near Downpatrick: attacked and killed his Irish neighbours, February 1643 after murders of mother and sister previous summer (Depositions of Grany Nee Mullan, 25 May 1653 [TCD MS 837, 101r–102v], John Litle, 20 May 1653 [ibid. f.103r], and John Irvin, 3 May 1653 [ibid. fols 105r–106v]).

[17] Two men are named John West elder (numbers 142 and 180) and two are named John West younger (numbers 320 and 427); two families called West were therefore resident on the estate.

[18] Son of number 429.

[19] English was identified as an assailant of the Irish at Magheramorne, near Larne, January 1642 (Depositions of Phelemye Magee, 5 May 1653 [TCD MS 837, fols 107r–107v] and Donnell McLester [McAllister], 20 May 1653 [ibid. fols 108r–108v]); English blamed others for the killings (Deposition of Andrew English, 20 April 1653 [ibid. fols 111r–111v]). Magee and McLester were living at Castlereagh and English was resident at Ballyedward, near Magheramorne, 1653.

[20] Killed near Downpatrick, 1641 (Deposition of William Gore, 1 July 1653 [ibid. fols 025r–025v] and Examination of Rowland Browne, 3 June 1653 [ibid. fols 164r–164v]).

219. John Hodgson
220. Thomas Hodgson younger
221. Alexander Boyd
222. Thomas Adams
223. Henry Clarke
224. Thomas Adamson
225. James Crookehead
226. Thomas Osbesson
227. William Steele
228. John Broadfoote
229. John McKenan
230. William Edgger
231. Symond Scott
232. Patrick Anderson
233. Miles Ramson
234. James Taylor
235. William Arbiston
236. Thomas Carter
237. John Dixon

[f. 210v]

238. Thomas Pardisse
239. Ralph Smyth
240. Robert Clencross
241. Symon Athy
242. William Davis
243. William Morris
244. William Bordlad
245. Essacary Brute
246. Robert Wilson
247. John Humphrey
248. John Reed
249. Harbert Young
250. Alexander Sincleer
251. John mcKee
252. Thomas Kenedy
253. John Kenedy
254. Robert Browne
255. John Johnston
256. Robert Lattimor
257. Abraham Lenton
258. Thomas Smyth
259. Thomas Standise
260. John Kelly
261. Thomas Kelly
262. Arthur Patterson
263. William Con

264. Walter Chambers
265. James mcKee
266. Peter Jefferey

[f. 211]

267. Thomas Johnston
268. Robert Carradhowse
269. John Black
270. Robert Maxwell
271. John Shanke
272. George Carsan
273. Robert Carsan
274. John Fensell
275. Alexander Keoghy
276. Alexander Jenkinson
277. John Maxwell
278. William Grace
279. Thomas Maxwell
280. Alexander Armestrong
281. Robert Harris
282. Edward Bigham
283. George Bell
284. Arthur Broadfoat
285. John McCartney
286. Edward Foster
287. William Burley[21]
288. William Wardlaw
289. John Humfrey
290. William Maglow
291. John Wilson
292. Mungo Wilson
293. George Armestrang
294. William Young [Deleted]
295. Thomas Rea[22]
296. Thomas Rea younger

[f. 211v]

297. John Pringle
298. Arthur Fynestowne
299. James Dungan
300. Robert Stoen
301. Henry Jackson
302. Danyell Merryman[23]
303. Robert Nixon
304. Richard Russell[24]
305. William Russell
306. Robert Black

307. John Stewart
308. Richard Davis
309. James Black
310. Neall mcMaister
311. George Purdenn
312. Patrick Cachy
313. John Johnston
314. William Bell
315. Robert McConn
316. Rowland Griffin
317. Nathaniell Bleston
318. James Bleston
319. Richard Reedward
320. John West
321. Henry Carse
322. James Crag
323. William Naught

[f. 212]

Pike only

324. Thomas Ward
325. Robert Dixon younger[25]
326. Richard Foster
327. George Walker
328. John Wynrin
329. William Dixon
330. John Kelly
331. Robert Gibson
332. Alexander Hana
333. James Symond
334. Alexander Cammell
335. John Bowman
336. James Atkinson
337. Thomas Close
338. Rowland Taylor
339. John Hutchon[26]

Halberds

340. John Roger
341. John Hutchen younger
342. William Dronry
343. James Tayllyane
344. James Crookart
345. James Steele
346. John McKenan
347. William Turner
348. Patrick Anderson

[21] High sheriff of Down, 1640 (*Montgomery MSS*, p. 138); described himself as 'sergeant major William Burley of Magheralagan, one of his majesty's justices of the peace and quorum within the county of Down'; losses £8,000 0s 0d (Deposition of William Burley, 10 August 1644 [TCD MS 837, fols 029r–029v]).

[22] Numbers 295 and 296 are father and son.

[23] Daniel Merriman may be a son of Robert Merriman, who described himself as 'of Ballyhornan in the county of Down, gentleman aged seventy-two years' when he made his deposition, 18 May 1653 (TCD MS 837, fols 079r–080v). Nicholas Merriman of Ardglass was another of his sons (ibid. f. 132r]). George Merriman, who escorted the English prisoners to Newcastle, December 1641 and who was living at Dundrum, 1653 and William Merriman of Bishopscourt were probably also relatives (Deposition of Edmund Doran, 8 June 1653 [ibid. fols 092r–092v]; *Montgomery MSS*, p. 315).

[24] Richard Russell was the son of Christopher Russell, died 22 June 1619 (*Montgomery MSS*, p. 315); the Russells, barons of Killough, were related to the Merrimans.

[25] Son of Robert Dixon (number 60) and possibly brother of Thomas Dixon of Bishopscourt (Cromwell, number 63); resident in Ardglass, 1641 (Examination of Thomas Dixon, 7 May 1653 [TCD MS 837, fols 148r–149v]).

349. Edward Wanderon
350. John Maxwell

No Arms

351. Richard Kill
352. John Dixon
353. Richard Turner
354. William Morriss
355. John Coop
356. Andrew Young elder[27]
357. John Carsan
358. John Maxwell
359. John Lyndsay
360. Robert Froud
361. William Maxwell[28]
362. Thomas Maxwell
363. George Carrudhouse
364. Alexander Armestrong
365. John McCartney
366. John Law
367. John Bell
368. John Robinson
369. Francis Houdgate
370. David Thompson
371. Hugh Gill
372. Peter Smith
373. Robert Odall
374. Richard Kelsay
375. Nicholas Fitz Symonds[29]
376. John Flood
377. Ralph Smyth
378. William Preston
379. John Kirkam
380. John Raymentoun

[f. 213]

Swords and Muskets

381. Robert Claney
382. William Roberts
383. James Preston
384. Quinton Agnew
385. William Agnew
386. William Clappertowne
387. Robert Clapperton
388. William Oustin
389. John Oustin
390. Robert Crafford
391. Hugh Crafford
392. Hugh Russell
393. James Murphe
394. James Russell
395. William Labby
396. John Crassan
397. Donnell McIlroy
398. William Waughan
399. John McBrid
400. John Graham
401. John Wast younger
402. John Messenger[30]
403. John Messenger younger

Pikes only

404. James Cornnell
405. William Gore[31]
406. Symond Swell
407. Joseph Thomson
408. Thomas Crone
409. Thomas Barther

[f. 213v]

410. William Adares
411. Thomas Butler
412. Robert Heild
413. John Goody
414. John Mc McCub
415. Ralph Littleane
416. John Kirkonne
417. John Ringneton
418. William Hosting
419. John Loughead
420. William Lamb
421. Robert Sterling
422. Richard Gredall[32]
423. John Carsan
424. Thomas Wildony
425. James Cornewell
426. Symond Swell
427. John West younger
428. Robert Ogton
429. John McMathew elder[33]
430. James Upritt
431. John McCaghey
432. John Biggon
433. Henry Wallace
434. Robert Borthick
435. Peter Smith
436. William Cahlell
437. John Killaspy

438. John Nicholson
439. Peter Taylor
440. George Robinson

[f. 214]

441. Symond Johnston
442. John Peterson
443. William Taylor
444. John Jenkinson
445. Hugh Price
446. Thomas Roberts
447. John Styles
448. Henry Gower
449. Myles Yare
450. Thomas Stenison
451. Peter Colf
452. Steaphen Hall
453. Robert Rowland
454. John Hughes
455. Gilbert Raylton
456. John Brothait
457. Thomas Tarne
458. Symond Simpson
459. Paul Robertson
460. George Nealson
461. Peter Hayes
462. William Weltch

[f. 214v]

463. Hugh Hobson
464. Steven Garrat
465. Henry Hudson
466. Gilbert Fryer
467. Thomas Faynesay
468. John Nichols
469. Richard Richardson
470. Peter Wiggat
471. Thomas Nealson
472. William Turner
473. Henry Gray
474. George Nevison
475. Humphrey Goudyere
476. James Johnston
477. Thomas Baly[34]
478. Gregory Mason
479. John Turner
480. Gyles Heiron

---

[26] Numbers 339 and 341 are father and son.
[27] Father of number 87 above.
[28] Killed at Ballee church in January 1642 (Deposition of John Kimming, 19 May 1653 [TCD MS 837, fols 072r–072v]).
[29] Possibly son of Redmond Fitzsimmons (Deposition of Phellymy Smith, 1 June 1653 [ibid. fols 061r–062v]); described himself as 'of the castle of Kilclief in the county of Down, gentleman' (Deposition of Nicholas Fitzsymons, 11 May 1642 [ibid. fols 129r–129v]).
[30] Numbers 402 and 403 are father and son.
[31] 'Of Ballintogher …, gentleman'; losses £500 0s 0d (Deposition of William Gore, 1 July 1643 [TCD MS 837, fols 025r–025v]).
[32] Resident Downpatrick; wife, Katherine, killed, February 1642 (Deposition of Richard Cradell, 3 May 1653 [ibid. fols 095r–096v] and Examination of John Smith, 10 June 1653 [ibid. fols 167r–167v]).
[33] Father of number 183.
[34] Named as a burgess in the charter of Killyleagh, 10 March 1613 (*Hamilton MSS*, general appendix, p. lxv).

[f. 215]

Down

The Lord Viscount of Ards,
his men and arms

No Arms

1. John McNeise[35]
2. John Milmorrow
3. Edward Johnston[36]
4. John Dabbin
5. Patrick Cample
6. John Neally
7. Andrew McIlwrath[37]
8. Thomas McMaster
9. John mcEnestry
10. Thomas McEnestry
11. Thomas Walker
12. John Law
13. Patrick Patterson
14. David McMaiester
15. Ralph Farnam
16. John Creighton
17. George Patterson
18. Robert Carrudhowse
19. John Nicholl
20. John Wilson
21. Robert Nealson
22. John McClelan
23. James Sheill
24. Hugh Mountgomery
25. Robert Rorison
26. William Capert
27. Robert Graham
28. John Kenedy

[f. 215v]

29. George Cornock
30. John Sandeland
31. John Kayle
32. John Gibby
33. William Johnston
34. John Browne
35. Patrick Orr
36. John Peacock[38]
37. Adam Coline

38. Patrick Hanna
39. William Farge
40. John Taylor
41. John Paul
42. Alexander Smith
43. Patrick McLarg
44. John Old
45. Gilbert McHyre
46. High McBrid
47. Roger McMurry
48. William Walker
49. John Milligen
50. Patrick Purse
51. James Willson
52. Robert Thompson
53. John Alson
54. John Martyn[39]
55. John Holliday
56. William Burges[40]
57. John Gilmore
58. John Kenedy

[f. 216]

59. Robert Mountgomery
60. David McGill[41]
61. Andrew Harvy
62. William Scot
63. Hugh Clarke
64. Thomas Jameson younger[42]
65. John Scot
66. William McNabin
67. James Kenedy
68. John Parsly
69. William Henderson
70. Alexander Coushey
71. John Gibson
72. David Gibson
73. William Cant
74. John Thompson[43]
75. John Martyne
76. Walter Robson
77. James McIlmorrow
78. John Forsith
79. Mathew Robertson
80. John Howston
81. John McCullagh
82. William Galbreath
83. Robert Jabson

84. John Jarden
85. Alexander Gilmoore

[f. 216v]

86. Martin Shellene
87. David Beggs
88. John Sprot
89. John mcCrere
90. Michaell Maghine
91. John Alexander
92. Gilbert Steward
93. John Shallene
94. John Henderson
95. William Rogerson
96. Patrick Edger
97. John Browne
98. Andrew Browne
99. James Hamilton
100. Patrick McMaiester

Swords only

101. Andrew Black
102. Thomas Mulligan
103. James McCrery
104. James Parker
105. Alexander McGusoke
106. John Jackson
107. John Moore[44]
108. John Alexander
109. John Mountgomery
110. Alexander Earle
111. James McKee
112. John Smart
113. James Kinkirk

[f. 217]

114. William Skells
115. Alexander McBryny
116. John Grane
117. Thomas McCamlees
118. John Haning
119. John Osten
120. Andrew Forsith
121. James Moore
122. John Gourden
123. Andrew Carsan
124. John Conningham[45]

---

35 Swords only deleted until number 94.

36 Edward Johnston of Greengraves was one of the mourners at the funeral of viscount Ards, 1636 (*Montgomery MSS*, p. 132).

37 Resident Ballymaglaff before 1641 (Deposition of William MacGillwrath, 2 May 1653 [TCD MS 837, fols 055r–056v]).

38 'John Peacocke of Ballydoonan', near Carrowdore, received letters of denization, 1617 (*Calendar of patent rolls, Ireland, James I*, pp 326–39; *Montgomery MSS*, p. 56).

39 One of the John Martins in this list is 'John Marten of Dunnevilly' who received letters of denization, 1617 (*Calendar of patent rolls, Ireland, James I*, pp 326–39; *Montgomery MSS*, p. 56).

40 William Burgess and John Gilmore of Newtown appear among the servants in the cortege of viscount Ards, 1636 (ibid. p. 135).

41 Son of David Magill, chaplain at Greyabbey since 1607 (ibid. p. 61).

42 Son of number 1028.

43 'Of Blackabbey'; denization, 1617 (*Calendar of patent rolls, Ireland, James I*, pp 326–39; *Montgomery MSS*, p. 56).

44 Resident Donaghadee; denization, 1617 (*Calendar of patent rolls, Ireland, James I*, pp 326–39; *Montgomery MSS*, p. 56).

45 Possibly 'John Cunningham of Rinchrivie'; denization, 1617 (*Calendar of patent rolls, Ireland, James I*, pp 326–39; *Montgomery MSS*, p. 56).

125. John Steinson
126. Alexander McDonnell
127. John Grayne
128. Gilbert Begs
129. Alexander Beggs
130. James Anderson
131. John McIlvian[46]
132. Patrick McCarmont
133. Gilbert McTeare
134. Peter Phillip
135. William Granie
136. Robert Kenedy
137. James Jarden
138. James Wilson
139. John Orr
140. Richard Thompson
141. Robert McClenan
142. Adam Rutherfoord

[f. 217v]

143. John Shenane
144. Thomas McNaryne
145. John McMurry
146. John Latimer
147. John Spence
148. Robert Coary
149. John Craye
150. William Bothwene
151. James Anderson
152. John Mulligan
153. William Kenedy
154. Cuthbert McNeally
155. Robert Kirkpatrick
156. Robert Martyne
157. John Martyne
158. Michaell Wakeson
159. Michaell Scot
160. Alexander Gillespicke
161. John Ellot
162. Andrew Smyth
163. James Orr
164. John Donnalson
165. Gilbert McLyne
166. John Barkly[47]
167. Hugh Knock
168. James Steward
169. Alexander McCaly
170. Henry Coltor

[f. 218]

171. Thomas Scot
172. Michaell McCallyne
173. Robert Steward
174. John Ross
175. John Trumble
176. John Cawell
177. James Davison
178. Humphrey mcCollyne
179. William Catherwood[48]
180. John mcClune
181. John Tynning
182. Gilbert mcCay
183. Hugh Montgomery
184. Mathew Hislack
185. Adam Wilson
186. Edward McGilton
187. James McKenny
188. John Wandrick
189. John Welly
190. John Patterson
191. Thomas Donagh
192. Patrick Agneill
193. Alexander Milligan
194. Thomas Gillmoore
195. Robert Christiaill
196. David Crafford

[f. 218v]

197. William Wilby
198. James Moore
199. John mcKnely
200. Thomas Scot elder[49]
201. John McConnell
202. Thomas Kilpatrick
203. John Milling
204. Mathew Mountgomery
205. Mathew Scot
206. Andrew Roresteill
207. James Johnston

Swords and Pikes
208. William Kenedy
209. David Kenedy[50]
210. John Moran
211. Gilbert Crossan
212. John Howston

213. Fynlay Dalyell
214. John Dalyell
215. Edward Irwing
216. John Irwing
217. Thomas Orr
218. Anthony McNeally
219. Alexander McGuffog
220. John Willson
221. John Scot
222. John McNealy younger[51]
223. John McNealy elder

[f. 219]

224. Richard Irwing
225. Adam Grange
226. Hugh Caddon
227. Robert Grange
228. George Scot
229. John Gibson[52]
230. John Gibson younger
231. John mcClelan
232. John mcIlwayne
233. John McWaugh
234. John McCarnock
235. Patrick mcCullagh
236. William Murragh
237. Edward Sceit
238. Robert Read
239. William Jackson
240. Nynian mcHaff
241. John Brewhouse
242. William Brewhowse
243. William Keabry
244. Andrew Read
245. John Moore
246. John Murry
247. Andrew Garnen
248. Robert Dury
249. Mungo McGea
250. Jo. Montgoumry
251. Adam Montgumry[53]
252. John Gourdon

[f. 219v]

253. Gilbert Johnston
254. Thomas Scot[54]
255. Adam Murry

---

[46] Andrew McIlveen – possibly the son of John McIlveen – escorted Irish refugees from Holywood to the Ards, February 1642 (Examination of Daniell MacThomas O Gilmore, 28 April 1653 [TCD MS 838, fols 249r–250v]).

[47] Resident Ballyrolly, near Millisle; denization, 1617 (*Calendar of patent rolls, Ireland, James I*, pp 326–39; *Montgomery MSS*, p. 56).

[48] Catherwood was one of the original settlers on the Montgomery estate; his denization papers (1617) describe him as 'of Ballyfrench, near Portavogie (*Calendar of patent rolls, Ireland, James I*, pp 326–39; *Montgomery MSS*, p. 56). He purchased Ballyvester, near Donaghadee from William and Archibald Edmonston, 1 October 1630 and was one of the mourners at the funeral of viscount Ards, 1636 (ibid. p. 54).

[49] Father of number 254.

[50] 'David Kennedy of Gortivillan' received letters of denization, 1617 (*Calendar of patent rolls, Ireland, James I*, pp 326–39; *Montgomery MSS*, p. 56).

[51] Numbers 222 and 223 are father and son.

[52] Numbers 229 and 230 are father and son.

[53] Carpenter; licenced to fell timber around Comber, 1610 (*Calendar of patent rolls, Ireland, James I*, pp 254–5; *Inquisitions of Ulster, Down* (105), Charles I; Morrin, *Patent rolls, Charles I*, 1–8, p. 65).

[54] Son of number 200.

256. John Anderson
257. Adam Gamill
258. David Gibson
259. John Parke
260. James mcHuthdene
261. Cuthbert mcMeellan
262. Robert McMullen
263. John mcHutchden
264. Andrew Kaig
265. William Mountgomery
266. John mcKitrick
267. William Orr
268. James Edire   Headpiece
269. John Gourden
270. Wm mcCullagh
271. Robert Knox
272. David Wallace
273. Alexander Cogheran
274. James mcCullen
275. Thomas mcCullen
276. Fynlay Cogheran
277. Alexander Gourdan
278. Robert Montgoomry
279. Robert Kenedy
280. Henry mcGlessen
281. James Moore

[f. 220]

282. Thomas mcLymond
283. James mcCallow
284. William Dunlop
285. William Weltch
286. William Morin
287. Symond Graham
288. James Miller
289. John Dickee
290. William Russell
291. Robert Steward
292. Neall McGill
293. William Deniston
294. Thomas mcQuahan
295. Alexander Speere[55]
296. John Millen[56]

297. Thomas mcCannan
298. William Bires
299. John mcQuoyd
300. Robert Boyd[57]
301. Thomas Cambell
302. John Cogheran
303. William Allen
304. James Patten
305. William Buchan
306. John McThomson
307. John Cowet
308. Patrick Allen[58]
309. Mathew Ekleene
310. Robert Moore
311. James Michell

[f. 220v]

312. Thomas More
313. John Dunlap
314. Thomas Hudye
315. John Frizell
316. Robert Davyson
317. Thomas Hoghan
318. John James
319. James mcKee
320. Gawen Henderson
321. William Stone
322. John Edgar
323. George Byner
324. John Fayres
325. John Gynnan
326. John Guyman
327. John Shaw[59]
328. Robert Cogheran
329. Nynyan McRobert
330. James Browne
331. James Dobbison
332. John mcCligham
333. William mcKillin
334. Francis Irwing
335. John Irwing
336. David Kenedy
337. John mcTully

338. Mathew Lewis
339. Thomas mcTaggat
340. Edward Irwing

[f. 221]

341. Richard Harris
342. Andrew mcTyre
343. Nichol: Dynn
344. John Spere elder[60]
345. Thomas Dunkan
346. William Might
347. Thomas Montgumery[61]
348. James Willy
349. James Biggin
350. David McAdam
351. Robert Wilson[62]
352. William Callender
353. John Frasser[63]
354. William Buyes
355. Alexander Jameson
356. John Alleson
357. John Jordane[64]
358. John Bane
359. John Browne
360. Andrew Fargison
361. Alexander Maxwell
362. Malcome Napa
363. James Wilson
364. John Rogerson
365. Mathew Thompson
366. Thomas Fargussonn
367. George Read
368. William Cunning
369. William Shaw[65]

[f. 221v]

370. Edward Cantart
371. John Richy
372. John Fargusson
373. Thomas London
374. Allen Sympson
375. Robert Curry

---

55 'Of Grey Abbey'; denization in 1617 (*Calendar of patent rolls, Ireland, James I*, pp 326–39; *Montgomery MSS*, p. 56).

56 'John Millen of Greyabbey' appears among the servants in the cortege of viscount Ards, 1636 (*Montgomery MSS*, p. 135).

57 One of the Robert Boyds in this list was the son of Colonel David Boyd, one of the original settlers in North Down. Boyd purchased Ballymacarret from Conn O'Neill, 1609 and passed it to James Cathcart. Cathcart, who was resident at Ballycroghan when he received denization, 1617 (*Calendar of patent rolls, Ireland, James I*, pp 326–39; *Montgomery MSS*, p. 56), sold the townland to Lord Clandeboy in 1623 (ibid. p. 41). Boyd became a tenant of viscount Ards at Castletown [Ballycastle townland, near Mountstewart] and his son, Robert, inherited the property, 22 March 1625 (*Montgomery MSS*, p. 53; *Calendar of patent rolls, Ireland, James I*, p. 582; Inquisitions of Ulster, Down (40) and (75), Charles I).

58 Resident Ballydoonan; denization, 1617 (*Calendar of patent rolls, Ireland, James I*, pp 326–39; *Montgomery MSS*, p. 56).

59 John Shaw of Greenock was the brother-in-law of Sir High Montgomery and Patrick Montgomery. Shaw took possession of two townlands, 1616 and still held them, 1623 (*Montgomery MSS*, pp 51–2).

60 Father of number 656.

61 This (or number 794) may be Thomas Montgomery of Blacktown, a distant relative of viscount Ards and brother-in-law to William and Alexander Dobbin (numbers 774 and 1098): Thomas Montgomery was a resident of Newtownards (*Montgomery MSS*, p. 26).

62 Resident Newtown; denization, 1617 (*Calendar of patent rolls, Ireland, James I*, pp 326–39; *Montgomery MSS*, p. 56).

63 Denization, 1617; resident Donaghadee (*Calendar of patent rolls, Ireland, James I*, pp 326–39; *Montgomery MSS*, p. 56).

64 'John Jerden' appears among the servants in the cortege of viscount Ards, 1636 (*Montgomery MSS*, p. 135).

65 Resident Ballycullen; denization, 1617 (*Calendar of patent rolls, Ireland, James I*, pp 326–39; *Montgomery MSS*, p. 56).

376. William Coussen
377. John Coussen
378. William Smyth
379. Robert Rod
380. Robert Gibson
381. Gilbert Ekally
382. John mcNeight
383. John Lowry
384. William Cockbourn
385. Andrew Michaell
386. John Dunkan
387. James Orr
388. John mcConie
389. George Willson
390. William Ouston
391. James Conningham
392. John Conffee
393. Mungo Jabson
394. Walter mcClure
395. Thomas Japhrey
396. John Porter[66]
397. James Boyd
398. David Smyth
399. John Hanna

[f. 222]

400. Patrick Bonatin
401. James Sincleare
402. Richard Maxwell
403. Robert Winkerston
404. Robert mcCoullees
405. David Roger
406. John Bell
407. John mcClenan
408. John Hughnan
409. John Dayell
410. William Gledry
411. James mcClish
412. John Fargusson
413. Robert Grane
414. John mcNeary
415. Richard mcBrid
416. James Wallace
417. John Stroyane
418. Alexander Read
419. David Alexander
420. John Rootherfoord
421. Roger Ireland
422. Patrick Black
423. David Wilson
424. Robert Browne
425. Henry Browne
426. James Michell
427. John Michell

[f. 222v]

428. James Mulligan
429. William Grere
430. Hugh Eglene
431. John Stroyen
432. Andrew Skilling
433. William Skilling
434. Dunkan mcWilliam
435. William Wilson
436. John McDonnell
437. Alexander Herron
438. Daniell McDonnell
439. Downey McDonnell
440. John mcCowtrone
441. Alexander Rose
442. Robert Jarden
443. John McGill
444. John Steward
445. William Parker
446. George Habberson
447. Gilbert mcGea
448. Patrick Gibson
449. John McKee
450. Allan Makee
451. John Makey
452. John Stroyan
453. David Knight
454. Adam Jackson
455. Thomas Stoup
456. John Gourdan
457. Thomas Nell
458. Robert Neill

[f. 223]

459. Robert Steaphen
460. Michaell Gibson
461. John Gamill
462. John mcCanlees
463. Alexander Ross
464. James mcKeen
465. James Browne
466. Thomas McDonnell
467. Harbert mcCullagh
468. Thomas Lundy
469. John Martin
470. John Walker
471. Symond mcCarle
472. John Daire
473. William Haning
474. Robert Eskine
475. James McCullagh
476. Robert Gourden
477. Andrew Gourden
478. John McDonnell

479. Andrew Bell
480. William Read
481. James Skilling
482. John Beggs
483. William McCarby
484. Andrew Bannantyne
485. Robert Creighton
486. Michael Hooke
487. James Ingram[67]
488. Gilbert Moonie

[f. 233v]

489. William Jordan
490. John Steane
491. John Rorison
492. Patrick McDonnell
493. Gilbert Wallice
494. Gilbert McCrery
495. John Dungan
496. John Thompson
497. John Davy
498. John Howet
499. John Dunlap
500. Alexander mcCalla
501. James Murdorgh
502. John Boyd[68]
503. Robert Boyd
504. Thomas mcRobert
505. John Jarden
506. Patrick Heron
507. John Anderson
508. James Jarden
509. Thomas Jarden
510. Alexander Jarden
511. John Latimer
512. Andrew Young
513. Thomas Torly
514. James Dalrumple
515. Andrew mcAlexander
516. John Parke
517. Alexander Rowcastle
518. Robert Edger
519. Archbald Cowtronie
520. Robert Gourden

[f. 224]

521. John Bryneione
522. Cuthbert Orr
523. Patrick mcKelly
524. Thomas Adam
525. Thomas Browne
526. William Browne
527. David Herrot
528. Adam Farly

---

66 Killed, 1641 [Examination of Patricke o Hoiland, 5 May 1653 [TCD MS 838, fols 169r–169v]).

67 Possibly the father of Thomas and Leonard Ingram: the former was killed around 1642 and the latter was one of George Rawdon's troopers (Examination of Bryan McIlcrany, 5 May 1653 [TCD MS 838, fols 168r–168v]).

68 John Boyd, grandson of Colonel David Boyd, was one of the mourners at the funeral of viscount Ards, 1636 (*Montgomery MSS*, p. 132).

529. John McKillouffe
530. Robert Allen
531. James Neill
532. James Geimmell
533. James Egleson
534. Mathew Glascoe
535. Robert Allen
536. John Douglass
537. Thomas Steward
538. William McCre
539. Andrew McDowgall
540. Andrew Read
541. James Kelso
542. Robert Matlan
543. Robert Calwell
544. William Powell
545. Daniell Powell
546. John Park
547. Archbald Kelso
548. Alexander Kelso
549. Andrew Slane

[f. 224v]

550. James Bagster
551. John Johnston
552. Thomas White
553. John Read
554. David Trumble
555. William Wilson
556. John mcIlhew
557. John Wilson
558. Robert Scot
559. Robert Calwell
560. Thomas Gourden
561. John Powell
562. Patrick mcGall
563. James Bell
564. John Candelom
565. John Baton
566. Andrew Bowne
567. Thomas Gord
568. James Dobby
569. Michaell Dobby
570. William Cord
571. Archbald Cord
572. Robert Peacock
573. Thomas Browne
574. William Browne
575. John McIlgared
576. Charles Skilling

577. John McIlhugh
578. Hugh Montgumry

[f. 225]

579. Thomas Fargusson
580. Hugh Montgumery
581. William McHallen
582. Andrew Boweene
583. Symond McWalter
584. Andrew Willson
585. Robert Hisluck
586. John Monteeth
587. John Maccord
588. John Wilson
589. Hugh Nesbit
590. William Patrick
591. Charles Davison
592. John mcBriall
593. John Harp
594. James Kirkpatrick
595. Patrick Patterson
596. Patrick Moore[69]
597. Andrew Rogerson
598. John mcMaister
599. John McCord
600. Alexander McGilduff
601. James Scot
602. James Anderson
603. John Montgumry[70]
604. John Moody
605. John Coolum
606. Nynyne McMurry

[f. 225v]

Swords and Muskets
607. James Steelbirt
608. Hugh Montgomery
609. John Labrow
610. John McConnell
611. Henry Moody
612. William Monteeth
613. John Scot
614. Adam Montgumry
615. William Hany
616. John Conningham[71]
617. Mathew Ramsay
618. Henry Oakburne
619. John Harper[72]
620. John Softley
621. John Atkinhead

622. Robert Johnston
623. John Shewane
624. James Kirkwood
625. John mcCulyne
626. Hugh Stilly
627. James Wight
628. William Small
629. James McKenahan
630. William Spot
631. John Scot

[f. 226]

632. Thomas Mcilmorrow
633. William Moore[73]
634. Thomas Willson
635. Robert Smart
636. Robert Dunkan
637. Thomas McCarnock
638. John Frizell
639. John Montgomery
640. Neill Montgumry
641. Robert Montgomry[74]
642. Lawrence Rootherfoord
643. William Montgumry
644. James Crones
645. John McCornock
646. James Arnott
647. James Orr
648. Allyn Syd
649. Alexander Shawe
650. John McMeaghan
651. John Clarke
652. Patrick Akin
653. John Orr
654. Mathew Ryddle
655. Archbald Turner
656. John Spere[75]
657. John Loggan
658. John Read
659. John Fargusson
660. John Micheallson

[f. 266v]

661. Robert Willson
662. Hugh Willson
663. David Blany
664. Robert mcCrery
665. James Dunkan
666. John mcIlno
667. John Frowe

[69] Patrick Moore of Aughneil was one of the mourners at the funeral of viscount Ards, 1636 (*Montgomery MSS.*, p. 53).

[70] Resident Roddans; denization, 1617 (ibid. p 56; *Calendar of patent rolls, Ireland, James I*, pp 326–39).

[71] 'John Cunningham of Newtown' was one of the gentlemen and esquire mourners at the funeral of viscount Ards, 1636 (*Montgomery MSS*, p. 136)

[72] Two men named John Harper – one resident at Donaghadee and the other at Ballyhay – received letters of denization in 1617 (*Calendar of patent rolls, Ireland, James I*, pp 326–39; *Montgomery MSS*, p. 56).

[73] 'William Moore of Milntowne [Millisle]'; denization, 1617 (*Calendar of patent rolls, Ireland, James I*, pp 326–39; *Montgomery MSS*, p. 56).

[74] Robert and William Montgomery of Donaghadee (numbers 641 and 643) received denization, 1617 (*Calendar of patent rolls, Ireland, James I*, pp 326–39; *Montgomery MSS*, p. 56).

[75] Son of number 344.

668. John Cample
669. Thomas Moore
670. Robert Montgumry
671. James Chalmers
672. Alexander Crafford
673. Andrew Makee
674. John Michaelson
675. John Farguson
676. John Barkley
677. Gilbert Kenedy
678. Robert Dunkan
679. Robert Smart
680. John Boyd[76]
681. James Couff
682. John Boyd younger[77]
683. Alexander mcClenan
684. Patrick Sprot
685. Robert McClish
686. William Douglass
687. John Grane
688. William Ireland
689. James Willson

[f. 227]

690. Robert Mulligan
691. Fargus McIlmovet
692. John Kenedy
693. John McBurney
694. John Story
695. Robert Phillip
696. David McCamlees
697. Adam Lyndy
698. David Templeton
699. William Eskin
700. William McAlexander
701. Alexander McBrid
702. James Button
703. Thomas Kenedy[78]
704. Samuell Roe
705. John Gourden
706. Robert Marshall
707. John Hurrin
708. John Yeoman
709. John Forbus
710. Andrew Jordan
711. John McGerr
712. William Magee
713. William Jarden
714. Gilbert Alexander

715. Gilbert Kirke
716. John Walker
717. Edward Blaire
718. Marmaduke Houle
719. Robert Torly

[f. 227v]

Swords only
720. John Barnet
721. John Dickye
722. William Brynean
723. John McClingan
724. Robert Allen younger
725. John Brisland
726. William Long
727. William Calwell
728. David Read
729. Andrew Catherwood
730. Hugh Montgumry
731. Andrew Forrester
732. James Montgomery
733. Alexander Boyd
734. John mcIlmont
735. Rynyan Barkeley
736. William Scot
737. Robert Arkin
738. Robert More
739. John Dermont
740. Andrew Dermoote
741. James McLaughlin[79]
742. Mathew Thompson
743. John Milling
744. George Milling
745. Archbald Millinge
746. John Montgomery
747. William Wilson

[f. 228]

748. Roger mcKirdney
749. James Whirk
750. William Gray
751. John mcCormock
752. John Spere
753. John Steinson
754. John Drisdall
755. Adam Montgumry
756. William mcNabene
757. Robert Conningham

758. William Forsith
759. James Lockhartt
760. William McBirny
761. John Kelton
762. John Haning
763. George Watson
764. George Galbreath
765. Christopher Jardan
766. Thomas Hana
767. John McClenan
768. Thomas Coadan
769. Michaell mcIlmeane
770. John Tate
771. John Rae
772. William Moore
773. John Little
774. William Dobbin[80]
775. John Doneld
776. John Steele
777. James Arkinhead

[f. 228v]

Swords and Halberds
778. Adam Carby
779. James Mackee
780. John Johnston
781. John mcDill
782. John mcCallen
783. John Crag
784. John Rabe
785. James mcIllmorrow
786. Neal Catherwood
787. Andrew mcQuirk
788. John Wood
789. James Greasly
790. Adam Gibson
791. Thomas Brice

Swords and Snaphances
792. James Steinson
793. John Cample

Sword and Caliver
794. Thomas Montgumry[81]

Swords and Targets
795. Allen Conningham
796. James mcPerson
797. John Lockert

---

[76] Father of number 682.

[77] Son of number 680.

[78] 'Thomas Kennedy of Cumber [Comber]' was one of viscount Ards's representatives in the arbitration of his dispute with Lord Clandeboy in 1633 (*Montgomery MSS*, p. 81).

[79] This may be the father of Patrick McLaughlin of Ballinderry, who was born around 1627 and who identified some of the Scots responsible for the killings of the Irish in North Down in 1641: the McLaughlins were living at Galwally, 1641 (Examination of Pattrick McLoughlin, 9 May 1653 [TCD MS 838, fols 162r and 229r–229v]).

[80] See numbers 347 and 1098: 'Lieutenant William Dobbin doth acknowledge himself to have had a hand therein [the killings at Island Magee in 1642]' (Examination of James Collogh, 1 June 1653 [ibid. fols 208r–209v]).

[81] See number 347.

Swords and Headpieces

798. Thomas mcMillen
799. Gawen Boyle[82]

Sword and Drum

800. Robert Trundle

Swords only

801. Gilbert Heiron
802. John Bowen
803. George Rogerson
804. James Mulligan

[f. 229]

805. John Chalmers
806. Andrew Montgomry
807. James Richy
808. John Jamyson
809. Patrick Hanna
810. Thomas Torbers
811. Patrick Wright
812. Richard Ga
813. Thomas Webster
814. William Old
815. George Kelso
816. John Farly
817. Andrew Slayne
818. George Or
819. Andrew mcKilwarnock
820. Robert Hood
821. John Montgomry
822. George Gibs
823. George Metland
824. John Gibson
825. Robert Kenly
826. Robert Jenisy
827. Thomas mcCay
828. Fynlay McCay
829. James Robinson
830. John Cuthcert
831. Robert Granchee

[f. 229v]

832. Robert Gurrow
833. Thomas McHutchon
834. James Sympson
835. John McMynns
836. Patrick Sympson
837. John Hodg
838. John Miller
839. Thomas Hany
840. John Beaty

841. William Smyth
842. Gilbert mcWilly
843. Robert Hood
844. Patrick Callan
845. James Curry
846. Robert Hood
847. Quinton Moore[83]
848. John Calbreath
849. Thomas Gillmoore
850. Gilbert Mclure
851. James mcWhirk
852. James Harp
853. Dunkan mcHallan
854. James Hood
855. Edward Slit
856. John Beaty
857. William Smyth

[f. 230]

No Arms

858. Robert Eddier
859. William Lawder
860. James Lawder
861. John Reed
862. Robert Cat
863. William Car
864. Thomas Cogheran
865. John Wood
866. Andrew Patterson
867. John Templeton
868. George Gidds
869. Edward Hills
870. John Lurg
871. James McAmont
872. John Gibson
873. James English
874. Robert Sterling
875. John Kenedy
876. William Whitlaw
877. John Howet
878. John Gowerly
879. Edward Makee
880. Alexander Guthery
881. Thomas McMaister
882. John Kenedy
883. Michaell Black
884. James Boyd
885. Thomas Kirkpatrick
886. James Cornock
887. Robert Milton

[f. 230v]

888. William Robinson
889. George Gourden
890. John Gourden
891. John Montgumry[84]
892. Wm. Steaphenson
893. James Steill
894. John Cutbert
895. John Buchanan
896. William McHaffy
897. Patrick Montgumry[85]
898. Dunkan Brice
899. William Rae
900. George Makee
901. Michaell Makee
902. James Makee
903. Neall Gamble
904. John Dixon
905. Alexander Canilin
906. Gilbert mcCullo
907. John mcKirk
908. Thomas McBrid
909. John McNeise
910. John McChemny
911. John Edier
912. John Knox
913. James Henryson
914. Fargus mcLaughen
915. Walter McCard
916. Gilbert Cogheran

[f. 231]

917. Nynyan mcCullo
918. Nicholl Martyn
919. John Hadney
920. John Reede
921. Charles Moorehead
922. William Johnston
923. Andrew Crafford
924. Robert Crag
925. James Gibson
926. Robert Shenan
927. Robert Coop
928. Robert Barkly
929. Robert Gray
930. Andrew McWalter
931. Adam Hyeron
932. Robert Glass
933. John Coates
934. James Tate
935. Thomas Gourly
936. John McCay

---

[82] Possibly the son of Robert Boyle of Drumfad, who received denization in 1617 (*Calendar of patent rolls, Ireland, James I*, pp 326–39; *Montgomery MSS*, p. 56); Drumfad is near Millisle.

[83] 'Quintene Moore of Aughneill'; denization, 1617 (*Calendar of patent rolls, Ireland, James I*, p. 329).

[84] Second son of Patrick Montgomery, the brother-in-law of Sir James Montgomery, viscount Ards (*Montgomery MSS*, p.27): Patrick Montgomery senior from Largs; attorney for Con O'Neill, 1605 (*Hamilton MSS*, p. 18); denization, 1617; died, 1629; lands Craigboy, near Donaghadee (*Montgomery MSS*, pp 51–2, 56).

[85] Youngest son of Patrick Montgomery and brother of John Montgomery (number 891).

937. Adam White
938. Robert Beaty
939. John Montgumry
940. James Cron
941. Patrick Lewis
942. John Royne
943. William Stote
944. Thomas Ognew[86]
945. Robert Speere

[f. 231v]

946. Andrew McWilliam
947. James Maggee
948. Roger Bell
949. Robert Boyd
950. Patrick Pearce
951. Mathew Galway
952. Alexander Palmer
953. David Smith
954. John Makee
955. John Wright
956. John Blackwood
957. George Dunlap
958. John Berkeley
959. John Browne
960. John McQuharre
961. Alexander Harper
962. Adam Fullerton
963. John Thomson
964. Allan Wilson[87]
965. John Drisdall
966. John McDoypall
967. David Smyth
968. Thomas Blackwood
969. James Sorbid
970. Alexander Montgumry
971. William Montgumry
972. John Montgumry

[f. 232]

973. John Conningham
974. Hugh Montgumry[88]
975. Alexander Dobison
976. Hugh Fraser
977. Alexander Wans
978. John Black
979. Thomas McGea
980. Hugh McAlexander

981. John McAlexander
982. Alexander Orr
983. Nynyan McConnell
984. Alexander mcKennell
985. William Edgar
986. William Reeve
987. Hugh Vaus
988. John Clarke
989. John Carnes
990. James Allet
991. William Scot
992. John Hendry
993. Gilbert mcBrid
994. Robert Chirres
995. James Cammock
996. Charles Guyman
997. Herbert Jarden
998. James Johnston
999. John Payne

[f. 232v]

1000. James Watson
1001. John Boyd
1002. Archbald Fynlay
1003. Wm. Glendining
1004. Thomas McChesney
1005. John Harris
1006. John Scot
1007. James Catherwood
1008. William Carnes
1009. John McKillue
1010. George Miller
1011. William Fariss
1012. John McIlmorrow
1013. John Caldwell
1014. William Hana
1015. Thomas Frassall
1016. John Grange
1017. James Stoup
1018. Adam Orr
1019. George Armestrang
1020. Walter Scot
1021. Hugh Dynn
1022. William Barkely
1023. William Hammilton
1024. John Yeates
1025. David Irwing
1026. David Gibson

[f. 233]

1027. John Clarck
1028. Thomas Jamison[89]
1029. Hugh Kenedy[90]
1030. James Delap
1031. John Potter
1032. Daniell McCoul
1033. John Kennydy
1034. John Dunkan
1035. John Johnston
1036. John Vaugh
1037. James Steel
1038. Thomas Moody
1039. John Logtowne
1040. John Frass[91]
1041. John McNaught
1042. Thomas Reed
1043. John Bell
1044. Robert Irwing
1045. David Weere
1046. David Prats
1047. Hugh Catherwood
1048. Gilbert McClure
1049. Gilbert McGibbone
1050. William Darrigh
1051. John Kilpatrick
1052. William Henderson
1053. Robert Porter
1054. David Richy
1055. James Smart

[f. 233v]

1056. Alexander Weere
1057. William Guttery
1058. John Harris
1059. Adam Carr
1060. John McBryne
1061. Patrick Naper
1062. John Scot
1063. John Smyth
1064. David Maxwell
1065. Hugh Lowe
1066. James Douglass
1067. John Milligan
1068. William Gourden
1069. John Wylly[92]
1070. Hugh Montgumry
1071. Thomas Dowell
1072. John Marshall[93]

86   'Thomas Agnew of Greyabbey'; denization, 1617 (*Calendar of patent rolls, Ireland, James I*, pp 326–39; *Montgomery MSS*, p. 56).
87   'Allen Wilson of Newton'; denization, 1617 (*Calendar of patent rolls, Ireland, James I*, pp 326–39; *Montgomery MSS*, p. 56).
88   Hugh Montgomery (died 1630) was the eldest son of Patrick Montgomery of Craigboy (*Montgomery MSS*, pp 51–2): there are several Hugh Montgomerys in this list and I have annotated the one nearest to Patrick Montgomery junior.
89   Father of number 64.
90   Hugh Kennedy of Greengraves and Hugh Kennedy of Drumawhy were among the mourners at viscount Ards's funeral, 1636 (*Montgomery MSS*, pp 131, 138).
91   Shortening of Frasser [RJH].
92   Resident Ballyhay since 1607; denization, 1617 (*Calendar of patent rolls, Ireland, James I*, pp 326–39; *Montgomery MSS*, p. 56).
93   One of the assailants of the Irish Island Magee, January 1642 (see, for example, Examination of Aney Nygill, 9 April 1653 [TCD MS 838, fols 236r–236v]).

1073. John Thyrry
1074. John Stroyane
1075. Hector McKey
1076. Robert McFye
1077. John Lawdone
1078. Rowland Michaell
1079. Robert Smyth
1080. John Cant
1081. Hugh Montgumry
1082. John Jarden
1083. John Heiron
1084. Thomas Adamson
1085. John Bayty
1086. John Colphen

[f. 234]

1087. John Conningham
1088. William Ridbich
1089. Andrew Alexander
1090. George McCartney
1091. John McCapene
1092. Alexander Jarden
1093. Patrick Carsan
1094. Adam Fargusson
1095. Alexander Hary
1096. John Clingen
1097. Thomas Rosse
1098. Alexander Dobbin[94]
1099. John Cathcart
1100. James Martyn[95]
1101. Robert Martyn
1102. William Wakeson
1103. John Kinzen
1104. Archbald Latimer
1105. John Gillespike
1106. John Murry
1107. Phillip Moore
1108. John Edgar
1109. Robert Browne
1110. William Egleson
1111. Archbald Moore
1112. Mungo Holmes[96]
1113. John Neal
1114. Hugh Glasgowe[97]
1115. David Steward

1116. John Delfer
1117. Adam Rawlstone

[f. 234v]

1118. John Leggan
1119. John Hopes
1120. William Reed
1121. John Bell
1122. John Cord
1123. Thomas mcCrackan
1124. Alexander Baly
1125. Alexander McGarrogh
1126. John McGarrogh
1127. William Palmer[98]
1128. John Galway
1129. James Steaphenson
1130. Thomas Downwoodders
1131. John Montgumry
1132. William Montgumry
1133. James Steele
1134. John Bell
1135. Thomas Wilson
1136. Cormock Ogilmoore
1137. Patrick Omilligan
1138. Ogen Ogilmore
1139. Brian McClarimore
1140. James Cuddy
1141. James Read
1142. John mcCullagh
1143. John Crag
1144. John Lyndsay
1145. John Cant
1146. George Creighton
1147. Thomas Murphey[99]
1148. Thomas Murphey younger

[f. 235]

1149. John Foster[100]
1150. William Welly
1151. John Thomson
1152. James Moore
1153. Hugh Legat
1154. John Foster younger[101]
1155. John Agneill
1156. Allan Hislop

1157. John Ross
1158. Robert Montgumry
1159. John Davison
1160. Thomas Atkin
1161. Guy Scot
1162. John Reed
1163. Patrick Alleson
1164. John Richy
1165. John Small
1166. Robert Montgumry
1167. John Montgumry
1168. James Broadeshaw
1169. John Steward
1170. Patrick Wright
1171. Alexander Wause
1172. Fargus Thomson
1173. Thomas Thomson
1174. John Breitch
1175. Ninian Calwell
1176. Alexander Harp
1177. James Harper

[f. 235v]

1178. George Machone
1179. John Moore
1180. Robert Cragg
1181. Patrick mcFarlan
1182. James McCullagh
1183. John McOwen[102]
1184. William Reed
1185. Alexander mcKey
1186. Alexander McCoole
1187. John mcKeogh
1188. John Clarke
1189. Alexander mcMurra
1190. William Smyth
1191. James Moody
1192. Robert Harper[103]
1193. John mcKeallan
1194. John Clarke
1195. Robert Clarke
1196. Alexander Monteeth
1197. Gilbert Cord
1198. John Barkly
1199. John Barkeley
1200. John Montgumry

[94] See numbers 347 and 774; Alexander Dobbin junior was involved in the killing of the Irish at Ballydavey, near Holywood, February 1642 (Examination of Daniell MacThomas O Gilmore, 28 April 1653 [ibid. fols 249r–250v]).

[95] Identified as one of the killers of the Irish at Ballydavey, February 1642; moved to Munster before 1653 (Examination of James Gourdan, 3 May 1653 [TCD MS 837, fols 155r–155v]).

[96] 'Corrected from William' [RJH].

[97] Hugh and Matthew Glasgow were probably related and may be close relatives of Robert Glasgow, one of the perpetrators of the massacre of the Irish on Island Magee, January 1641 (See, for example, Examination of William Willson, 1 June 1653 [TCD MS 838, fols 218r–219v]).

[98] Palmer was named as one of the killers of the Irish near Holywood, February 1642 (Examination of Daniell MacThomas O Gilmore, 28 April 1653 [ibid. fols 249r–250v]).

[99] Numbers 1147 and 1148 are father and son.

[100] Father of number 1154.

[101] Son of number 1149.

[102] 'A soldier in Captain McCullough's company'; implicated in the killings of the Irish on Island Magee, January 1642 (Confession of John McOwen, 3 April 1653 [TCD MS 838, fols 215r–215v]).

[103] 'Of Provostoun'; denization, 1617 (Calendar of patent rolls, Ireland, James I, pp 326–39; Montgomery MSS, p. 56).

1201. John Frizell
1202. Alexander Shankeland
1203. John Kirkpatrick
1204. Hugh Bounty
1205. David Adam
1206. John McAlexander

[f. 236]

1207. John Scot
1208. Alexander Rybourne
1209. John Jammison
1210. Danald Cample
1211. Robert Kile
1212. Alexand: Boyd
1213. Thomas Huery
1214. James Hogg
1215. John Scot
1216. Gilbert Claughton
1217. John Kenedy[104]
1218. John Kenedy younger
1219. Wm Montgumry
1220. William Johnston
1221. William Osburne
1222. William Christy
1223. John mcKentcheon
1224. John Scot
1225. Alexander Harvye
1226. John Smily
1227. James Montgumry
1228. James Shewer
1229. John Galbreath
1230. John Adam
1231. John Johnston
1232. Walter Grimble
1233. Charles Grimble
1234. John Rayne
1235. John Hutchon
1236. Christell Coole
1237. Thomas Coyne
1238. John Kelly
1239. Wm. Kerbery

[f. 236v]

1240. Patrick Moore
1241. William Scot
1242. Robert Jannyson
1243. John Wilson
1244. John Griere
1245. Robert Davyson
1246. John McNaught
1247. Hugh Reed
1248. John mcCleland

1249. Patrick Bonatan
1250. James Sinklere
1251. Martyn Shallene
1252. Richard Maxwell
1253. John mcClenan
1254. Alexander mcClenan
1255. John Hughnan
1256. John Dayell
1257. Richard Gay
1258. David Beggs
1259. Patrick Sprot
1260. John Sprot[105]
1261. John mcCrere
1262. Thomas Cowdan
1263. Mighell Maghire
1264. John Alexander
1265. Gilbert Stewart
1266. John Shallan
1267. Patrick Edger
1268. John Browne

[f. 237]

1269. Andrew Browne
1270. Robert Clish
1271. Joh: Fargusson
1272. James Hammilton
1273. Patrick McMaister
1274. John Neary
1275. William Douglas
1276. John Gran
1277. Richard McBrid
1278. James Wallace
1279. William Ireland
1280. John Stroyan
1281. Alexander Reed
1282. David Alexander
1283. John Rutherfoord
1284. Roger Ireland
1285. Patrick Black
1286. David Wilson
1287. James Wilson
1288. Robert Browne
1289. James Milligan
1290. William Grere
1291. Andrew Skillin
1292. John McDonnell
1293. James McCrey
1294. John McCoultron
1295. Robert Jarden
1296. John Kenedy
1297. John Henryson
1298. John Marshall
1299. William Dunlap[106]

[f. 237v]

1300. Christopher Irwing
1301. Fynlay McIlman
1302. John mcNeally
1303. John Moore
1304. Christopher Steel
1305. James Hunter
1306. James McConnell
1307. George Carr
1308. John McCarr
1309. David Chalmes
1310. Robert Browne
1311. Patrick Conningham
1312. Michaell Ligat
1313. David Michaell
1314. John Montgumry[107]
1315. John Montgumry younger
1316. John Crafford

[f. 238]

Down
The town of Bangor

The names of the Lord Viscount Clannaboyes men and arms as followeth

Pikes Completely Armed

1. John Stilly
2. Andrew Clark
3. Henry Jerdg
4. James Black
5. John Pattercrew
6. William Fynlay
7. Luke Smyth
8. John Dawes
9. Andrew Henderson
10. John Johnston
11. James Gibson
12. William McDowgall
13. Robert Moore
14. William Cowen
15. William Hammilton[108]
16. William Whitlawe
17. John Black
18. Thomas Adam
19. James Johnston
20. Thomas Thompson
21. Symond Gilmoore
22. Alexander McConnell
23. Thomas Wilkinett
24. John McConnell

---

[104] Father and son.
[105] 'John Spratt' was stripped near Moira, 1641 (Examination of Lenas Oge O Haghiran, 5 May 1653 [TCD MS 838, fols 147r]).
[106] Shown as 1300 in the original MS: Graham appears to have miscounted.
[107] Father and son.
[108] Tenant since 1616 (*Montgomery MSS*, pp 51–2).

25. Thomas Lowry
26. John Patton
27. Quinton McGill
28. Alexander Gillies
29. Robert Hammilton
30. John Willy
31. Robert Hammilton

[f. 238v]

32. Mathew Thorn
33. John Creighton
34. Andrew Forsith
35. John Wilson
36. Thomas Murchie
37. William Fynlay
38. Robert Gibson
39. James Haddon
40. Thomas Clarke
41. James Patterson
42. Thomas Harris
43. Thomas McCartney
44. Robert Edger
45. John Louke
46. Robert Fynlay
47. John Young
48. James Rosse
49. John McCray
50. William Fynlay
51. Alexander Pirry
52. John McNaught[109]
53. John McNaught younger
54. James McCrew
55. John Bisset
56. John Warnock
57. Andrew Clarke
58. James Clarke
59. Mathew Nicholson
60. Cuthbert Donnell
61. Alexander Maxwell
62. Walter Purdy
63. John Purdy
64. Stephen Crafford
65. John Miller
66. David Donnell

[f. 239]

67. John Blackwood
68. George Wilson
69. William Rea

70. John Moore
71. James Hammelton
72. Gilbert Boyd
73. John McKelly
74. John Donnell
75. David Montgumry
76. William Grea
77. Hugh McWalter
78. John Patton
79. William Barkley
80. Wm. McGleddery
81. Alexander Forrest
82. Gilbert Neilson
83. John McBryd
84. James Browne
85. James Woodrow[110]
86. James Woodrow younger
87. John Wilson
88. George Whoam
89. Alexander Berry
90. Alexander Hammilton
91. Robert Wyly
92. Donell McKelvey
93. James Hammilton
94. William Young
95. Andrew Miller
96. George Moore
97. James Steward
98. William Galt[111]
99. William Galt younger
100. Adam McCaghaghen
101. William Aykin
102. David Drenan
103. John Richard
104. Sampson Callingwood

[f. 239v]

105. William McMighan
106. Gilbert Agnew
107. Andrew McConnell
108. Andrew Anderson
109. John Anderson
110. Thomas Howne
111. Owthry Camble
112. William Parrons
113. Ninian Martyn
114. Richard Browne
115. John Donnell
116. Robert Shane
117. William Bayly[112]

118. George McComb
119. James McCullagh[113]
120. Patrick McMeoghan
121. Robert McGill
122. Gilbert Bartran
123. William McQuhoull
124. Andrew McFarran
125. Gilbert McFarran
126. James Whitlaw
127. William Boyd
128. Andrew Camble
129. Quinton Law
130. Allen Smyth
131. George Torbeene
132. Andrew McQuhoul
133. John Wright
134. Constantyne Kenedy
135. Owthred McDowgall[114]
136. George Miller
137. John Nealson
138. Gilbert Logan
139. William Nixon
140. John McGowne
141. William Hyndman
142. George Lawe

[f. 240]

143. James McMurtree
144. Alexander McCamont
145. Andrew Shenan
146. John McCarrlye
147. John Camble
148. Anthony McCracken
149. Adam McCullen
150. John Moscamble
151. George Camble
152. Andrew McTeir
153. Ninian Whoam
154. Adam Broadffoote
155. Dowgall McMicheall
156. Thomas McMaister
157. William Steaphenson[115]
158. James Rea
159. James Johnston
160. Gilbert Rowans
161. John Rowans
162. Robert Hammilton
163. Alester oge McConnell
164. William Steward
165. John McClarkan

---

[109] Numbers 52 and 53 are father and son.
[110] Father and son.
[111] Father and son.
[112] Named as a burgess of Bangor in the town's charter, 18 March 1613 (*Hamilton MSS*, general appendix, p. lxxix).
[113] Captain of one of the companies of foot responsible for killing the Irish on Island Magee, January 1642 (Confession of John McOwen, 3 April 1653 [TCD MS 838, fols 215r–215v] and Examination of Richard Kelly, 31 May 1653 [ibid. fols 216r–217v]); McCullough died before 1653 (Examination of James Gourdan, 3 May 1653 [TCD MS 837, fols 155r–155v]).
[114] Probably Cothered McDougall, named as a burgess of Bangor in the town's charter, 18 March 1613 (*Hamilton MSS*, general appendix, p. lxxix); 'Uthred M'Dowgall of Ballimaconnell [Ballymaconnell]' received denization in 1617 (*Calendar of patent rolls, Ireland, James I*, pp 326–39; *Montgomery MSS*, p, 56).
[115] Numbers 157 and 162 named as burgesses of Bangor in the town's charter, 18 March 1613 (*Hamilton MSS*, general appendix, p. lxxix).

166. James McFarren
167. Patrick Peebles
168. Thomas Boyd
169. Gilbert McGassock
170. Gillaspeck McKelwy
171. James Parker
172. Thomas Bole[116]
173. William Hunter[117]
174. John McCairley
175. James McCairley
176. John McLumpert
177. William McIlno
178. John McMeaghand
179. Thomas McCoshee
180. James Steavenson

[f. 240v]

181. James Cleland
182. James Nicholson
183. William Nicholson
184. William Pollock
185. John Wyly
186. William Neilson
187. John Neilson
188. Alexander Wylly[118]
189. Alexander Wylly younger
190. Hugh Camble
191. George Maccullo
192. Thomas Pollock
193. William Donnell
194. John McMeaghan
195. Nynyan McNeilly
196. Patrick McNeilly
197. James McNeilly
198. Patrick Lennox
199. William Lennox
200. John Lennox

Swords, Muskets, and bandoliers
201. Mungo McCullo[119]
202. Fynlay McMeaghan
203. Andrew Carins
204. Andrew Hammilton[120]
205. John Pots
206. Andrew Sympson
207. John Sympson

208. Robert Murrey[121]
209. Robert Murrey younger
210. John Gemill
211. Thomas Knox
212. Archbald Black
213. John Hammilton[122]
214. Alexander McDowgall
215. David Reed
216. James Reed
217. John Fynley
218. Andrew Lyndsay

[f. 241]

219. John Lyndsay
220. Robert Curry
221. James McKelly
222. Michaell Blanye
223. Robert Blanye
224. Archbald Miller
225. Robert Howy
226. William Applin
227. Arthur Cleland
228. William Carnes
229. Patrick Hutcheson
230. Robert Hutcheson
231. James McConnell
232. Alexander Steavenson
233. John Steavenson
234. Patrick Wyly
235. Alexander Galstone
236. John Black
237. Robert Black
238. William Irwing
239. Thomas Kyle
240. Patrick Gourden
241. Andrew Johnston[123]
242. David Miller
243. John McCooke
244. Alexander Gay
245. John McCardy
246. James Jefferey
247. David Laughlin
248. John Laghlin[124]
249. Adam Laghlin
250. Thomas Kile
251. John Laghlin younger

252. John McDowgall
253. John Anderson
254. John Bryson
255. John Moore[125]
256. John Moore younger
257. David Rosse
258. John Armor

[f. 241v]

259. Andrew Browne
260. Robert Ross[126]
261. John Ross
262. Robert Ross younger
263. Thomas Craig
264. John Agnew
265. John McCormick
266. James Browne
267. Robert Moore
268. John McCartney
269. Andrew McCartney
270. James Pollock
271. Rowland Lyndsay
272. Alester Agnew
273. John McCartney
274. John Harp
275. William Browne
276. John Browne
277. Dunkan McCullan
278. John McWilliam
279. Robert Carrudes
280. John McWhingy
281. Owtry McCosh
282. Patrick Slonen
283. John Hanna
284. John Anderson
285. William McCoole
286. Owtry McDowgall
287. John Paterson
288. Gilbert Moscamble
289. John McCamont
290. Quinton McDowgall
291. Owthay McDowgall
292. John McDowgall
293. William Bromley
294. Andrew McConnell
295. John Fargusson

---

[116] Son or nephew of John Bole, minister at Killyleagh; John Bole took out a lease for six acres of land near Killyleagh for the life of his daughter, Jane, 1632; Jane Bole married William Murdoch, who predeceased her (*Hamilton MSS*, p. 34). William Bole, possibly the son of Thomas Bole, rented part of Balloo townland at Killinchy for £4 0s 0d in 1689–91 and for £2 0s 0d in 1692 (ibid. p. 129).

[117] Denization, 1617; then resident at Dunover (*Calendar of patent rolls, Ireland, James I*, pp 326–39; *Montgomery MSS*, p. 56).

[118] Father and son.

[119] 'Macin Macollagh in the Ards', one of the killers of the Irish near Holywood in 1642 (Examination of Daniell MacThomas O Gilmore, 28 April 1653 [TCD MS 838, fols 249r–250v]).

[120] One of the killers of the Irish near Holywood in 1642 (Examination of Katerine McGarry, 10 May 1653 [ibid, fols 247r–248v]).

[121] Father and son.

[122] Named as a burgess of Bangor and appointed provost in the town's charter, 18 March 1613 (*Hamilton MSS*, general appendix, pp lxxix–lxxx).

[123] 'John Johnson, son to Andrew Jonson of Balledavey' was one 'of the murderers' of the Irish near Holywood, February 1642 (Examination of Daniell MacThomas O Gilmore, 28 April 1653 [TCD MS 838, fols 249r–250v]).

[124] Numbers 248, 249, and 251 are a father and two sons.

[125] Father and son.

[126] Father and two sons.

296. John Sinckler
297. John McGarroth

[f. 242]

298. Richard Morrison
299. Gilbert McKitrick
300. James Rosse
301. Patrick Roxbrough
302. Thomas Sterret
303. John mcIlwayne[127]
304. John McIlwayne younger
305. Patrick Slowen
306. Andrew Hammilton
307. Robert Barkeley
308. Robert Gibb
309. John Ballentyne
310. James Mawe
311. John Kearnes
312. Thomas McCracken
313. Alexander Smyth
314. Hugh Stilly
315. Anthony Kenedy
316. Alexander Kenedy
317. John Killy
318. Alexander Kilpatrick
319. David Camble
320. William Anderson
321. Gawen Roxburgh
322. Patrick mcKennen
323. John Forrest
324. John McBlanie
325. Robert McBlanie
326. Gilbert Templeton
327. Downie Davison
328. John Read
329. John McBlanie
330. Mathew Davison
331. Mathew Kinney

[f. 242v]

332. John Parke
333. James Davyson
334. Gawen Hamilton[128]
335. John Martin
336. John McIlwaine
337. Robert Campell
338. John Campell

339. William Campell
340. Alexander Campell

Swords and Calivers

341. Fynlay Campell
342. Patrick Campell
343. David Smyth
344. John McCallon
345. John Corse
346. Charles Campbell[129]
347. Robert Campbell
348. George Campbell
349. Hugh Campbell
350. Hugh White
351. John McCargall
352. John McMichan
353. Peter Browne
354. John Curry
355. Andrew Donnell[130]
356. Cullo McIcrinye
357. James McIcrinye
358. Andrew Pallein
359. John McCrackan
360. George Monnsis
361. James Girthrig
362. James Girthrig
363. James Aclan
364. David Campbell
365. James Murrey
366. Bryan Dornan[131]

[f. 243]

367. Donnell O Dornan
368. John McWilliam
369. William Old[132]
370. William Whitley
371. Robert Ray
372. Patrick Campbell
373. William Old younger[133]
374. John McCare
375. Stephen Lorrymer
376. John Lorrymer
377. James Gray
378. Mungo Richy
379. Gilbert Campbell
380. John McKenney
381. Robert McCleland
382. Andrew Miller

383. John Gray
384. Gilbert Gray
385. John Gray younger
386. Gilbert Glanine
387. James Gray
388. Cuthbert Campbell
389. John Campbell
390. John Clanny
391. Gilbert Clanny
392. Andrew Cassan
393. Robert Tuit[134]
394. Robert Tuit younger
395. James Lawe
396. John McComb
397. William McComb
398. Alexander Colvanie
399. Hugh Baird

[f. 243v]

Swords and Pikes

400. Andrew McCleland
401. James Browne
402. James Arbaucle
403. Andrew Agnell
404. John Forsith
405. John McNechen
406. Alexander McNechen
407. Fynlay McMikin
408. Andrew McNeally
409. George Mimmock
410. John McClelan
411. James Rodger
412. John Rodger
413. George Roger
414. Adam Thomson
415. Archbald McKirrogh
416. Robert Hammilton
417. Robert Dunlop
418. Andrew Hunter
419. David McMurry
420. Hugh Hammilton
421. James Shaw
422. Robert Corbert
423. Robert Steward
424. Michaell Campbell
425. John Kinning[135]
426. John Kinning younger
427. John McCleland[136]

---

[127] Father and son.
[128] Gavin Hamilton of Ballymonestragh was one of viscount Clandeboye's representatives in the arbitration of the dispute with viscount Ards in 1633 (*Montgomery MSS*, p. 81).
[129] Numbers 346 to 349 probably members of the same family.
[130] 'Of Ballynagross, late of Ballyhornan, in the county of Down, yeoman, aged 53 years' (Deposition of Andrew Daniel, 18 May 1653 [TCD MS 837, fols 075r–075v]); surname spelled Donnell on the recognisance (ibid. fols 076r–076v).
[131] Bryan and Donnell O'Dornan may be the sons of James O'Dornan, one of Sir James Hamilton's tenants in 1616 (*Hamilton MSS*, p. 55).
[132] Father of number 373.
[133] Son of number 369.
[134] Father and son.
[135] Numbers 424, 425, and 431 are a father and two sons.
[136] A father and two sons.

428. John McCleland younger
429. Alexander McCleland
430. Andrew McKee
431. Thomas Kinning
432. James McGagnon

[f. 244]

433. Patrick McClennoghan
434. William Lorrimer
435. Robert Wightman
436. George mcClelan
437. Fargus McDowgall
438. John Dunlop
439. George Gibson
440. John Gemmill
441. William Gemmill
442. James Logan
443. James Neisbit
444. William Moore
445. William Gemmill
446. Gilbert Dunlap
447. William Hammilton
448. Gawen Hammilton
449. Andrew Hammilton
450. Michaell Montgumry
451. Thomas Cocheane
452. Thomas Dormond
453. Thomas McClelan
454. John Browne
455. James Browne
456. Hugh Browne
457. Andrew Haitly
458. Thomas Carr
459. George Reed
460. George Gemmill
461. William Browne
462. James Conningham
463. Andrew Hammilton
464. James Hammilton

[f. 244v]

465. James Crawford
466. Alexander Porter
467. John Campbell
468. Andrew Campbell
469. John Tod
470. James Tod
471. James Tod younger
472. Alexander Cassen
473. Thomas Tod
474. Robert Greir[137]
475. Andrew Greir
476. William Greir
477. Gilbert Greir

478. Gilbert Greir younger
479. John McQuhill
480. Andrew Bartran
481. Nicholl Campbell
482. Francis Porter
483. William Richard
484. Alexander Russell
485. Hugh White
486. John Russell
487. Gilbert Ray
488. William Fynlay
489. Donnell McAlester
490. John Barnard
491. Thomas McClelan
492. George James
493. William Twynan
494. Thomas Smyth
495. John Smyth
496. William Smyth
497. Gilbert McGibbon
498. Niven McCullogh

[f. 245]

499. John Gelston
500. Moyses Browre
501. William Miller
502. John Miller
503. Robert Miller
504. John Browne
505. George Little
506. Alexander Parke
507. Cuthbert Neilson
508. John Anderson
509. John Beaty
510. David Miller
511. Wm. McGaguhon
512. William Wright
513. John Johnston[138]
514. Symond Dixon
515. John Harshaw
516. Robert Harshaw
517. James Harper
518. Robert Shawe
519. Robert Archbald
520. Andrew Shawe
521. John Still
522. Alexander Wilson[139]
523. Thomas McBryd
524. James Adam
525. John Hockills
526. John Ray
527. Alexander Fyndlay
528. George Fyndlay
529. Symon Wall

530. John Davie
531. William Davie
532. Alexander Davye
533. William Snodgrass

[f. 245v]

534. John Watt
535. Thomas Wilson
536. John Boyd
537. Robert Gibson
538. Andrew McIllvenie
539. Adam Browne
540. Quinton Hammilton
541. John Hall
542. William McGie
543. John Kilpatrick
544. William Potts
545. James Potts
546. James Cogheran
547. Robert Wray
548. William Snodgrass
549. Walter Fyndley
550. John Dun
551. John Lorrimer
552. Robert Crawfford
553. John Buy
554. John Latimer
555. William Patterson
556. John Caderwood
557. William Greir
558. Robert Greir
559. James Greir

Swords and Snaphances
560. William Palmer
561. John Greir
562. Archbald Scot
563. Alester Carleill
564. Andrew McGaguhen
565. John McKinne
566. Andrew McKinne
567. John Mosman
568. William Raven
569. John Dixon

[f. 246]

570. Robert Hongen
571. John McFyrren
572. Patrick Fyndley
573. John Fyndley
574. John McWhirke
575. William McCosh
576. Richard Gibson
577. John McCosh

---

[137] Number 474 to 478 are a family group.

[138] 'Son to Andrew Jonson of Balledavy' and one 'of the murderers' of the Irish near Holywood, February 1642 (Examination of Daniell MacThomas O Gilmore, 28 April 1653 [TCD MS 838, fols 249r–250v]).

[139] Daniell MacThomas O Gilmore, 'being informed by one Sandy Wilson that there was a hole broken in the end of the house' where he was held, escaped the killing of the Irish at Ballydavey, February 1642 (ibid.).

578. Robert Browne
579. John Nicholl
580. Thomas McCrackan
581. Andrew Crawford
582. John Crawford
583. Mallcome Crawford
584. John Henderson
585. Mungo Weir
586. John McCawen
587. John Carsan
588. Andrew McGill
589. Patrick Coyne
590. Thomas Higgis
591. John Campbell
592. John Hannay
593. Hugh McTeir
594. John Borland
595. John Moore
596. William Allen
597. James Blair[140]
598. William Gilmoore[141]
599. William Gilmoore younger
600. John Blayre
601. William Smyth
602. Hugh Miller
603. John Steward
604. John Watson

[f. 246v]

605. Richard Michelson
606. Archbald Mowet
607. Patrick McDowgall[142]
608. Alexander Dunlap
609. Nathaniell Cockroger
610. James Wyly
611. John Wyly
612. Alaster Wyly
613. James Logan
614. Donnell McClowie
615. George Fergusshill
616. Addam Harris
617. Thomas Hannay
618. Alexander Binnice
619. William Gardner

The Lordship of Duffrin

Swords and Pikes
620. James Dunbar
621. Hugh Dunbar
622. John Dunbar
623. Fynlay Shaw

624. James McCutcheon
625. Thomas Dixon
626. Thomas Sprot
627. Andrew Corby
628. David Johnston
629. John Dixon
630. Cawen Alliett
631. William Harvye
632. Peter Wallace
633. John Wallace
634. John O Brat
635. James Wallace
636. William Wallace[143]
637. William Cadan
638. William Kney
639. Cuthbert Kney

[f. 247]

640. Michaell Cowtart
641. James Cowan
642. William Lowry
643. David Fish
644. John McBlein
645. John Lawry
646. Alexander Lawry
647. David Cratch
648. Andrew Bran
649. Edward Lanrick
650. William Lanrick
651. John Carrudhous
652. William Kirke[144]
653. Robert Sommerrill
654. John Campbell
655. John Campbell
656. Adam Browne
657. Andrew Howat
658. William Dowgan
659. John Crawford
660. William Gourdon
661. Thomas Makee
662. William Brengen
663. Andrew Walker
664. John Walker
665. William Maxwell
666. John Asteck
667. Andrew McGuffock
668. Humfrey Burdeene
669. James Fisher
670. Thomas Moorehead
671. Peter Scott
672. Hugh Fargushill
673. George Moyerland
674. Thomas Steele

[f. 247v]

675. Alexander McCremont
676. John McCleland
677. David Hynnenge
678. Outhrie Bittle
679. Thomas Bradeley
680. Edward Bradeley
681. John Hammilton
682. Thomas Dixon
683. George Johnston
684. Robert Mywourne
685. James Stell
686. Thomas Shorton
687. Richard Bair
688. David Johnston
689. George Richardson
690. David Richardson
691. George Johnston
692. John Moore
693. John Byrd
694. David Hughman
695. Thomas Dixon
696. Adam Wallace
697. George Meeke
698. John Meeke
699. John Baninton
700. Thomas Aickin[145]
701. Alexander Lowry
702. James Cassills
703. William Cassills
704. Robert Williamson
705. Richard Byrd
706. James Chambers
707. William Weir
708. Alexander McDowgall
709. John McCann
710. William Coop
711. Alaster Biers

[f. 246]

712. Andrew Byers
713. Gilbert McWhartor
714. John McCartney
715. John Dongelson
716. William Harknes
717. George McCairtney
718. George Wilson
719. William Morison
720. William McDowgall
721. Patrick McDowgall
722. John McDowgall
723. James Vaus

---

[140] Named as a burgess of Bangor in the town's charter, 18 March 1613 (*Hamilton MSS*, general appendix, p. lxxix).

[141] Numbers 598 and 599 are father and son.

[142] Named as a burgess of Bangor in the town's charter, 18 March 1613 (*Hamilton MSS*, general appendix, p. lxxix); Patrick McDowell junior mustered in Dufferin.

[143] Tenant in 1616 (*Hamilton MSS*, p. 54).

[144] Moved to Marlacoo, county Armagh before 1641 (Examination of his wife, Christian Hunter, 6 May 1653 [TCD MS 836, fols 212r–213v]).

[145] Thomas Aitkin appears among the servants in the cortege of the viscount Ards, 1636 (*Montgomery MSS*, p. 135).

724. Edward Wallace
725. John McCarnoghan
726. James McKee
727. John Neper
728. Thomas Oliver
729. John Strowan
730. Robert Mathey
731. Anthony Mirrie
732. Andrew Dick
733. James Conninham
734. John Swynsin
735. John Sample
736. Robert Fynlay
737. Thomas Fynlay
738. Andrew Jesom
739. Robert Johnston
740. James Cloughston
741. James Dunlap
742. Adam Conninham
743. William McKee
744. John McCatcheon
745. Thomas Egleston[146]
746. John Egleston
747. John Egleston younger

[f. 248v]

748. John McKee
749. John McRobert[147]
750. John McRobert younger
751. Robert Willy
752. Emer Wilson
753. Winnin Hopkin
754. John Hopkin
755. William Sloane
756. John Sloane
757. George Gray
758. Thomas Caddan
759. Thomas Robinson
760. James McWhirke
761. Mathew Warren
762. Thomas Thompson
763. Cuthbert Thompson
764. Robert Christian
765. Malcolme Steavenson
766. Edward Lucas
767. Morris Fisher
768. Hugh Fisher
769. Thomas Maisterton
770. Michaell Gray
771. John Masterton
772. William Weir

773. Robert Grosert
774. Robert Sym
775. James Miller
776. John Hunter
777. Thomas Purdy
778. Hugh Purdy
779. Robert Williamson

[f. 249]

780. John Williamson
781. John McCleland
782. John Wyly
783. Thomas Lawson
784. James Young
785. Hugh Thomson
786. Gilbert McKenleyes
787. John McKenleys
788. David Bell
789. John Bell
790. John McConnell
791. Symond Williamson
792. Robert Williamson
793. Walter Johnston
794. Adam Glendining
795. James Johnston[148]
796. James Johnston younger
797. John Pennington
798. John Holyday
799. John Williamson[149]
800. Alexander Williamson
801. George Cogheran
802. Thomas Blacklock
803. James Gilchrist
804. Robert McMichaell
805. John Cogheran
806. John Steward
807. John Gilpatrick
808. James Camble
809. Donell Caure
810. David Irwin
811. Walter Williamson
812. John Skillan
813. Andrew Sympson
814. William Sympson

[f. 249v]

815. William Rae
816. Patrick Kelly
817. David McKena
818. Robert Hyeron

819. Robert Mofat
820. Robert Hogg
821. James Aickin
822. William Dixon
823. Archbald Corse
824. John Browne
825. Robert Steele
826. Thomas Anderson
827. John Howy
828. John Stewerd
829. Gilbert Morkid
830. John Howie
831. George Scot
832. John Dickye
833. Alexander McCobragh
834. George Torbron
835. Martin Mordagh
836. Robert Hamilton
837. William Spotswood
838. John Morrison
839. John Lader
840. William Whitlaw
841. John Cullons
842. John Williamson
843. John Henry
844. Alexander Wancis
845. Mr John Ramsay
846. Thomas Moore
847. John Moore
848. John Banantyne

[f. 250]

849. George Cornewall
850. Mathew Wyly
851. Hugh Begg
852. George Aikin
853. John Anderson
854. Thomas Fish
855. Thomas Moore
856. John Reed
857. Robert Welsh[150]
858. Thomas Donwooddy
859. David Wallace
860. Robert Wallace
861. Patrick Shane   papist
862. Francis Shane
863. Thomas Irwyn
864. James Forrest
865. Hugh Wallace
866. John Butler
867. John Wilson

---

[146] Numbers 745 to 747: father and two sons.

[147] Numbers 749 and 750 are father and son.

[148] These are probably the 'James Johnson elder and younger' who were among the killers of the Irish near Holywood, 1642 (Examinations of Katerine McGarry, 10 May 1653 [TCD MS 838, fols 247r–248v] and Daniell MacThomas O Gilmore, 28 April 1653 [ibid. fols 249r–250v]). They were alive and living at Ballydavey, 1653 (Examination of Hugh McGee, 21 April 1653 [ibid. fols 251r–252v]).

[149] Williamson appears as 800 in the original manuscript: Graham seems to have miscounted.

[150] Welsh may have moved to Saul before 1641 (Examination of Robert Welch, 3 May 1653 [TCD MS 837, fols 180r–180v]).

The town and Parish of Killegleagh

868. Alaster Lockhart
869. William Hamilton[151]
870. John Hamilton
871. James McMeaghan[152]
872. Walter Robinson
873. James Shortwright
874. John Payeyan
875. Andrew Golly
876. William McKee
877. John Darumple
878. John Easton
879. John McCullogh[153]
880. John Bradfoote

[f. 250v]

881. John Stroyan
882. John Pidgeon
883. Thomas Robinson
884. Alexander Broadfoote
885. John McCluire
886. Thomas Stroyan
887. William Forrest
888. James Lockhart
889. James Lowden
890. James Henry
891. Thomas Rowans
892. Nevin Steward
893. Mathew Stein
894. Hugh Warden
895. Thomas Rosse
896. Thomas Robinson
897. John Rosse
898. Andrew Lanses
899. John Hendry
900. William Nixon
901. John Maxwell[154]
902. James Reed[155]
903. James Reed younger
904. William Lockhart
905. John Reed
906. John McKenne
907. John Pettecrell
908. James Telfer

909. James Reed
910. William Henderson
911. William Welch
912. William Allison
913. John McAllen
914. John Hanelawe

[f. 251]

915. Robert Lynton
916. John Young
917. Alexander Hasty
918. John Boyd
919. Patrick Reed
920. John Johnston
921. William Rodger
922. James Boyle
923. James Geddes
924. Gilbert Greir
925. James Morrison
926. John Boyle
927. John Steward
928. Mungo Carmighell[156]
929. John Ireland[157]
930. Emmer Tullons
931. John Ireland younger
932. Poncane Read
933. George Alexander
934. William Purdy
935. John Strawbridg
936. Abraham Porter
937. Adam Hunter
938. Andrew Taylor
939. John Fynlay
940. Thomas Watson
941. Cullen Fynlay
942. George Hamilton
943. John Forrest[158]
944. John Forrest younger
945. John Hunter
946. John Pudgeon
947. William Kinge
948. Henry Corse

[f. 251v]

949. John Marvell
950. James Anderson

951. John Watson
952. Thomas Joanes
953. John Lyndsay
954. George Williamson
955. John Bradefoote
956. Michaell Purbouse
957. John Weltch
958. Robert Croft
959. William Wast
960. John Robinson
961. William Cambell
962. John Weltch younger[159]
963. David Weltch
964. Andrew Kers
965. James Miller
966. Andrew Reynold
967. John Weltch   saddler
968. John Ramsey
969. William Bradley
970. John Kilpatrick
971. John Moore[160]
972. John Goffock
973. Richard Pearson[161]
974. John Shirdall
975. George Slowan
976. William Holyday
977. John Williamson
978. David Read
979. Thomas Hamelton
980. Patrick Anderson
981. John McKee

[f. 252]

982. Mathew Hendry
983. James Hendry
984. Richard Fasset
985. Patrick o Kan
986. Alexander McGill

In the Iland Maghee

Swords and Snaphances
987. Robert Conninham
988. Alexander Conninham[162]
989. John Heiron
990. Alexander Rowcastle

---

[151] Possibly one of the killers of the Irish at Ballydavey, near Holywood, February 1642 (Examination of Owen O Gilmore, undated [ibid. fols 157r–158v]).

[152] 'James McMakene' of Donaghadee received letters of denization 1617 (*Calendar of patent rolls, Ireland, James I*, pp 326–29).

[153] Identified as one of the killers of the Irish at Ballydavey, February 1642 (Examination of James Gourdan, 3 May 1653 [TCD MS 837, fols 155r–155v]).

[154] One of the John Maxwells in this list was a tenant of Sir James Hamilton in 1616 (*Hamilton MSS*, p. 54).

[155] Numbers 902 and 903 are father and son.

[156] Possibly related to Rachael Carmichael, second wife of Archibald Hamilton, Lord Clandeboy's brother (*Hamilton MSS*, p. 43).

[157] Numbers 929 and 931 are father and son.

[158] Numbers 943 and 944 are father and son.

[159] Son of either number 957 or number 967.

[160] Named as a burgess in the charter of Killyleagh, 10 March 1613 (*Hamilton MSS*, general appendix, p. lxv).

[161] Pearson was resident 'in Galwally, being below Castlereagh' in 1641, according to his servant, Patrick McLaughlin [Examination of Patrick McLaughlin, 9 May 1653 [TCD MS 838, fols 229r–230v]].

[162] Named as a burgess in the charter of Killyleagh, 10 March 1613 (*Hamilton MSS*, general appendix, p. lxv).

991. William McCartney
992. John Turner
993. Alexander McCullo
994. James Hunter
995. James Sloan
996. Hugh Conninham[163]
997. William Steward
998. William Little
999. George Jackson
1000. Robert Harper
1001. John McMeighan
1002. Alexander McClaire
1003. John Smyth
1004. John McCullo
1005. John McSlibberries[164]
1006. John McSlibberries younger
1007. James McCanine
1008. David Steavenson
1009. Thomas Ross
1010. Michaell McCalwey
1011. John Steavenson
1012. Edward Steavenson
1013. John Heiron

[f. 252v]

1014. John McKee
1015. Alexander Hillhouse
1016. Thomas McCleland
1017. John Fargusson
1018. James Miller
1019. William Hillhowse
1020. Mathew Fargushill
1021. John Jackson
1022. William Bell
1023. James Tait
1024. James Browne
1025. James Banantyne
1026. William Tait
1027. Alexander Weir
1028. William Campbell
1029. William Oar
1030. Patrick Oar
1031. Patrick Reed
1032. James Boyd
1033. John Freind
1034. Downy Bony
1035. John Steele
1036. William McTyr

1037. William Watson
1038. John Heiron
1039. John Mathew
1040. Malcolme Rogers
1041. John Hawthorne
1042. John Wilson
1043. John Campbell
1044. Thomas Stanhop
1045. James McKea
1046. John Greene
1047. Mathew Fargushill
1048. John Casset
1049. Patrick Browne

[f. 253]

Down

The barony of great Ardes

Swords and Pikes

1050. Thomas Boyd
1051. John Irwing
1052. Robert Clark
1053. James McAlexander
1054. Thomas McCamont
1055. William Blaire
1056. Andrew Armestong
1057. George McAdam
1058. Alexander Couper
1059. Thomas McKidridg
1060. John McNeisy
1061. Thomas Boyd
1062. Malcolme Donald
1063. Robert Donald
1064. Collin Waghop
1065. John Armor
1066. Thomas McTyer
1067. William Hammilton
1068. John Keirney
1069. William Johnston
1070. David Lewis
1071. Archbald Kerney
1072. Archbald Johnston[165]
1073. Edward Irwin
1074. George Donnell
1075. John McKennet
1076. Thomas Blain

1077. John Irwin
1078. James Maxwell[166]
1079. James Hammilton
1080. Gilbert McNeill
1081. William Johnston
1082. Thomas Robinson
1083. John Cassan[167]
1084. Robert Cassan
1085. Robert Irwing

[f. 253v]

1086. James Irwing
1087. John Murdogh[168]
1088. Gilbert Edger
1089. John Murdogh younger[169]
1090. James Montgumry
1091. John Maxwell
1092. John Martin
1093. John Martin younger
1094. Robert Martin
1095. Robert Irwing
1096. James McWharry
1097. John Crage
1098. William Crage
1099. Collin Crage
1100. William Clarke
1101. Andrew Wilson
1102. Mighell Crage[170]
1103. John Maxwell
1104. Collen Maxwell
1105. William McCoffye
1106. John Graghame
1107. James Mosmanie
1108. Andrew Hammilton
1109. Michaell Nasmith
1110. John McConnell
1111. Archbald McCall
1112. John Roger
1113. Cuthbert Irwin
1114. John Maxwell
1115. Saunders Maxwell
1116. John McCoffye
1117. John Clarke
1118. Thomas McCoffye
1119. Michaell Crage
1120. Patrick Cassan
1121. John Holliday

---

[163] Resident Castle Espie; denization, 1617 (*Calendar of patent rolls, Ireland, James I*, pp 326–39; *Montgomery MSS*, p. 56).

[164] Numbers 1005 and 1006 are father and son.

[165] 'Archbell Johnson' was 'aged five and fifty years' and resident at 'Bleary in Clanconnell in county Down' in 1653 (Examination of Archbell Johnson, 2 May 1653 [TCD MS 837, fols 140r–141v]); he had probably moved to the Magheralin area before 1641.

[166] James Maxwell of Gransha received letters of denization in 1617 (*Calendar of patent rolls, Ireland, James I*, pp 326–39; *Montgomery MSS*, p. 56).

[167] John Cashan or McHassan was an attorney for Con O'Neill, 1605 (*Hamilton MSS*, p. 18) and was a tenant of Sir Hugh Montgomery at Ballynacroie, 1607–23; his son, Hugh, held Ballygrangee townland, near Carrowdore, 1629 (*Montgomery MSS*, pp 41–2).

[168] Father of number 1089.

[169] Son of number 1087.

[170] Tenant of Sir James Hamilton, 1616 (*Hamilton MSS*, p. 54); resident Roddans, near Ballywalter; denization, 1617 (*Calendar of patent rolls, Ireland, James I*, pp 326–39; *Montgomery MSS*, p. 56).

[f. 254]

1122. Andrew Clarke
1123. Dunkan McKee
1124. William Deglish
1125. George Fairly
1126. John Warnock
1127. Patrick Maxwell
1128. Charles McCratton
1129. John Irwing
1130. Gilbert Cavan
1131. Robert Clyde
1132. John Thompson
1133. John Gourdon
1134. Michaell Marshall
1135. Thomas Gourdon
1136. John McCullen
1137. David Reed
1138. Gilbert Weir
1139. John McCreiry
1140. John McKellin
1141. John McKeddy
1142. David Boyd
1143. John McComb
1144. William Crawford[171]
1145. James Copeland
1146. John McNish
1147. Alexander Bigham
1148. John McCans
1149. Andrew Hogg
1150. Thomas Crawfford
1151. John Quater
1152. John Copeland[172]
1153. Robert Crag
1154. John Copeland younger
1155. Andrew McCullen
1156. John McCullen
1157. Robert Hammilton
1158. Thomas Mackbryn

[f. 254v]

Pikes only
1159. John Moore
1160. William Moore
1161. John McAdam
1162. John O Lyne
1163. Dunkan Mulligan
1164. Adam Chesny
1165. Thomas Douglas
1166. Gilbert Henderson
1167. Alexander McIllduff
1168. John Lewis

1169. Archbald Steward
1170. Andrew McCrattin
1171. Adam Kee
1172. Alexander Dods
1173. Thomas McMurphew
1174. David Bayly
1175. Robert Donnelson
1176. John George
1177. Robert Kennydee
1178. Alexander Hannagh
1179. John McClery
1180. Alexander Bayly
1181. William Bayly[173]
1182. John Bayly
1183. William Hannagh
1184. Anthony Kee
1185. Oswell Wright
1186. Gilbert Conningham
1187. William Bayly younger
1188. John Baly
1189. David Hammilton
1190. David McCullum
1191. William Patterson
1192. Martin Robinson
1193. Patrick Howye

[f. 255]

1194. Thomas Pattrowne
1195. William Gubeland
1196. Patrick McConles

Swords and Pikes
1197. John Barkley
1198. John Clarke
1199. William Cragg
1200. John Blaine[174]
1201. John Montgumry
1202. Neal Montgumry
1203. John Moffet
1204. Walter Hunter
1205. Patrick Hannagh
1206. John Conningham
1207. John Neil[175]
1208. John Gilchrist
1209. Robert Throw
1210. Robert Neal
1211. Symon Biggam
1212. John Biggam
1213. James Biggam
1214. William Wallace[176]
1215. Hugh Wallace

1216. Thomas Harper
1217. Alexander Clarke
1218. John Steward
1219. John Leniston
1220. James Gemill
1221. James Carnoghan
1222. John Thompson
1223. Cuthbert Thompson
1224. John Par
1225. Thomas McEnnis
1226. William Irwing
1227. John Carley
1228. Bryan o Kelly
1229. Adam Coningham

[f. 255v]

1230. Hugh Young
1231. John Young
1232. John Warnock
1233. Donald McCratten
1234. John Calwell
1235. John Byers
1236. Thomas Byers
1237. John Pollock
1238. John McCullod
1239. John Crawfford
1240. William Crawfford
1241. Thomas Crawfford
1242. James Cowy
1243. John Barkley
1244. John Martin
1245. John McGeoghan
1246. John Hammilton
1247. David Irwin

Swords and Muskets
1248. John Beck
1249. Adam Beck
1250. Thomas Andrew
1251. John Allen
1252. Gilbert Martin
1253. John Bryan
1254. John Patton
1255. Mathew Johnston
1256. Thomas Johnston
1257. Martin Humphrey
1258. Robert McWhirke
1259. Edward Maxwell[177]
1260. Alexander Meaghan
1261. Patrick Sempell
1262. Adam Beck

---

[171] 'William Crawford of Cuningburn [near Mount Stewart]'; denization, 1617 (*Calendar of patent rolls, Ireland, James I*, pp 326–39; *Montgomery MSS*, p. 56).
[172] Numbers 1152 and 1154 are father and son; number 1145 is probably a relation.
[173] Numbers 1181 and 1187 are father and son.
[174] Resident at Ballynafeagh, 1641; married to 'Mary McGaghy' (Deposition of Donell Rush, 2 May 1653 [TCD MS 837, fols 057r–058v]).
[175] John and Archibald Neil were among the original settlers on the Montgomery estate (*Montgomery MSS*, p. 54).
[176] Tenant, 1616 (*Hamilton MSS*, p. 54).
[177] Tenant, 1616 (*Hamilton MSS*, p. 54).

1263. William Carr
1264. John Irwing
1265. John Tolly
1266. Alexander Swan

[f. 256]

1267. John McCullen
1268. James How
1269. Ninian Paseley[178]
1270. Walter Loggan[179]
1271. John Rutherfoord
1272. Edward Perry
1273. James Love
1274. Robert Passeley
1275. Andrew Passeley
1276. John McChoyn
1277. James Truill
1278. John Peacock
1279. Alexander Coop
1280. Patrick Spruill
1281. William Hillhowse
1282. John Hillhowse[180]
1283. Robert Moore
1284. William Pettron
1285. John Wallace
1286. John Neilson
1287. James Neilson
1288. Edward Irwing
1289. Sanders Crum
1290. Archbald Spere
1291. Thomas Barkley
1292. John Callwell
1293. Williams Biggs
1294. John Carr
1295. Adam Irwin
1296. John Barkley
1297. William Britch
1298. Nevin Flack
1299. John Loud
1300. Joseph Biggot
1301. Mathew Biggot
1302. John Barkeley
1303. William Blackstock

[f. 256v]

1304. John Browne
1305. John White
1306. Alexander Boyd

1307. Hugh Hammilton[181]
1308. Alexander Hammilton
1309. William Boyd
1310. Hugh Boyd
1311. William Glen
1312. Archbald Rinlan
1313. William Gilmoore
1314. John McCratten

Swords and Snaphances
1315. John Browne
1316. Archbald Barnet
1317. John Ore
1318. David Hay
1319. John Lynton
1320. Mathew Jeffreyes
1321. William Gray
1322. Edward Hoghen
1323. James Birs
1324. Mathew McCrad
1325. Robert Hunter
1326. Thomas Browne
1327. James Waltomson
1328. Robert Andrew
1329. Robert Irwing
1330. Adam Aird
1331. James Brown
1332. William Patterson
1333. John Carr
1334. Alexander Boyd
1335. Paul Wilson
1336. James Birs   miller
1337. James Robinson
1338. James Neilson
1339. Donnell Morrison

[f. 257]

1340. John McIlwoorth
1341. James Robinson
1342. Robert Long
1343. John Wilson
1344. Robert Love
1345. John Marshall
1346. John Kerny
1347. Robert Orr
1348. John Christwell
1349. John Love
1350. Ninian Adam

1351. John Jackson
1352. James Micclesjohn
1353. David Michaell
1354. Tobyas Knox
1355. James Gay
1356. Thomas Scot
1357. William Irwin
1358. Archbald Scot
1359. John Orr
1360. Sandy Orr
1361. Robert Long
1362. George Robinson
1363. Sandy Sympson

The Towne and Lands of Holliwood

Swords and Pikes
1364. John McGill[182]
1365. John McGill younger
1366. Thomas McGill
1367. Ninian Girly
1368. John McFarren
1369. Nynyan McCarr
1370. Hugh McCarr
1371. John McCarr
1372. James Rankin
1373. Andrew Scot[183]

[f. 257v]

1374. Andrew McBrid
1375. John McCar
1376. John Thompson
1377. Andrew McCullogh
1378. Patrick Rowan
1379. James Johnston
1380. Patrick Macferrin
1381. John McCleland
1382. Adam Breges
1383. John Woodsyde
1384. John Thompson
1385. Robert Kels
1386. Thomas Thompson
1387. Robert Hunter
1388. Robert Thompson
1389. John Thompson
1390. James Slose

---

[178] The Paisleys lived near Portaferry (Deposition of Thomas Paseley, 3 May 1653 [TCD MS 837, fols 130r–130v]).

[179] Denization, 1617; then resident at 'Proveston' (*Calendar of patent rolls, Ireland, James I*, pp 326–39; *Montgomery MSS*, p. 56).

[180] The only John Hillhouse to be mentioned in the 1641 depositions was resident at Gortycavan, near Coleraine in county Londonderry. He was killed on 20 December 1641. If this is the same man, he took his sword with him (Examination of Jane Todd, Hillhouse's widow, 18 March 1653 [TCD MS 838, fols 079v–080r]).

[181] Named as a burgess in the charter of Killyleagh, 10 March 1613 (*Hamilton MSS*, general appendix, p. lxv).

[182] Father of number 1365 and probably of number 1366; the family was resident at Ballyrobert and were among the killers of the Irish, February 1642; Thomas Magill died before 1653 (Examination of Daniell MacThomas O Gilmore, 28 April 1653 [TCD MS 838, fols 249r–250v]).

[183] Andrew Scott senior was the parish constable in 1642 and 'did endeavour to save the lives of such Irish as were there' when the killings started near Holywood (Examinations of Katerine McGarry, 10 May 1653 [ibid. fols 247r–247v] and Hugh McGee, 21 April 1653 [ibid. fols 251r–252v]). However, 'Andrew Scott [now] dead [but] then constable' and 'Andrew Scott Junior' were named as among 'the murderers' of the Irish near Holywood (Examination of Daniell MacThomas O Gilmore, 28 April 1653 [ibid. fols 249r–250v]).

1391. Robert Slose
1392. Thomas Little
1393. Daniell Coop
1394. William Bridges[184]
1395. Nynian McGlaney
1396. Thomas Nealson
1397. James Flyn
1398. Thomas McMullan
1399. Archbald Caruth[185]
1400. William Shaw
1401. John Fleming
1402. John Carbrath
1403. Christopher Porter
1404. John McCormack
1405. John Cuddy
1406. George Fish
1407. James Ross
1408. Archbald Lyndsay
1409. Robert Ross
1410. Alexander Loggan
1411. Patrick Goodlet

[f. 258]

1412. Henry Frame
1413. George Browne
1414. Walter Scot
1415. John Patomy
1416. Alexander Caruth
1417. John Gibson
1418. John Lyon
1419. John Pettecrew
1420. Robert Steele
1421. Thomas Thomson
1422. James Thompson
1423. Mathew Magowine
1424. John Wright[186]
1425. John Wright younger
1426. Frauncis Wright
1427. Thomas Bell
1428. William Liniston
1429. Andrew Short
1430. James Richy
1431. William Little
1432. William Davidson
1433. John Ranton[187]
1434. John Ranton younger

1435. Thomas Creswell[188]
1436. John Creswell
1437. John Creswell younger
1438. Malcolm Creswell
1439. William Creswell
1440. Andrew McNab
1441. James McIlman
1442. William Allan
1443. Robert Allan
1444. James Allan
1445. William McConnell
1446. William McCormick
1447. Martyn Beatty
1448. James Robye

[f. 258v]

1449. John McMillen
1450. William Steward
1451. Gilbert Slowan
1452. William Smyth
1453. Thomas Graham
1454. George Gragham
1455. Alexander Brand
1456. Henry Coshcry
1457. Patrick Hume
1458. Archbald Frow
1459. John Barclay
1460. John Fargushill
1461. Adam Gibson
1462. Walter Pearcy
1463. Thomas Kirkpatrick
1464. John Michaell[189]
1465. John Barkeley
1466. Thomas McCrerie
1467. John Crawfoord[190]
1468. Steaphen Crawford
1469. Robert Neall
1470. Donald McAllan
1471. Andrew Miller
1472. John Patterson
1473. William Dunbar[191]
1474. James Browne
1475. John Miller
1476. William McClene
1477. Frauncis Moffatt
1478. James Mathy

1479. William Carlill
1480. Gilbert Johnston
1481. Robert Little
1482. William Watt
1483. William Miltowne
1484. William Taylor
1485. Archbald McGibbone
1486. John McMillen

[f. 259]

1487. Allan Russell
1488. James Curry
1489. Fargus Drennan
1490. Alexander Reed
1491. Hugh Watt
1492. Robert Warden
1493. John Warden
1494. David Sympson
1495. John Kenedy
1496. George Cant
1497. Thomas McTyne
1498. William Cowye
1499. John Little
1500. John Lowdon[192]
1501. George Kennydye
1502. Patrick Thomson
1503. John Moorehead
1504. James Wilson
1505. Gilbert McTyre
1506. John Drysdall
1507. John Greswell
1508. John Love
1509. Andrew Reed
1510. Mathew Ranton
1511. John Rowen
1512. George Cowie
1513. Patrick Martin
1514. William Curry
1515. George Curry
1516. William London
1517. John Robe
1518. Thomas Moorehead
1519. Robert Miltowne
1520. Dunkan Hawthorne
1521. Alexander Hawthorne
1522. Richard Armestrong
1523. Patrick McWhaw

[184] Bridges, a weaver, was one of the killers of the Irish at Ballydavey in February 1642; he was still alive and living at Dromore in 1653 (Examination of Hugh McGee, 21 April 1653 [ibid. fols 251r–252v]).

[185] Caruth appears as 1400 in the original MS. The number is in a different ink. The original number was written against James Johnston (number 1379) but was deleted. The totals were therefore checked after the muster was completed.

[186] Father of number 1425; possibly 'John Wright of Holywood … Merchant', robbed at Wexford, February 1642 (Deposition of John Wright, 8 October 1642 [TCD MS 837, fols 018r–018v]).

[187] Numbers 1433 and 1434 are father and son.

[188] Numbers 1435 to 1439 are a family group.

[189] John Mitchell of Ballyhackamore was one of viscount Clandeboye's representatives in the arbitration of the dispute with viscount Ards in 1633 (*Montgomery MSS*, p. 81).

[190] John Crawford of Crawfordsburn was one of the killers of the Irish near Holywood, February 1642 (Examination of Daniell MacThomas O Gilmore, 28 April 1653 [TCD MS 838, fols 249r–250v]).

[191] Named as a burgess in the charter for Killyleagh, 10 March 1613 (*Hamilton MSS*, general appendix, p. lxv).

[192] 'John Loudon, clerk' was one of the servants in the cortege at the funeral of viscount Ards, 1636 (*Montgomery MSS*, p. 135).

[f. 259v]

1524. John McChaghan
1525. John Smyth
1526. John Milton
1527. Alexander Sympson
1528. John Sinckler
1529. Thomas Drynam
1530. James McClatchie
1531. John Cragg
1532. John Bran
1533. Richard Roddin
1534. John Dunber
1535. John Alexander
1536. John McClatchie
1537. James Lanarick
1538. William Porter
1539. James McClatchie
1540. Patrick Gibson
1541. John Chalmeris
1542. Alexander McIlwaine
1543. Hector Peacock

Sword and Musket

1544. William Grossard
1545. Archbald Miller
1546. Ninian McClairy
1547. Robert Hunter
1548. David Shaw[193]
1549. David Shaw younger[194]
1550. Gilbert Shaw
1551. James Nesbit
1552. William McCar
1553. Archbald Wright
1554. Robert Hunter
1555. Charles Dunn
1556. Thomas Carlell
1557. John McClennoghan
1558. Hugh Fargushill
1559. John McMillen
1560. Thomas Carlell
1561. William Fargusson
1562. Thomas Ranton

[f. 260]

1563. Jn: Breddagh
1564. William Mullen
1565. Edward Purdy
1566. Thomas Purdy
1567. John Watson
1568. William Herslop
1569. Cuthbert McMullen
1570. Alexander McCar
1571. Alexander McMerry
1572. John Williamson

1573. Henry Whitesyde
1574. Thomas Whitesyde
1575. William Shortridg
1576. Allen Claghston
1577. John Martyn
1578. Robert Robinson
1579. Michaell Bangs
1580. Robert Gnasson
1581. James Addysson
1582. Robert Jordane
1583. John Addyson
1584. Thomas Booman

Swords and Pikes

1585. Arthur Nixon
1586. William Johnston
1587. John McMurray
1588. John Harknes
1589. Thomas Smyth
1590. Alexander Campbell
1591. John Smith elder
1592. George Smyth
1593. John Hammilton[195]
1594. Patrick McMullan
1595. Anthony McMullan
1596. Gilbert Browne

[f. 260v]

1597. Gilbert McConnell
1598. John McMeane
1599. John Dixon
1600. John McMurdenne
1601. Christopher Lason
1602. John McAlexander
1603. Robert Graham
1604. John Spence
1605. Daniell Little
1606. George Bell
1607. Robert Lason
1608. John Kirkpatrick
1609. Ignatius Little
1610. Walter Beaty
1611. Archbald Lyttle
1612. Andrew Warwick
1613. James Steavenson
1614. John Kirkpatrick[196]
1615. John Kirkpatrick younger
1616. John Johnston
1617. Thomas Kirkpatrick
1618. John Martin
1619. Thomas Martin
1620. Daniell Beatty
1621. James McCartney
1622. Andrew Ranton

1623. James Copeland
1624. Neale McNish
1625. Andrew Cullan
1626. Robert Hammilton
1627. Dunkan Milligan
1628. Thomas McMurphew
1629. David Baly
1630. Gilbert Henderson

[f. 261]

1631. David Boyd
1632. Collen Maxwell
1633. Michaell Cragg
1634. James Holliday
1635. Robert Irwin
1636. Charles McCratten
1637. Collin Maxwell
1638. James Mosmaine
1639. Robert Donald
1640. Alexander Coop
1641. Thomas Blainie
1642. Gilbert McNeal
1643. Thomas McKidridg
1644. John Armor

No Arms

1645. David Lewis
1646. Downie Bonnie
1647. William Car
1648. David Steavenson
1649. William Hillhowse
1650. Malcolme Rogers
1651. John Heiron
1652. James Sloane
1653. James Bannantyne
1654. George Slowan
1655. Gilbert Bradley
1656. John Weltch
1657. David Reed
1658. James Telfer
1659. John Pidgion
1660. Thomas Rowans
1661. John Easton
1662. John Miller
1663. James Forrest
1664. Andrew Golly
1665. John Lader

[f. 261v]

1666. David Irwin
1667. John Skillan
1668. Patrick Kelly
1669. John McConnell
1670. John Penington

[193] Numbers 1548 to 1549 are father and two sons.
[194] Identified as one of the assailants of the Irish, 1642 (Depositions of Donell Rush, 2 May 1653 [TCD MS 837, fols 057r–058v] and Gorre Rush, undated [ibid. fols 114r–114v]).
[195] Younger brother of Lord Clandeboy and leaseholder of Ballyrobert and Ballydavey townlands, 1616 (*Hamilton MSS*, pp 56–7).
[196] Father of number 1615 and possibly of number 1617.

1671. George Scot
1672. James Camble
1673. David Bell
1674. James Miller
1675. Robert Wyly
1676. James Dunlap
1677. John Masterton
1678. George Gray
1679. John McRobert
1680. Hugh Fisher
1681. James Miller
1682. Edward Lucas
1683. Thomas Oliver
1684. William Were
1685. John Wilson
1686. Alexander Lowry
1687. John McDowgall
1688. Andrew Byers
1689. James Chambers
1690. William Cashell
1691. John Neper
1692. David Johnston
1693. Andrew Walker
1694. Thomas Dixon[197]
1695. William Gourden
1696. James Fisher
1697. John Moore
1698. Peter Scot
1699. Thomas Dixon younger
1700. Richard Baird

[f. 262]

1701. David Fish
1702. James Dunbar
1703. Peter Wallace
1704. John Campbell
1705. Andrew Corby
1706. William Caddon
1707. James Wallace
1708. Thomas Hanna
1709. Alexander Lowry
1710. John Dunbar
1711. William Gardner
1712. James Logan

1713. John Carsan
1714. Mungo Weir
1715. Hugh Miller
1716. John Borland
1717. John McCosh
1718. Patrick Fyndley
1719. James Pots
1720. William Roven[198]
1721. William Greir
1722. John Watt[199]
1723. John Hall
1724. George Fyndley
1725. John Ray
1726. James Greir
1727. Quinton Hammilton
1728. John Still
1729. William Twynan
1730. Symond Dixon
1731. Robert Miller
1732. Andrew Bartran
1733. James Harper
1734. George Innes

[f. 262v]

1735. Patrick Goodlet
1736. Patrick McFirren
1737. James Slose
1738. Hugh McCar
1739. Andrew Scot
1740. Robert Kels
1741. John Cuddy
1742. Andrew McBrid
1743. Robert Allen
1744. John Lyon
1745. John Wright
1746. Henry Frame
1747. William McCormick
1748. Thomas Bell
1749. Mathew McCrade
1750. Archbald Barnet
1751. Robert Long
1752. David Hay
1753. James Birrs
1754. Donnell Morison

1755. Robert Andrew
1756. John Lyndon
1757. John Smyth
1758. James Reed
1759. Gilbert McIlwrath
1760. John Reed
1761. John Smyth

[f. 263]

1762. Andrew Reed
1763. Adam Hunter
1764. Gawen Kirkpatrick
1765. David Spence
1766. John Murray
1767. Robert Calmeris
1768. James Kirkpatrick
1769. Robert McCartney
1770. Robert Blake
1771. John Satlington
1772. William Glendinning
1773. James McKee
1774. John Hooke
1775. Thomas Pott
1776. William McGawen[200]

[f. 264]

Down

The Lord General his workmen at his Iron Mills[201]

No Arms
1. David Sawyer
2. Thomas Guly[202]
3. Thomas Guly younger
4. Robert Buller
5. James Buller
6. Robert Barnes[203]
7. Thomas Bowman[204]
8. William Jones
9. John Shaw
10. Robert Shaw
11. William Coole[205]

---

[197] Numbers 1694 and 1699 are father and son.

[198] Identified as one of the killers of the Irish near Holywood in February 1642; died before 1653; James Rowen, the constable of Bangor in 1653, who was also involved in the killing of the Irish in 1642, may have been one of his sons (Examination of Daniell MacThomas O Gilmore, 28 April 1653 [TCD MS 838, fols 249r–250v]).

[199] John Watt was one of the killers of the Irish near Holywood in February 1642 (Examinations of Katerine McGarry, 10 May 1653 [ibid. fols 247r–247v] and Daniell MacThomas O Gilmore, 28 April 1653 [ibid. fols 249r–250v]). Watt was still alive in 1653 and living at 'Carne bally hill in kilmakeuitt' (Examination of Hugh McGill, 21 April 1653 [ibid. fols 251r–252v]).

[200] Shown as 1778 in original MS.

[201] The notes marked [RJH] are taken directly from Robert Hunter's working papers and refer to the Blaris parish registers (PRONI, D1823/5, CR1/35/A, and MIC1/3/1) [JJ].

[202] Gully may possibly be Bill in the parish register, 1637–46, p. 25 [RJH].

[203] Robert Barnes was one of the killers of the Irish near Holywood, 1642 (Examination of Katerine McGarry, 10 May 1653 [TCD MS 838, fols 247r–248v]); he died before 1653 (Examination of Daniell MacThomas O Gilmore, 28 April 1653 [ibid. fols 249r–250v]). RJH cross-references him to 'Robert Brownes', number 49 on the 'Plotte'.

[204] 'Mary, daughter of Thomas Bodman', was 'baptised 7 June 1640' and 'buried 1641' (Parish Register, pp 19, 23) [RJH].

[205] Cross-referenced to Cullin [RJH].

12. Henry Goodwin
13. Thomas Wilson[206]
14. Thomas Walker[207]
15. William Coop
16. Bryan McGee
17. Thomas Sameton
18. Phillime Gridy
19. Robert Sympson[208]
20. Robert Gotier
21. James Wilson[209]
22. William Sympson[210]
23. Robert Cartwright[211]
24. John Turly
25. Henry Toppin[212]
26. Thomas Addyson
27. Frauncis Wermane
28. John Bickerston

[f. 264v]

Down

The Lord Bishop of Down his tenants and Mr Patrick Savage and Mr Rowland Savage: their tenants, their names and arms as followeth

Swords only

1. William Wahop
2. James White
3. John Maxwell[213]
4. William Chagstone
5. John Dunbar
6. John Thompson
7. John Montgumry
8. William Ramsay[214]
9. Jonn Machellon
10. William Ramsay younger
11. Thomas McMurray
12. William Donaldson
13. George Deary
14. Alexander Chambers
15. John Jeniy

16. John Irwyn
17. Alexander Gowen
18. George Carell
19. William McNeally
20. Fargus McDonnell
21. Robert Maxwell
22. Gilbert Adaire[215]
23. Gilbert Makeir
24. John Bell
25. Walter Kernes
26. John Kerneyes
27. William Gilmoore
28. John Tenant[216]
29. John Tate

[f. 265]

30. John Edger
31. James Edger
32. Thomas McCleland
33. Alexander Agnew
34. Paul Reed

No Arms

35. John Dixon
36. George Steward
37. Gilbert Tenant
38. John Gely
39. John McIlnagh
40. John Collyne
41. William Clarke
42. William Kenne
43. John Dungalsan
44. Rynyon Clinblock

Swords and Pikes

45. Walter Scot
46. John McNish
47. John McRobert
48. John Robinson
49. Andrew Agnew[217]
50. John McKeir
51. Thomas Dronan
52. Alexander Dungelson
53. William Harvye

Swords and Halberds

54. John McCrery
55. Thomas McClenan

Sword and Musket

56. Alexander Steward

Sword and Snaphance

57. Cuthbert Boyd

[f. 265v]

No Arms

58. James Tomson
59. Nevin McWilliam
60. William Dunbar
61. George Johnston
62. Gilbert McHelen
63. Neivin McCormick
64. Andrew McCormick
65. Outhrid McCormick
66. Gilbert McCormick
67. John Crawford
68. John Cragg
69. John Small
70. John Fargye
71. James Edger
72. Gilbert Cutbert
73. Alexander Creckin
74. Andrew McBrid
75. Fargus McKee
76. John Bradfoote
77. Thomas Glansy
78. Robert Martyn
79. Patrick Glass
80. William Kenedy
81. John McClynd
82. Robert Smyth
83. William Collynd
84. Rynyon McDonnell
85. Adam Kenedy
86. John McMurra
87. Patrick Well
88. John McWell
89. James McRynyon

---

[206] Cross-referenced to Henry Wilson; Robert, the son of Thomas Wilson, was baptised, 19 November 1639 (Parish Register, 1637–46, p. 16) [RJH].

[207] Cross-referenced to Richard Walker; Thomas Walker was buried, 3 August 1640 (Parish Register, 1637–46, p. 19) [RJH].

[208] Cross-referenced to Thomas Symonson [RJH].

[209] Cross-referenced to Henry Wilson [RJH].

[210] Cross-referenced to Tomas Symonson [RJH].

[211] Son of J [...] Cartwright [RJH].

[212] Cross-referenced to Henry Wilson [RJH].

[213] 'John Maxwell of Ballihalberd' was the father-in-law of Hugh Cunningham of 'Downburge', county Antrim and was held prisoner in Newry until exchanged for another prisoner in late 1641 or early 1642 (Deposition of Hugh Cunningham, 21 April 1642 [TCD MS 836, fols 080r–081v]). Maxwell settled on the Montgomery estate around 1607 and received denization, 1617 (*Calendar of patent rolls, Ireland, James I*, pp 326–39; *Montgomery MSS*, p. 56).

[214] Numbers 8 and 10 are father and son.

[215] Denization, 1617; resident Ardkeen (*Calendar of patent rolls, Ireland, James I*, pp 326–39; *Montgomery MSS*, p. 56).

[216] Resident in Lecale and aged fifty-four, 1653 (Deposition of John Tennent, 3 May 1653 [TCD MS 837, f. 131r]).

[217] Resident Carney Hill, near Carrowdore; denization, 1617 (*Calendar of patent rolls, Ireland, James I*, pp 326–39; *Montgomery MSS*, p. 56).

90. Thomas Kintart
91. Barnaby Carman
92. John Cullan[218]
93. John Cullan younger

47 Swords, 9 Pikes, 1 Musket, 1 Snaphance, 2 Halberds

[f. 266]

Down

The British of the Lord Bishop of Dromore dwelling on his land and in the town of Dunmoore, with others residing in the Lower Euvagh

Pikes only

1. John Adamson
2. David Sybid
3. Robert Johnston
4. William McRichard
5. John Lowry
6. Thomas Makee
7. James Wilson
8. William Walker

Halberd only

9. John Rosbragh

Snaphances only

10. John McCrery
11. James Hartnes
12. William Bayly
13. Alexander McNaynin
14. James Richy
15. William Cardene
16. John McNarrin
17. George Hill
18. John McJohnsy
19. George Johnston
20. Alexander Gourden
21. John Gynenes
22. Thomas Turner
23. William Cassan
24. James Wadfell
25. Robert Montgumry
26. Thomas Davyson
27. Thomas Johnston
28. William Johnston
29. Gawen Johnston
30. William Johnston

31. James Hamelton
32. John McCarly

[f. 266v]

33. James Maxwell
34. John Wright
35. William Douglas
36. Archbald Thompson
37. Archbald Thomson
38. Patrick Makin
39. John Greir
40. Malcolme Farris
41. Guy Horner
42. James Douglas
43. Robert Turner
44. John Campbell
45. David McCail
46. Robert Conningham
47. John Williamson
48. David Crawfford
49. John Coward
50. John Younger
51. Robert English
52. Robert Wallace
53. George Formont
54. Thomas McWilliam
55. John Clarke
56. John Milling
57. Richy McMorland
58. William Dixon
59. David O Keife
60. William Crafford
61. John Wilson[219]
62. John Wilson younger
63. David McCrohart
64. James Kenedy
65. George Bosell

[f. 267]

66. William Browne
67. Robert Sprot
68. James McGowen
69. Thomas Sprot
70. Alexander McKina
71. Donnell Roodell
72. Hugh Roodell
73. David Makee
74. Mathew Galloway
75. James Payden
76. Adam Conningham
77. George Shaw[220]
78. George Wilson

79. Robert Richmont
80. Robert McCully
81. John Douglas
82. William Olie
83. William Ridle
84. John Money
85. George Shaw
86. William Cory[221]
87. John Tate
88. Donnell Hamill
89. William Smyth
90. George Murry
91. John Potter
92. Hugh Glasford
93. Richard Archbalson
94. Alexander Ross
95. John Bayle
96. Robert Smyth
97. William Smyth
98. Steaphen Hughin
99. Olver Toller
100. William Ryller
101. John Wright
102. John Smyth

[f. 267v]

103. John Bryeth
104. Thomas McKilnay
105. Thomas Haventry
106. William Searle
107. Richard Knox
108. John Sanderson
109. Robert Beaty
110. George Halso
111. Cutbert Wids
112. Alexander McCoppin
113. Nicholas Carrally
114. John McDonnell
115. Robert Wallace
116. John McWilliam
117. Constant Coghreny
118. John Mulligan
119. Walter McMulligan
120. David Crawford
121. John Weilly
122. John Johnston
123. William Copeland
124. David Richie
125. John Thompson
126. George Bell
127. John McCachallon
128. James Nicholson
129. John Hathorne

[218] Numbers 92 and 93 are father and son.
[219] Numbers 61 and 62 are father and son.
[220] The Shaws (numbers 77 and 85) are probably father and son: their property near Magheralin was plundered in October 1641 (Examination of George Shawe, junior, of Lurgan, 21 May 1653 [TCD MS 838, fols 231r–231v] and Deposition of George Shaw, 2 May 1653 [ibid. fols 065r–065v]).
[221] Corry's property was plundered, October 1641; he was living at Drombo, 1653 (Examination of George Shawe, junior, of Lurgan, 21 May 1653 [ibid. fols 231r–231v]).

130. George Costyne
131. John Lyne
132. John Montgumery
133. John Makee
134. Andrew Tate
135. William Wilson
136. John Gibson

[f. 268]

137. William Toder
138. William Depaw
139. John Scot
140. Thomas Irwing
141. William Porter
142. Robert Martiall

No Arms

143. Christopher Marsell
144. Roger Blackbrow
145. John Shaw
146. William Turner
147. John Beltin
148. James Doran
149. John Clyfford
150. Nicholas Harty
151. James Obison
152. Thomas Hale
153. Roger Bell
154. William Dixon
155. John Kennedy
156. Alexander Carssan

133 Swords, 8 Pikes, 1 halberd

[f. 268v]

Down

Robert Melvin esquire
his British tenants

Swords and Pikes
1. Thomas Milwell esquire
2. Thomas Milwell
3. William Millwell

Pike only
4. David Taylor

Swords only
5. Archbald Rea
6. Francis Little
7. John Parke
8. Gerry Johnston
9. John Wright
10. William Slowan
11. John Glendininy
12. John Black
13. James Rea
14. George Dobid
15. John Bell
16. John Rose
17. John Edwards

No Arms
18. David Blemish
19. John Lyndsay
20. Robert Annanhill
21. John Berry
22. James Trumble
23. John Gray
24. David Johnston
25. James Johnston
26. William Clercag
27. James Watson

[f. 269]

28. John Glascag
29. Michaell Boyd
30. James Little
31. John Wiggan
32. James Clarke
33. John Anthony
34. Thomas Benson
35. Walter Benson
36. Walter Johnston
37. William Haddock
38. John Fisher
39. James Clerson
40. Ralph Bolton
41. Robert Stobire

42. Thomas Johnston
43. Roger Denton
44. Bartholemew Drinker
45. Myles Wildman
46. Richard Wildman
47. William Moss
48. Alexander Barran
49. James Reed
50. Frauncis Houlden
51. Hugh Williams
52. Lawrence Robinson

16 Swords, 4 Pikes

[f. 269v]

Down

Mr Ward his tenants
on his Churchlands

No Arms
1. Nicholas Ward[222]
2. Barnard Ward
3. William Welsman
4. John Hammelton
5. Robert Butler
6. James Davis
7. William Conningham[223]
8. John McMakine

Lieutenant Burris his tenants
dwelling on the lands of
Castle Reagh

No Arms
1. James Reed
2. Robert McCarter
3. Alexander Porter
4. Robert Gryne
5. Patrick McMullan
6. John McMurry
7. Alexander Cannell
8. John Montgumry

---

[222] Nicholas Ward 'took to lease from Patrick Macartan one quarter of the townland of Loughinisland [in May 1641], where he with his family and goods were resident at the beginning of the rebellion' (Examination of Nicholas Ward, 9 June 1653 [TCD MS 837, fols 177r–178v]).

[223] Named as a burgess of Bangor in the town's charter, 18 March 1613 (*Hamilton MSS*, general appendix, p. lxxix).

County Monaghan

[f. 270]

The Outrisings of the County of Monaghan[1]

Barony de Darty

Sir Robert Loftus: his British tenants on his abbey lands: their names and arms

Swords only
1. Richard Cutler
2. Joseph Bryan

Pikes only
3. Richard Bradshaw
4. George Foster
5. Robert Johnston[2]
6. Robert Aldridg[3]

[No arms][4]
7. John Johnston
8. John Moore
9. Bryan Browney
10. James Dungeon[5]
11. Robert Richardson
12. Richard Beaty
13. Nicholas Wilson
14. Symond Graham

14 Men; 2 swords; 4 pikes

[f. 270v]

Mr Art oge Mc. Maghan: his men and arms out of his outrisings[6]

3 Horse, 3 Swords, and 3 Lances
1. Patrick Moore[7]
2. Hugh McEdmund oge McMaghan[8]
3. William Moore[9]

Swords and Pikes
4. Patrick Conally
5. Dinagh McCab
6. Thomas O Bryan
7. Patrick McBrian OConnall

Sword and Musket
8. Bryan O Mulcoyle

Sword only
9. Owen Ro OCarrin

9 Men; 3 horses; 9 swords; 3 Lances; 4 Pikes; 1 Musket

[f. 271]

Cullo McEver McMaghan out of his outrisings

Horses, Swords, Lances, and Headpieces
1. Patrick McMaghan[10]
2. Art McMaghan
3. Patrick McMaghan
4. Henry O Callan

Swords, Pikes, and Headpieces
5. Morricett McWard
6. Patrick McMaghan
7. Bryan McWard
8. Phillip McWard[11]
9. Cullo McMaghan[12]
10. Art McMaghan

Swords and Snaphances
11. Patrick McMaghan
12. William O Carrier

---

1 I am grateful to the Clogher Historical Society for permission to reproduce this transcript (John Johnston, 'An Irish county in 1630: the muster roll of county Monaghan', in *Clogher Record*, **20** (2010) [hereafter, Johnston, 'Monaghan'], pp 233–42) [JJ].

2 Killed Clones, 1641 (Deposition of Robert Aldrich, 10 February 1644 [TCD MS 834, fols 168r–169v]).

3 Robert Aldridge, the 'son and heir of Edward Aldrich', organised the defence of Clones in 1641. He was taken prisoner by the Irish when the town fell but managed to escape (Examination of Charles Camble, undated [TCD MS 816, fols 008r–009v] and deposition of Robert Aldrich, 10 February 1644 [TCD MS 834, fols 168r–169v]).

4 The first six men are shown in the original manuscript as carrying weapons: no weapons are shown against the remaining men and so they are assumed to have been unarmed.

5 Killed Clones, 1641 (Depositions of Mathew Browne, 24 March 1642 [TCD MS 834, fols 100r–101v] and Robert Aldrich, 10 February 1644 [ibid. fols 168r–169v]).

6 The will of 'Art oge McMahon of Ballynun, county Monaghan esquire' was written, 3 July and proved, 19 September 1635 (NAI, BET1/41, p. 142) [RJH].

7 According to his deposition, Moore 'was born in the Queen's County, and is of the banished sept of the Moores there and … hath lived these twenty years in the county of Monaghan.' He 'lived with Art oge McMahan' for about ten years. After the death of Art Óg and having failed to become a soldier in the Low Countries, 'he hath lived in Clownish and Cloncurrin', where he 'kept an ale house until of late May last [1641].' In October 1641, hearing that their brother, James, had returned from service in France, Patrick and his brother, William (number 3), went to Dublin to enlist as soldiers in Roger Moore's company (Examination of Patrick Moore, 30 October 1641 [TCD MS 809, fols 036r–037v]).

8 Possibly the 'Hugh mcEdmond oge mcMahone', who was one of those who captured Clones in October 1641 (Deposition of Mathew Browne, 24 March 1642 [TCD MS 834, fols 100r–101v]).

9 Brother of Patrick Moore (number 1), he 'lived the most part of his life at Clownish in the county of Monaghan' and accompanied his brother to Dublin in October 1641 'to gain some preferment under the captains which he heard were then going into Spain' (Examination of William Moore, 3 November 1641 [TCD MS 809, fols 079r–080v]).

10 One of the four men named Patrick McMahon is the son and heir of Art oge McMahon (NAI BET1/41, p. 142) [RJH].

11 'Phelom McWard … yeoman' was one of those who captured Glaslough, 23 October 1641 (Deposition of Alexander Creichton, 28 February 1642 [TCD MS 834, fols 108r–109v]).

12 'Collo oge mcMahon' captured Castleblaney, 1641 (Deposition of Joseph Bury, 5 March 1642 [ibid. fols 102r–102v]).

13 His son, Hugh, was one of those who seized the towns of Clones and Monaghan in October 1641 (Depositions of Mathew Browne, 24 March 1642 [ibid. fols 100r–101v] and Henry Lord Blany, 11 July 1642 [ibid. fols 171r–172v]).

[f. 271v]

Patrick Duff McCullo McMaghan[13] out of his outrisings

Horses, Sword, Lance, and Headpiece
1. Brian O Duff

Swords, Pikes, and Headpieces
2. James Cardell
3. Neal McKenedy

[f. 272]

Rosse Bane McMaghan his outrisings

Horse, Lance, Sword, and Headpiece
Reedman McMahon[14]

The above said Rosse bane mcMahon should have appeared with 3 horse and 6 footmen

[f. 272v]

Art Roe McMahon:[15] out of his outrisings, being heir to Patrick mcArt Moyle McMahone

[f. 273]

Neall McKenna,[16] son and heir to Patrick McKenna: out of his outrisings

Horses, Swords, and Lances
1. William Griffin
2. Thomas Griffin

Sword only
3. Laughline McKenna

Sword and Caliver
4. Edmond McKena

Sword and Pike
5. Towell O meallan

No Arms
6. Thomas Bellyes

2 Horses; 5 Swords; 1 Pike; 1 Caliver; 2 Lances

[f. 273v]

The British of the town of Monnaghan[17]

Pikes only
1. Thomas Bloxan
2. Richard Phillips
3. Thomas Barrones
4. William Vaughan

Swords only
5. Archibald Griffin
6. William Griffin

No Arms
7. Richard Ballard[18]
8. David Faulltes
9. George Sparkes[19]
10. Richard Ballard[20]

11. Evan Phillips
12. Andrew Edmonds
13. Thomas Sareitsa[21]
14. Robert Moorehead

4 Pikes; 2 Swords

[f. 274]

Mr Aikelyns British tenants on his churchlands[22]

[f. 274v]

Edward Auldridg[23] esquire: his men and arms residing in Dartry

Swords and Pikes
1. Franncis Johnston
2. Robert Johnston
3. Hugh Johnston
4. Andrew Johnston[24]
5. Andrew Johnston younger
6. William Graham
7. William Cadman
8. John Walker
9. Robert Deglis
10. John Martyn[25]
11. William Wilson
12. John Larfoord
13. Pearce Rupton
14. William Ginlyn
15. John Gynlin
16. Robert Beattison
17. Arch: Glendining
18. John Little
19. William Little
20. John Acheson
21. William Walreach

---

14 One of the 'captains of rebels', 1641 (Deposition of John Mountgomery, 26 January 1642 [TCD MS 834, fols 130r–135v; responsible for the deaths of Richard Squire and his eldest son (Deposition of Elizabeth Northope, 3 February 1642 [ibid. fols 136r–136v]).

15 Art Roe McMahon was one of those who captured Monaghan town, 23 October 1641 (Deposition of George Cottingham, 4 March 1642 [TCD MS 834, fols 106r–107v]). His son, Hugh, and his brother, Bryan, captured Clones (Deposition of Mathew Browne, 24 March 1642 [ibid. fols 100r–101v]).

16 Neil McKenna – 'a notorious captain of the rebels' (Deposition of John Mountgomery, 26 January 1642 [ibid. fols 130r–135v]) – was one of those who took Monaghan town, 23 October 1641 (Deposition of George Cottingham, 4 March 1642 [ibid. fols 106r–107v]).

17 There are some Welsh names amongst 'the British of the town of Monaghan' because Lord Blaney, the town's proprietor, came from the principality [RJH].

18 Richard Bollard was captured by the Irish, 1641 and subsequently escaped (Deposition of George Cottingham, 4 March 1642 [TCD MS 834, fols 106r–107v]).

19 Resident Cornecassa, 1641 (Deposition of Jane Watson, 24 November 1642 [ibid. fols 177r–177v]).

20 Killed Monaghan, 1641 (Deposition of Brigitt Lee, 24 November 1642 [ibid. fols 162r–162v]).

21 This is RJH's transliteration: Thomas Sargent was one of several 'rich farmers' who were killed near Magheraveely, county Fermanagh, 1641 (Deposition of Robert Aldrich, 10 February 1644 [ibid. fols 168r–169v]).

22 Ackland was killed, 1641 (Examination of Michaell Harrison, 4 January 1642 [TCD MS 836, fols 127r–128v]).

23 Edward Aldridge became 'a captain on his majesty's part [in 1641] and [was] slain at Julianstown near Drogheda' (Deposition of Robert Aldrich, 10 February 1644 [TCD MS 834, fols 168r–169v]).

24 Numbers 4 and 5 are father and son.

25 Resident Corrinary, county Cavan, 1641 (Deposition of his wife, Dorras Martin, 14 January 1642 [TCD MS 835, fol. 048v]); losses of livestock, goods, and money amounted to £44 0s 0d (Deposition of John Marten, 14 January 1642 [ibid. MS 834, fols 127r]).

Swords only

22. George Cotman
23. Edward Johnston
24. Anthony Walker
25. Anthony de Brume
26. Richard Woodgreese
27. John Browne[26]
28. George Dey[27]
29. Robert Slack
30. Michael Allan[28]

[f. 275]

Sword and Musket

31. George Irwing

Sword and Caliver

32. Hugh Williams[29]

No Arms

33. Richard Scot
34. Thomas Scot
35. Robert Doughty
36. Robert Edgar
37. John Johnston
38. Thomas Guin
39. James Johnston
40. Thomas Jones[30]
41. Thomas Kiniston
42. Frauncis Ward[31]
43. Bartholemew Ward
44. John Williams
45. George Cotman

32 Swords; 1 Musket; 1 Caliver;
21 Pikes

---

[26] Possibly father of Matthew Browne, 'gentleman' (Deposition of Mathew Browne [ibid. fols 100r–101v]), who was captured by the Irish, 1641 (Examination of Charles Camble, undated [TCD MS 816, fols 008r–009v]).

[27] Killed near Clones, 1641 (Deposition of John Marten, 14 January 1642 [TCD MS 834, fols 127r]).

[28] Resident Grangeboy; farmed Killenenagh; losses £645 0s 0d; killed, 1641 (Deposition of his widow, Katherin Allen, 12 February 1642 [ibid. fols 095r–096v]).

[29] Hugh Williams was killed Mountjoy, county Tyrone with his wife, October 1641 (Examination of John Morris, 27 May 1653 [TCD MS 838, fols 296r–296v]).

[30] Relation of William Jones, who was killed Monaghan, 1641 (Deposition of Brigitt Lee, 24 November 1642 [TCD MS 834, fols 162r–162v]).

[31] Possibly a brother of Luke Ward, who was hanged Monaghan, 1641 (Deposition of George Cottingham [TCD MS 834, fols 106r–107v]); Francis Ward was a blacksmith, resident near Drum; losses £168 0s 0d (Deposition of Dorothy Ward, 18 January 1642 [ibid. fols 146r–146v]). Another member of the family, Bartholomew, had leased Annareagh for 49 years from Thomas Fleming, father-in-law of Connor Maguire, Lord Enniskillen (Deposition of Mary Ward, 2 April 1642 [ibid. fols 176r–176v]).

Breviate

[f. 276]

A breviate of the whole book, wherein you shall find the leaf in the first column wherein every chief tenant's men are placed, the next showeth the quantity of ground they hold, [and thereafter] the numbers of their men and their arms.[1]

[f. 277]
The County of Cavan

		Acres	Men	Swords	Pikes	Muskets	Calivers	Snaphances	Halberds
[3][2]	Sir Steaphen Butler his undertaker's lands	2,000	164	31	7				
[7]	Sir Frauncis Hammilton out of his undertaker's lands	3,000	113	24	25	6	1	9	
[10]	Sir James Cragg out of his undertaker's lands	2,000	54	16	15	6			1
[11v]	Sir Archbald Atchison out of his undertaker's lands	1,000	20	14	8			5	
[12]	Sir Edward Bagshaw out of his undertaker's lands	1,500	32	5	3	1		4	
[13]	The Lady Waldrum out of her undertaker's lands	2,000	54	5	4			1	
[14]	Mr Taylor out of his undertaker's lands	1,500	85	15	11	1		10	1
[16]	Mr Moynes out of his undertaker's lands	2,000	28	4	1	1	3	1	
[16v]	Mr Amis and Mr Greenham out of their undertaker's lands	1,500	9	5	4	1		[1]	
[17]	Sir Henry Pearce out of his undertaker's lands	3,000	16	7	6		2		
[17v]	Mr John Hammelton out of his undertaker's lands	1,000	44	10	3	1	1	6	
[18v]	Mr William Bayly out of his undertaker's lands	1,000	34	5	3			2	
[19v]	Mrs Hammilton Widow out of her undertaker's lands	1,000	5	5	3			2	
[20]	Sir Edward Fish out of his undertaker's lands	2,000	48	7	2			5	
[21]	Servitors and Churchlands: the Earle of Fyngall	1,500	28	4					1
[21v]	The Bishop of Killmoore: his Churchlands	2,000	36	4	2		1		1
[22v]	The town of Cavan	1,000	18	3	1			1	
[23]	The Churchlands of Drumgowne	300	7	2	2				
	[Total]		795	166	100	17	8	46	3

---

[1] The numbers of men who mustered on each estate, apart from those in county Monaghan, have been published in Robinson, *Plantation of Ulster*, pp 212–24.

[2] The folio numbering is that conventionally used and not the original numbering.

[f. 277v]
The County of Armagh

		Acres	Men	Swords	Pikes	Muskets	Calivers	Snaphances	Halberds
[24]	Anthony Coope Esquire out of his undertaker's lands	3,000	155	18	7	5	2	4	
[27]	Mr John Dillon out of his undertaker's lands	1,500	34	6	2	2	2		
[27v]	Mr Waldrum out of his undertaker's lands	2,000	45	9		2		5	
[28v]	Mr Stanway out of his undertaker's lands	1,500	16	2	1			9	
[29]	Mr Satcheuerall out of his undertaker's lands	2,000	104	3	8		1	9	
[31]	Mr Richard Cope and Mr Obbins their undertakers' lands	2,000	24	8	2		3	4	
[31v]	Sir William Brumlagh out of his undertaker's lands	2,500	42	27	16	1	8	4	
[32v]	The Lord Mountnorrice his undertaker's lands	1,000	33	11	3		3	4	
[33v]	Sir Archbald Aitchison out of his undertaker's lands	3,000	56	4	28		7	2	
[35]	Mr John Hammelton out of his undertaker's lands	2,500	113	53	42	2	7	9	
[37v]	The Lord Grandison out of his undertaker's lands	1,000	31	9	1		3	3	
	Servitors and Churchlands								
[38v]	The Lord Grandison	1,500	21	5		1		2	
[39]	Sir Henry Boocer	2,000	10	4					
[39v]	Sir Charles Poynes	500	27	9	2		1		
	Churchlands								
[40v]	The Lord Primate	5,000	127	70	11	3	4	15	
[43v]	The Lord Calfeild	3,000	56	56	23	12	9		
[45]	Mr Richardson Minister	300	8						
	[Total]		902	295	146	28	50	70	

[f. 278]
The County of Fermanagh

		Acres	Men	Swords	Pikes	Muskets	Calivers	Snaphances	Halberds
[46]	The Lord Ballfoure out of his undertaker's lands	5,000	95	37	11			3	
[48]	Sir William Coale out of his undertaker's lands	1,000	58	49	14	3	7		
[50]	Mr Archdall out of his undertaker's lands	2,000	41	20	1	3	7	2	

[51]	Mrs Hammilton, widow of the late archbishop of Cashell, out of her undertaker's lands	1,500	24	22	14		1		
[51]	Sir John Humes out of his undertaker's lands	3,000	88	52	37		1	5	2
[53]	Mr George Hume out of his undertaker's lands	1,000	28	21	7	1		7	
[54]	Sir Gerrard Lowther out of his undertaker's lands	2,000	47	40	17	9	13		
[55]	Mr Hannings out of his undertaker's lands	1,000	24	12	8	1	2	2	
[56]	Mr Flowerdew out of his undertaker's lands	2,000	30	10	7	1	3	2	
[57]	Mr Franncis Blennerhasset out of his undertaker's lands	1,500	24	4				1	
[57]	Mr Leonard Blennerhasset out of his undertaker's lands	2,000	21	8	6			2	
[58]	Sir Hugh Woorrell out of his undertaker's lands	1,000	19	6	1			2	
[58v]	The Bishop of Kilfenora out of his undertaker's lands	1,000	22	13	10			3	
[59]	Mr Waterhouse out of his undertaker's lands	1,000	12	3	3				
[59v]	Mr Hatton out of his undertaker's lands	1,000	24	15	19		2	3	
[60]	Mr Sudburroh out of his undertaker's lands	1,000	16	6	11		1	3	
[61]	Sir John Dunbar out of his undertaker's lands	1,000	10	10	5	4		1	
[61]	Mr Adwick out of his undertaker's lands	1,000	6	1	2			3	
[62]	Sir Steaphen Butler out of his undertaker's lands	3,000	92	22	9			12	1
[64]	The town of Enniskillen		32	32	10		5	1	2
	The servitors, natives, and churchlands planted with British								
[65]	The Lord Dillon out of his servitor's lands	1,500	27	16	5				
[66]	Sir William Coale out of his servitor's Lands	1,000	13	13	5			1	
[67]	Captain Roger Atkinson out of his servitor's lands	1,000	25	8					
[67]	Sir Ralph Gower out of his servitor's lands	1,000	31						
	Churchlands								
[67]	The Lord Hastings out of his Churchlands	1,500	41	15	4		2		
[68]	Mr Archdall his Churchlands	1,000	14	5	4				

[69]	Mr Leonard Blennerhasset out of his Churchlands	500	7						
[69]	The Lady Browerton out of her Churchlands	2,000	15	11	6				
[71]	Lieuftenant Graham out of his Churchlands	200	8	8	3	2	2	1	
[71]	Mr Fullerton out of his Churchlands	120	2	2				2	
[71]	Mr Willobye out of his Churchlands	500	6	4	3				
[71]	Mr Hugh Montgumery out of his Churchlands	500	11	7	2				
	[Total]		913	476	224	24	46	56	5

[ff 279r–279v]

The County of Tyrone

		Acres	Men	Swords	Pikes	Muskets	Calivers	Snaphances	Halberds
[72]	Sir James Erskin out of his undertaker's lands	3,000	138	58	27	3	7	4	
[75]	Sir William Steward out of his undertaker's lands	4,000	130	64	32	7	11	8	
[77v]	Sir Henry Tychbourne out of his undertaker's lands	2,200	54	28	13		4	4	
[78v]	Sir William Parsons out of his undertaker's lands	1,500	59	31	18	1		2	2
[79v]	Mr Richard Coape out of his undertaker's lands	1,500	28	16	15		1	1	
[80]	Mr John Leigh out of his undertaker's lands	2,000	17	8	4	3		1	
[80v]	Mr Archbald Hammilton out of his undertaker's lands	1,000	25	21	5	2	3		
[81]	Sir Andrew Steward out of his undertaker's lands	4,500	93	86	45			20	
[83]	Mr Henry Steward out of his undertaker's lands	1,500	46	27	7	3	3	7	
[84]	Captain Sanderson out of his undertaker's lands	1,000	34	18	9		1	4	
[85]	Mr Symmonton out of his undertaker's lands	1,000	28	8	3			4	
[85v]	Mr Richardson out of his undertaker's lands	1,000	26	10	4			4	
[86]	Mr Lyndsey out of his undertaker's lands	1,000	65	22	7		1	7	
[87]	The Lord Hastings out of his undertaker's lands	2,000	25	18	3	2	1	8	

		Acres	Men	Swords	Pikes	Muskets	Calivers	Snaphances	Halberds
[87v]	Sir Pearce Crosby out of his undertaker's lands	3,000	47	28	5			4	
[88v]	Captain Mervin, out of his undertaker's lands	6,000	57	38	16	8	2	9	
[90]	Mr Dromond out of his undertaker's lands	1,000	15	15	11		1	2	
[90v]	Sir George Hamilton out of his undertaker's lands	2,500	54	50	8		3	7	
[91v]	The Countess of Abercorne out of her undertaker's lands	2,000	40	36	7		3	7	
[92v]	The Master of Abercorn	2,500	51	39	10	1	1	14	
[93v]	Sir William Hammilton out of his undertaker's lands	2,750	43	42	22		1	18	
[94v]	The town of Strabane		208	121	43	5	8	47	2
	Servitors and Churchlands								
[98v]	The Lord Primate's Churchlands	4,000	58	18	5			8	
[100]	The Bishop of Clogher out of his Churchlands	3,000	64	22	10	4		4	2
[101v]	Mr William Hammilton out of his Churchlands	1,000	14						
[102]	The Lord Viscount Chichester out of his town of Dungannon and the rest of his servitor's lands	2,000	31	10		1		1	
[103]	The Lord Viscount Powerscourt out of his servitor's lands	1,220	46	33	1	1	4	10	
[104]	The Lord Calfeild out of his servitor's lands	1,240	12	12	1		2	2	
[104v]	Sir Bawerley Newcom out of his servitor's lands	2,000	30	15	10	1	4	5	
	[Total]		1,538	896	341	42	53	197	7

[f. 280]
Londonderry

		Acres	Men	Swords	Pikes	Muskets	Calivers	Snaphances	Halberds
	The names of the chief tenants who hold the plantation lands in the county of Londonderry belonging to the Companies of the City of London								
[105]	The City and Liberties of Londonderry	2,000	599	333	55	77		6	4
[117]	Sir Robert Macklelan	6,000	192	118	54	1	14	20	1
[121]	Mr Harrington	3,000	57	44	11	1	10	18	1
[122]	Mr Freeman the elder: his men appeared with the City and Liberties of Londonderry								

[123]	Mr Freeman the younger	3,000	42	19	6		2	12	
[124v]	The Lady Cooke	3,000							
[124v]	Mr Wall, Mr Hartopsson in tow	3,000	48	29	9	15	1		1
[125v]	Mr Caning	3,000	122	85	61	26	1		3
[128]	Mr Church	3,000	87	52	21	2	30	3	
[130]	Mr Conway	3,000	102	52	12	1	6	6	
[132]	Mr Barker	3,000	45	16	1		2	1	
	Mr Whistler	3,000							
[133v]	The town and Liberties of Coleraine	1,500	357	251	69	48	38	53	8
	The Servitors, Natives, and Churchlands in the County of Derry where the British inhabit								
[140]	Sir Thomas Phillips's Servitor's Lands	3,000	121	89	16	3	44	25	
[142v]	Mr Graidy, his Natives Lands	1,000	10	3				3	
[143]	The Lady Maccleland's Churchlands	2,000	48	35	12	4			
[144]	Mr Barrasfoord's natives lands	1,000	36	6	4			1	
[145]	The Lord Primate's Churchlands	1,000	11	4					
[145v]	Mr Dawson's Churchlands	500	13	3	1		1	2	
[146]	Magharrah and Desert Martin out of Servitors and Churchlands	700	40	25	3			2	
	[Total]		1,930	1,164	335	178	149	152	18

[f. 279v]

The County of Antrim[3]

	The numbers of men mustered in the above said county, but the particular quantity of lands there are not divided into thousands of acres as in the six escheated Counties	Men	Swords	Pikes	Muskets	Calivers	Snaphances	Halberds
[145]	The Earl of Antrim out of his lands, being half that county	947	418	6	1	3	1	1
[165]	Out of Mr Adare's lands, Lord of Kinhilt there appeared	135	76	36	2	1	15	
[168]	Out of Mr Edmonston's Lands there appeared	151	79	56			1	
[168]	Out of Mr Peter Hill his Lands there appeared	11						
[171]	Out of Mr Redding's lands there appeared	15						

[3] Published in Gillespie, Colonial Ulster, p. 231.

[171v]	Out of Mr Dallway's lands there appeared	38						
[172v]	Out of Sir John Clotwoorthy his lands there appeared	229						
[177]	Out of Mr Upton's lands there appeared	92	2	4				
	[Total]	1,618	575	102	3	4	17	1

[f. 280]

The County of Donegal

		Acres	Men	Swords	Pikes	Muskets	Calivers	Snaphances	Halberds
[179]	The Duke of Lennox out of his undertaker's lands	4,000	166	100	14			25	
[182]	Sir John Conningham out of his undertaker's lands	2,000	124	70	38	3	2	8	
[184v]	The Lady Conningham out of her undertaker's lands	2,000	66	33	10		1	8	1
[186]	Sir John Kingmell out of his undertaker's lands	2,270	45	40	8			1	
[187]	Captain Mansfeild out of his undertaker's lands	1,000	16	10	2		1		
[187v]	Sir John Willson out of his undertaker's lands	2,550	66	52	9	1	2	5	
[189]	Mr Benson out of his undertaker's lands	1,500	39	21	4	1		2	3
[190]	Mr Steward Lord of Dunduff out of his undertaker's lands	1,000	61	44	14	1		8	
[191]	Mr Cahoune Lord of Luce out of his undertaker's lands	1,000	9	6	4			8	1
[191v]	Captain Davis out of his undertaker's lands	2,000	25	13	5		1	3	
[192]	Mr Harrington out of his undertaker's lands	4,000	57	55	16	7	1	18	
[193]	Mr Alexander Steward out of his undertaker's lands	1,000	32	17	9	1		5	
[193v]	Mr John Conningham, out of his undertaker's lands	1,000	59	28	10			14	2
[194v]	Mr John Steward out of his undertaker's lands	1,000	13	8	1				
[195]	The Earle of Annandall out of his undertaker's lands	10,000	143	4				1	
[197v]	Mr William Farrell out of his undertaker's lands	1,500							
	Servitors and Churchlands							
[198]	The Bishop of Rapho his churchlands	2,700	150	95	12	1	1	14	

[200v]	The Deane of Rapho his churchlands	300	7	5				1	
[200v]	Churchlands of Tayboyne		6						
[201]	The Lo: Chichester his servitors lands in the barony of Eneshone		174	128	4	5		8	3
	[Total]		1,258	746	162	20	8	119	8
	All the rest of the servitors in the County of Donegal, who inhabit the barony of Kilmacrenan and the barony of Tirhugh, caused not their British to appear at the general muster at the time and places appointed according to the warning given them.								

[f. 281v]

The County of Down[4]

	The number of men and their arms mustered in the county of Down, but there is no division into thousands of acres of the lands of that county.	**Men**	**Swords**	**Pikes**	**Muskets**	**Calivers**	**Snaphances**	**Halberds**
[204]	The Earle of Kildare out of his Lands there appeared	125	78					
[206v]	The Lord Crumwell out of his Lands there appeared	480	229	106	25	2	2	10
[215]	The Lord Viscount of Ardes his men and arms	1,317	757	399	113	1	2	14
[238]	The Lord Viscount of Clannyboyes his men and arms	1,778	1,588	1,107	247	60	172	
[264]	The Lord General belonging to his ironworks there appeared	28						
[264v]	The Bishop of Down out of his lands and out of the Savages lands being natives there appeared	93	47	9	1		1	2
[266]	The Bishop of Drummoore out of his lands there appeared	156	133	8				
[268v]	Mr Robert Melvin out of his lands there appeared	52	16	4				
[269v]	Mr Ward out of his lands there appeared	8						
[269v]	Lieuftenant Burris out of his lands there appeared	8						
	6 great horse and men completely armed out of the Lord Clannaboyes his outrisings	4,045	2,848	1,633	386	63	177	27

[4] Published in Gillespie, *Colonial Ulster*, p. 231.

[f. 282]
The County of Monaghan[5]

	Natives, Servitors, and Churchlands	Men	Swords	Pikes	Muskets	Snaphances	Calivers	Lances
[270]	Sir Robert Loftus out of his Abbey Lands in Clones	14	2	4				
[270v]	Mr Art Oge McMaughen out of his outrisings	6 foot 3 horses	9	4	1			3
[271]	Cullo McEver McMaughen out of his outrisings	8 foot 4 horse	8	6		2		4
[271v]	Patrick Duff McCullo McMaughen out of his outrisings	2 foot 1 horse	2	2				1
[272]	Ross Bann McMaughan out of his outrisings	1 horse						1
[272v]	Art Roe McMaughan out of his outrisings							
[273]	Neal McKenny out of his outrisings	4 foot 2 horse	5	1			1	2
[273v]	The British of the town of Monaghan	14	2	4				
[274]	Mr Acklish British tenants out of his Churchlands							
[274v]	Mr Auldridg his British tenants out of his natives' lands	45	32	21	1		1	
	11 horse	93	60	42	2	2	2	11

[f. 283]
The total of every particular county within the province of Ulster

In the County of	Men	Swords	Pikes	Muskets	Calivers	Snaphances	Halberds	Lances
Cavan	795	166	100	17	8	46	3	
Armagh	902	295	146	28	50	70		
Fermanagh	913	476	224	24	46	56	5	
Tyrone	1,538	896	341	42	53	197	7	
Londonderry	1,930	1164	335	178	149	152	18	
Antrim	1,618	575	102	3	4	17	1	
Donegal	1,258	746	162	20	9	119	8	
Down	4,045	2848	1633	386	63	177	27	
Monaghan	93	60	42	2	2	2		11
The Total	13,092	7,226	3,085	700	384	836	69	11

---

5   The summary for county Monaghan has been published in Shirley, *Some account of Farney*, pp 124–5 and Johnston, 'Monaghan'.

BIBLIOGRAPHY

Manuscripts
British Library, London
Additional Manuscript (BL, Add. MS)
    4770: Muster roll of the province of Ulster, *c.* 1630

Public Record Office of Northern Ireland, Belfast (PRONI)
Earl of Erne Estate Papers
    D/1939/21/6/1: The rental book of … Lord Balfour, 1632 (cited as Balfour Rental, 1632)
    D/1939/20/6/2: A true rental of … Sir William [Balfour's] lands in the county of Fermanagh, 10 May 1636
    (cited as Balfour Rental, 1636)

R.J. Hunter Papers
    D4446

Blaris Parish Registers (Lisburn, county Antrim)
    D1823/5
    CR1/35/A
    MIC1/3/1

Trinity College, Dublin (TCD)
Depositions, 1641–53
    MSS 809–39

Sheffield City Council: Libraries, Archives, and Information
Wentworth Woodhouse Papers[1]

    WWM/StrP: Strafford Papers

Printed Materials
Boynton, Lindsay, *The Elizabethan militia, 1558–1633* (London, 1967)
Burke, Bernard, *Vicissitudes of families*, third series (London, 1863)
Canny, Nicholas, *Making Ireland British, 1580–1650* (Oxford, 2001)
Calendar of Carew MSS, 1603–24
Calendar of state papers, Ireland, 1615–25 and *1625–32*
Cotton, Henry, *Fasti ecclesiae Hiberniae*, 1 (2nd edition, Dublin, 1851)
Gillespie, Raymond, 'The origins and development of an Ulster urban network, 1600–41', in *Irish Historical Studies*, 24 (1984), pp 15–29
— , *Colonial Ulster: the settlement of east Ulster, 1600–41* (Cork, 1986)
Historical Manuscripts Commission, *Report on the Hastings manuscripts*, 4 (London, 1947)
Hill, George, *An historical account of the plantation in Ulster at the commencement of the seventeenth century, 1608–20* (Belfast, 1877)
Hunter, R.J., 'The settler population of an Ulster plantation county', in *Donegal Annual*, 10 (1972), pp 124–54
— , 'The Fishmongers' Company of London and the Londonderry plantation, 1609-41', in Gerard O'Brien (ed.), *Derry and Londonderry: history and society* (Dublin, 1999), pp 205–58
— , 'The Bible and the bawn: an Ulster planter inventorised', in Ciaran Brady and Jane Ohlmeyer (eds.), *British interventions in early modern Ireland* (Cambridge, 2005), pp 116–43
— and Perceval-Maxwell, Michael, 'The muster roll of *c.* 1630: county Cavan', in *Breifne*, 5 (1978), pp 206–21
Inquisitionum in cancellariae rotolorum Hiberniae asservatarum reportorium, 2: Ultonia (Dublin, 1827) (cited as Inquisitions of Ulster)

Irish Manuscripts Commission, *The Irish patent rolls of James I: a facsimile of the calendar prepared before 1630*, (Dublin, 1966)

Johnston, John, 'The plantation of county Fermanagh, 1610–41: an archaeological and historical survey' (unpublished M.A. thesis, Queen's University Belfast, 1976)

— , 'Settlement on an Ulster estate: the Balfour rentals of 1632 and 1636', in *Clogher Record*, 12 (1985), pp 92–102

— , 'An Irish county in 1630: the muster roll of county Monaghan', in *Clogher Record*, 20 (2010), pp 233–42

Leslie, J.B., *Clogher clergy and parishes* (Enniskillen, 1929)

Loeber, Rolf, *A biographical dictionary of architects in Ireland, 1600–1720* (London, 1981)

Macafee, W.A., 'The movement of British settlers into Ulster during the seventeenth century', in *Familia: Ulster Genealogical Review*, 2 (1992), pp 94–111

Moody, T.W. (ed.), 'The revised articles of the Ulster plantation, 1610', in *Bulletin of the Institute for Historical Research*, 12 (1935), pp 178–83

— , 'Ulster plantation papers, no. 18', in *Analecta Hibernica*, 8

— , *The Londonderry plantation: the City of London and the plantation in Ulster, 1607–41* (Belfast, 1939)

Morrin, James (ed.), *A calendar of the patent and close rolls of chancery in Ireland for the reign of Charles I, years 1 to 8 inclusive* (Dublin, 1863)

Paterson, T.G.F., 'An unpublished early seventeenth-century census of the men and arms on the estates of English and Scotch settlers in county Armagh', in *Seanchas Ard Mhacha*, 5 (1970), pp 401–17

Perceval-Maxwell, Michael, *The Scottish migration to Ulster in the reign of James I* (London, 1973)

Robinson, Philip, *The plantation of Ulster: British settlement in an Irish landscape, 1600–70* (Dublin, 1984)

Shirley, Evelyn Philip, *Some account of the territory or dominion of Farney in the province and earldom of Ulster* (London, 1845)

Treadwell, Victor (ed.), *The Irish commission of 1622: an investigation of the Irish administration, 1615–22 and its consequences, 1623–4*, Irish Manuscripts Commission (Dublin, 2006)

Trimble, William Copeland, *The history of Enniskillen, with references to some manors in county Fermanagh and other local subjects*, 1 (Enniskillen, 1919)

[1] The Wentworth Woodhouse Papers have been accepted in lieu of inheritance tax by H.M. Government and allocated to Sheffield City Council.

INDEX

Surname	Forename	Estate	Co.	Page	Surname	Forename	Estate	Co.	Page
Allen	Henry	Bagshaw	Cv	7	Anderson	James	Crag	Cv	7
Allen	James	Antrim	An	117	Anderson	James	Ards	Dn	148
Allen	James	Brownlow	Ar	26	Anderson	James	Ards	Dn	148
Allen younger	James	Bp Rapho	Dl	138	Anderson	James	Ards	Dn	151
Allen	John	Hammelton	Ar	30	Anderson	James	Clannaboyes	Dn	163
Allen	John	Lord Primate	Ar	33	Anderson	James	Sir J. Hume	Fe	42
Allen	John	Fish	Cv	14	Anderson	James	Grocers	Ly	91
Allen	John	Lynox	Dl	128	Anderson	James	Erskin	Ty	57
Allen	John	Clannaboyes	Dn	165	Anderson	John	Crumwell	Dn	144
Allen	John	Sir J. Hume	Fe	42	Anderson	John	Ards	Dn	149
Allen	John	Londonderry	Ly	83	Anderson	John	Ards	Dn	150
Allen	John	Londonderry	Ly	87	Anderson	John	Clannaboyes	Dn	157
Allen	John	Londonderry	Ly	88	Anderson	John	Clannaboyes	Dn	158
Allen	John	Clothworkers	Ly	90	Anderson	John	Clannaboyes	Dn	158
Allen younger	John	Lord Primate	Ar	33	Anderson	John	Clannaboyes	Dn	160
Allen	Jonathan	Butler	Fe	50	Anderson	John	Clannaboyes	Dn	162
Allen	Patrick	Ards	Dn	149	Anderson	John	Londonderry	Ly	83
Allen	Patrick	Londonderry	Ly	83	Anderson	John	Haberdashers	Ly	89
Allen	Robert	Antrim	An	115	Anderson	John	Grocers	Ly	91
Allen	Robert	Adare	An	119	Anderson	John	Ironmongers	Ly	94
Allen	Robert	Taylor	Cv	10	Anderson	John	Coleraine	Ly	102
Allen	Robert	Ards	Dn	151	Anderson	John	Crosby	Ty	69
Allen	Robert	Ards	Dn	151	Anderson	John	Crosby	Ty	69
Allen	Robert	Clannaboyes	Dn	169	Anderson	John	Mervin	Ty	70
Allen	Robert	Butler	Fe	49	Anderson	John	M. of Abbercorne	Ty	72
Allen younger	Robert	Ards	Dn	152	Anderson	Patrick	Crumwell	Dn	145
Allen	Rowland	Mercers	Ly	96	Anderson	Patrick	Crumwell	Dn	145
Allen	Thomas	Butler	Fe	50	Anderson	Patrick	Clannaboyes	Dn	163
Allen	Thomas	Coleraine	Ly	103	Anderson	Robert	Antrim	An	110
Allen	William	Antrim	An	113	Anderson	Robert	Antrim	An	112
Allen	William	Ards	Dn	149	Anderson	Robert	Sir F. Hammelton	Cv	5
Allen	William	Clannaboyes	Dn	161	Anderson	Robert	Haberdashers	Ly	89
Allen	William	Londonderry	Ly	83	Anderson	Roger	Vintners	Ly	97
Allen	William	Londonderry	Ly	87	Anderson	Symond	Crag	Cv	7
Allen	William	Maghera & Desert Martin	Ly	107	Anderson	Thomas	Waldrum	Ar	22
Allert	Gilbert	Lord Primate	Ar	34	Anderson	Thomas	Clannaboyes	Dn	162
Alleson	John	Ards	Dn	149	Anderson	Thomas	Archdall	Fe	41
Alleson	Patrick	Ards	Dn	155	Anderson	William	Clannaboyes	Dn	159
Allet	James	Ards	Dn	154	Anderson	William	Londonderry	Ly	83
Allicock	Henry	Chichester	Dl	139	Anderson	William	Londonderry	Ly	88
Alliett	Cawen	Clannaboyes	Dn	161	Anderson	William	Lady McCleland	Ly	105
Allison	John	Cahoune	Dl	134	Anderson	William	Parsons	Ty	61
Allison	John	Londonderry	Ly	87	Anderson	William	Parsons	Ty	62
Allison	William	Clannaboyes	Dn	163	Anderson	William	Newton	Ty	80
Allson	John	Coleraine	Ly	102	Anderson	Wm	Kildare	Dn	142
Allwell	Alexander	Coleraine	Ly	101	Andrew	James	Strabane T.	Ty	74
Allwell	George	Coleraine	Ly	101	Andrew	John	Antrim	An	110
Ally	Art	Chichester	Ty	78	Andrew	Robert	Antrim	An	118
Ally	Thomas	Cope	Ar	25	Andrew	Robert	Clannaboyes	Dn	166
Allyson	George	Lynox	Dl	129	Andrew	Robert	Clannaboyes	Dn	169
Allyson	James	Londonderry	Ly	87	Andrew	Thomas	Clannaboyes	Dn	165
Allyson	John	W. Steward	Dl	133	Andrew	Thomas	Coleraine	Ly	102
Allyson	John	Londonderry	Ly	87	Andrewes	Robert	Coleraine	Ly	101
Allyson	Robert	Grocers	Ly	92	Andrewes	Roger	Sir A. Steward	Ty	64
Alman	Thomas	Lord Primate	Ar	34	Andrewes	Thomas	Coleraine	Ly	104
Alpher	Thomas	Londonderry	Ly	87	Andrews younger	Thomas	Coleraine	Ly	103
Alson	John	Ards	Dn	147	Anes	William	Cavan T.	Cv	16
Alson	John	Londonderry	Ly	88	Angleson	Robert	Benson	Dl	133
Amcres	William	Hannings	Fe	44	Angret	Ralph	Crumwell	Dn	144
Amerson	John	Enniskillen T.	Fe	51	Annanhill	Robert	Melvin	Dn	172
Amerson	Michaell	Woorell	Fe	45	Anson	Christopher	Butler	Cv	2
Amerson	William	Woorell	Fe	46	Anson	William	Lord Primate	Ar	33
Amis	Silvester	Lord Primate	Ar	33	Anston	William	Butler	Cv	3
Amon	Cuthbert	Crumwell	Dn	143	Anthony	John	Melvin	Dn	172
Anderson	Adam	Sir F. Hammelton	Cv	5	Anthony	John	Mervin	Ty	70
Anderson	Alexander	J. Hammelton	Cv	12	Antryn	William	Butler	Fe	50
Anderson	Alexander	J. Hammelton	Cv	12	Aphy	Anthony	Butler	Cv	2
Anderson	Alexander	Sir J. Hume	Fe	42	Aphy	Anthony	Butler	Cv	4
Anderson elder	Alexander	Sir J. Hume	Fe	42	Apievin	John	Davis	Dl	134
Anderson	Andrew	Clannaboyes	Dn	157	Appleby	George	Coleraine	Ly	103
Anderson	Christopher	Sir J. Hume	Fe	42	Appleton	William	Londonderry	Ly	85
Anderson	David	Sir J. Hume	Fe	42	Applin	William	Clannaboyes	Dn	158
Anderson	George	Sir F. Hammelton	Cv	5	Arbarhale	John	C. of Abbercorne	Ty	71
Anderson	George	Lady McCleland	Ly	105	Arbaucle	James	Clannaboyes	Dn	159
Anderson	James	Poyntes	Ar	33	Arbiston	William	Crumwell	Dn	145
Anderson	James	Sir F. Hammelton	Cv	5	Arbuch	James	Abp Armagh	Ty	76

Surname	Forename	Estate	Co.	Page
Atkinson	Alexander	Londonderry	Ly	87
Atkinson	George	Sir J. Hume	Fe	42
Atkinson	James	Brownlow	Ar	26
Atkinson	James	Crumwell	Dn	145
Atkinson	Robert	Grandison	Ar	32
Atkinson	Thomas	Sir J. Hume	Fe	42
Atkinson	Thomas	Atkinson	Fe	52
Atkinson	William	Grandison	Ar	32
Atterew	James	Bp Rapho	Dl	138
Atterew	James	Bp Rapho	Dl	138
Atwill	Thomas	Gower	Fe	53
Avary	Edward	Powerscourt	Ty	79
Avery	Henry	H. Steward	Ty	65
Avery	Henry	H. Steward	Ty	66
Avery elder	Richard	Mercers	Ly	96
Avery younger	Richard	Mercers	Ly	96
Avery	Thomas	H. Steward	Ty	65
Awerd	John	Harrington	Dl	134
Awnes	Robert	Cavan T.	Cv	16
Awnes	Thomas	Cavan T.	Cv	16
Ayer	John	Taylor	Cv	9
Aykin	William	Clannaboyes	Dn	157
Ayre	William	Sir J. Hume	Fe	42
Babbington	Edward	Benson	Dl	133
Babbington	Richard	Benson	Dl	133
Baber	Edward	Londonderry	Ly	87
Bably	John	Sanderson	Ty	66
Bacehanon	Duncan	Sir W. Steward	Ty	60
Bachanan	Robert	Bp Rapho	Dl	138
Bacraby	Francis	Merchant Taylors	Ly	92
Baddaly	Richard	Lord Primate	Ar	35
Badlock	James	Calfield	Ar	35
Baety	David	Lowther	Fe	43
Baety	Hugh	Lowther	Fe	43
Baety	James	Newton	Ty	80
Baety	John	Lowther	Fe	44
Baety	John	Hatton	Fe	47
Baety	Walter	Lowther	Fe	43
Baety	William	Newton	Ty	80
Bagan	Thomas	Kildare	Dn	142
Bagster	James	Ards	Dn	151
Bagster	John	Annandall	Dl	137
Bair	Richard	Clannaboyes	Dn	161
Baird	Hugh	Clannaboyes	Dn	159
Baird	Richard	Clannaboyes	Dn	169
Baird	Robert	Haberdashers	Ly	89
Baird	Robert	Sanderson	Ty	66
Baiteye	Gawin	Dillon	Fe	52
Baity	Richard	Lowther	Fe	43
Bakane	Godfrey	Coleraine	Ly	99
Baker	Cyprian	Erskin	Ty	57
Baker	Edward	Londonderry	Ly	88
Baker	John	Upton	An	125
Baker	John	Crag	Cv	7
Baker	John	Fish	Cv	14
Baker	John	Fish	Cv	14
Baker	John	Londonderry	Ly	83
Baker	Richard	Crag	Cv	6
Baker	Thomas	Londonderry	Ly	88
Baker	William	Butler	Cv	2
Balfoare	James	C. of Abbercorne	Ty	72
Balfoore	James	Ballfowre	Fe	39
Balfoure	Alexander	Ballfowre	Fe	39
Balfoure	John	Antrim	An	110
Balie	John	Balye	Cv	13
Baliff	Alexander	Antrim	An	112
Baliff	Alexander	Antrim	An	114
Baliff	Humfrey	Londonderry	Ly	85
Baliff	Thomas	Antrim	An	113
Ball	Godfrey	Coleraine	Ly	103
Ball	Richard	Boocer	Ar	32
Ball	Thomas	Boocer	Ar	32
Ball	William	Gaidy	Ly	105
Ballantyne	John	Adare	An	120
Ballard	Richard	Monnaghan T.	Mo	175
Ballard	Richard	Monnaghan T.	Mo	175
Ballas younger	John	Londonderry	Ly	84
Ballentyne	John	Clannaboyes	Dn	159
Ballfoure	James	Tychborne	Ty	60
Ballfoure	John	Antrim	An	114
Ballintyne	Archbald	Lynox	Dl	129
Balls	William	Archdal	Fe	53
Ballyntyn	John	Crosby	Ty	69
Ballyntyn	William	Crosby	Ty	69
Balmanner	Alexander	Sir J. Conningham	Dl	129
Balmanner	Andrew	Sir J. Conningham	Dl	129
Balmanner	Andrew	Sir J. Conningham	Dl	130
Balmer	Robert	Grandison	Ar	31
Baly	Alexander	Ards	Dn	155
Baly	David	Clannaboyes	Dn	168
Baly	Edward	Leigh	Ty	63
Baly	James	Antrim	An	118
Baly	John	Clannaboyes	Dn	165
Baly	John	Abp Armagh	Ty	76
Baly	Thomas	Balye	Cv	13
Baly	Thomas	Crumwell	Dn	146
Baly	William	Bp Clougher	Ty	77
Baly	William	Powerscourt	Ty	79
Bampton	Edward	Hannings	Fe	44
Ban	Henry	Sir F. Hammelton	Cv	5
Ban	James	Sir F. Hammelton	Cv	5
Banantyne	James	Clannaboyes	Dn	164
Banantyne	John	Clannaboyes	Dn	162
Bane	John	Ards	Dn	149
Bangs	Michaell	Clannaboyes	Dn	168
Baninton	John	Clannaboyes	Dn	161
Bankehead	James	Antrim	An	113
Bannantyne	Andrew	Ards	Dn	150
Bannantyne	James	Clannaboyes	Dn	168
Bar	Cuthbert	Ironmongers	Ly	93
Bar	John	Londonderry	Ly	83
Bar younger	Robert	Antrim	An	111
Bar	William	Londonderry	Ly	88
Barber	Gabby	Clatworthy	An	122
Barber	James	Clatworthy	An	122
Barber	John	Clatworthy	An	122
Barber	Robert	Clatworthy	An	122
Barber	Thomas	Calfield	Ar	35
Barber	William	Newton	Ty	80
Barbie	John	Cope	Ar	20
Barbor	David	Clatworthy	An	123
Barbor	David	Balye	Cv	13
Barbor	David	Strabane T.	Ty	74
Barbor	Edward	Clatworthy	An	123
Barbor	Gabby	Clatworthy	An	123
Barbor	John	Clatworthy	An	123
Barbor	John	Lady Conningham	Dl	130
Barbor	William	Clatworthy	An	123
Barclay	John	Clannaboyes	Dn	167
Bard	George	Antrim	An	110
Bard	John	Antrim	An	112
Bard	John	Haberdashers	Ly	90
Bard	John	Dromond	Ty	70
Bard	Ninian	Antrim	An	112
Bard	Thomas	Edmonston	An	121
Barde	John	Haberdashers	Ly	89
Barefoote	Thomas	Flowerdew	Fe	44
Barefoote	William	Flowerdew	Fe	44
Barhill	James	Sir G. Hammilton	Ty	71
Barkedyes	Robert	H. Steward	Ty	65
Barkeley	John	Ards	Dn	155
Barkeley	John	Clannaboyes	Dn	166
Barkeley	John	Clannaboyes	Dn	167
Barkeley	Robert	Clannaboyes	Dn	159
Barkeley	Rynyan	Ards	Dn	152
Barkely	William	Ards	Dn	154
Barker	George	Londonderry	Ly	83
Barker	Peter	Drapers	Ly	98
Barkley	John	Ards	Dn	152
Barkley	John	Clannaboyes	Dn	165
Barkley	John	Clannaboyes	Dn	165
Barkley	John	Clannaboyes	Dn	166

Surname	Forename	Estate	Co.	Page
Beaty	John	Ards	Dn	153
Beaty	John	Clannaboyes	Dn	160
Beaty	John	Ballfowre	Fe	38
Beaty	John	Ballfowre	Fe	38
Beaty	John	Ballfowre	Fe	38
Beaty	John	Ballfowre	Fe	39
Beaty	John	Hatton	Fe	48
Beaty	John	Gower	Fe	53
Beaty	John	Hastings	Fe	53
Beaty	John	Brewerton	Fe	54
Beaty	John	Sir W. Steward	Ty	59
Beaty	John	Sir W. Steward	Ty	59
Beaty	John	Tychborne	Ty	60
Beaty	John	Leigh	Ty	63
Beaty elder	John	Parsons	Ty	62
Beaty younger	John	Hatton	Fe	47
Beaty younger	John	Parsons	Ty	62
Beaty	Matthew	Ballfowre	Fe	39
Beaty	Mungo	Kildare	Dn	142
Beaty	Richard	Cole	Fe	40
Beaty	Richard	Loftus	Mo	174
Beaty	Robert	Ards	Dn	154
Beaty	Robert	Bp Dromore	Dn	171
Beaty	Robert	Mervin	Ty	69
Beaty	Thomas	Cole	Fe	39
Beaty	Thomas	Gower	Fe	53
Beaty	Thomas	Hastings	Fe	53
Beaty	Thomas	Brewerton	Fe	54
Beaty	Thomas	Bp Clougher	Ty	78
Beaty	Walter	Clannaboyes	Dn	168
Beaty	Walter	Brewerton	Fe	54
Beaty	William	Ballfowre	Fe	39
Beaty	William	Mrs Hammelton	Fe	41
Beaty	William	Lowther	Fe	44
Beaty	William	Hatton	Fe	47
Beaty	William	Clothworkers	Ly	91
Beck	Adam	Clannaboyes	Dn	165
Beck	Adam	Clannaboyes	Dn	165
Beck	John	Clannaboyes	Dn	165
Beckwith	Leonard	Fyngall	Cv	15
Beckworth	Lawrence	Fyngall	Cv	15
Bedgs	Gilbert	Edmonston	An	121
Bedlock younger	James	Calfield	Ar	35
Begard	Shane	Londonderry	Ly	87
Begart	Robert	Crumwell	Dn	144
Begat	Robert	Crumwell	Dn	144
Begg	Georg	Londonderry	Ly	86
Begg	Hugh	Clannaboyes	Dn	162
Beggs	Alexander	Ards	Dn	148
Beggs	David	Ards	Dn	147
Beggs	David	Ards	Dn	156
Beggs	John	Ards	Dn	150
Beggy	George	Goldsmiths	Ly	92
Begis	George	Edmonston	An	121
Begs	Gilbert	Ards	Dn	148
Begs	John	Clatworthy	An	122
Begs	John	Clatworthy	An	124
Beier	John	Dromond	Ty	70
Beke	John	Cope	Ar	21
Belfeild	William	Fyngall	Cv	15
Bell	Adam	Sir A. Steward	Ty	65
Bell	Adam	Lyndsay	Ty	68
Bell	Alexander	Sir J. Hume	Fe	42
Bell	Andrew	Hammelton	Ar	31
Bell	Andrew	Ards	Dn	150
Bell	Andrew	Haberdashers	Ly	90
Bell	David	Clannaboyes	Dn	162
Bell	David	Clannaboyes	Dn	169
Bell	David	Erskin	Ty	56
Bell	David	Erskin	Ty	58
Bell	Enias	Dawson	Ly	106
Bell	Francis	Erskin	Ty	58
Bell	George	Clatworthy	An	123
Bell	George	Hammelton	Ar	30
Bell	George	Hammelton	Ar	30
Bell	George	Hammelton	Ar	31

Surname	Forename	Estate	Co.	Page
Bell	George	Crumwell	Dn	145
Bell	George	Clannaboyes	Dn	168
Bell	George	Bp Dromore	Dn	171
Bell	George	Clothworkers	Ly	90
Bell	James	Kildare	Dn	142
Bell	James	Ards	Dn	151
Bell	Jenkin	Lyndsay	Ty	67
Bell	Jenkin	Lyndsay	Ty	68
Bell	John	Antrim	An	111
Bell	John	Edmonston	An	121
Bell	John	Clatworthy	An	123
Bell	John	Butler	Cv	3
Bell	John	Sir F. Hammelton	Cv	4
Bell	John	Sir F. Hammelton	Cv	5
Bell	John	J. Hammelton	Cv	12
Bell	John	Mansfield	Dl	131
Bell	John	Crumwell	Dn	143
Bell	John	Crumwell	Dn	146
Bell	John	Ards	Dn	150
Bell	John	Ards	Dn	154
Bell	John	Ards	Dn	155
Bell	John	Ards	Dn	155
Bell	John	Clannaboyes	Dn	162
Bell	John	Bp Down etc	Dn	170
Bell	John	Melvin	Dn	172
Bell	John	Woorell	Fe	46
Bell	John	Graham	Fe	54
Bell	John	Londonderry	Ly	83
Bell	John	Erskin	Ty	58
Bell	John	Sir W. Steward	Ty	58
Bell	John	A. Hammelton	Ty	63
Bell	John	Symonton	Ty	67
Bell younger	John	Kildare	Dn	142
Bell younger	John	Kildare	Dn	142
Bell	Patrick	Erskin	Ty	56
Bell	Roger	Ards	Dn	154
Bell	Roger	Bp Dromore	Dn	172
Bell	Rynyon	Sir J. Hume	Fe	42
Bell	Thomas	Clatworthy	An	123
Bell	Thomas	Upton	An	124
Bell	Thomas	Crumwell	Dn	143
Bell	Thomas	Clannaboyes	Dn	167
Bell	Thomas	Clannaboyes	Dn	169
Bell	Thomas	Butler	Fe	50
Bell	Thomas	Erskin	Ty	57
Bell	Thomas	Leigh	Ty	63
Bell	Walter	Crumwell	Dn	143
Bell	Walter	Parsons	Ty	62
Bell	William	Hammelton	Ar	29
Bell	William	Sir F. Hammelton	Cv	4
Bell	William	Kildare	Dn	142
Bell	William	Crumwell	Dn	145
Bell	William	Clannaboyes	Dn	164
Bell	William	Hannings	Fe	44
Bell	William	Haberdashers	Ly	89
Bell	William	Vintners	Ly	98
Bell	William	Erskin	Ty	56
Bell	William	Erskin	Ty	56
Bell	William	Erskin	Ty	58
Bell	William	Coape	Ty	62
Bellison	Archball	Sir A. Steward	Ty	65
Bellyes	Thomas	Neall McKenna	Mo	175
Belshes	Thomas	Pearce	Cv	12
Belstes	Thomas	J. Hammelton	Cv	12
Beltin	John	Bp Dromore	Dn	172
Ben	John	Londonderry	Ly	88
Ben	John	Coleraine	Ly	102
Bene	John	Mercers	Ly	96
Benidict	Richard	Moynes	Cv	11
Benner	Henry	Coleraine	Ly	100
Bennet	John	Ironmongers	Ly	93
Bennet elder	John	Erskin	Ty	57
Bennet younger	John	Erskin	Ty	58
Bennet	Richard	Bagshaw	Cv	8
Bennet	Richard	Londonderry	Ly	84
Bennet	Richard	Phillips	Ly	104

Surname	Forename	Estate	Co.	Page
Blaire	Robert	Antrim	An	116
Blaire	William	Clannaboyes	Dn	164
Blake	Robert	Clannaboyes	Dn	169
Blakeborone	William	Lord Primate	Ar	35
Blakelock	Gyles	Waldrum	Ar	22
Blanchet	John	Mercers	Ly	96
Bland	Edward	Londonderry	Ly	83
Blane	James	Annandall	Dl	136
Blane	John	Annandall	Dl	136
Blane	Thomas	Annandall	Dl	136
Blankett	Richard	Antrim	An	110
Blany	David	Ards	Dn	151
Blany	John	Enniskillen T.	Fe	51
Blany	John	Coleraine	Ly	102
Blanye	Michaell	Benson	Dl	133
Blanye	Michaell	Clannaboyes	Dn	158
Blanye	Robert	Clannaboyes	Dn	158
Blare	George	Phillips	Ly	105
Blare	Hugh	Merchant Taylors	Ly	93
Blare	Hugh	Coleraine	Ly	103
Blare	James	Antrim	An	116
Blare	James	Upton	An	124
Blare	James	Merchant Taylors	Ly	93
Blare	John	Antrim	An	112
Blare	John	Sir J. Conningham	Dl	129
Blare	John	Cahoune	Dl	133
Blare	Peter	Lowther	Fe	43
Blare	Robert	Merchant Taylors	Ly	92
Blare	William	Coleraine	Ly	100
Blayne	James	Strabane T.	Ty	74
Blayney	Thomas	Hastings	Fe	53
Blayre	Bevis	Antrim	An	116
Blayre	John	Clannaboyes	Dn	161
Blemish	David	Melvin	Dn	172
Bleston	James	Crumwell	Dn	145
Bleston	Nathaniell	Crumwell	Dn	145
Blomer	Andrew	Powerscourt	Ty	79
Blomer	Edmond	Powerscourt	Ty	79
Blomer	Edmond	Powerscourt	Ty	79
Blomer	Nicholas	Powerscourt	Ty	79
Bloxan	Thomas	Monnaghan T.	Mo	175
Bloxholme	William	Butler	Cv	4
Blundell	Richard	Calfield	Ar	36
Blunket	Edward	Londonderry	Ly	85
Blythe	John	Antrim	An	112
Bochanan	James	Antrim	An	114
Bochanan	John	Strabane T.	Ty	74
Bochanan	William	M. of Abbercorne	Ty	72
Bochanan	William	M. of Abbercorne	Ty	72
Bochonan	George	Enniskillen T.	Fe	51
Bochonan	John	Coleraine	Ly	100
Bockham	Bartholemew	Sir F. Hammelton	Cv	6
Bog	Patrick	Londonderry	Ly	87
Bog	William	Clothworkers	Ly	91
Bogg	James	Londonderry	Ly	86
Bole	Thomas	Clannaboyes	Dn	158
Bolton	Ralph	Melvin	Dn	172
Bonatan	Patrick	Ards	Dn	156
Bonatin	Patrick	Ards	Dn	150
Bond	John	Abp Armagh	Ty	76
Bone	John	Vintners	Ly	97
Boner	William	Harrington	Dl	134
Bonner	Robert	Waldrum	Ar	22
Bonner	William	Satcheuerall	Ar	24
Bonnie	Downie	Clannaboyes	Dn	168
Bonnty	Alexander	Sir W. Steward	Ty	59
Bony	Downy	Clannaboyes	Dn	164
Boochanan	Patrick	Cahoune	Dl	133
Boochanan	Robert	Bp Rapho	Dl	137
Boochannan	William	Enniskillen T.	Fe	51
Booman	Thomas	Clannaboyes	Dn	168
Boone	Edward	Brownlow	Ar	27
Boordlaine	Andrew	Antrim	An	110
Bootes	William	Butler	Fe	50
Booth younger	James	Butler	Fe	50
Booth	John	Butler	Fe	50
Booth	Steaphen	Grandison	Ar	32
Booth	Thomas	Londonderry	Ly	87
Booth	Thomas	Londonderry	Ly	88
Bord	John	Chichester	Dl	139
Bord	John	Chichester	Dl	140
Bordlad	William	Crumwell	Dn	145
Bordland	John	Kingsmell	Dl	131
Bores	John	Londonderry	Ly	82
Borkeberry	Thomas	Butler	Cv	2
Borland	John	Antrim	An	116
Borland	John	Clannaboyes	Dn	161
Borland	John	Clannaboyes	Dn	169
Borrell	Robert	Hastings	Ty	68
Borrowes	John	Vintners	Ly	97
Borthick	Robert	Crumwell	Dn	146
Bosell	George	Bp Dromore	Dn	171
Boston	Jeremy	Sir F. Hammelton	Cv	5
Bothwene	William	Ards	Dn	148
Botkine	Thomas	Lord Primate	Ly	106
Boucher	James	Antrim	An	118
Bougham	David	Londonderry	Ly	86
Boulton	John	Powerscourt	Ty	79
Bountaine	Thomas	Berresfourd	Ly	106
Bounty	Hugh	Ards	Dn	156
Bourston	Angaies	Phillips	Ly	104
Bouth	William	Powerscourt	Ty	79
Boward	Humphry	Sanderson	Ty	66
Boware	John	Mountnorrice	Ar	27
Boweene	Andrew	Ards	Dn	151
Bowell	Cuthbert	Antrim	An	111
Bowen	John	Ards	Dn	153
Bowen	Randall	Dunbar	Fe	48
Bowen	Thomas	Coleraine	Ly	103
Bower	James	Edmonston	An	121
Bowhadan	William	Antrim	An	112
Bowmaker	John	G. Hume	Fe	43
Bowmaker	Robert	G. Hume	Fe	43
Bowman	John	Crumwell	Dn	145
Bowman	Thomas	Lord General	Dn	169
Bowne	Andrew	Ards	Dn	151
Bowser	Christopher	Waldrune	Cv	8
Bowser	Christopher	Waterhouse	Fe	46
Box	Edward	Cope	Ar	18
Box	Philip	Cope	Ar	18
Boy	James	Satcheuerall	Ar	24
Boy	James	Satcheuerall	Ar	25
Boy	John	Satcheuerall	Ar	23
Boy	Walter	Chichester	Dl	140
Boyd	Adam	Antrim	An	111
Boyd	Adam	Antrim	An	117
Boyd	Alexand:	Ards	Dn	156
Boyd	Alexander	Crumwell	Dn	145
Boyd	Alexander	Ards	Dn	152
Boyd	Alexander	Clannaboyes	Dn	166
Boyd	Alexander	Clannaboyes	Dn	166
Boyd	Andrew	Crumwell	Dn	143
Boyd	Andrew	Londonderry	Ly	84
Boyd	Archbald	Antrim	An	111
Boyd	Cuthbert	Bp Down etc	Dn	170
Boyd	David	Upton	An	124
Boyd	David	Clannaboyes	Dn	165
Boyd	David	Clannaboyes	Dn	168
Boyd	Gilbert	Clannaboyes	Dn	157
Boyd	Hugh	Clannaboyes	Dn	166
Boyd	James	Antrim	An	117
Boyd	James	Ards	Dn	150
Boyd	James	Ards	Dn	153
Boyd	James	Clannaboyes	Dn	164
Boyd	James	Londonderry	Ly	82
Boyd	James	C. of Abbercorne	Ty	72
Boyd	John	Antrim	An	113
Boyd	John	Antrim	An	114
Boyd	John	Antrim	An	115
Boyd	John	Antrim	An	116
Boyd	John	Antrim	An	117
Boyd	John	Antrim	An	117

Surname	Forename	Estate	Co.	Page
Bridges	Robert	Calfield	Ar	36
Bridges	William	Crumwell	Dn	143
Bridges	William	Clannaboyes	Dn	167
Bridghowse	Otywll	Adwick	Fe	48
Briding	William	Antrim	An	114
Bridome	Thomas	Hammelton	Ar	31
Bridon	Christopher	Butler	Fe	50
Briers	William	Londonderry	Ly	84
Bright	John	Coleraine	Ly	103
Bright	Patrick	Sir J. Conningham	Dl	130
Brinan	James	Cole	Fe	40
Bringbranke	Henry	Dawson	Ly	106
Brisland	John	Ards	Dn	152
Bristo	Robert	Coleraine	Ly	100
Bristow	William	Moynes	Cv	11
Britch	William	Clannaboyes	Dn	166
Brittaine	Robert	Crumwell	Dn	144
Brittein	John	Lynox	Dl	129
Broad	William	Chichester	Ty	78
Broadeshaw	James	Ards	Dn	155
Broadffoote	Adam	Clannaboyes	Dn	157
Broadfoat	Arthur	Crumwell	Dn	145
Broadfoote	Alexander	Clannaboyes	Dn	163
Broadfoote	John	Crumwell	Dn	143
Broadfoote	John	Crumwell	Dn	145
Broadfull	Adam	Reding	An	121
Broadhead	Mathew	Lord Primate	Ar	33
Broadshaw	George	Butler	Fe	50
Brock	James	Sir J. Hume	Fe	42
Brock	John	Sir J. Hume	Fe	42
Brock	William	Sir J. Hume	Fe	42
Brocker	George	Fish	Cv	14
Brocker	William	Coleraine	Ly	104
Brocter	John	Mercers	Ly	96
Brodhorse	John	Waldrune	Cv	8
Brome	John	Powerscourt	Ty	79
Bromley	William	Clannaboyes	Dn	158
Bromside	Robert	Willson	Dl	132
Bron	Georg	Sir G. Hammilton	Ty	71
Bronstones	George	Clatworthy	An	122
Bront	Nicholas	Mervin	Ty	69
Brooke	Archbald	Sir G. Hammilton	Ty	71
Brooke	Eluathain	Cavan T.	Cv	16
Brooke	John	Antrim	An	116
Brooker younger	George	Fish	Cv	14
Brooker	Nicholas	Butler	Cv	2
Brookes	Charles	Gower	Fe	52
Brookes	Edmond	Lord Primate	Ar	33
Brookes	Edward	Lord Primate	Ar	33
Brookes	George	Dillon	Ar	21
Brookes	George	Butler	Cv	2
Brookes	George	Coleraine	Ly	99
Brookes	Henry	Taylor	Cv	9
Brookes	John	Taylor	Cv	10
Brookes	Joseph	Coleraine	Ly	100
Brookes	Richard	Coleraine	Ly	100
Brookes	Thomas	Londonderry	Ly	85
Brookes	William	Dillon	Ar	22
Brookes	William	Lord Primate	Ar	33
Brop	Gilbert	Mercers	Ly	95
Broster	Edward	Londonderry	Ly	85
Broster	John	Londonderry	Ly	85
Brothait	John	Crumwell	Dn	146
Brotherton	Thomas	Coleraine	Ly	99
Brouchas	Humphrey	Cope	Ar	20
Brown	James	Clannaboyes	Dn	166
Brown younger	George	Cope	Ar	20
Browne	Adam	Clannaboyes	Dn	160
Browne	Adam	Clannaboyes	Dn	161
Browne	Adam	Cole	Fe	39
Browne	Adam	Bp Clougher	Ty	78
Browne	Alexander	Antrim	An	113
Browne	Alexander	Hammelton	Ar	30
Browne	Alexander	Grandison	Ar	32
Browne	Alexander	Kingsmell	Dl	131
Browne	Alexander	Chichester	Dl	139

Surname	Forename	Estate	Co.	Page
Browne	Alexander	Phillips	Ly	105
Browne	Alexander	Sir G. Hammilton	Ty	71
Browne	Alexander	C. of Abbercorne	Ty	71
Browne	Andrew	Antrim	An	110
Browne	Andrew	W. Steward	Dl	133
Browne	Andrew	J. Cunningham	Dl	135
Browne	Andrew	Ards	Dn	147
Browne	Andrew	Ards	Dn	156
Browne	Andrew	Clannaboyes	Dn	158
Browne	Andrew	Coleraine	Ly	100
Browne	Andrew	Sir G. Hammilton	Ty	71
Browne	Archbald	Coleraine	Ly	103
Browne	Christopher	Mervin	Ty	70
Browne	Cormick	Antrim	An	114
Browne	Daniell	Antrim	An	118
Browne	Daniell	Sir G. Hammilton	Ty	70
Browne	David	Antrim	An	115
Browne	David	Sir J. Hume	Fe	42
Browne	Edward	Butler	Cv	3
Browne	Edward	Hannings	Fe	44
Browne	George	Cope	Ar	20
Browne	George	Clannaboyes	Dn	167
Browne	George	Mervin	Ty	70
Browne	Gilbert	Clannaboyes	Dn	168
Browne	Henry	Ards	Dn	150
Browne	Hugh	Antrim	An	116
Browne	Hugh	Upton	An	124
Browne	Hugh	Chichester	Dl	139
Browne	Hugh	Clannaboyes	Dn	160
Browne	James	Antrim	An	113
Browne	James	Antrim	An	114
Browne	James	Antrim	An	117
Browne	James	Adare	An	119
Browne	James	Adare	An	120
Browne	James	Sir J. Conningham	Dl	130
Browne	James	J. Conningham	Dl	136
Browne	James	Ards	Dn	149
Browne	James	Ards	Dn	150
Browne	James	Clannaboyes	Dn	157
Browne	James	Clannaboyes	Dn	158
Browne	James	Clannaboyes	Dn	159
Browne	James	Clannaboyes	Dn	160
Browne	James	Clannaboyes	Dn	164
Browne	James	Clannaboyes	Dn	167
Browne	James	Sir J. Hume	Fe	42
Browne	James	Londonderry	Ly	88
Browne	James	Clothworkers	Ly	90
Browne	James	Grocers	Ly	91
Browne	James	Coleraine	Ly	102
Browne	James	Mervin	Ty	69
Browne	James	C. of Abbercorne	Ty	71
Browne	James	Strabane T.	Ty	75
Browne younger	James	Adare	An	119
Browne	John	Antrim	An	115
Browne	John	Antrim	An	117
Browne	John	Clatworthy	An	123
Browne	John	Upton	An	124
Browne	John	Hammelton	Ar	30
Browne	John	Poyntes	Ar	32
Browne	John	Cavan T.	Cv	16
Browne	John	Willson	Dl	132
Browne	John	W. Steward	Dl	133
Browne	John	J. Conningham	Dl	135
Browne	John	Chichester	Dl	140
Browne	John	Crumwell	Dn	143
Browne	John	Crumwell	Dn	143
Browne	John	Ards	Dn	147
Browne	John	Ards	Dn	147
Browne	John	Ards	Dn	149
Browne	John	Ards	Dn	154
Browne	John	Ards	Dn	156
Browne	John	Clannaboyes	Dn	158
Browne	John	Clannaboyes	Dn	160
Browne	John	Clannaboyes	Dn	160
Browne	John	Clannaboyes	Dn	162
Browne	John	Clannaboyes	Dn	166

Surname	Forename	Estate	Co.	Page	Surname	Forename	Estate	Co.	Page
Butler	George	Chichester	Dl	140	Calles	Gilbert	Kildare	Dn	142
Butler	Izack	Butler	Cv	4	Callet	David	Waldrune	Cv	8
Butler	John	Moynes	Cv	10	Callhown	Andrew	J. Conningham	Dl	136
Butler	John	Clannaboyes	Dn	162	Callingwood	Sampson	Clannaboyes	Dn	157
Butler	Robert	Crumwell	Dn	144	Callwell	George	Adare	An	119
Butler	Robert	Ward	Dn	172	Callwell	Hugh	Lady McCleland	Ly	105
Butler	Thomas	Cope	Ar	20	Callwell	James	Antrim	An	112
Butler	Thomas	Stanhow	Ar	23	Callwell	John	Clannaboyes	Dn	166
Butler	Thomas	Crumwell	Dn	146	Callwell	Robert	Churchlands of Tayboyne	Dl	139
Butler	William	Butler	Cv	4	Cally	Archbald	Phillips	Ly	104
Butter	Richard	Cope	Ar	20	Calmeris	Andrew	Lynox	Dl	129
Button	James	Ards	Dn	152	Calmeris	Robert	Lynox	Dl	129
Button	James	Abp Armagh	Ty	76	Calmeris	Robert	Clannaboyes	Dn	169
Buy	John	Clannaboyes	Dn	160	Calore	Daniell	Kildare	Dn	142
Buyes	William	Ards	Dn	149	Calore	Henry	Kildare	Dn	142
Byers	Andrew	Clannaboyes	Dn	161	Calquahan	James	Lady Conningham	Dl	130
Byers	Andrew	Clannaboyes	Dn	169	Calson	William	Clothworkers	Ly	91
Byers	David	Archdall	Fe	41	Calsy	James	Antrim	An	117
Byers	John	Clannaboyes	Dn	165	Calveill	John	Londonderry	Ly	83
Byers	Richard	Crosby	Ty	69	Calveill	William	Londonderry	Ly	83
Byers	Thomas	Clannaboyes	Dn	165	Calvert	Christopher	Lowther	Fe	43
Bygon	Edward	Crumwell	Dn	144	Calvert	Christopher	Flowerdew	Fe	44
Bylands	Hugh	Londonderry	Ly	87	Calvert	Edward	Grandison	Ar	31
Byner	George	Ards	Dn	149	Calvert	Robert	Grandison	Ar	32
Byngham	John	Berresfourd	Ly	106	Calwater	Robert	Crumwell	Dn	144
Byny	James	Ballfowre	Fe	39	Calweill	John	Sir W. Steward	Ty	60
Byrd	John	Clannaboyes	Dn	161	Calwel	John	Sir W. Steward	Ty	60
Byrd	Richard	Clannaboyes	Dn	161	Calwell	John	J. Conningham	Dl	136
Byrnye	George	H. Steward	Ty	65	Calwell	John	Bp Rapho	Dl	138
Cabbard	Robert	Clatworthy	An	123	Calwell	John	Clannaboyes	Dn	165
Cabbin	John	Clothworkers	Ly	91	Calwell	John	Londonderry	Ly	83
Cabeine	John	Clothworkers	Ly	90	Calwell	Ninian	Ards	Dn	155
Cachy	Patrick	Crumwell	Dn	145	Calwell	Robert	Antrim	An	111
Cacone	James	Sir W. Steward	Ty	59	Calwell	Robert	Ards	Dn	151
Cadan	William	Clannaboyes	Dn	161	Calwell	Robert	Ards	Dn	151
Cadarisse	William	Richardson	Ty	67	Calwell	Robert	Ballfowre	Fe	38
Cadash	Patrick	Lyndsay	Ty	68	Calwell	Robert	M. of Abbercorne	Ty	72
Caddan	Thomas	Clannaboyes	Dn	162	Calwell	Thomas	Haberdashers	Ly	90
Caddon	Hugh	Ards	Dn	148	Calwell	Thomas	Sir W. Steward	Ty	59
Caddon	William	Clannaboyes	Dn	169	Calwell	William	Ards	Dn	152
Cade	Richard	Fyngall	Cv	15	Caman	John	Phillips	Ly	104
Cade	Richard	Fyngall	Cv	15	Cambell	Alexander	Willson	Dl	132
Cadell	William	Sir F. Hammelton	Cv	6	Cambell	Alexander	A. Steward	Dl	135
Cader	William	Strabane T.	Ty	76	Cambell	Alexander	A. Steward	Dl	135
Caderwood	John	Clannaboyes	Dn	160	Cambell	Andrew	A. Steward	Dl	135
Cadman	William	Auldridg	Mo	175	Cambell	Andrew	J. Conningham	Dl	136
Cadwalder	Robert	Crumwell	Dn	144	Cambell	Andrew	J. Steward	Dl	136
Cadwell	Alexander	Chichester	Dl	139	Cambell	Donnell	W. Steward	Dl	133
Cadwell	Andrew	Chichester	Dl	139	Cambell	Dunkan	Lynox	Dl	128
Cadwell	Mathew	Chichester	Dl	139	Cambell	Dunkan	Dean of Rapho	Dl	139
Cady	Thomas	Parsons	Ty	62	Cambell	George	Balye	Cv	13
Cahawin	Robert	Antrim	An	118	Cambell	George	Londonderry	Ly	85
Cahlell	William	Crumwell	Dn	146	Cambell	George	Vintners	Ly	97
Cahowne	James	Antrim	An	118	Cambell	James	A. Steward	Dl	135
Cahowne	Patrick	Adare	An	119	Cambell	John	Antrim	An	111
Cahowne	Richard	Butler	Cv	3	Cambell	John	Antrim	An	118
Cahowne	Thomas	Antrim	An	118	Cambell	John	Lynox	Dl	128
Cakrell	Adam	Bp Clougher	Ty	77	Cambell	John	Sir J. Conningham	Dl	129
Calagh	Alexander	Hammelton	Ar	30	Cambell	John	W. Steward	Dl	133
Calbreath	John	Ards	Dn	153	Cambell	John	W. Steward	Dl	133
Calbreath	Thomas	Atkinson	Fe	52	Cambell	John	A. Steward	Dl	135
Calbreath	Thomas	Atkinson	Fe	52	Cambell	John	Londonderry	Ly	85
Calder	George	Sir J. Hume	Fe	41	Cambell	John	Vintners	Ly	98
Calder	Hugh	Strabane T.	Ty	75	Cambell elder	John	Lynox	Dl	128
Calder	Hugh	Strabane T.	Ty	76	Cambell younger	John	Lynox	Dl	128
Caldwell	John	Antrim	An	118	Cambell	Robert	Lynox	Dl	129
Caldwell	John	Ards	Dn	154	Cambell	Robert	Crumwell	Dn	144
Caldwell	John	Enniskillen T.	Fe	51	Cambell	Thomas	Ards	Dn	149
Caldwell	Robert	Antrim	An	116	Cambell	William	Antrim	An	118
Cale	Christopher	Willson	Dl	132	Cambell	William	A. Steward	Dl	135
Callam	John	Antrim	An	112	Cambell	William	J. Steward	Dl	136
Callan	Patrick	Ards	Dn	153	Cambell	William	Clannaboyes	Dn	163
Callen	James	Clatworthy	An	122	Camble	Andrew	Clannaboyes	Dn	157
Callender	Thomas	Adare	An	120	Camble	David	Clannaboyes	Dn	159
Callender	William	Ards	Dn	149	Camble	George	Clannaboyes	Dn	157
Callendyn	Henry	Amis & Greeneham	Cv	11	Camble	Hugh	Clannaboyes	Dn	158

Surname	Forename	Estate	Co.	Page
Carness	John	Parsons	Ty	61
Carnington	Nathaniell	Ironmongers	Ly	94
Carnog	Hugh	Kingsmell	Dl	131
Carnoghan	James	Clannaboyes	Dn	165
Carr	Adam	Ards	Dn	154
Carr	Alexander	Sir J. Hume	Fe	41
Carr	Andrew	M. of Abbercorne	Ty	72
Carr	Francis	Lyndsay	Ty	68
Carr	George	Ards	Dn	156
Carr	George	Lyndsay	Ty	67
Carr	George	Lyndsay	Ty	68
Carr	John	Antrim	An	111
Carr	John	Butler	Cv	2
Carr	John	Clannaboyes	Dn	166
Carr	John	Clannaboyes	Dn	166
Carr	Marke	Clatworthy	An	124
Carr	Rober	Antrim	An	111
Carr	Robert	Coleraine	Ly	103
Carr	Robert	Coleraine	Ly	104
Carr	Roger	Satcheuerall	Ar	25
Carr	Storiment	A. Steward	Dl	135
Carr	Thomas	Dalloway	An	122
Carr	Thomas	Clatworthy	An	124
Carr	Thomas	Clannaboyes	Dn	160
Carr	Thomas	Richardson	Ty	67
Carr	Thomas	M. of Abbercorne	Ty	72
Carr	Walter	Willson	Dl	132
Carr	William	Edmonston	An	120
Carr	William	Clannaboyes	Dn	166
Carradhouse	John	Crumwell	Dn	144
Carradhowse	Robert	Crumwell	Dn	145
Carrally	Nicholas	Bp Dromore	Dn	171
Carran	Owen	Leigh	Ty	63
Carrat	John	Crumwell	Dn	144
Carrington	Ralph	Bp Clougher	Ty	77
Carroll	John	Enniskillen T.	Fe	51
Carrous	Henry	Kildare	Dn	142
Carrudas	Francis	Hammelton	Ar	29
Carrudas	William	Hammelton	Ar	29
Carruddas	Christopher	Ballfowre	Fe	38
Carruddas	Francis	Sir W. Steward	Ty	59
Carruddas	John	Satcheuerall	Ar	24
Carruddas	Robert	Satcheuerall	Ar	25
Carruddas	Thomas	Crumwell	Dn	143
Carrudes	Robert	Clannaboyes	Dn	158
Carrudhous	John	Clannaboyes	Dn	161
Carrudhouse	George	J. Hammelton	Cv	12
Carrudhouse	George	Crumwell	Dn	146
Carrudhouse	Herbert	Phillips	Ly	104
Carrudhouse	John	J. Hammelton	Cv	12
Carrudhowse	John	Erskin	Ty	56
Carrudhowse	Robert	Ards	Dn	147
Carrudhowse	Thomas	Crumwell	Dn	144
Carsall	William	Edmonston	An	121
Carsan	Alexander	Crumwell	Dn	144
Carsan	Andrew	Ards	Dn	147
Carsan	George	Crumwell	Dn	145
Carsan	John	Kildare	Dn	142
Carsan	John	Crumwell	Dn	143
Carsan	John	Crumwell	Dn	143
Carsan	John	Crumwell	Dn	146
Carsan	John	Crumwell	Dn	146
Carsan	John	Clannaboyes	Dn	161
Carsan	John	Clannaboyes	Dn	169
Carsan	Patrick	Ards	Dn	155
Carsan	Robert	Crumwell	Dn	145
Carsby	Robert	Churchlands of Tayboyne	Dl	139
Carse	Henry	Crumwell	Dn	145
Carson	George	Coape	Ty	62
Carson	John	Sir W. Steward	Ty	58
Carson	Richard	Bp Rapho	Dl	138
Carsonne	William	Clatworthy	An	124
Carssan	Alexander	Bp Dromore	Dn	172
Carssan	John	Crumwell	Dn	143
Carssar'es	Wm	Bp Rapho	Dl	138
Carsson	John	Clatworthy	An	124

Surname	Forename	Estate	Co.	Page
Carter	Andrew	Maghera & Desert Martin	Ly	107
Carter	Henry	Maghera & Desert Martin	Ly	107
Carter	John	Cope	Ar	25
Carter	Thomas	Butler	Cv	4
Carter	Thomas	Waldrune	Cv	9
Carter	Thomas	Crumwell	Dn	145
Carter	William	Londonderry	Ly	87
Carthers	Symond	Hammelton	Ar	31
Cartwright	Richard	Berresfourd	Ly	106
Cartwright	Robert	Lord General	Dn	170
Caruth	Alexander	Clannaboyes	Dn	167
Caruth	Archbald	Clannaboyes	Dn	167
Carver	John	Hatton	Fe	47
Carwer	John	Edmonston	An	120
Cary	Edward	Sir F. Hammelton	Cv	5
Cary	Edward	Mercers	Ly	95
Cary	George	Chichester	Dl	140
Cary	James	C. of Abbercorne	Ty	71
Cary	Robert	Chichester	Dl	139
Cashell	William	Clannaboyes	Dn	169
Cass	George	M. of Abbercorne	Ty	72
Cass	John	Hammelton	Ar	30
Cass	John	Londonderry	Ly	82
Cass	John	Lyndsay	Ty	68
Cassan	Andrew	Clannaboyes	Dn	159
Cassan	John	Reding	An	121
Cassan	John	Upton	An	124
Cassan	John	Clannaboyes	Dn	164
Cassan	Patrick	Clannaboyes	Dn	164
Cassan	Robert	Clannaboyes	Dn	164
Cassan	Rowland	Upton	An	124
Cassan	William	Bp Dromore	Dn	171
Casse	Thomas	Antrim	An	115
Casselden	Richard	Waldrune	Cv	8
Casselden	William	Waldrune	Cv	8
Cassen	Alexander	Clannaboyes	Dn	160
Cassen	Andrew	Strabane T.	Ty	75
Casset	John	Clannaboyes	Dn	164
Cassills	James	Clannaboyes	Dn	161
Cassills	William	Clannaboyes	Dn	161
Cassment	Phillip	Grandison	Ar	32
Casson	John	Londonderry	Ly	83
Casson	William	Reding	An	122
Cassrone	John	Londonderry	Ly	88
Cassydon	John	Leigh	Ty	63
Cat	Robert	Ards	Dn	153
Catcherd	George	Sir A. Steward	Ty	64
Cathcart	Allen	Adare	An	120
Cathcart	John	Ards	Dn	155
Catheron	Alexander	Clatworthy	An	123
Catherson	William	Strabane T.	Ty	75
Catherwood	Andrew	Ards	Dn	152
Catherwood	Hugh	Ards	Dn	154
Catherwood	James	Ards	Dn	154
Catherwood	Neal	Ards	Dn	152
Catherwood	William	Ards	Dn	148
Catnam	Benedict	Bagshaw	Cv	7
Catnam	Sammuell	Bagshaw	Cv	7
Caugh	Robert	Kildare	Dn	142
Caughide	John	Kildare	Dn	142
Caughton	John	Erskin	Ty	57
Caulfield	Robert	Waldrum	Ar	22
Caure	Donell	Clannaboyes	Dn	162
Cavan	Gilbert	Clannaboyes	Dn	165
Cawarty	Christopher	Lowther	Fe	43
Caweill	Patrick	Strabane T.	Ty	73
Cawell	John	Ards	Dn	148
Cawlian	John	Londonderry	Ly	85
Cawtart	Andrew	W. Hammilton	Ty	78
Cawtart	Archbell	W. Hammilton	Ty	78
Cawtart	John	W. Hammilton	Ty	78
Caxanell	George	Chichester	Ty	78
Caxorne	Francis	Calfield	Ty	79
Cayl	William	C. of Abbercorne	Ty	71
Cayle	Andrew	Abp Armagh	Ty	76
Cerruddas	John	Atchison	Ar	28

Surname	Forename	Estate	Co.	Page	Surname	Forename	Estate	Co.	Page
Clayton	Roger	Crag	Cv	7	Cogheran	Gilbert	Ards	Dn	153
Clearetowne	Robert	Sedburrogh	Fe	48	Cogheran	James	Clannaboyes	Dn	160
Cleary	John	Clothworkers	Ly	90	Cogheran	James	Londonderry	Ly	88
Cleckhorne	Wm	Antrim	An	110	Cogheran	John	Antrim	An	111
Clegg	Eskill	Londonderry	Ly	85	Cogheran	John	Ards	Dn	149
Cleid	John	Londonderry	Ly	83	Cogheran	John	Clannaboyes	Dn	162
Cleid	Robert	Londonderry	Ly	87	Cogheran	John	Londonderry	Ly	86
Cleland	Arthur	Clannaboyes	Dn	158	Cogheran	Robert	Ards	Dn	149
Cleland	James	Clannaboyes	Dn	158	Cogheran	Robert	Londonderry	Ly	86
Clements	William	Londonderry	Ly	84	Cogheran	Robert	Londonderry	Ly	88
Clemmell	John	Merchant Taylors	Ly	93	Cogheran	Thomas	Ards	Dn	153
Clemments	John	Reding	An	121	Cogherin	Henry	Antrim	An	113
Clemments	John	Clatworthy	An	124	Coghrayne	John	C. of Abbercorne	Ty	71
Clencross	Robert	Crumwell	Dn	145	Coghreny	Constant	Bp Dromore	Dn	171
Clencross	Roger	Tychborne	Ty	61	Cokeran	William	Lynox	Dl	128
Clene	Johne	Chichester	Dl	139	Cole	John	Waldrum	Ar	22
Clenny	Alexander	Sir G. Hammilton	Ty	71	Cole	John	Londonderry	Ly	87
Clenny	James	Sir G. Hammilton	Ty	71	Cole	John	Londonderry	Ly	88
Clenton	John	Mercers	Ly	96	Cole	Robert	Crumwell	Dn	144
Clercag	William	Melvin	Dn	172	Cole	Robert	Londonderry	Ly	87
Clerke	George	Stanhow	Ar	23	Cole	Robert	Berresfourd	Ly	106
Clerson	James	Melvin	Dn	172	Colemore	George	Coleraine	Ly	100
Clifford	William	Cavan T.	Cv	16	Coleston	Richard	Sir A. Steward	Ty	64
Clinblock	Rynyon	Bp Down etc	Dn	170	Coleston	Robert	Sir A. Steward	Ty	64
Clingen	John	Ards	Dn	155	Coleston	Thomas	H. Steward	Ty	65
Clish	Robert	Ards	Dn	156	Coleston	William	Sir A. Steward	Ty	64
Cloff	Thomas	Butler	Cv	3	Colf	Peter	Crumwell	Dn	146
Clogheron	Georg	Goldsmiths	Ly	92	Coline	Adam	Ards	Dn	147
Cloheron younger	James	Goldsmiths	Ly	92	Colinn	Thomas	Strabane T.	Ty	73
Clogheron	Robert	Goldsmiths	Ly	92	Collagh	Morymont	Antrim	An	118
Clogherone	John	Goldsmiths	Ly	92	Collaghan	Archbald	Chichester	Dl	140
Clohorone	James	Goldsmiths	Ly	92	Collins	Richard	Calfield	Ar	35
Cloney	William	Antrim	An	112	Collins	Richard	Mercers	Ly	96
Close	Thomas	Crumwell	Dn	143	Collins	Richard	Drapers	Ly	98
Close	Thomas	Crumwell	Dn	145	Collom	Moyle	Ironmongers	Ly	94
Cloughan	John	Mervin	Ty	70	Collome	William	Ironmongers	Ly	94
Cloughan	Thomas	Bp Rapho	Dl	138	Collynd	William	Bp Down etc	Dn	170
Cloughston	James	Clannaboyes	Dn	162	Collyne	John	Bp Down etc	Dn	170
Cluny	John	Abp Armagh	Ty	76	Colmories	George	Lynox	Dl	128
Clyde	Robert	Clannaboyes	Dn	165	Colning	Thomas	Antrim	An	118
Clyfford	John	Bp Dromore	Dn	172	Coloston	Alexander	Crosby	Ty	69
Clyfton	Richard	Coleraine	Ly	101	Colphen	John	Ards	Dn	155
Clyfton	William	Grocers	Ly	91	Colquphone	Humfrey	Lynox	Dl	128
Clynton	Francis	Mercers	Ly	96	Coltor	Henry	Ards	Dn	148
Coadan	Thomas	Ards	Dn	152	Colvanie	Alexander	Clannaboyes	Dn	159
Coary	Robert	Ards	Dn	148	Colwell	William	Sir J. Conningham	Dl	130
Coates	John	Ards	Dn	153	Colyer	James	Antrim	An	112
Coay	John	Clatworthy	An	122	Come	John	Coleraine	Ly	102
Coborn	Gilbert	Clatworthy	An	123	Coming	James	Strabane T.	Ty	75
Coch	Thomas	Coleraine	Ly	103	Comlyne	John	Kildare	Dn	142
Cochan	John	Crumwell	Dn	143	Comyn	Robert	Strabane T.	Ty	73
Cocheane	Thomas	Clannaboyes	Dn	160	Con	James	Kildare	Dn	142
Cocherah	Robert	Haberdashers	Ly	90	Con	John	Kildare	Dn	142
Cocheran	James	Strabane T.	Ty	75	Con	William	Crumwell	Dn	145
Cocheran	John	Lynox	Dl	128	Conally	Patrick	Art oge Mc Maghan	Mo	174
Cocheran	John	Bp Rapho	Dl	138	Conchoy	Neelly	Antrim	An	112
Cocheran	Robert	Lynox	Dl	128	Condall	Thomas	Abp Armagh	Ty	76
Cocheran	William	Annandall	Dl	137	Conffee	John	Ards	Dn	150
Cocherone	John	Haberdashers	Ly	90	Coningham	Adam	Clannaboyes	Dn	165
Cochras	John	Coleraine	Ly	103	Coningham	David	Sir J. Conningham	Dl	129
Cock	Andrew	Lynox	Dl	128	Coningham	David	Strabane T.	Ty	75
Cock	Henry	Mercers	Ly	96	Coningham	Gabrahell	Sir J. Hume	Fe	42
Cock	James	Lynox	Dl	128	Coningham	Patrick	Sir J. Conningham	Dl	129
Cock	John	Lynox	Dl	128	Coningham	Thomas	Sir J. Hume	Fe	42
Cockbourn	William	Ards	Dn	150	Coningham	William	Strabane T.	Ty	73
Cocking	Vincent	Sir J. Hume	Fe	42	Conley	William	Kildare	Dn	142
Cockraine	Andrew	Archdal	Fe	53	Conn	Thomas	Phillips	Ly	104
Cockroger	Nathaniell	Clannaboyes	Dn	161	Connaghy	Fynlay	Antrim	An	115
Cody	Martin	Parsons	Ty	61	Connaway	John	Dawson	Ly	106
Coe	Thomas	Cope	Ar	25	Conne	Hector	Bp Rapho	Dl	138
Cofeild	John	Coleraine	Ly	101	Connell	James	Phillips	Ly	105
Cogheran	Alexander	Ards	Dn	149	Connell	Thomas	Phillips	Ly	104
Cogheran	Fynlay	Ards	Dn	149	Connerly	Thomas	Lord Primate	Ar	33
Cogheran	George	Clatworthy	An	122	Conningham	Adam	Bp Dromore	Dn	171
Cogheran	George	Clannaboyes	Dn	162	Conningham	Alexander	Clatworthy	An	122
Cogheran	George	Londonderry	Ly	86	Conningham	Alexander	Lady Conningham	Dl	131

Surname	Forename	Estate	Co.	Page	Surname	Forename	Estate	Co.	Page
Cordiner	John	Sir W. Steward	Ty	60	Cowtart	Michaell	Clannaboyes	Dn	161
Cormack	John	Crumwell	Dn	143	Cowterd	John	Hammelton	Ar	31
Cormack	John	Crumwell	Dn	143	Cowtronie	Archbald	Ards	Dn	150
Cormack	William	Crumwell ·	Dn	143	Cowy	James	Clannaboyes	Dn	165
Cormack	William	Crumwell	Dn	143	Cowye	William	Clannaboyes	Dn	167
Cornell	James	Crumwell	Dn	144	Cowyn	Thomas	Edmonston	An	121
Cornewall	George	Clannaboyes	Dn	162	Cox	John	Lord Primate	Ar	34
Cornewell	James	Crumwell	Dn	146	Cox	Nicholas	Lord Primate	Ar	34
Cornnell	James	Crumwell	Dn	146	Cox	Richard	Bagshaw	Cv	8
Cornock	George	Ards	Dn	147	Cox	Thomas	Mercers	Ly	96
Cornock	James	Ards	Dn	153	Cox	William	F. Blennerhasset	Fe	45
Corrington	Richard	Moynes	Cv	11	Coxes	John	Butler	Cv	4
Cors	John	Maghera & Desert Martin	Ly	107	Coyne	Patrick	Clannaboyes	Dn	161
Corsby	John	Haberdashers	Ly	89	Coyne	Thomas	Ards	Dn	156
Corse	Archbald	Clannaboyes	Dn	162	Cracton	William	Clothworkers	Ly	90
Corse	Henry	Clannaboyes	Dn	163	Crafford	Alexander	Ards	Dn	152
Corse	John	Clannaboyes	Dn	159	Crafford	Andrew	J. Conningham	Dl	135
Corson	George	Clatwoorthy	An	123	Crafford	Andrew	Ards	Dn	153
Corson	George	Clatwoorthy	An	123	Crafford	David	Ards	Dn	148
Corvinn	Henry	Lord Primate	Ar	34	Crafford	Dunkan	Lynox	Dl	129
Cory	Duncan	Sir A. Steward	Ty	64	Crafford	George	Mountnorrice	Ar	27
Cory	Robert	A. Hammelton	Ty	63	Crafford	Hugh	Antrim	An	116
Cory	Sammuell	A. Hammelton	Ty	63	Crafford	Hugh	Antrim	An	117
Cory younger	Robert	A. Hammelton	Ty	63	Crafford	Hugh	Clatwoorthy	An	122
Cory	William	Bp Dromore	Dn	171	Crafford	Hugh	Crumwell	Dn	146
Cory	William	Parsons	Ty	62	Crafford	James	Antrim	An	118
Coshcry	Henry	Clannaboyes	Dn	167	Crafford	James	Kingsmell	Dl	131
Coskey	Andrew	Dromond	Ty	70	Crafford	James	Annandall	Dl	136
Cosly	John	Kildare	Dn	143	Crafford	John	Antrim	An	117
Costenden	George	Coleraine	Ly	99	Crafford	John	Upton	An	124
Coster	Francis	Phillips	Ly	104	Crafford	John	Lady Conningham	Dl	131
Costyne	George	Bp Dromore	Dn	172	Crafford	John	Ards	Dn	156
Cotes	Christopher	Butler	Fe	50	Crafford	Patrick	Sir J. Conningham	Dl	130
Cothers	Archball	Atchison	Ar	29	Crafford	Quintan	Clatwoorthy	An	123
Cotle	Thomas	Cope	Ar	20	Crafford	Robert	Antrim	An	117
Cotman	George	Auldridg	Mo	176	Crafford	Robert	Edmonston	An	120
Cotman	George	Auldridg	Mo	176	Crafford	Robert	Lady Conningham	Dl	131
Cotnam	Benedict	Moynes	Cv	11	Crafford	Robert	Crumwell	Dn	146
Cottingham	Bastyn	Hatton	Fe	47	Crafford	Stephen	Clannaboyes	Dn	157
Couch	Nathaniel	Chichester	Dl	139	Crafford	Thomas	Edmonston	An	121
Couch	Richard	Bagshaw	Cv	7	Crafford	Thomas	Lynox	Dl	129
Couff	James	Ards	Dn	152	Crafford	William	Antrim	An	119
Cougheron	Wm	Chichester	Dl	139	Crafford	William	Clatwoorthy	An	122
Coulden	John	A. Hammelton	Ty	63	Crafford	William	Sir J. Conningham	Dl	130
Coult	Richard	Flowerdew	Fe	44	Crafford	William	Chichester	Dl	140
Coulter	James	Archdall	Fe	40	Crafford	William	Bp Dromore	Dn	171
Coulton	William	Phillips	Ly	104	Craffourd	John	Edmonston	An	120
Couper	Alexander	Clannaboyes	Dn	164	Craoford	Mathew	Sir W. Hammilton	Ty	72
Courser	George	Cole	Fe	40	Craoford	Peter	Londonderry	Ly	88
Coushey	Alexander	Ards	Dn	147	Craford	Allen	Londonderry	Ly	88
Coussen	John	Ards	Dn	150	Craford	George	G. Hume	Fe	43
Coussen	William	Ards	Dn	150	Craford	Hugh	Sanderson	Ty	66
Coussings	Francis	Sir F. Hammelton	Cv	6	Craford	John	Hastings	Fe	53
Coussings	William	Sir F. Hammelton	Cv	6	Craford	John	Vintners	Ly	98
Coutch	Christopher	Londonderry	Ly	84	Craford	Thomas	Londonderry	Ly	85
Covert	Robert	Brownlow	Ar	27	Craford	William	Sir W. Steward	Ty	59
Cowan	James	Adare	An	119	Crag younger	Gawen	Londonderry	Ly	83
Cowan	James	Clannaboyes	Dn	161	Crag	James	Crumwell	Dn	145
Cowan	John	Londonderry	Ly	86	Crag	James	Londonderry	Ly	87
Coward	John	Bp Dromore	Dn	171	Crag	John	Ards	Dn	152
Cowayne	John	Sanderson	Ty	66	Crag	John	Ards	Dn	155
Cowbrone	John	Chichester	Dl	139	Crag	John	Londonderry	Ly	84
Cowdan	Thomas	Ards	Dn	156	Crag	John	Coleraine	Ly	101
Coweene	Robert	Chichester	Dl	139	Crag	John	Erskin	Ty	58
Cowell	Andrew	Crag	Cv	6	Crag	John	Strabane T.	Ty	74
Cowelson	Richard	Sir A. Steward	Ty	65	Crag	Robert	Ards	Dn	153
Cowen	John	Adare	An	119	Crag	Robert	Clannaboyes	Dn	165
Cowen	John	Adare	An	120	Crag	Thomas	Erskin	Ty	58
Cowen	John	Sir F. Hammelton	Cv	5	Crag	Thomas	Sir W. Steward	Ty	58
Cowen	Robert	Edmonston	An	121	Crag	William	Antrim	An	110
Cowen	William	Clannaboyes	Dn	156	Crag	William	Sir J. Conningham	Dl	130
Cowert	Thomas	Brownlow	Ar	26	Crag	William	Strabane T.	Ty	75
Cowet	John	Ards	Dn	149	Crage	Collin	Clannaboyes	Dn	164
Cowey	James	Londonderry	Ly	87	Crage	Gawen	Londonderry	Ly	88
Cowie	George	Clannaboyes	Dn	167	Crage	John	Clannaboyes	Dn	164
Cowtard	David	Hammelton	Ar	31	Crage	Michaell	Clannaboyes	Dn	164

Surname	Forename	Estate	Co.	Page
Crucks	John	Lady McCleland	Ly	105
Crum	Sanders	Clannaboyes	Dn	166
Cruse	Henry	Lynox	Dl	129
Cuddy	James	Ards	Dn	155
Cuddy	John	Clannaboyes	Dn	167
Cuddy	John	Clannaboyes	Dn	169
Cuddy	Thomas	Upton	An	124
Culiland	William	Londonderry	Ly	87
Cullan	Andrew	Clannaboyes	Dn	168
Cullan	John	Bp Down etc	Dn	171
Cullan younger	John	Bp Down etc	Dn	171
Cullons	John	Clannaboyes	Dn	162
Culpar	Robert	Antrim	An	113
Culum	Anthony	Bp Kilmore	Cv	15
Cumell	Arch:	Vintners	Ly	98
Cumell	Robert	Vintners	Ly	98
Cuming	James	Strabane T.	Ty	74
Cummell	Hugh	Londonderry	Ly	87
Cunaston	Edward	Crumwell	Dn	144
Cunaston	Frauncis	Crumwell	Dn	144
Cuningham	Barnard	Sir J. Conningham	Dl	130
Cuningham	Mathew	Sir J. Conningham	Dl	130
Cunning	William	Ards	Dn	149
Cunningham	John	J. Conningham	Dl	136
Cunningham	John	Strabane T.	Ty	76
Cunny	Alexander	Sir A. Steward	Ty	64
Cuomes	John	Coleraine	Ly	103
Cuoston	John	Waldrune	Cv	8
Cup	George	Antrim	An	112
Cupar	David	Clothworkers	Ly	90
Cupper	George	Antrim	An	114
Curly	Alexander	Sir W. Steward	Ty	59
Curly	George	Sir W. Steward	Ty	59
Curratt	John	Kildare	Dn	142
Currne	Gilbert	Edmonston	An	121
Curry	George	Clannaboyes	Dn	167
Curry	James	Ards	Dn	153
Curry	James	Clannaboyes	Dn	167
Curry	John	Clannaboyes	Dn	159
Curry	John	Lady McCleland	Ly	106
Curry	John	Strabane T.	Ty	74
Curry	Robert	Ards	Dn	149
Curry	Robert	Clannaboyes	Dn	158
Curry	William	Clannaboyes	Dn	167
Curtis	Ingram	Mountnorrice	Ar	27
Curtis	Richard	Powerscourt	Ty	79
Curtis	Thomas	Powerscourt	Ty	79
Curtis	Thomas	Powerscourt	Ty	79
Curtis	William	Lord Primate	Ar	35
Custis	Thomas	Hammelton	Ar	29
Cutberson	James	Balye	Cv	13
Cutberson	John	Balye	Cv	13
Cutberson	Robert	Balye	Cv	13
Cutberson	William	Sir J. Conningham	Dl	130
Cutbert	Francis	Coleraine	Ly	100
Cutbert	George	Antrim	An	115
Cutbert	Gilbert	Bp Down etc	Dn	170
Cutbert	John	Ards	Dn	153
Cutbertson	James	M. of Abbercorne	Ty	72
Cutbertson	John	Londonderry	Ly	86
Cutbertson	Robert	Londonderry	Ly	87
Cutbertson	William	Londonderry	Ly	87
Cute	Charles	Archdall	Fe	41
Cuthbert	Allan	Strabane T.	Ty	74
Cuthbert	John	Antrim	An	117
Cuthbert	William	Strabane T.	Ty	75
Cuthcert	John	Ards	Dn	153
Cutler	Edward	L. Blennerhasset	Fe	53
Cutler	Henry	Kildare	Dn	142
Cutler	James	Maghera & Desert Martin	Ly	107
Cutler	Richard	Loftus	Mo	174
Cutris	John	Calfield	Ar	36
Dabbin	John	Ards	Dn	147
Dabsyre	Edward	Vintners	Ly	97
Daire	John	Ards	Dn	150
Dale	John	Grandison	Ar	32

Surname	Forename	Estate	Co.	Page
Dale	John	Sir A. Steward	Ty	64
Dale	William	Sir A. Steward	Ty	65
Dallaway	Francis	Londonderry	Ly	84
Dallson	Christopher	Adwick	Fe	48
Dally	William	Adare	An	119
Dalmore	Henry	Butler	Fe	49
Dalrumple	James	Ards	Dn	150
Dalton	Henry	Calfield	Ar	36
Dalyell	Fynlay	Ards	Dn	148
Dalyell	John	Ards	Dn	148
Damson	Thomas	Edmonston	An	121
Danes	William	Haberdashers	Ly	89
Dannet	Robert	Cavan T.	Cv	16
Daragh	Henry	H. Steward	Ty	65
Daragh	Robert	Symonton	Ty	67
Daragh	William	Sir G. Hammilton	Ty	71
Darbishere	John	Cope	Ar	20
Darbishere	Lawrance	Cope	Ar	20
Darbishere	Thomas	Satcheuerall	Ar	25
Dardes	Nathaniell	Cavan T.	Cv	16
Dards	Lawrance	Cavan T.	Cv	16
Darlin	Thomas	Moynes	Cv	11
Darling	Thomas	Grocers	Ly	91
Darlington	Robert	Coleraine	Ly	102
Darlington	Thomas	Coleraine	Ly	102
Darrigh	William	Ards	Dn	154
Darson	James	Harrington	Dl	134
Darumple	John	Clannaboyes	Dn	163
Darwin	Sammuell	Mercers	Ly	95
Daskins	George	Lord Primate	Ar	33
Davenport	Thomas	Chichester	Dl	140
David	John	Upton	An	125
David	Mungo	W. Steward	Dl	133
David	Robert	Calfield	Ty	79
Davidson	Alexander	J. Hammelton	Cv	12
Davidson	John	W. Steward	Dl	133
Davidson	Michaell	Parsons	Ty	62
Davidson	William	Clannaboyes	Dn	167
Davie	John	Clannaboyes	Dn	160
Davie	William	Clannaboyes	Dn	160
Davis	Edward	Butler	Cv	2
Davis	Edward	Butler	Cv	2
Davis	Edward	Butler	Cv	3
Davis	Henry	Calfield	Ar	35
Davis	James	Crumwell	Dn	144
Davis	James	Crumwell	Dn	144
Davis	James	Ward	Dn	172
Davis	James	Gaidy	Ly	105
Davis	John	Clatworthy	An	122
Davis	John	Willson	Dl	132
Davis	John	Benson	Dl	133
Davis	John	Enniskillen T.	Fe	51
Davis	John	Gaidy	Ly	105
Davis	Leonard	Londonderry	Ly	84
Davis	Lewis	Londonderry	Ly	87
Davis	Martin	Grocers	Ly	92
Davis	Mathew	Crumwell	Dn	144
Davis	Nathaniell	Coleraine	Ly	99
Davis	Richard	Davis	Dl	134
Davis	Richard	Crumwell	Dn	145
Davis	Rise	Kingsmell	Dl	131
Davis	Robert	Antrim	An	113
Davis	Thomas	Willson	Dl	132
Davis	Thomas	Gaidy	Ly	105
Davis	William	Cope	Ar	19
Davis	William	Cope	Ar	20
Davis	William	Kingsmell	Dl	131
Davis	William	Crumwell	Dn	144
Davis	William	Crumwell	Dn	145
Davis	William	Parsons	Ty	62
Davison	Ambross	Coleraine	Ly	100
Davison	Andrew	Sir W. Hammilton	Ty	73
Davison	Charles	Ards	Dn	151
Davison	Downie	Clannaboyes	Dn	159
Davison	Henry	Londonderry	Ly	83
Davison	James	Ards	Dn	148

Surname	Forename	Estate	Co.	Page	Surname	Forename	Estate	Co.	Page
Dixon	John	Crag	Cv	7	Doone	William	Sir J. Conningham	Dl	130
Dixon	John	Kildare	Dn	142	Doory	Andrew	Antrim	An	112
Dixon	John	Crumwell	Dn	144	Doran	James	Bp Dromore	Dn	172
Dixon	John	Crumwell	Dn	145	Dormond	Thomas	Clannaboyes	Dn	160
Dixon	John	Crumwell	Dn	146	Dornan	Bryan	Clannaboyes	Dn	159
Dixon	John	Ards	Dn	153	Dory	John	Calfield	Ty	79
Dixon	John	Clannaboyes	Dn	160	Doughty	Robert	Auldridg	Mo	176
Dixon	John	Clannaboyes	Dn	161	Douglas	Alexander	Londonderry	Ly	86
Dixon	John	Clannaboyes	Dn	168	Douglas	Archbald	Crosby	Ty	69
Dixon	John	Bp Down etc	Dn	170	Douglas	David	Antrim	An	118
Dixon	John	Erskin	Ty	57	Douglas	Gawen	Abp Armagh	Ty	77
Dixon	Joseph	Sedburrogh	Fe	48	Douglas	George	Antrim	An	112
Dixon	Michael	Sir J. Hume	Fe	42	Douglas	George	Edmonston	An	121
Dixon	Richard	Taylor	Cv	9	Douglas	George	Londonderry	Ly	86
Dixon	Richard	Ironmongers	Ly	94	Douglas	George	Sanderson	Ty	66
Dixon	Robert	Crumwell	Dn	143	Douglas	Hector	Annandall	Dl	136
Dixon younger	Robert	Crumwell	Dn	145	Douglas	James	Bp Dromore	Dn	171
Dixon	Symond	Clannaboyes	Dn	160	Douglas	John	Moynes	Cv	10
Dixon	Symond	Clannaboyes	Dn	169	Douglas	John	Lynox	Dl	129
Dixon	Thomas	Kildare	Dn	142	Douglas	John	Bp Dromore	Dn	171
Dixon	Thomas	Clannaboyes	Dn	161	Douglas	John	Londonderry	Ly	86
Dixon	Thomas	Clannaboyes	Dn	161	Douglas	John	Haberdashers	Ly	88
Dixon	Thomas	Clannaboyes	Dn	161	Douglas	John	Erskin	Ty	57
Dixon	Thomas	Clannaboyes	Dn	169	Douglas	John	Sanderson	Ty	66
Dixon younger	Thomas	Clannaboyes	Dn	169	Douglas	John	Strabane T.	Ty	76
Dixon	William	Willson	Dl	132	Douglas	Richard	Abp Armagh	Ty	77
Dixon	William	Crumwell	Dn	145	Douglas	Robert	Londonderry	Ly	86
Dixon	William	Clannaboyes	Dn	162	Douglas	Thomas	Clannaboyes	Dn	165
Dixon	William	Bp Dromore	Dn	171	Douglas	William	Lynox	Dl	128
Dixon	William	Bp Dromore	Dn	172	Douglas	William	Annandall	Dl	137
Doake	William	Londonderry	Ly	86	Douglas	William	Chichester	Dl	139
Dobbin	Alexander	Ards	Dn	155	Douglas	William	Ards	Dn	156
Dobbin	William	Ards	Dn	152	Douglas	William	Bp Dromore	Dn	171
Dobbison	James	Ards	Dn	149	Douglass	James	Ards	Dn	154
Dobby	James	Ards	Dn	151	Douglass	John	Ards	Dn	151
Dobby	John	Antrim	An	115	Douglass	Robert	Antrim	An	118
Dobby	Michaell	Ards	Dn	151	Douglass	William	Ards	Dn	152
Dobby	Robert	Merchant Taylors	Ly	92	Dow	John	Mountnorrice	Ar	28
Dobid	George	Melvin	Dn	172	Doway	Sammuell	Londonderry	Ly	84
Dobison	Alexander	Ards	Dn	154	Dowdall	John	Cavan T.	Cv	16
Dobson	Jacob	Cope	Ar	19	Dowdall	Randall	Londonderry	Ly	87
Dobson	Thomas	Sir A. Steward	Ty	64	Dowe	Allen	Moynes	Cv	10
Dod	William	Poyntes	Ar	32	Dowe	Henry	Satcheuerall	Ar	24
Dods	Alexander	Clannaboyes	Dn	165	Dowell	Thomas	Ards	Dn	154
Doggin	William	Mercers	Ly	96	Dower	William	Satcheuerall	Ar	25
Donagh	Thomas	Ards	Dn	148	Dowgan	William	Clannaboyes	Dn	161
Donald	Malcolme	Clannaboyes	Dn	164	Dowglas	William	Mountnorrice	Ar	27
Donald	Robert	Clannaboyes	Dn	164	Dowkes	William	Amis & Greeneham	Cv	11
Donald	Robert	Clannaboyes	Dn	168	Downes	Robert	Grocers	Ly	91
Donaldson	John	Londonderry	Ly	83	Downwoodders	Thomas	Ards	Dn	155
Donaldson	William	Bp Down etc	Dn	170	Dowxkes	John	Bp Kilmore	Cv	15
Donan	John	Edmonston	An	120	Dowxkes	Thomas	Bp Kilmore	Cv	15
Donan	John	Edmonston	An	121	Dragford	Richard	Mercers	Ly	96
Donan	John	Edmonston	An	121	Drakefoord	Thomas	Coleraine	Ly	100
Doneld	John	Ards	Dn	152	Dranan	James	Antrim	An	113
Dongelson	John	Clannaboyes	Dn	161	Dranan	Mathew	Antrim	An	114
Donnalson	John	Ards	Dn	148	Draper	Henry	Calfield	Ar	35
Donne	William	Satcheuerall	Ar	24	Draydon	William	Bp Clougher	Ty	78
Donnell	Alexander	Adare	An	119	Draydon younger	William	Bp Clougher	Ty	78
Donnell	Andrew	Clannaboyes	Dn	159	Drayton	Richard	Mercers	Ly	95
Donnell	Andrew	Erskin	Ty	56	Drenan	David	Clannaboyes	Dn	157
Donnell younger	Andrew	Antrim	An	116	Drennan	Fargus	Clannaboyes	Dn	167
Donnell	Cuthbert	Clannaboyes	Dn	157	Drinker	Bartholemew	Melvin	Dn	172
Donnell	Cuthbert	Maghera & Desert Martin	Ly	107	Drisdall	John	Ards	Dn	152
Donnell	David	Clannaboyes	Dn	157	Drisdall	John	Ards	Dn	154
Donnell	George	Clannaboyes	Dn	164	Drody	Edward	Edmonston	An	120
Donnell	John	Clannaboyes	Dn	157	Drody	Edward	Edmonston	An	121
Donnell	John	Clannaboyes	Dn	157	Dromeed	James	Sir W. Steward	Ty	60
Donnell	William	Clannaboyes	Dn	158	Dromfeild	Hector	Chichester	Ty	78
Donnelson	John	Antrim	An	117	Dromond	James	Lynox	Dl	128
Donnelson	John	Londonderry	Ly	86	Dronan	Thomas	Bp Down etc	Dn	170
Donnelson	Robert	Clannaboyes	Dn	165	Dronry	William	Crumwell	Dn	145
Donniell	Claud	Bp Rapho	Dl	138	Drowry	Gerrard	Drapers	Ly	98
Donnold	William	Edmonston	An	121	Drune	John	Antrim	An	118
Donwooddy	Thomas	Clannaboyes	Dn	162	Drury	Thomas	Londonderry	Ly	82
Dony	David	Mervin	Ty	69	Drynam	Thomas	Clannaboyes	Dn	168

Surname	Forename	Estate	Co.	Page
Edmonston	John	Edmonston	An	121
Edmonston	Robert	Edmonston	An	121
Edward	John	Bp Rapho	Dl	137
Edward	Robert	Clothworkers	Ly	90
Edwards	John	Melvin	Dn	172
Edwards	Morgan	Abp Armagh	Ty	77
Edwards	William	Hastings	Ty	68
Egells	William	Upton	An	124
Eglene	Hugh	Ards	Dn	150
Egleson	James	Ards	Dn	151
Egleson	John	Vintners	Ly	97
Egleson	William	Ards	Dn	155
Egleston	John	Clannaboyes	Dn	162
Egleston younger	John	Clannaboyes	Dn	162
Egleston	Thomas	Clannaboyes	Dn	162
Ekally	Gilbert	Ards	Dn	150
Ekey	Robert	Atchison	Ar	28
Ekleene	Mathew	Ards	Dn	149
Elcock	John	Cope	Ar	20
Elcock	Richard	Cope	Ar	20
Elder	Peter	Chichester	Dl	140
Eling	John	Londonderry	Ly	85
Elipham	William	Antrim	An	112
Ellcock younger	John	Cope	Ar	19
Ellet	Arthur	Newton	Ty	80
Ellet	Symond	Lord Primate	Ar	35
Elliot	Paul	Chichester	Dl	139
Elliott	Adam	Sir F. Hammelton	Cv	5
Ellis	Edward	Mercers	Ly	96
Ellis	John	Hannings	Fe	44
Ellis	Robert	Mercers	Ly	96
Ellis	Thomas	Mansfield	Dl	131
Ellot	Andrew	Erskin	Ty	57
Ellot	Andrew	Parsons	Ty	62
Ellot	Andrew	Richardson	Ty	67
Ellot	Andrew	Richardson	Ty	67
Ellot	Arch	Newton	Ty	80
Ellot	Archbald	Richardson	Ty	67
Ellot	Archbald	Lyndsay	Ty	67
Ellot	Archbald	Lyndsay	Ty	68
Ellot	Archball	Poyntes	Ar	32
Ellot	Archball	Lord Primate	Ar	33
Ellot	Archball	Hastings	Fe	53
Ellot	Archball	A. Hammelton	Ty	63
Ellot	Archbell	Gower	Fe	53
Ellot younger	Archbell	Gower	Fe	53
Ellot	Christopher	Bp Kilmore	Cv	15
Ellot	David	Cole	Fe	52
Ellot	Francis	Richardson	Ty	67
Ellot	Francis	Richardson	Ty	67
Ellot	Gawen	Mrs Hammelton	Fe	41
Ellot	Gawen	Newton	Ty	80
Ellot	Gawyn	Butler	Cv	2
Ellot	Gawyn	Waldrune	Cv	8
Ellot	George	Annandall	Dl	136
Ellot	George	Annandall	Dl	137
Ellot	Gilbert	Berresfourd	Ly	106
Ellot	Hector	Sanderson	Ty	66
Ellot	Herbert	Sir W. Steward	Ty	59
Ellot	James	G. Hume	Fe	43
Ellot	James	Richardson	Ty	67
Ellot	James	Chichester	Ty	78
Ellot	John	Hammelton	Ar	30
Ellot	John	Ards	Dn	148
Ellot	John	Cole	Fe	40
Ellot	John	Dillon	Fe	52
Ellot	John	Atkinson	Fe	52
Ellot	John	Gower	Fe	52
Ellot	John	Hastings	Fe	53
Ellot	John	A. Hammelton	Ty	63
Ellot	John	Lyndsay	Ty	67
Ellot	John	Strabane T.	Ty	76
Ellot	John	Abp Armagh	Ty	76
Ellot	John	Chichester	Ty	78
Ellot younger	John	Gower	Fe	53
Ellot	Lancelot	Sir A. Steward	Ty	64
Ellot	Marke	Mrs Hammelton	Fe	41
Ellot	Marke	Richardson	Ty	67
Ellot	Marke	Richardson	Ty	67
Ellot	Martin	Sir J. Hume	Fe	42
Ellot	Martin	Dillon	Fe	52
Ellot elder	Martin	Dillon	Fe	52
Ellot	Mungo	Mrs Hammelton	Fe	41
Ellot	Nynyan	Waldrune	Cv	8
Ellot	Randall	Dillon	Fe	51
Ellot	Robert	Hammelton	Ar	30
Ellot	Robert	Richardson	Ar	36
Ellot	Robert	Mrs Hammelton	Fe	41
Ellot	Robert	Dillon	Fe	52
Ellot	Robert	L. Blennerhasset	Fe	53
Ellot	Robert	Erskin	Ty	57
Ellot	Robert	Sir A. Steward	Ty	65
Ellot	Robert	Richardson	Ty	67
Ellot	Robert	Lyndsay	Ty	68
Ellot	Robert	Lyndsay	Ty	68
Ellot	Robert	Abp Armagh	Ty	77
Ellot younger	Robert	Dillon	Fe	52
Ellot	Rynyon	Moynes	Cv	11
Ellot	Thomas	Gower	Fe	53
Ellot	Thomas	Hastings	Fe	53
Ellot	Thomas	Hastings	Fe	53
Ellot	Thomas	Sir A. Steward	Ty	64
Ellot	William	Mountnorrice	Ar	27
Ellot	William	Poyntes	Ar	33
Ellot	William	Annandall	Dl	136
Ellot	William	Ballfowre	Fe	39
Ellot	William	Archdall	Fe	40
Ellot	William	Archdall	Fe	40
Ellot	William	Archdall	Fe	40
Ellot	William	Mrs Hammelton	Fe	41
Ellot	William	Gower	Fe	53
Ellot	William	Hastings	Fe	53
Ellot	William	Lord Primate	Ly	106
Ellot	William	Erskin	Ty	57
Ellot	William	A. Hammelton	Ty	63
Ellot	William	Lyndsay	Ty	67
Ellot	William	Lyndsay	Ty	68
Ellot	William	Newton	Ty	80
Ellott	William	Mrs Hammelton	Fe	41
Elly	John	Chichester	Dl	139
Elman	James	Antrim	An	115
Elshinter	Andrew	Bp Rapho	Dl	138
Elshinter	Symon	Bp Rapho	Dl	138
Elshintor	Thomas	Bp Rapho	Dl	137
Elton	Michaell	Erskin	Ty	57
Elwood	George	Butler	Cv	3
Emery	Jeremy	L. Blennerhasset	Fe	45
Enerat	James	Fullerton	Fe	54
Enerrington	Mathew	Butler	Cv	2
Enery	John	J. Conningham	Dl	135
English	Andrew	Crumwell	Dn	144
English	David	Lyndsay	Ty	67
English	Henry	Chichester	Dl	140
English	James	Ards	Dn	153
English	John	Sir A. Steward	Ty	64
English	John	Sir A. Steward	Ty	65
English	Robert	Bp Dromore	Dn	171
Enman	Thomas	Satcheuerall	Ar	25
Eorill	Ralph	Harrington	Dl	134
Epfall	John	Ironmongers	Ly	95
Epfull	Robert	Ironmongers	Ly	94
Erd	Hugh	Antrim	An	113
Eridgson	Robert	Maghera & Desert Martin	Ly	107
Erskin	Mathew	F. Blennerhasset	Fe	45
Erskin	William	Erskin	Ty	56
Erskin	William	Erskin	Ty	58
Eskin	William	Ards	Dn	152
Eskine	Robert	Ards	Dn	150
Esson	Richard	Lord Primate	Ar	34
Estone	John	Adare	An	120
Ethington	David	Lord Primate	Ar	34
Euance	Edward	Davis	Dl	134

Surname	Forename	Estate	Co.	Page	Surname	Forename	Estate	Co.	Page
Fitzpatrick	Gawin	Crag	Cv	6	Foster	David	Adare	An	120
Fixter	Richard	Erskin	Ty	56	Foster	Edward	Crumwell	Dn	145
Fixter	William	Londonderry	Ly	85	Foster	Gabraehell	Drapers	Ly	98
Flack	Fergus	Hammelton	Ar	30	Foster	George	Loftus	Mo	174
Flack	John	Crumwell	Dn	143	Foster	James	Lyndsay	Ty	68
Flack	Nevin	Clannaboyes	Dn	166	Foster	John	Cahoune	Dl	134
Flaintstone	Alexander	Kildare	Dn	142	Foster	John	Ards	Dn	155
Flamming	James	Strabane T.	Ty	74	Foster	John	Coleraine	Ly	100
Fleck	John	Hammelton	Ar	30	Foster	John	H. Steward	Ty	66
Flecker	Gregory	Moynes	Cv	11	Foster younger	John	Ards	Dn	155
Fleete	Robert	Antrim	An	116	Foster	Lancelot	Drapers	Ly	98
Fleming	Adam	Sir J. Conningham	Dl	129	Foster	Nicholas	Sir W. Steward	Ty	59
Fleming	Archbald	Sir J. Conningham	Dl	130	Foster	Patrick	Haberdashers	Ly	89
Fleming	Gibert	Sir J. Conningham	Dl	130	Foster	Richard	Crumwell	Dn	145
Fleming	James	Antrim	An	113	Foster	Richard	Archdall	Fe	41
Fleming	James	Harrington	Dl	134	Foster	Robert	Waldrum	Ar	22
Fleming	James	M. of Abbercorne	Ty	72	Foster	Robert	Atchison	Ar	28
Fleming	John	Sir J. Conningham	Dl	130	Foster	Robert	Mrs Hammelton	Fe	41
Fleming	John	Willson	Dl	132	Foster	Robert	Maghera & Desert Martin	Ly	107
Fleming	John	Clannaboyes	Dn	167	Foster younger	Robert	Crumwell	Dn	143
Fleming	Patt:	Sir J. Conningham	Dl	130	Foster	Thomas	Waldrum	Ar	22
Fleming	Robert	Bp Rapho	Dl	138	Foster	Thomas	Drapers	Ly	98
Flemming	James	Londonderry	Ly	83	Foster	Zacary	Stanhow	Ar	23
Flemming	James	Goldsmiths	Ly	92	Fouchon	Richard	Coleraine	Ly	100
Flemming	William	Londonderry	Ly	84	Foud	John	Antrim	An	117
Flent	William	Butler	Fe	49	Fould	Patrick	Sir J. Conningham	Dl	129
Flesher	James	Antrim	An	112	Foulton	Ninian	Lady Conningham	Dl	130
Fletcher	Patrick	Phillips	Ly	104	Foulton	Robert	Bp Rapho	Dl	138
Flewry	John	Hammelton	Ar	29	Fourber	Anthony	Butler	Cv	4
Flock	John	Dalloway	An	122	Fourber	John	Butler	Cv	4
Flood	John	Crumwell	Dn	146	Fowell	John	Londonderry	Ly	84
Florry	John	Waldrum	Ar	22	Fowler elder	John	Coleraine	Ly	103
Florry	Thomas	Hammelton	Ar	30	Frag	Steaphen	Sir J. Conningham	Dl	130
Flowery	Sampson	Cope	Ar	20	Frame	Henry	Clannaboyes	Dn	167
Flyn	James	Clannaboyes	Dn	167	Frame	Henry	Clannaboyes	Dn	169
Flyng	John	Chichester	Dl	139	Francis	Richard	Lord Primate	Ar	34
Foord	John	Phillips	Ly	105	Francye	William	Antrim	An	116
Foothey	John	Antrim	An	112	Frankley	George	Kildare	Dn	142
Foothey	Robert	Antrim	An	112	Franklin	Arnold	Cope	Ar	25
Foothey	Robert	Antrim	An	114	Franncis	Richard	Chichester	Dl	140
Forbee	Richard	Hammelton	Ar	30	Frasch	Symon	Haberdashers	Ly	90
Forbes	William	Londonderry	Ly	83	Fraser	Hugh	Ards	Dn	154
Forborne	Anthony	Butler	Cv	3	Fraser	Thomas	J. Hammelton	Cv	12
Forborne	Jaly	Butler	Cv	3	Frass	John	Ards	Dn	154
Forborne	Thomas	Butler	Cv	3	Frassall	Thomas	Ards	Dn	154
Forbus	Edward	Sir W. Steward	Ty	59	Frasser	John	Ards	Dn	149
Forbus	John	Ards	Dn	152	Frasser	William	Haberdashers	Ly	89
Ford	John	Enniskillen T.	Fe	51	Fray	Nicholas	Vintners	Ly	98
Foreman	David	Clatworthy	An	122	Free	Walter	Butler	Fe	50
Forker	John	Sir F. Hammelton	Cv	5	Freeman	Edward	Londonderry	Ly	86
Forkhead	Thomas	Clatworthy	An	124	Freeman	Henry	Londonderry	Ly	86
Forley	David	Crosby	Ty	69	Freeman	Thomas	Powerscourt	Ty	79
Forman	Robert	Clatworthy	An	122	Freind	John	Clannaboyes	Dn	164
Formont	George	Bp Dromore	Dn	171	Freman	Mathew	Butler	Fe	50
Forrest	Alexander	Clannaboyes	Dn	157	Freman	Thomas	Butler	Fe	50
Forrest	Charles	Cole	Fe	39	Freman	Thomas	Londonderry	Ly	88
Forrest	James	Clannaboyes	Dn	162	French	James	Clatworthy	An	123
Forrest	James	Clannaboyes	Dn	168	Frezell	John	Tychborne	Ty	60
Forrest	John	Clannaboyes	Dn	159	Frezell	William	Mervin	Ty	69
Forrest	John	Clannaboyes	Dn	163	Frihall	George	Ballfowre	Fe	38
Forrest younger	John	Clannaboyes	Dn	163	Frissell	Alexander	Sir F. Hammelton	Cv	5
Forrest	Thomas	Cole	Fe	40	Frissell	George	Sir F. Hammelton	Cv	5
Forrest	William	Clannaboyes	Dn	163	Frith	John	Enniskillen T.	Fe	51
Forrest	William	Sir W. Steward	Ty	59	Frizell	Andrew	Crag	Cv	6
Forrester	Andrew	Ards	Dn	152	Frizell	Archbald	Coleraine	Ly	102
Forret	John	Sir J. Conningham	Dl	129	Frizell	James	Annandall	Dl	137
Forsith	Andrew	Edmonston	An	121	Frizell	John	Antrim	An	118
Forsith	Andrew	Ards	Dn	147	Frizell	John	Sir J. Conningham	Dl	130
Forsith	Andrew	Clannaboyes	Dn	157	Frizell	John	Willson	Dl	132
Forsith	John	Ards	Dn	147	Frizell	John	Annandall	Dl	137
Forsith	John	Clannaboyes	Dn	159	Frizell	John	Ards	Dn	149
Forsith	William	Ards	Dn	152	Frizell	John	Ards	Dn	151
Forsyth	James	Sir J. Conningham	Dl	130	Frizell	John	Ards	Dn	156
Fortick	William	Coleraine	Ly	103	Frizell younger	John	Sir J. Conningham	Dl	129
Fostall	James	Sanderson	Ty	66	Frizell	Patrick	Hastings	Fe	53
Foster	Arthur	Higget	Fe	46	Frizell	Walter	Dillon	Fe	52

Surname	Forename	Estate	Co.	Page
Gardner	William	Londonderry	Ly	82
Gardner younger	William	Londonderry	Ly	82
Garlebang	James	Antrim	An	115
Garlick	Edward	H. Steward	Ty	66
Garlick	Edward	H. Steward	Ty	66
Garnen	Andrew	Ards	Dn	148
Garnor	William	Clatworthy	An	122
Garrald	Donnogh	Phillips	Ly	104
Garrat	John	Satcheuerall	Ar	23
Garrat	Sammuell	Satcheuerall	Ar	24
Garrat	Steven	Crumwell	Dn	146
Garthy	William	Phillips	Ly	104
Garvan	John	Antrim	An	111
Garvance	Adam	Lady Conningham	Dl	130
Garven	James	Ironmongers	Ly	95
Garvin	Robert	Clothworkers	Ly	90
Garvye	Henry	Crag	Cv	6
Garvye	Neyman	Coleraine	Ly	102
Garwen	Thomas	Antrim	An	115
Garyner	John	Sir F. Hammelton	Cv	6
Gass	David	Hammelton	Ar	30
Gasse	George	Hammelton	Ar	31
Gasse	Peter	Clothworkers	Ly	91
Gassron	William	Hill	An	121
Gate	Adam	Grocers	Ly	91
Gate	John	Goldsmiths	Ly	92
Gate	John	Goldsmiths	Ly	92
Gate	Thomas	Ironmongers	Ly	94
Gate	William	Antrim	An	112
Gate	William	Clothworkers	Ly	90
Gates	Thomas	Satcheuerall	Ar	25
Gath	George	Sanderson	Ty	66
Gath	George	Symonton	Ty	67
Gath	James	Symonton	Ty	66
Gath younger	John	Sanderson	Ty	66
Gather	William	Butler	Cv	2
Gaut	Paul	Ironmongers	Ly	94
Gaute	Paul	Coleraine	Ly	101
Gawen	George	Chichester	Dl	140
Gawhones	Gilbert	Lord Primate	Ar	33
Gawnes	Thomas	Antrim	An	112
Gay	Alexander	Clannaboyes	Dn	158
Gay	James	Clannaboyes	Dn	166
Gay	John	Londonderry	Ly	88
Gay	Richard	Ards	Dn	156
Gay	William	Phillips	Ly	105
Gealton	John	Crumwell	Dn	144
Geat	Christopher	Bp Rapho	Dl	138
Geddes	James	Clannaboyes	Dn	163
Geimmell	James	Ards	Dn	151
Gelard	John	Coleraine	Ly	101
Gelderson	William	Coleraine	Ly	100
Gellaspy	John	Sir F. Hammelton	Cv	6
Gelly	Gawen	Crumwell	Dn	143
Gelly	Guy	Kildare	Dn	142
Gelston	John	Clannaboyes	Dn	160
Gely	John	Bp Down etc	Dn	170
Gemell	Gilbert	Antrim	An	115
Gemell	James	Antrim	An	116
Gemell	Robert	Antrim	An	118
Gemell	William	Antrim	An	115
Gemill	James	Clannaboyes	Dn	165
Gemill	John	Antrim	An	113
Gemill	John	Clannaboyes	Dn	158
Gemmell	James	J. Hammelton	Cv	12
Gemmell	Mathew	J. Hammelton	Cv	12
Gemmell	William	Antrim	An	111
Gemmill	Alexander	Antrim	An	110
Gemmill	George	Clannaboyes	Dn	160
Gemmill	John	Clannaboyes	Dn	160
Gemmill	William	Antrim	An	110
Gemmill	William	Clannaboyes	Dn	160
Gemmill	William	Clannaboyes	Dn	160
Gennivill	John	J. Hammelton	Cv	12
Gennivill	William	J. Hammelton	Cv	12
Genniwill	James	J. Hammelton	Cv	12

Surname	Forename	Estate	Co.	Page
Genvill	Mathew	J. Hammelton	Cv	12
George	Alexander	Antrim	An	115
George	Andrew	Antrim	An	113
George	Andrew	Lady Conningham	Dl	131
George	John	Clannaboyes	Dn	165
George	John	Haberdashers	Ly	88
George	John	Phillips	Ly	104
George	John	Phillips	Ly	105
Geratt	Robert	Dillon	Ar	21
Gercen	Robert	Atchison	Ar	28
Gerin	John	Sir A. Steward	Ty	65
German	Mathew	Hammelton	Ar	30
German	Symond	Lord Primate	Ar	33
Gerr	William	Antrim	An	110
Gesson	William	Mercers	Ly	95
Getty	George	Antrim	An	114
Getty	John	Antrim	An	111
Getty	John	Antrim	An	114
Gety	John	Antrim	An	118
Ghasright	Robert	Sir A. Steward	Ty	64
Ghay	Martyn	Edmonston	An	121
Gib	James	Strabane T.	Ty	73
Gibb	Allen	Hannings	Fe	44
Gibb	David	Lynox	Dl	129
Gibb	John	Sir A. Steward	Ty	65
Gibb	Robert	Clannaboyes	Dn	159
Gibbins	John	Newton	Ty	80
Gibbins	William	Newton	Ty	80
Gibbon	Robert	Waldrum	Ar	22
Gibbone	Patrick	Phillips	Ly	105
Gibbs	John	Cole	Fe	39
Gibbs	John	Powerscourt	Ty	79
Gibbs	Robert	Brownlow	Ar	26
Gibbs	Roger	Brownlow	Ar	26
Gibbs	William	Butler	Cv	3
Gibby	John	Ards	Dn	147
Gibs	George	Ards	Dn	153
Gibson	Adam	Ards	Dn	152
Gibson	Adam	Clannaboyes	Dn	167
Gibson	Alexander	Bp Rapho	Dl	138
Gibson	David	Clatworthy	An	123
Gibson	David	Ards	Dn	147
Gibson	David	Ards	Dn	149
Gibson	David	Ards	Dn	154
Gibson	Edward	Atchison	Ar	29
Gibson	Gabrarll	Ballfowre	Fe	39
Gibson	George	Clannaboyes	Dn	160
Gibson	George	Sir J. Hume	Fe	42
Gibson	James	Ards	Dn	153
Gibson	James	Clannaboyes	Dn	156
Gibson	James	Ironmongers	Ly	94
Gibson	James	Coleraine	Ly	103
Gibson	John	Antrim	An	112
Gibson	John	Antrim	An	117
Gibson	John	Reding	An	121
Gibson	John	Dalloway	An	122
Gibson	John	Dalloway	An	122
Gibson	John	Clatworthy	An	124
Gibson	John	Atchison	Ar	28
Gibson	John	J. Hammelton	Cv	12
Gibson	John	Mrs Hammelton	Cv	14
Gibson	John	Ards	Dn	147
Gibson	John	Ards	Dn	148
Gibson	John	Ards	Dn	153
Gibson	John	Ards	Dn	153
Gibson	John	Clannaboyes	Dn	167
Gibson	John	Bp Dromore	Dn	172
Gibson	John	G. Hume	Fe	43
Gibson	John	Londonderry	Ly	82
Gibson	John	Sir W. Steward	Ty	58
Gibson	John	Abp Armagh	Ty	77
Gibson younger	John	Ards	Dn	148
Gibson	Michaell	Ards	Dn	150
Gibson	Patrick	Ards	Dn	150
Gibson	Patrick	Clannaboyes	Dn	168
Gibson	Peter	Chichester	Dl	140

Surname	Forename	Estate	Co.	Page	Surname	Forename	Estate	Co.	Page
Gibson	Richard	Benson	Dl	132	Gilpatrick	John	Clannaboyes	Dn	162
Gibson	Richard	Clannaboyes	Dn	160	Gilpatricke	Alexander	Crosby	Ty	69
Gibson	Robert	Crumwell	Dn	143	Gilpatricke	Francis	Erskin	Ty	57
Gibson	Robert	Crumwell	Dn	145	Gilsoe	Gawin	Phillips	Ly	104
Gibson	Robert	Ards	Dn	150	Ginlyn	William	Auldridg	Mo	175
Gibson	Robert	Clannaboyes	Dn	157	Girlie	Robert	Fish	Cv	14
Gibson	Robert	Clannaboyes	Dn	160	Girly	Ninian	Clannaboyes	Dn	166
Gibson	Thomas	Ironmongers	Ly	94	Girthrig	James	Clannaboyes	Dn	159
Gibson	Thomas	Coleraine	Ly	102	Girthrig	James	Clannaboyes	Dn	159
Gibson	William	Atchison	Cv	7	Girwan	John	Sir A. Steward	Ty	64
Gibson	William	Benson	Dl	133	Gisley	Arthur	Lord Primate	Ar	34
Gibson	William	Londonderry	Ly	84	Glandoney	John	Chichester	Dl	140
Gidds	George	Ards	Dn	153	Glanine	Gilbert	Clannaboyes	Dn	159
Gieffe	Mathew	J. Conningham	Dl	135	Glansy	Thomas	Bp Down etc	Dn	170
Giffeinge	David	Goldsmiths	Ly	92	Glascag	John	Melvin	Dn	172
Giffen elder	John	Chichester	Dl	139	Glascoe	Mathew	Ards	Dn	151
Giffin	Sallomon	Lady Conningham	Dl	131	Glaser	Tymothy	Fish	Cv	14
Gifford	Christopher	Londonderry	Ly	85	Glasford	Hugh	Bp Dromore	Dn	171
Gilbert	John	Antrim	An	110	Glasgowe	Hugh	Ards	Dn	155
Gilchrist	James	Clannaboyes	Dn	162	Glasier	Thomas	Fish	Cv	14
Gilchrist	John	Clannaboyes	Dn	165	Glaspeck	Andrew	Sir F. Hammelton	Cv	6
Gildony	William	Parsons	Ty	62	Glaspeck	William	Sir F. Hammelton	Cv	6
Gilespy	Andrew	Sir F. Hammelton	Cv	5	Glass	Alexander	Londonderry	Ly	87
Gill	Edward	Cope	Ar	26	Glass	Patrick	Bp Down etc	Dn	170
Gill	Francis	Merchant Taylors	Ly	92	Glass	Robert	Lynox	Dl	128
Gill	Hugh	Crumwell	Dn	146	Glass	Robert	Ards	Dn	153
Gill	Nicholas	Merchant Taylors	Ly	92	Glass	William	Londonderry	Ly	82
Gill	Thomas	Coleraine	Ly	103	Gledony	Nynyan	Coape	Ty	62
Gillaspeck	John	Crumwell	Dn	144	Gledry	William	Ards	Dn	150
Gillaspick	John	Vintners	Ly	97	Gledston	John	Bp Clougher	Ty	77
Gillaspy	James	Antrim	An	113	Gleen	John	Haberdashers	Ly	89
Gillaspy	James	Parsons	Ty	62	Gleene	James	J. Hammelton	Cv	12
Gillaspy	John	Antrim	An	110	Gleene	Jeremy	Enniskillen T.	Fe	51
Gillaspy	John	A. Steward	Dl	135	Gleene	John	Haberdashers	Ly	88
Gillaspy	John	Parsons	Ty	61	Glen	Alexander	Sir W. Hammilton	Ty	73
Gillaspy	Richard	Sanderson	Ty	66	Glen	Archbald	Sir W. Hammilton	Ty	73
Gillaspy	Thomas	Parsons	Ty	61	Glen	James	J. Hammelton	Cv	12
Gillaspy	William	Sanderson	Ty	66	Glen	John	Atchison	Cv	7
Gilleland	John	Phillips	Ly	104	Glen	William	Mansfield	Dl	131
Gillerson	James	Antrim	An	110	Glen	William	Clannaboyes	Dn	166
Gillespi	John	J. Hammelton	Cv	12	Glencourse	Michaell	Antrim	An	117
Gillespicke	Alexander	Ards	Dn	148	Glendidge	George	Haberdashers	Ly	88
Gillespike	John	Ards	Dn	155	Glendidge	William	Haberdashers	Ly	88
Gillespy	Thomas	Erskin	Ty	56	Glendining	Adam	Clannaboyes	Dn	162
Gillespy	William	Sir F. Hammelton	Cv	6	Glendining	Arch:	Auldridg	Mo	175
Gillies	Alexander	Clannaboyes	Dn	157	Glendining	Wm	Ards	Dn	154
Gilliner	John	Clothworkers	Ly	90	Glendininne	John	Maghera & Desert Martin	Ly	107
Gillinows	Robert	Parsons	Ty	62	Glendininne	Walter	Maghera & Desert Martin	Ly	107
Gillis	Thomas	Sir A. Steward	Ty	64	Glendininy	John	Melvin	Dn	172
Gillispick	John	Sir F. Hammelton	Cv	4	Glendinning	William	Clannaboyes	Dn	169
Gillmoore	Robert	Phillips	Ly	104	Glendonagh	Andrew	Coape	Ty	62
Gillmoore	Thomas	Ards	Dn	148	Glendonagh	Archball	Coape	Ty	62
Gillmoore	Thomas	Ards	Dn	153	Glendonagh	John	Coape	Ty	62
Gillmore	David	Harrington	Dl	134	Glendonagh	William	Coape	Ty	62
Gillmore	James	J. Conningham	Dl	135	Glendoney	Adam	Coape	Ty	63
Gillmore	Robert	Sir A. Steward	Ty	65	Glendony	Gawen	Atchison	Ar	28
Gillpatrick	John	Antrim	An	110	Glendony	John	Boocer	Ar	32
Gillpatrick	John	Cole	Fe	39	Glenduning	James	Lyndsay	Ty	68
Gillrew	Mathew	Lynox	Dl	129	Glendunning	Adam	Lyndsay	Ty	67
Gills	John	J. Conningham	Dl	135	Glene	John	Haberdashers	Ly	90
Gills	Robert	Clatworthy	An	124	Glene	William	Ballfowre	Fe	39
Gilmoore	Alexander	Ards	Dn	147	Glenn	William	Haberdashers	Ly	88
Gilmoore	Andrew	Clothworkers	Ly	90	Glentrot	Robert	Crumwell	Dn	144
Gilmoore	James	Clothworkers	Ly	90	Glover	Edward	Coleraine	Ly	99
Gilmoore	Symond	Clannaboyes	Dn	156	Glover	John	Clatworthy	An	123
Gilmoore	Thomas	Clothworkers	Ly	90	Glover	Richard	Vintners	Ly	97
Gilmoore	William	Clannaboyes	Dn	161	Glover	Rowland	Flowerdew	Fe	44
Gilmoore	William	Clannaboyes	Dn	166	Glyne	Thomas	Chichester	Dl	139
Gilmoore	William	Bp Down etc	Dn	170	Glynon	George	Lyndsay	Ty	68
Gilmoore younger	William	Clannaboyes	Dn	161	Gnasson	Robert	Clannaboyes	Dn	168
Gilmore	John	Ards	Dn	147	Gnesse	John	Antrim	An	115
Gilmore	John	Dunbar	Fe	48	Goathead	Thomas	Butler	Cv	3
Gilmore	Thomas	Edmonston	An	121	Goathead	Thomas	Butler	Cv	4
Gilmour	James	C. of Abbercorne	Ty	71	Gobbet	John	Grandison	Ar	32
Gilpatrick	Daniell	Erskin	Ty	57	Goddar	Nicholas	Stanhow	Ar	23
Gilpatrick	John	Atchison	Cv	7	Goddy	John	Crumwell	Dn	144

Surname	Forename	Estate	Co.	Page	Surname	Forename	Estate	Co.	Page
Godfrey	Edward	Calfield	Ar	36	Gourden	William	Ards	Dn	154
Godfrey	George	Berresfourd	Ly	106	Gourden	William	Clannaboyes	Dn	169
Godfrey	Humphrey	Chichester	Ty	78	Gourdner	Archball	Crag	Cv	6
Godfrey	John	Chichester	Ty	78	Gourdon	Alexander	Antrim	An	113
Godfrey	Steaphen	Londonderry	Ly	84	Gourdon	Andrew	Antrim	An	114
Goffock	John	Clannaboyes	Dn	163	Gourdon	George	Atchison	Ar	28
Goldsmith	John	Londonderry	Ly	87	Gourdon	James	Crumwell	Dn	143
Golly	Andrew	Clannaboyes	Dn	163	Gourdon	John	Annandall	Dl	136
Golly	Andrew	Clannaboyes	Dn	168	Gourdon	John	Ards	Dn	148
Good younger	John	Lowther	Fe	44	Gourdon	John	Clannaboyes	Dn	165
Good	Richard	Lowther	Fe	43	Gourdon	John	Lyndsay	Ty	68
Good	Robert	Lowther	Fe	43	Gourdon	Patrick	J. Hammelton	Cv	12
Goodbody	John	Bagshaw	Cv	7	Gourdon	Thomas	Clannaboyes	Dn	165
Goodbody	John	Moynes	Cv	11	Gourdon	William	Clannaboyes	Dn	161
Goodfellow	John	Sir J. Hume	Fe	42	Gourly	Thomas	Ards	Dn	153
Goodfellow	John	Sir J. Hume	Fe	42	Gout	Allen	Ironmongers	Ly	94
younger					Gouthwet	Thomas	Taylor	Cv	10
Goodfellow	Thomas	Sir J. Hume	Fe	42	Gowen	Alexander	Bp Down etc	Dn	170
Goodlad	David	H. Steward	Ty	65	Gowen	John	Adare	An	119
Goodlad	William	H. Steward	Ty	65	Gower	Henry	Crumwell	Dn	146
Goodlet	Patrick	Clannaboyes	Dn	167	Gower	Robert	Brewerton	Fe	54
Goodlet	Patrick	Clannaboyes	Dn	169	Gower	Symond	Cope	Ar	18
Goodman	John	Ballfowre	Fe	38	Gowerly	John	Ards	Dn	153
Goodman	William	Waldrune	Cv	8	Grace	Henry	Lord Primate	Ar	35
Goodman elder	William	Mercers	Ly	96	Grace	William	Crumwell	Dn	145
Goodman	William	Mercers	Ly	96	Grace	William	L. Blennerhasset	Fe	45
younger					Gracy	John	Antrim	An	113
Goodwin	Christopher	Butler	Cv	2	Gracye	John	Kildare	Dn	142
Goodwin	Henry	Lord General	Dn	170	Gradell	Richard	Crumwell	Dn	144
Goodwin	Richard	Mercers	Ly	95	Gradin	Robert	Ballfowre	Fe	39
Goodwin	Thomas	Fish	Cv	14	Gragham	George	Clannaboyes	Dn	167
Goodwin elder	Robert	Londonderry	Ly	85	Graghame	John	Clannaboyes	Dn	164
Goodwin	Robert	Londonderry	Ly	85	Graham	Alexander	A. Hammelton	Ty	63
younger					Graham	Archbald	Coape	Ty	62
Goody	John	Crumwell	Dn	146	Graham	Arthur	Lord Primate	Ar	34
Goody	John	Coleraine	Ly	103	Graham	Arthur	Woorell	Fe	46
Goody	John	Coleraine	Ly	104	Graham	David	Clatworthy	An	123
Goody	William	Strabane T.	Ty	75	Graham	Dunkan	Lynox	Dl	128
Goodyeer	Edward	Londonderry	Ly	82	Graham	Edward	Woorell	Fe	46
Gord	Thomas	Ards	Dn	151	Graham	Edward	Graham	Fe	54
Gordan	Andrew	Mercers	Ly	96	Graham	Fargus	Antrim	An	115
Gordan	John	Upton	An	124	Graham	Fargus	Cole	Fe	40
Gorden	Alexander	Calfield	Ar	36	Graham	Fargus	Erskin	Ty	57
Gorden	John	Sir A. Steward	Ty	64	Graham	Francis	Lord Primate	Ar	34
Gorden	Patrick	Hammelton	Ar	30	Graham	Francis	Graham	Fe	54
Gorden	Roger	Adare	An	119	Graham	Frauncis	Calfield	Ar	36
Gordon	George	Sir W. Steward	Ty	59	Graham	Frauncis	J. Hammelton	Cv	12
Gordon	James	Erskin	Ty	57	Graham	Frauncis	Drowmgowne	Cv	16
Gore	Francis	Powerscourt	Ty	79	Graham younger	Frauncis	Drowmgowne	Cv	16
Gore	James	Lord Primate	Ar	34	Graham	George	Cole	Fe	40
Gore	John	Powerscourt	Ty	79	Graham	George	Sir J. Hume	Fe	42
Gore elder	John	Powerscourt	Ty	79	Graham	George	Woorell	Fe	46
Gore	Robert	Powerscourt	Ty	79	Graham	Herbert	Graham	Fe	54
Gore	William	Crumwell	Dn	146	Graham	Hugh	Graham	Fe	54
Goslop	William	Crag	Cv	7	Graham	James	Butler	Cv	2
Gotier	Robert	Lord General	Dn	170	Graham	James	Taylor	Cv	10
Gouchom	John	Strabane T.	Ty	76	Graham	James	Ballfowre	Fe	38
Goudyere	Humphrey	Crumwell	Dn	146	Graham	James	Sir J. Hume	Fe	42
Gould	Alexander	Ironmongers	Ly	93	Graham	James	Sir W. Steward	Ty	59
Gourdan	Alexander	Ards	Dn	149	Graham	James	Tychborne	Ty	61
Gourdan	John	Ards	Dn	150	Graham	James	Parsons	Ty	62
Gourden	Alexander	Bp Dromore	Dn	171	Graham	James	Newton	Ty	80
Gourden	Andrew	Ards	Dn	150	Graham	John	Antrim	An	113
Gourden	George	Ards	Dn	153	Graham	John	Hammelton	Ar	30
Gourden	James	Crumwell	Dn	144	Graham	John	Sir F. Hammelton	Cv	5
Gourden	John	J. Hammelton	Cv	12	Graham	John	Bp Rapho	Dl	138
Gourden	John	J. Hammelton	Cv	12	Graham	John	Crumwell	Dn	146
Gourden	John	Ards	Dn	147	Graham	John	Mrs Hammelton	Fe	41
Gourden	John	Ards	Dn	149	Graham	John	Lowther	Fe	43
Gourden	John	Ards	Dn	152	Graham	John	Graham	Fe	54
Gourden	John	Ards	Dn	153	Graham	John	Clothworkers	Ly	90
Gourden	John	Mervin	Ty	69	Graham	John	Erskin	Ty	57
Gourden	Patrick	Clannaboyes	Dn	158	Graham	John	Erskin	Ty	57
Gourden	Robert	Ards	Dn	150	Graham	John	Sir W. Steward	Ty	58
Gourden	Robert	Ards	Dn	150	Graham	John	Tychborne	Ty	60
Gourden	Thomas	Ards	Dn	151	Graham	John	Tychborne	Ty	61

Surname	Forename	Estate	Co.	Page
Hammilton	John	Strabane T.	Ty	74
Hammilton	Patrick	Strabane T.	Ty	75
Hammilton	Quinton	Clannaboyes	Dn	160
Hammilton	Quinton	Clannaboyes	Dn	169
Hammilton	Robert	Clatworthy	An	123
Hammilton	Robert	Chichester	Dl	140
Hammilton	Robert	Kingsmell	Dl	131
Hammilton	Robert	Clannaboyes	Dn	157
Hammilton	Robert	Clannaboyes	Dn	157
Hammilton	Robert	Clannaboyes	Dn	157
Hammilton	Robert	Clannaboyes	Dn	159
Hammilton	Robert	Clannaboyes	Dn	165
Hammilton	Robert	Clannaboyes	Dn	168
Hammilton	Robert	Crosby	Ty	69
Hammilton	Robert	Crosby	Ty	69
Hammilton	Robert	Mervin	Ty	70
Hammilton	Robert	M. of Abbercorne	Ty	72
Hammilton	Robert	Sir W. Hammilton	Ty	72
Hammilton	Walter	Londonderry	Ly	84
Hammilton	William	Kildare	Dn	142
Hammilton	William	Ards	Dn	154
Hammilton	William	Clannaboyes	Dn	156
Hammilton	William	Clannaboyes	Dn	160
Hammilton	William	Clannaboyes	Dn	164
Hammilton	William	Strabane T.	Ty	75
Hammilton	Wm	Crumwell	Dn	143
Hamond	Alexander	Lynox	Dl	129
Hamons	John	Berresfourd	Ly	106
Hampton	Henry	Satcheuerall	Ar	24
Hamwell	Robert	Calfield	Ty	79
Hana	Alexander	Crumwell	Dn	145
Hana	Thomas	Ards	Dn	152
Hana	William	Ards	Dn	154
Hanan	Patrick	Crumwell	Dn	144
Hancely	Alford	Londonderry	Ly	88
Hanck	William	Butler	Cv	3
Hancock	Roger	Londonderry	Ly	83
Hancock	Thomas	Butler	Fe	50
Handbridg	Thomas	Butler	Fe	50
Handley	Robert	Coleraine	Ly	102
Hanelawe	John	Clannaboyes	Dn	163
Hanford	John	Londonderry	Ly	88
Haning	John	Ards	Dn	147
Haning	John	Ards	Dn	152
Haning	William	Ards	Dn	150
Hankes	John	Londonderry	Ly	84
Hanley	Joseph	Cope	Ar	18
Hanly	Robert	Coleraine	Ly	103
Hanmor	Thomas	Ironmongers	Ly	95
Hanna	James	Crumwell	Dn	143
Hanna	James	Strabane T.	Ty	75
Hanna	James	Strabane T.	Ty	76
Hanna	John	Crumwell	Dn	143
Hanna	John	Ards	Dn	150
Hanna	John	Clannaboyes	Dn	158
Hanna	John	Erskin	Ty	56
Hanna	John	Erskin	Ty	58
Hanna	Patrick	Crumwell	Dn	144
Hanna	Patrick	Ards	Dn	147
Hanna	Patrick	Ards	Dn	153
Hanna	Thomas	Clannaboyes	Dn	169
Hanna	William	Bp Clougher	Ty	77
Hannagh	Alexander	Clannaboyes	Dn	165
Hannagh	Patrick	Clannaboyes	Dn	165
Hannagh	William	Clannaboyes	Dn	165
Hannay	John	Clannaboyes	Dn	161
Hannay	Thomas	Clannaboyes	Dn	161
Hanny	John	Coleraine	Ly	102
Hanny	William	Coleraine	Ly	102
Hantsworth	Robert	Hannings	Fe	44
Hany	Andrew	Haberdashers	Ly	89
Hany	John	Haberdashers	Ly	89
Hany	Thomas	Ards	Dn	153
Hany	William	Ards	Dn	151
Harbertson	Thomas	Adare	An	119
Harcough	Thomas	Londonderry	Ly	84
Harderson	John	Sir A. Steward	Ty	65
Hardy	Gilbert	Sanderson	Ty	66
Hardyn	Thomas	Clatworthy	An	123
Hare	George	Antrim	An	118
Hare	John	Londonderry	Ly	84
Hare	John	Haberdashers	Ly	89
Hare	John	Haberdashers	Ly	90
Hare	Symond	Londonderry	Ly	83
Hare	Symond	Londonderry	Ly	86
Hargrave	Thomas	Coleraine	Ly	101
Harkalls	George	Benson	Dl	132
Harknes	John	Hammelton	Ar	29
Harknes	John	Clannaboyes	Dn	168
Harknes	William	Clannaboyes	Dn	161
Harland	Peter	Brownlow	Ar	26
Harlore	Christopher	Cole	Fe	40
Harlore	Thomas	Cole	Fe	40
Harnor	John	Dromond	Ty	70
Harp	Alexander	Ards	Dn	155
Harp	James	Ards	Dn	153
Harp	John	Ards	Dn	151
Harp	John	Clannaboyes	Dn	158
Harper	Alexander	Ards	Dn	154
Harper	James	Ards	Dn	155
Harper	James	Clannaboyes	Dn	160
Harper	James	Clannaboyes	Dn	169
Harper	James	Lyndsay	Ty	67
Harper	John	Clatworthy	An	123
Harper	John	J. Conningham	Dl	135
Harper	John	Bp Rapho	Dl	138
Harper	John	Ards	Dn	151
Harper	John	Londonderry	Ly	86
Harper	John	Grocers	Ly	91
Harper	Robert	Adare	An	119
Harper	Robert	Ards	Dn	155
Harper	Robert	Clannaboyes	Dn	164
Harper	Thomas	Clannaboyes	Dn	165
Harper	William	Clatworthy	An	122
Harre	Cutbeart	Adare	An	119
Harrelton	Roger	Adare	An	120
Harrington	John	Londonderry	Ly	87
Harris	Addam	Clannaboyes	Dn	161
Harris	Christopher	Sir A. Steward	Ty	64
Harris	John	Cope	Ar	21
Harris	John	Ards	Dn	154
Harris	John	Ards	Dn	154
Harris	Richard	Ards	Dn	149
Harris	Richard	Vintners	Ly	97
Harris	Robert	Crumwell	Dn	144
Harris	Robert	Crumwell	Dn	145
Harris	Thomas	Satcheuerall	Ar	24
Harris	Thomas	Satcheuerall	Ar	25
Harris	Thomas	Clannaboyes	Dn	157
Harris	Thomas	Powerscourt	Ty	79
Harris	William	Powerscourt	Ty	79
Harrison	Charles	Ironmongers	Ly	95
Harrison	George	F. Blennerhasset	Fe	45
Harrison	Gilbert	Satcheuerall	Ar	25
Harrison	James	Hammelton	Ar	29
Harrison	John	Enniskillen T.	Fe	51
Harrison	John	Londonderry	Ly	84
Harrison	John	Lord Primate	Ar	34
Harrison younger	John			
Harrison	Nathaniell	Maghera & Desert Martin	Ly	106
Harrison	Robert	Brownlow	Ar	27
Harrison	Thomas	Flowerdew	Fe	44
Harrison	William	Dillon	Ar	22
Harrison	William	Ironmongers	Ly	95
Harrison	William	Maghera & Desert Martin	Ly	107
Harshaw	John	Clannaboyes	Dn	160
Harshaw	Robert	Clannaboyes	Dn	160
Harshon	James	Drapers	Ly	98
Hartland	Andrew	Tychborne	Ty	60
Hartnes	James	Bp Dromore	Dn	171
Hartup	Valentyne	Mercers	Ly	95
Harty	Nicholas	Bp Dromore	Dn	172

Surname	Forename	Estate	Co.	Page	Surname	Forename	Estate	Co.	Page
Henry	Alexander	Antrim	An	112	Hill	William	Taylor	Cv	10
Henry	Alexander	Antrim	An	114	Hill	William	Berresfourd	Ly	106
Henry	Gawin	Londonderry	Ly	82	Hillhouse	Alexander	Clannaboyes	Dn	164
Henry	James	Clannaboyes	Dn	163	Hillhowse	John	Clannaboyes	Dn	166
Henry	John	Antrim	An	114	Hillhowse	William	Clannaboyes	Dn	164
Henry	John	Clannaboyes	Dn	162	Hillhowse	William	Clannaboyes	Dn	166
Henry	John	Ironmongers	Ly	93	Hillhowse	William	Clannaboyes	Dn	168
Henry	Walter	Lynox	Dl	129	Hills	Edward	Ards	Dn	153
Henry	William	Bp Rapho	Dl	138	Hilman	Thomas	Coleraine	Ly	103
Henry	William	Londonderry	Ly	86	Hilton	John	Coleraine	Ly	104
Henryson	James	Ards	Dn	153	Hilton	Peter	Butler	Cv	3
Henryson	John	Ards	Dn	156	Hilton	Peter	Butler	Cv	4
Herbert	Sammuell	Lord Primate	Ar	33	Hingson	William	Mercers	Ly	96
Herbert	Walter	Lord Primate	Ar	34	Hinkeson	John	Londonderry	Ly	84
Herbert	William	Waldrum	Ar	22	Hinman	Hector	Lynox	Dl	128
Hercus	John	Sir A. Steward	Ty	65	Hislack	Mathew	Ards	Dn	148
Herit	Andrew	G. Hume	Fe	43	Hislat	Thomas	Sir J. Conningham	Dl	129
Hermidston	James	G. Hume	Fe	42	Hislop	Allan	Ards	Dn	155
Hermiston	James	Sir J. Hume	Fe	42	Hisluck	Robert	Ards	Dn	151
Heron	John	Butler	Cv	2	Hitchcock	Mathew	Moynes	Cv	11
Heron	Patrick	Ards	Dn	150	Hitchins	John	Mercers	Ly	96
Herper	James	Clatworthy	An	123	Hitchins	Nathaniell	Lord Primate	Ly	106
Herret	George	Edmonston	An	121	Hitchins	Robert	Vintners	Ly	98
Herring	Archbald	Edmonston	An	121	Hitchins	Thomas	Mercers	Ly	96
Herring	David	Edmonston	An	120	Hitchins	William	Mercers	Ly	96
Herriot	James	Edmonston	An	120	Hobkin	Archbald	Antrim	An	112
Herriott	Andrew	Sir F. Hammelton	Cv	5	Hobkin	John	Antrim	An	113
Herrod	George	Satcheuerall	Ar	24	Hobkin	Robert	Antrim	An	110
Herron	Alexander	Ards	Dn	150	Hobkins	John	Satcheuerall	Ar	25
Herron	John	Balye	Cv	13	Hobs	James	Satcheuerall	Ar	24
Herron	Patrick	Annandall	Dl	136	Hobson	Frauncis	Lord Primate	Ar	33
Herron	Patrick	Richardson	Ty	67	Hobson	Hugh	Crumwell	Dn	146
Herrot	David	Ards	Dn	150	Hobson	John	Brownlow	Ar	26
Herslop	William	Clannaboyes	Dn	168	Hockills	John	Clannaboyes	Dn	160
Hervy	James	Bp Rapho	Dl	138	Hodg	James	Hammelton	Ar	29
Hesee	Gilbert	Benson	Dl	132	Hodg	John	Hammelton	Ar	29
Hesket	Richard	F. Blennerhasset	Fe	45	Hodg	John	Ards	Dn	153
Heslet	John	Bp Rapho	Dl	138	Hodg	Thomas	Hammelton	Ar	30
Hetherrington	George	Lyndsay	Ty	67	Hodgenson	Trynion	Satcheuerall	Ar	24
Hettels	John	Sir J. Conningham	Dl	130	Hodges	Thomas	Chichester	Dl	140
Hettels younger	John	Sir J. Conningham	Dl	130	Hodgkins	John	Londonderry	Ly	82
Hetton	Sammuel	Montgomery	Fe	54	Hodgson	John	Crumwell	Dn	144
Hewes	Owen	Londonderry	Ly	83	Hodgson	John	Crumwell	Dn	145
Hewes	William	Lynox	Dl	129	Hodgson	Lancelot	Grandison	Ar	32
Hexter	John	Bp Kilmore	Cv	15	Hodgson	Robert	Kildare	Dn	142
Hexter	Thomas	Bp Kilmore	Cv	15	Hodgson younger	Thomas	Crumwell	Dn	145
Heyden	John	Calfield	Ar	36	Hodleston	Andrew	Adare	An	119
Heyland	Teige	Phillips	Ly	104	Hog	Bartholemew	Chichester	Dl	140
Hibbots	Daniell	Taylor	Cv	9	Hog	James	H. Steward	Ty	66
Hibbots	John	Taylor	Cv	9	Hog	Richard	Coleraine	Ly	101
Hibbots	Moyses	Taylor	Cv	9	Hog	Thomas	Hastings	Ty	68
Hibbots	William	Chichester	Dl	140	Hog	Walter	H. Steward	Ty	66
Hickman	John	Butler	Cv	2	Hog	William	Coleraine	Ly	103
Hide	Ganther	Cope	Ar	25	Hog	William	Coleraine	Ly	104
Higard	Andrew	Antrim	An	117	Hogg	Alexander	G. Hume	Fe	42
Higat	Alexander	Chichester	Dl	139	Hogg	Andrew	Clannaboyes	Dn	165
Higgins	Anthony	Coleraine	Ly	103	Hogg	James	Antrim	An	113
Higgis	Thomas	Clannaboyes	Dn	161	Hogg	James	Ards	Dn	156
Highgate	Gilbert	Lady Conningham	Dl	131	Hogg	John	Antrim	An	115
Higs	John	Satcheuerall	Ar	24	Hogg	Robert	Clannaboyes	Dn	162
Hilbot	John	Chichester	Dl	140	Hogg	Thomas	Flowerdew	Fe	44
Hill	Danniell	Sir G. Hammilton	Ty	71	Hogg	Thomas	Enniskillen T.	Fe	51
Hill	Edward	Harrington	Dl	134	Hogg	Thomas	Lord Primate	Ly	106
Hill	George	Bp Dromore	Dn	171	Hogg	Walter	Clatworthy	An	123
Hill	Hugh	Antrim	An	116	Hogg	William	Dalloway	An	122
Hill	John	Cope	Ar	21	Hogg	William	Enniskillen T.	Fe	51
Hill	John	Cavan T.	Cv	16	Hogg	William	Londonderry	Ly	87
Hill	John	Bp Clougher	Ty	77	Hoggard	David	Londonderry	Ly	86
Hill	Peter	Crumwell	Dn	143	Hoggard	Thomas	Kingsmell	Dl	131
Hill	Ralph	Satcheuerall	Ar	25	Hogge	John	Mervin	Ty	69
Hill	Richard	F. Blennerhasset	Fe	45	Hoggin	John	Adare	An	120
Hill	Robert	Antrim	An	116	Hoggshead	James	M. of Abbercorne	Ty	72
Hill	Thomas	Antrim	An	116	Hogguyre	John	Chichester	Dl	140
Hill	Thomas	Taylor	Cv	9	Hoghan	Thomas	Ards	Dn	149
Hill	Thomas	Enniskillen T.	Fe	51	Hoghen	Edward	Clannaboyes	Dn	166
Hill	Thomas	Londonderry	Ly	88	Holan	Robert	Sir W. Hammilton	Ty	73

Surname	Forename	Estate	Co.	Page
Huggins	John	Sir J. Hume	Fe	42
Hugh	Thomas	Coleraine	Ly	103
Hughes	John	Crumwell	Dn	146
Hughey	Patrick	Antrim	An	117
Hughin	Steaphen	Bp Dromore	Dn	171
Hughman	David	Clannaboyes	Dn	161
Hughnan	John	Ards	Dn	150
Hughnan	John	Ards	Dn	156
Hughston	James	Merchant Taylors	Ly	93
Hughston	John	Merchant Taylors	Ly	93
Hughston	John	Ironmongers	Ly	94
Hughston	Mathew	Merchant Taylors	Ly	93
Hughston	Robert	Goldsmiths	Ly	92
Hughstone	John	Goldsmiths	Ly	92
Hughye	Robert	Coleraine	Ly	103
Hugones	James	Annandall	Dl	137
Hully	William	Coleraine	Ly	102
Hume	Alexand	Antrim	An	112
Hume	Alexander	Sir F. Hammelton	Cv	5
Hume	Alexander	Sir J. Hume	Fe	42
Hume	Andrew	G. Hume	Fe	43
Hume	David	Cahoune	Dl	133
Hume	John	Clatworthy	An	124
Hume	Patrick	Clannaboyes	Dn	167
Hume	Patrick	Sir J. Hume	Fe	42
Hume	Thomas	Sir A. Steward	Ty	64
Humes	John	Clatworthy	An	123
Humes	John	Strabane T.	Ty	75
Humes	Walter	Waldrune	Cv	9
Humfrey	John	Clatworthy	An	123
Humfrey	John	Crumwell	Dn	145
Humfrey	John	Hastings	Fe	53
Humfrey	Thomas	Hastings	Fe	53
Humfreyes	Zachary	Powerscourt	Ty	79
Hummersly	John	Upton	An	125
Humphrey	John	Crumwell	Dn	145
Humphrey	John	Sir A. Steward	Ty	64
Humphrey	Martin	Clannaboyes	Dn	165
Humphreyes	John	Taylor	Cv	9
Humphreys	Henry	Cope	Ar	19
Humphreys	Richard	Cope	Ar	20
Hund	William	Londonderry	Ly	83
Hunkinson	George	Satcheuerall	Ar	25
Hunston	Mathew	Coleraine	Ly	102
Hunt	Arthur	Cope	Ar	20
Hunt	Christopher	Crag	Cv	6
Hunt	Henry	Cope	Ar	18
Hunt	Henry	Cope	Ar	21
Hunt	Henry	Cavan T.	Cv	16
Hunt	Robert	Sir F. Hammelton	Cv	4
Hunt	Robert	Cavan T.	Cv	16
Hunt	William	Sir F. Hammelton	Cv	4
Hunter	Adam	Clannaboyes	Dn	163
Hunter	Adam	Clannaboyes	Dn	169
Hunter	Andrew	Antrim	An	115
Hunter	Andrew	Clannaboyes	Dn	159
Hunter	Andrew	Ironmongers	Ly	94
Hunter	Archbald	Sir J. Conningham	Dl	130
Hunter	Archbald	Harrington	Dl	134
Hunter	David	Antrim	An	114
Hunter	David	Willson	Dl	132
Hunter	David	Londonderry	Ly	87
Hunter	David	Londonderry	Ly	88
Hunter	David	Clothworkers	Ly	90
Hunter	George	Hill	An	121
Hunter	George	Clatworthy	An	124
Hunter	George	Londonderry	Ly	84
Hunter	Henry	Brownlow	Ar	27
Hunter	Henry	Boocer	Ar	32
Hunter	Henry	Lady Conningham	Dl	131
Hunter younger	Henry	Boocer	Ar	32
Hunter	Hugh	Antrim	An	112
Hunter	Hugh	M. of Abbercorne	Ty	72
Hunter	James	Clatworthy	An	122
Hunter	James	Clatworthy	An	123
Hunter	James	Ards	Dn	156

Surname	Forename	Estate	Co.	Page
Hunter	James	Clannaboyes	Dn	164
Hunter	James	Londonderry	Ly	85
Hunter	John	Antrim	An	110
Hunter	John	Antrim	An	113
Hunter	John	Antrim	An	114
Hunter	John	Antrim	An	114
Hunter	John	Antrim	An	115
Hunter	John	Antrim	An	115
Hunter	John	Upton	An	124
Hunter	John	Upton	An	124
Hunter	John	Sir J. Conningham	Dl	130
Hunter	John	Lady Conningham	Dl	131
Hunter	John	Lady Conningham	Dl	131
Hunter	John	Chichester	Dl	140
Hunter	John	Clannaboyes	Dn	162
Hunter	John	Clannaboyes	Dn	163
Hunter	John	Atkinson	Fe	52
Hunter	John	Clothworkers	Ly	90
Hunter	John	Coleraine	Ly	102
Hunter	Nicholas	Antrim	An	112
Hunter	Nynyan	Antrim	An	110
Hunter	Patrick	Sir G. Hammilton	Ty	71
Hunter	Robert	Antrim	An	115
Hunter	Robert	Clatworthy	An	123
Hunter	Robert	Clannaboyes	Dn	166
Hunter	Robert	Clannaboyes	Dn	166
Hunter	Robert	Clannaboyes	Dn	168
Hunter	Robert	Clannaboyes	Dn	168
Hunter	Robert	Londonderry	Ly	83
Hunter	Robert	Haberdashers	Ly	89
Hunter younger	Robert	Boocer	Ar	32
Hunter	Steaphen	Bp Clougher	Ty	77
Hunter	Thomas	Antrim	An	110
Hunter	Thomas	Butler	Cv	2
Hunter	Walter	Clannaboyes	Dn	165
Hunter	William	Antrim	An	114
Hunter	William	Brownlow	Ar	27
Hunter	William	Chichester	Dl	140
Hunter	William	Clannaboyes	Dn	158
Hunter	William	Strabane T.	Ty	74
Hurd	Archbell	Londonderry	Ly	88
Hurly	Leonard	Adare	An	119
Hurn	John	Clatworthy	An	122
Hurran	Robert	Kildare	Dn	142
Hurrin	John	Ards	Dn	152
Hurslurgh	Robert	Edmonston	An	121
Hururence	John	J. Conningham	Dl	135
Huscock	Nathaniell	Londonderry	Ly	85
Husselton	William	Powerscourt	Ty	79
Huston	Fyndlay	Bp Rapho	Dl	138
Huston	James	Londonderry	Ly	87
Huston	John	Haberdashers	Ly	89
Huston	Phillomy	Kingsmell	Dl	131
Huston	William	Londonderry	Ly	87
Hustone	James	Lynox	Dl	128
Hutchen younger	John	Crumwell	Dn	145
Hutcheson	Patrick	Clannaboyes	Dn	158
Hutcheson	Robert	Clannaboyes	Dn	158
Hutchison	Andrew	Dillon	Ar	21
Hutchison	James	Sir J. Conningham	Dl	130
Hutchison	James	Kildare	Dn	142
Hutchison	John	Butler	Cv	3
Hutchison	Robert	Crumwell	Dn	144
Hutchon	Alexander	Londonderry	Ly	87
Hutchon	John	Crumwell	Dn	145
Hutchon	John	Ards	Dn	156
Hutchon	Patrick	Antrim	An	113
Hutchon	William	Antrim	An	111
Hutchone	John	Bp Rapho	Dl	138
Hutton	Francis	Clatworthy	An	123
Hutton	John	Clatworthy	An	123
Hutton	John	Strabane T.	Ty	76
Hutton	Thomas	Annandall	Dl	137
Hyde	John	Hannings	Fe	44
Hyeron	Adam	Ards	Dn	153

Surname	Forename	Estate	Co.	Page
Hyeron	Robert	Clannaboyes	Dn	162
Hyll	William	Coleraine	Ly	100
Hymphil	James	Sir W. Hammilton	Ty	73
Hymphill	James	Ironmongers	Ly	93
Hynde	William	Atchison	Ar	28
Hyndman	William	Clannaboyes	Dn	157
Hyndze	James	Parsons	Ty	62
Hyndze	William	Parsons	Ty	61
Hyneman	James	Coleraine	Ly	102
Hyneman	John	Coleraine	Ly	102
Hynes	John	Strabane T.	Ty	74
Hyng	William	Leigh	Ty	63
Hynnenge	David	Clannaboyes	Dn	161
Iesack	William	Sir J. Conningham	Dl	130
Ignawe	Patrick	Antrim	An	118
Illiner	Walter	Chichester	Dl	140
Impson	James	Mountnorrice	Ar	27
Inch younger	John	Coleraine	Ly	103
Ingle	William	Dawson	Ly	106
Ingledene	Robert	Grandison	Ar	31
Ingram	James	Ards	Dn	150
Innes	George	Clannaboyes	Dn	169
Inpske	Alexander	Coleraine	Ly	102
Ireland	John	Clannaboyes	Dn	163
Ireland younger	John	Clannaboyes	Dn	163
Ireland	Roger	Ards	Dn	150
Ireland	Roger	Ards	Dn	156
Ireland	William	Ards	Dn	152
Ireland	William	Ards	Dn	156
Irwin	Adam	Clannaboyes	Dn	166
Irwin	Andrew	Ballfowre	Fe	38
Irwin	Arthur	Mercers	Ly	96
Irwin	Christopher	Hammelton	Ar	31
Irwin	Christopher	Poyntes	Ar	32
Irwin	Christopher	Flowerdew	Fe	44
Irwin	Christopher	Sir W. Hammilton	Ty	73
Irwin	Cuthbert	Clannaboyes	Dn	164
Irwin	David	Clannaboyes	Dn	162
Irwin	David	Clannaboyes	Dn	165
Irwin	David	Clannaboyes	Dn	168
Irwin	David	Ballfowre	Fe	39
Irwin	Edward	Clannaboyes	Dn	164
Irwin	Edwin	Erskin	Ty	57
Irwin	Francis	Lowther	Fe	44
Irwin	Francis	Flowerdew	Fe	44
Irwin	Francis	Drapers	Ly	98
Irwin	Francis	Sir W. Hammilton	Ty	73
Irwin	George	J. Hammelton	Cv	12
Irwin	George	Archdall	Fe	40
Irwin	George	Archdall	Fe	41
Irwin	George	L. Blennerhasset	Fe	53
Irwin	George	Parsons	Ty	62
Irwin	Hugh	W. Hammilton	Ty	78
Irwin	James	Lowther	Fe	43
Irwin	James	Hastings	Fe	53
Irwin	James	Coleraine	Ly	103
Irwin	John	Atchison	Ar	29
Irwin	John	Poyntes	Ar	32
Irwin	John	Clannaboyes	Dn	164
Irwin	John	Ballfowre	Fe	39
Irwin	John	Archdall	Fe	40
Irwin	John	Archdall	Fe	40
Irwin	John	Flowerdew	Fe	44
Irwin	John	Hatton	Fe	47
Irwin	John	Haberdashers	Ly	89
Irwin	John	Clothworkers	Ly	90
Irwin	John	Lyndsay	Ty	68
Irwin younger	John	Poyntes	Ar	32
Irwin	Mathew	Drapers	Ly	98
Irwin	Richard	L. Blennerhasset	Fe	53
Irwin	Richard	Parsons	Ty	62
Irwin	Robert	Adare	An	120
Irwin	Robert	Clannaboyes	Dn	168
Irwin	Robert	Londonderry	Ly	86
Irwin	Robert	Londonderry	Ly	86
Irwin	Robert	Parsons	Ty	62
Irwin	Thomas	Abp Armagh	Ty	77
Irwin	Walter	Drapers	Ly	98
Irwin	William	Mountnorrice	Ar	27
Irwin	William	Atchison	Ar	28
Irwin	William	Poyntes	Ar	32
Irwin	William	Lord Primate	Ar	35
Irwin	William	Clannaboyes	Dn	166
Irwin	William	Lowther	Fe	43
Irwing	Christopher	Ards	Dn	156
Irwing	David	Ards	Dn	154
Irwing	Edward	Ards	Dn	148
Irwing	Edward	Ards	Dn	149
Irwing	Edward	Clannaboyes	Dn	166
Irwing	Francis	Ards	Dn	149
Irwing	George	Willson	Dl	132
Irwing	George	Auldridg	Mo	176
Irwing	James	Clannaboyes	Dn	164
Irwing	James	Coleraine	Ly	104
Irwing	John	Crumwell	Dn	144
Irwing	John	Ards	Dn	148
Irwing	John	Ards	Dn	149
Irwing	John	Clannaboyes	Dn	164
Irwing	John	Clannaboyes	Dn	165
Irwing	John	Clannaboyes	Dn	166
Irwing	Richard	Ards	Dn	148
Irwing	Robert	Ards	Dn	154
Irwing	Robert	Clannaboyes	Dn	164
Irwing	Robert	Clannaboyes	Dn	164
Irwing	Robert	Clannaboyes	Dn	166
Irwing	Thomas	Bp Dromore	Dn	172
Irwing	William	Clannaboyes	Dn	158
Irwing	William	Clannaboyes	Dn	165
Irwyn	John	Bp Down etc	Dn	170
Irwyn	Thomas	Clannaboyes	Dn	162
Itson	Edward	Ironmongers	Ly	95
Jabe	John	Antrim	An	115
Jabson	Mungo	Ards	Dn	150
Jabson	Robert	Ards	Dn	147
Jack	Hugh	Phillips	Ly	104
Jack	John	Londonderry	Ly	88
Jack	Thomas	Lord Primate	Ar	34
Jacket	Walter	Londonderry	Ly	85
Jacks	John	Phillips	Ly	104
Jackson	Adam	Ards	Dn	150
Jackson	Arthur	Clatworthy	An	123
Jackson	David	Annandall	Dl	136
Jackson	David	Annandall	Dl	137
Jackson younger	David	Annandall	Dl	136
Jackson	Francis	Chichester	Ty	78
Jackson	George	Clannaboyes	Dn	164
Jackson	George	Coleraine	Ly	100
Jackson	Gregory	Satcheuerall	Ar	23
Jackson	Henry	Crumwell	Dn	145
Jackson	James	Newton	Ty	80
Jackson	John	Satcheuerall	Ar	24
Jackson	John	Ards	Dn	147
Jackson	John	Clannaboyes	Dn	164
Jackson	John	Clannaboyes	Dn	166
Jackson	John	Archdall	Fe	40
Jackson	John	Hastings	Fe	53
Jackson	John	Symonton	Ty	66
Jackson	John	Strabane T.	Ty	75
Jackson	Patrick	Phillips	Ly	104
Jackson	Patrick	Sir A. Steward	Ty	64
Jackson	Ralph	Mountnorrice	Ar	28
Jackson	Ralph	Grandison	Ar	31
Jackson	Richard	Coleraine	Ly	103
Jackson	Robert	Stanhow	Ar	23
Jackson	Stephen	Brownlow	Ar	27
Jackson	William	Ards	Dn	148
James	George	Clannaboyes	Dn	160
James	John	Ards	Dn	149
James	Roger	Calfield	Ar	36
Jameson	Alexander	Ards	Dn	149
Jameson	James	Antrim	An	118
Jameson	John	Antrim	An	118

Surname	Forename	Estate	Co.	Page
Kee	Anthony	Clannaboyes	Dn	165
Kee	Frauncis	Sir F. Hammelton	Cv	5
Kee	William	Bp Clougher	Ty	77
Keemyn	John	Londonderry	Ly	86
Keemyng	John	Ironmongers	Ly	94
Keene	Henry	Londonderry	Ly	82
Keere	Andrew	Antrim	An	118
Keg	John	Sir W. Steward	Ty	59
Keil	Walter	Crumwell	Dn	144
Keine	John mcJohn	J. Conningham	Dl	136
Keirney	John	Clannaboyes	Dn	164
Keirs	Andrew	Annandall	Dl	137
Kell	Robert	Adare	An	119
Kellane	Bryan	F. Blennerhasset	Fe	45
Kellogh	John	Phillips	Ly	105
Kellum	William	Taylor	Cv	10
Kelly	Andrew	Strabane T.	Ty	73
Kelly	Daniell	Antrim	An	113
Kelly	James	Kildare	Dn	142
Kelly	James	Crumwell	Dn	144
Kelly	John	W. Steward	Dl	133
Kelly	John	Crumwell	Dn	145
Kelly	John	Crumwell	Dn	145
Kelly	John	Ards	Dn	156
Kelly	Patrick	Crumwell	Dn	143
Kelly	Patrick	Clannaboyes	Dn	162
Kelly	Patrick	Clannaboyes	Dn	168
Kelly	Thomas	Crumwell	Dn	145
Kelly	Thomas	Londonderry	Ly	83
Kelly	Walter	Kildare	Dn	142
Kelly	William	Londonderry	Ly	87
Kels	Robert	Clannaboyes	Dn	166
Kels	Robert	Clannaboyes	Dn	169
Kelsa	Gawen	Haberdashers	Ly	88
Kelsay	Richard	Crumwell	Dn	146
Kelso	Alexander	Ards	Dn	151
Kelso	Archbald	Ards	Dn	151
Kelso	George	Ards	Dn	153
Kelso	Henry	Haberdashers	Ly	90
Kelso	James	Ards	Dn	151
Kelson	John	Antrim	An	115
Kelson	Thomas	Bp Rapho	Dl	138
Kelson	Thomas	Grocers	Ly	91
Kelsy	Richard	Crumwell	Dn	144
Kelton	John	Ards	Dn	152
Kendrick	Jud	Londonderry	Ly	84
Kenedy	Adam	Bp Down etc	Dn	170
Kenedy	Alexander	Clannaboyes	Dn	159
Kenedy	Anthony	Antrim	An	116
Kenedy	Anthony	W. Steward	Dl	133
Kenedy	Anthony	Clannaboyes	Dn	159
Kenedy	Constantyne	Clannaboyes	Dn	157
Kenedy	David	W. Steward	Dl	133
Kenedy	David	Ards	Dn	148
Kenedy	David	Ards	Dn	149
Kenedy	Gilbert	Antrim	An	110
Kenedy	Gilbert	Ards	Dn	152
Kenedy	Hector	Clatworthy	An	122
Kenedy	Hugh	Ards	Dn	154
Kenedy	James	Ards	Dn	147
Kenedy	James	Bp Dromore	Dn	171
Kenedy	John	Antrim	An	111
Kenedy	John	Antrim	An	112
Kenedy	John	Antrim	An	114
Kenedy	John	Bp Rapho	Dl	138
Kenedy	John	Crumwell	Dn	145
Kenedy	John	Ards	Dn	147
Kenedy	John	Ards	Dn	147
Kenedy	John	Ards	Dn	152
Kenedy	John	Ards	Dn	153
Kenedy	John	Ards	Dn	153
Kenedy	John	Ards	Dn	156
Kenedy	John	Ards	Dn	156
Kenedy	John	Clannaboyes	Dn	167
Kenedy	John	Bp Clougher	Ty	77
Kenedy younger	John	Ards	Dn	156

Surname	Forename	Estate	Co.	Page
Kenedy	Robert	Antrim	An	115
Kenedy	Robert	Ards	Dn	148
Kenedy	Robert	Ards	Dn	149
Kenedy	Thomas	Crumwell	Dn	143
Kenedy	Thomas	Crumwell	Dn	145
Kenedy	Thomas	Ards	Dn	152
Kenedy	William	Adare	An	119
Kenedy	William	Annandall	Dl	137
Kenedy	William	Ards	Dn	148
Kenedy	William	Ards	Dn	148
Kenedy	William	Bp Down etc	Dn	170
Kenedye	David	W. Steward	Dl	133
Kenellye	James	W. Steward	Dl	133
Kenly	Robert	Ards	Dn	153
Kennan	John	A. Steward	Dl	135
Kenne	William	Bp Down etc	Dn	170
Kennedy	John	Bp Dromore	Dn	172
Kennedy	Neele	Adare	An	119
Kennedy	Thomas	Upton	An	124
Kennety	David	Antrim	An	114
Kennitee	Oliver	Mountnorrice	Ar	27
Kennitee	Oliver	Boocer	Ar	32
Kennittee	Adam	Strabane T.	Ty	73
Kennittee	William	Strabane T.	Ty	74
Kenny	James	Sir W. Hammilton	Ty	73
Kennydee	Robert	Clannaboyes	Dn	165
Kennydy	John	Ards	Dn	154
Kennydye	George	Clannaboyes	Dn	167
Kent	Edward	Butler	Fe	50
Kent	Richard	Coleraine	Ly	103
Keoghy	Alexander	Crumwell	Dn	145
Ker	Daniell	Coleraine	Ly	103
Kerbery	Wm	Ards	Dn	156
Kerfoote	Henry	Stanhow	Ar	23
Kerfoote	Thomas	Stanhow	Ar	23
Kerne	Barnaby	Ironmongers	Ly	95
Kernes	David	Annandall	Dl	136
Kernes	Robert	Annandall	Dl	136
Kernes	Robert	Annandall	Dl	137
Kernes	Walter	Bp Down etc	Dn	170
Kerney	Archbald	Clannaboyes	Dn	164
Kerneyes	John	Bp Down etc	Dn	170
Kerny	John	Clannaboyes	Dn	166
Kerny	Thomas	Dalloway	An	122
Kerr	Alexander	Edmonston	An	121
Kers	Andrew	Clannaboyes	Dn	163
Kersone	James	Haberdashers	Ly	89
Keth	Francis	Kildare	Dn	142
Kettagh	Daniell	Sir W. Steward	Ty	60
Kettle	John	Butler	Fe	49
Kettle	William	Waterhouse	Fe	47
Kettymoore	John	Clatworthy	An	123
Key	David	Benson	Dl	133
Key	James	Hammelton	Ar	30
Key	John	Bp Rapho	Dl	137
Key	Mathew	Vintners	Ly	98
Key	Roger	Lord Primate	Ar	35
Keymyn	James	Londonderry	Ly	86
Keyye	John	Edmonston	An	121
Kid	John	Antrim	An	114
Kidd	Hugh	Antrim	An	110
Kidd	William	Antrim	An	110
Kidly	John	Gower	Fe	53
Kiell	John	Strabane T.	Ty	75
Kilcrag	James	Sir F. Hammelton	Cv	5
Kile	Robert	Ards	Dn	156
Kile	Thomas	Clannaboyes	Dn	158
Kill	Archbald	Richardson	Ty	67
Kill	Mungo	Londonderry	Ly	88
Kill	Richard	Crumwell	Dn	146
Kill	Robert	Londonderry	Ly	85
Kill	Rynyon	Kildare	Dn	142
Killaspy	John	Crumwell	Dn	146
Killer	Roger	Moynes	Cv	11
Killet	David	Bp Kilmore	Cv	15
Killhare	Roger	Bagshaw	Cv	8

Surname	Forename	Estate	Co.	Page	Surname	Forename	Estate	Co.	Page
Krick	John	Hammelton	Ar	30	Latay	John	Bp Rapho	Dl	138
Kunningham	William	M. of Abbercorne	Ty	72	Latham	John	Phillips	Ly	104
Kyd	Robert	Antrim	An	114	Latham	John	Phillips	Ly	105
Kyle	Thomas	Clannaboyes	Dn	158	Latimer	Archbald	Ards	Dn	155
Kymin	John	Lady McCleland	Ly	105	Latimer	John	Ards	Dn	148
Kynard	John	M. of Abbercorne	Ty	72	Latimer	John	Ards	Dn	150
Kyng	Alexander	Londonderry	Ly	82	Latimer	John	Clannaboyes	Dn	160
Labby	William	Crumwell	Dn	146	Lattar	James	Antrim	An	118
Labrow	John	Ards	Dn	151	Lattar	Robert	Antrim	An	118
Lacillis	Francis	Bp Rapho	Dl	138	Lattimor	Robert	Crumwell	Dn	145
Lackbone	William	Sedburrogh	Fe	48	Lattimore	Edward	Clatwoorthy	An	123
Lacker	Alexander	Chichester	Dl	139	Latty	Robert	Strabane T.	Ty	74
Lacker	John	Chichester	Dl	140	Laughlan	William	Lynox	Dl	128
Lackye	Andrew	Lynox	Dl	128	Laughlane	Thomas	Flowerdew	Fe	44
Lackye	Robert	Lynox	Dl	128	Laughlayne	John	Drapers	Ly	98
Laden	Richard	Maghera & Desert Martin	Ly	106	Laughlin	David	Clannaboyes	Dn	158
Lader	John	Clannaboyes	Dn	162	Laughlin	William	Sir W. Hammilton	Ty	73
Lader	John	Clannaboyes	Dn	168	Laughlyne	Patrick	Phillips	Ly	105
Ladly	Patrick	Antrim	An	114	Laughlyne	Peter	Sir G. Hammilton	Ty	70
Lagan	Robert	Vintners	Ly	97	Laughry	John	Clothworkers	Ly	90
Laghlin	Adam	Clannaboyes	Dn	158	Law	John	Crumwell	Dn	146
Laghlin	John	Clannaboyes	Dn	158	Law	John	Ards	Dn	147
Laghlin younger	John	Clannaboyes	Dn	158	Law	Quinton	Clannaboyes	Dn	157
Laine	Thomas	Antrim	An	112	Lawader	Henry	Butler	Cv	2
Laird	John	Bp Rapho	Dl	138	Lawander	Henry	Butler	Cv	4
Lairmounth	George	Atchison	Cv	7	Lawder	Alexander	Lynox	Dl	128
Laker	James	A. Hammelton	Ty	63	Lawder	George	Sir F. Hammelton	Cv	6
Laky	Thomas	Edmonston	An	120	Lawder	James	Sir F. Hammelton	Cv	6
Laman	Mathew	Londonderry	Ly	87	Lawder	James	Ards	Dn	153
Lamb	Michaell	Phillips	Ly	104	Lawder	William	Ards	Dn	153
Lamb	William	Crumwell	Dn	146	Lawdone	John	Ards	Dn	155
Lambert	William	Grandison	Ar	31	Lawe	Edward	Antrim	An	110
Lamberton	John	Coleraine	Ly	103	Lawe	George	Clannaboyes	Dn	157
Lamond	John	Antrim	An	117	Lawe	James	Clannaboyes	Dn	159
Lanarick	James	Clannaboyes	Dn	168	Lawesdall	George	Willoby	Fe	54
Landels	Andrew	Sir A. Steward	Ty	64	Lawhart	Thomas	Sir J. Hume	Fe	42
Landles	Andrew	Sir A. Steward	Ty	64	Lawrance	William	Lord Primate	Ar	34
Landsey	Alexander	Londonderry	Ly	83	Lawrence	Thomas	Butler	Fe	50
Landy	Thomas	Hastings	Ty	68	Lawrences	James	Sir W. Steward	Ty	60
Lane	Thomas	Higget	Fe	46	Lawry	Alexander	Clannaboyes	Dn	161
Lane	Walter	Bp Rapho	Dl	139	Lawry	John	Clannaboyes	Dn	161
Lang	Arthur	Clothworkers	Ly	90	Lawson	Alexander	Sir J. Conningham	Dl	129
Lang	George	Clothworkers	Ly	90	Lawson	James	Newton	Ty	80
Lang	James	Bp Rapho	Dl	137	Lawson	John	Crag	Cv	7
Lang	James	Clothworkers	Ly	90	Lawson	John	J. Hammelton	Cv	12
Lang	John	Harrington	Dl	134	Lawson	John	Haberdashers	Ly	89
Lang	John	Clothworkers	Ly	90	Lawson	John	Haberdashers	Ly	90
Langdell	Charles	Phillips	Ly	104	Lawson	John	Phillips	Ly	105
Lange	George	Coleraine	Ly	102	Lawson	John	C. of Abbercorne	Ty	71
Langmoor	John	Londonderry	Ly	86	Lawson	Thomas	Clannaboyes	Dn	162
Lanrick	Edward	Clannaboyes	Dn	161	Lawson	Thomas	Haberdashers	Ly	89
Lanrick	William	Clannaboyes	Dn	161	Lawson	Thomas	Haberdashers	Ly	90
Lanses	Andrew	Clannaboyes	Dn	163	Lawsonn	Anthony	Londonderry	Ly	86
Laply	George	Edmonston	An	121	Lawsonn	Phillip	Londonderry	Ly	86
Lard	James	Bp Rapho	Dl	138	Laxton	Bernard	Vintners	Ly	97
Larfoord	John	Auldridg	Mo	175	Layfield	John	Grandison	Ar	32
Large	Gabraell	Londonderry	Ly	84	Layne	George	Dalloway	An	122
Large	John	Dromond	Ty	70	Layser	William	Annandall	Dl	137
Larges	Robert	Sir J. Conningham	Dl	130	Leach	David	Hammelton	Ar	29
Largg	William	Sir W. Steward	Ty	59	Leach	James	Cahoune	Dl	133
Lars	Thomas	J. Conningham	Dl	135	Leach	Nathaniell	Satcheuerall	Ar	25
Lasillis	Wm	Bp Rapho	Dl	138	Leach	Patrick	Cahoune	Dl	134
Lason	Christopher	Clannaboyes	Dn	168	Leach	William	Hammelton	Ar	29
Lason	Robert	Clannaboyes	Dn	168	Leacklen	Thomas	Londonderry	Ly	87
Lassels	Luke	Chichester	Dl	140	Leackye	Robert	Lynox	Dl	128
Lassilles	Thomas	Bp Rapho	Dl	138	Leadley	William	Atchison	Ar	28
Lassles	James	Willson	Dl	132	Leadson	John	Vintners	Ly	98
Lassles	Thomas	Willson	Dl	132	Leadstone	Thomas	Erskin	Ty	56
Lassles	William	Willson	Dl	132	Leag	Andrew	J. Conningham	Dl	135
Lasson	Adam	Dalloway	An	122	Leag	Hugh	J. Conningham	Dl	135
Lasson	Adam	Clatwoorthy	An	124	Leag	Hugh	J. Conningham	Dl	136
Lasson	Robert	Londonderry	Ly	85	Leagh	Hugh	Vintners	Ly	97
Lassy	John	Sir F. Hammelton	Cv	5	Leake	Edward	Crag	Cv	6
Lastly	Daniell	Crosby	Ty	69	Leake	William	Crag	Cv	6
Lastly	William	Haberdashers	Ly	90	Leakin elder	Thomas	Pearce	Cv	12
Lasy	Danyell	Sir W. Steward	Ty	59	Leakin younger	Thomas	Pearce	Cv	12

Surname	Forename	Estate	Co.	Page	Surname	Forename	Estate	Co.	Page
Marke	John	Upton	An	124	Mason	William	Coleraine	Ly	101
Marke	Robert	Kingsmell	Dl	131	Masson	Thomas	Dillon	Ar	21
Markham	Henry	Lord Primate	Ar	35	Massy	John	Cope	Ar	20
Markham	Thomas	Waldrum	Ar	22	Massy	John	Cope	Ar	20
Markhand	Roger	Butler	Fe	50	Massy	Robert	Lord Primate	Ar	34
Marriot	William	Cope	Ar	20	Masterton	John	Clannaboyes	Dn	162
Marsell	Christopher	Bp Dromore	Dn	172	Masterton	John	Clannaboyes	Dn	169
Marshall	Donnell	Clothworkers	Ly	90	Maston	James	Crosby	Ty	69
Marshall	James	Merchant Taylors	Ly	93	Maston	John	Crosby	Ty	69
Marshall	John	Ards	Dn	154	Mastoune	Michaell	Satcheuerall	Ar	25
Marshall	John	Ards	Dn	156	Matchet	Donnell	Satcheuerall	Ar	25
Marshall	John	Clannaboyes	Dn	166	Mathers	William	Mercers	Ly	96
Marshall	Michaell	Clannaboyes	Dn	165	Mathew	Alexander	Antrim	An	113
Marshall	Robert	Ards	Dn	152	Mathew	Anthony	Phillips	Ly	105
Marshall	William	Sir J. Conningham	Dl	130	Mathew	Gabraell	Strabane T.	Ty	75
Marshall	William	Archdall	Fe	40	Mathew	James	Antrim	An	114
Marshell	Steaphen	W. Steward	Dl	133	Mathew	James	Sir G. Hammilton	Ty	70
Marson	John	Haberdashers	Ly	88	Mathew	James	Strabane T.	Ty	75
Marston	Edward	Butler	Cv	3	Mathew	James	Strabane T.	Ty	76
Martcall	Phillip	Coleraine	Ly	103	Mathew	John	Antrim	An	113
Martiall	Robert	Bp Dromore	Dn	172	Mathew	John	Sir J. Conningham	Dl	130
Martin	Cutbert	Bp Clougher	Ty	77	Mathew	John	Clannaboyes	Dn	164
Martin	Edward	L. Blennerhasset	Fe	45	Mathew	John	Lady McCleland	Ly	105
Martin	Gilbert	Clannaboyes	Dn	165	Mathew	John	Sir W. Hammilton	Ty	73
Martin	James	Harrington	Dl	134	Mathew	Michaell	Antrim	An	110
Martin	John	Lord Primate	Ar	35	Mathew	William	Londonderry	Ly	83
Martin	John	Lynox	Dl	128	Mathewes	James	Londonderry	Ly	86
Martin	John	Crumwell	Dn	143	Mathewes	James	Berresfourd	Ly	106
Martin	John	Ards	Dn	150	Mathewes	Robert	Coleraine	Ly	103
Martin	John	Clannaboyes	Dn	159	Mathews	Ralph	Vintners	Ly	97
Martin	John	Clannaboyes	Dn	164	Mathewson	John	C. of Abbercorne	Ty	71
Martin	John	Clannaboyes	Dn	165	Mathey	Gylaspick	Merchant Taylors	Ly	93
Martin	John	Clannaboyes	Dn	168	Mathey	James	Bp Rapho	Dl	138
Martin	John	Haberdashers	Ly	88	Mathey	James	Bp Rapho	Dl	138
Martin	John	Erskin	Ty	57	Mathey	James	Bp Rapho	Dl	138
Martin	John	Newton	Ty	80	Mathey	Robert	Clannaboyes	Dn	162
Martin elder	John	Phillips	Ly	104	Mathy	James	Clannaboyes	Dn	167
Martin younger	John	Clannaboyes	Dn	164	Matlan	Robert	Ards	Dn	151
Martin younger	John	Phillips	Ly	104	Matlo	William	Dillon	Ar	21
Martin younger	John	Phillips	Ly	105	Matty	John	Antrim	An	114
Martin	Mathew	Dillon	Ar	22	Maughan	Archbald	Crosby	Ty	69
Martin	Patrick	Clannaboyes	Dn	167	Maughan	James	Crosby	Ty	69
Martin	Peter	Annandall	Dl	137	Maughan	Thomas	Crosby	Ty	69
Martin	Robert	Clannaboyes	Dn	164	Maure	John	Waldrum	Ar	22
Martin elder	Robert	Phillips	Ly	104	Maure	Richard	Waldrum	Ar	22
Martin younger	Robert	Phillips	Ly	104	Mawe	James	Clannaboyes	Dn	159
Martin	Thomas	Cope	Ar	20	Mawe	William	F. Blennerhasset	Fe	45
Martin	Thomas	Clannaboyes	Dn	168	Mawitie	James	Sir F. Hammelton	Cv	5
Martin	Thomas	Bp Clougher	Ty	77	Mawitie	John	Sir F. Hammelton	Cv	5
Marting	Walter	Edmonston	An	120	Mawitie	Nathaniell	Sir F. Hammelton	Cv	5
Martyn	James	Ards	Dn	155	Mawitie elder	Thomas	Sir F. Hammelton	Cv	5
Martyn	John	Ards	Dn	147	Maxfeild	Alexander	Benson	Dl	133
Martyn	John	Clannaboyes	Dn	168	Maxon	William	Lyndsay	Ty	68
Martyn	John	Auldridg	Mo	175	Maxwell	Alexander	Benson	Dl	133
Martyn	Nicholl	Ards	Dn	153	Maxwell	Alexander	Ards	Dn	149
Martyn	Ninian	Clannaboyes	Dn	157	Maxwell	Alexander	Clannaboyes	Dn	157
Martyn	Robert	Ards	Dn	155	Maxwell	Archbald	M. of Abbercorne	Ty	72
Martyn	Robert	Bp Down etc	Dn	170	Maxwell	Archbold	Antrim	An	114
Martyne	John	Ards	Dn	147	Maxwell	Arthur	Strabane T.	Ty	75
Martyne	John	Ards	Dn	148	Maxwell	Collen	Clannaboyes	Dn	164
Martyne	Robert	Ards	Dn	148	Maxwell	Collen	Clannaboyes	Dn	168
Marvell	John	Clannaboyes	Dn	163	Maxwell	Collin	Clannaboyes	Dn	168
Marvin	Edward	Mervin	Ty	69	Maxwell	David	Ards	Dn	154
Mase	Robert	H. Steward	Ty	65	Maxwell	Edward	Kildare	Dn	142
Mase	Robert	H. Steward	Ty	66	Maxwell	Edward	Clannaboyes	Dn	165
Mase younger	Robert	H. Steward	Ty	65	Maxwell	Edward	Gower	Fe	52
Mason	Francis	Ironmongers	Ly	95	Maxwell	Gabraell	Bp Rapho	Dl	138
Mason	Gilbert	Coleraine	Ly	103	Maxwell	Homer	M. of Abbercorne	Ty	72
Mason	Gilbert	Coleraine	Ly	104	Maxwell	Hugh	Strabane T.	Ty	74
Mason	Gregory	Crumwell	Dn	146	Maxwell	Hugh	Strabane T.	Ty	76
Mason	John	Londonderry	Ly	85	Maxwell	James	Clannaboyes	Dn	164
Mason	Richard	Kildare	Dn	142	Maxwell	James	Bp Dromore	Dn	171
Mason	Robert	Antrim	An	114	Maxwell	James	Lowther	Fe	44
Mason	Thomas	Haberdashers	Ly	89	Maxwell	James	Londonderry	Ly	87
Mason	Thomas	Sir W. Steward	Ty	59	Maxwell	John	Antrim	An	114
Mason	William	Flowerdew	Fe	44	Maxwell	John	Adare	An	120

Surname	Forename	Estate	Co.	Page	Surname	Forename	Estate	Co.	Page
McCala	John	Crosby	Ty	69	mcCarr	Thomas	Adare	An	119
McCala	John	Crosby	Ty	69	McCarrdy	John	Upton	An	124
mcCall	Allyn	Kingsmell	Dl	131	McCarrlye	John	Clannaboyes	Dn	157
McCall	Archbald	Clannaboyes	Dn	164	McCarroll	Robert	Antrim	An	115
McCall	John	Hammelton	Ar	30	McCarroll	William	Londonderry	Ly	87
mcCalla	Alexander	Ards	Dn	150	mcCarslaire	Donnell	W. Steward	Dl	133
mcCalla	Archbald	Bp Rapho	Dl	138	McCartan	George	Tychborne	Ty	60
mcCalla	John	Bp Rapho	Dl	138	McCartan	Thomas	Enniskillen T.	Fe	51
McCallan	Quintan	Clatworthy	An	124	younger				
mcCallen	Allen	Antrim	An	114	McCarteney	John	Clatworthy	An	123
mcCallen	John	Ards	Dn	152	McCarteney	Thomas	Clatworthy	An	123
McCallen	Thomas	Sir W. Steward	Ty	58	mcCarter	James	Berresfourd	Ly	106
McCallon	John	Clannaboyes	Dn	159	McCarter	James	Berresfourd	Ly	106
McCallow	Alexander	Upton	An	124	McCarter	Robert	Burris	Dn	172
mcCallow	James	Ards	Dn	149	McCartney	Andrew	Clannaboyes	Dn	158
mcCallow	William	Upton	An	124	McCartney	Donnell	Atchison	Ar	28
McCallyne	Michaell	Ards	Dn	148	McCartney	George	Ards	Dn	155
McCalman	Thomas	Antrim	An	118	McCartney	James	Clannaboyes	Dn	168
M'Calstander	James	Mrs Hammelton	Fe	41	McCartney	John	Annandall	Dl	136
McCalwey	Michaell	Clannaboyes	Dn	164	McCartney	John	Crumwell	Dn	145
McCaly	Alexander	Ards	Dn	148	McCartney	John	Crumwell	Dn	146
McCamer	Gillcolm	Antrim	An	117	McCartney	John	Clannaboyes	Dn	158
McCamer	Mourgh	Antrim	An	117	McCartney	John	Clannaboyes	Dn	158
McCamlees	David	Ards	Dn	152	McCartney	John	Clannaboyes	Dn	161
McCamlees	Thomas	Ards	Dn	147	McCartney	Robert	Clannaboyes	Dn	169
McCamond	James	Clatworthy	An	122	McCartney	Thomas	Clannaboyes	Dn	157
McCamont	Alexander	Clannaboyes	Dn	157	McCartney	William	Clannaboyes	Dn	164
McCamont	John	Clannaboyes	Dn	158	McCarton	Robert	Atchison	Ar	28
McCamont	Thomas	Clannaboyes	Dn	164	McCary	Art	Sir J. Conningham	Dl	129
mcCamy	Robert	J. Conningham	Dl	136	McCaslane	Alexander	Sir W. Steward	Ty	60
mcCamy	Robert	J. Conningham	Dl	136	McCatcheon	John	Clannaboyes	Dn	162
younger					McCauke	Neal	Antrim	An	116
mcCan	Gilbert	A. Steward	Dl	135	mcCauley	Fynlay	Annandall	Dl	137
McCan	John	Crumwell	Dn	144	mcCaw	Donnell Roe	Antrim	An	115
McCanine	James	Clannaboyes	Dn	164	mcCaw	Gilnew	Antrim	An	116
mcCanlees	John	Ards	Dn	150	McCaw	James	Londonderry	Ly	84
McCann	John	Clannaboyes	Dn	161	mcCawe	Alexander	Antrim	An	115
mcCannan	Thomas	Ards	Dn	149	mcCawe	Donnell	Antrim	An	116
McCanny	Gilbert	Hammelton	Ar	31	McCawe	Donnell Mor	Antrim	An	116
McCans	John	Clannaboyes	Dn	165	McCawe	Hugh	Coleraine	Ly	103
McCapein	John	Edmonston	An	121	McCawe	John	Antrim	An	116
McCapene	John	Ards	Dn	155	McCawen	John	Clannaboyes	Dn	161
McCappin	Thomas	Edmonston	An	121	mcCawly	John	Lynox	Dl	128
younger					McCay	Fynlay	Ards	Dn	153
McCapy	John	Edmonston	An	121	mcCay	Gilbert	Ards	Dn	148
McCapy	Thomas	Edmonston	An	121	McCay	John	Ards	Dn	153
McCar	Alexander	Clannaboyes	Dn	168	mcCay	Thomas	Ards	Dn	153
McCar	Hugh	Clannaboyes	Dn	169	McChaghan	John	Clannaboyes	Dn	168
McCar	John	Clannaboyes	Dn	166	McChapy	John	Sir A. Steward	Ty	64
McCar	William	Clannaboyes	Dn	168	McChemny	John	Ards	Dn	153
McCarby	William	Ards	Dn	150	McChench	George	Balye	Cv	13
McCard	Walter	Ards	Dn	153	mcCheney	Andrew	Benson	Dl	133
McCardy	Alexander	Antrim	An	110	mcCheney	John	Benson	Dl	133
McCardy	John	Clannaboyes	Dn	158	McChesney	Thomas	Ards	Dn	154
mcCardy	Robert	Antrim	An	112	McChonchoy	John	Antrim	An	112
McCare	John	Clannaboyes	Dn	159	McChower	Gilbert	Bp Clougher	Ty	77
McCargall	John	Clannaboyes	Dn	159	McChoyn	John	Clannaboyes	Dn	166
McCarkan	Donnell	Londonderry	Ly	88	McChristian	Gilbert	Adare	An	120
McCarket	John	Edmonston	An	120	McClaire	Alexander	Clannaboyes	Dn	164
mcCarle	Symond	Ards	Dn	150	McClairy	Ninian	Clannaboyes	Dn	168
McCarly	John	Bp Dromore	Dn	171	McClanakan	John	Antrim	An	111
McCarmack	Thomas	Erskin	Ty	57	mcClanes	John	Annandall	Dl	136
McCarmack	Thomas	Erskin	Ty	57	mcClaney	Alexander	W. Steward	Dl	133
McCarmont	Patrick	Ards	Dn	148	McClarimore	Brian	Ards	Dn	155
McCarney	James	Sir W. Hammilton	Ty	72	McClarkan	John	Clannaboyes	Dn	157
McCarnid	David	Antrim	An	118	McClarty	Gillcrist	Antrim	An	117
McCarnock	John	Ards	Dn	148	McClarty	John	Haberdashers	Ly	89
McCarnock	Thomas	Ards	Dn	151	McClatchie	James	Clannaboyes	Dn	168
McCarnoghan	John	Clannaboyes	Dn	162	McClatchie	James	Clannaboyes	Dn	168
McCarny	Adam	Adare	An	119	McClatchie	John	Clannaboyes	Dn	168
McCarny	Thomas	Adare	An	119	mcClaughey elder	John	Annandall	Dl	137
McCarr	Hugh	Clannaboyes	Dn	166	mcClaughry	James	Annandall	Dl	137
McCarr	John	Adare	An	119	mcClaughry	William	Annandall	Dl	137
McCarr	John	Ards	Dn	156	McClaydd	Donnell	Merchant Taylors	Ly	92
McCarr	John	Clannaboyes	Dn	166	McCleane	Donnell	Strabane T.	Ty	75
McCarr	Nynyan	Clannaboyes	Dn	166	mcCleane	Roary	W. Steward	Dl	133

Surname	Forename	Estate	Co.	Page	Surname	Forename	Estate	Co.	Page
McCord	John	Edmonston	An	120	mcCrere	John	Ards	Dn	147
McCord	John	Ards	Dn	151	mcCrere	John	Ards	Dn	156
McCordall	William	Londonderry	Ly	87	McCrerie	Thomas	Clannaboyes	Dn	167
McCordy	Gilbert	Tychborne	Ty	61	McCrery	Andrew	Erskin	Ty	56
McCordy	John	Tychborne	Ty	61	McCrery	Gilbert	Ards	Dn	150
McCordy	Thomas	Tychborne	Ty	61	McCrery	James	Ards	Dn	147
mcCorkey	Aghey	Chichester	Dl	139	McCrery	John	Bp Down etc	Dn	170
mcCorkill	Andrew	Lady Conningham	Dl	130	McCrery	John	Bp Dromore	Dn	171
mcCorkill	John	Lady Conningham	Dl	130	McCrery	John	Sir W. Steward	Ty	58
McCormack	Andrew	Erskin	Ty	56	mcCrery	Robert	Ards	Dn	151
McCormack	John	Clannaboyes	Dn	167	McCrery	Thomas	Edmonston	An	121
McCormick	Andrew	Bp Down etc	Dn	170	McCrerye	John	Edmonston	An	121
McCormick	Gilbert	Bp Down etc	Dn	170	McCrew	James	Clannaboyes	Dn	157
mcCormick	John	Annandall	Dl	137	McCrey	James	Ards	Dn	156
McCormick	John	Clannaboyes	Dn	158	McCroch	James	Sir A. Steward	Ty	64
McCormick	Neivin	Bp Down etc	Dn	170	McCroch	Neekeed	Sir A. Steward	Ty	64
McCormick	Outhrid	Bp Down etc	Dn	170	McCrohart	David	Bp Dromore	Dn	171
McCormick	William	Clannaboyes	Dn	167	McCronill	John	Haberdashers	Ly	88
McCormick	William	Clannaboyes	Dn	169	McCroych	James	Sir A. Steward	Ty	64
mcCormock	John	Ards	Dn	152	McCru younger	John	Mervin	Ty	70
McCornock	John	Ards	Dn	151	McCrue	John	Crosby	Ty	69
McCosh	John	Clannaboyes	Dn	160	McCulaph	Peter	Mountnorrice	Ar	27
McCosh	John	Clannaboyes	Dn	169	McCuler	James	Strabane T.	Ty	74
McCosh	Owtry	Clannaboyes	Dn	158	M'Culin	William	Brewerton	Fe	54
McCosh	William	Clannaboyes	Dn	160	McCull	Archbold	Reding	An	121
McCoshee	Thomas	Clannaboyes	Dn	158	McCullagh	Bartholemew	Dalloway	An	122
McCoskery	Thomas	Adare	An	119	mcCullagh	Harbert	Ards	Dn	150
mcCostune	Dunkan	Sir J. Conningham	Dl	130	McCullagh	James	Ards	Dn	150
McCoul	Daniell	Ards	Dn	154	McCullagh	James	Ards	Dn	155
mcCoullees	Robert	Ards	Dn	150	McCullagh	James	Clannaboyes	Dn	157
McCoultron	John	Ards	Dn	156	McCullagh	John	Antrim	An	110
McCourty	John	Kildare	Dn	142	McCullagh	John	Edmonston	An	121
McCourty	John	Crumwell	Dn	144	McCullagh	John	Dalloway	An	122
McCourty younger	John	Coleraine	Ly	102	mcCullagh	John	W. Steward	Dl	133
					McCullagh	John	Ards	Dn	147
McCourty	Robert	Coleraine	Ly	104	mcCullagh	John	Ards	Dn	155
McCowan	John	Londonderry	Ly	87	McCullagh	Patrick	Dalloway	An	122
mcCowene	Walter	Chichester	Dl	139	mcCullagh	Patrick	Ards	Dn	148
mcCowr	Alexander	Willson	Dl	132	McCullagh	Robert	Dalloway	An	122
mcCowr	John	Willson	Dl	132	mcCullagh	Wm	Ards	Dn	149
mcCowtrone	John	Ards	Dn	150	mcCullam	Hugh	Antrim	An	113
McCrabb	James	Sir W. Steward	Ty	60	mcCullan	Dunkan	Antrim	An	112
McCracane	Thomas	Haberdashers	Ly	89	McCullan	Dunkan	Clannaboyes	Dn	158
McCracharan	Gilbert	C. of Abbercorne	Ty	71	McCullane	John	Antrim	An	112
McCrackan	John	Clannaboyes	Dn	159	McCullen	Adam	Clannaboyes	Dn	157
mcCrackan	Thomas	Ards	Dn	155	McCullen	Andrew	Clannaboyes	Dn	165
McCrackan	Thomas	Clannaboyes	Dn	161	mcCullen	James	Ards	Dn	149
McCracken	Anthony	Clannaboyes	Dn	157	McCullen	John	Clannaboyes	Dn	165
McCracken	Archbald	Londonderry	Ly	83	McCullen	John	Clannaboyes	Dn	165
McCracken	Thomas	Clannaboyes	Dn	159	McCullen	John	Clannaboyes	Dn	166
McCrad	Mathew	Clannaboyes	Dn	166	mcCullen	Thomas	Ards	Dn	149
McCrade	Mathew	Clannaboyes	Dn	169	McCullo	Alexander	Clannaboyes	Dn	164
McCraigh	Andrew	Clatworthy	An	123	mcCullo	Gilbert	Ards	Dn	153
McCraigh	John	Clatworthy	An	123	McCullo	John	Clannaboyes	Dn	164
McCraigh	Patrick	Clatworthy	An	123	McCullo	Mungo	Clannaboyes	Dn	158
McCraise	John	Coleraine	Ly	103	mcCullo	Nynyan	Ards	Dn	153
mcCranny	Martin	Coleraine	Ly	102	McCullod	John	Clannaboyes	Dn	165
McCrary	John	Kildare	Dn	142	mcCullog	Alexander	Annandall	Dl	137
McCratten	Charles	Clannaboyes	Dn	168	McCullogh	Andrew	Clannaboyes	Dn	166
McCratten	Donald	Clannaboyes	Dn	165	mcCullogh	Archbold	Edmonston	An	120
McCratten	John	Clannaboyes	Dn	166	McCullogh	Bartholemew	Dalloway	An	122
McCrattin	Andrew	Clannaboyes	Dn	165	McCullogh	David	Edmonston	An	121
McCratton	Charles	Clannaboyes	Dn	165	mcCullogh	George	Annandall	Dl	137
McCray	John	Clannaboyes	Dn	157	McCullogh	John	Clannaboyes	Dn	163
McCre	William	Ards	Dn	151	McCullogh	Niven	Clannaboyes	Dn	160
McCreary	Adam	Kildare	Dn	142	McCullogh	Robert	Adare	An	120
mcCreary	James	Benson	Dl	132	mcCullogh	Thomas	Annandall	Dl	137
mcCreary	John	Benson	Dl	132	McCullum	David	Clannaboyes	Dn	165
McCreary	John	Kildare	Dn	142	McCully	Robert	Bp Dromore	Dn	171
mcCreay	James	Sir J. Conningham	Dl	129	M'Culm	John	Brewerton	Fe	54
mcCredy	Fynlay	J. Conningham	Dl	135	McCuloe	Gylernew	Antrim	An	118
McCredy	John	Reding	An	121	mcCulver	Alexander	Bp Rapho	Dl	138
M'Creeke	John	Mrs Hammelton	Fe	41	mcCulver	Richard	Bp Rapho	Dl	138
McCreiry	John	Clannaboyes	Dn	165	mcCulyne	John	Ards	Dn	151
McCremont	Alexander	Clannaboyes	Dn	161	McCupein	Alexander	Edmonston	An	121
mcCrere	John	Edmonston	An	120	mcCurdin	Alexander	Antrim	An	112

Surname	Forename	Estate	Co.	Page	Surname	Forename	Estate	Co.	Page
McGill younger	John	Clannaboyes	Dn	166	McIlgared	John	Ards	Dn	151
McGill	Neall	Ards	Dn	149	mcIlhew	John	Ards	Dn	151
McGill	Quinton	Clannaboyes	Dn	157	mcIlhome	John	Lady Conningham	Dl	131
McGill	Robert	Clannaboyes	Dn	157	mcIlhome	John	Lady Conningham	Dl	131
McGill	Thomas	Clannaboyes	Dn	166	McIlhugh	John	Ards	Dn	151
McGill	William	Ironmongers	Ly	95	mcIllcrylin	Donnell	Antrim	An	113
mcGillapsey	Neil	Coleraine	Ly	103	McIllduff	Alexander	Clannaboyes	Dn	165
McGillbredy	Owen	Ironmongers	Ly	93	McIllhench	Alexander	Balye	Cv	13
mcGillione	John	Lynox	Dl	129	mcIllmorrow	James	Ards	Dn	152
mcGillmane	Gilbert	Antrim	An	115	McIlltough	William	Parsons	Ty	61
McGillowse	Robert	Hill	An	121	McIllvenie	Andrew	Clannaboyes	Dn	160
McGillure	Patrick	Clatwoorthy	An	123	mcIlman	Donnell	Sir J. Conningham	Dl	130
McGillurne	John	Cahoune	Dl	133	McIlman	Fynlay	Ards	Dn	156
mcGilmartin	Donnell	Antrim	An	116	mcIlman	James	Lady Conningham	Dl	131
mcGilmichill	Dunkan	Bp Rapho	Dl	138	McIlman	James	Clannaboyes	Dn	167
McGilpyne	John	Bp Clougher	Ty	77	McIlman	John	Lynox	Dl	128
McGilray	John	Lady McCleland	Ly	105	mcilmartin	Mathew	Antrim	An	113
mcGilrouse	Neece	Lynox	Dl	129	McIlmartin	Patrick	Lady McCleland	Ly	106
McGilroy	Andrew	Clatwoorthy	An	123	mcIlmeane	Michaell	Ards	Dn	152
McGilroy	John	Bp Clougher	Ty	78	mcIlmont	John	Ards	Dn	152
McGilroy	Robert	Hill	An	121	McIlmorrow	James	Ards	Dn	147
McGilton	Edward	Ards	Dn	148	McIlmorrow	John	Ards	Dn	154
mcGiltorane	John	Antrim	An	116	Mcilmorrow	Thomas	Ards	Dn	151
mcGilwory	John	Harrington	Dl	134	McIlmovet	Fargus	Ards	Dn	152
McGir	John	J. Hammelton	Cv	12	McIlnagh	John	Bp Down etc	Dn	170
McGir	John	J. Hammelton	Cv	12	mcIlno	John	Ards	Dn	151
McGlaney	Nynian	Clannaboyes	Dn	167	McIlno	William	Clannaboyes	Dn	158
McGleddery	Wm	Clannaboyes	Dn	157	McIlroy	Donnell	Crumwell	Dn	146
mcGlessen	Henry	Ards	Dn	149	mcIltherne	William	Lady Conningham	Dl	130
McGlower	Andrew	Antrim	An	110	mcIlvaine	Andrew	Bp Rapho	Dl	138
McGlyn	Alexander	Upton	An	124	McIlvian	John	Ards	Dn	148
mcGourden	John	Lynox	Dl	128	McIlwaine	Alexander	Clannaboyes	Dn	168
McGowen	James	Bp Dromore	Dn	171	McIlwaine	Danniall	Sir G. Hammilton	Ty	71
mcGowen	John	Antrim	An	110	McIlwaine	John	Clannaboyes	Dn	159
McGower	John	Edmonston	An	120	mcIlwane	John	A. Steward	Dl	135
McGowne	John	Clannaboyes	Dn	157	mcIlwayne	John	Ards	Dn	148
McGowne	Thomas	Dromond	Ty	70	mcIlwayne	John	Clannaboyes	Dn	159
McGoy	John	Mercers	Ly	96	McIlwayne	John	Clannaboyes	Dn	159
McGragan	Thomas	Antrim	An	112	younger				
McGrame	James	Edmonston	An	121	McIlwayne	Noel	Strabane T.	Ty	73
mcGreere	Donnell	Antrim	An	116	McIlwoorth	John	Clannaboyes	Dn	166
McGreere	Gillorish	Antrim	An	112	McIlwrath	Andrew	Ards	Dn	147
McGreere	John	Antrim	An	113	McIlwrath	Gilbert	Clannaboyes	Dn	169
McGreere	John Dow	Antrim	An	110	McInch	William	Coleraine	Ly	99
McGregor	John	Dromond	Ty	70	mcIntch	John	Coleraine	Ly	99
MíGregor	John	Montgomery	Fe	54	mcIntch	Mathew	Coleraine	Ly	99
McGriffin	Robert	Lyndsay	Ty	68	mcInteer	Robert	Sir J. Conningham	Dl	129
mcGrowder	Neal	Antrim	An	112	mcIthaney	John	Upton	An	125
McGrowder	Thomas	Antrim	An	113	McJanet	John	Antrim	An	112
McGuffock	Andrew	Clannaboyes	Dn	161	McJohnsy	John	Bp Dromore	Dn	171
McGuffog	Alexander	Ards	Dn	148	McJury	John	Erskin	Ty	57
mcGumberry	James	Willson	Dl	132	McKahan	Gillcollum	Antrim	An	113
mcGuney	Robert	Coleraine	Ly	100	mcKaine	John	Lynox	Dl	128
McGusoke	Alexander	Ards	Dn	147	mcKaine	Killime	J. Steward	Dl	136
mcHaff	Nynian	Ards	Dn	148	mcKan	David	Lynox	Dl	129
McHaffy	William	Ards	Dn	153	McKanly	Adam	Londonderry	Ly	88
McHale	Mortah	Vintners	Ly	97	McKarmick	John	Strabane T.	Ty	75
mcHallan	Dunkan	Ards	Dn	153	McKarnes	John	M. of Abbercorne	Ty	72
McHallen	William	Ards	Dn	151	McKasby	James	Strabane T.	Ty	76
McHelen	Gilbert	Bp Down etc	Dn	170	McKea	James	Clannaboyes	Dn	164
McHellan	George	Maghera & Desert Martin	Ly	107	McKea	Patrick	Kildare	Dn	142
McHennet	Wm	Antrim	An	112	McKeag	John	Clatwoorthy	An	124
McHenry	John	Antrim	An	116	McKeag	Mark	Clatwoorthy	An	124
mcHilheney	John	Antrim	An	112	mcKeag	Thomas	Dean of Rapho	Dl	139
McHillan	John	Maghera & Desert Martin	Ly	107	mcKeallan	John	Ards	Dn	155
mcHutchden	John	Ards	Dn	149	McKean	Donnell	Sir J. Conningham	Dl	130
mcHutchen	Robert	Annandall	Dl	137	McKean	James	Sir W. Steward	Ty	59
mcHutchin	Patrick	Annandall	Dl	137	McKean	William	Kildare	Dn	142
mcHutchon	John	Lady Conningham	Dl	131	McKeaugh	John	Kildare	Dn	142
McHutchon	Thomas	Ards	Dn	153	McKeddy	John	Clannaboyes	Dn	165
mcHuthdene	James	Ards	Dn	149	McKedyon	Andrew	Lyndsay	Ty	68
McHyre	Gilbert	Ards	Dn	147	McKee	Alexander	Willson	Dl	132
McIcrinye	Cullo	Clannaboyes	Dn	159	McKee	Alexander	Londonderry	Ly	86
McIcrinye	James	Clannaboyes	Dn	159	McKee	Andrew	Clannaboyes	Dn	160
mcIldonagh	John	Lynox	Dl	129	McKee	Andrew	Londonderry	Ly	83
mcIldony	Nole	M. of Abbercorne	Ty	72	McKee	Donnell	Sir J. Conningham	Dl	129

Surname	Forename	Estate	Co.	Page	Surname	Forename	Estate	Co.	Page
McTeare	Patrick	Merchant Taylors	Ly	92	Merryman	Edmond	Mervin	Ty	69
McTeere	William	Merchant Taylors	Ly	92	Mervin	Thomas	Mervin	Ty	70
mcTeere	Andrew	Clannaboyes	Dn	157	Mervin	John	Crumwell	Dn	146
McTeir	Hugh	Clannaboyes	Dn	161	Messenger	John	Crumwell	Dn	146
McTeir	John	Adare	An	120	Messenger younger	Richard	Satcheuerall	Ar	24
McTeraghan	Andrew	Adare	An	119	Messenger	George	Londonderry	Ly	87
McTernaghan	John	Adare	An	120	Messongor	Edward	Lord Primate	Ar	35
McTernaghan	John	Ards	Dn	149	Messy	David	Antrim	An	110
McThomson	John	Ards	Dn	149	Metland	David	Antrim	An	111
mcTully	Thomas	Clannaboyes	Dn	164	Metland	George	Ards	Dn	153
McTyer	Thomas	Clannaboyes	Dn	167	Metland	Patrick	Sir F. Hammelton	Cv	5
McTyne	William	Clannaboyes	Dn	164	Mewres	James	Clatworthy	An	123
McTyr	Andrew	Lynox	Dl	128	Meyns	James	Clannaboyes	Dn	166
mcTyre	Andrew	Ards	Dn	149	Micclesjohn	Andrew	Ards	Dn	150
mcTyre	Gilbert	Clannaboyes	Dn	167	Michaell	David	Ards	Dn	156
McTyre	Robert	Strabane T.	Ty	76	Michaell	David	Clannaboyes	Dn	166
McTyre	John	Chichester	Ty	78	Michaell	Gilbert	Antrim	An	113
McVaugh	John	W. Steward	Dl	133	Michaell	John	Clannaboyes	Dn	167
mcWalker	Andrew	Ards	Dn	153	Michaell	John	Haberdashers	Ly	89
McWalter	Hugh	Clannaboyes	Dn	157	Michaell	John	Mervin	Ty	70
McWalter	Symond	Ards	Dn	151	Michaell	John	Sir G. Hammilton	Ty	70
McWalter	Bryan	Cullo McEver McMaghan	Mo	174	Michaell	Robert	Sir A. Steward	Ty	64
McWard	Morricett	Cullo McEver McMaghan	Mo	174	Michaell	Robert	Sir A. Steward	Ty	65
McWard	Phillip	Cullo McEver McMaghan	Mo	174	Michaell	Rowland	Ards	Dn	155
McWard	Donnell	Clatworthy	An	124	Michaell	John	Ards	Dn	152
McWaugh	John	Ards	Dn	148	Michaelson	John	Gower	Fe	52
McWaugh	John	Bp Down etc	Dn	170	Micheall	John	Ards	Dn	151
McWell	James	Clannaboyes	Dn	164	Micheallson	Andrew	Clatworthy	An	123
McWharry	Gilbert	Clannaboyes	Dn	161	Michell	Gawen	Sir J. Conningham	Dl	129
McWhartor	Patrick	Clannaboyes	Dn	167	Michell	George	Harrington	Dl	134
McWhaw	Danyell	Coleraine	Ly	103	Michell	George	Sir W. Steward	Ty	59
McWhery	John	Clannaboyes	Dn	158	Michell	Gilbert	Antrim	An	113
McWhingy	James	Ards	Dn	153	Michell	Gilbert	Crumwell	Dn	143
mcWhirk	James	Clannaboyes	Dn	162	Michell	Hugh	Londonderry	Ly	87
McWhirke	John	Clannaboyes	Dn	160	Michell	James	Antrim	An	115
McWhirke	Robert	Clannaboyes	Dn	165	Michell	James	Chichester	Dl	140
McWhirke	Alexander	W. Steward	Dl	133	Michell	James	Ards	Dn	149
mcWilliam	Andrew	Ards	Dn	154	Michell	James	Ards	Dn	150
McWilliam	Dunkan	Ards	Dn	150	Michell	James	Clothworkers	Ly	90
mcWilliam	James	Antrim	An	115	Michell	James	Coleraine	Ly	103
mcWilliam	James	Haberdashers	Ly	89	Michell	James	Coleraine	Ly	104
McWilliam	John	Antrim	An	115	Michell	John	Antrim	An	115
McWilliam	John	Clannaboyes	Dn	158	Michell	John	Dalloway	An	122
McWilliam	John	Clannaboyes	Dn	159	Michell	John	Sir F. Hammelton	Cv	4
McWilliam	John	Bp Dromore	Dn	171	Michell	John	Willson	Dl	132
McWilliam	Nevin	Bp Down etc	Dn	170	Michell	John	Benson	Dl	133
McWilliam	Robert	Antrim	An	114	Michell	John	Chichester	Dl	140
McWilliam	Thomas	Bp Dromore	Dn	171	Michell	John	Kildare	Dn	142
McWilliam	John	Crumwell	Dn	144	Michell	John	Ards	Dn	150
McWilliams	Andrew	Grocers	Ly	91	Michell	John	Ballfowre	Fe	38
McWilly	Gilbert	Ards	Dn	153	Michell	John	Mercers	Ly	96
mcWilly	Dunkan	J. Conningham	Dl	136	Michell	John	Coleraine	Ly	99
mcWrick	Alexander	Clannaboyes	Dn	165	Michell	Patt	Chichester	Dl	140
Meaghan	John	Cope	Ar	20	Michell	Richard	Mercers	Ly	95
Meallaway	John	Adare	An	119	Michell	Robert	Lynox	Dl	128
Mean	Thomas	Butler	Fe	49	Michell	Robert	Ballfowre	Fe	38
Meanese	John	Butler	Fe	49	Michell	Robert	Vintners	Ly	98
Meanse	John	Upton	An	124	Michell	Robert	Lady McCleland	Ly	105
Meare	Roger	Satcheuerall	Ar	25	Michell	Thomas	Hatton	Fe	48
Medcalf	John	Mercers	Ly	96	Michell	William	Harrington	Dl	134
Medley	George	Clannaboyes	Dn	161	Michell	William	G. Hume	Fe	43
Meeke	John	Clannaboyes	Dn	161	Michell	William	Londonderry	Ly	85
Meeke	David	Erskin	Ty	57	Michell	William	Londonderry	Ly	87
Meliken	James	Erskin	Ty	57	Michell	William	Vintners	Ly	98
Meliken	John	Erskin	Ty	57	Michell	William	Phillips	Ly	105
Meliken	James	Adare	An	119	Michell	Richard	Clannaboyes	Dn	161
Melikin	Andrew	Antrim	An	112	Michelson	Symond	Lord Primate	Ar	34
Melvill	Andrew	Antrim	An	114	Michelson	James	Tychborne	Ty	61
Melvin	James	Kildare	Dn	142	Mickle	Gilbert	Parsons	Ty	62
Melvin	Duncan	H. Steward	Ty	66	Middiken	Thomas	Butler	Fe	50
Meny	John	Annandall	Dl	136	Middlebroke	Morrish	Higget	Fe	46
Menzes	Anthony	Londonderry	Ly	84	Middlebrooke	Robert	Sir W. Steward	Ty	59
Mercer	Evance	Calfield	Ar	35	Middleton	Thomas	Butler	Fe	49
Meredeth	John	Grandison	Ar	32	Midlebrooke	William	Ards	Dn	149
Meredeth	Edward	Satcheuerall	Ar	24	Might	John	Willoby	Fe	54
Meres	Danyell	Crumwell	Dn	145					

Surname	Forename	Estate	Co.	Page	Surname	Forename	Estate	Co.	Page
Monteeth	William	Ards	Dn	151	Moore	George	Mercers	Ly	96
Montgomery	Hugh	Ards	Dn	148	Moore	Gilbert	Antrim	An	112
Montgomery	Hugh	Ards	Dn	151	Moore	Gilbert	Antrim	An	114
Montgomery	James	Ards	Dn	152	Moore	Hamlet	Powerscourt	Ty	79
Montgomery	John	Lord Primate	Ar	33	Moore	Henry	Mountnorrice	Ar	27
Montgomery	John	Ards	Dn	151	Moore	Henry	Lady McCleland	Ly	105
Montgomery	John	Ards	Dn	152	Moore	Hugh	Satcheuerall	Ar	25
Montgomery	Neal	Montgomery	Fe	54	Moore	James	Antrim	An	113
Montgomery	William	Atchison	Ar	28	Moore	James	Antrim	An	113
Montgomery	William	Montgomery	Fe	54	Moore	James	Antrim	An	114
Montgomry	Andrew	Ards	Dn	153	Moore	James	Antrim	An	114
Montgomry	John	Ards	Dn	153	Moore	James	Antrim	An	116
Montgomry	Robert	Ards	Dn	151	Moore	James	Antrim	An	118
Montgoomry	Robert	Ards	Dn	149	Moore	James	Clatwoorthy	An	123
Montgoumry	Jo	Ards	Dn	148	Moore	James	Ards	Dn	147
Montgumery	Hugh	Ards	Dn	151	Moore	James	Ards	Dn	148
Montgumery	John	Bp Dromore	Dn	172	Moore	James	Ards	Dn	149
Montgumery	Thomas	Ards	Dn	149	Moore	James	Ards	Dn	155
Montgumry	Adam	Ards	Dn	148	Moore	James	Londonderry	Ly	83
Montgumry	Adam	Ards	Dn	151	Moore	John	Antrim	An	110
Montgumry	Adam	Ards	Dn	152	Moore	John	Antrim	An	111
Montgumry	Alexander	Ards	Dn	154	Moore	John	Antrim	An	112
Montgumry	David	Clannaboyes	Dn	157	Moore	John	Antrim	An	112
Montgumry	Hugh	Ards	Dn	151	Moore	John	Antrim	An	113
Montgumry	Hugh	Ards	Dn	152	Moore	John	Antrim	An	114
Montgumry	Hugh	Ards	Dn	154	Moore	John	Antrim	An	116
Montgumry	Hugh	Ards	Dn	154	Moore	John	Antrim	An	117
Montgumry	Hugh	Ards	Dn	155	Moore	John	Antrim	An	117
Montgumry	James	Ards	Dn	156	Moore	John	Antrim	An	117
Montgumry	James	Clannaboyes	Dn	164	Moore	John	Antrim	An	118
Montgumry	John	Ards	Dn	151	Moore	John	Adare	An	119
Montgumry	John	Ards	Dn	153	Moore	John	Upton	An	124
Montgumry	John	Ards	Dn	154	Moore	John	W. Steward	Dl	133
Montgumry	John	Ards	Dn	154	Moore	John	Bp Rapho	Dl	138
Montgumry	John	Ards	Dn	155	Moore	John	Ards	Dn	147
Montgumry	John	Ards	Dn	155	Moore	John	Ards	Dn	148
Montgumry	John	Ards	Dn	155	Moore	John	Ards	Dn	155
Montgumry	John	Ards	Dn	156	Moore	John	Ards	Dn	156
Montgumry	John	Clannaboyes	Dn	165	Moore	John	Clannaboyes	Dn	157
Montgumry	John	Bp Down etc	Dn	170	Moore	John	Clannaboyes	Dn	158
Montgumry	John	Burris	Dn	172	Moore	John	Clannaboyes	Dn	161
Montgumry	John	Ards	Dn	156	Moore	John	Clannaboyes	Dn	161
	younger				Moore	John	Clannaboyes	Dn	162
Montgumry	Michaell	Clannaboyes	Dn	160	Moore	John	Clannaboyes	Dn	163
Montgumry	Neal	Clannaboyes	Dn	165	Moore	John	Clannaboyes	Dn	165
Montgumry	Neill	Ards	Dn	151	Moore	John	Clannaboyes	Dn	169
Montgumry	Patrick	Ards	Dn	153	Moore	John	Brewerton	Fe	54
Montgumry	Robert	Ards	Dn	152	Moore	John	Haberdashers	Ly	89
Montgumry	Robert	Ards	Dn	155	Moore	John	Haberdashers	Ly	90
Montgumry	Robert	Ards	Dn	155	Moore	John	Goldsmiths	Ly	92
Montgumry	Robert	Bp Dromore	Dn	171	Moore	John	Coleraine	Ly	101
Montgumry	Thomas	Ards	Dn	152	Moore	John	Berresfourd	Ly	106
Montgumry	William	Ards	Dn	151	Moore	John	Loftus	Mo	174
Montgumry	William	Ards	Dn	154	Moore	John	Parsons	Ty	61
Montgumry	William	Ards	Dn	155	Moore	John	Parsons	Ty	61
Montgumry	Wm	Ards	Dn	156	Moore younger	John	Clannaboyes	Dn	158
Montieth	William	Haberdashers	Ly	89	Moore	Lawrence	Cavan T.	Cv	16
Montsod	Robert	Antrim	An	117	Moore	Michaell	Antrim	An	116
Monzy	Thomas	Dromond	Ty	70	Moore	Patrick	Ards	Dn	151
Moody	Henry	Ards	Dn	151	Moore	Patrick	Ards	Dn	156
Moody	James	Lord Primate	Ar	34	Moore	Patrick	Coleraine	Ly	103
Moody	James	Ards	Dn	155	Moore	Patrick	Art oge Mc Maghan	Mo	174
Moody	John	Lord Primate	Ar	35	Moore	Phillip	Ards	Dn	155
Moody	John	Ards	Dn	151	Moore	Quinton	Ards	Dn	153
Moody	Patrick	Lord Primate	Ar	34	Moore	Richard	Mountnorrice	Ar	27
Moody	Thomas	Ards	Dn	154	Moore	Richard	Richardson	Ar	36
Moonie	Gilbert	Ards	Dn	150	Moore	Rist	Woorell	Fe	46
Moore	Allen	Erskin	Ty	58	Moore	Robert	Antrim	An	111
Moore	Archbald	Ards	Dn	155	Moore	Robert	Antrim	An	117
Moore	Christopher	Phillips	Ly	104	Moore	Robert	Upton	An	125
Moore	David	Haberdashers	Ly	90	Moore	Robert	Ards	Dn	149
Moore	Dunkan	Adare	An	119	Moore	Robert	Clannaboyes	Dn	156
Moore	Edward	Hastings	Ty	68	Moore	Robert	Clannaboyes	Dn	158
Moore	Edward	Hastings	Ty	68	Moore	Robert	Clannaboyes	Dn	166
Moore	Gabrahell	Coleraine	Ly	103	Moore	Robert	Woorell	Fe	45
Moore	George	Clannaboyes	Dn	157	Moore	Robert	Goldsmiths	Ly	92

Surname	Forename	Estate	Co.	Page	Surname	Forename	Estate	Co.	Page
Mosman	John	Clannaboyes	Dn	160	Murer	Archbald	Antrim	An	114
Mosmanie	James	Clannaboyes	Dn	164	Murer	Quintan	Antrim	An	114
Moss	William	Melvin	Dn	172	Muriall	William	Haberdashers	Ly	89
Mosser	Alexander	Lord Primate	Ar	34	Murmon	John	Hammelton	Ar	30
Mountgomery	Dunkan	Bp Rapho	Dl	138	Murphe	James	Crumwell	Dn	146
Mountgomery	Edward	Antrim	An	113	Murphey	Thomas	Ards	Dn	155
Mountgomery	Hugh	Antrim	An	110	Murphey	Thomas	Ards	Dn	155
Mountgomery	Hugh	Antrim	An	113	younger				
Mountgomery	Hugh	Antrim	An	115	Murragh	William	Ards	Dn	148
Mountgomery	Hugh	Ards	Dn	147	Murray	Charles	Montgomery	Fe	54
Mountgomery	Humphrey	Cahoune	Dl	133	Murray	David	Sir G. Hammilton	Ty	70
Mountgomery	James	Ballfowre	Fe	39	Murray	George	Haberdashers	Ly	89
Mountgomery	James	Bp Clougher	Ty	77	Murray	Guy	Dalloway	An	122
Mountgomery	John	Antrim	An	111	Murray	John	Clannaboyes	Dn	169
Mountgomery	John	Antrim	An	118	Murray	John	Lady McCleland	Ly	105
Mountgomery	John	Dalloway	An	122	Murray	Richard	Annandall	Dl	136
Mountgomery	John	Chichester	Dl	139	Murray	Richard	Ballfowre	Fe	38
Mountgomery	John	Ards	Dn	147	Murray	Robert	Lady McCleland	Ly	105
Mountgomery	John	Phillips	Ly	104	Murray	Walter	Ballfowre	Fe	38
Mountgomery	Mathew	Ards	Dn	148	Murray	William	Ballfowre	Fe	38
Mountgomery	Robert	Antrim	An	112	Murray	William	Londonderry	Ly	86
Mountgomery	Robert	Ards	Dn	147	Murrey	David	Antrim	An	118
Mountgomery	Thomas	Clatworthy	An	124	Murrey	David	Hammelton	Ar	29
Mountgomery	William	Chichester	Dl	140	Murrey	James	Adare	An	120
Mountgomery	William	Ards	Dn	149	Murrey	James	Kildare	Dn	142
Moure	John	Clatworthy	An	124	Murrey	James	Clannaboyes	Dn	159
Moure	Mathew	Clatworthy	An	124	Murrey	John	Sir G. Hammilton	Ty	70
Moure	Walter	Clatworthy	An	124	Murrey	Patrick	Coleraine	Ly	103
Mouse	James	Vintners	Ly	97	Murrey	Robert	Clannaboyes	Dn	158
Mouse	John	Enniskillen T.	Fe	51	Murrey	Robert	Clannaboyes	Dn	158
Mowberry	Arch:	Benson	Dl	132	younger				
Mowet	Archbald	Clannaboyes	Dn	161	Murrey	William	Hammelton	Ar	29
Moyerland	George	Clannaboyes	Dn	161	Murroch	Andrew	Crumwell	Dn	144
Muckle	James	Antrim	An	117	Murrow	Thomas	Sir F. Hammelton	Cv	4
Muddy	Patrick	Strabane T.	Ty	74	Murrow	William	Erskin	Ty	57
Muffes	Thomas	Sir F. Hammelton	Cv	6	Murrowes	Gilbert	Sir F. Hammelton	Cv	4
Mullan	Iver	Phillips	Ly	104	Murrowes	Patrick	Sir F. Hammelton	Cv	4
Mullen	William	Clannaboyes	Dn	168	Murry	Adam	Ards	Dn	148
Mulligan	Dunkan	Clannaboyes	Dn	165	Murry	Alexander	Annandall	Dl	137
Mulligan	James	Ards	Dn	150	Murry	George	Bp Dromore	Dn	171
Mulligan	James	Ards	Dn	153	Murry	James	Annandall	Dl	137
Mulligan	John	Ards	Dn	148	Murry	John	Sir F. Hammelton	Cv	6
Mulligan	John	Bp Dromore	Dn	171	Murry	John	Annandall	Dl	137
Mulligan	Robert	Ards	Dn	152	Murry	John	Ards	Dn	148
Mulligan	Thomas	Ards	Dn	147	Murry	John	Ards	Dn	155
Mulnes	Alexander	Edmonston	An	120	Murryne	Thomas	Ironmongers	Ly	94
Mumberson	Thomas	Sir F. Hammelton	Cv	5	Murtagh	William	Clatworthy	An	122
Mund	James	Coleraine	Ly	103	Murteant	Melchesedeck	Grandison	Ar	31
Mund	James	Coleraine	Ly	104	Murthee	Alexander	Dalloway	An	122
Mundall	John	Ballfowre	Fe	38	Murtough	Steaphen	Coleraine	Ly	101
Mungomery	Alexander	Lord Primate	Ar	33	Muthey	James	Lynox	Dl	129
Mungomery	Gilbert	Bp Clougher	Ty	78	Muthray	John	Edmonston	An	121
elder					Myles	William	Powerscourt	Ty	79
Mungomery	Gilbert	Bp Clougher	Ty	78	Myllikin	William	Sanderson	Ty	66
younger					Myn	Allyn	Coleraine	Ly	99
Mungomery	James	Bp Clougher	Ty	77	Myn	James	Sir W. Steward	Ty	59
Mungomery	John	Montgomery	Fe	54	Myn	John	Sir W. Steward	Ty	59
Mungomery	John	Coape	Ty	62	Myn	John	Sir W. Steward	Ty	59
Mungomery	John	Bp Clougher	Ty	77	Myn	William	Sir W. Steward	Ty	58
Mungomery	Robert	Ironmongers	Ly	95	Myning	James	Sir W. Steward	Ty	59
Mungomery	Robert	Bp Clougher	Ty	77	Mynne	John	Sir W. Steward	Ty	58
Mungomery	Thomas	Haberdashers	Ly	89	Mynne	Roger	Sir W. Steward	Ty	58
Munnings	Clemment	Grocers	Ly	91	Mynne	William	Sir W. Steward	Ty	58
Muntgomery	Robert	Lady Conningham	Dl	131	Mynnes	George	Merchant Taylors	Ly	93
Murchie	Thomas	Clannaboyes	Dn	157	Mynnis	John	Richardson	Ty	67
Murdaugh	John	Antrim	An	115	Mywourne	Robert	Clannaboyes	Dn	161
Murdo	John	Hastings	Fe	53	Napa	Malcome	Ards	Dn	149
Murdo	William	J. Hammelton	Cv	12	Naper	Patrick	Ards	Dn	154
Murdogh	John	Clannaboyes	Dn	164	Narath	Richard	Butler	Cv	3
Murdogh	John	Clannaboyes	Dn	164	Nasmith	Michaell	Clannaboyes	Dn	164
younger					Natley	Richard	F. Blennerhasset	Fe	45
Murdorgh	James	Ards	Dn	150	Natley	Walter	F. Blennerhasset	Fe	45
Mure	Adam	Antrim	An	115	Naught	George	J. Conningham	Dl	136
Mure	Hugh	Cahoune	Dl	134	Naught	William	Kildare	Dn	142
Mure	Hugh	J. Conningham	Dl	136	Naught	William	Crumwell	Dn	145
Mure	Robert	Antrim	An	118	Naylor	George	Taylor	Cv	10

Surname	Forename	Estate	Co.	Page
Nixon	George	Sir F. Hammelton	Cv	4
Nixon	Hugh	Dillon	Fe	52
Nixon	John	Satcheuerall	Ar	23
Nixon	John	Lowther	Fe	44
Nixon	John	Dillon	Fe	52
Nixon	John	Dillon	Fe	52
Nixon	Quinton	Atchison	Ar	29
Nixon	Quinton	Dillon	Fe	52
Nixon	Robert	Sir F. Hammelton	Cv	5
Nixon	Robert	Crumwell	Dn	145
Nixon	Robert	Hastings	Fe	53
Nixon	Robert	Lyndsay	Ty	67
Nixon	Robert	Lyndsay	Ty	68
Nixon	William	Mountnorrice	Ar	27
Nixon	William	Clannaboyes	Dn	157
Nixon	William	Clannaboyes	Dn	163
Noble	John	Coleraine	Ly	101
Noble	Quintan	Ballfowre	Fe	38
Noble	Thomas	Lowther	Fe	44
Noble	Thomas	Dillon	Fe	52
Noble elder	Thomas	Dillon	Fe	52
Noble	Walter	Erskin	Ty	58
Noble	William	Lynox	Dl	129
Noble	William	Erskin	Ty	57
Noble	William	Parsons	Ty	62
Nordus	William	Cole	Fe	39
Norrice	George	Maghera & Desert Martin	Ly	106
Norrice	Robert	Bagshaw	Cv	8
Norris	George	Cope	Ar	19
Norris	John	Londonderry	Ly	87
Norris	Nicholas	Upton	An	124
North	John	Mercers	Ly	95
North	Richard	Butler	Cv	4
North	Thomas	Taylor	Cv	10
North	William	Taylor	Cv	10
Norton	Edward	Mercers	Ly	96
Norton	James	Satcheuerall	Ar	24
Nortyn	Thomas	Antrim	An	114
Norwich	Thomas	Hammelton	Ar	29
Nother	Cuthbert	Vintners	Ly	97
Notley	Richard	L. Blennerhasset	Fe	45
Notley	William	F. Blennerhasset	Fe	45
Nuson	Anthony	Coleraine	Ly	101
Nygrone	David	Edmonston	An	121
Nyst	Richard	Enniskillen T.	Fe	51
O ? rines	James	Benson	Dl	132
O Brat	John	Clannaboyes	Dn	161
O Bryan	Thomas	Art oge Mc Maghan	Mo	174
O Callan	Henry	Cullo McEver McMaghan	Mo	174
O Carrier	William	Cullo McEver McMaghan	Mo	174
O Crag	Gilbert	Crosby	Ty	69
O Dare	Rynyon	Kildare	Dn	142
O Dornan	Donnell	Clannaboyes	Dn	159
O Duff	Brian	Patrick Duff McCullo McMaghan	Mo	175
O Gordon	John	Drapers	Ly	98
O Gyleire	Owen	Coleraine	Ly	103
o Kan	Patrick	Clannaboyes	Dn	163
O Kat	Turlo	Ironmongers	Ly	95
O Keife	David	Bp Dromore	Dn	171
o Kelly	Bryan	Clannaboyes	Dn	165
O Lyne	John	Clannaboyes	Dn	165
O meallan	Towell	Neall McKenna	Mo	175
O Mory	John	A. Hammelton	Ty	63
O Mulcoyle	Bryan	Art oge Mc Maghan	Mo	174
Oakburne	Henry	Ards	Dn	151
Oar	Patrick	Clannaboyes	Dn	164
Oar	William	Clannaboyes	Dn	164
Oathes	Bryan	Lord Primate	Ar	34
Obison	James	Bp Dromore	Dn	172
Obyne	John	Dalloway	An	122
Ocane	Hugh	Mercers	Ly	96
OCarrin	Owen Ro	Art oge Mc Maghan	Mo	174
OConnall	Patrick McBrian	Art oge Mc Maghan	Mo	174
Odall	Robert	Crumwell	Dn	146

Surname	Forename	Estate	Co.	Page
Odomes	Thomas	Satcheuerall	Ar	25
Odoylson	Marcus	Sir J. Conningham	Dl	130
Oge	William	Coleraine	Ly	103
Oghterson	John	Maghera & Desert Martin	Ly	107
Oghterson	William	Maghera & Desert Martin	Ly	107
Ogill	John	Butler	Cv	2
Ogilmoore	Cormock	Ards	Dn	155
Ogilmore	Ogen	Ards	Dn	155
Ogle	Alexander	Cole	Fe	40
Ogle	William	Hannings	Fe	44
Oglee	John	Cole	Fe	39
Ogleshew	Richard	Drapers	Ly	98
Ognew	Thomas	Ards	Dn	154
Ognewe	Gilbert	Antrim	An	117
Ognewe	John	Antrim	An	116
Ognewe	Patt	Antrim	An	118
Ogton	Robert	Crumwell	Dn	146
Okelly	John	Sir W. Steward	Ty	60
Okenhead	John	Cahoune	Dl	134
Okes	Elias	Vintners	Ly	98
Old	Adam	Antrim	An	113
Old	John	Ards	Dn	147
Old	Thomas	Antrim	An	112
Old	William	Ards	Dn	153
Old	William	Clannaboyes	Dn	159
Old younger	William	Clannaboyes	Dn	159
Olfeard	Olfeard	Londonderry	Ly	84
Olfords	Patrick	Londonderry	Ly	87
Olie	William	Bp Dromore	Dn	171
Oliver	James	Phillips	Ly	104
Oliver	John	Haberdashers	Ly	90
Oliver	Thomas	Moynes	Cv	11
Oliver	Thomas	Clannaboyes	Dn	162
Oliver	Thomas	Clannaboyes	Dn	169
Olly	John	Powerscourt	Ty	79
Omilligan	Patrick	Ards	Dn	155
Omolldarg	Donal	Antrim	An	113
Or	Donnell	W. Steward	Dl	133
Or	George	Ards	Dn	153
Ore	Andrew	Strabane T.	Ty	75
Ore	Andrew	Strabane T.	Ty	76
Ore	John	Clannaboyes	Dn	166
Ore	John	Brewerton	Fe	54
Ore	John	M. of Abbercorne	Ty	72
Ore	John	M. of Abbercorne	Ty	72
Ore	John	Strabane T.	Ty	75
Ore elder	John	Sir G. Hammilton	Ty	71
Ore younger	John	Sir G. Hammilton	Ty	71
Ore	Patrick	Londonderry	Ly	86
Orme	Richard	Hannings	Fe	44
Ormoyle	John	Londonderry	Ly	86
Orr	Adam	Ards	Dn	154
Orr	Alexander	Ards	Dn	154
Orr	Cuthbert	Ards	Dn	150
Orr	James	Antrim	An	115
Orr	James	Ards	Dn	148
Orr	James	Ards	Dn	150
Orr	James	Ards	Dn	151
Orr	John	Ards	Dn	148
Orr	John	Ards	Dn	151
Orr	John	Clannaboyes	Dn	166
Orr	Patrick	Ards	Dn	147
Orr	Robert	Clannaboyes	Dn	166
Orr	Sandy	Clannaboyes	Dn	166
Orr	Thomas	Antrim	An	112
Orr	Thomas	Antrim	An	118
Orr	Thomas	Chichester	Dl	140
Orr	Thomas	Ards	Dn	148
Orr	William	Ards	Dn	149
Orre	James	Antrim	An	111
Orum	William	Enniskillen T.	Fe	51
Osbesson	Thomas	Crumwell	Dn	145
Osborne	Henry	Londonderry	Ly	85
Osborne	James	Londonderry	Ly	88
Osborne	John	Chichester	Dl	139
Osburne	William	Ards	Dn	156

Surname	Forename	Estate	Co.	Page	Surname	Forename	Estate	Co.	Page
Patterson	James	Antrim	An	115	Peares	Zachary	Londonderry	Ly	85
Patterson	James	Sir J. Conningham	Dl	129	Pearse	Randall	Cole	Fe	40
Patterson	James	Clannaboyes	Dn	157	Pearse	Roger	Cole	Fe	40
Patterson	James	Coleraine	Ly	103	Pearson	George	Clatworthy	An	123
Patterson	John	Antrim	An	113	Pearson	Lancelot	Brownlow	Ar	26
Patterson	John	Kingsmell	Dl	131	Pearson	Leonard	Brownlow	Ar	26
Patterson	John	Cahoune	Dl	133	Pearson	Nicholas	Drapers	Ly	98
Patterson	John	Ards	Dn	148	Pearson	Quinton	Clatworthy	An	123
Patterson	John	Clannaboyes	Dn	167	Pearson	Richard	Grandison	Ar	32
Patterson	John	Haberdashers	Ly	88	Pearson	Richard	Clannaboyes	Dn	163
Patterson	John	Lady McCleland	Ly	105	Pearson	Rynyon	Lyndsay	Ty	68
Patterson elder	John	Strabane T.	Ty	76	Pearson	Thomas	Sedburrogh	Fe	48
Patterson	Mathew	Bp Rapho	Dl	137	Pearson	William	Cope	Ar	18
Patterson	Patrick	Ards	Dn	147	Peate	Arthur	Sir W. Steward	Ty	60
Patterson	Patrick	Ards	Dn	151	Peate	Robert	Sir W. Steward	Ty	60
Patterson	Patrick	Londonderry	Ly	87	Pebult	James	Antrim	An	115
Patterson	Robert	Lord Primate	Ar	35	Pecock	John	Lynox	Dl	129
Patterson	Robert	J. Conningham	Dl	136	Peebles	Patrick	Clannaboyes	Dn	158
Patterson	Robert	Strabane T.	Ty	76	Peeke	Thomas	Coleraine	Ly	103
Patterson	William	Clannaboyes	Dn	160	Peirce	Evaine	Davis	Dl	134
Patterson	William	Clannaboyes	Dn	165	Pelog	John	Adare	An	120
Patterson	William	Clannaboyes	Dn	166	Pench	Henry	Sir F. Hammelton	Cv	6
Patterson	William	Coleraine	Ly	103	Penington	John	Clannaboyes	Dn	168
Patterson	William	Coleraine	Ly	104	Penne	John	Butler	Fe	49
Pattisn	John	Waldrum	Ar	22	Penney elder	Thomas	Erskin	Ty	58
Patton	Alexander	Haberdashers	Ly	89	Penney younger	Thomas	Erskin	Ty	58
Patton	James	Erskin	Ty	58	Pennington	John	Clannaboyes	Dn	162
Patton	John	Clannaboyes	Dn	157	Pennington	William	Butler	Cv	2
Patton	John	Clannaboyes	Dn	157	Penny	William	Crumwell	Dn	143
Patton	John	Clannaboyes	Dn	165	Penny	William	Crumwell	Dn	143
Patton	Robert	Phillips	Ly	104	Peoples	Cuthbert	Antrim	An	118
Pattowne	James	Strabane T.	Ty	74	Peoples	John	Antrim	An	114
Pattrowne	Thomas	Clannaboyes	Dn	165	Peoples	John	Adare	An	119
Paul	Claudius	Sir G. Hammilton	Ty	70	Peoples	Robert	Antrim	An	110
Paul	John	Ards	Dn	147	Peoples	Robert	Antrim	An	118
Paul	Robert	Edmonston	An	120	Peoples	Thomas	Antrim	An	116
Pay	Archbald	Clatworthy	An	124	Peoples	Thomas	Londonderry	Ly	86
Payden	Alexander	Antrim	An	118	Pepells	John	Harrington	Dl	134
Payden	James	Bp Dromore	Dn	171	Pepells	John	Harrington	Dl	134
Paye	John	Sir W. Steward	Ty	59	Pepper	Alexander	Haberdashers	Ly	89
Payeyan	John	Clannaboyes	Dn	163	Pepper	Edward	Calfield	Ty	79
Payne	David	Davis	Dl	134	Pepper	Phillip	Taylor	Cv	10
Payne	Edward	Haberdashers	Ly	89	Pepper	Richard	Taylor	Cv	10
Payne	James	Grocers	Ly	91	Pepper	Robert	Haberdashers	Ly	89
Payne	John	Atchison	Ar	28	Pepper	Robert	Haberdashers	Ly	90
Payne	John	Lord Primate	Ar	34	Perdy	Robert	Sir A. Steward	Ty	64
Payne	John	Ards	Dn	154	Perkin	John	Calfield	Ar	36
Payne	John	Haberdashers	Ly	89	Perkin	William	Calfield	Ar	36
Payne	John	Haberdashers	Ly	90	Perkins	William	Taylor	Cv	10
Payne	John	Sir W. Steward	Ty	59	Perkins	William	Butler	Fe	51
Payne	Peter	Davis	Dl	134	Perkinson	Thomas	Taylor	Cv	9
Payne	Robert	Lord Primate	Ar	34	Perpoynt	James	Londonderry	Ly	85
Payne	Robert	Grocers	Ly	91	Perry	Alexandre	Leigh	Ty	63
Payne	Thomas	Sir W. Steward	Ty	59	Perry	Edward	Clannaboyes	Dn	166
Payne	Valentine	Kildare	Dn	142	Perry	Francis	Crosby	Ty	69
Peacock	Hector	Clannaboyes	Dn	168	Perry	James	Mervin	Ty	69
Peacock	John	Ards	Dn	147	Perry	Thomas	Cole	Fe	40
Peacock	John	Clannaboyes	Dn	166	Person	James	Mervin	Ty	70
Peacock	John	Lowther	Fe	43	Pert	William	Cope	Ar	20
Peacock	Morrice	Lynox	Dl	129	Peter	Andrew	Butler	Cv	4
Peacock	Richard	Cope	Ar	21	Peter	John	Antrim	An	118
Peacock	Robert	Ards	Dn	151	Peteroul	Mathew	Sanderson	Ty	66
Peacok	Richard	Cope	Ar	19	Peterson	John	Crumwell	Dn	146
Peale	Thomas	Coleraine	Ly	103	Petfeild	John	Londonderry	Ly	85
Peale	Richard	Taylor	Cv	10	Petfeild	Richard	Londonderry	Ly	85
Pearance	Richard	Coleraine	Ly	103	Petfeild	Walter	Londonderry	Ly	85
Pearath	James	Berresfourd	Ly	106	Pettecrell	John	Clannaboyes	Dn	163
Pearce	Gilbert	Upton	An	125	Pettecrew	John	Clannaboyes	Dn	167
Pearce	John	Lynox	Dl	129	Pettegson	Thomas	Sir W. Hammilton	Ty	73
Pearce	Patrick	Ards	Dn	154	Petterson	Robert	Antrim	An	117
Pearce	Robert	Erskin	Ty	56	Pettron	William	Clannaboyes	Dn	166
Pearce	Thomas	Butler	Fe	49	Phare	John	Erskin	Ty	56
Pearcy	Richard	Coleraine	Ly	103	Philbye	Marke	Clatworthy	An	123
Pearcy	Walter	Clannaboyes	Dn	167	Phillicote	William	Goldsmiths	Ly	92
Peareman	John	Londonderry	Ly	87	Phillip	Peter	Ards	Dn	148
Peareman	Thomas	Londonderry	Ly	87	Phillip	Robert	Ards	Dn	152

Surname	Forename	Estate	Co.	Page	Surname	Forename	Estate	Co.	Page
Price	John	Londonderry	Ly	83	Ramsay	Mathew	Ards	Dn	151
Price	Steaphen	Annandall	Dl	137	Ramsay	William	Bp Down etc	Dn	170
Price	Thomas	Butler	Cv	3	Ramsay younger	William	Bp Down etc	Dn	170
Price	Thomas	Crumwell	Dn	144	Ramsey	David	Clothworkers	Ly	90
Price	Thomas	Lord Primate	Ly	106	Ramsey	James	Antrim	An	118
Price	William	Pearce	Cv	11	Ramsey	John	Clannaboyes	Dn	163
Prick	Richard	Davis	Dl	134	Ramsey	John	Erskin	Ty	58
Pridion	Henry	Londonderry	Ly	87	Ramsey	Thomas	Lynox	Dl	128
Prier	David	Bp Rapho	Dl	138	Ramson	Andrew	Chichester	Dl	140
Prigeon	John	Londonderry	Ly	85	Ramson	Miles	Crumwell	Dn	145
Prince	Alexander	Clatworthy	An	123	Ramson	Richard	Antrim	An	114
Pringle	James	Satcheuerall	Ar	25	Ramson	Thomas	Antrim	An	115
Pringle	James	Grandison	Ar	32	Ramswey	James	Clatworthy	An	124
Pringle	James	Grandison	Ar	32	Ramsy	Andrew	Edmonston	An	121
Pringle	John	Crumwell	Dn	145	Ramsy	John	Edmonston	An	121
Pringle	Robert	Grandison	Ar	32	Ramsy	Silvester	Lord Primate	Ar	35
Prior	Anthony	Hastings	Fe	53	Ranag	James	Harrington	Dl	134
Prison	Edward	Calfield	Ar	35	Ranckeln	Costyme	Lynox	Dl	128
Pritchard	Morrise	Satcheuerall	Ar	25	Randall	Robert	Abp Armagh	Ty	76
Propter	Nicholas	Londonderry	Ly	85	Randell	John	Antrim	An	113
Prowden	Lancelot	Drapers	Ly	98	Raney	David	Clatworthy	An	122
Prowdlow	Andrew	Fish	Cv	14	Raney	John	Clatworthy	An	122
Prowing	Robert	Atkinson	Fe	52	Ranick	Walter	Ballfowre	Fe	39
Pudgeon	John	Clannaboyes	Dn	163	Rankin	George	Sir J. Hume	Fe	42
Purbouse	Michaell	Clannaboyes	Dn	163	Rankin	James	Lady Conningham	Dl	131
Purdenn	George	Crumwell	Dn	145	Rankin	James	Clannaboyes	Dn	166
Purdon	Daniell	Strabane T.	Ty	75	Rankin	John	Londonderry	Ly	82
Purdy	Edward	Clannaboyes	Dn	168	Rankin	William	Lady Conningham	Dl	130
Purdy	Hugh	Clannaboyes	Dn	162	Rankin	William	Bp Rapho	Dl	139
Purdy	John	Clannaboyes	Dn	157	Rankine	Phillip	Londonderry	Ly	88
Purdy	Thomas	Clannaboyes	Dn	162	Rankyn	John	Antrim	An	110
Purdy	Thomas	Clannaboyes	Dn	168	Rankyne	John	Sir F. Hammelton	Cv	5
Purdy	Walter	Clannaboyes	Dn	157	Rannell	John	Antrim	An	115
Purdy	William	Clannaboyes	Dn	163	Rannick	David	Londonderry	Ly	84
Purris	David	Abp Armagh	Ty	76	Rannick	John	Sir J. Hume	Fe	42
Purse	Patrick	Ards	Dn	147	Ranny	William	Atchison	Cv	7
Py	Thomas	Cope	Ar	20	Ranolds	William	Lord Primate	Ar	34
Pyman	Richard	Butler	Cv	2	Ranson	Robert	Crumwell	Dn	143
Pyman	Richard	Butler	Cv	3	Ranton	Andrew	Clannaboyes	Dn	168
Pyman	Thomas	Butler	Cv	2	Ranton	John	Clannaboyes	Dn	167
Pyn	Richard	Chichester	Dl	139	Ranton younger	John	Clannaboyes	Dn	167
Pyper	James	Haberdashers	Ly	89	Ranton	Mathew	Clannaboyes	Dn	167
Quahone	Adam	Lynox	Dl	129	Ranton	Thomas	Clannaboyes	Dn	168
Qualane	Edward	Londonderry	Ly	87	Rany	William	Clatworthy	An	123
Quater	John	Clannaboyes	Dn	165	Rasedeyhe	John	Mervin	Ty	70
Queenton	John	Sir W. Hammilton	Ty	73	Rasid	John	Antrim	An	110
Quhally	John	Tychborne	Ty	61	Rassell	James	Clatworthy	An	123
Quin	James	Upton	An	124	Rastoll	Thomas	Waldrune	Cv	9
Quinton	Alexander	Sir W. Hammilton	Ty	72	Rastoll	William	Waldrune	Cv	9
Quinton	James	Sir W. Hammilton	Ty	72	Rathborne	John	Ballfowre	Fe	39
Quisy	William	Taylor	Cv	9	Rattall	William	Waldrune	Cv	8
Qwenton	Peter	Hill	An	121	Ratty	John	Antrim	An	115
Rabe	John	Ards	Dn	152	Raven	William	Clannaboyes	Dn	160
Raborne	John	Hammelton	Ar	31	Rawlins	Thomas	Coleraine	Ly	99
Rackins	Robert	L. Blennerhasset	Fe	45	Rawlstone	Adam	Ards	Dn	155
Radcliff	John	Enniskillen T.	Fe	51	Ray	Gilbert	Clannaboyes	Dn	160
Rae	John	Ards	Dn	152	Ray	John	Clannaboyes	Dn	160
Rae	Michell	Hammelton	Ar	31	Ray	John	Clannaboyes	Dn	169
Rae	William	Ards	Dn	153	Ray	Robert	Drowmgowne	Cv	16
Rae	William	Clannaboyes	Dn	162	Ray	Robert	Willson	Dl	132
Raeffearne	John	Cope	Ar	20	Ray	Robert	Willson	Dl	132
Ragdall	Thomas	Pearce	Cv	11	Ray	Robert	Clannaboyes	Dn	159
Raikie	James	Cole	Fe	40	Ray	William	Balye	Cv	13
Rakin	John	Strabane T.	Ty	74	Raying	Thomas	Grocers	Ly	91
Ralf	John	Grandison	Ar	32	Raylton	Gilbert	Crumwell	Dn	146
Ralph	Ephraim	Butler	Cv	4	Rayman	Steaphen	Londonderry	Ly	87
Ralph	Izack	Butler	Cv	4	Rayman	Thomas	Butler	Cv	2
Ralph	John	Butler	Cv	4	Raymentoun	John	Crumwell	Dn	146
Ralston	John	Lynox	Dl	128	Rayne	John	Ards	Dn	156
Ramfrey	James	Londonderry	Ly	86	Raynick	Richard	Hannings	Fe	44
Rampayne	Zachary	Atkinson	Fe	52	Raynick	Thomas	Coleraine	Ly	101
Ramsay	Daniell	Lady Conningham	Dl	130	Rayny	Water	Abp Armagh	Ty	76
Ramsay	David	Sir J. Conningham	Dl	129	re	Archbald	Londonderry	Ly	86
Ramsay	David	Lady Conningham	Dl	131	Rea	Archbald	Melvin	Dn	172
Ramsay	Gilbert	Bp Clougher	Ty	78	Rea	George	Sir A. Steward	Ty	65
Ramsay	John	Clannaboyes	Dn	162	Rea	James	Antrim	An	110

Surname	Forename	Estate	Co.	Page
Rosse	John	Clannaboyes	Dn	163
Rosse	John	Phillips	Ly	104
Rosse	John	Sanderson	Ty	66
Rosse	Laughlyne	Londonderry	Ly	86
Rosse	Robert	Balye	Cv	13
Rosse	Thomas	Ards	Dn	155
Rosse	Thomas	Clannaboyes	Dn	163
Rotes	Michaell	Lady Conningham	Dl	131
Rotherfield	Mungo	Enniskillen T.	Fe	51
Round	Thomas	Waldrune	Cv	9
Roven	William	Clannaboyes	Dn	169
Rowan	Patrick	Clannaboyes	Dn	166
Rowans	Gilbert	Clannaboyes	Dn	157
Rowans	John	Clannaboyes	Dn	157
Rowans	Thomas	Clannaboyes	Dn	163
Rowans	Thomas	Clannaboyes	Dn	168
Rowcastle	Alexander	Ards	Dn	150
Rowcastle	Alexander	Clannaboyes	Dn	163
Rowchester	Robert	Harrington	Dl	134
Rowe	John	Londonderry	Ly	82
Rowelly	Thomas	Coleraine	Ly	103
Rowelly	William	Vintners	Ly	98
Rowen	John	Crumwell	Dn	143
Rowen	John	Clannaboyes	Dn	167
Roweth	George	Phillips	Ly	105
Rowkins	John	Taylor	Cv	10
Rowl	William	Lyndsay	Ty	68
Rowland	Robert	Crumwell	Dn	146
Rowle	William	Lyndsay	Ty	68
Rowles	Richard	Butler	Cv	3
Rowlstone	David	C. of Abbercorne	Ty	71
Rowly	Thomas	Mercers	Ly	96
Rowsell	John	Willson	Dl	132
Roxbrough	Patrick	Clannaboyes	Dn	159
Roxburgh	Gawen	Clannaboyes	Dn	159
Royare	Andrew	Lynox	Dl	128
Royer	John	Lynox	Dl	129
Royne	John	Ards	Dn	154
Rud	John	Lyndsay	Ty	68
Ruddall	Archbald	Goldsmiths	Ly	92
Ruddell	William	Crag	Cv	6
Rudderfoord	Thomas	C. of Abbercorne	Ty	72
Ruddock	Israell	Grocers	Ly	91
Ruddock	Tymothy	Londonderry	Ly	87
Rudson	Edward	Chichester	Dl	140
Rupton	Pearce	Auldridg	Mo	175
Russell	Alexander	Antrim	An	116
Russell	Alexander	Clannaboyes	Dn	160
Russell	Allan	Clannaboyes	Dn	167
Russell	David	Lady McCleland	Ly	105
Russell	Edward	Waldrum	Ar	22
Russell	Edward	Londonderry	Ly	87
Russell	Francis	Richardson	Ty	67
Russell	George	Harrington	Dl	134
Russell	George	Coape	Ty	63
Russell	Hugh	Antrim	An	110
Russell	Hugh	Crumwell	Dn	146
Russell	Hugh	Lord Primate	Ly	106
Russell	James	Crumwell	Dn	144
Russell	James	Crumwell	Dn	146
Russell	John	Antrim	An	112
Russell	John	Dillon	Ar	21
Russell	John	Waldrum	Ar	22
Russell	John	Taylor	Cv	10
Russell	John	Crumwell	Dn	144
Russell	John	Crumwell	Dn	144
Russell	John	Clannaboyes	Dn	160
Russell	Richard	Crumwell	Dn	145
Russell	Richard	Drapers	Ly	98
Russell	Robert	Antrim	An	118
Russell	Robert	Londonderry	Ly	82
Russell	Robert	Drapers	Ly	98
Russell	Robert	Strabane T.	Ty	75
Russell	Thomas	Coleraine	Ly	102
Russell	William	Crumwell	Dn	145
Russell	William	Ards	Dn	149
Russell	William	Sir W. Steward	Ty	59
Russell	William	Richardson	Ty	67
Russell	William	Richardson	Ty	67
Rust	Thomas	Londonderry	Ly	87
Rust	Thomas	Londonderry	Ly	88
Rutherfoord	Adam	Ards	Dn	148
Rutherfoord	John	Ards	Dn	156
Rutherfoord	John	Clannaboyes	Dn	166
Rutledg	Jeffery	Lord Primate	Ar	35
Rutleidg	Symond	Cole	Fe	52
Rutter	Robert	Londonderry	Ly	82
Rybourne	Alexander	Ards	Dn	156
Rycroft	Robert	L. Blennerhasset	Fe	45
Ryddle	Mathew	Ards	Dn	151
Rydick	William	Edmonston	An	121
Rydings	Daniell	Antrim	An	110
Rydley	John	Clothworkers	Ly	90
Ryller	William	Bp Dromore	Dn	171
Sadler	John	Londonderry	Ly	84
Sadock	John	Londonderry	Ly	85
Safftin	Robert	Vintners	Ly	98
Saintson	Christopher	Bp Clougher	Ty	78
Salder	Water	Chichester	Dl	140
Sallowes	John	Sir F. Hammelton	Cv	6
Salsmond	Hugh	Bp Rapho	Dl	138
Salterston	John	Dillon	Ar	21
Samcock	Edward	Amis & Greeneham	Cv	11
Sameton	Thomas	Lord General	Dn	170
Sammuell	William	Lyndsay	Ty	67
Sample	John	Clannaboyes	Dn	162
Sampson	Alexander	Clothworkers	Ly	90
Sampson	John	Chichester	Dl	139
Sampson	John	Londonderry	Ly	82
Sampson	John	Coleraine	Ly	100
Sampson	Richard	Chichester	Dl	139
Sampson	William	Londonderry	Ly	82
Sams	Francis	Satcheuerall	Ar	24
Samson	William	Clatwoorthy	An	124
Sandeland	John	Ards	Dn	147
Sandelands	William	Antrim	An	117
Sanderson	Archbald	Sanderson	Ty	66
Sanderson	Edward	Merchant Taylors	Ly	93
Sanderson	James	Sir A. Steward	Ty	64
Sanderson	James	Lyndsay	Ty	68
Sanderson	James	Bp Clougher	Ty	77
Sanderson	John	Bp Dromore	Dn	171
Sanderson	Thomas	Cole	Fe	40
Sanderson	Thomas	G. Hume	Fe	43
Sanderson	Thomas	Butler	Fe	51
Sanderson	William	H. Steward	Ty	65
Sanderson	William	Lyndsay	Ty	68
Sandyes	Christopher	Londonderry	Ly	87
Saner	William	Sir J. Conningham	Dl	129
Sareitsa	Thomas	Monnaghan T.	Mo	175
Satcheverall	Francis	Satcheuerall	Ar	25
Satcheverall	Henry	Satcheuerall	Ar	24
Satcheverall	Wm	Satcheuerall	Ar	24
Satcheverell	Thomas	L. Blennerhasset	Fe	45
Satlington	John	Clannaboyes	Dn	169
Savage	William	Sir J. Hume	Fe	42
Savage	William	L. Blennerhasset	Fe	45
Sawer	Hugh	Sir J. Conningham	Dl	130
Sawson	John	Butler	Cv	3
Sawyer	David	Lord General	Dn	169
Saywell	Christopher	Crumwell	Dn	144
Scahane	Roger	Haberdashers	Ly	89
Scammell younger	Edward	Hannings	Fe	44
Sceit	Edward	Ards	Dn	148
Scersby	John	Sir W. Steward	Ty	59
Scot	Alexander	Atchison	Ar	28
Scot	Alexander	Annandall	Dl	137
Scot	Alexander	Erskin	Ty	58
Scot	Alexander	Erskin	Ty	58
Scot	Allen	Antrim	An	110
Scot	Andrew	Clannaboyes	Dn	166
Scot	Andrew	Clannaboyes	Dn	169

Surname	Forename	Estate	Co.	Page	Surname	Forename	Estate	Co.	Page
Sharp	Thomas	Butler	Cv	4	Shinan	Alexander	Antrim	An	117
Sharp	William	Adare	An	119	Shippheard	Roger	Crumwell	Dn	143
Sharp	William	Sir F. Hammelton	Cv	4	Shirdall	John	Clannaboyes	Dn	163
Sharp	William	Coleraine	Ly	100	Sholes	Arch:	Crosby	Ty	69
Sharpe	William	Dromond	Ty	70	Short	Andrew	Clannaboyes	Dn	167
Shaw	Anthony	Annandall	Dl	137	Short	John	Chichester	Ty	78
Shaw	David	Clannaboyes	Dn	168	Short	Thomas	Mercers	Ly	96
Shaw younger	David	Clannaboyes	Dn	168	Shorton	Thomas	Clannaboyes	Dn	161
Shaw	Fynlay	Clannaboyes	Dn	161	Shortridg	William	Clannaboyes	Dn	168
Shaw	George	Bp Dromore	Dn	171	Shortwright	James	Clannaboyes	Dn	163
Shaw	George	Bp Dromore	Dn	171	Shpent	John	Antrim	An	116
Shaw	Gilbert	Annandall	Dl	136	Shynean	Roger	Antrim	An	118
Shaw	Gilbert	Clannaboyes	Dn	168	Sidbert	Patrick	Londonderry	Ly	83
Shaw	James	Antrim	An	117	Sill	Edward	Bp Rapho	Dl	139
Shaw	James	Annandall	Dl	137	Simble	John	Lowther	Fe	43
Shaw	James	Clannaboyes	Dn	159	Simmes	James	Cope	Ar	19
Shaw	James	Sanderson	Ty	66	Simpson	Symond	Crumwell	Dn	146
Shaw	James	Sanderson	Ty	66	Sinckler	John	Clannaboyes	Dn	159
Shaw younger	James	Annandall	Dl	137	Sinckler	John	Clannaboyes	Dn	168
Shaw	John	Antrim	An	117	Sincleare	David	Antrim	An	113
Shaw	John	Waldrum	Ar	22	Sincleare	David	Antrim	An	114
Shaw	John	Ards	Dn	149	Sincleare	James	Antrim	An	114
Shaw	John	Lord General	Dn	169	Sincleare	James	Ards	Dn	150
Shaw	John	Bp Dromore	Dn	172	Sincleare	James	Sir W. Steward	Ty	59
Shaw	John	Sanderson	Ty	66	Sincleare	James	Lyndsay	Ty	68
Shaw	John	C. of Abbercorne	Ty	71	Sincleare	John	Antrim	An	114
Shaw	Lancelot	Antrim	An	118	Sincleare	John	Sir W. Steward	Ty	58
Shaw	Robert	Lord General	Dn	169	Sincleer	Thomas	Sir A. Steward	Ty	65
Shaw	Robert	Londonderry	Ly	85	Sincleer	Alexander	Crumwell	Dn	145
Shaw	William	Ards	Dn	149	Singcleare	George	Tychborne	Ty	61
Shaw	William	Clannaboyes	Dn	167	Singcock	Edward	Bp Kilmore	Cv	15
Shaw	William	Mervin	Ty	69	Singleton	George	Lord Primate	Ar	34
Shawe	Alexander	Ards	Dn	151	Sinkclere	James	Ards	Dn	156
Shawe	Andrew	Clannaboyes	Dn	160	Skales	Roger	Cole	Fe	39
Shawe younger	John	Annandall	Dl	137	Skandall	William	Lord Primate	Ar	35
Shawe	Robert	Sir F. Hammelton	Cv	5	Skarlet elder	John	Atkinson	Fe	52
Shawe	Robert	Clannaboyes	Dn	160	Skarlet younger	John	Atkinson	Fe	52
Shawe	William	Mountnorrice	Ar	27	Skarlet	Marke	Cope	Ar	19
Sheall	James	Lord Primate	Ar	34	Skayles	William	Cole	Fe	52
Sheano	George	Dunbar	Fe	48	Skeares	Alexander	Cole	Fe	40
Sheapheard	David	Crosby	Ty	69	Skells	William	Ards	Dn	147
Shearerton	John	Atkinson	Fe	52	Skelton	Philip	Butler	Fe	50
Shearly	Robert	Cope	Ar	18	Skeogh	Allen	Antrim	An	118
Sheat	George	Cope	Ar	20	Skerlet	Thomas	Londonderry	Ly	88
Sheath	Henry	Cope	Ar	18	Skillan	John	Clannaboyes	Dn	162
Shedy	Bryan	Sir F. Hammelton	Cv	5	Skillan	John	Clannaboyes	Dn	168
Sheill	James	Ards	Dn	147	Skillin	Andrew	Ards	Dn	156
Sheirley	John	Phillips	Ly	104	Skilling	Andrew	Ards	Dn	150
Sheirtt	James	Edmonston	An	121	Skilling	Charles	Ards	Dn	151
Shella	Andrew	Annandall	Dl	136	Skilling	James	Ards	Dn	150
Shellan	Martin	Annandall	Dl	136	Skilling	William	Ards	Dn	150
Shellene	Martin	Ards	Dn	147	Skrest	James	Sir J. Hume	Fe	41
Shelly	Thomas	Coleraine	Ly	102	Skynner	Latham	Londonderry	Ly	87
Shelson	William	Sir F. Hammelton	Cv	5	Skynner	Thomas	Londonderry	Ly	82
Shelton	William	Waldrum	Ar	22	Slack	John	Hatton	Fe	48
Shenan	Andrew	Clannaboyes	Dn	157	Slack	Robert	Auldridg	Mo	176
Shenan	Robert	Ards	Dn	153	Slack	Thomas	Hastings	Fe	53
Shenane	John	Ards	Dn	148	Slane	Andrew	Ards	Dn	151
Shepy	Richard	Cavan T.	Cv	16	Slark	John	Crumwell	Dn	143
Shere	Alexander	Ballfowre	Fe	39	Slater	Leonard	Lowther	Fe	43
Sherewood	William	Coleraine	Ly	99	Slater	William	Lord Primate	Ar	33
Sherin	Edmond	Butler	Cv	3	Slater	William	F. Blennerhasset	Fe	45
Sherington	Edward	Londonderry	Ly	87	Slayne	Andrew	Ards	Dn	153
Sherley	John	Hammelton	Ar	30	Sleman	John	Londonderry	Ly	86
Sherley elder	John	Phillips	Ly	104	Sligh	Steaphen	Waldrune	Cv	8
Sherlocke	Sammuell	Waldrum	Ar	22	Slit	Edward	Ards	Dn	153
Sherly	Francis	Cope	Ar	20	Sloan	James	Clannaboyes	Dn	164
Sherly	Peter	Londonderry	Ly	83	Sloane	James	Clannaboyes	Dn	168
Sherwood	Hugh	Adwick	Fe	48	Sloane	John	Clannaboyes	Dn	162
Sherwood	Thomas	Adwick	Fe	49	Sloane	William	Clannaboyes	Dn	162
Sherynd	Edward	Butler	Cv	2	Sloane	William	Haberdashers	Ly	90
Shewane	John	Ards	Dn	151	Slone	Andrew	Kildare	Dn	142
Shewer	James	Ards	Dn	156	Slonen	Patrick	Clannaboyes	Dn	158
Shewernam	Georg	Atchison	Cv	7	Slonne	James	Upton	An	125
Shewers	Patrick	Vintners	Ly	98	Slortenant	Anthony	Bp Kilmore	Cv	15
Shilan	Alexander	Annandall	Dl	137	Slortenant	William	Bp Kilmore	Cv	15

Surname	Forename	Estate	Co.	Page
Smyth younger	John	H. Steward	Ty	66
Smyth	Luke	Clannaboyes	Dn	156
Smyth elder	Michaell	Lord Primate	Ar	33
Smyth	Nicholas	Butler	Cv	3
Smyth	Oliver	Butler	Cv	3
Smyth	Ralph	Crumwell	Dn	144
Smyth	Ralph	Crumwell	Dn	145
Smyth	Ralph	Crumwell	Dn	146
Smyth	Richard	Enniskillen T.	Fe	51
Smyth	Robert	Antrim	An	110
Smyth	Robert	Antrim	An	113
Smyth	Robert	Ards	Dn	155
Smyth	Robert	Bp Down etc	Dn	170
Smyth	Robert	Bp Dromore	Dn	171
Smyth	Robert	Ironmongers	Ly	94
Smyth	Robert	Lord Primate	Ly	106
Smyth	Sammuell	Antrim	An	115
Smyth	Sampson	Butler	Cv	3
Smyth	Thomas	Antrim	An	110
Smyth	Thomas	Crumwell	Dn	145
Smyth	Thomas	Clannaboyes	Dn	160
Smyth	Thomas	Clannaboyes	Dn	168
Smyth	Thomas	Ballfowre	Fe	39
Smyth	Thomas	Vintners	Ly	98
Smyth	Thomas	Coleraine	Ly	100
Smyth	Thomas	Powerscourt	Ty	79
Smyth	William	Antrim	An	115
Smyth	William	Antrim	An	117
Smyth	William	Antrim	An	118
Smyth	William	Clatworthy	An	123
Smyth	William	Butler	Cv	2
Smyth	William	Ards	Dn	150
Smyth	William	Ards	Dn	153
Smyth	William	Ards	Dn	153
Smyth	William	Ards	Dn	155
Smyth	William	Clannaboyes	Dn	160
Smyth	William	Clannaboyes	Dn	161
Smyth	William	Clannaboyes	Dn	167
Smyth	William	Bp Dromore	Dn	171
Smyth	William	Bp Dromore	Dn	171
Smyth	William	Londonderry	Ly	84
Smyth	William	Coleraine	Ly	103
Smyth	William	Phillips	Ly	104
Smyth	William	Lady McCleland	Ly	106
Smyth	William	Berresfourd	Ly	106
Smyth	William	Maghera & Desert Martin	Ly	107
Smyth	William	Erskin	Ty	57
Smythe	John	Brownlow	Ar	27
Smythe	John	Lowther	Fe	44
Smythson	Richard	Bp Clougher	Ty	77
Snadgarse	John	Lynox	Dl	128
Snoden	Sammuell	Vintners	Ly	97
Snodgrass	John	Bp Rapho	Dl	138
Snodgrass	William	Clannaboyes	Dn	160
Snodgrass	William	Clannaboyes	Dn	160
Snoeland	John	Londonderry	Ly	84
Snort	William	Clatworthy	An	123
Snowball	Symond	Erskin	Ty	58
Snyp	William	Sir J. Conningham	Dl	130
Softley	John	Ards	Dn	151
Sollers	John	Londonderry	Ly	85
Solspey	Francis	Upton	An	125
Somerwell	Robert	Ballfowre	Fe	39
Sommerell	James	Calfield	Ar	35
Sommerrill	Robert	Clannaboyes	Dn	161
Sommerscall	Richard	Waldrum	Ar	22
Sommervil	Hugh	Strabane T.	Ty	75
Sommervil	Hugh	Strabane T.	Ty	76
Sommervile	James	Lyndsay	Ty	67
Sommervile	John	Lyndsay	Ty	68
Sommervill	Adam	Richardson	Ty	67
Sommervill	James	H. Steward	Ty	65
Sommervill	William	Strabane T.	Ty	75
Sommerville	James	Sir A. Steward	Ty	65
Sommerville	Walter	Richardson	Ty	67
Sommerwell	James	Mrs Hammelton	Fe	41
Sorbid	James	Ards	Dn	154
Sorerd	James	Chichester	Dl	140
Sorlow	Robert	Chichester	Ty	78
Sothersan	Robert	H. Steward	Ty	65
Southerne	John	Abp Armagh	Ty	76
Sovage younger	William	Cole	Fe	40
Sowerty	Adam	Mervin	Ty	70
Sowgdan	John	Fish	Cv	14
Sowgdan	Thomas	Fish	Cv	14
Sparckle	Archbald	Symonton	Ty	67
Sparke	James	Drapers	Ly	98
Sparkes	George	Monnaghan T.	Mo	175
Sparrowes	Thomas	Vintners	Ly	97
Speare	George	J. Conningham	Dl	136
Speare	James	Merchant Taylors	Ly	93
Speare	John	Kingsmell	Dl	131
Speare	John	Londonderry	Ly	86
Speareman	John	Phillips	Ly	104
Speere	Alexander	Ards	Dn	149
Speere	James	Antrim	An	112
Speere	John	Antrim	An	113
Speere	Robert	Ards	Dn	154
Speere	William	Antrim	An	117
Speire	David	Antrim	An	117
Spence	Alexander	Antrim	An	114
Spence	Alexander	Sir J. Hume	Fe	42
Spence	Andrew	Crumwell	Dn	143
Spence	David	Clannaboyes	Dn	169
Spence	Fynlay	Antrim	An	113
Spence	John	Ards	Dn	148
Spence	John	Clannaboyes	Dn	168
Spence	John	Sir J. Hume	Fe	42
Spence	Nicholl	Edmonston	An	121
Spence	Robert	Antrim	An	113
Spence	Thomas	Brownlow	Ar	26
Spence	Thomas	Crumwell	Dn	143
Spence	Thomas	Sir J. Hume	Fe	42
Spencer	Alexander	Antrim	An	112
Spencer	Christopher	Cope	Ar	18
Spencer	John	Cope	Ar	20
Spencer	Thomas	Cope	Ar	19
Spencer	William	Cope	Ar	18
Speney	Dunkan	Lynox	Dl	128
Spent	Andrew	Crumwell	Dn	144
Spere	Archbald	Clannaboyes	Dn	166
Spere	John	Ards	Dn	151
Spere	John	Ards	Dn	152
Spere elder	John	Ards	Dn	149
Sperling	James	Antrim	An	113
Spery	William	Satcheuerall	Ar	24
Spike	Walter	Vintners	Ly	97
Spire elder	Adam	Ironmongers	Ly	94
Spire elder	Lawrence	Ironmongers	Ly	94
Spire younger	James	Ironmongers	Ly	95
Spire	Robert	Ironmongers	Ly	95
Spire	William	Ironmongers	Ly	94
Spole	John	Crumwell	Dn	144
Spot	William	Ards	Dn	151
Spotswood	William	Clannaboyes	Dn	162
Spotwood	John	Coleraine	Ly	101
Sprag	Thomas	Butler	Fe	50
Spreckly	Thomas	Fyngall	Cv	15
Spreull	James	Bp Rapho	Dl	138
Sprockes	Thomas	Fyngall	Cv	15
Sprot	Andrew	Atchison	Ar	28
Sprot	John	Atchison	Ar	28
Sprot	John	Ards	Dn	147
Sprot	John	Ards	Dn	156
Sprot	Patrick	Ards	Dn	152
Sprot	Patrick	Ards	Dn	156
Sprot	Robert	Bp Dromore	Dn	171
Sprot	Thomas	Clannaboyes	Dn	161
Sprot	Thomas	Bp Dromore	Dn	171
Sprouse	Gabraell	Londonderry	Ly	85
Sprowell	Clawdius	Phillips	Ly	104
Sproyle	John	Crumwell	Dn	144

Surname	Forename	Estate	Co.	Page	Surname	Forename	Estate	Co.	Page
Steward	Alexander	Bp Down etc	Dn	170	Steward	John Duff	Antrim	An	116
Steward	Alexander	Vintners	Ly	97	Steward	Lodwick	Ballfowre	Fe	38
Steward	Alexander	Berresfourd	Ly	106	Steward	Mathew	Antrim	An	113
Steward	Alexander	Berresfourd	Ly	106	Steward	Nevin	Clannaboyes	Dn	163
Steward	Alexander	Sir W. Hammilton	Ty	73	Steward	Ninian	A. Steward	Dl	135
Steward	Andrew	Antrim	An	110	Steward	Patrick	W. Steward	Dl	133
Steward	Andrew	Sir A. Steward	Ty	64	Steward	Patrick	W. Hammilton	Ty	78
Steward	Andrew	Sir A. Steward	Ty	65	Steward	Ralph	Grandison	Ar	32
Steward	Anthony	Lynox	Dl	129	Steward	Robert	Antrim	An	111
Steward	Anthony	W. Steward	Dl	133	Steward	Robert	Antrim	An	115
Steward	Arch	Antrim	An	114	Steward	Robert	A. Steward	Dl	135
Steward	Arch	J. Steward	Dl	136	Steward	Robert	J. Steward	Dl	136
Steward	Archbald	Antrim	An	112	Steward	Robert	Ards	Dn	148
Steward	Archbald	W. Steward	Dl	133	Steward	Robert	Ards	Dn	149
Steward	Archbald	A. Steward	Dl	135	Steward	Robert	Clannaboyes	Dn	159
Steward	Archbald	Clannaboyes	Dn	165	Steward	Robert	Sir W. Steward	Ty	60
Steward	David	Antrim	An	113	Steward	Robert	Calfield	Ty	79
Steward	David	Antrim	An	115	Steward	Thomas	Ards	Dn	151
Steward	David	Antrim	An	118	Steward	Thomas	Londonderry	Ly	84
Steward	David	Ards	Dn	155	Steward	Thomas	Mercers	Ly	96
Steward	David	Sir A. Steward	Ty	64	Steward	Thomas	Coape	Ty	62
Steward	Davyd	Antrim	An	117	Steward	William	Antrim	An	112
Steward	Donnell	Antrim	An	110	Steward	William	Clatwoorthy	An	122
Steward	Donnell	Antrim	An	111	Steward	William	Lady Conningham	Dl	131
Steward	George	W. Steward	Dl	133	Steward	William	Kildare	Dn	142
Steward	George	Bp Down etc	Dn	170	Steward	William	Crumwell	Dn	144
Steward	George	Coape	Ty	62	Steward	William	Clannaboyes	Dn	157
Steward	Gilbert	Ards	Dn	147	Steward	William	Clannaboyes	Dn	164
Steward	Henry	Coleraine	Ly	99	Steward	William	Clannaboyes	Dn	167
Steward	James	Antrim	An	111	Steward	William	Londonderry	Ly	83
Steward	James	Antrim	An	112	Steward	William	Sir A. Steward	Ty	64
Steward	James	Antrim	An	113	Steward	William	Calfield	Ty	79
Steward	James	Antrim	An	118	Stewart	Gilbert	Ards	Dn	156
Steward	James	Cope	Ar	20	Stewart	John	Crumwell	Dn	145
Steward	James	Poyntes	Ar	32	Stewerd	John	Clannaboyes	Dn	162
Steward	James	Pearce	Cv	12	Steyne	John	J. Hammelton	Cv	12
Steward	James	Sir J. Conningham	Dl	130	Still	John	Crumwell	Dn	144
Steward	James	Ards	Dn	148	Still	John	Clannaboyes	Dn	160
Steward	James	Clannaboyes	Dn	157	Still	John	Clannaboyes	Dn	169
Steward	James	Hatton	Fe	47	Stilly	Hugh	Ards	Dn	151
Steward	James	Londonderry	Ly	84	Stilly	Hugh	Clannaboyes	Dn	159
Steward	James	Coleraine	Ly	102	Stilly	John	Clannaboyes	Dn	156
Steward	James	Sir A. Steward	Ty	63	Stiught	Robert	Antrim	An	117
Steward	James	Sir A. Steward	Ty	64	Stobire	Robert	Melvin	Dn	172
Steward	James	Abp Armagh	Ty	76	Stockdal	George	Grandison	Ar	32
Steward	John	Antrim	An	111	Stocker	William	Waldrum	Ar	22
Steward	John	Antrim	An	112	Stockes	Richard	Londonderry	Ly	84
Steward	John	Antrim	An	114	Stockkin	Richard	Drapers	Ly	98
Steward	John	Antrim	An	115	Stockman	John	Coleraine	Ly	102
Steward	John	Upton	An	124	Stockwood	Trypinion	Cope	Ar	18
Steward	John	Cope	Ar	21	Stoen	Robert	Crumwell	Dn	145
Steward	John	Poyntes	Ar	32	Stokes	Hugh	Sedburrogh	Fe	48
Steward	John	Balye	Cv	13	Stole	Thomas	J. Conningham	Dl	135
Steward	John	Lynox	Dl	128	Stone	William	Ards	Dn	149
Steward	John	Lynox	Dl	129	Stonehouse	James	Kildare	Dn	142
Steward	John	W. Steward	Dl	133	Stones	John	Cope	Ar	19
Steward	John	A. Steward	Dl	135	Stones	John	Haberdashers	Ly	90
Steward	John	J. Steward	Dl	136	Stones	Nathaniell	Cope	Ar	19
Steward	John	Bp Rapho	Dl	138	Stones	Robert	Cope	Ar	20
Steward	John	Ards	Dn	150	Stoniford	John	Taylor	Cv	9
Steward	John	Ards ·	Dn	155	Stoodman	Thomas	Cope	Ar	20
Steward	John	Clannaboyes	Dn	161	Storagh	David	Antrim	An	117
Steward	John	Clannaboyes	Dn	162	Storagh	David	Antrim	An	118
Steward	John	Clannaboyes	Dn	163	Storourt	Robert	Antrim	An	115
Steward	John	Clannaboyes	Dn	165	Storret	John	Chichester	Dl	139
Steward	John	Londonderry	Ly	82	Stortvant	Anthony	Waldrune	Cv	8
Steward	John	Londonderry	Ly	83	Stortwant	William	Waldrune	Cv	8
Steward	John	Phillips	Ly	105	Story	David	Ballfowre	Fe	39
Steward	John	Sir A. Steward	Ty	63	Story	George	Sir F. Hammelton	Cv	6
Steward	John	Sir A. Steward	Ty	65	Story	John	Ards	Dn	152
Steward	John	Sir A. Steward	Ty	65	Story	Robert	Atkinson	Fe	52
Steward	John	Symonton	Ty	67	Story	William	Lord Primate	Ar	33
Steward	John	Hastings	Ty	68	Stosbany	George	Waldrune	Cv	8
Steward	John	Crosby	Ty	69	Stote	William	Ards	Dn	154
Steward	John	W. Hammilton	Ty	78	Stotesbury	William	Mercers	Ly	95
Steward younger	John	Antrim	An	115	Stoub	John	Reding	An	121

Surname	Forename	Estate	Co.	Page	Surname	Forename	Estate	Co.	Page
Taylor	John	Cope	Ar	19	Thompson	Cuthbert	Clannaboyes	Dn	165
Taylor	John	Cope	Ar	21	Thompson	David	Crumwell	Dn	146
Taylor	John	Poyntes	Ar	33	Thompson	David	Bp Clougher	Ty	77
Taylor	John	Moynes	Cv	11	Thompson	Hugh	Antrim	An	113
Taylor	John	Fish	Cv	14	Thompson	James	Adare	An	119
Taylor	John	Fish	Cv	14	Thompson	James	Brownlow	Ar	26
Taylor	John	Dean of Rapho	Dl	139	Thompson	James	Davis	Dl	134
Taylor	John	Kildare	Dn	142	Thompson	James	Clannaboyes	Dn	167
Taylor	John	Crumwell	Dn	144	Thompson	John	Mountnorrice	Ar	27
Taylor	John	Ards	Dn	147	Thompson	John	Poyntes	Ar	32
Taylor	John	Cole	Fe	40	Thompson	John	Ards	Dn	147
Taylor	John	Goldsmiths	Ly	92	Thompson	John	Ards	Dn	150
Taylor	John	Hastings	Ty	68	Thompson	John	Clannaboyes	Dn	165
Taylor	Nynan	Antrim	An	118	Thompson	John	Clannaboyes	Dn	165
Taylor	Peter	Crumwell	Dn	146	Thompson	John	Clannaboyes	Dn	166
Taylor	Randall	Crumwell	Dn	144	Thompson	John	Clannaboyes	Dn	166
Taylor	Richard	Cope	Ar	20	Thompson	John	Clannaboyes	Dn	166
Taylor	Robert	Taylor	Cv	9	Thompson	John	Bp Down etc	Dn	170
Taylor	Rowland	Crumwell	Dn	145	Thompson	John	Bp Dromore	Dn	171
Taylor	Thomas	Butler	Cv	4	Thompson	John	Sir J. Hume	Fe	41
Taylor	Thomas	Bp Kilmore	Cv	15	Thompson	John	Sir J. Hume	Fe	42
Taylor	Thomas	Coleraine	Ly	103	Thompson	John	Coleraine	Ly	99
Taylor	Thomas	Coleraine	Ly	104	Thompson	John	Lady McCleland	Ly	105
Taylor	William	Waldrum	Ar	22	Thompson	John	Coape	Ty	62
Taylor	William	Butler	Cv	3	Thompson	John	Strabane T.	Ty	75
Taylor	William	Bp Kilmore	Cv	15	Thompson	John	Strabane T.	Ty	76
Taylor	William	Crumwell	Dn	146	Thompson	Martin	Erskin	Ty	57
Taylor	William	Clannaboyes	Dn	167	Thompson	Mathew	Ards	Dn	149
Tayre	Robert	Coleraine	Ly	99	Thompson	Mathew	Ards	Dn	152
Tayres	Richard	Coleraine	Ly	100	Thompson	Ninian	Bp Rapho	Dl	138
Tayres	Thomas	Coleraine	Ly	100	Thompson	Richard	Ards	Dn	148
Te Grome	John	Coleraine	Ly	103	Thompson	Robert	Atchison	Ar	28
Teat	Nathaniell	Taylor	Cv	9	Thompson	Robert	Kildare	Dn	142
Teckison	Robert	Hastings	Fe	53	Thompson	Robert	Ards	Dn	147
Tedder	Thomas	Lord Primate	Ar	35	Thompson	Robert	Clannaboyes	Dn	166
Teddy	George	Lord Primate	Ar	34	Thompson	Thomas	Antrim	An	114
Tegard	James	Clatworthy	An	122	Thompson	Thomas	Brownlow	Ar	27
Tegard	John	Clatworthy	An	122	Thompson	Thomas	Clannaboyes	Dn	156
Teich	Dono	Haberdashers	Ly	89	Thompson	Thomas	Clannaboyes	Dn	162
Teig	Thomas	Berresfourd	Ly	106	Thompson	Thomas	Clannaboyes	Dn	166
Telfer	Hugh	Edmonston	An	121	Thompson	William	Clatworthy	An	123
Telfer	Hugh	Edmonston	An	121	Thompson	William	Mountnorrice	Ar	28
Telfer	James	Clannaboyes	Dn	163	Thompson	William	Lowther	Fe	43
Telfer	James	Clannaboyes	Dn	168	Thompson	William	Londonderry	Ly	87
Tellyfeare	Robert	Ballfowre	Fe	38	Thompson	William	Sir A. Steward	Ty	64
Temple	Henry	Chichester	Dl	139	Thomson	Archbald	W. Steward	Dl	133
Temple	Robert	Butler	Fe	50	Thomson	Adam	Clannaboyes	Dn	159
Templeton	David	Ards	Dn	152	Thomson	Alexander	Londonderry	Ly	88
Templeton	David	M. of Abbercorne	Ty	72	Thomson	Alexander	Londonderry	Ly	88
Templeton	Gilbert	Clannaboyes	Dn	159	Thomson	Andrew	Clothworkers	Ly	90
Templeton	James	Antrim	An	112	Thomson	Arch	Londonderry	Ly	87
Templeton	John	Upton	An	124	Thomson	Archbald	Antrim	An	114
Templeton	John	Ards	Dn	153	Thomson	Archbald	Bp Dromore	Dn	171
Templeton	John	Coleraine	Ly	101	Thomson	David	Hammelton	Ar	29
Templeton	John	M. of Abbercorne	Ty	72	Thomson	David	Lyndsay	Ty	67
Tenant	Gilbert	Bp Down etc	Dn	170	Thomson	David	Lyndsay	Ty	68
Tenant	John	Upton	An	125	Thomson	Edward	Flowerdew	Fe	44
Tenant	John	Bp Down etc	Dn	170	Thomson	Edward	Londonderry	Ly	88
Teus	Alexander	Harrington	Dl	134	Thomson	Fargus	Ards	Dn	155
Tewdor	Jenken	Coleraine	Ly	101	Thomson	George	Coape	Ty	62
That	James	Benson	Dl	132	Thomson	Hugh	Antrim	An	110
Thom	John	Antrim	An	113	Thomson	Hugh	Sir J. Conningham	Dl	130
Thomas	Arch	Antrim	An	110	Thomson	Hugh	Sir J. Conningham	Dl	130
Thomas	David	Crumwell	Dn	144	Thomson	Hugh	Clannaboyes	Dn	162
Thomas	Griffin	Vintners	Ly	98	Thomson	James	Antrim	An	113
Thomas	John	Antrim	An	114	Thomson	James	Antrim	An	115
Thomas	John	Clatworthy	An	124	Thomson	James	Coleraine	Ly	101
Thomas	Kinrick	Davis	Dl	134	Thomson	James	Sir A. Steward	Ty	64
Thomas	Thomas ap	Powerscourt	Ty	79	Thomson	James	Sir A. Steward	Ty	65
Thomas	Tymothy	Coleraine	Ly	99	Thomson	John	Antrim	An	110
Thompson	Alexander	Mountnorrice	Ar	28	Thomson	John	Antrim	An	110
Thompson	Alexander	Sir J. Conningham	Dl	130	Thomson	John	Clatworthy	An	123
Thompson	Andrew	W. Steward	Dl	133	Thomson	John	Upton	An	125
Thompson	Andrew	Lady McCleland	Ly	105	Thomson	John	Sir F. Hammelton	Cv	6
Thompson	Archbald	Bp Dromore	Dn	171	Thomson	John	Ards	Dn	154
Thompson	Cuthbert	Clannaboyes	Dn	162	Thomson	John	Ards	Dn	155

Surname	Forename	Estate	Co.	Page	Surname	Forename	Estate	Co.	Page
Turner	Richard	Kildare	Dn	142	Wacker	George	Tychborne	Ty	60
Turner	Richard	Crumwell	Dn	146	Wacker	Thomas	Tychborne	Ty	60
Turner	Richard	Dromond	Ty	70	Wadare	William	Waldrune	Cv	8
Turner	Robert	Atchison	Ar	28	Waddell	James	Erskin	Ty	56
Turner	Robert	Bp Dromore	Dn	171	Waddell	James	Erskin	Ty	58
Turner	Robert	Crosby	Ty	69	Waddell	James	Erskin	Ty	58
Turner	Thomas	Bp Dromore	Dn	171	Waden	John	Londonderry	Ly	87
Turner	Thomas	Mercers	Ly	96	Wadfell	James	Bp Dromore	Dn	171
Turner	Thomas	Vintners	Ly	98	Wadsworth	Abraham	Cole	Fe	40
Turner	William	Cope	Ar	20	Waghop	Collin	Clannaboyes	Dn	164
Turner	William	Crumwell	Dn	143	Wahop	William	Bp Down etc	Dn	170
Turner	William	Crumwell	Dn	143	Waker	John	Annandall	Dl	137
Turner	William	Crumwell	Dn	143	Wakeson	Michaell	Ards	Dn	148
Turner	William	Crumwell	Dn	145	Wakeson	William	Ards	Dn	155
Turner	William	Crumwell	Dn	146	Wakey	Richard	Grocers	Ly	91
Turner	William	Bp Dromore	Dn	172	Wakis	Robert	Coleraine	Ly	101
Turnor	Thomas	Butler	Fe	49	Wald	William	Mansfield	Dl	131
Turnstall	William	Londonderry	Ly	85	Walker	Alexander	Antrim	An	112
Tutle	Thomas	Butler	Fe	50	Walker	Andrew	Antrim	An	113
Tuttle	John	Butler	Fe	50	Walker	Andrew	Clatworthy	An	123
Tutton	William	Vintners	Ly	98	Walker	Andrew	Clannaboyes	Dn	161
Tuttorr	Thomas	Fullerton	Fe	54	Walker	Andrew	Clannaboyes	Dn	169
Twedy	Thomas	Sir F. Hammelton	Cv	5	Walker	Anthony	Auldridg	Mo	176
Tweed	John	Antrim	An	113	Walker	Christopher	Sir J. Conningham	Dl	130
Tweed	John	Antrim	An	119	Walker	David	Lady Conningham	Dl	130
Twig	Alexander	Harrington	Dl	134	Walker	Edward	Lord Primate	Ar	34
Twig	Jefferey	Waldrune	Cv	9	Walker	Edward	Londonderry	Ly	88
Twig	Jeremy	Waldrune	Cv	8	Walker	George	Crumwell	Dn	145
Twig	John	Waldrune	Cv	8	Walker	Guy	A. Hammelton	Ty	63
Twig	Robert	Waldrune	Cv	9	Walker	James	Lyndsay	Ty	68
Twigg	Thomas	Sir F. Hammelton	Cv	5	Walker	John	Antrim	An	113
Twilly	Martin	Cope	Ar	19	Walker	John	Antrim	An	114
Twilly	Thomas	Cope	Ar	19	Walker	John	Antrim	An	114
Twynan	William	Clannaboyes	Dn	160	Walker	John	Antrim	An	118
Twynan	William	Clannaboyes	Dn	169	Walker	John	Butler	Cv	4
Tybbeall	Thomas	Sedburrogh	Fe	48	Walker	John	Harrington	Dl	134
Tyllyfley	Henry	Stanhow	Ar	23	Walker	John	Annandall	Dl	137
Tylor	William	Coleraine	Ly	101	Walker	John	Annandall	Dl	137
Tymeyng	John	Flowerdew	Fe	44	Walker	John	Bp Rapho	Dl	138
Tyming	Richard	Ironmongers	Ly	95	Walker	John	Bp Rapho	Dl	138
Tyndall	Alexander	Balye	Cv	13	Walker	John	Ards	Dn	150
Tyndy	Alexander	Annandall	Dl	136	Walker	John	Ards	Dn	152
Tyngle	Richard	Dawson	Ly	106	Walker	John	Clannaboyes	Dn	161
Tynning	John	Ards	Dn	148	Walker	John	Auldridg	Mo	175
Tynsley	Robert	Grandison	Ar	31	Walker	John	Tychborne	Ty	61
Typar	Richard	Butler	Cv	3	Walker	John	Sir W. Hammilton	Ty	73
Typpyne	William	Leigh	Ty	63	Walker	John	Sir W. Hammilton	Ty	73
Typpyr	Richard	Leigh	Ty	63	Walker	Nichol	Annandall	Dl	136
Tyrell	Ralph	Lord Primate	Ar	35	Walker	Richard	Brownlow	Ar	26
Underwood	Robert	Butler	Cv	3	Walker	Richard	Calfield	Ar	36
Upperry	Thomas	Cole	Fe	39	Walker	Richard	Butler	Fe	50
Uprichard	Griffin	Hastings	Ty	68	Walker	Richard	Vintners	Ly	97
Uprichard	William	Harrington	Dl	134	Walker	Robert	Antrim	An	113
Upritt	James	Crumwell	Dn	146	Walker	Robert	Annandall	Dl	136
Usher	Mathew	Lord Primate	Ar	34	Walker	Robert	Butler	Fe	50
Usher	Peter	Cavan T.	Cv	16	Walker	Robert	Butler	Fe	50
Valentyne	John	Lynox	Dl	128	Walker	Thomas	Antrim	An	111
Valintyne	Robert	Drapers	Ly	98	Walker	Thomas	Butler	Cv	2
Vananker	Hugh	Calfield	Ar	35	Walker	Thomas	Ards	Dn	147
Vannanker	Thomas	Calfield	Ar	35	Walker	Thomas	Lord General	Dn	170
Vaugh	John	Ards	Dn	154	Walker	Thomas	Butler	Fe	49
Vaughan	Hugh	Vintners	Ly	97	Walker	William	Ards	Dn	147
Vaughan	William	Monnaghan T.	Mo	175	Walker	William	Bp Dromore	Dn	171
Vaus	Hugh	Ards	Dn	154	Walker	William	Abp Armagh	Ty	76
Vaus	James	Clannaboyes	Dn	161	Walkey	John	Antrim	An	114
Vaus	John	Butler	Cv	3	Wall	Symon	Clannaboyes	Dn	160
Vaux	John	Annandall	Dl	137	Wallace	Adam	Clannaboyes	Dn	161
Vaux	Robert	Annandall	Dl	137	Wallace	David	Ards	Dn	149
Venables	William	Butler	Cv	2	Wallace	David	Clannaboyes	Dn	162
Vernam	John	L. Blennerhasset	Fe	45	Wallace	Edward	Clannaboyes	Dn	162
Vich	John	Hatton	Fe	47	Wallace	Henry	Crumwell	Dn	146
Vincent	George	Poyntes	Ar	33	Wallace	Hugh	Clannaboyes	Dn	162
Vincent	John	Ironmongers	Ly	93	Wallace	Hugh	Clannaboyes	Dn	165
Vincent	Leonard	Mercers	Ly	96	Wallace	James	Ards	Dn	150
Vincent	William	Ironmongers	Ly	94	Wallace	James	Ards	Dn	156
Vynables	Thomas	Butler	Cv	2	Wallace	James	Clannaboyes	Dn	161

Surname	Forename	Estate	Co.	Page	Surname	Forename	Estate	Co.	Page
Watson	John	Londonderry	Ly	87	Welshman	William	Crumwell	Dn	144
Watson	Joseph	Coleraine	Ly	103	Welsman	William	Ward	Dn	172
Watson	Peter	Newton	Ty	80	Welson	William	Coleraine	Ly	99
Watson	Robert	Londonderry	Ly	83	Weltch	David	Clannaboyes	Dn	163
Watson	Rynyon	Enniskillen T.	Fe	51	Weltch	John	Clannaboyes	Dn	163
Watson	Thomas	Crumwell	Dn	143	Weltch	John	Clannaboyes	Dn	163
Watson	Thomas	Clannaboyes	Dn	163	Weltch	John	Clannaboyes	Dn	168
Watson	William	Crumwell	Dn	143	Weltch younger	John	Clannaboyes	Dn	163
Watson	William	Clannaboyes	Dn	164	Weltch	William	Crumwell	Dn	146
Watt	David	Antrim	An	113	Weltch	William	Ards	Dn	149
Watt	Hugh	Clannaboyes	Dn	167	Wen	Adam	Sir G. Hammilton	Ty	71
Watt	James	Adare	An	119	Wenge	Gilbert	Antrim	An	115
Watt	John	Sir J. Conningham	Dl	130	Wentfoord	Symond	Butler	Fe	51
Watt	John	Clannaboyes	Dn	160	Wentworth	Thomas	Bagshaw	Cv	8
Watt	John	Clannaboyes	Dn	169	Were	William	Clannaboyes	Dn	169
Watt	John	Haberdashers	Ly	90	Weredy	Denis	Mercers	Ly	96
Watt	Robert	Erskin	Ty	57	Werlyne	John	Upton	An	124
Watt	Thomas	Antrim	An	112	Wermane	Frauncis	Lord General	Dn	170
Watt	William	Clannaboyes	Dn	167	Wernogh	Robert	Sir J. Conningham	Dl	129
Watters	John	Vintners	Ly	97	Wesscoat	John	Londonderry	Ly	87
Watters	Nynean	Phillips	Ly	105	Wesson	John	Woorell	Fe	46
Watterson	John	Sir J. Hume	Fe	42	Wessy	John	Tychborne	Ty	61
Watterson	John	Symonton	Ty	67	West	John	Butler	Cv	4
Watts	Straford	Londonderry	Ly	85	West	John	Crumwell	Dn	145
Watty	John	Antrim	An	112	West	John	Butler	Fe	50
Waugh	James	G. Hume	Fe	43	West	John	Butler	Fe	50
Waugh	John	Clatwoorthy	An	123	West elder	John	Crumwell	Dn	144
Waugh	Thomas	Clatwoorthy	An	123	West elder	John	Crumwell	Dn	144
Waughan	William	Crumwell	Dn	146	West younger	John	Crumwell	Dn	146
Waus	John	Annandall	Dl	136	West	Joseph	Goldsmiths	Ly	92
Wause	Alexander	Ards	Dn	155	West	Thomas	Atkinson	Fe	52
Wause	John	Bp Rapho	Dl	138	West	Thomas	Vintners	Ly	98
Wawigh	David	Sir F. Hammelton	Cv	5	West	William	Butler	Fe	50
Waynes	John	Willson	Dl	132	Westby	Robert	L. Blennerhasset	Fe	45
Wayst	John	Hatton	Fe	47	Westby elder	Thomas	L. Blennerhasset	Fe	45
Wear	Edward	Montgomery	Fe	54	Westby younger	Thomas	L. Blennerhasset	Fe	45
Weare	Andrew	Clatwoorthy	An	124	Westen	Edward	Mercers	Ly	96
Weare	James	Antrim	An	116	Westhead	Evance	Hannings	Fe	44
Weare	John	Edmonston	An	120	Wetherowe	William	Londonderry	Ly	86
Weasworth	Thomas	Satcheuerall	Ar	25	Wetten	Richard	Butler	Cv	4
Web	Edward	Ironmongers	Ly	94	Wheatlow	William	Enniskillen T.	Fe	51
Web	Richard	Vintners	Ly	97	Wheeler	Humphrey	Butler	Fe	50
Webster	Richard	Taylor	Cv	9	Wheler	John	Moynes	Cv	11
Webster	Thomas	Ards	Dn	153	Whilly	John	Antrim	An	116
Weere	Alexander	Ards	Dn	154	Whirk	James	Ards	Dn	152
Weere	David	Ards	Dn	154	Whirwoods	Lucke	Cavan T.	Cv	16
Weere	John	A. Hammelton	Ty	63	Whit	Alexander	Clatwoorthy	An	122
Weere	John	Sir A. Steward	Ty	64	Whit	Thomas	Edmonston	An	121
Weilding	Thomas	Crumwell	Dn	144	Whit	William	Clatwoorthy	An	123
Weilly	John	Bp Dromore	Dn	171	Whitakers	Thomas	Lord Primate	Ar	35
Wein	David	C. of Abbercorne	Ty	72	Whitby	Thomas	Archdall	Fe	41
Weir	Alexander	Clannaboyes	Dn	164	White	Adam	Ards	Dn	154
Weir	Gilbert	Clannaboyes	Dn	165	White	Adam	Sanderson	Ty	66
Weir	Mungo	Clannaboyes	Dn	161	White	Alexander	Haberdashers	Ly	90
Weir	Mungo	Clannaboyes	Dn	169	White	Alexander	Coleraine	Ly	101
Weir	William	Clannaboyes	Dn	161	White	David	Strabane T.	Ty	75
Weir	William	Clannaboyes	Dn	162	White	George	J. Conningham	Dl	135
Weire	John	Coleraine	Ly	103	White	Gilbert	Coleraine	Ly	101
Weire	William	Antrim	An	113	White	Henry	Lady McCleland	Ly	105
Weiton	John	Willson	Dl	132	White	Hugh	Antrim	An	117
Welch	James	Erskin	Ty	57	White	Hugh	Clannaboyes	Dn	159
Welch	William	Clannaboyes	Dn	163	White	Hugh	Clannaboyes	Dn	160
Weldon	Francis	Calfield	Ar	35	White	Hugh	Phillips	Ly	104
Well	John	Londonderry	Ly	87	White	James	Atchison	Ar	29
Well	Patrick	Bp Down etc	Dn	170	White	James	Bp Down etc	Dn	170
Well	William	Londonderry	Ly	87	White	John	Antrim	An	110
Welles	Andrew	Newton	Ty	80	White	John	Antrim	An	117
Wells	John	Newton	Ty	80	White	John	Antrim	An	118
Wells	Lawrence	Ironmongers	Ly	93	White	John	Clatwoorthy	An	123
Welly	John	Ards	Dn	148	White	John	Bp Rapho	Dl	138
Welly	William	Ards	Dn	155	White	John	Clannaboyes	Dn	166
Welsh	John	Londonderry	Ly	85	White	John	Londonderry	Ly	86
Welsh	Peter	Grandison	Ar	32	White	John	Goldsmiths	Ly	92
Welsh	Robert	Pearce	Cv	12	White	John	Phillips	Ly	104
Welsh	Robert	Clannaboyes	Dn	162	White	John	Berresfourd	Ly	106
Welshen	William	Crumwell	Dn	144	White	John	Sir A. Steward	Ty	64

Surname	Forename	Estate	Co.	Page	Surname	Forename	Estate	Co.	Page
Willson	James	Tychborne	Ty	60	Wilson	John	Edmonston	An	120
Willson	John	Antrim	An	112	Wilson	John	Dalloway	An	122
Willson	John	Willson	Dl	132	Wilson	John	Cope	Ar	21
Willson	John	Bp Rapho	Dl	138	Wilson	John	Taylor	Cv	10
Willson	John	Crumwell	Dn	144	Wilson	John	Taylor	Cv	10
Willson	John	Ards	Dn	148	Wilson	John	Lady Conningham	Dl	131
Willson	John	Coleraine	Ly	100	Wilson	John	Kingsmell	Dl	131
Willson	John	Coleraine	Ly	103	Wilson	John	Kildare	Dn	143
Willson	John	Coleraine	Ly	104	Wilson	John	Crumwell	Dn	143
Willson	John	M. of Abbercorne	Ty	72	Wilson	John	Crumwell	Dn	145
Willson	Nathaniell	Chichester	Dl	140	Wilson	John	Ards	Dn	147
Willson	Richard	Sir A. Steward	Ty	65	Wilson	John	Ards	Dn	151
Willson	Robert	Ards	Dn	151	Wilson	John	Ards	Dn	151
Willson	Robert	Archdall	Fe	40	Wilson	John	Ards	Dn	156
Willson	Robert	Archdall	Fe	40	Wilson	John	Clannaboyes	Dn	157
Willson	Robert	Butler	Fe	50	Wilson	John	Clannaboyes	Dn	157
Willson	Roger	Antrim	An	117	Wilson	John	Clannaboyes	Dn	162
Willson	Thomas	Antrim	An	110	Wilson	John	Clannaboyes	Dn	164
Willson	Thomas	Ards	Dn	151	Wilson	John	Clannaboyes	Dn	166
Willson	Thomas	Coleraine	Ly	100	Wilson	John	Clannaboyes	Dn	169
Willson	William	Hill	An	121	Wilson	John	Bp Dromore	Dn	171
Willson	William	Clatworthy	An	124	Wilson	John	Archdall	Fe	41
Willson	William	Parsons	Ty	62	Wilson	John	Mrs Hammelton	Fe	41
Willson	William	M. of Abbercorne	Ty	72	Wilson	John	Londonderry	Ly	83
Willy	George	Antrim	An	112	Wilson	John	Mercers	Ly	95
Willy	James	Edmonston	An	121	Wilson	John	Phillips	Ly	104
Willy	James	Ards	Dn	149	Wilson	John	Sir W. Steward	Ty	59
Willy	John	Antrim	An	113	Wilson	John	Sir W. Steward	Ty	59
Willy	John	J. Hammelton	Cv	12	Wilson	John	Coape	Ty	62
Willy	John	Balye	Cv	13	Wilson	John	Sir G. Hammilton	Ty	71
Willy	John	Bp Rapho	Dl	138	Wilson	John	C. of Abbercorne	Ty	71
Willy	John	Clannaboyes	Dn	157	Wilson	John	Strabane T.	Ty	75
Willy	Mungo	J. Conningham	Dl	136	Wilson	John	Abp Armagh	Ty	76
Willy	Robert	Clannaboyes	Dn	162	Wilson	John	Bp Clougher	Ty	77
Willy	Thomas	Antrim	An	118	Wilson younger	John	Bp Dromore	Dn	171
Willy	William	Kildare	Dn	142	Wilson younger	John	Sir W. Steward	Ty	59
Wilson	Adam	Ards	Dn	148	Wilson	Michael	Ballfowre	Fe	39
Wilson	Alexander	Clannaboyes	Dn	160	Wilson	Mungo	Crumwell	Dn	145
Wilson	Allan	Ards	Dn	154	Wilson	Nicholas	Loftus	Mo	174
Wilson	Andrew	Clatworthy	An	122	Wilson	Patrick	Drapers	Ly	98
Wilson	Andrew	Clannaboyes	Dn	164	Wilson	Paul	Clannaboyes	Dn	166
Wilson	Archbald	Coape	Ty	62	Wilson	Quistirne	Adare	An	119
Wilson	Archball	Antrim	An	117	Wilson	Ralph	Atchison	Cv	7
Wilson	Archball	Hatton	Fe	48	Wilson	Richard	Archdall	Fe	41
Wilson	Christopher	Poyntes	Ar	33	Wilson	Richard	Sir A. Steward	Ty	64
Wilson	Christopher	Chichester	Ty	78	Wilson	Robert	Antrim	An	113
Wilson	David	Annandall	Dl	137	Wilson	Robert	Kingsmell	Dl	131
Wilson	David	Ards	Dn	150	Wilson	Robert	Crumwell	Dn	145
Wilson	David	Ards	Dn	156	Wilson	Robert	Ards	Dn	149
Wilson	David	Coleraine	Ly	101	Wilson	Robert	Ironmongers	Ly	94
Wilson	Dunkan	Edmonston	An	120	Wilson	Robert	Coape	Ty	62
Wilson	Edward	Tychborne	Ty	61	Wilson	Robert	Strabane T.	Ty	75
Wilson	Emer	Clannaboyes	Dn	162	Wilson	Robert	Strabane T.	Ty	76
Wilson	Francis	Hammelton	Ar	30	Wilson	Thomas	Grandison	Ar	31
Wilson	Gabraell	Harrington	Dl	134	Wilson	Thomas	Poyntes	Ar	32
Wilson	Gabraell	Londonderry	Ly	83	Wilson	Thomas	Ards	Dn	155
Wilson	George	Clannaboyes	Dn	157	Wilson	Thomas	Clannaboyes	Dn	160
Wilson	George	Clannaboyes	Dn	161	Wilson	Thomas	Lord General	Dn	170
Wilson	George	Bp Dromore	Dn	171	Wilson	Thomas	Bp Clougher	Ty	77
Wilson	George	Atkinson	Fe	52	Wilson	William	Edmonston	An	120
Wilson	James	Antrim	An	113	Wilson	William	Edmonston	An	121
Wilson	James	Clatworthy	An	123	Wilson	William	Poyntes	Ar	32
Wilson	James	Atchison	Ar	29	Wilson	William	Atchison	Cv	7
Wilson	James	Sir J. Conningham	Dl	130	Wilson	William	Sir J. Conningham	Dl	130
Wilson	James	Kingsmell	Dl	131	Wilson	William	Willson	Dl	132
Wilson	James	Ards	Dn	148	Wilson	William	Kildare	Dn	143
Wilson	James	Ards	Dn	149	Wilson	William	Ards	Dn	150
Wilson	James	Ards	Dn	156	Wilson	William	Ards	Dn	151
Wilson	James	Clannaboyes	Dn	167	Wilson	William	Ards	Dn	152
Wilson	James	Lord General	Dn	170	Wilson	William	Bp Dromore	Dn	172
Wilson	James	Bp Dromore	Dn	171	Wilson	William	Hatton	Fe	47
Wilson	James	Coleraine	Ly	100	Wilson	William	Coleraine	Ly	101
Wilson	John	Antrim	An	110	Wilson	William	Auldridg	Mo	175
Wilson	John	Antrim	An	113	Wilson	William	Sir W. Steward	Ty	58
Wilson	John	Antrim	An	116	Wilson	William	Strabane T.	Ty	75
Wilson	John	Antrim	An	117	Win	George	Cope	Ar	25

Surname	Forename	Estate	Co.	Page	Surname	Forename	Estate	Co.	Page
Wyly	Robert	Clannaboyes	Dn	169	Young	James	Symonton	Ty	67
Wyndser younger	Oliver	Butler	Fe	49	Young	John	Antrim	An	115
					Young	John	Antrim	An	116
Wyndstandby	Ralph	Archdal	Fe	53	Young	John	Antrim	An	117
Wyndstones	Ralph	Lowther	Fe	44	Young	John	Antrim	An	118
Wyne	Robert	Harrington	Dl	134	Young	John	Edmonston	An	121
Wyne	Wylliam	Clothworkers	Ly	91	Young	John	J. Hammelton	Cv	12
Wynrin	John	Crumwell	Dn	145	Young	John	Drowmgowne	Cv	16
Wynter	Thomas	Cope	Ar	21	Young	John	Lynox	Dl	129
Wyre	John	Phillips	Ly	104	Young	John	Clannaboyes	Dn	157
Wyre	John	Phillips	Ly	105	Young	John	Clannaboyes	Dn	163
Wytty	William	Ironmongers	Ly	95	Young	John	Clannaboyes	Dn	165
Yare	Myles	Crumwell	Dn	146	Young	John	Mrs Hammelton	Fe	41
Yarrow	Edward	Powerscourt	Ty	79	Young	John	Coleraine	Ly	103
Yate	John	Londonderry	Ly	86	Young	John	Symonton	Ty	67
Yates	John	Strabane T.	Ty	76	Young	Mathew	Edmonston	An	120
Yates	Richard	Brownlow	Ar	26	Young	Mungo	Antrim	An	118
Yates	Thomas	Brownlow	Ar	26	Young	Patrick	Adare	An	119
Yates	Thomas	Enniskillen T.	Fe	51	Young	Robert	Antrim	An	114
Yeates	John	Ards	Dn	154	Young	Robert	Sir J. Conningham	Dl	129
Yebells	John	Antrim	An	117	Young	Robert	Chichester	Dl	139
Yeddin	George	Flowerdew	Fe	44	Young	Robert	Londonderry	Ly	83
Yedding	John	Flowerdew	Fe	44	Young elder	Robert	Strabane T.	Ty	74
Yeoman	John	Ards	Dn	152	Young younger	Robert	Strabane T.	Ty	76
Yoole	John	Sir J. Conningham	Dl	130	Young	Thomas	Edmonston	An	120
Yorke	John	Londonderry	Ly	82	Young	Thomas	Symonton	Ty	67
Youghell	John	Richardson	Ar	36	Young	Thomas	Strabane T.	Ty	73
Youghell	Norman	Richardson	Ar	36	Young elder	Thomas	Strabane T.	Ty	73
Young	Adam	Atchison	Ar	29	Young	William	Sir F. Hammelton	Cv	6
Young	Alexander	Mrs Hammelton	Fe	41	Young	William	Sir J. Conningham	Dl	130
Young	Andrew	Chichester	Dl	140	Young	William	Sir J. Conningham	Dl	130
Young	Andrew	Crumwell	Dn	143	Young	William	Crumwell	Dn	143
Young	Andrew	Ards	Dn	150	Young	William	Crumwell	Dn	145
Young elder	Andrew	Crumwell	Dn	146	Young	William	Clannaboyes	Dn	157
Young younger	Andrew	Crumwell	Dn	143	Young	William	Londonderry	Ly	83
Young younger	Andrew	Crumwell	Dn	143	Young	William	Phillips	Ly	104
Young	Archball	Atchison	Ar	28	Young	William	Phillips	Ly	105
Young	David	Sir J. Conningham	Dl	130	Young	William	Sir W. Steward	Ty	59
Young	David	Londonderry	Ly	83	Young	William	Tychborne	Ty	60
Young	David	Londonderry	Ly	87	Young	William	Strabane T.	Ty	73
Young	David	Abp Armagh	Ty	76	Young	William	Strabane T.	Ty	74
Young	George	Kingsmell	Dl	131	Younger	John	Bp Dromore	Dn	171
Young	Harbert	Crumwell	Dn	145	Younger	John	Strabane T.	Ty	76
Young	Herbert	Crumwell	Dn	143	Younger	Robert	Sir J. Hume	Fe	42
Young	Hugh	Clannaboyes	Dn	165	Younger	Thomas	Sir J. Hume	Fe	42
Young	James	Sir J. Conningham	Dl	129	Yow	John	Phillips	Ly	105
Young	James	Chichester	Dl	140	Yury	Robert	Strabane T.	Ty	74
Young	James	Clannaboyes	Dn	162	Zack	Thomas	Atkinson	Fe	52
Young	James	Drapers	Ly	98	Zack	William	Atkinson	Fe	52